PLAYBOY'S®
Little Annie Fanny™

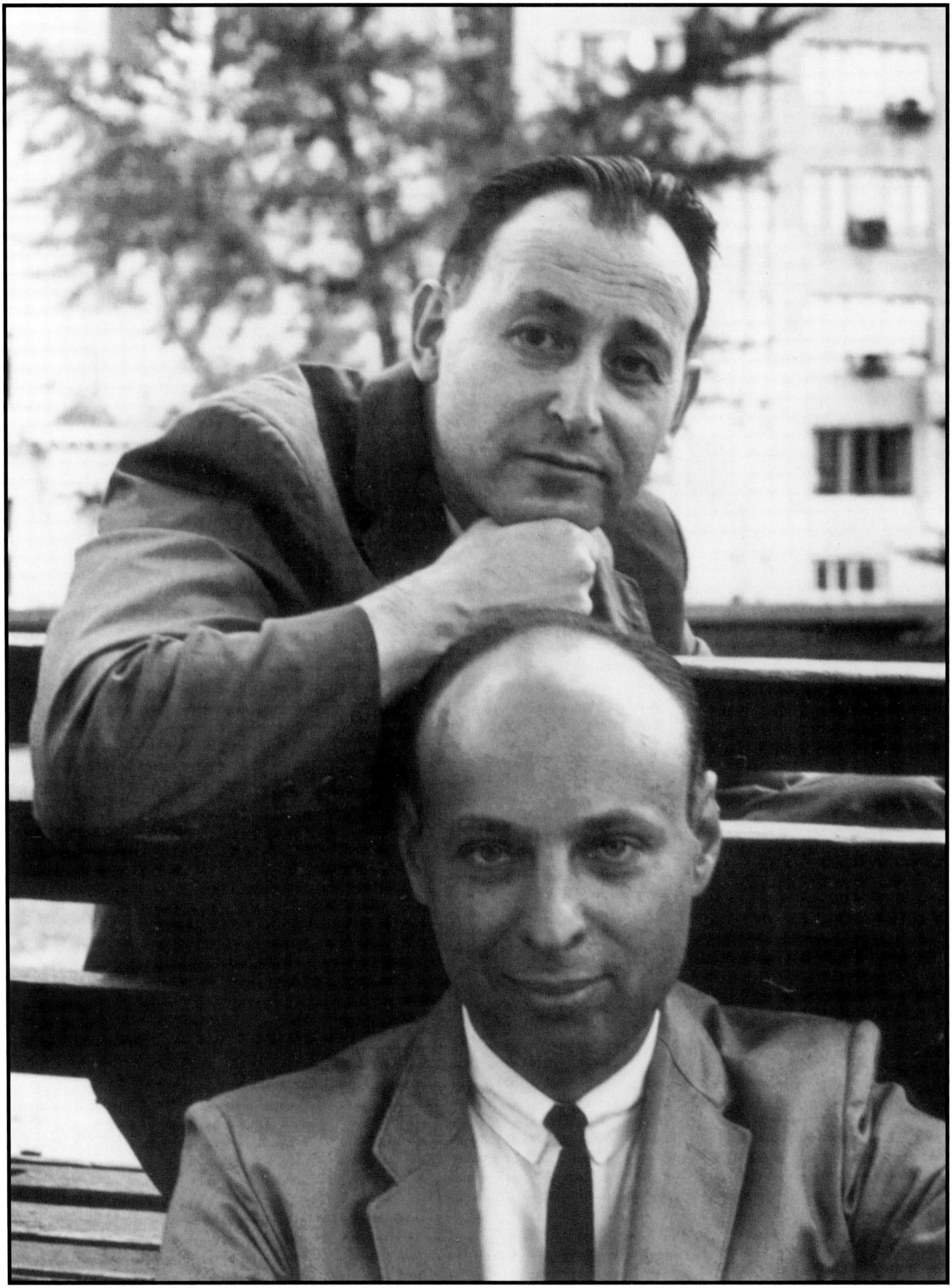

Will Elder (top) and **Harvey Kurtzman**, circa 1962

PLAYBOY'S
Little Annie Fanny ™

by **Harvey Kurtzman**
and **Will Elder**

Editor
Hugh Hefner

DARK HORSE COMICS®

Contributing Artists and Writers

Paul Coker, Jr.

Jack Davis

Frank Frazetta

Russ Heath

Al Jaffee

Bob Price

Arnold Roth

Larry Siegel

Overview and Annotations

Denis Kitchen

Dark Horse Editor

Scott Allie
with Adam Gallardo

Playboy Cartoon Editor

Michelle Urry

Assistant to Ms. Urry

Jennifer Thiele

Designers

Mark Cox
Jeremy Perkins

Publisher

Mike Richardson

Published by
Dark Horse Comics, Inc.
10956 SE Main Street
Milwaukie, OR 97222

First edition: November 2000
ISBN: 1-56971-519-X

1 3 5 7 9 10 8 6 4 2
Printed in Canada

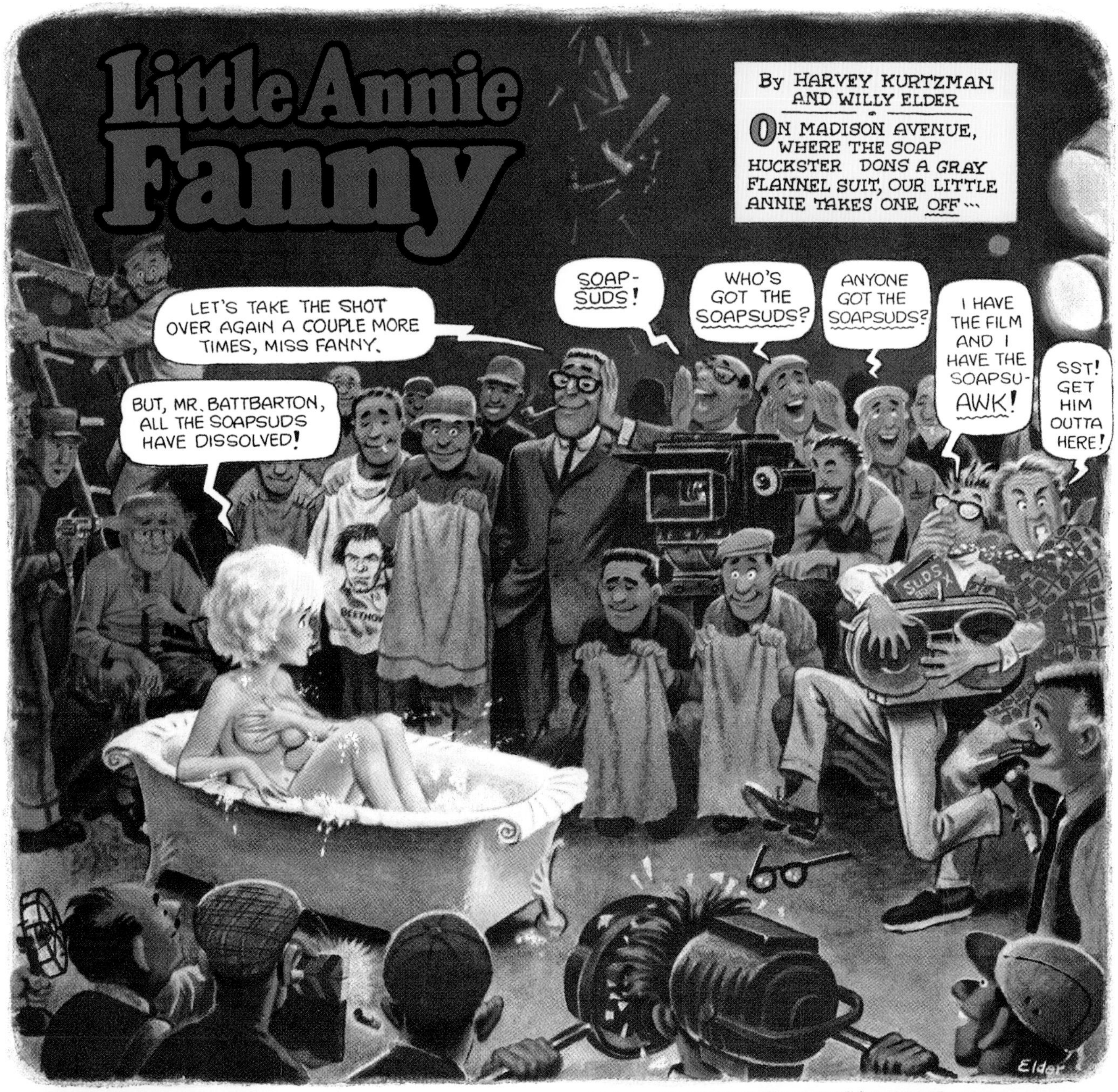
Little Annie Fanny
By HARVEY KURTZMAN AND WILLY ELDER
ON MADISON AVENUE, WHERE THE SOAP HUCKSTER DONS A GRAY FLANNEL SUIT, OUR LITTLE ANNIE TAKES ONE OFF…
LET'S TAKE THE SHOT OVER AGAIN A COUPLE MORE TIMES, MISS FANNY.
BUT, MR. BATTBARTON, ALL THE SOAPSUDS HAVE DISSOLVED!
SOAP-SUDS!
WHO'S GOT THE SOAPSUDS?
ANYONE GOT THE SOAPSUDS?
I HAVE THE FILM AND I HAVE THE SOAPSU-AWK!
SST! GET HIM OUTTA HERE!
BEETHOV
SUDS
Elder

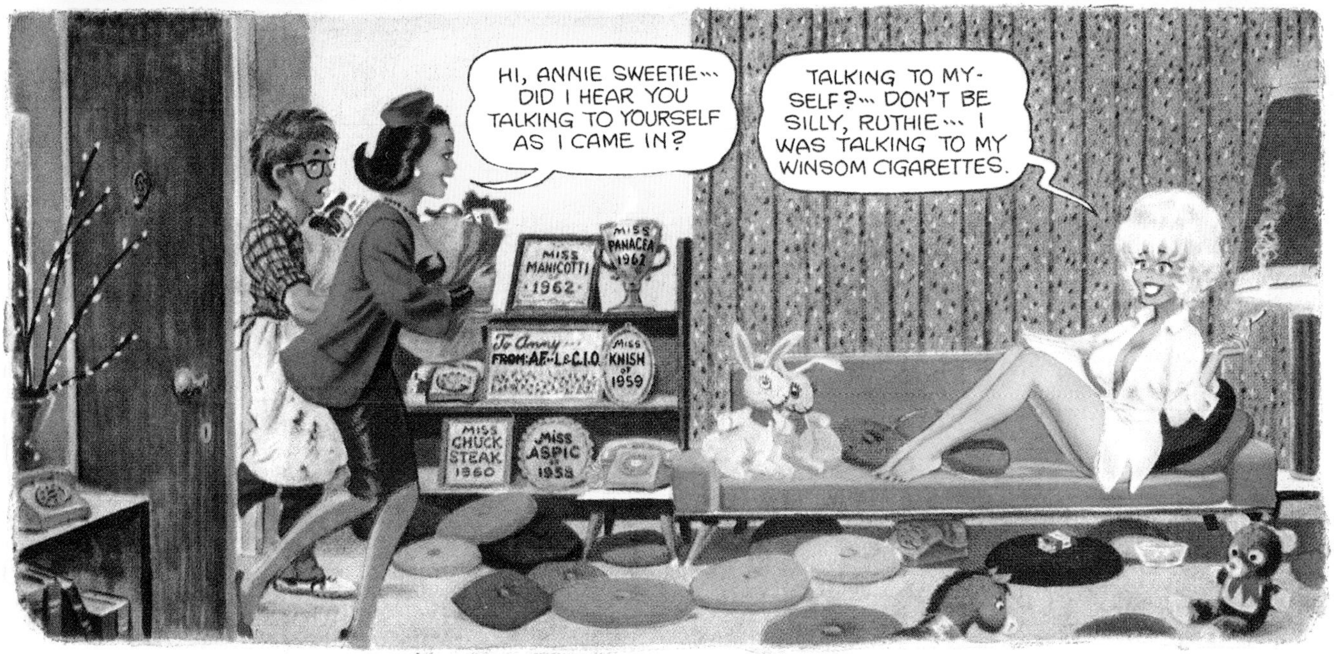
HI, ANNIE SWEETIE… DID I HEAR YOU TALKING TO YOURSELF AS I CAME IN?
TALKING TO MY-SELF?… DON'T BE SILLY, RUTHIE… I WAS TALKING TO MY WINSOM CIGARETTES.
MISS MANICOTTI 1962
MISS PANACEA 1962
To Annie… FROM: AF-L&C.I.O.
MISS KNISH OF 1959
MISS CHUCK STEAK 1960
MISS ASPIC OF 1958

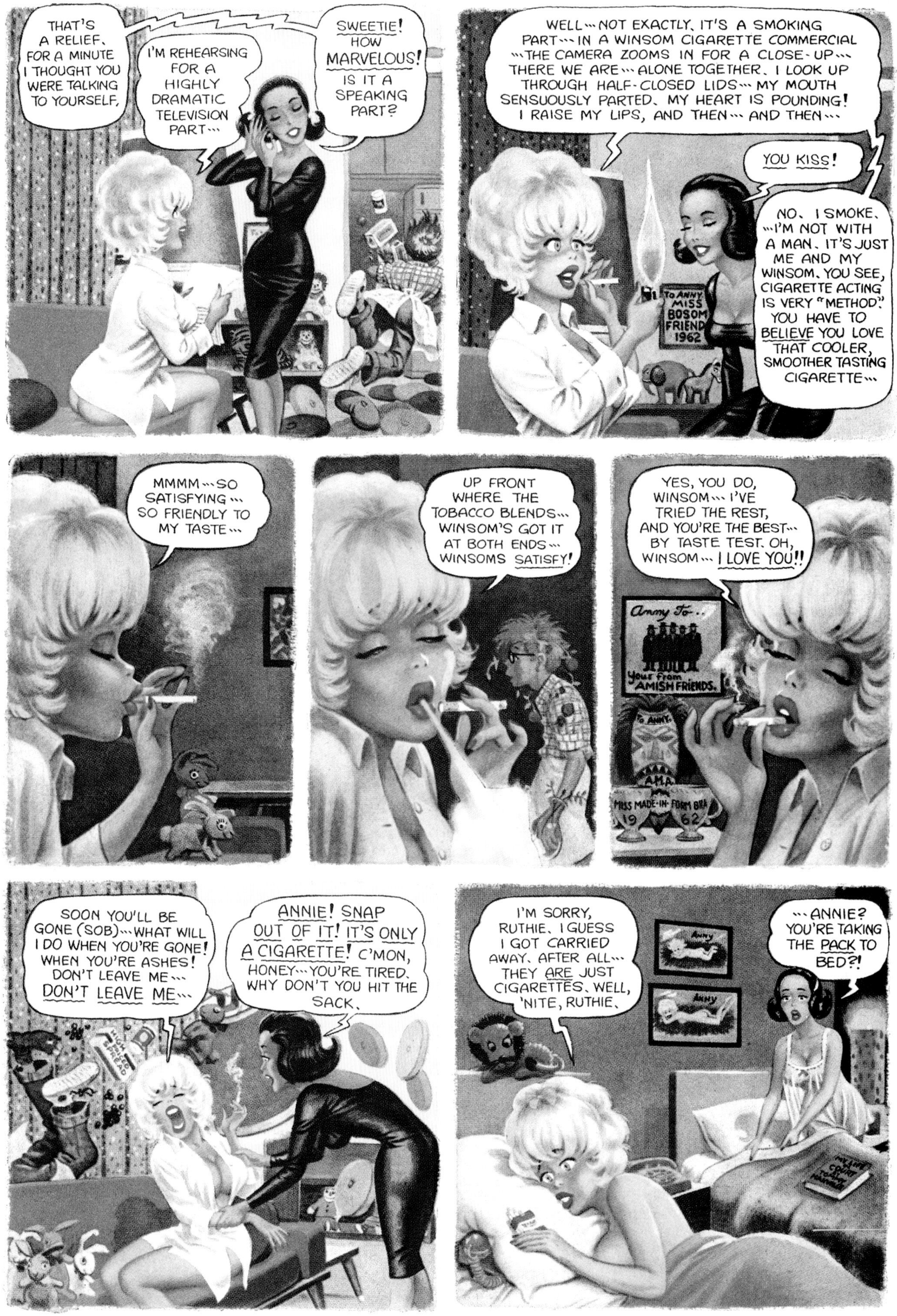
THAT'S A RELIEF. FOR A MINUTE I THOUGHT YOU WERE TALKING TO YOURSELF.
I'M REHEARSING FOR A HIGHLY DRAMATIC TELEVISION PART...
SWEETIE! HOW MARVELOUS! IS IT A SPEAKING PART?
WELL... NOT EXACTLY. IT'S A SMOKING PART... IN A WINSOM CIGARETTE COMMERCIAL ...THE CAMERA ZOOMS IN FOR A CLOSE-UP... THERE WE ARE... ALONE TOGETHER. I LOOK UP THROUGH HALF-CLOSED LIDS... MY MOUTH SENSUOUSLY PARTED. MY HEART IS POUNDING! I RAISE MY LIPS, AND THEN... AND THEN...
YOU KISS!
NO. I SMOKE. ...I'M NOT WITH A MAN. IT'S JUST ME AND MY WINSOM. YOU SEE, CIGARETTE ACTING IS VERY "METHOD." YOU HAVE TO BELIEVE YOU LOVE THAT COOLER, SMOOTHER TASTING CIGARETTE...
TO ANNY MISS BOSOM FRIEND 1962
MMMM... SO SATISFYING... SO FRIENDLY TO MY TASTE...
UP FRONT WHERE THE TOBACCO BLENDS... WINSOM'S GOT IT AT BOTH ENDS... WINSOMS SATISFY!
YES, YOU DO, WINSOM... I'VE TRIED THE REST, AND YOU'RE THE BEST... BY TASTE TEST. OH, WINSOM... I LOVE YOU!!
Anny To.. Yours from AMISH FRIENDS.
SOON YOU'LL BE GONE (SOB)... WHAT WILL I DO WHEN YOU'RE GONE! WHEN YOU'RE ASHES! DON'T LEAVE ME... DON'T LEAVE ME...
ANNIE! SNAP OUT OF IT! IT'S ONLY A CIGARETTE! C'MON, HONEY... YOU'RE TIRED. WHY DON'T YOU HIT THE SACK.
I'M SORRY, RUTHIE. I GUESS I GOT CARRIED AWAY. AFTER ALL... THEY ARE JUST CIGARETTES. WELL, 'NITE, RUTHIE.
...ANNIE? YOU'RE TAKING THE PACK TO BED?!

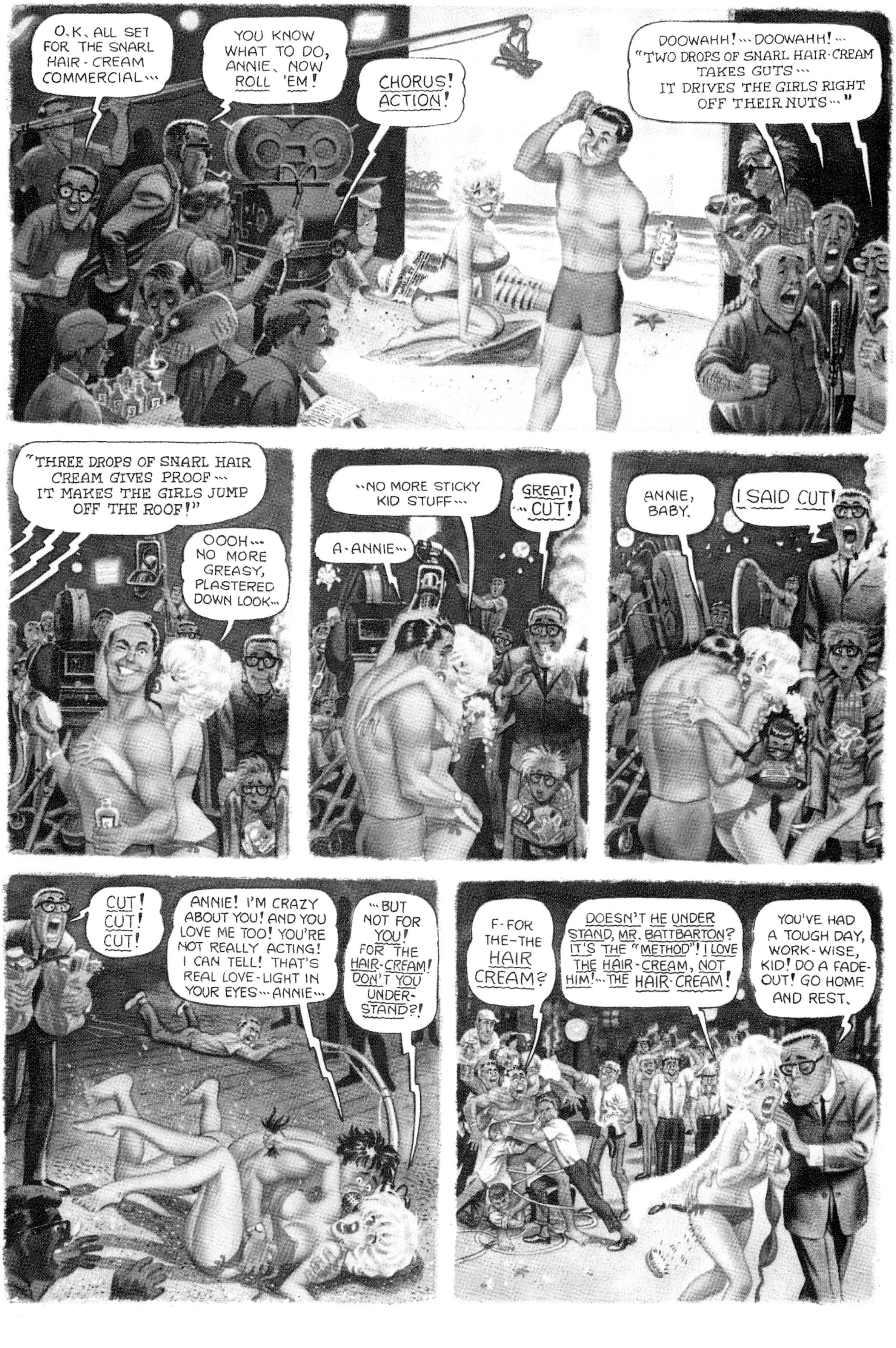
O.K. ALL SET FOR THE SNARL HAIR-CREAM COMMERCIAL...
YOU KNOW WHAT TO DO, ANNIE. NOW ROLL 'EM!
CHORUS! ACTION!
DOOWAHH!... DOOWAHH!... "TWO DROPS OF SNARL HAIR-CREAM TAKES GUTS... IT DRIVES THE GIRLS RIGHT OFF THEIR NUTS..."
"THREE DROPS OF SNARL HAIR CREAM GIVES PROOF... IT MAKES THE GIRLS JUMP OFF THE ROOF!"
OOOH... NO MORE GREASY, PLASTERED DOWN LOOK...
...NO MORE STICKY KID STUFF...
A-ANNIE...
GREAT! ...CUT!
ANNIE, BABY.
I SAID CUT!
CUT! CUT! CUT!
ANNIE! I'M CRAZY ABOUT YOU! AND YOU LOVE ME TOO! YOU'RE NOT REALLY ACTING! I CAN TELL! THAT'S REAL LOVE-LIGHT IN YOUR EYES... ANNIE...
...BUT NOT FOR YOU! FOR THE HAIR-CREAM! DON'T YOU UNDER-STAND?!
F-FOR THE-THE HAIR CREAM?
DOESN'T HE UNDER STAND, MR. BATTBARTON? IT'S THE "METHOD"! I LOVE THE HAIR-CREAM, NOT HIM!... THE HAIR-CREAM!
YOU'VE HAD A TOUGH DAY, WORK-WISE, KID! DO A FADE-OUT! GO HOME AND REST.

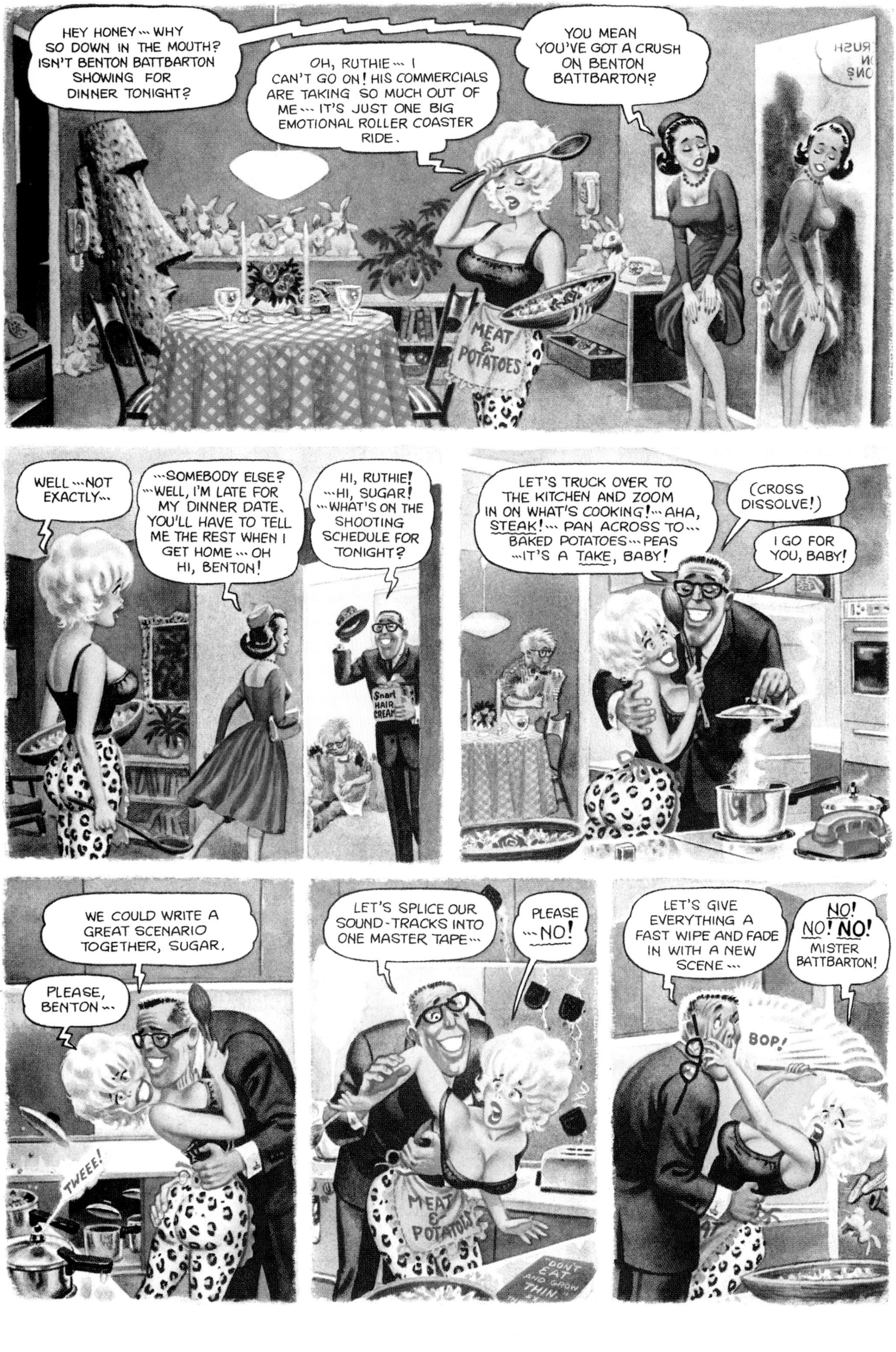
HEY HONEY ··· WHY SO DOWN IN THE MOUTH? ISN'T BENTON BATTBARTON SHOWING FOR DINNER TONIGHT?
OH, RUTHIE ··· I CAN'T GO ON! HIS COMMERCIALS ARE TAKING SO MUCH OUT OF ME ··· IT'S JUST ONE BIG EMOTIONAL ROLLER COASTER RIDE.
YOU MEAN YOU'VE GOT A CRUSH ON BENTON BATTBARTON?
MEAT & POTATOES
WELL ··· NOT EXACTLY···
···SOMEBODY ELSE? ···WELL, I'M LATE FOR MY DINNER DATE. YOU'LL HAVE TO TELL ME THE REST WHEN I GET HOME ··· OH HI, BENTON!
HI, RUTHIE! ···HI, SUGAR! ···WHAT'S ON THE SHOOTING SCHEDULE FOR TONIGHT?
Snarl HAIR CREAM
LET'S TRUCK OVER TO THE KITCHEN AND ZOOM IN ON WHAT'S COOKING! ··· AHA, STEAK! ··· PAN ACROSS TO ··· BAKED POTATOES ··· PEAS ··· IT'S A TAKE, BABY!
(CROSS DISSOLVE!)
I GO FOR YOU, BABY!
WE COULD WRITE A GREAT SCENARIO TOGETHER, SUGAR.
PLEASE, BENTON ···
TWEEE!
LET'S SPLICE OUR SOUND-TRACKS INTO ONE MASTER TAPE ···
PLEASE ··· NO!
MEAT & POTATOES
"DON'T EAT AND GROW THIN."
LET'S GIVE EVERYTHING A FAST WIPE AND FADE IN WITH A NEW SCENE ···
NO! NO! NO! MISTER BATTBARTON!
BOP!

8

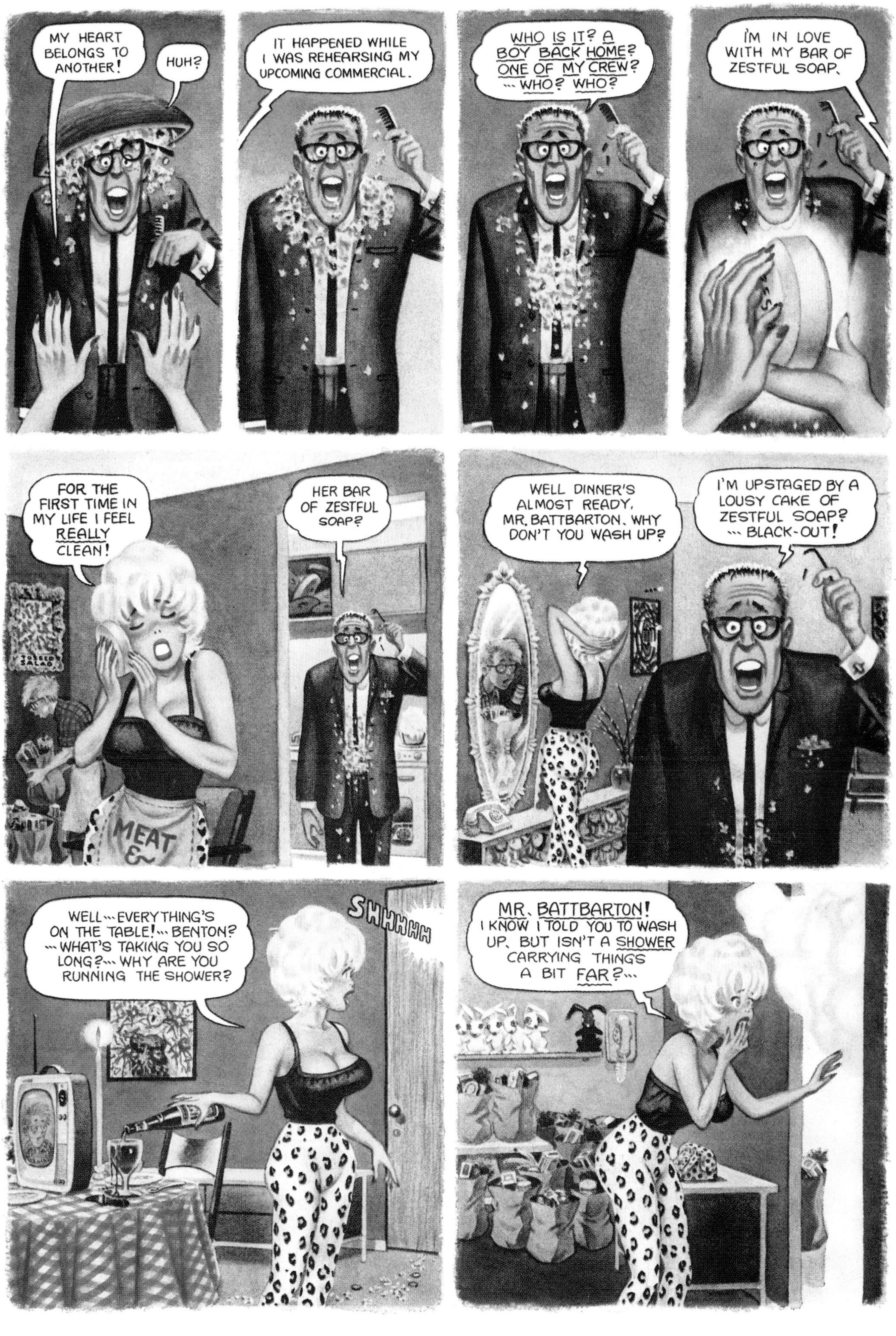
MY HEART BELONGS TO ANOTHER!
HUH?
IT HAPPENED WHILE I WAS REHEARSING MY UPCOMING COMMERCIAL.
WHO IS IT? A BOY BACK HOME? ONE OF MY CREW? ... WHO? WHO?
I'M IN LOVE WITH MY BAR OF ZESTFUL SOAP.
FOR THE FIRST TIME IN MY LIFE I FEEL REALLY CLEAN!
HER BAR OF ZESTFUL SOAP?
MEAT &
WELL DINNER'S ALMOST READY, MR. BATTBARTON. WHY DON'T YOU WASH UP?
I'M UPSTAGED BY A LOUSY CAKE OF ZESTFUL SOAP? ... BLACK-OUT!
WELL ... EVERYTHING'S ON THE TABLE! ... BENTON? ... WHAT'S TAKING YOU SO LONG? ... WHY ARE YOU RUNNING THE SHOWER?
SHHHHHH
MR. BATTBARTON! I KNOW I TOLD YOU TO WASH UP, BUT ISN'T A SHOWER CARRYING THINGS A BIT FAR? ...

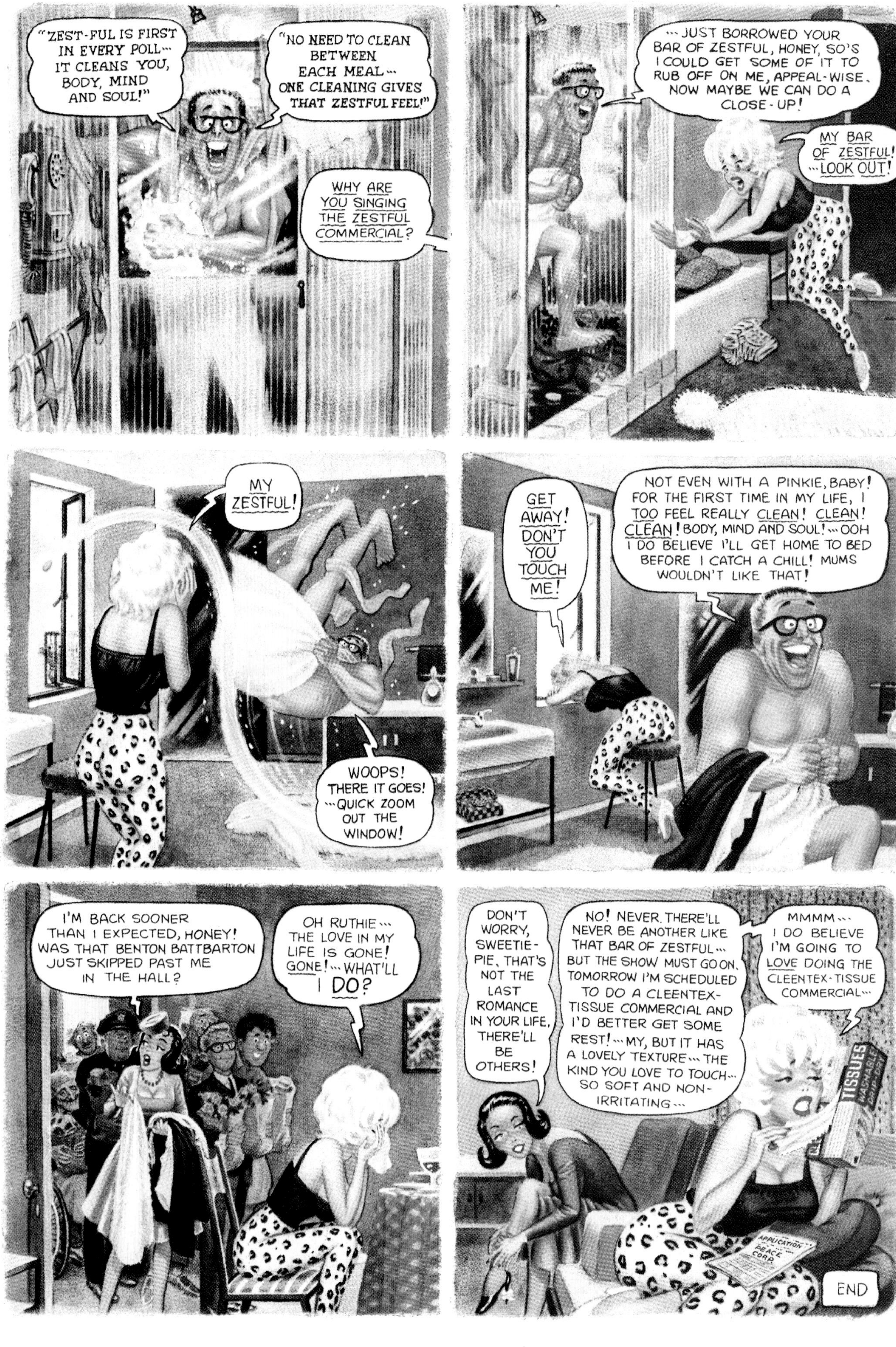
"ZEST-FUL IS FIRST IN EVERY POLL... IT CLEANS YOU, BODY, MIND AND SOUL!"
"NO NEED TO CLEAN BETWEEN EACH MEAL... ONE CLEANING GIVES THAT ZESTFUL FEEL!"
WHY ARE YOU SINGING THE ZESTFUL COMMERCIAL?
...JUST BORROWED YOUR BAR OF ZESTFUL, HONEY, SO'S I COULD GET SOME OF IT TO RUB OFF ON ME, APPEAL-WISE. NOW MAYBE WE CAN DO A CLOSE-UP!
MY BAR OF ZESTFUL! ...LOOK OUT!
MY ZESTFUL!
WOOPS! THERE IT GOES! ...QUICK ZOOM OUT THE WINDOW!
GET AWAY! DON'T YOU TOUCH ME!
NOT EVEN WITH A PINKIE, BABY! FOR THE FIRST TIME IN MY LIFE, I TOO FEEL REALLY CLEAN! CLEAN! CLEAN! BODY, MIND AND SOUL!...OOH I DO BELIEVE I'LL GET HOME TO BED BEFORE I CATCH A CHILL! MUMS WOULDN'T LIKE THAT!
I'M BACK SOONER THAN I EXPECTED, HONEY! WAS THAT BENTON BATTBARTON JUST SKIPPED PAST ME IN THE HALL?
OH RUTHIE... THE LOVE IN MY LIFE IS GONE! GONE!...WHAT'LL I DO?
DON'T WORRY, SWEETIE-PIE, THAT'S NOT THE LAST ROMANCE IN YOUR LIFE, THERE'LL BE OTHERS!
NO! NEVER. THERE'LL NEVER BE ANOTHER LIKE THAT BAR OF ZESTFUL... BUT THE SHOW MUST GO ON. TOMORROW I'M SCHEDULED TO DO A CLEENTEX-TISSUE COMMERCIAL AND I'D BETTER GET SOME REST!...MY, BUT IT HAS A LOVELY TEXTURE...THE KIND YOU LOVE TO TOUCH... SO SOFT AND NON-IRRITATING...
MMMM... I DO BELIEVE I'M GOING TO LOVE DOING THE CLEENTEX-TISSUE COMMERCIAL...
TISSUES
APPLICATION PEACE CORP.
END

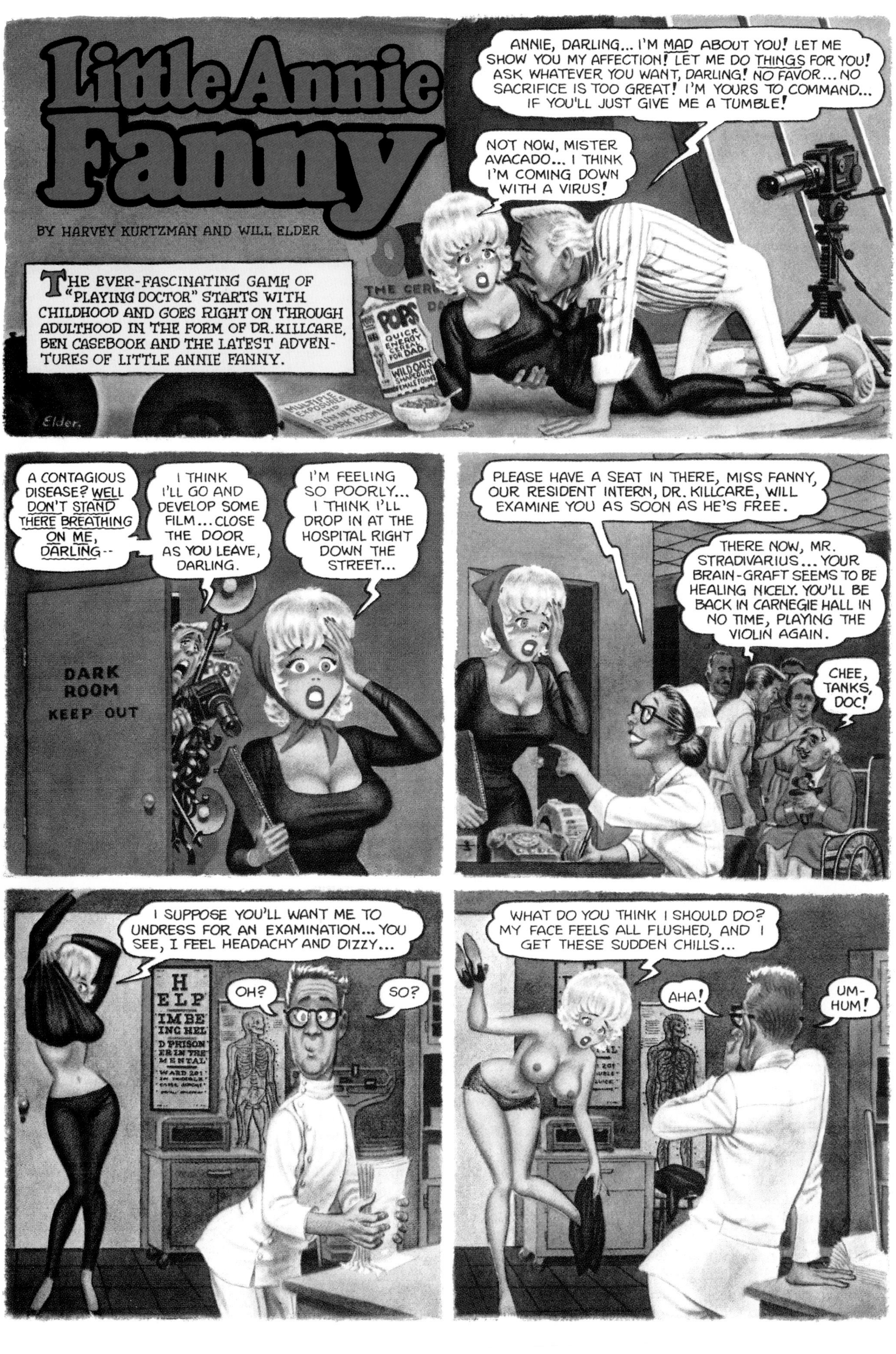

Little Annie Fanny
BY HARVEY KURTZMAN AND WILL ELDER
THE EVER-FASCINATING GAME OF "PLAYING DOCTOR" STARTS WITH CHILDHOOD AND GOES RIGHT ON THROUGH ADULTHOOD IN THE FORM OF DR. KILLCARE, BEN CASEBOOK AND THE LATEST ADVENTURES OF LITTLE ANNIE FANNY.
ANNIE, DARLING... I'M MAD ABOUT YOU! LET ME SHOW YOU MY AFFECTION! LET ME DO THINGS FOR YOU! ASK WHATEVER YOU WANT, DARLING! NO FAVOR... NO SACRIFICE IS TOO GREAT! I'M YOURS TO COMMAND... IF YOU'LL JUST GIVE ME A TUMBLE!
NOT NOW, MISTER AVACADO... I THINK I'M COMING DOWN WITH A VIRUS!
POPS QUICK ENERGY CEREAL FOR DAD.
WILD OATS
MULTIPLE EXPOSURES AND FUN IN THE DARK ROOM
Elder.
A CONTAGIOUS DISEASE? WELL DON'T STAND THERE BREATHING ON ME, DARLING--
I THINK I'LL GO AND DEVELOP SOME FILM... CLOSE THE DOOR AS YOU LEAVE, DARLING.
I'M FEELING SO POORLY... I THINK I'LL DROP IN AT THE HOSPITAL RIGHT DOWN THE STREET...
DARK ROOM KEEP OUT
PLEASE HAVE A SEAT IN THERE, MISS FANNY, OUR RESIDENT INTERN, DR. KILLCARE, WILL EXAMINE YOU AS SOON AS HE'S FREE.
THERE NOW, MR. STRADIVARIUS... YOUR BRAIN-GRAFT SEEMS TO BE HEALING NICELY. YOU'LL BE BACK IN CARNEGIE HALL IN NO TIME, PLAYING THE VIOLIN AGAIN.
CHEE, TANKS, DOC!
I SUPPOSE YOU'LL WANT ME TO UNDRESS FOR AN EXAMINATION... YOU SEE, I FEEL HEADACHY AND DIZZY...
OH?
SO?
WHAT DO YOU THINK I SHOULD DO? MY FACE FEELS ALL FLUSHED, AND I GET THESE SUDDEN CHILLS...
AHA!
UM-HUM!

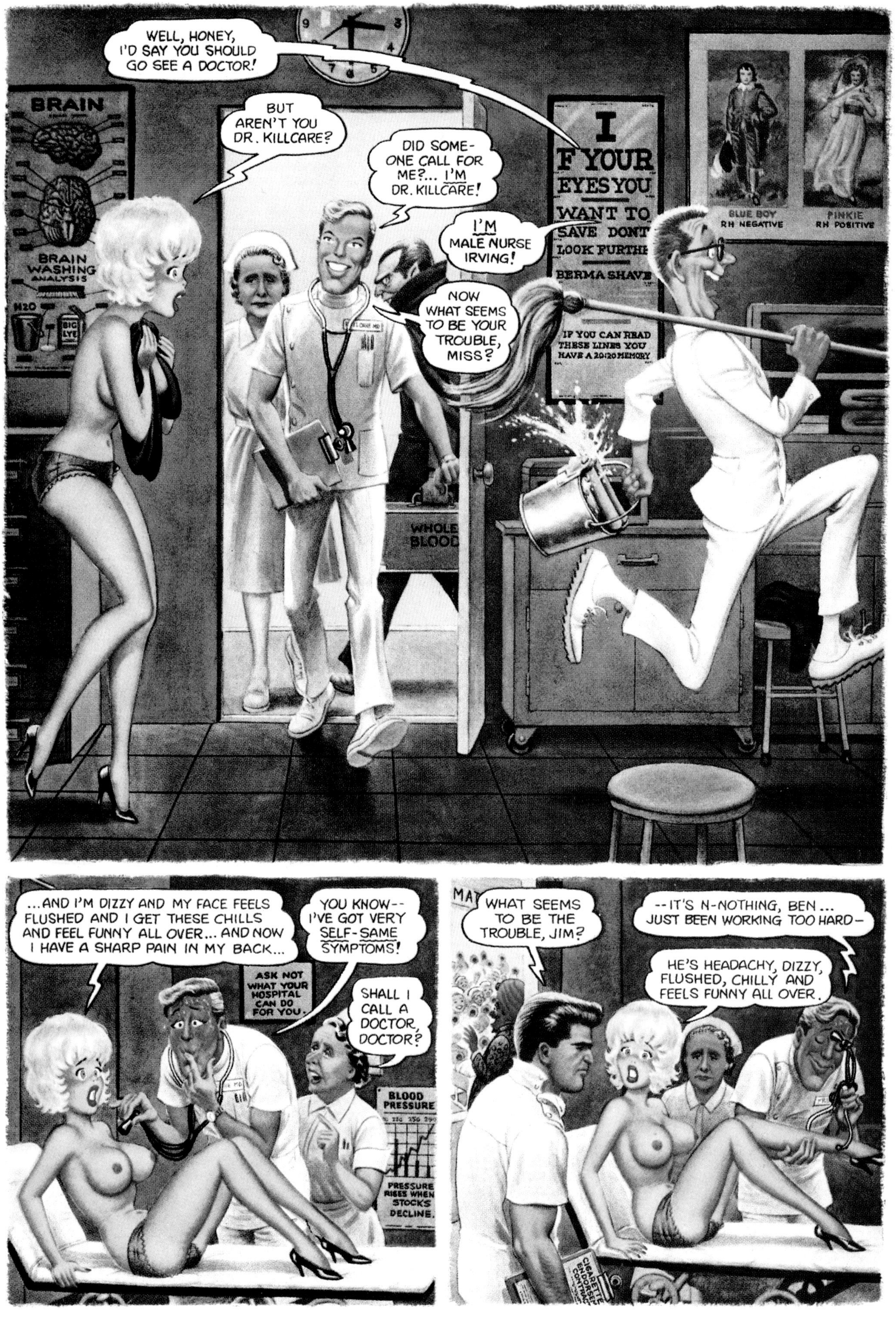
WELL, HONEY, I'D SAY YOU SHOULD GO SEE A DOCTOR!
BUT AREN'T YOU DR. KILLCARE?
DID SOME-ONE CALL FOR ME?... I'M DR. KILLCARE!
I'M MALE NURSE IRVING!
NOW WHAT SEEMS TO BE YOUR TROUBLE, MISS?
BRAIN
BRAIN WASHING ANALYSIS
I F YOUR EYES YOU WANT TO SAVE DONT LOOK FURTHE
BERMA SHAVE
IF YOU CAN READ THESE LINES YOU HAVE A 20/20 MEMORY
BLUE BOY RH NEGATIVE
PINKIE RH POSITIVE
WHOLE BLOOD
...AND I'M DIZZY AND MY FACE FEELS FLUSHED AND I GET THESE CHILLS AND FEEL FUNNY ALL OVER... AND NOW I HAVE A SHARP PAIN IN MY BACK...
YOU KNOW-- I'VE GOT VERY SELF-SAME SYMPTOMS!
SHALL I CALL A DOCTOR, DOCTOR?
ASK NOT WHAT YOUR HOSPITAL CAN DO FOR YOU.
BLOOD PRESSURE
PRESSURE RISES WHEN STOCKS DECLINE.
WHAT SEEMS TO BE THE TROUBLE, JIM?
--IT'S N-NOTHING, BEN... JUST BEEN WORKING TOO HARD--
HE'S HEADACHY, DIZZY, FLUSHED, CHILLY AND FEELS FUNNY ALL OVER.

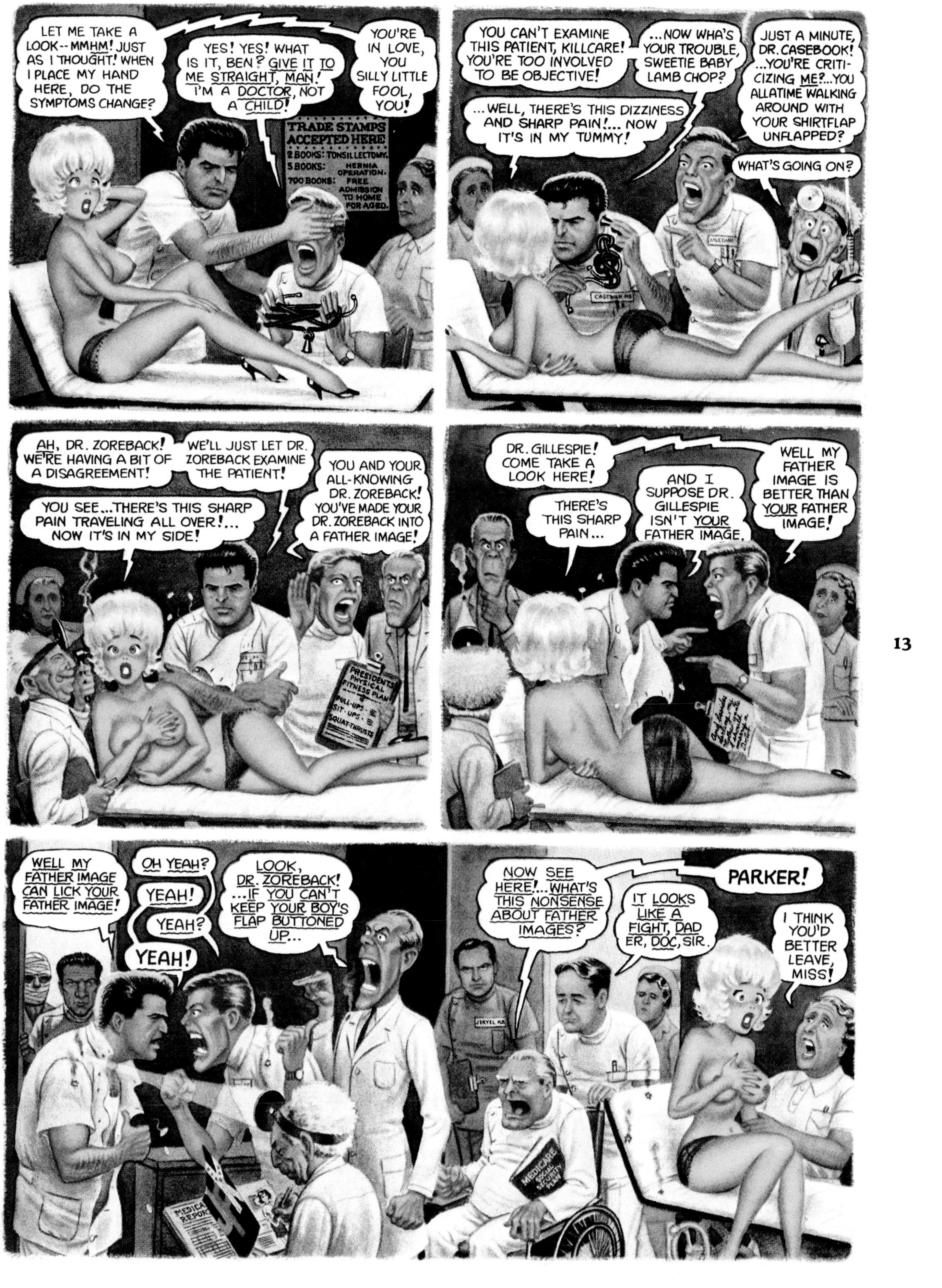
LET ME TAKE A LOOK--MMHM! JUST AS I THOUGHT! WHEN I PLACE MY HAND HERE, DO THE SYMPTOMS CHANGE?
YES! YES! WHAT IS IT, BEN? GIVE IT TO ME STRAIGHT, MAN! I'M A DOCTOR, NOT A CHILD!
YOU'RE IN LOVE, YOU SILLY LITTLE FOOL, YOU!
TRADE STAMPS ACCEPTED HERE!
2 BOOKS: TONSILLECTOMY.
5 BOOKS: HERNIA OPERATION.
700 BOOKS: FREE ADMISSION TO HOME FOR AGED.
YOU CAN'T EXAMINE THIS PATIENT, KILLCARE! YOU'RE TOO INVOLVED TO BE OBJECTIVE!
...NOW WHA'S YOUR TROUBLE, SWEETIE BABY LAMB CHOP?
...WELL, THERE'S THIS DIZZINESS AND SHARP PAIN!... NOW IT'S IN MY TUMMY!
JUST A MINUTE, DR. CASEBOOK! ...YOU'RE CRITICIZING ME?...YOU ALLATIME WALKING AROUND WITH YOUR SHIRTFLAP UNFLAPPED?
WHAT'S GOING ON?
AH, DR. ZOREBACK! WE'RE HAVING A BIT OF A DISAGREEMENT!
WE'LL JUST LET DR. ZOREBACK EXAMINE THE PATIENT!
YOU SEE...THERE'S THIS SHARP PAIN TRAVELING ALL OVER!... NOW IT'S IN MY SIDE!
YOU AND YOUR ALL-KNOWING DR. ZOREBACK! YOU'VE MADE YOUR DR. ZOREBACK INTO A FATHER IMAGE!
PRESIDENT'S PHYSICAL FITNESS PLAN
PULL-UPS
SIT-UPS
SQUAT-THRUSTS
DR. GILLESPIE! COME TAKE A LOOK HERE!
THERE'S THIS SHARP PAIN...
AND I SUPPOSE DR. GILLESPIE ISN'T YOUR FATHER IMAGE.
WELL MY FATHER IMAGE IS BETTER THAN YOUR FATHER IMAGE!
WELL MY FATHER IMAGE CAN LICK YOUR FATHER IMAGE!
OH YEAH?
YEAH!
YEAH?
YEAH!
LOOK, DR. ZOREBACK! ...IF YOU CAN'T KEEP YOUR BOY'S FLAP BUTTONED UP...
NOW SEE HERE!...WHAT'S THIS NONSENSE ABOUT FATHER IMAGES?
PARKER!
IT LOOKS LIKE A FIGHT, DAD ER, DOC, SIR.
I THINK YOU'D BETTER LEAVE, MISS!
MEDICARE

13

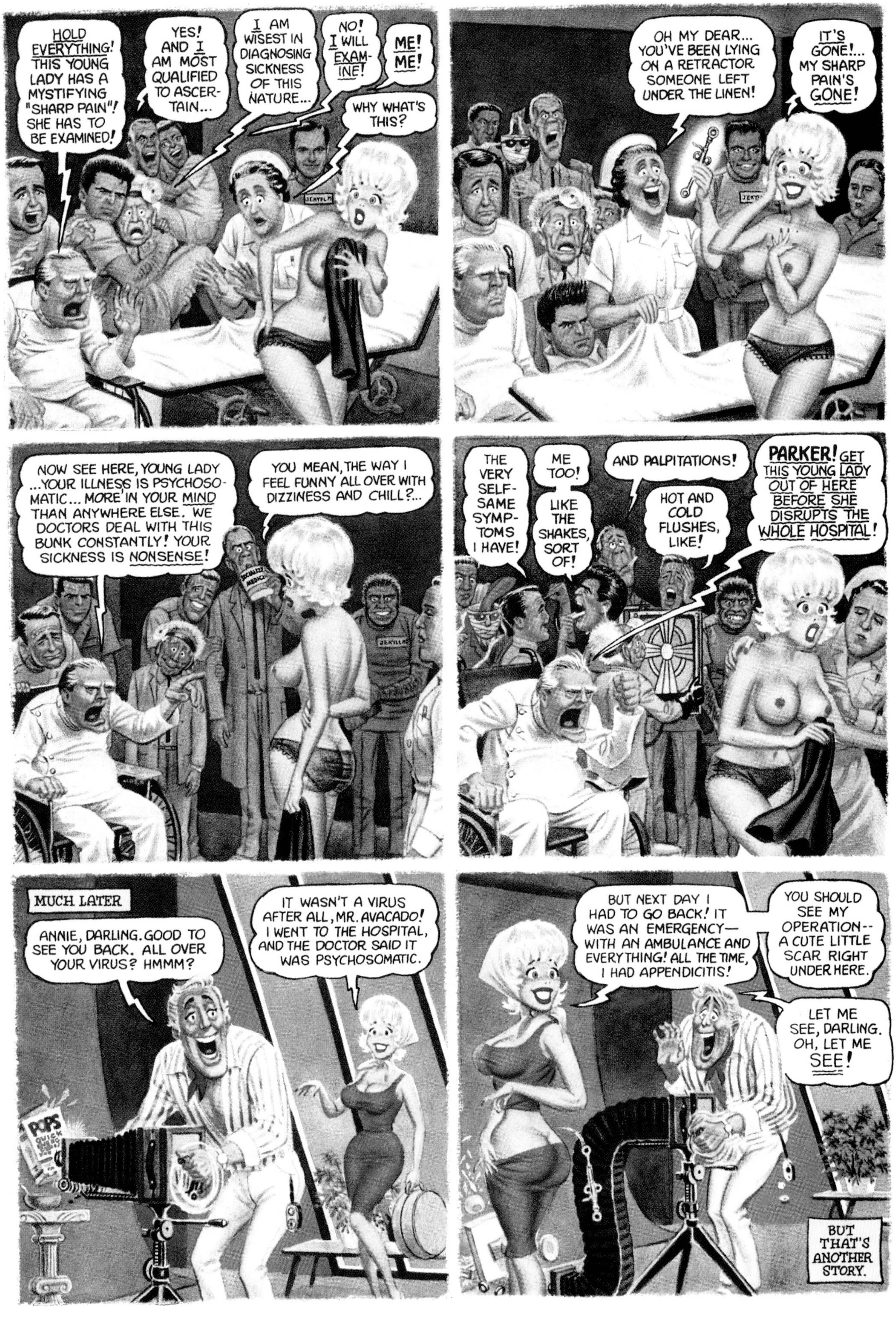

HOLD EVERYTHING! THIS YOUNG LADY HAS A MYSTIFYING "SHARP PAIN"! SHE HAS TO BE EXAMINED!
YES! AND I AM MOST QUALIFIED TO ASCERTAIN...
I AM WISEST IN DIAGNOSING SICKNESS OF THIS NATURE...
NO! I WILL EXAMINE!
ME! ME!
WHY WHAT'S THIS?
OH MY DEAR... YOU'VE BEEN LYING ON A RETRACTOR SOMEONE LEFT UNDER THE LINEN!
IT'S GONE!... MY SHARP PAIN'S GONE!
NOW SEE HERE, YOUNG LADY ...YOUR ILLNESS IS PSYCHOSOMATIC... MORE IN YOUR MIND THAN ANYWHERE ELSE. WE DOCTORS DEAL WITH THIS BUNK CONSTANTLY! YOUR SICKNESS IS NONSENSE!
YOU MEAN, THE WAY I FEEL FUNNY ALL OVER WITH DIZZINESS AND CHILL?...
THE VERY SELF-SAME SYMPTOMS I HAVE!
ME TOO!
LIKE THE SHAKES, SORT OF!
AND PALPITATIONS!
HOT AND COLD FLUSHES, LIKE!
PARKER! GET THIS YOUNG LADY OUT OF HERE BEFORE SHE DISRUPTS THE WHOLE HOSPITAL!
MUCH LATER
ANNIE, DARLING. GOOD TO SEE YOU BACK. ALL OVER YOUR VIRUS? HMMM?
IT WASN'T A VIRUS AFTER ALL, MR. AVACADO! I WENT TO THE HOSPITAL, AND THE DOCTOR SAID IT WAS PSYCHOSOMATIC.
BUT NEXT DAY I HAD TO GO BACK! IT WAS AN EMERGENCY— WITH AN AMBULANCE AND EVERYTHING! ALL THE TIME, I HAD APPENDICITIS!
YOU SHOULD SEE MY OPERATION-- A CUTE LITTLE SCAR RIGHT UNDER HERE.
LET ME SEE, DARLING. OH, LET ME SEE!
BUT THAT'S ANOTHER STORY.

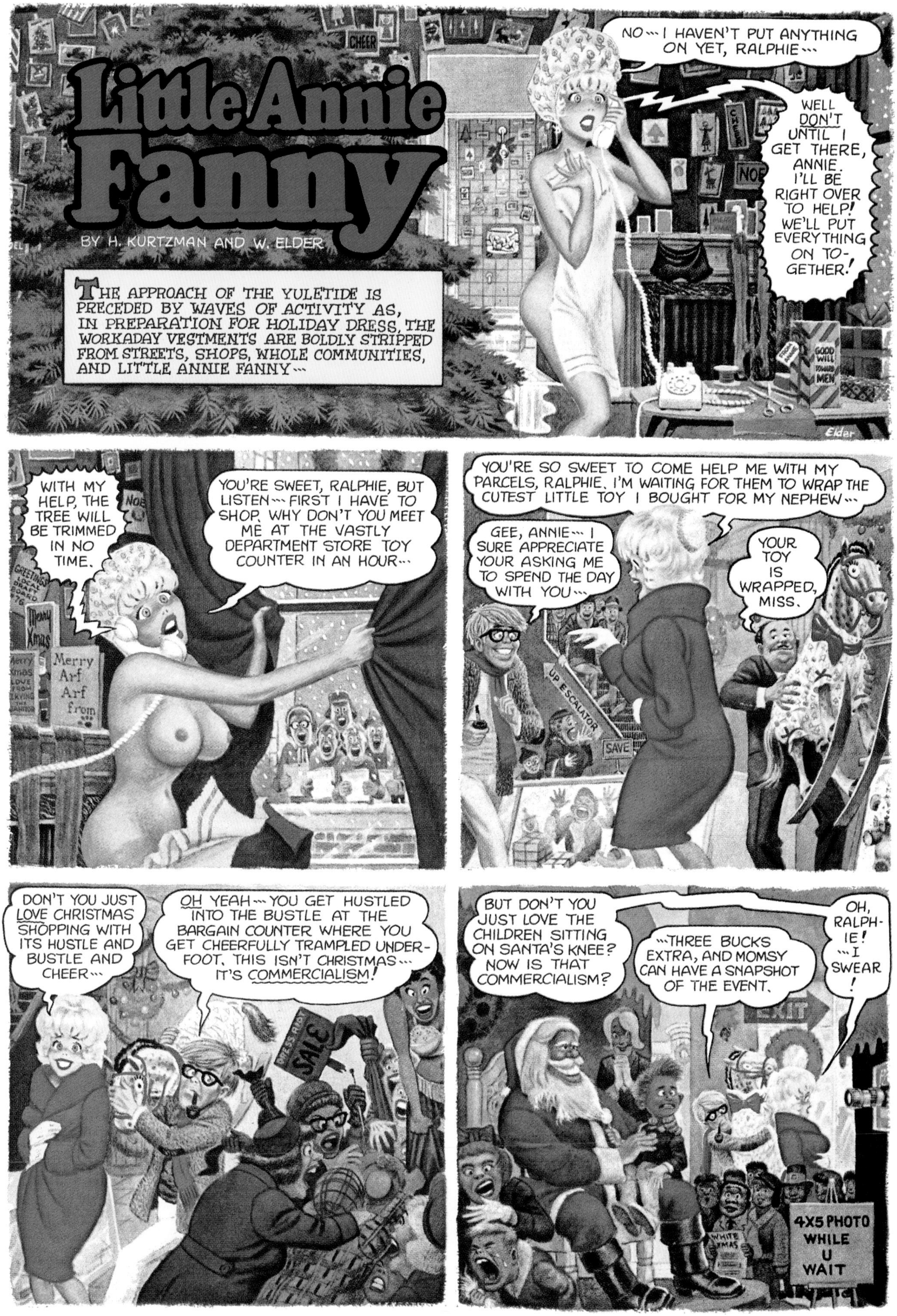

Little Annie Fanny
BY H. KURTZMAN AND W. ELDER
THE APPROACH OF THE YULETIDE IS PRECEDED BY WAVES OF ACTIVITY AS, IN PREPARATION FOR HOLIDAY DRESS, THE WORKADAY VESTMENTS ARE BOLDLY STRIPPED FROM STREETS, SHOPS, WHOLE COMMUNITIES, AND LITTLE ANNIE FANNY···
NO··· I HAVEN'T PUT ANYTHING ON YET, RALPHIE···
WELL DON'T UNTIL I GET THERE, ANNIE. I'LL BE RIGHT OVER TO HELP! WE'LL PUT EVERYTHING ON TO-GETHER!
CHEER
NOEL
GOOD WILL TOWARD MEN
Elder
WITH MY HELP, THE TREE WILL BE TRIMMED IN NO TIME.
YOU'RE SWEET, RALPHIE, BUT LISTEN··· FIRST I HAVE TO SHOP. WHY DON'T YOU MEET ME AT THE VASTLY DEPARTMENT STORE TOY COUNTER IN AN HOUR···
Merry Xmas
Merry Arf Arf from
YOU'RE SO SWEET TO COME HELP ME WITH MY PARCELS, RALPHIE. I'M WAITING FOR THEM TO WRAP THE CUTEST LITTLE TOY I BOUGHT FOR MY NEPHEW···
GEE, ANNIE··· I SURE APPRECIATE YOUR ASKING ME TO SPEND THE DAY WITH YOU···
YOUR TOY IS WRAPPED, MISS.
UP ESCALATOR
SAVE
DON'T YOU JUST LOVE CHRISTMAS SHOPPING WITH ITS HUSTLE AND BUSTLE AND CHEER···
OH YEAH··· YOU GET HUSTLED INTO THE BUSTLE AT THE BARGAIN COUNTER WHERE YOU GET CHEERFULLY TRAMPLED UNDER-FOOT. THIS ISN'T CHRISTMAS··· IT'S COMMERCIALISM!
SALE
BUT DON'T YOU JUST LOVE THE CHILDREN SITTING ON SANTA'S KNEE? NOW IS THAT COMMERCIALISM?
···THREE BUCKS EXTRA, AND MOMSY CAN HAVE A SNAPSHOT OF THE EVENT.
OH, RALPH-IE! ···I SWEAR!
EXIT
4X5 PHOTO WHILE U WAIT

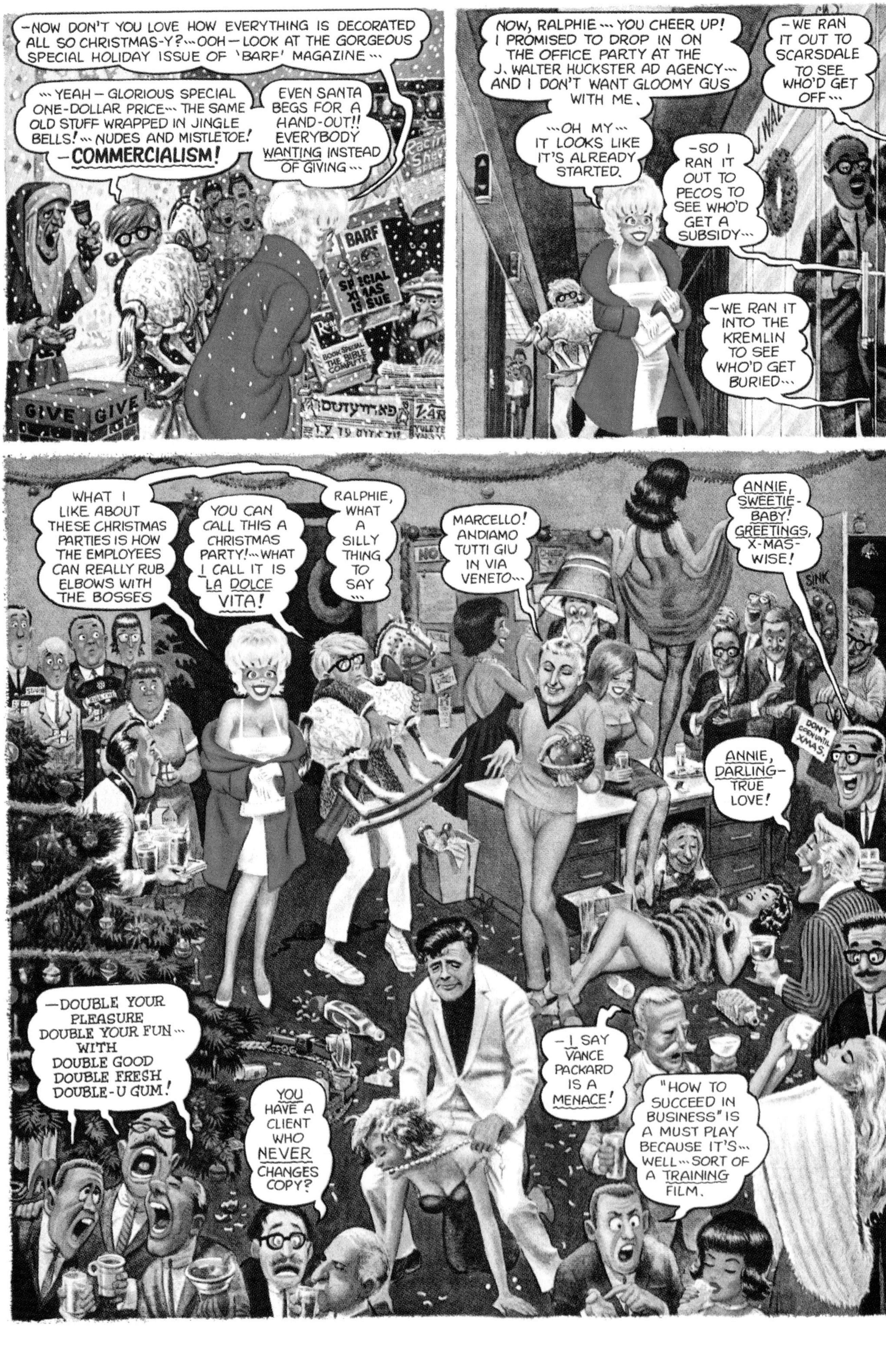
–NOW DON'T YOU LOVE HOW EVERYTHING IS DECORATED ALL SO CHRISTMAS-Y? ··· OOH – LOOK AT THE GORGEOUS SPECIAL HOLIDAY ISSUE OF 'BARF' MAGAZINE ···
··· YEAH – GLORIOUS SPECIAL ONE-DOLLAR PRICE ··· THE SAME OLD STUFF WRAPPED IN JINGLE BELLS! ··· NUDES AND MISTLETOE! – COMMERCIALISM!
EVEN SANTA BEGS FOR A HAND-OUT!! EVERYBODY WANTING INSTEAD OF GIVING ···
BARF
SPECIAL XMAS ISSUE
THE BIBLE COMPLETE
GIVE GIVE
NOW, RALPHIE ··· YOU CHEER UP! I PROMISED TO DROP IN ON THE OFFICE PARTY AT THE J. WALTER HUCKSTER AD AGENCY ··· AND I DON'T WANT GLOOMY GUS WITH ME.
···OH MY··· IT LOOKS LIKE IT'S ALREADY STARTED.
–WE RAN IT OUT TO SCARSDALE TO SEE WHO'D GET OFF ···
–SO I RAN IT OUT TO PECOS TO SEE WHO'D GET A SUBSIDY ···
–WE RAN IT INTO THE KREMLIN TO SEE WHO'D GET BURIED ···
WHAT I LIKE ABOUT THESE CHRISTMAS PARTIES IS HOW THE EMPLOYEES CAN REALLY RUB ELBOWS WITH THE BOSSES
YOU CAN CALL THIS A CHRISTMAS PARTY! ··· WHAT I CALL IT IS LA DOLCE VITA!
RALPHIE, WHAT A SILLY THING TO SAY
MARCELLO! ANDIAMO TUTTI GIU IN VIA VENETO ···
ANNIE, SWEETIE-BABY! GREETINGS, X-MAS-WISE!
SINK
DON'T OPEN UNTIL XMAS
ANNIE, DARLING– TRUE LOVE!
–DOUBLE YOUR PLEASURE DOUBLE YOUR FUN ··· WITH DOUBLE GOOD DOUBLE FRESH DOUBLE-U GUM!
YOU HAVE A CLIENT WHO NEVER CHANGES COPY?
–I SAY VANCE PACKARD IS A MENACE!
"HOW TO SUCCEED IN BUSINESS" IS A MUST PLAY BECAUSE IT'S ··· WELL ··· SORT OF A TRAINING FILM.

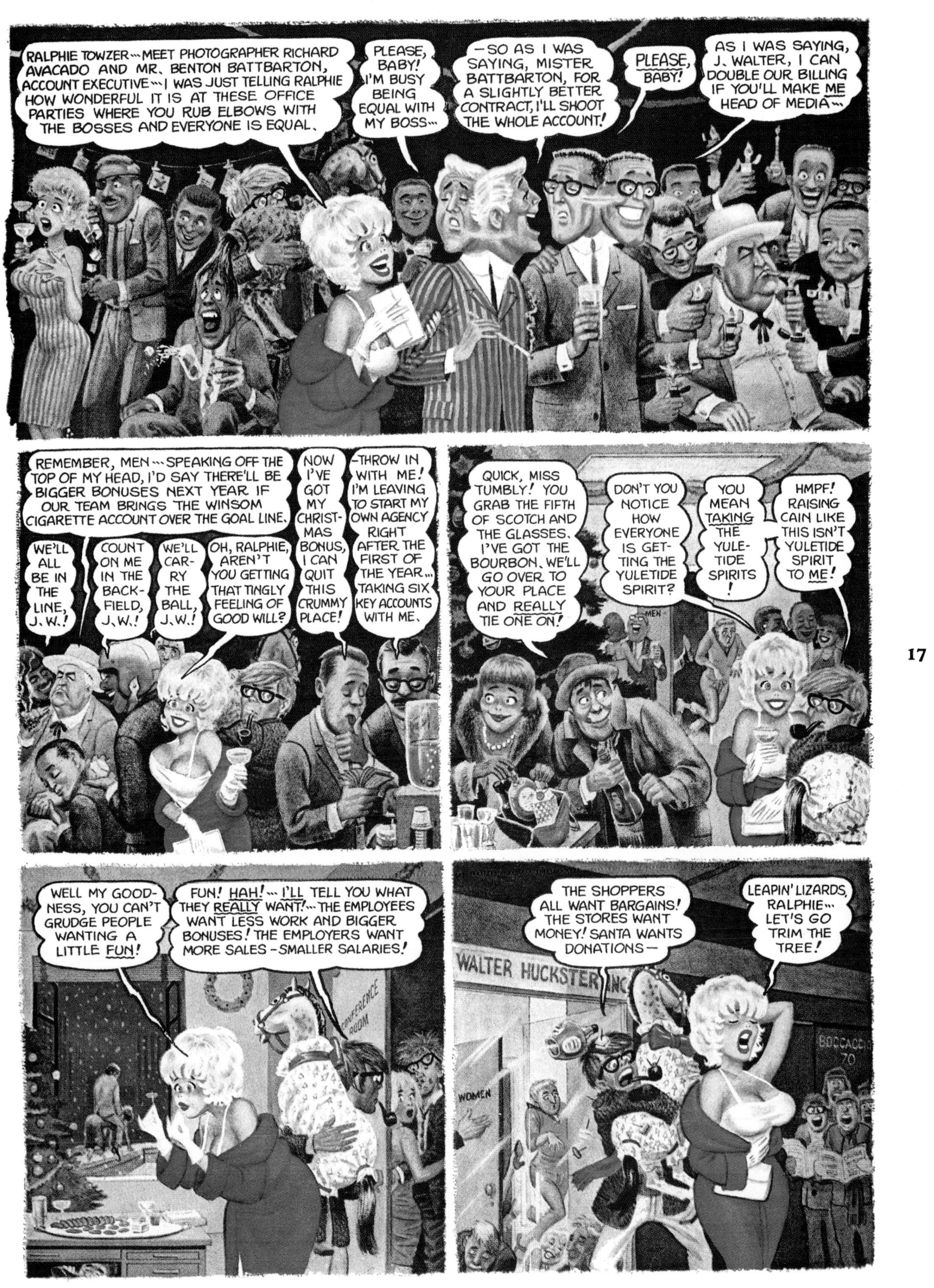
RALPHIE TOWZER ··· MEET PHOTOGRAPHER RICHARD AVACADO AND MR. BENTON BATTBARTON, ACCOUNT EXECUTIVE ··· I WAS JUST TELLING RALPHIE HOW WONDERFUL IT IS AT THESE OFFICE PARTIES WHERE YOU RUB ELBOWS WITH THE BOSSES AND EVERYONE IS EQUAL.
PLEASE, BABY! I'M BUSY BEING EQUAL WITH MY BOSS···
—SO AS I WAS SAYING, MISTER BATTBARTON, FOR A SLIGHTLY BETTER CONTRACT, I'LL SHOOT THE WHOLE ACCOUNT!
PLEASE, BABY!
AS I WAS SAYING, J. WALTER, I CAN DOUBLE OUR BILLING IF YOU'LL MAKE ME HEAD OF MEDIA···
REMEMBER, MEN ··· SPEAKING OFF THE TOP OF MY HEAD, I'D SAY THERE'LL BE BIGGER BONUSES NEXT YEAR IF OUR TEAM BRINGS THE WINSOM CIGARETTE ACCOUNT OVER THE GOAL LINE.
WE'LL ALL BE IN THE LINE, J.W.!
COUNT ON ME IN THE BACK-FIELD, J.W.!
WE'LL CAR-RY THE BALL, J.W.!
OH, RALPHIE, AREN'T YOU GETTING THAT TINGLY FEELING OF GOOD WILL?
NOW I'VE GOT MY CHRIST-MAS BONUS, I CAN QUIT THIS CRUMMY PLACE!
—THROW IN WITH ME! I'M LEAVING TO START MY OWN AGENCY RIGHT AFTER THE FIRST OF THE YEAR... TAKING SIX KEY ACCOUNTS WITH ME.
QUICK, MISS TUMBLY! YOU GRAB THE FIFTH OF SCOTCH AND THE GLASSES. I'VE GOT THE BOURBON. WE'LL GO OVER TO YOUR PLACE AND REALLY TIE ONE ON!
DON'T YOU NOTICE HOW EVERYONE IS GET-TING THE YULETIDE SPIRIT?
YOU MEAN TAKING THE YULE-TIDE SPIRITS!
HMPF! RAISING CAIN LIKE THIS ISN'T YULETIDE SPIRIT TO ME!
MEN
WELL MY GOOD-NESS, YOU CAN'T GRUDGE PEOPLE WANTING A LITTLE FUN!
FUN! HAH! ··· I'LL TELL YOU WHAT THEY REALLY WANT! ··· THE EMPLOYEES WANT LESS WORK AND BIGGER BONUSES! THE EMPLOYERS WANT MORE SALES - SMALLER SALARIES!
CONFERENCE ROOM
THE SHOPPERS ALL WANT BARGAINS! THE STORES WANT MONEY! SANTA WANTS DONATIONS—
LEAPIN' LIZARDS, RALPHIE··· LET'S GO TRIM THE TREE!
WALTER HUCKSTER INC
WOMEN

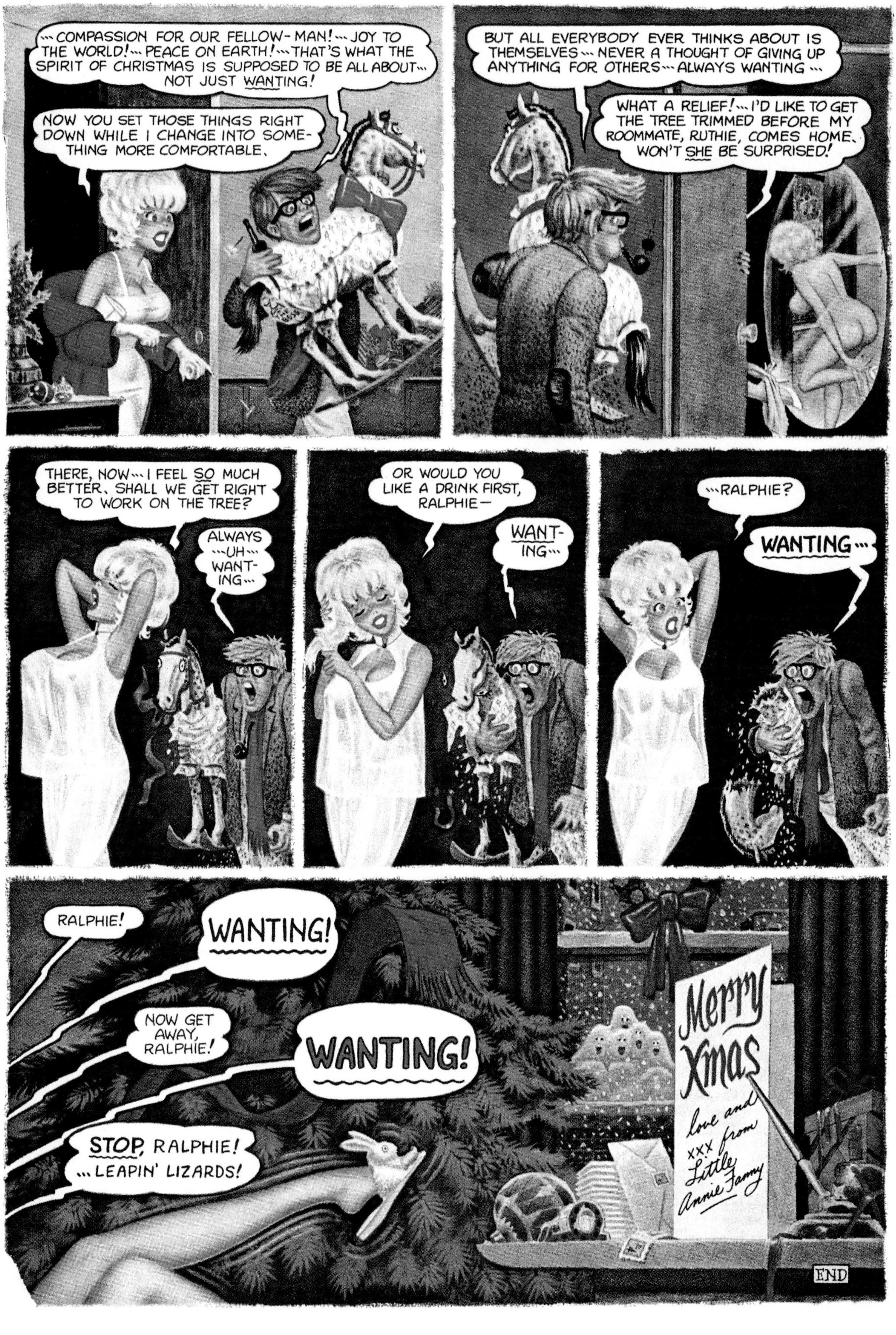
...COMPASSION FOR OUR FELLOW-MAN!...JOY TO THE WORLD!...PEACE ON EARTH!...THAT'S WHAT THE SPIRIT OF CHRISTMAS IS SUPPOSED TO BE ALL ABOUT... NOT JUST WANTING!
NOW YOU SET THOSE THINGS RIGHT DOWN WHILE I CHANGE INTO SOMETHING MORE COMFORTABLE.
BUT ALL EVERYBODY EVER THINKS ABOUT IS THEMSELVES... NEVER A THOUGHT OF GIVING UP ANYTHING FOR OTHERS... ALWAYS WANTING...
WHAT A RELIEF!...I'D LIKE TO GET THE TREE TRIMMED BEFORE MY ROOMMATE, RUTHIE, COMES HOME. WON'T SHE BE SURPRISED!
THERE, NOW... I FEEL SO MUCH BETTER. SHALL WE GET RIGHT TO WORK ON THE TREE?
ALWAYS ...UH... WANTING...
OR WOULD YOU LIKE A DRINK FIRST, RALPHIE—
WANTING...
...RALPHIE?
WANTING...
RALPHIE!
WANTING!
NOW GET AWAY, RALPHIE!
WANTING!
STOP, RALPHIE! ...LEAPIN' LIZARDS!
Merry Xmas love and xxx from Little Annie Fanny
END

18

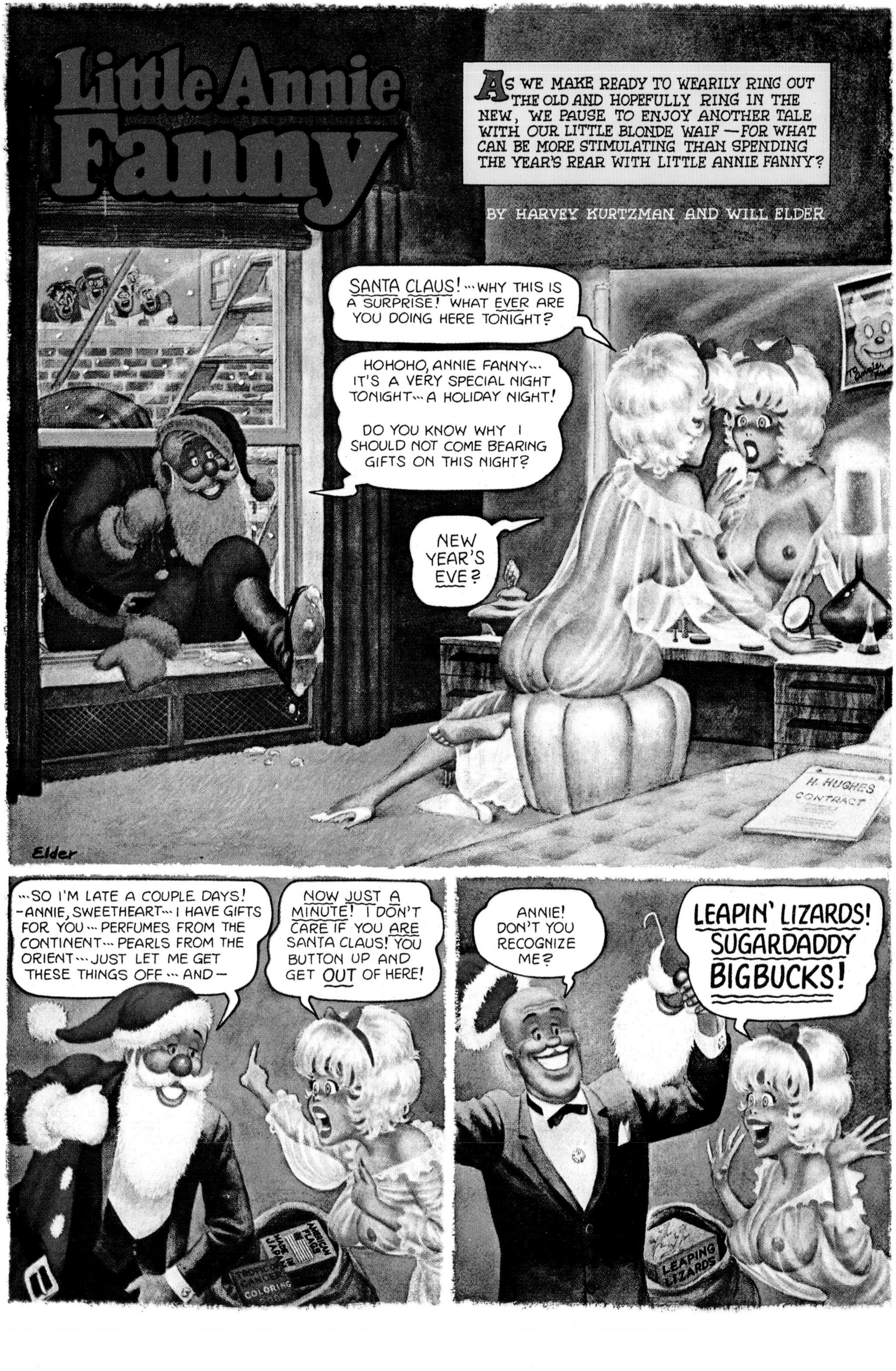
Little Annie Fanny
AS WE MAKE READY TO WEARILY RING OUT THE OLD AND HOPEFULLY RING IN THE NEW, WE PAUSE TO ENJOY ANOTHER TALE WITH OUR LITTLE BLONDE WAIF —FOR WHAT CAN BE MORE STIMULATING THAN SPENDING THE YEAR'S REAR WITH LITTLE ANNIE FANNY?
BY HARVEY KURTZMAN AND WILL ELDER
SANTA CLAUS! ··· WHY THIS IS A SURPRISE! WHAT EVER ARE YOU DOING HERE TONIGHT?
HOHOHO, ANNIE FANNY··· IT'S A VERY SPECIAL NIGHT TONIGHT··· A HOLIDAY NIGHT!
DO YOU KNOW WHY I SHOULD NOT COME BEARING GIFTS ON THIS NIGHT?
NEW YEAR'S EVE?
H. HUGHES CONTRACT
Elder
···SO I'M LATE A COUPLE DAYS! -ANNIE, SWEETHEART··· I HAVE GIFTS FOR YOU··· PERFUMES FROM THE CONTINENT··· PEARLS FROM THE ORIENT··· JUST LET ME GET THESE THINGS OFF··· AND—
NOW JUST A MINUTE! I DON'T CARE IF YOU ARE SANTA CLAUS! YOU BUTTON UP AND GET OUT OF HERE!
AMERICAN FLAGS
MADE IN JAPAN
COLORING
ANNIE! DON'T YOU RECOGNIZE ME?
LEAPIN' LIZARDS! SUGARDADDY BIGBUCKS!
LEAPING LIZARDS

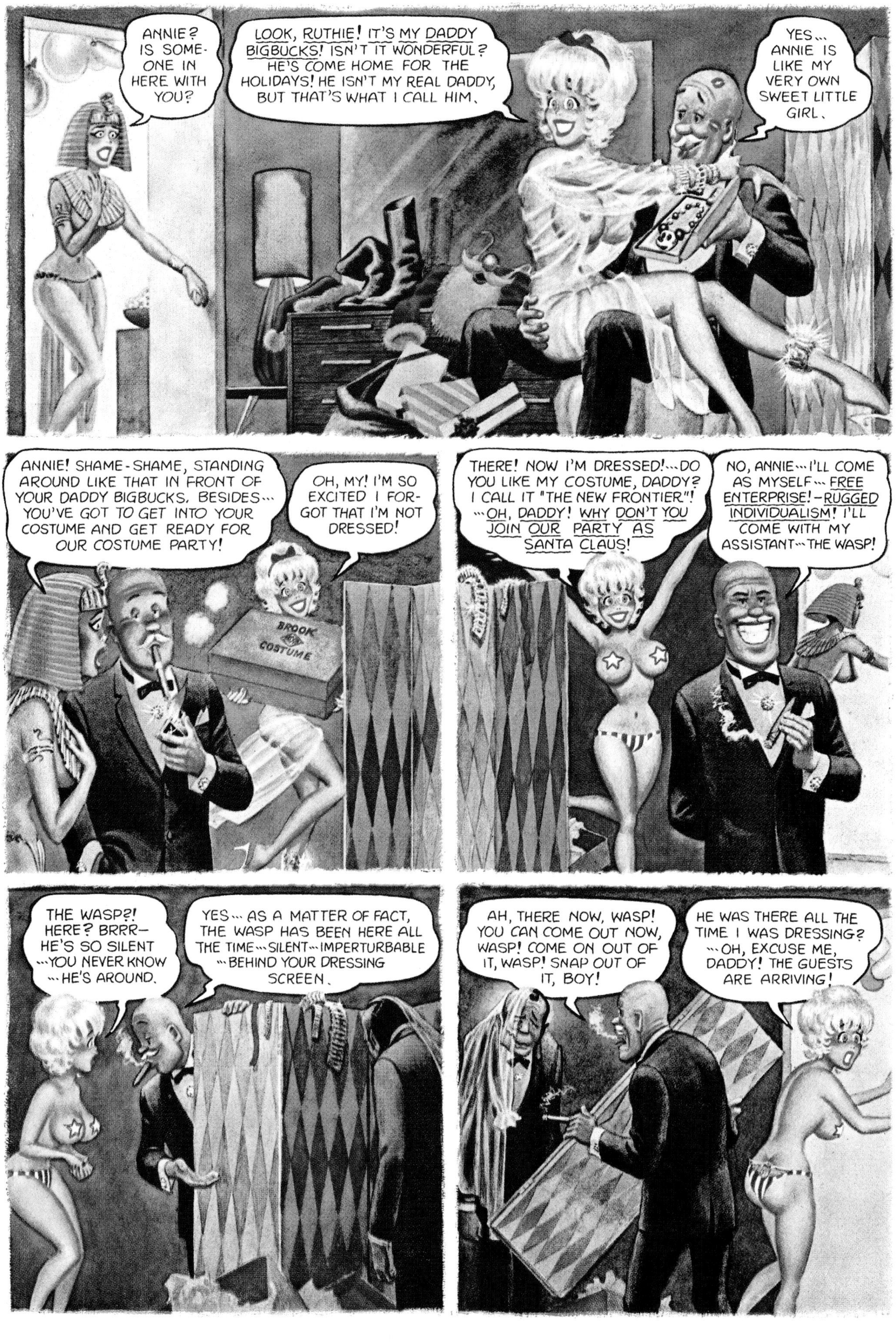
ANNIE? IS SOME-ONE IN HERE WITH YOU?
LOOK, RUTHIE! IT'S MY DADDY BIGBUCKS! ISN'T IT WONDERFUL? HE'S COME HOME FOR THE HOLIDAYS! HE ISN'T MY REAL DADDY, BUT THAT'S WHAT I CALL HIM.
YES... ANNIE IS LIKE MY VERY OWN SWEET LITTLE GIRL.
ANNIE! SHAME-SHAME, STANDING AROUND LIKE THAT IN FRONT OF YOUR DADDY BIGBUCKS. BESIDES... YOU'VE GOT TO GET INTO YOUR COSTUME AND GET READY FOR OUR COSTUME PARTY!
OH, MY! I'M SO EXCITED I FOR-GOT THAT I'M NOT DRESSED!
BROOK COSTUME
THERE! NOW I'M DRESSED!...DO YOU LIKE MY COSTUME, DADDY? I CALL IT "THE NEW FRONTIER"! ...OH, DADDY! WHY DON'T YOU JOIN OUR PARTY AS SANTA CLAUS!
NO, ANNIE...I'LL COME AS MYSELF... FREE ENTERPRISE!—RUGGED INDIVIDUALISM! I'LL COME WITH MY ASSISTANT...THE WASP!
THE WASP?! HERE? BRRR— HE'S SO SILENT ...YOU NEVER KNOW ...HE'S AROUND.
YES... AS A MATTER OF FACT, THE WASP HAS BEEN HERE ALL THE TIME...SILENT...IMPERTURBABLE ...BEHIND YOUR DRESSING SCREEN.
AH, THERE NOW, WASP! YOU CAN COME OUT NOW, WASP! COME ON OUT OF IT, WASP! SNAP OUT OF IT, BOY!
HE WAS THERE ALL THE TIME I WAS DRESSING? ...OH, EXCUSE ME, DADDY! THE GUESTS ARE ARRIVING!

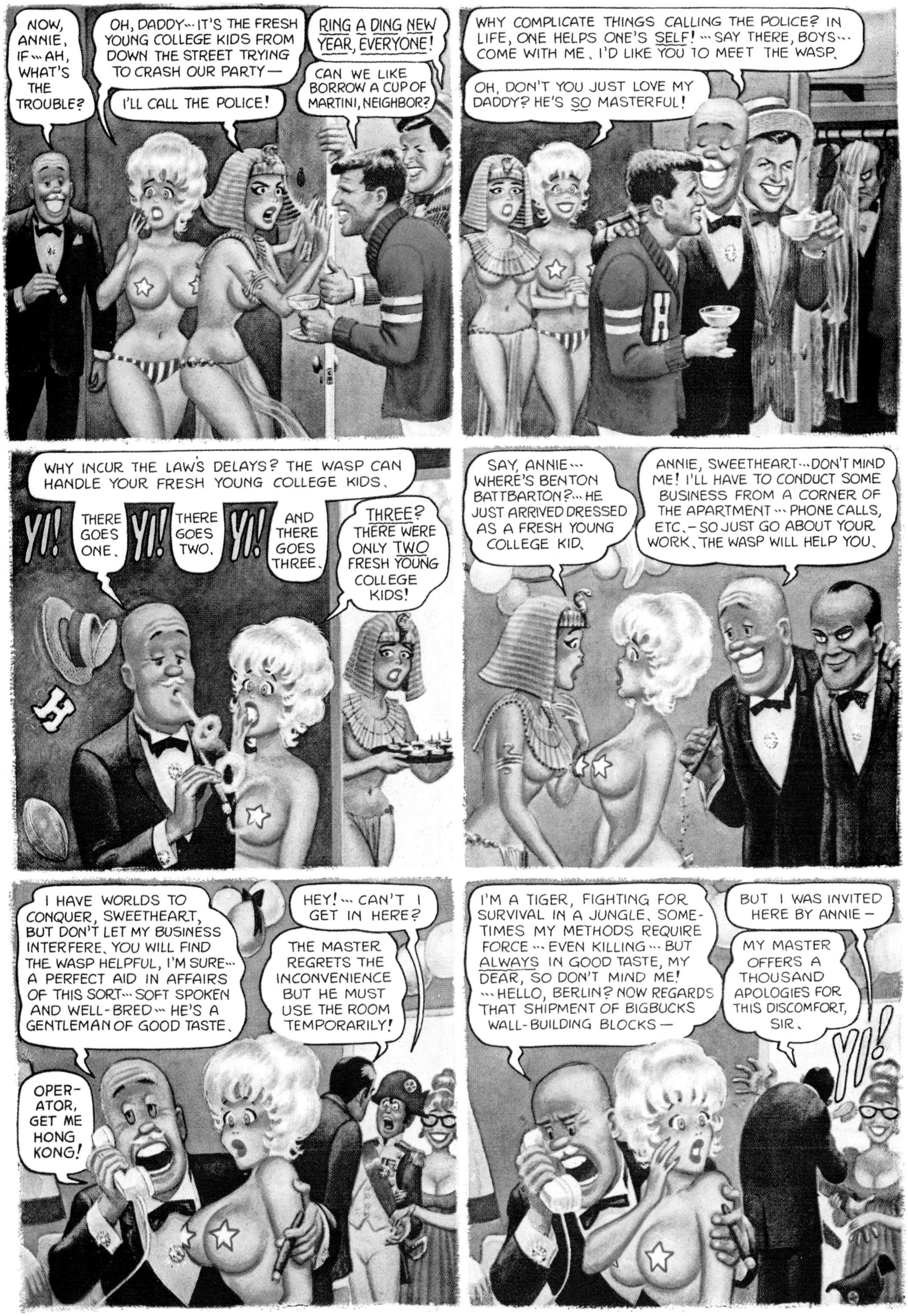
NOW, ANNIE, IF ··· AH, WHAT'S THE TROUBLE?
OH, DADDY ··· IT'S THE FRESH YOUNG COLLEGE KIDS FROM DOWN THE STREET TRYING TO CRASH OUR PARTY —
I'LL CALL THE POLICE!
RING A DING NEW YEAR, EVERYONE!
CAN WE LIKE BORROW A CUP OF MARTINI, NEIGHBOR?
WHY COMPLICATE THINGS CALLING THE POLICE? IN LIFE, ONE HELPS ONE'S SELF! ··· SAY THERE, BOYS ··· COME WITH ME. I'D LIKE YOU TO MEET THE WASP.
OH, DON'T YOU JUST LOVE MY DADDY? HE'S SO MASTERFUL!
WHY INCUR THE LAW'S DELAYS? THE WASP CAN HANDLE YOUR FRESH YOUNG COLLEGE KIDS.
YI!
THERE GOES ONE.
YI!
THERE GOES TWO.
YI!
AND THERE GOES THREE.
THREE? THERE WERE ONLY TWO FRESH YOUNG COLLEGE KIDS!
SAY, ANNIE ··· WHERE'S BENTON BATTBARTON? ··· HE JUST ARRIVED DRESSED AS A FRESH YOUNG COLLEGE KID.
ANNIE, SWEETHEART ··· DON'T MIND ME! I'LL HAVE TO CONDUCT SOME BUSINESS FROM A CORNER OF THE APARTMENT ··· PHONE CALLS, ETC. – SO JUST GO ABOUT YOUR WORK. THE WASP WILL HELP YOU.
I HAVE WORLDS TO CONQUER, SWEETHEART, BUT DON'T LET MY BUSINESS INTERFERE. YOU WILL FIND THE WASP HELPFUL, I'M SURE ··· A PERFECT AID IN AFFAIRS OF THIS SORT ··· SOFT SPOKEN AND WELL-BRED ··· HE'S A GENTLEMAN OF GOOD TASTE.
HEY! ··· CAN'T I GET IN HERE?
THE MASTER REGRETS THE INCONVENIENCE BUT HE MUST USE THE ROOM TEMPORARILY!
OPERATOR, GET ME HONG KONG!
I'M A TIGER, FIGHTING FOR SURVIVAL IN A JUNGLE. SOMETIMES MY METHODS REQUIRE FORCE ··· EVEN KILLING ··· BUT ALWAYS IN GOOD TASTE, MY DEAR, SO DON'T MIND ME! ··· HELLO, BERLIN? NOW REGARDS THAT SHIPMENT OF BIGBUCKS WALL-BUILDING BLOCKS —
BUT I WAS INVITED HERE BY ANNIE —
MY MASTER OFFERS A THOUSAND APOLOGIES FOR THIS DISCOMFORT, SIR.
YI!

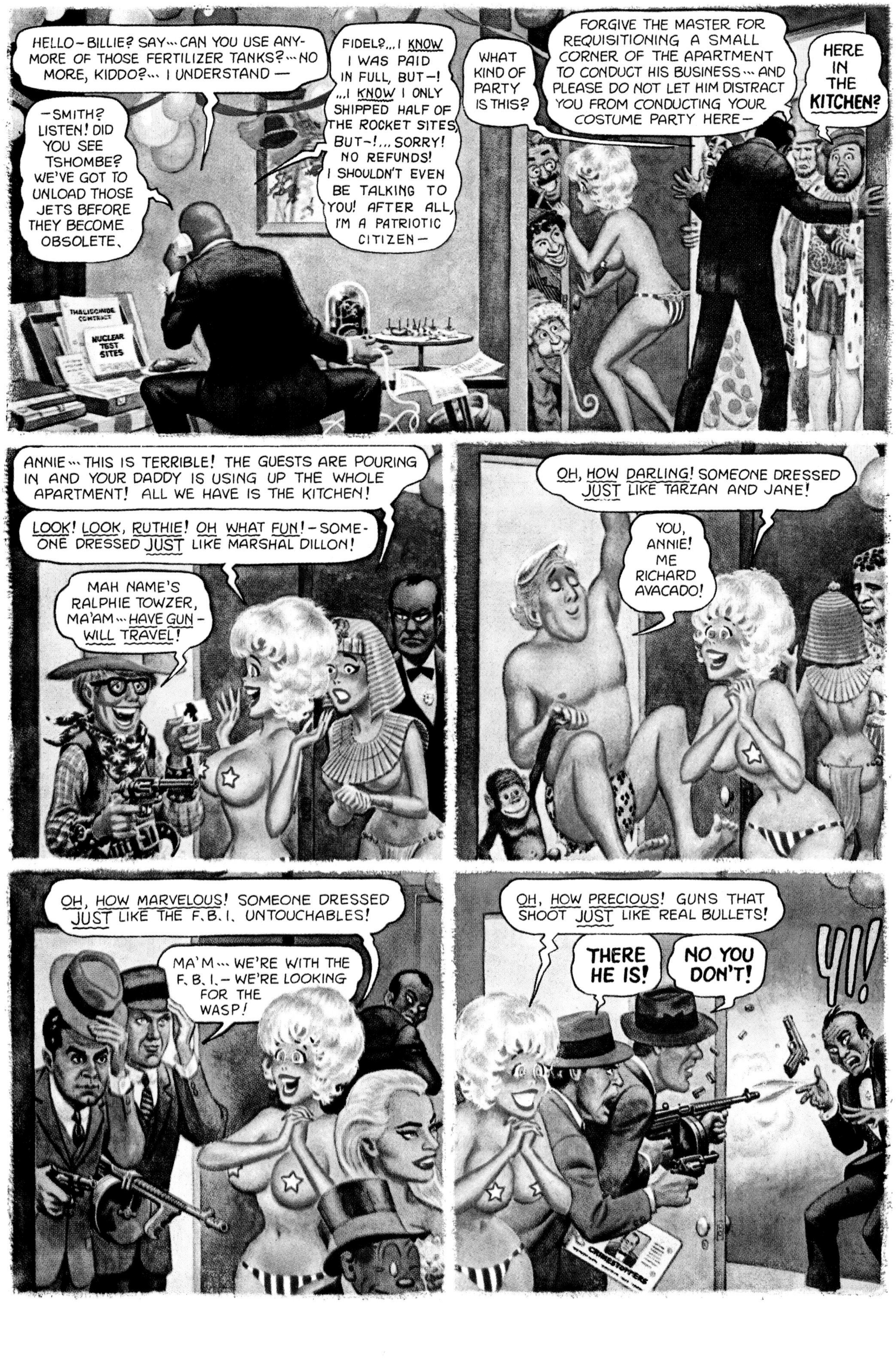
HELLO – BILLIE? SAY … CAN YOU USE ANY-MORE OF THOSE FERTILIZER TANKS? … NO MORE, KIDDO? … I UNDERSTAND —
— SMITH? LISTEN! DID YOU SEE TSHOMBE? WE'VE GOT TO UNLOAD THOSE JETS BEFORE THEY BECOME OBSOLETE.
FIDEL? … I KNOW I WAS PAID IN FULL, BUT –! … I KNOW I ONLY SHIPPED HALF OF THE ROCKET SITES, BUT –! … SORRY! NO REFUNDS! I SHOULDN'T EVEN BE TALKING TO YOU! AFTER ALL, I'M A PATRIOTIC CITIZEN —
NUCLEAR TEST SITES
WHAT KIND OF PARTY IS THIS?
FORGIVE THE MASTER FOR REQUISITIONING A SMALL CORNER OF THE APARTMENT TO CONDUCT HIS BUSINESS … AND PLEASE DO NOT LET HIM DISTRACT YOU FROM CONDUCTING YOUR COSTUME PARTY HERE —
HERE IN THE KITCHEN?
ANNIE … THIS IS TERRIBLE! THE GUESTS ARE POURING IN AND YOUR DADDY IS USING UP THE WHOLE APARTMENT! ALL WE HAVE IS THE KITCHEN!
LOOK! LOOK, RUTHIE! OH WHAT FUN! – SOME-ONE DRESSED JUST LIKE MARSHAL DILLON!
MAH NAME'S RALPHIE TOWZER, MA'AM … HAVE GUN – WILL TRAVEL!
OH, HOW DARLING! SOMEONE DRESSED JUST LIKE TARZAN AND JANE!
YOU, ANNIE! ME RICHARD AVACADO!
OH, HOW MARVELOUS! SOMEONE DRESSED JUST LIKE THE F.B.I. UNTOUCHABLES!
MA'M … WE'RE WITH THE F.B.I. – WE'RE LOOKING FOR THE WASP!
OH, HOW PRECIOUS! GUNS THAT SHOOT JUST LIKE REAL BULLETS!
THERE HE IS!
NO YOU DON'T!
YI!

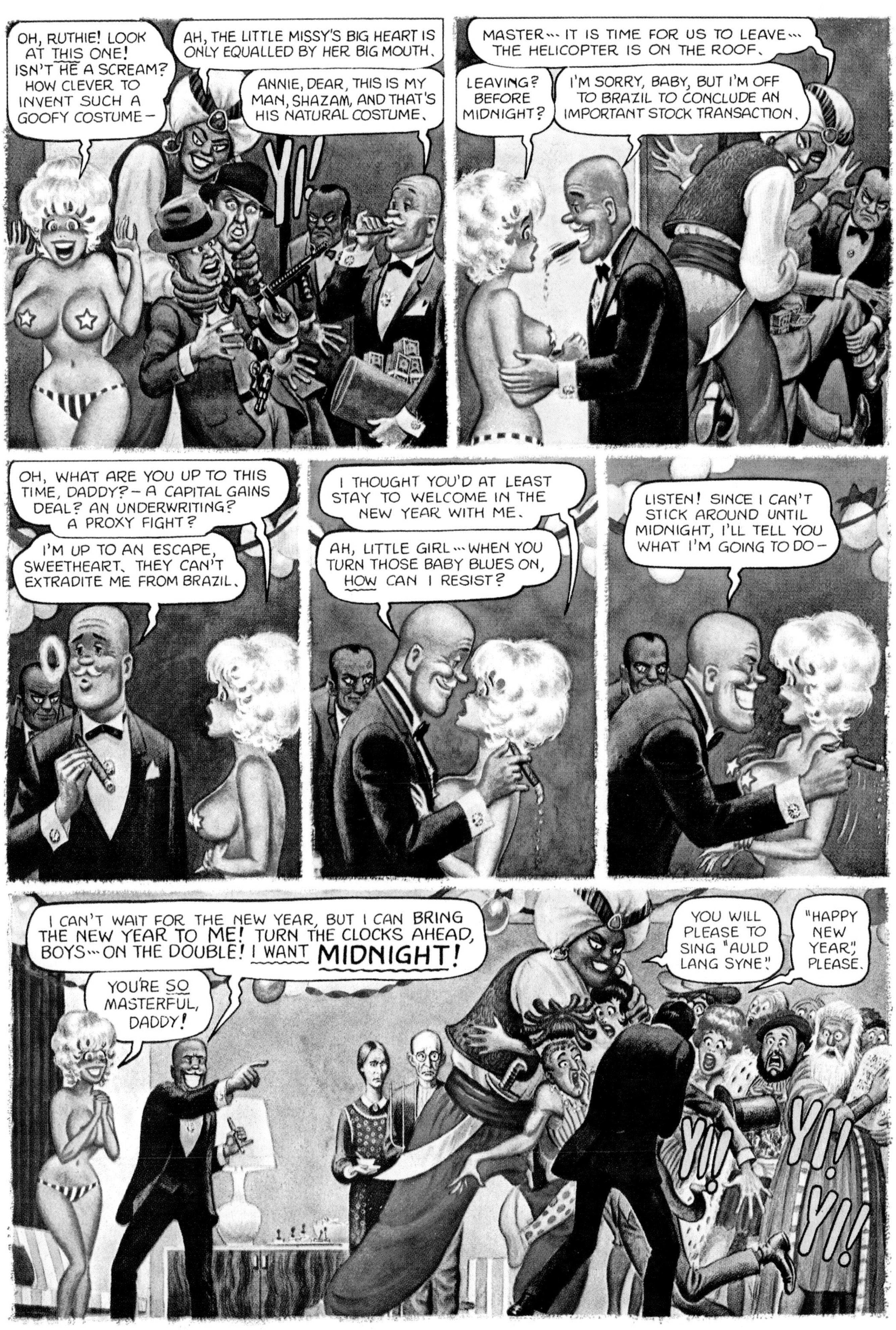
OH, RUTHIE! LOOK AT THIS ONE! ISN'T HE A SCREAM? HOW CLEVER TO INVENT SUCH A GOOFY COSTUME—
AH, THE LITTLE MISSY'S BIG HEART IS ONLY EQUALLED BY HER BIG MOUTH.
ANNIE, DEAR, THIS IS MY MAN, SHAZAM, AND THAT'S HIS NATURAL COSTUME.
YI!
MASTER... IT IS TIME FOR US TO LEAVE... THE HELICOPTER IS ON THE ROOF.
LEAVING? BEFORE MIDNIGHT?
I'M SORRY, BABY, BUT I'M OFF TO BRAZIL TO CONCLUDE AN IMPORTANT STOCK TRANSACTION.
OH, WHAT ARE YOU UP TO THIS TIME, DADDY?— A CAPITAL GAINS DEAL? AN UNDERWRITING? A PROXY FIGHT?
I'M UP TO AN ESCAPE, SWEETHEART. THEY CAN'T EXTRADITE ME FROM BRAZIL.
I THOUGHT YOU'D AT LEAST STAY TO WELCOME IN THE NEW YEAR WITH ME.
AH, LITTLE GIRL... WHEN YOU TURN THOSE BABY BLUES ON, HOW CAN I RESIST?
LISTEN! SINCE I CAN'T STICK AROUND UNTIL MIDNIGHT, I'LL TELL YOU WHAT I'M GOING TO DO—
I CAN'T WAIT FOR THE NEW YEAR, BUT I CAN BRING THE NEW YEAR TO ME! TURN THE CLOCKS AHEAD, BOYS... ON THE DOUBLE! I WANT MIDNIGHT!
YOU'RE SO MASTERFUL, DADDY!
YOU WILL PLEASE TO SING "AULD LANG SYNE."
"HAPPY NEW YEAR," PLEASE.
YI!!
YI!
YI!!

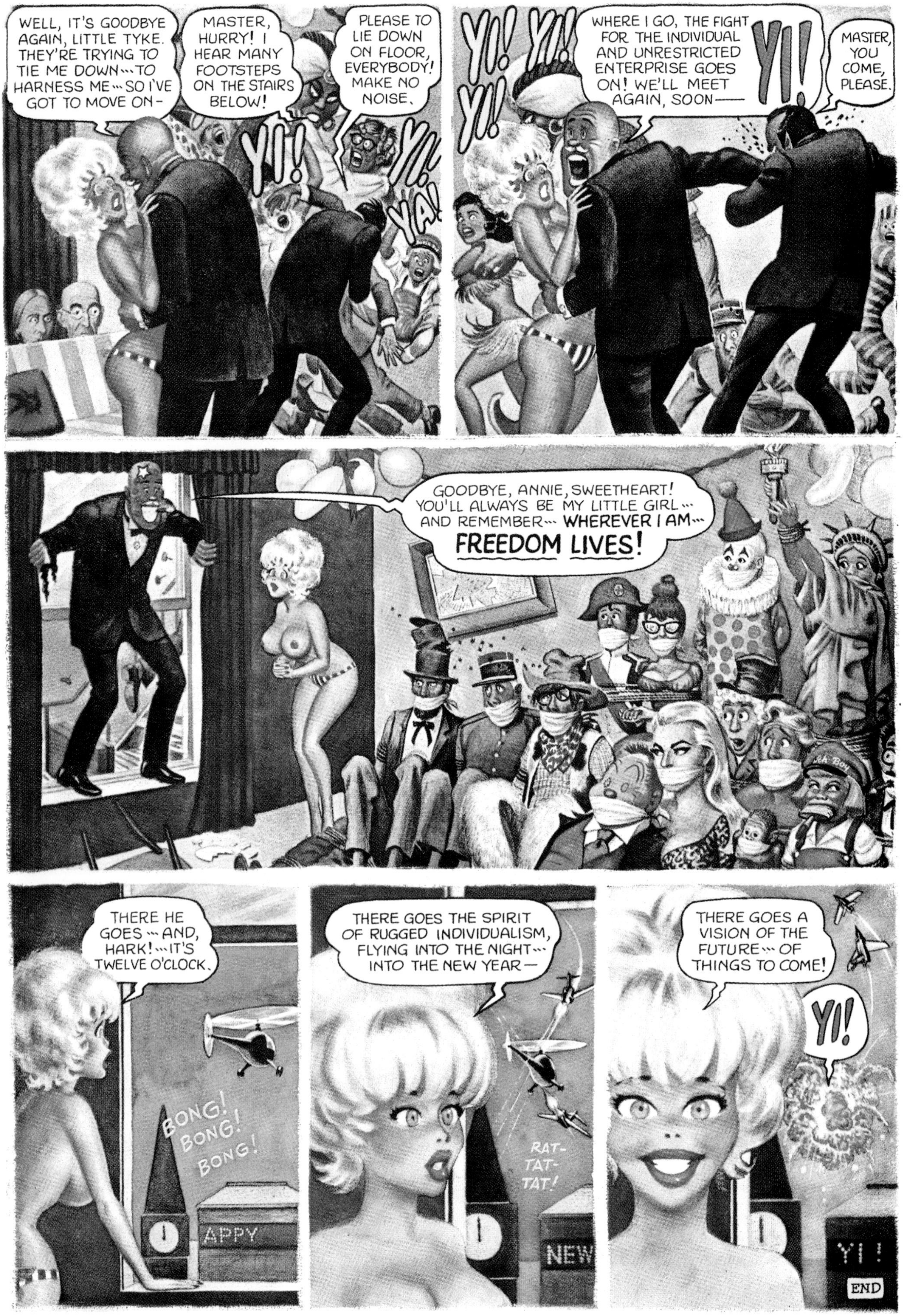
WELL, IT'S GOODBYE AGAIN, LITTLE TYKE. THEY'RE TRYING TO TIE ME DOWN··· TO HARNESS ME··· SO I'VE GOT TO MOVE ON–
MASTER, HURRY! I HEAR MANY FOOTSTEPS ON THE STAIRS BELOW!
PLEASE TO LIE DOWN ON FLOOR, EVERYBODY! MAKE NO NOISE.
YI!
YI!
YA!
YI! YI! YI!
WHERE I GO, THE FIGHT FOR THE INDIVIDUAL AND UNRESTRICTED ENTERPRISE GOES ON! WE'LL MEET AGAIN, SOON——
YI!
MASTER, YOU COME, PLEASE.
GOODBYE, ANNIE, SWEETHEART! YOU'LL ALWAYS BE MY LITTLE GIRL··· AND REMEMBER··· WHEREVER I AM··· FREEDOM LIVES!
THERE HE GOES··· AND, HARK!··· IT'S TWELVE O'CLOCK.
BONG! BONG! BONG!
APPY
THERE GOES THE SPIRIT OF RUGGED INDIVIDUALISM, FLYING INTO THE NIGHT··· INTO THE NEW YEAR—
RAT-TAT-TAT!
NEW
THERE GOES A VISION OF THE FUTURE··· OF THINGS TO COME!
YI!
YI!
END

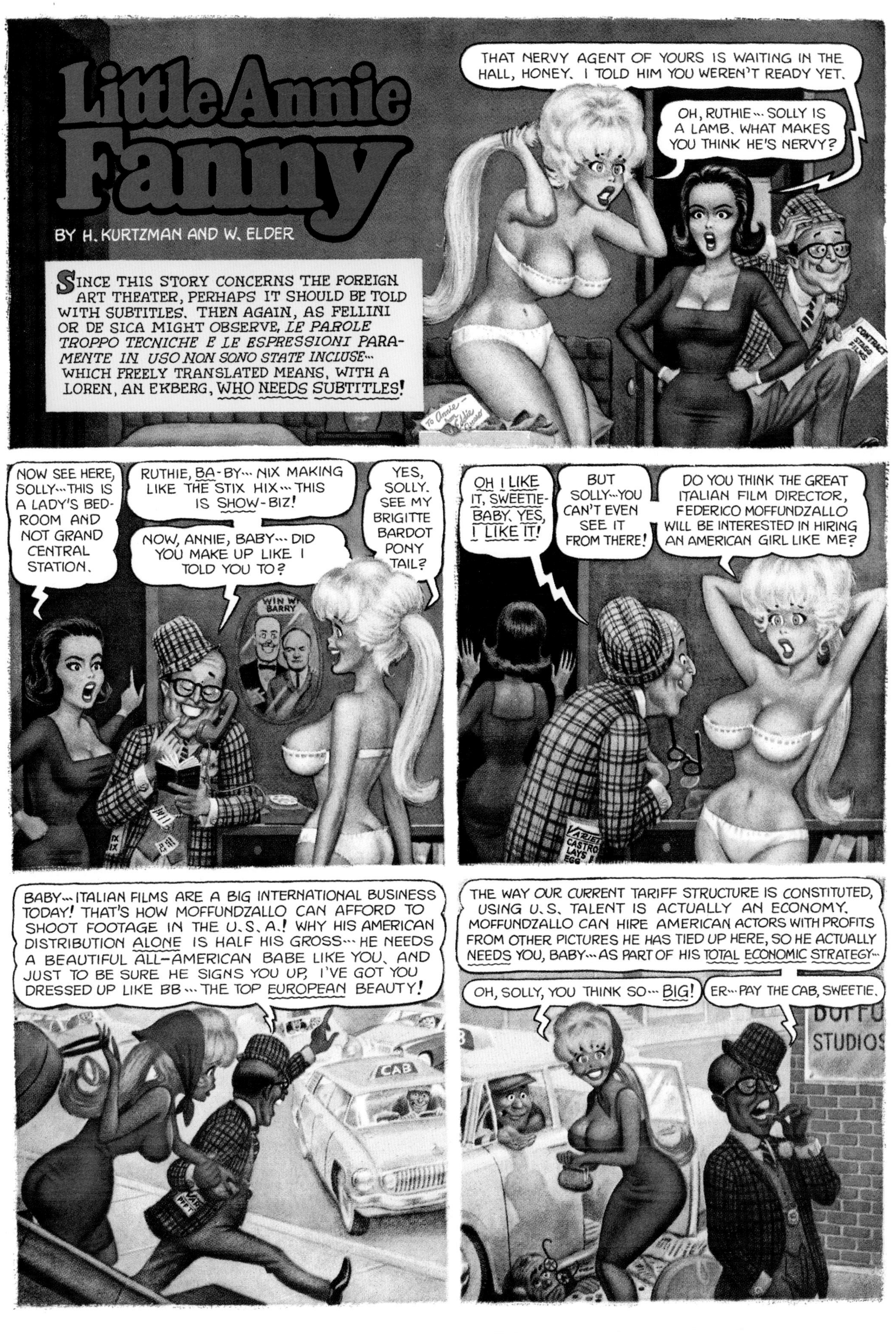
Little Annie Fanny
BY H. KURTZMAN AND W. ELDER
SINCE THIS STORY CONCERNS THE FOREIGN ART THEATER, PERHAPS IT SHOULD BE TOLD WITH SUBTITLES. THEN AGAIN, AS FELLINI OR DE SICA MIGHT OBSERVE, *LE PAROLE TROPPO TECNICHE E LE ESPRESSIONI PARAMENTE IN USO NON SONO STATE INCLUSE*··· WHICH FREELY TRANSLATED MEANS, WITH A LOREN, AN EKBERG, WHO NEEDS SUBTITLES!
THAT NERVY AGENT OF YOURS IS WAITING IN THE HALL, HONEY. I TOLD HIM YOU WEREN'T READY YET.
OH, RUTHIE··· SOLLY IS A LAMB. WHAT MAKES YOU THINK HE'S NERVY?
CONTRACT
NOW SEE HERE, SOLLY··· THIS IS A LADY'S BEDROOM AND NOT GRAND CENTRAL STATION.
RUTHIE, BA-BY··· NIX MAKING LIKE THE STIX HIX··· THIS IS SHOW-BIZ!
NOW, ANNIE, BABY··· DID YOU MAKE UP LIKE I TOLD YOU TO?
YES, SOLLY. SEE MY BRIGITTE BARDOT PONY TAIL?
WIN W/ BARRY
OH I LIKE IT, SWEETIE-BABY. YES, I LIKE IT!
BUT SOLLY··· YOU CAN'T EVEN SEE IT FROM THERE!
DO YOU THINK THE GREAT ITALIAN FILM DIRECTOR, FEDERICO MOFFUNDZALLO WILL BE INTERESTED IN HIRING AN AMERICAN GIRL LIKE ME?
VARIETY
CASTRO LAYS EGG
BABY··· ITALIAN FILMS ARE A BIG INTERNATIONAL BUSINESS TODAY! THAT'S HOW MOFFUNDZALLO CAN AFFORD TO SHOOT FOOTAGE IN THE U.S.A.! WHY HIS AMERICAN DISTRIBUTION ALONE IS HALF HIS GROSS··· HE NEEDS A BEAUTIFUL ALL-AMERICAN BABE LIKE YOU, AND JUST TO BE SURE HE SIGNS YOU UP, I'VE GOT YOU DRESSED UP LIKE BB··· THE TOP EUROPEAN BEAUTY!
CAB
THE WAY OUR CURRENT TARIFF STRUCTURE IS CONSTITUTED, USING U.S. TALENT IS ACTUALLY AN ECONOMY. MOFFUNDZALLO CAN HIRE AMERICAN ACTORS WITH PROFITS FROM OTHER PICTURES HE HAS TIED UP HERE, SO HE ACTUALLY NEEDS YOU, BABY··· AS PART OF HIS TOTAL ECONOMIC STRATEGY···
OH, SOLLY, YOU THINK SO··· BIG!
ER··· PAY THE CAB, SWEETIE.
STUDIOS

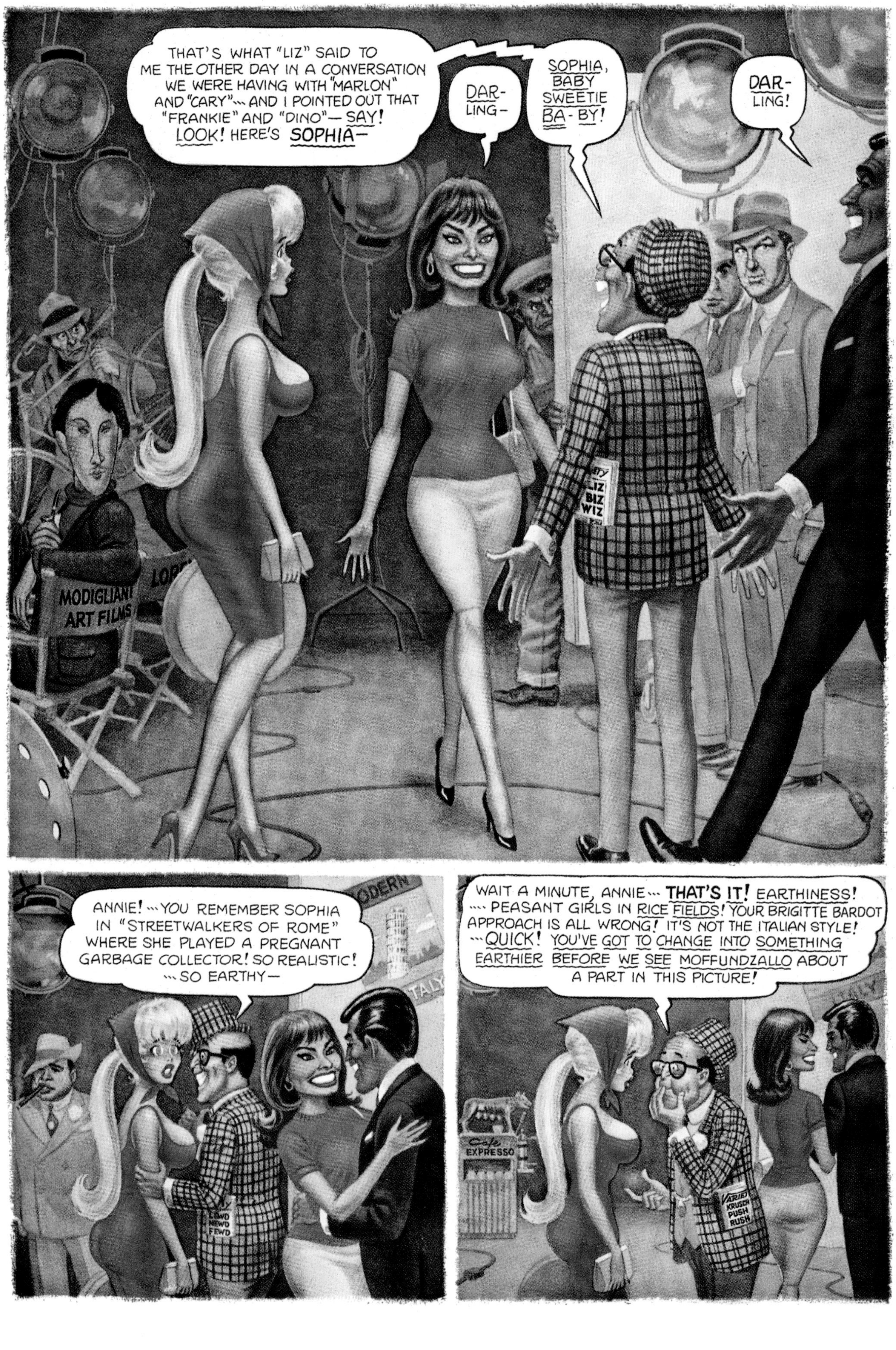
THAT'S WHAT "LIZ" SAID TO ME THE OTHER DAY IN A CONVERSATION WE WERE HAVING WITH "MARLON" AND "CARY" ··· AND I POINTED OUT THAT "FRANKIE" AND "DINO"— SAY! LOOK! HERE'S SOPHIA—
DAR-LING—
SOPHIA, BABY SWEETIE BA-BY!
DAR-LING!
MODIGLIANI ART FILMS
LIZ BIZ WIZ
ANNIE! ··· YOU REMEMBER SOPHIA IN "STREETWALKERS OF ROME" WHERE SHE PLAYED A PREGNANT GARBAGE COLLECTOR! SO REALISTIC! ··· SO EARTHY—
LEWD NEWD FEWD
WAIT A MINUTE, ANNIE ··· THAT'S IT! EARTHINESS! ···· PEASANT GIRLS IN RICE FIELDS! YOUR BRIGITTE BARDOT APPROACH IS ALL WRONG! IT'S NOT THE ITALIAN STYLE! ··· QUICK! YOU'VE GOT TO CHANGE INTO SOMETHING EARTHIER BEFORE WE SEE MOFFUNDZALLO ABOUT A PART IN THIS PICTURE!
Cafe EXPRESSO
Variety KRUSCH PUSH RUSH

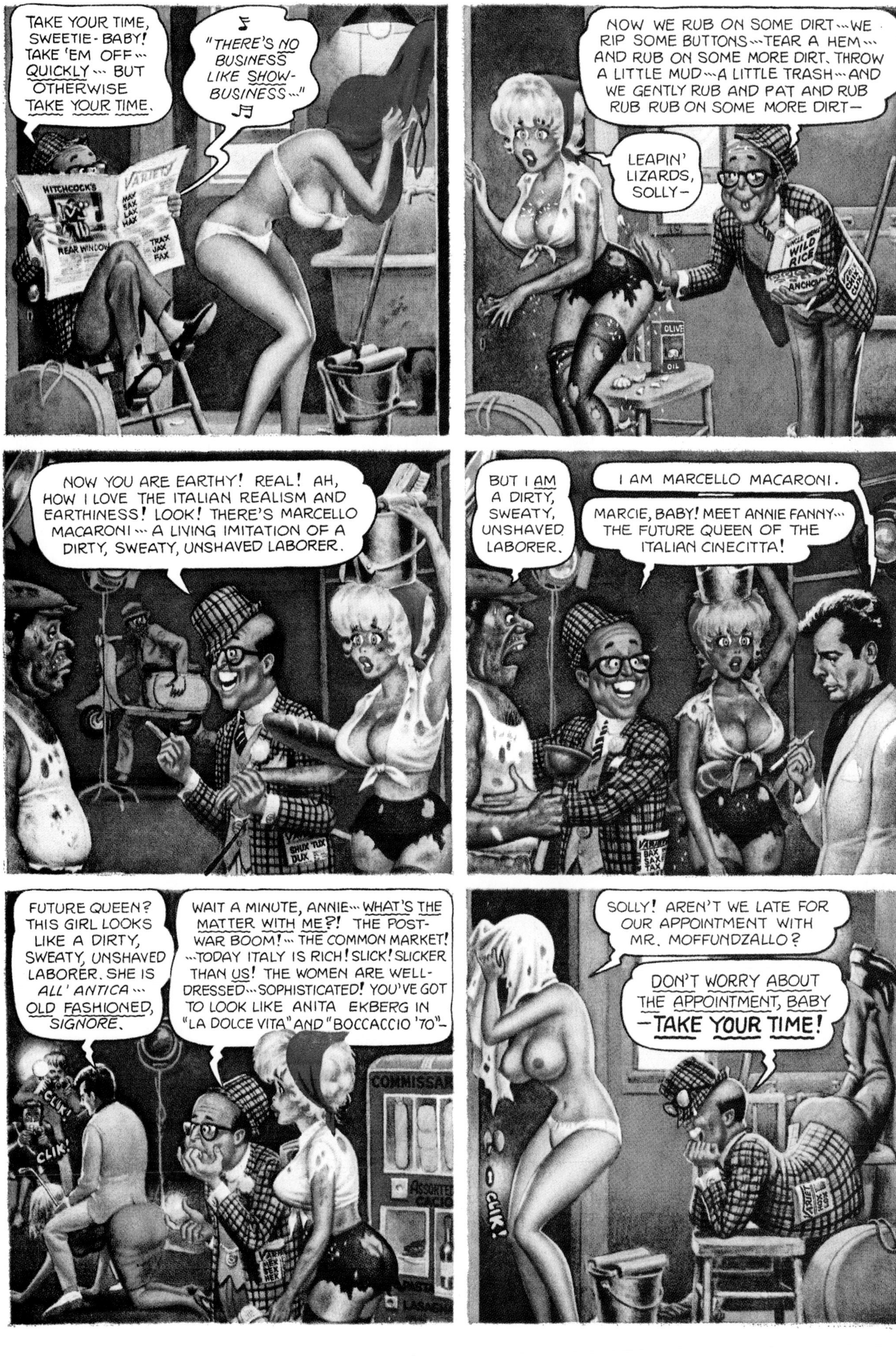
TAKE YOUR TIME, SWEETIE-BABY! TAKE 'EM OFF··· QUICKLY··· BUT OTHERWISE TAKE YOUR TIME.
"THERE'S NO BUSINESS LIKE SHOW-BUSINESS···"
HITCHCOCK'S REAR WINDOW
VARIETY
NOW WE RUB ON SOME DIRT··· WE RIP SOME BUTTONS··· TEAR A HEM··· AND RUB ON SOME MORE DIRT. THROW A LITTLE MUD··· A LITTLE TRASH··· AND WE GENTLY RUB AND PAT AND RUB RUB RUB ON SOME MORE DIRT—
LEAPIN' LIZARDS, SOLLY—
WILD RICE
OLIVE OIL
NOW YOU ARE EARTHY! REAL! AH, HOW I LOVE THE ITALIAN REALISM AND EARTHINESS! LOOK! THERE'S MARCELLO MACARONI··· A LIVING IMITATION OF A DIRTY, SWEATY, UNSHAVED LABORER.
BUT I AM A DIRTY, SWEATY, UNSHAVED LABORER.
I AM MARCELLO MACARONI.
MARCIE, BABY! MEET ANNIE FANNY··· THE FUTURE QUEEN OF THE ITALIAN CINECITTA!
FUTURE QUEEN? THIS GIRL LOOKS LIKE A DIRTY, SWEATY, UNSHAVED LABORER. SHE IS ALL' ANTICA··· OLD FASHIONED, SIGNORE.
WAIT A MINUTE, ANNIE··· WHAT'S THE MATTER WITH ME?! THE POST-WAR BOOM!··· THE COMMON MARKET! ···TODAY ITALY IS RICH! SLICK! SLICKER THAN US! THE WOMEN ARE WELL-DRESSED··· SOPHISTICATED! YOU'VE GOT TO LOOK LIKE ANITA EKBERG IN "LA DOLCE VITA" AND "BOCCACCIO '70"—
CLIK!
CLIK!
SOLLY! AREN'T WE LATE FOR OUR APPOINTMENT WITH MR. MOFFUNDZALLO?
DON'T WORRY ABOUT THE APPOINTMENT, BABY —TAKE YOUR TIME!
CLIK!

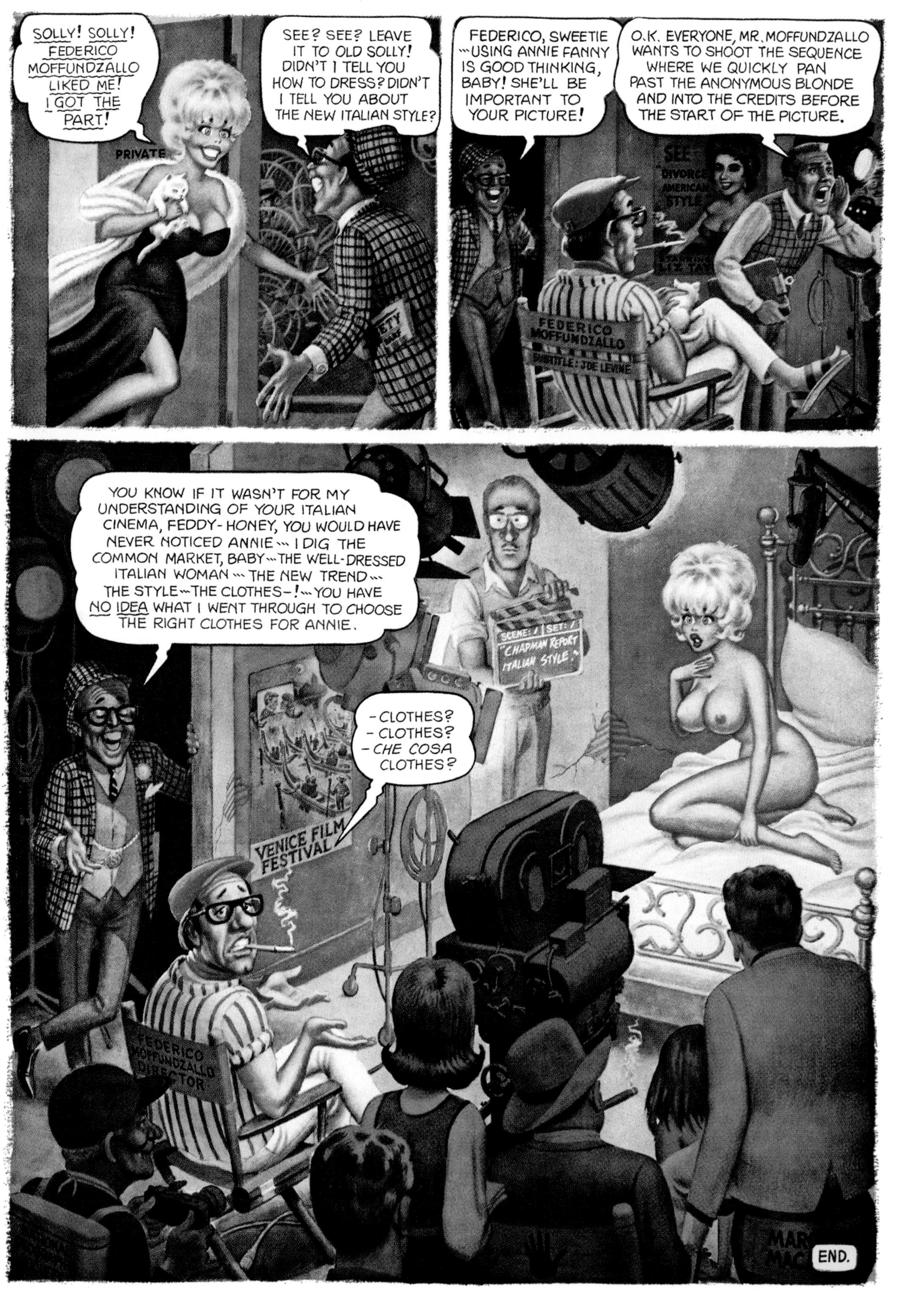
SOLLY! SOLLY! FEDERICO MOFFUNDZALLO LIKED ME! I GOT THE PART!
PRIVATE
SEE? SEE? LEAVE IT TO OLD SOLLY! DIDN'T I TELL YOU HOW TO DRESS? DIDN'T I TELL YOU ABOUT THE NEW ITALIAN STYLE?
FEDERICO, SWEETIE ··· USING ANNIE FANNY IS GOOD THINKING, BABY! SHE'LL BE IMPORTANT TO YOUR PICTURE!
O.K. EVERYONE, MR. MOFFUNDZALLO WANTS TO SHOOT THE SEQUENCE WHERE WE QUICKLY PAN PAST THE ANONYMOUS BLONDE AND INTO THE CREDITS BEFORE THE START OF THE PICTURE.
SEE
FEDERICO MOFFUNDZALLO
SUBTITLE: JOE LEVINE
YOU KNOW IF IT WASN'T FOR MY UNDERSTANDING OF YOUR ITALIAN CINEMA, FEDDY-HONEY, YOU WOULD HAVE NEVER NOTICED ANNIE ··· I DIG THE COMMON MARKET, BABY ··· THE WELL-DRESSED ITALIAN WOMAN ··· THE NEW TREND ··· THE STYLE ··· THE CLOTHES–! ··· YOU HAVE NO IDEA WHAT I WENT THROUGH TO CHOOSE THE RIGHT CLOTHES FOR ANNIE.
SCENE: 1 SET: 1
"CHAPMAN REPORT ITALIAN STYLE"
-CLOTHES? -CLOTHES? -CHE COSA CLOTHES?
VENICE FILM FESTIVAL
FEDERICO MOFFUNDZALLO DIRECTOR
END.

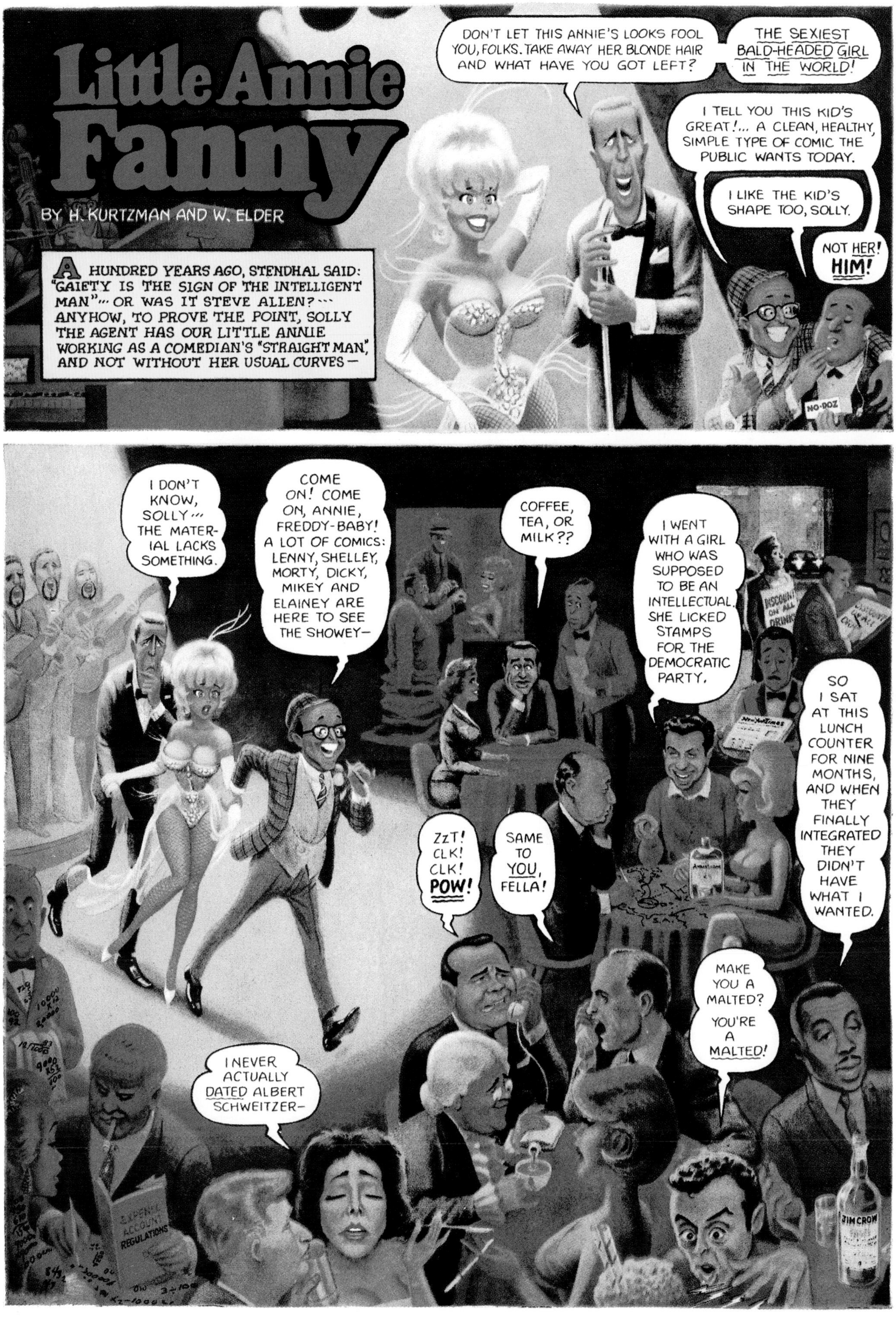

Little Annie Fanny
BY H. KURTZMAN AND W. ELDER
A HUNDRED YEARS AGO, STENDHAL SAID: "GAIETY IS THE SIGN OF THE INTELLIGENT MAN"... OR WAS IT STEVE ALLEN?... ANYHOW, TO PROVE THE POINT, SOLLY THE AGENT HAS OUR LITTLE ANNIE WORKING AS A COMEDIAN'S "STRAIGHT MAN", AND NOT WITHOUT HER USUAL CURVES—
DON'T LET THIS ANNIE'S LOOKS FOOL YOU, FOLKS. TAKE AWAY HER BLONDE HAIR AND WHAT HAVE YOU GOT LEFT?
THE SEXIEST BALD-HEADED GIRL IN THE WORLD!
I TELL YOU THIS KID'S GREAT!... A CLEAN, HEALTHY, SIMPLE TYPE OF COMIC THE PUBLIC WANTS TODAY.
I LIKE THE KID'S SHAPE TOO, SOLLY.
NOT HER! HIM!
NO-DOZ
I DON'T KNOW, SOLLY... THE MATERIAL LACKS SOMETHING.
COME ON! COME ON, ANNIE, FREDDY-BABY! A LOT OF COMICS: LENNY, SHELLEY, MORTY, DICKY, MIKEY AND ELAINEY ARE HERE TO SEE THE SHOWEY—
COFFEE, TEA, OR MILK??
I WENT WITH A GIRL WHO WAS SUPPOSED TO BE AN INTELLECTUAL. SHE LICKED STAMPS FOR THE DEMOCRATIC PARTY.
SO I SAT AT THIS LUNCH COUNTER FOR NINE MONTHS, AND WHEN THEY FINALLY INTEGRATED THEY DIDN'T HAVE WHAT I WANTED.
ZzT! CLK! CLK! POW!
SAME TO YOU, FELLA!
MAKE YOU A MALTED?
YOU'RE A MALTED!
I NEVER ACTUALLY DATED ALBERT SCHWEITZER—
EXPENSE ACCOUNT REGULATIONS
JIM CROW

29

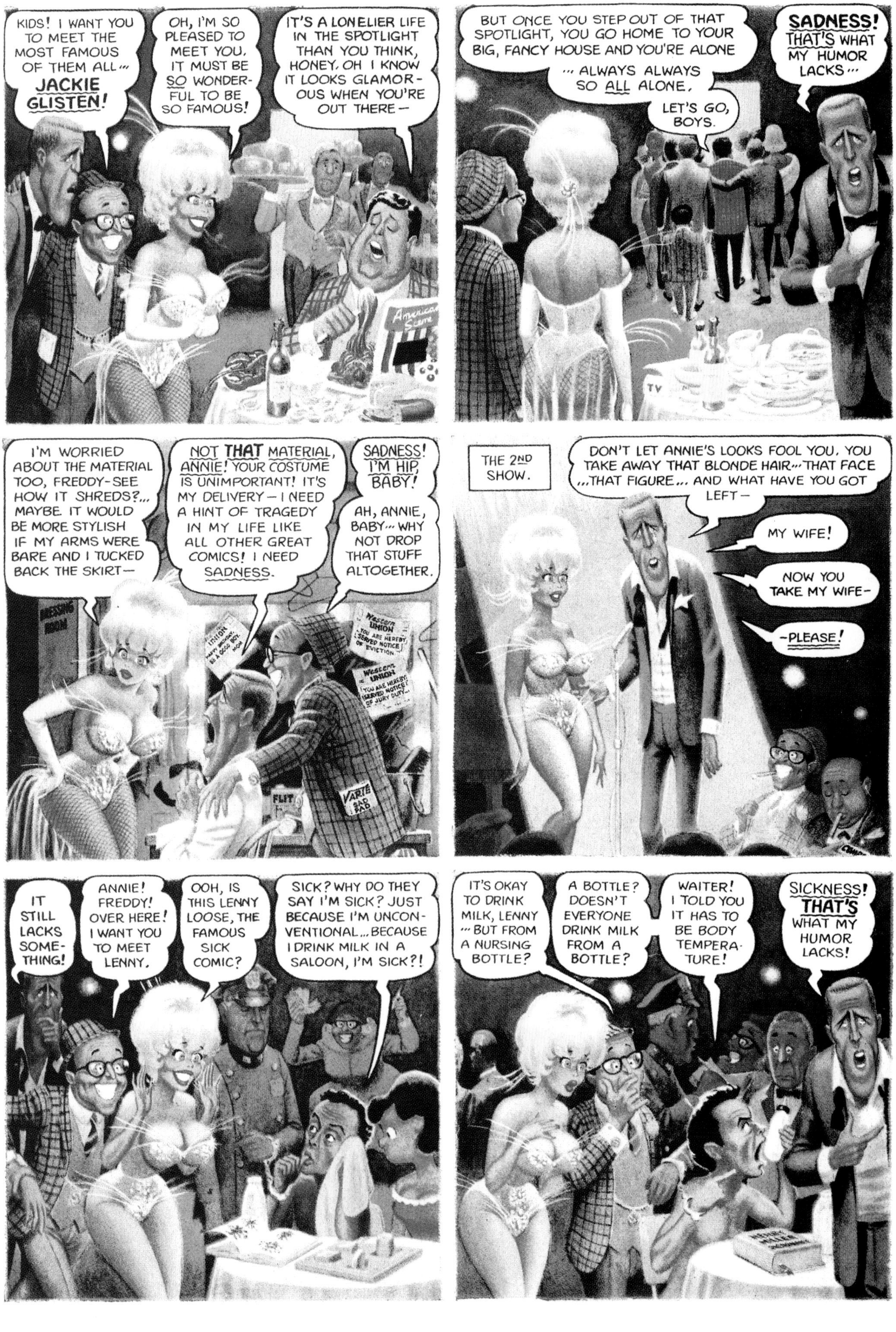

KIDS! I WANT YOU TO MEET THE MOST FAMOUS OF THEM ALL... JACKIE GLISTEN!
OH, I'M SO PLEASED TO MEET YOU. IT MUST BE SO WONDERFUL TO BE SO FAMOUS!
IT'S A LONELIER LIFE IN THE SPOTLIGHT THAN YOU THINK, HONEY. OH I KNOW IT LOOKS GLAMOROUS WHEN YOU'RE OUT THERE—
BUT ONCE YOU STEP OUT OF THAT SPOTLIGHT, YOU GO HOME TO YOUR BIG, FANCY HOUSE AND YOU'RE ALONE
... ALWAYS ALWAYS SO ALL ALONE.
LET'S GO, BOYS.
SADNESS! THAT'S WHAT MY HUMOR LACKS...
TV
I'M WORRIED ABOUT THE MATERIAL TOO, FREDDY-SEE HOW IT SHREDS?... MAYBE IT WOULD BE MORE STYLISH IF MY ARMS WERE BARE AND I TUCKED BACK THE SKIRT—
NOT THAT MATERIAL, ANNIE! YOUR COSTUME IS UNIMPORTANT! IT'S MY DELIVERY — I NEED A HINT OF TRAGEDY IN MY LIFE LIKE ALL OTHER GREAT COMICS! I NEED SADNESS.
SADNESS! I'M HIP, BABY!
AH, ANNIE, BABY... WHY NOT DROP THAT STUFF ALTOGETHER.
THE 2ND SHOW.
DON'T LET ANNIE'S LOOKS FOOL YOU. YOU TAKE AWAY THAT BLONDE HAIR... THAT FACE ... THAT FIGURE... AND WHAT HAVE YOU GOT LEFT —
MY WIFE!
NOW YOU TAKE MY WIFE-
-PLEASE!
IT STILL LACKS SOMETHING!
ANNIE! FREDDY! OVER HERE! I WANT YOU TO MEET LENNY.
OOH, IS THIS LENNY LOOSE, THE FAMOUS SICK COMIC?
SICK? WHY DO THEY SAY I'M SICK? JUST BECAUSE I'M UNCONVENTIONAL... BECAUSE I DRINK MILK IN A SALOON, I'M SICK?!
IT'S OKAY TO DRINK MILK, LENNY ... BUT FROM A NURSING BOTTLE?
A BOTTLE? DOESN'T EVERYONE DRINK MILK FROM A BOTTLE?
WAITER! I TOLD YOU IT HAS TO BE BODY TEMPERATURE!
SICKNESS! THAT'S WHAT MY HUMOR LACKS!

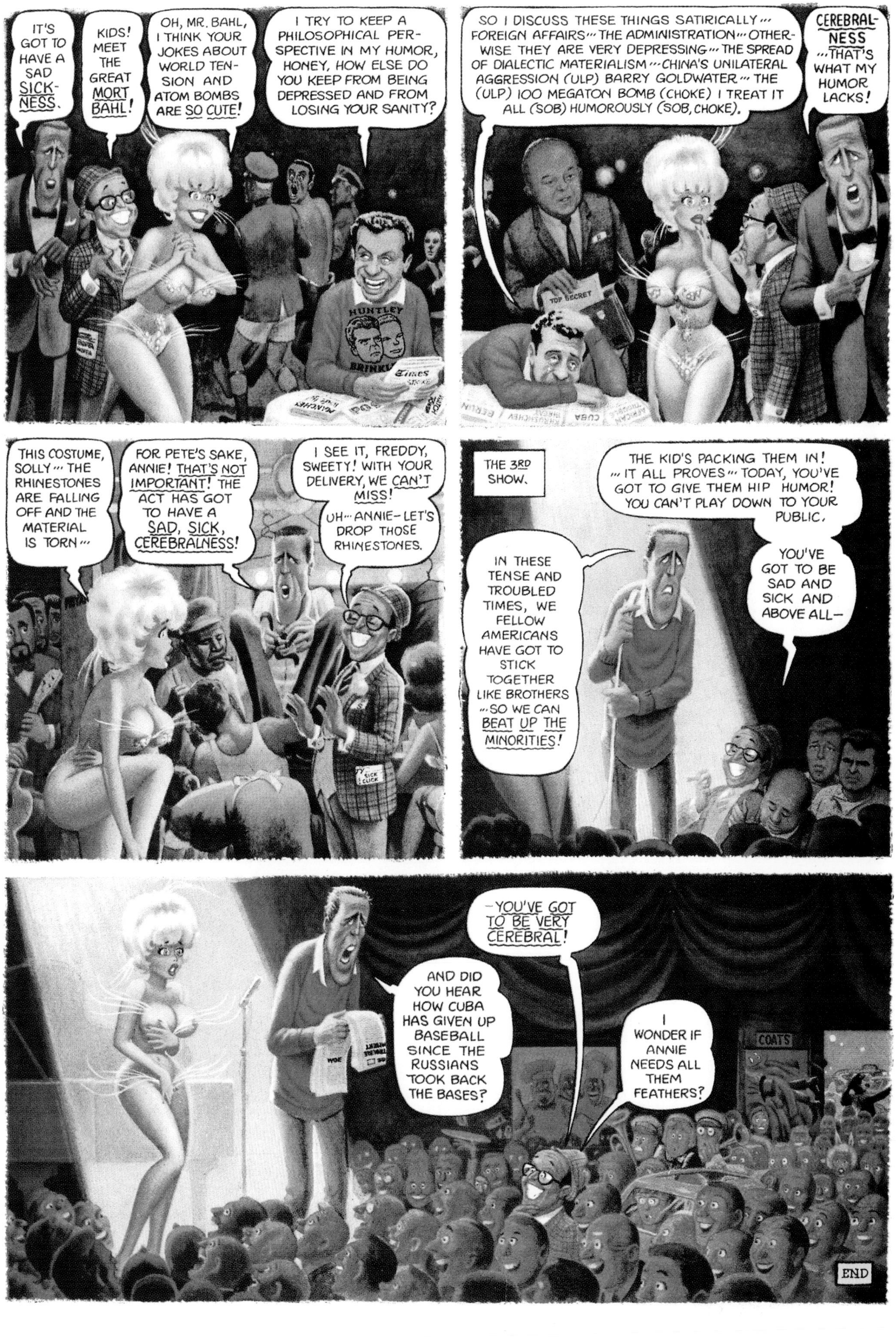
IT'S GOT TO HAVE A SAD SICKNESS.
KIDS! MEET THE GREAT MORT BAHL!
OH, MR. BAHL, I THINK YOUR JOKES ABOUT WORLD TENSION AND ATOM BOMBS ARE SO CUTE!
I TRY TO KEEP A PHILOSOPHICAL PERSPECTIVE IN MY HUMOR, HONEY, HOW ELSE DO YOU KEEP FROM BEING DEPRESSED AND FROM LOSING YOUR SANITY?
SO I DISCUSS THESE THINGS SATIRICALLY ... FOREIGN AFFAIRS ... THE ADMINISTRATION ... OTHERWISE THEY ARE VERY DEPRESSING ... THE SPREAD OF DIALECTIC MATERIALISM ... CHINA'S UNILATERAL AGGRESSION (ULP) BARRY GOLDWATER ... THE (ULP) 100 MEGATON BOMB (CHOKE) I TREAT IT ALL (SOB) HUMOROUSLY (SOB, CHOKE).
CEREBRALNESS ... THAT'S WHAT MY HUMOR LACKS!
TOP SECRET
THIS COSTUME, SOLLY ... THE RHINESTONES ARE FALLING OFF AND THE MATERIAL IS TORN ...
FOR PETE'S SAKE, ANNIE! THAT'S NOT IMPORTANT! THE ACT HAS GOT TO HAVE A SAD, SICK, CEREBRALNESS!
I SEE IT, FREDDY, SWEETY! WITH YOUR DELIVERY, WE CAN'T MISS!
UH ... ANNIE- LET'S DROP THOSE RHINESTONES.
THE 3RD SHOW.
THE KID'S PACKING THEM IN! ... IT ALL PROVES ... TODAY, YOU'VE GOT TO GIVE THEM HIP HUMOR! YOU CAN'T PLAY DOWN TO YOUR PUBLIC.
IN THESE TENSE AND TROUBLED TIMES, WE FELLOW AMERICANS HAVE GOT TO STICK TOGETHER LIKE BROTHERS ... SO WE CAN BEAT UP THE MINORITIES!
YOU'VE GOT TO BE SAD AND SICK AND ABOVE ALL-
-YOU'VE GOT TO BE VERY CEREBRAL!
AND DID YOU HEAR HOW CUBA HAS GIVEN UP BASEBALL SINCE THE RUSSIANS TOOK BACK THE BASES?
I WONDER IF ANNIE NEEDS ALL THEM FEATHERS?
COATS
END

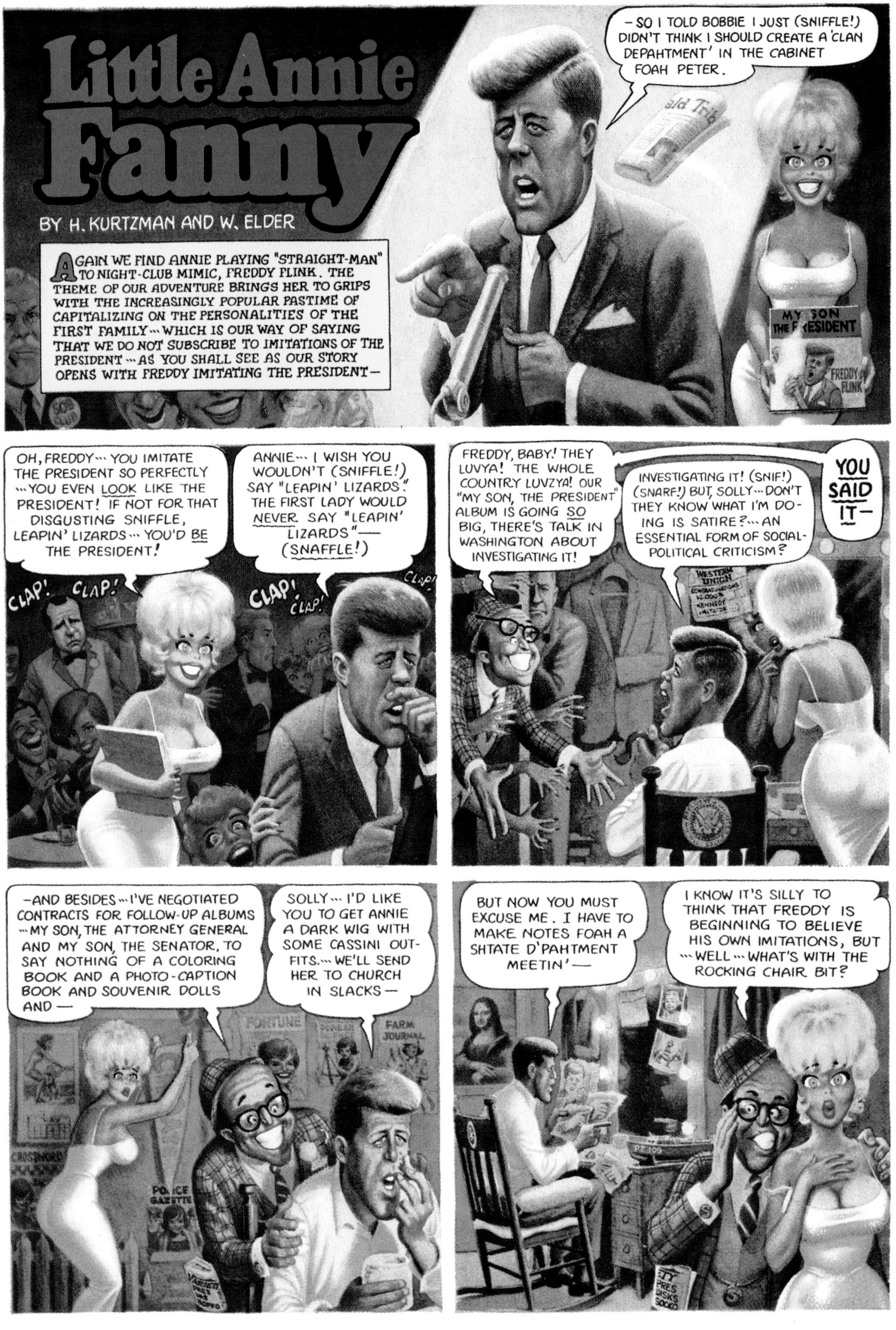
Little Annie Fanny
BY H. KURTZMAN AND W. ELDER
AGAIN WE FIND ANNIE PLAYING "STRAIGHT-MAN" TO NIGHT-CLUB MIMIC, FREDDY FLINK. THE THEME OF OUR ADVENTURE BRINGS HER TO GRIPS WITH THE INCREASINGLY POPULAR PASTIME OF CAPITALIZING ON THE PERSONALITIES OF THE FIRST FAMILY ··· WHICH IS OUR WAY OF SAYING THAT WE DO NOT SUBSCRIBE TO IMITATIONS OF THE PRESIDENT ··· AS YOU SHALL SEE AS OUR STORY OPENS WITH FREDDY IMITATING THE PRESIDENT—
—SO I TOLD BOBBIE I JUST (SNIFFLE!) DIDN'T THINK I SHOULD CREATE A 'CLAN DEPAHTMENT' IN THE CABINET FOAH PETER.
MY SON THE PRESIDENT
FREDDY FLINK
OH, FREDDY ··· YOU IMITATE THE PRESIDENT SO PERFECTLY ··· YOU EVEN LOOK LIKE THE PRESIDENT! IF NOT FOR THAT DISGUSTING SNIFFLE, LEAPIN' LIZARDS ··· YOU'D BE THE PRESIDENT!
ANNIE ··· I WISH YOU WOULDN'T (SNIFFLE!) SAY "LEAPIN' LIZARDS." THE FIRST LADY WOULD NEVER SAY "LEAPIN' LIZARDS"— (SNAFFLE!)
CLAP! CLAP! CLAP! CLAP! CLAP!
FREDDY, BABY! THEY LUVYA! THE WHOLE COUNTRY LUVZYA! OUR "MY SON, THE PRESIDENT" ALBUM IS GOING SO BIG, THERE'S TALK IN WASHINGTON ABOUT INVESTIGATING IT!
INVESTIGATING IT! (SNIF!) (SNARF!) BUT, SOLLY ··· DON'T THEY KNOW WHAT I'M DOING IS SATIRE? ··· AN ESSENTIAL FORM OF SOCIAL-POLITICAL CRITICISM?
YOU SAID IT—
WESTERN UNION
—AND BESIDES ··· I'VE NEGOTIATED CONTRACTS FOR FOLLOW-UP ALBUMS ··· MY SON, THE ATTORNEY GENERAL AND MY SON, THE SENATOR, TO SAY NOTHING OF A COLORING BOOK AND A PHOTO-CAPTION BOOK AND SOUVENIR DOLLS AND —
SOLLY ··· I'D LIKE YOU TO GET ANNIE A DARK WIG WITH SOME CASSINI OUT-FITS. ··· WE'LL SEND HER TO CHURCH IN SLACKS —
FORTUNE
FARM JOURNAL
POLICE GAZETTE
BUT NOW YOU MUST EXCUSE ME. I HAVE TO MAKE NOTES FOAH A SHTATE D'PAHTMENT MEETIN'—
I KNOW IT'S SILLY TO THINK THAT FREDDY IS BEGINNING TO BELIEVE HIS OWN IMITATIONS, BUT ··· WELL ··· WHAT'S WITH THE ROCKING CHAIR BIT?
PRES DISKS SOCKO

32

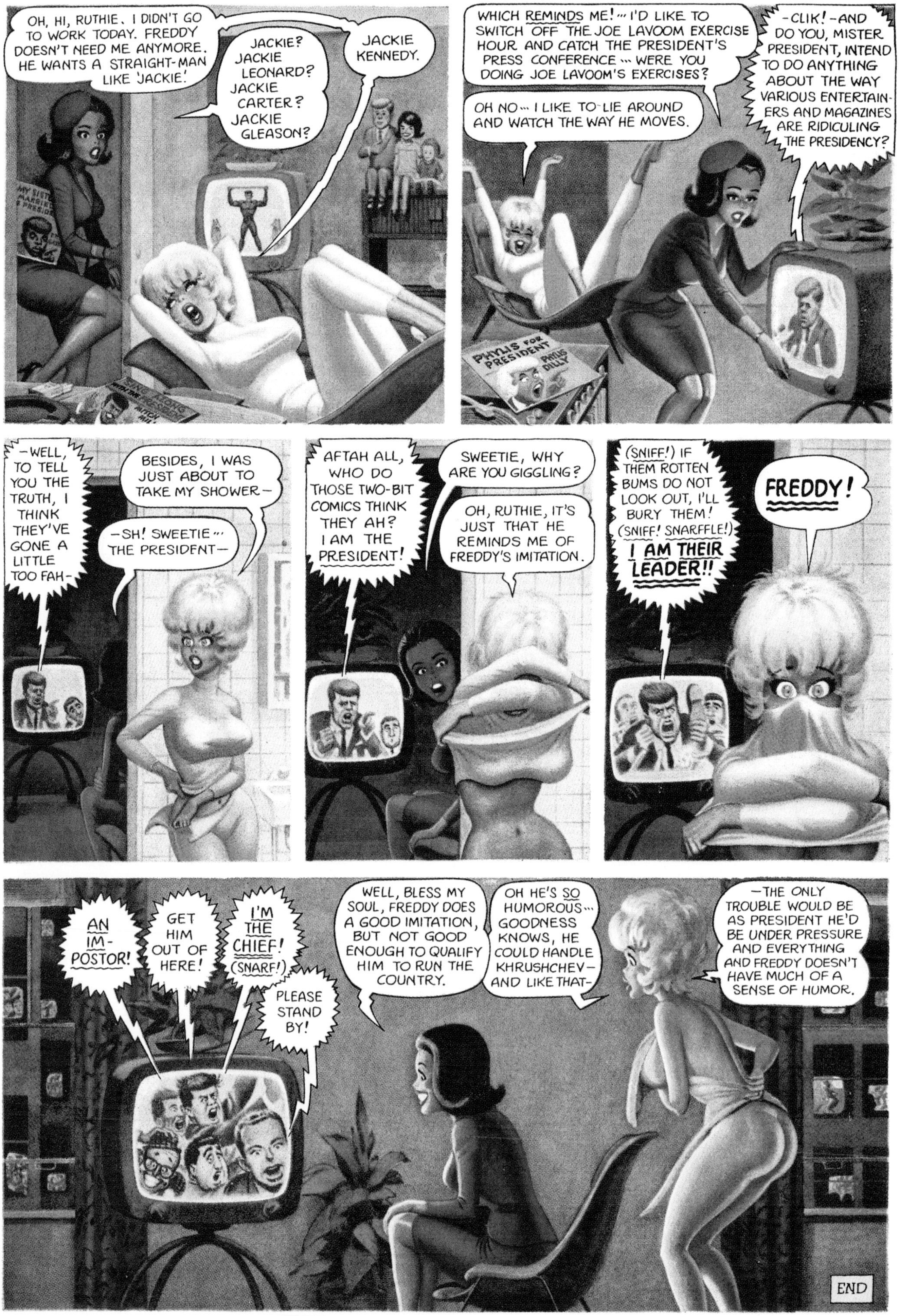
OH, HI, RUTHIE. I DIDN'T GO TO WORK TODAY. FREDDY DOESN'T NEED ME ANYMORE. HE WANTS A STRAIGHT-MAN LIKE 'JACKIE.'
JACKIE? JACKIE LEONARD? JACKIE CARTER? JACKIE GLEASON?
JACKIE KENNEDY.
WHICH REMINDS ME!... I'D LIKE TO SWITCH OFF THE JOE LAVOOM EXERCISE HOUR AND CATCH THE PRESIDENT'S PRESS CONFERENCE... WERE YOU DOING JOE LAVOOM'S EXERCISES?
OH NO... I LIKE TO LIE AROUND AND WATCH THE WAY HE MOVES.
-CLIK!-AND DO YOU, MISTER PRESIDENT, INTEND TO DO ANYTHING ABOUT THE WAY VARIOUS ENTERTAINERS AND MAGAZINES ARE RIDICULING THE PRESIDENCY?
PHYLIS FOR PRESIDENT
PHYLIS DILLY
-WELL, TO TELL YOU THE TRUTH, I THINK THEY'VE GONE A LITTLE TOO FAH-
BESIDES, I WAS JUST ABOUT TO TAKE MY SHOWER-
-SH! SWEETIE... THE PRESIDENT-
AFTAH ALL, WHO DO THOSE TWO-BIT COMICS THINK THEY AH? I AM THE PRESIDENT!
SWEETIE, WHY ARE YOU GIGGLING?
OH, RUTHIE, IT'S JUST THAT HE REMINDS ME OF FREDDY'S IMITATION.
(SNIFF!) IF THEM ROTTEN BUMS DO NOT LOOK OUT, I'LL BURY THEM! (SNIFF! SNARFFLE!) I AM THEIR LEADER!!
FREDDY!
AN IM-POSTOR!
GET HIM OUT OF HERE!
I'M THE CHIEF! (SNARF!)
PLEASE STAND BY!
WELL, BLESS MY SOUL, FREDDY DOES A GOOD IMITATION, BUT NOT GOOD ENOUGH TO QUALIFY HIM TO RUN THE COUNTRY.
OH HE'S SO HUMOROUS... GOODNESS KNOWS, HE COULD HANDLE KHRUSHCHEV- AND LIKE THAT-
-THE ONLY TROUBLE WOULD BE AS PRESIDENT HE'D BE UNDER PRESSURE AND EVERYTHING AND FREDDY DOESN'T HAVE MUCH OF A SENSE OF HUMOR.
END

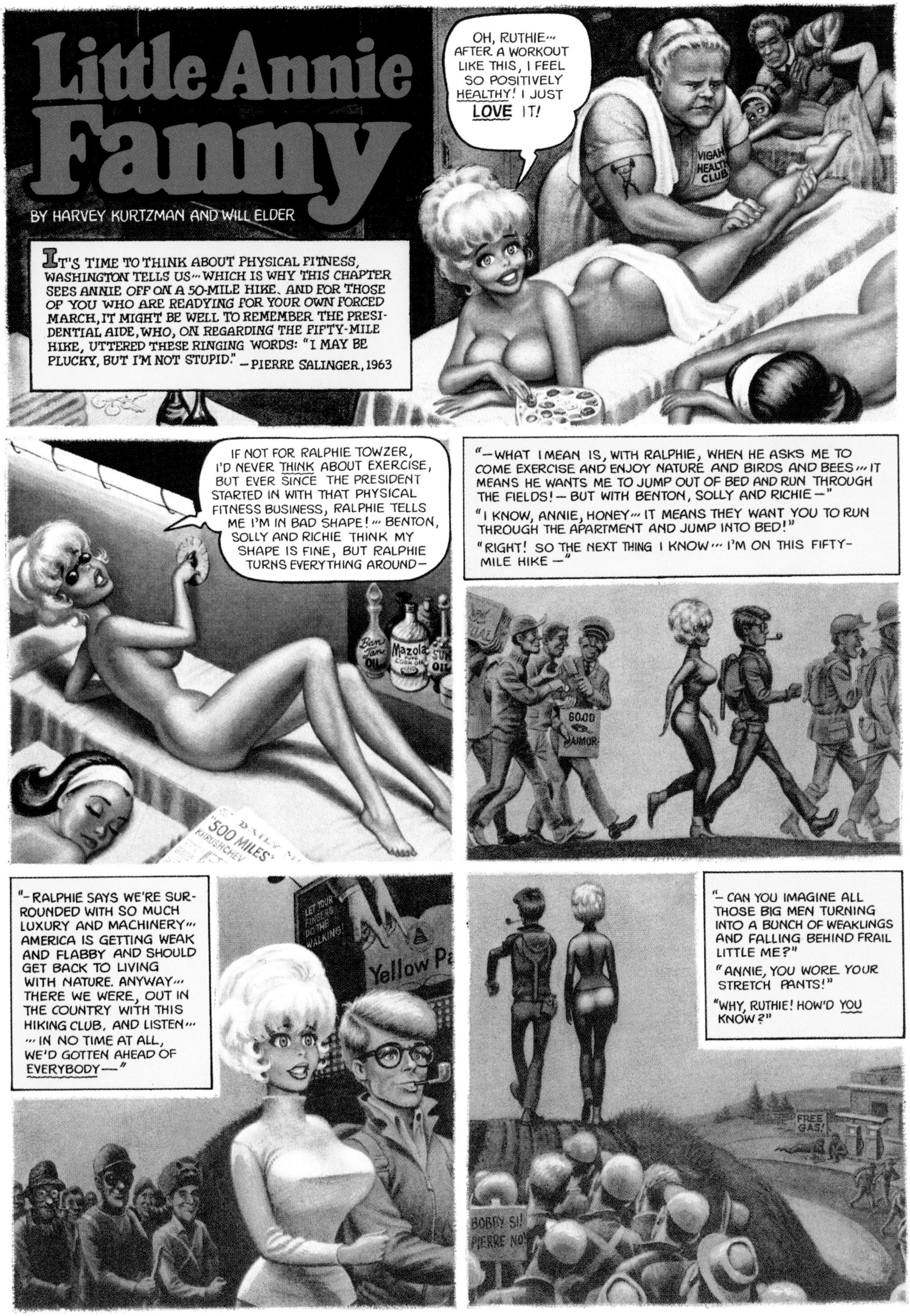
Little Annie Fanny
BY HARVEY KURTZMAN AND WILL ELDER
IT'S TIME TO THINK ABOUT PHYSICAL FITNESS, WASHINGTON TELLS US··· WHICH IS WHY THIS CHAPTER SEES ANNIE OFF ON A 50-MILE HIKE. AND FOR THOSE OF YOU WHO ARE READYING FOR YOUR OWN FORCED MARCH, IT MIGHT BE WELL TO REMEMBER THE PRESIDENTIAL AIDE, WHO, ON REGARDING THE FIFTY-MILE HIKE, UTTERED THESE RINGING WORDS: "I MAY BE PLUCKY, BUT I'M NOT STUPID." —PIERRE SALINGER, 1963
OH, RUTHIE··· AFTER A WORKOUT LIKE THIS, I FEEL SO POSITIVELY HEALTHY! I JUST LOVE IT!
VIGAH HEALTH CLUB
IF NOT FOR RALPHIE TOWZER, I'D NEVER THINK ABOUT EXERCISE, BUT EVER SINCE THE PRESIDENT STARTED IN WITH THAT PHYSICAL FITNESS BUSINESS, RALPHIE TELLS ME I'M IN BAD SHAPE! ··· BENTON, SOLLY AND RICHIE THINK MY SHAPE IS FINE, BUT RALPHIE TURNS EVERYTHING AROUND—
Mazola
"500 MILES"
"—WHAT I MEAN IS, WITH RALPHIE, WHEN HE ASKS ME TO COME EXERCISE AND ENJOY NATURE AND BIRDS AND BEES··· IT MEANS HE WANTS ME TO JUMP OUT OF BED AND RUN THROUGH THE FIELDS! — BUT WITH BENTON, SOLLY AND RICHIE —"
"I KNOW, ANNIE, HONEY··· IT MEANS THEY WANT YOU TO RUN THROUGH THE APARTMENT AND JUMP INTO BED!"
"RIGHT! SO THE NEXT THING I KNOW··· I'M ON THIS FIFTY-MILE HIKE —"
"— RALPHIE SAYS WE'RE SURROUNDED WITH SO MUCH LUXURY AND MACHINERY··· AMERICA IS GETTING WEAK AND FLABBY AND SHOULD GET BACK TO LIVING WITH NATURE. ANYWAY··· THERE WE WERE, OUT IN THE COUNTRY WITH THIS HIKING CLUB, AND LISTEN··· ··· IN NO TIME AT ALL, WE'D GOTTEN AHEAD OF EVERYBODY—"
LET YOUR FINGERS DO THE WALKING!
Yellow Pa
"— CAN YOU IMAGINE ALL THOSE BIG MEN TURNING INTO A BUNCH OF WEAKLINGS AND FALLING BEHIND FRAIL LITTLE ME?"
"ANNIE, YOU WORE YOUR STRETCH PANTS!"
"WHY, RUTHIE! HOW'D YOU KNOW?"
FREE GAS!
BOBBY SI! PIERRE NO!

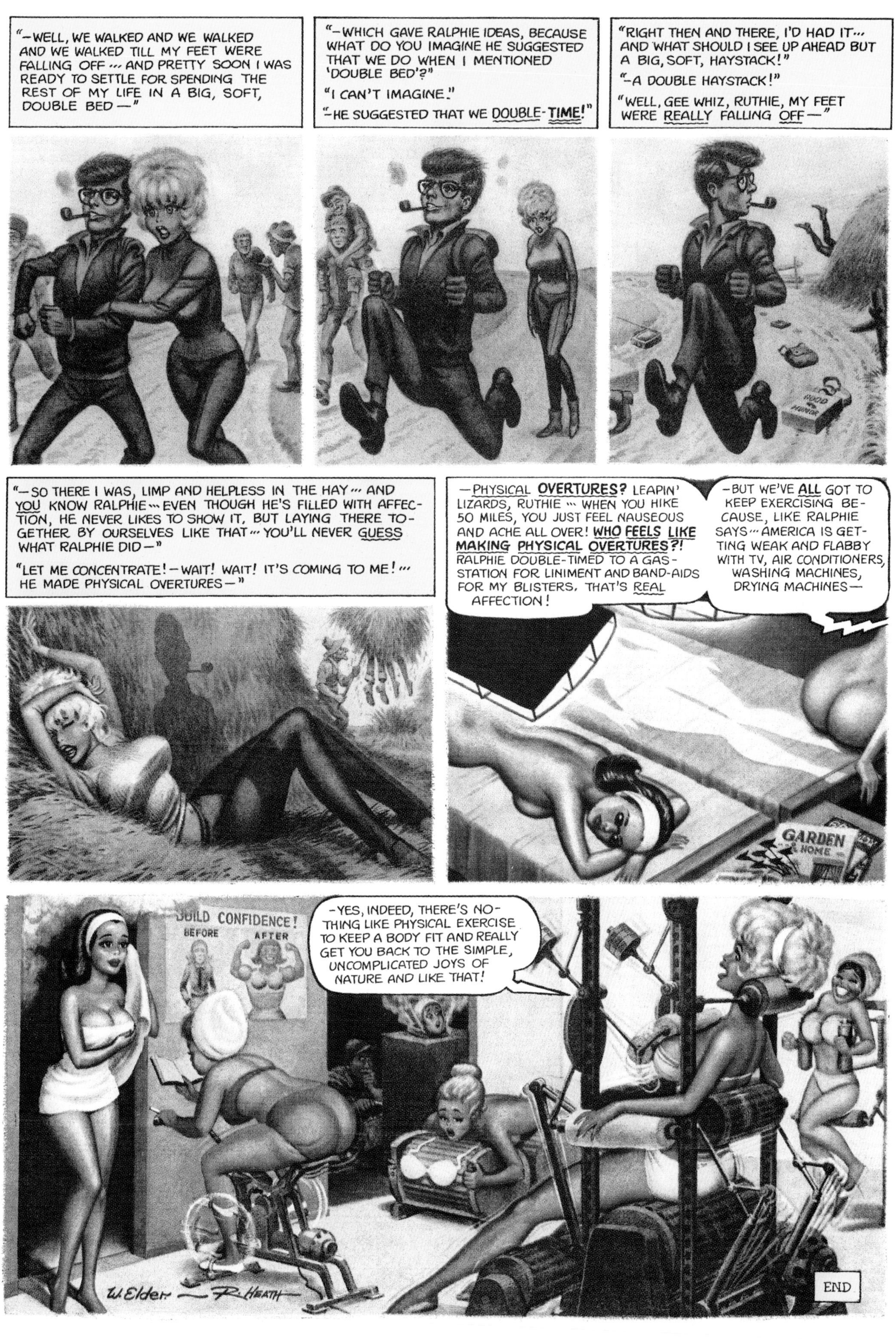
"—WELL, WE WALKED AND WE WALKED AND WE WALKED TILL MY FEET WERE FALLING OFF ··· AND PRETTY SOON I WAS READY TO SETTLE FOR SPENDING THE REST OF MY LIFE IN A BIG, SOFT, DOUBLE BED —"
"—WHICH GAVE RALPHIE IDEAS, BECAUSE WHAT DO YOU IMAGINE HE SUGGESTED THAT WE DO WHEN I MENTIONED 'DOUBLE BED'?"
"I CAN'T IMAGINE."
"—HE SUGGESTED THAT WE DOUBLE-TIME!"
"RIGHT THEN AND THERE, I'D HAD IT··· AND WHAT SHOULD I SEE UP AHEAD BUT A BIG, SOFT, HAYSTACK!"
"—A DOUBLE HAYSTACK!"
"WELL, GEE WHIZ, RUTHIE, MY FEET WERE REALLY FALLING OFF—"
"—SO THERE I WAS, LIMP AND HELPLESS IN THE HAY ··· AND YOU KNOW RALPHIE ··· EVEN THOUGH HE'S FILLED WITH AFFECTION, HE NEVER LIKES TO SHOW IT, BUT LAYING THERE TOGETHER BY OURSELVES LIKE THAT ··· YOU'LL NEVER GUESS WHAT RALPHIE DID—"
"LET ME CONCENTRATE! — WAIT! WAIT! IT'S COMING TO ME! ··· HE MADE PHYSICAL OVERTURES—"
—PHYSICAL OVERTURES? LEAPIN' LIZARDS, RUTHIE ··· WHEN YOU HIKE 50 MILES, YOU JUST FEEL NAUSEOUS AND ACHE ALL OVER! WHO FEELS LIKE MAKING PHYSICAL OVERTURES?! RALPHIE DOUBLE-TIMED TO A GAS-STATION FOR LINIMENT AND BAND-AIDS FOR MY BLISTERS. THAT'S REAL AFFECTION!
—BUT WE'VE ALL GOT TO KEEP EXERCISING BECAUSE, LIKE RALPHIE SAYS ··· AMERICA IS GETTING WEAK AND FLABBY WITH TV, AIR CONDITIONERS, WASHING MACHINES, DRYING MACHINES—
GARDEN & HOME
UILD CONFIDENCE!
BEFORE
AFTER
—YES, INDEED, THERE'S NOTHING LIKE PHYSICAL EXERCISE TO KEEP A BODY FIT AND REALLY GET YOU BACK TO THE SIMPLE, UNCOMPLICATED JOYS OF NATURE AND LIKE THAT!
W. Elder — R. Heath
END

35

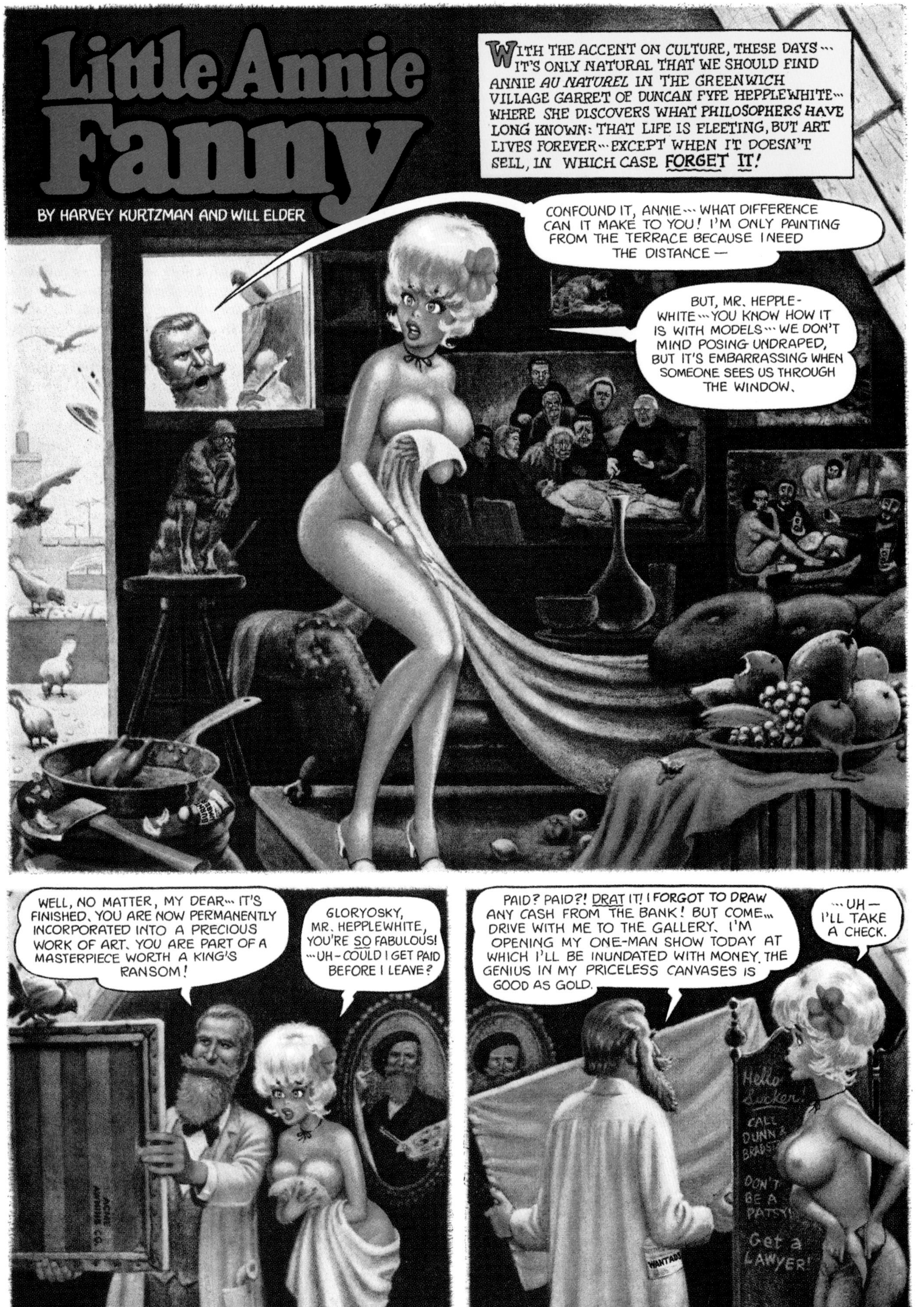

Little Annie Fanny
BY HARVEY KURTZMAN AND WILL ELDER
WITH THE ACCENT ON CULTURE, THESE DAYS... IT'S ONLY NATURAL THAT WE SHOULD FIND ANNIE *AU NATUREL* IN THE GREENWICH VILLAGE GARRET OF DUNCAN FYFE HEPPLEWHITE... WHERE SHE DISCOVERS WHAT PHILOSOPHERS HAVE LONG KNOWN: THAT LIFE IS FLEETING, BUT ART LIVES FOREVER... EXCEPT WHEN IT DOESN'T SELL, IN WHICH CASE FORGET IT!
CONFOUND IT, ANNIE... WHAT DIFFERENCE CAN IT MAKE TO YOU! I'M ONLY PAINTING FROM THE TERRACE BECAUSE I NEED THE DISTANCE —
BUT, MR. HEPPLE-WHITE... YOU KNOW HOW IT IS WITH MODELS... WE DON'T MIND POSING UNDRAPED, BUT IT'S EMBARRASSING WHEN SOMEONE SEES US THROUGH THE WINDOW.
WELL, NO MATTER, MY DEAR... IT'S FINISHED. YOU ARE NOW PERMANENTLY INCORPORATED INTO A PRECIOUS WORK OF ART. YOU ARE PART OF A MASTERPIECE WORTH A KING'S RANSOM!
GLORYOSKY, MR. HEPPLEWHITE, YOU'RE SO FABULOUS! ...UH—COULD I GET PAID BEFORE I LEAVE?
PAID? PAID?! DRAT IT! I FORGOT TO DRAW ANY CASH FROM THE BANK! BUT COME... DRIVE WITH ME TO THE GALLERY. I'M OPENING MY ONE-MAN SHOW TODAY AT WHICH I'LL BE INUNDATED WITH MONEY. THE GENIUS IN MY PRICELESS CANVASES IS GOOD AS GOLD.
...UH— I'LL TAKE A CHECK.
Hello Sucker!
DON'T BE A PATSY!
Get a LAWYER!
WANTADS

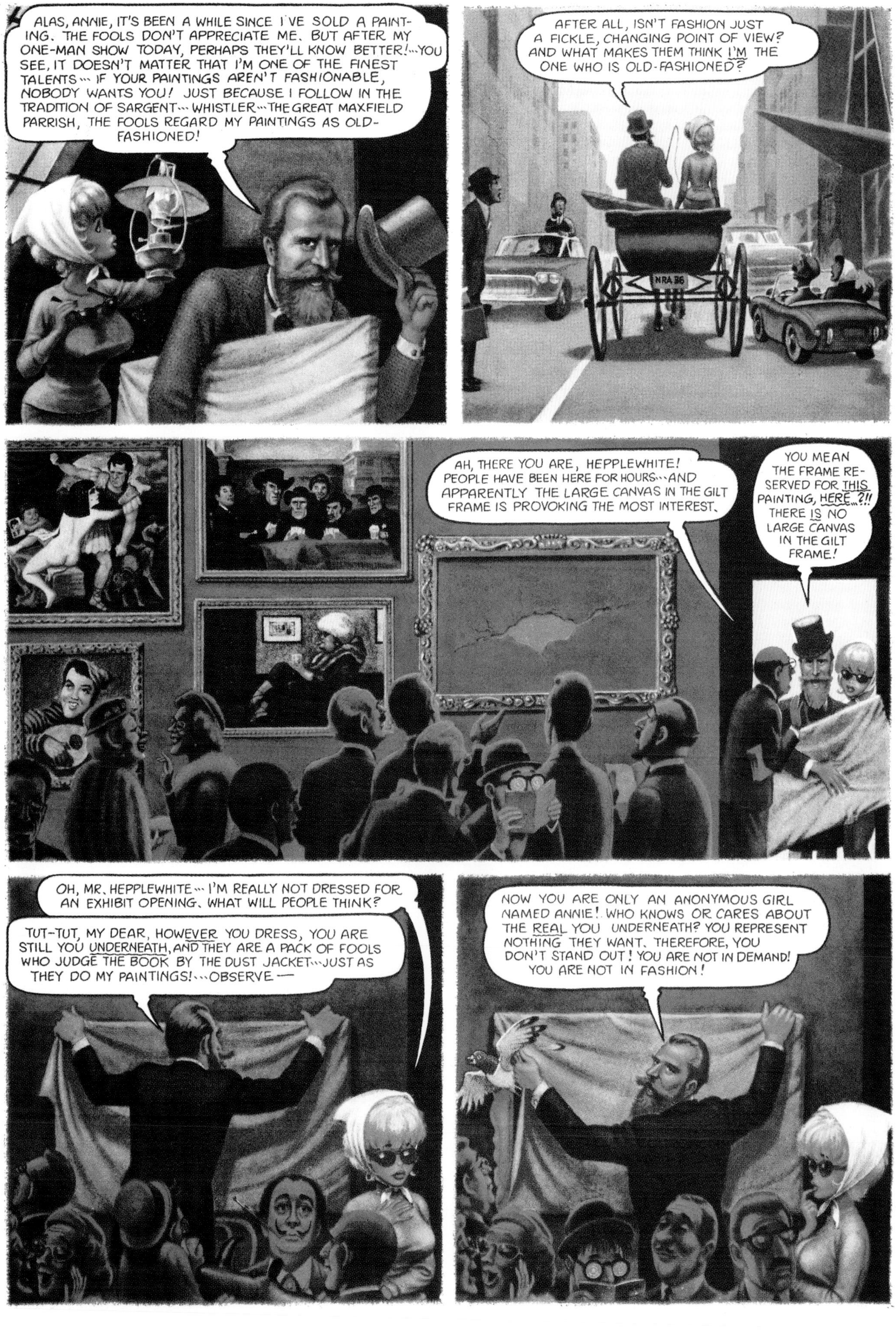

ALAS, ANNIE, IT'S BEEN A WHILE SINCE I'VE SOLD A PAINTING. THE FOOLS DON'T APPRECIATE ME. BUT AFTER MY ONE-MAN SHOW TODAY, PERHAPS THEY'LL KNOW BETTER!...YOU SEE, IT DOESN'T MATTER THAT I'M ONE OF THE FINEST TALENTS... IF YOUR PAINTINGS AREN'T FASHIONABLE, NOBODY WANTS YOU! JUST BECAUSE I FOLLOW IN THE TRADITION OF SARGENT... WHISTLER...THE GREAT MAXFIELD PARRISH, THE FOOLS REGARD MY PAINTINGS AS OLD-FASHIONED!
AFTER ALL, ISN'T FASHION JUST A FICKLE, CHANGING POINT OF VIEW? AND WHAT MAKES THEM THINK I'M THE ONE WHO IS OLD-FASHIONED?
NRA 86
AH, THERE YOU ARE, HEPPLEWHITE! PEOPLE HAVE BEEN HERE FOR HOURS...AND APPARENTLY THE LARGE CANVAS IN THE GILT FRAME IS PROVOKING THE MOST INTEREST.
YOU MEAN THE FRAME RESERVED FOR THIS PAINTING, HERE...?!! THERE IS NO LARGE CANVAS IN THE GILT FRAME!
OH, MR. HEPPLEWHITE... I'M REALLY NOT DRESSED FOR AN EXHIBIT OPENING. WHAT WILL PEOPLE THINK?
TUT-TUT, MY DEAR, HOWEVER YOU DRESS, YOU ARE STILL YOU UNDERNEATH, AND THEY ARE A PACK OF FOOLS WHO JUDGE THE BOOK BY THE DUST JACKET...JUST AS THEY DO MY PAINTINGS!...OBSERVE—
NOW YOU ARE ONLY AN ANONYMOUS GIRL NAMED ANNIE! WHO KNOWS OR CARES ABOUT THE REAL YOU UNDERNEATH? YOU REPRESENT NOTHING THEY WANT. THEREFORE, YOU DON'T STAND OUT! YOU ARE NOT IN DEMAND! YOU ARE NOT IN FASHION!

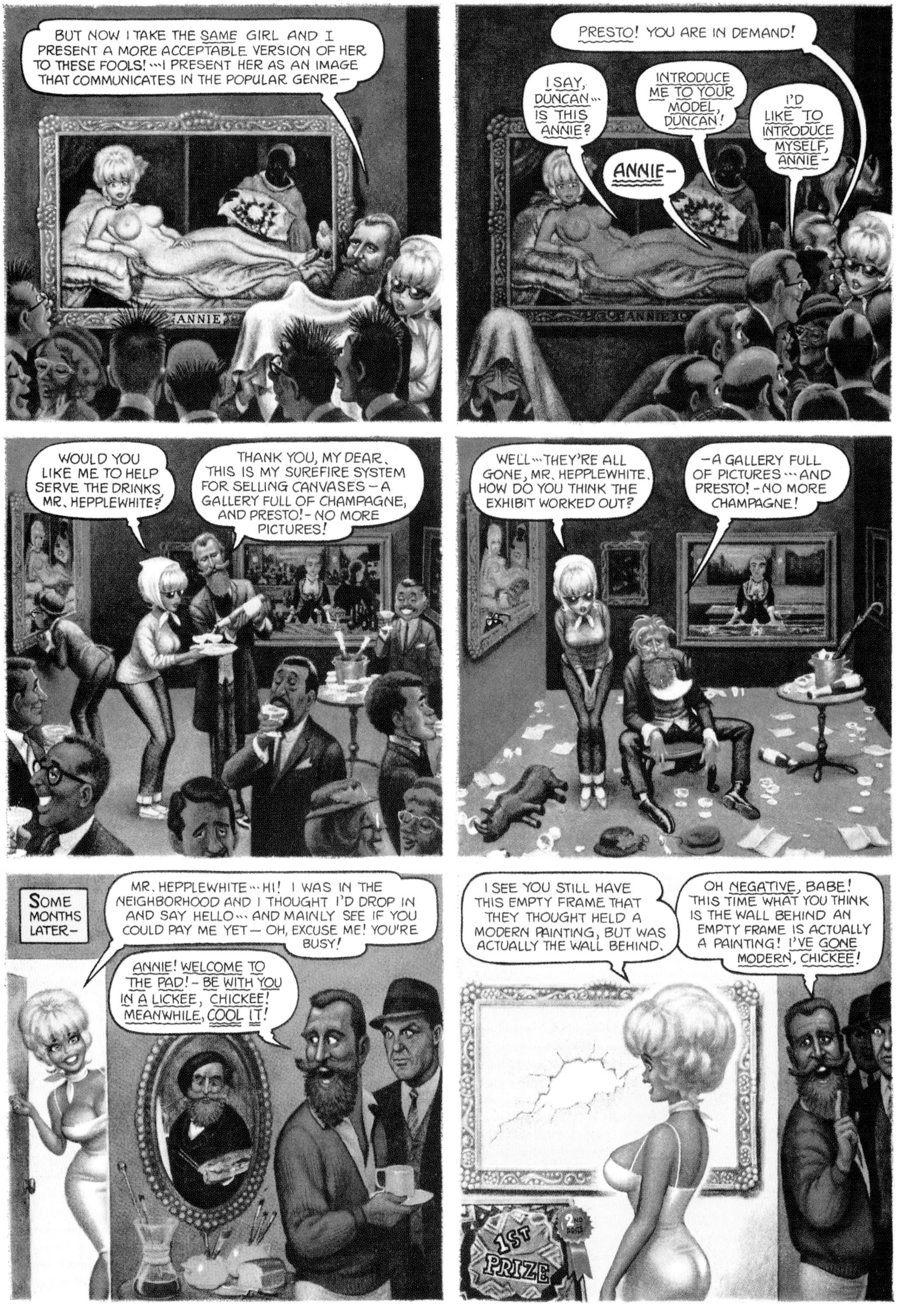
BUT NOW I TAKE THE SAME GIRL AND I PRESENT A MORE ACCEPTABLE VERSION OF HER TO THESE FOOLS! ···I PRESENT HER AS AN IMAGE THAT COMMUNICATES IN THE POPULAR GENRE—
ANNIE
PRESTO! YOU ARE IN DEMAND!
I SAY, DUNCAN··· IS THIS ANNIE?
INTRODUCE ME TO YOUR MODEL, DUNCAN!
I'D LIKE TO INTRODUCE MYSELF, ANNIE—
ANNIE—
WOULD YOU LIKE ME TO HELP SERVE THE DRINKS, MR. HEPPLEWHITE?
THANK YOU, MY DEAR. THIS IS MY SUREFIRE SYSTEM FOR SELLING CANVASES—A GALLERY FULL OF CHAMPAGNE, AND PRESTO!—NO MORE PICTURES!
WELL···THEY'RE ALL GONE, MR. HEPPLEWHITE. HOW DO YOU THINK THE EXHIBIT WORKED OUT?
—A GALLERY FULL OF PICTURES···AND PRESTO!—NO MORE CHAMPAGNE!
SOME MONTHS LATER—
MR. HEPPLEWHITE···HI! I WAS IN THE NEIGHBORHOOD AND I THOUGHT I'D DROP IN AND SAY HELLO··· AND MAINLY SEE IF YOU COULD PAY ME YET—OH, EXCUSE ME! YOU'RE BUSY!
ANNIE! WELCOME TO THE PAD!—BE WITH YOU IN A LICKEE, CHICKEE! MEANWHILE, COOL IT!
I SEE YOU STILL HAVE THIS EMPTY FRAME THAT THEY THOUGHT HELD A MODERN PAINTING, BUT WAS ACTUALLY THE WALL BEHIND.
OH NEGATIVE, BABE! THIS TIME WHAT YOU THINK IS THE WALL BEHIND AN EMPTY FRAME IS ACTUALLY A PAINTING! I'VE GONE MODERN, CHICKEE!
1ST PRIZE

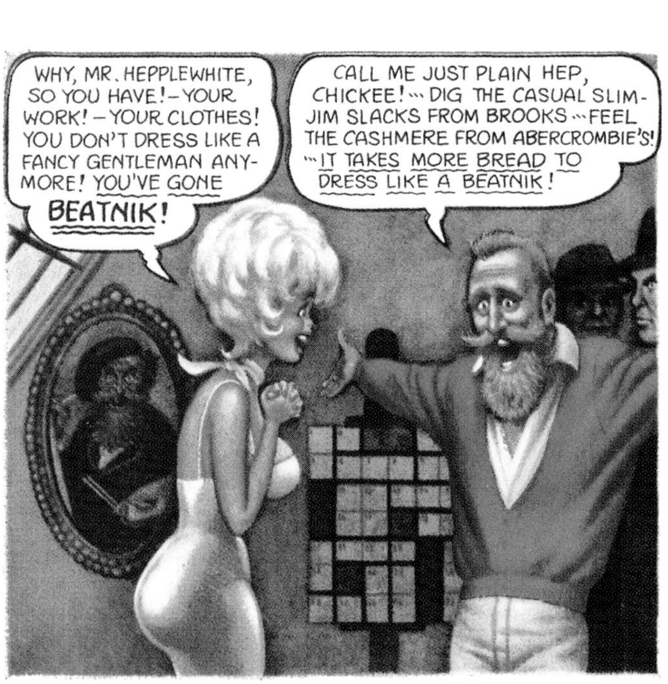
WHY, MR. HEPPLEWHITE, SO YOU HAVE! – YOUR WORK! – YOUR CLOTHES! YOU DON'T DRESS LIKE A FANCY GENTLEMAN ANYMORE! YOU'VE GONE BEATNIK!
CALL ME JUST PLAIN HEP, CHICKEE! ··· DIG THE CASUAL SLIM-JIM SLACKS FROM BROOKS ··· FEEL THE CASHMERE FROM ABERCROMBIE'S! ··· IT TAKES MORE BREAD TO DRESS LIKE A BEATNIK!

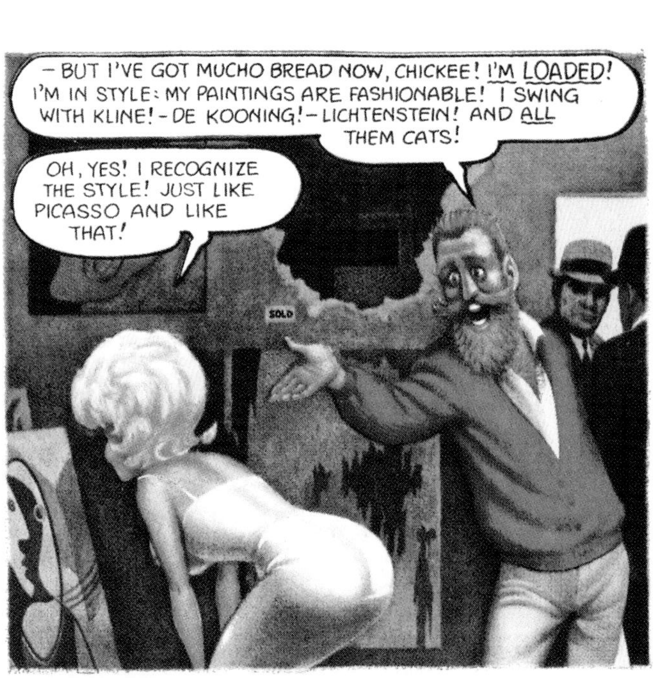
– BUT I'VE GOT MUCHO BREAD NOW, CHICKEE! I'M LOADED! I'M IN STYLE: MY PAINTINGS ARE FASHIONABLE! I SWING WITH KLINE! – DE KOONING! – LICHTENSTEIN! AND ALL THEM CATS!
OH, YES! I RECOGNIZE THE STYLE! JUST LIKE PICASSO AND LIKE THAT!
SOLD

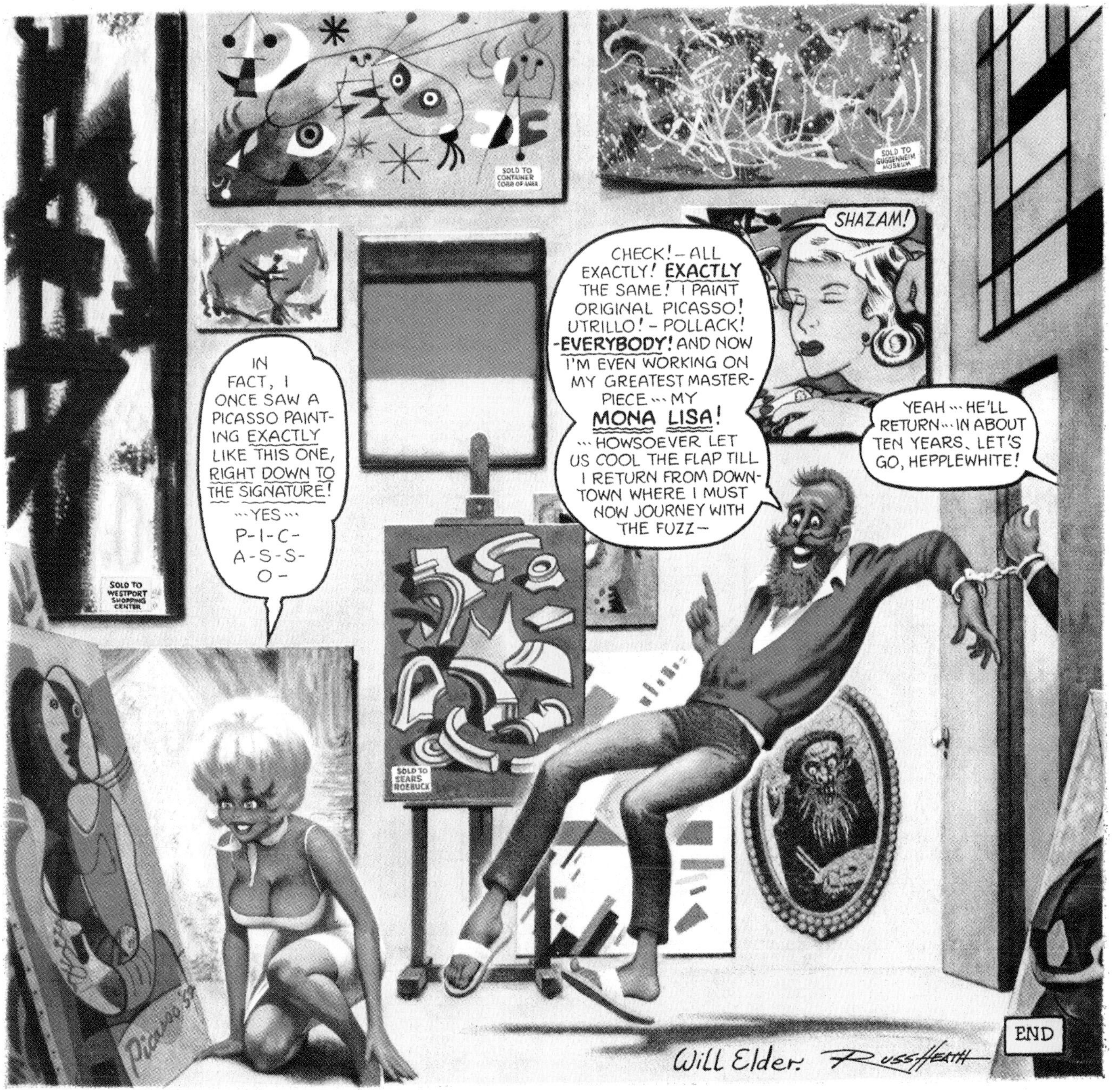
SOLD TO CONTAINER CORP OF AMER
SOLD TO GUGGENHEIM MUSEUM
SHAZAM!
IN FACT, I ONCE SAW A PICASSO PAINTING EXACTLY LIKE THIS ONE, RIGHT DOWN TO THE SIGNATURE! ··· YES ··· P-I-C-A-S-S-O –
CHECK! – ALL EXACTLY! EXACTLY THE SAME! I PAINT ORIGINAL PICASSO! UTRILLO! – POLLACK! – EVERYBODY! AND NOW I'M EVEN WORKING ON MY GREATEST MASTERPIECE ··· MY MONA LISA! ··· HOWSOEVER LET US COOL THE FLAP TILL I RETURN FROM DOWNTOWN WHERE I MUST NOW JOURNEY WITH THE FUZZ –
YEAH ··· HE'LL RETURN ··· IN ABOUT TEN YEARS. LET'S GO, HEPPLEWHITE!
SOLD TO WESTPORT SHOPPING CENTER
SOLD TO SEARS ROEBUCK
Picasso '59
Will Elder. Russ Heath
END

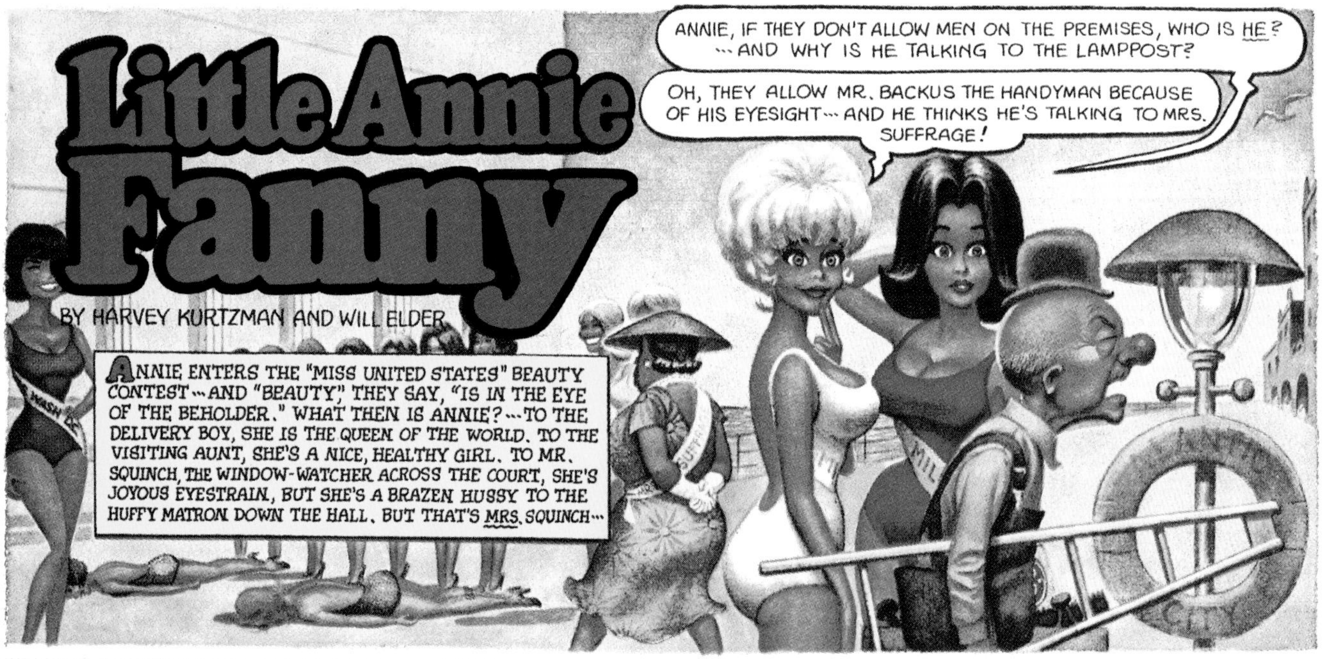

Little Annie Fanny
BY HARVEY KURTZMAN AND WILL ELDER
ANNIE ENTERS THE "MISS UNITED STATES" BEAUTY CONTEST... AND "BEAUTY," THEY SAY, "IS IN THE EYE OF THE BEHOLDER." WHAT THEN IS ANNIE?... TO THE DELIVERY BOY, SHE IS THE QUEEN OF THE WORLD. TO THE VISITING AUNT, SHE'S A NICE, HEALTHY GIRL. TO MR. SQUINCH, THE WINDOW-WATCHER ACROSS THE COURT, SHE'S JOYOUS EYESTRAIN, BUT SHE'S A BRAZEN HUSSY TO THE HUFFY MATRON DOWN THE HALL. BUT THAT'S MRS. SQUINCH...
ANNIE, IF THEY DON'T ALLOW MEN ON THE PREMISES, WHO IS HE? ... AND WHY IS HE TALKING TO THE LAMPPOST?
OH, THEY ALLOW MR. BACKUS THE HANDYMAN BECAUSE OF HIS EYESIGHT... AND HE THINKS HE'S TALKING TO MRS. SUFFRAGE!

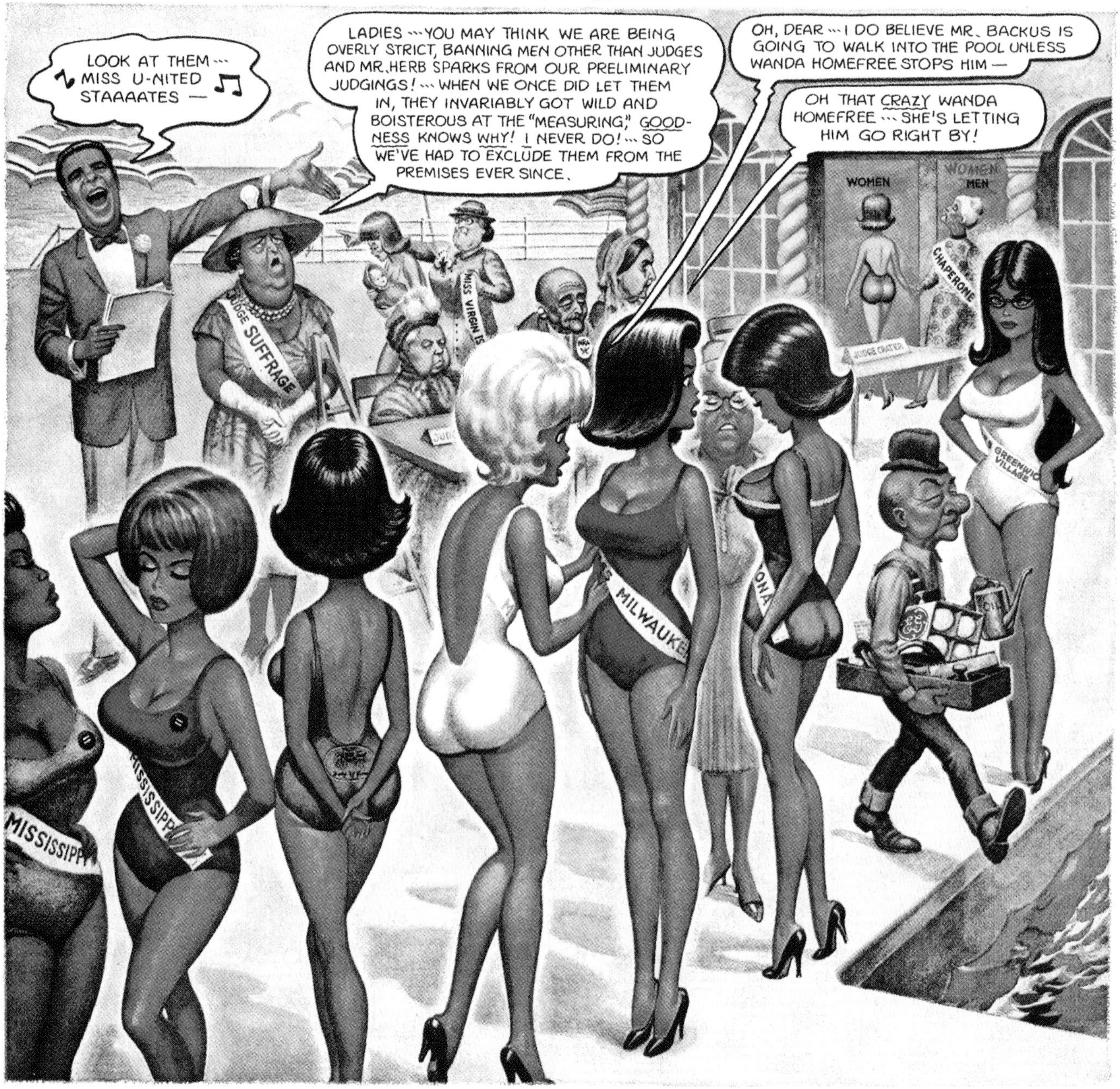

LOOK AT THEM... MISS U-NITED STAAAATES —
LADIES... YOU MAY THINK WE ARE BEING OVERLY STRICT, BANNING MEN OTHER THAN JUDGES AND MR. HERB SPARKS FROM OUR PRELIMINARY JUDGINGS! ... WHEN WE ONCE DID LET THEM IN, THEY INVARIABLY GOT WILD AND BOISTEROUS AT THE "MEASURING," GOODNESS KNOWS WHY! I NEVER DO! ... SO WE'VE HAD TO EXCLUDE THEM FROM THE PREMISES EVER SINCE.
OH, DEAR... I DO BELIEVE MR. BACKUS IS GOING TO WALK INTO THE POOL UNLESS WANDA HOMEFREE STOPS HIM —
OH THAT CRAZY WANDA HOMEFREE... SHE'S LETTING HIM GO RIGHT BY!
WOMEN
WOMEN MEN
JUDGE SUFFRAGE
CHAPERONE
MISS VIRGIN IS
MISSISSIPPI
MISSISSIPPI
MILWAUKEE
GREENWICH VILLAGE

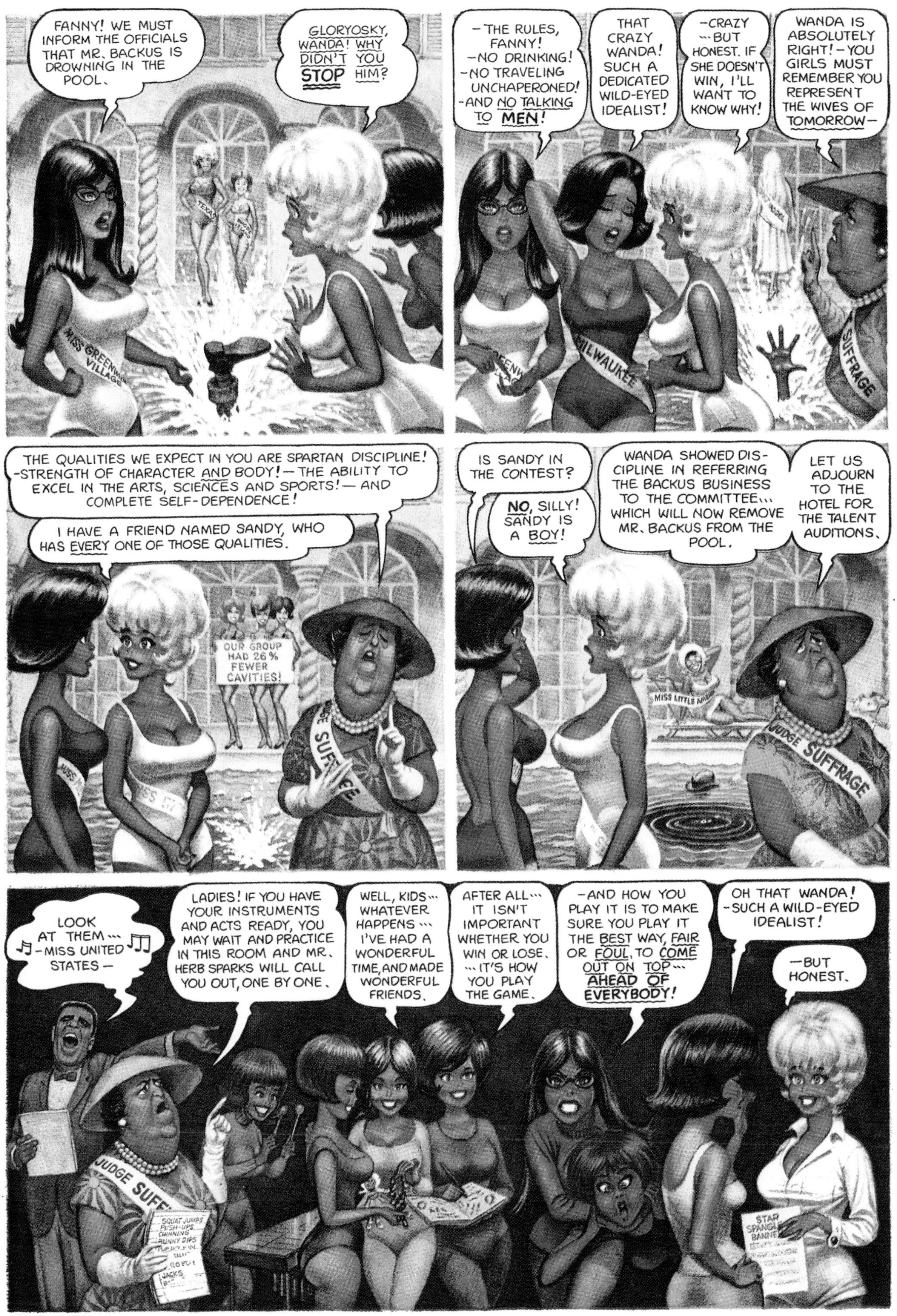

FANNY! WE MUST INFORM THE OFFICIALS THAT MR. BACKUS IS DROWNING IN THE POOL.
GLORYOSKY, WANDA! WHY DIDN'T YOU STOP HIM?
MISS GREENWICH VILLAGE
TEXAS
– THE RULES, FANNY! –NO DRINKING! –NO TRAVELING UNCHAPERONED! –AND NO TALKING TO MEN!
THAT CRAZY WANDA! SUCH A DEDICATED WILD-EYED IDEALIST!
–CRAZY ··· BUT HONEST. IF SHE DOESN'T WIN, I'LL WANT TO KNOW WHY!
WANDA IS ABSOLUTELY RIGHT! – YOU GIRLS MUST REMEMBER YOU REPRESENT THE WIVES OF TOMORROW –
MILWAUKEE
SUFFRAGE
THE QUALITIES WE EXPECT IN YOU ARE SPARTAN DISCIPLINE! –STRENGTH OF CHARACTER AND BODY! – THE ABILITY TO EXCEL IN THE ARTS, SCIENCES AND SPORTS! – AND COMPLETE SELF-DEPENDENCE!
I HAVE A FRIEND NAMED SANDY, WHO HAS EVERY ONE OF THOSE QUALITIES.
OUR GROUP HAD 26% FEWER CAVITIES!
IS SANDY IN THE CONTEST?
NO, SILLY! SANDY IS A BOY!
WANDA SHOWED DISCIPLINE IN REFERRING THE BACKUS BUSINESS TO THE COMMITTEE... WHICH WILL NOW REMOVE MR. BACKUS FROM THE POOL.
LET US ADJOURN TO THE HOTEL FOR THE TALENT AUDITIONS.
JUDGE SUFFRAGE
LOOK AT THEM ··· –MISS UNITED STATES –
LADIES! IF YOU HAVE YOUR INSTRUMENTS AND ACTS READY, YOU MAY WAIT AND PRACTICE IN THIS ROOM AND MR. HERB SPARKS WILL CALL YOU OUT, ONE BY ONE.
WELL, KIDS ··· WHATEVER HAPPENS ··· I'VE HAD A WONDERFUL TIME, AND MADE WONDERFUL FRIENDS.
AFTER ALL ··· IT ISN'T IMPORTANT WHETHER YOU WIN OR LOSE. ··· IT'S HOW YOU PLAY THE GAME.
–AND HOW YOU PLAY IT IS TO MAKE SURE YOU PLAY IT THE BEST WAY, FAIR OR FOUL, TO COME OUT ON TOP ··· AHEAD OF EVERYBODY!
OH THAT WANDA! –SUCH A WILD-EYED IDEALIST!
–BUT HONEST.
SQUAT JUMPS
PUSH-UPS
CHINNING
BUNNY DIPS

41

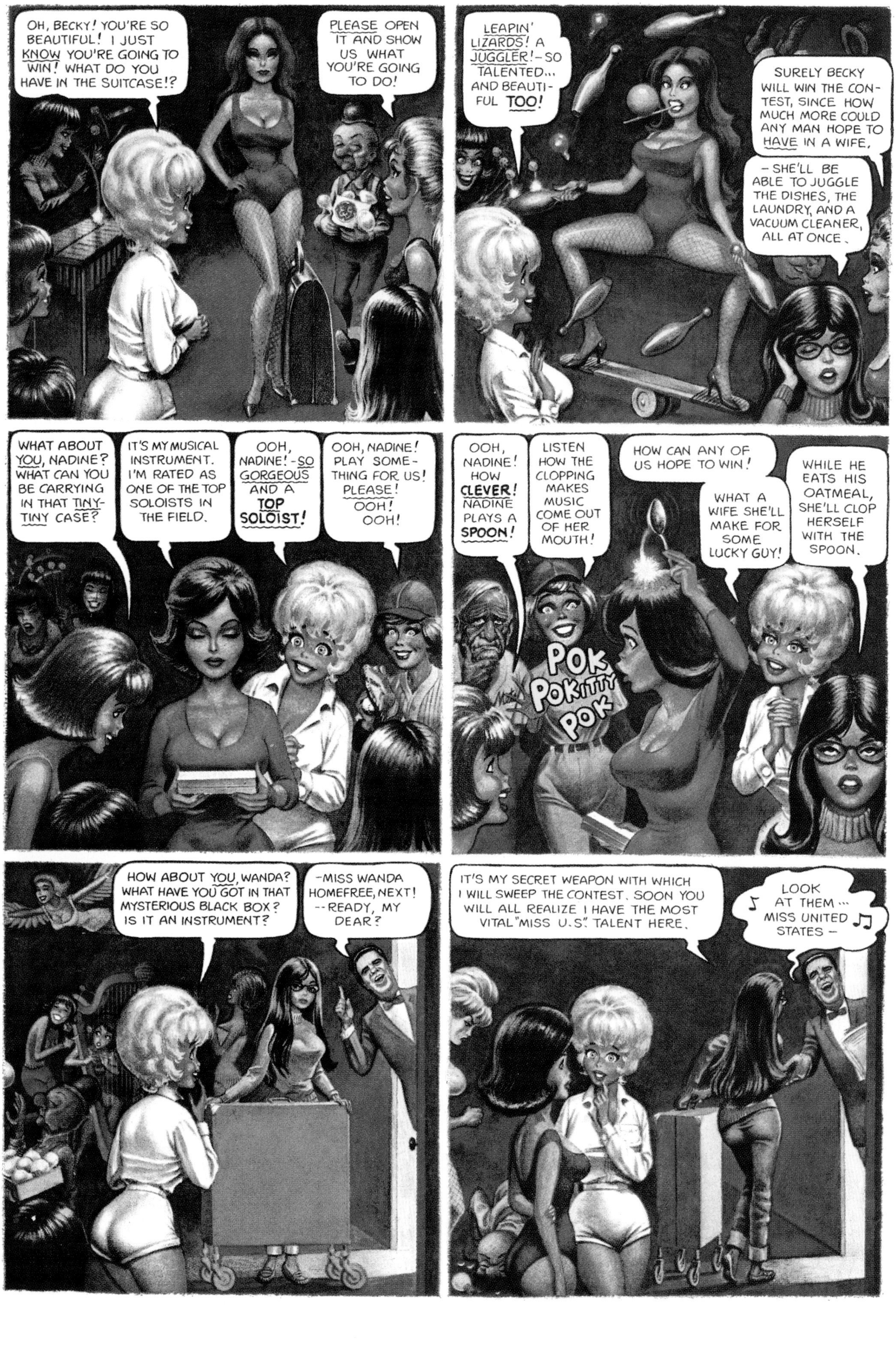
OH, BECKY! YOU'RE SO BEAUTIFUL! I JUST KNOW YOU'RE GOING TO WIN! WHAT DO YOU HAVE IN THE SUITCASE!?
PLEASE OPEN IT AND SHOW US WHAT YOU'RE GOING TO DO!
LEAPIN' LIZARDS! A JUGGLER!—SO TALENTED... AND BEAUTIFUL TOO!
SURELY BECKY WILL WIN THE CONTEST, SINCE HOW MUCH MORE COULD ANY MAN HOPE TO HAVE IN A WIFE,
—SHE'LL BE ABLE TO JUGGLE THE DISHES, THE LAUNDRY, AND A VACUUM CLEANER, ALL AT ONCE.
WHAT ABOUT YOU, NADINE? WHAT CAN YOU BE CARRYING IN THAT TINY-TINY CASE?
IT'S MY MUSICAL INSTRUMENT. I'M RATED AS ONE OF THE TOP SOLOISTS IN THE FIELD.
OOH, NADINE!—SO GORGEOUS AND A TOP SOLOIST!
OOH, NADINE! PLAY SOMETHING FOR US! PLEASE! OOH! OOH!
OOH, NADINE! HOW CLEVER! NADINE PLAYS A SPOON!
LISTEN HOW THE CLOPPING MAKES MUSIC COME OUT OF HER MOUTH!
HOW CAN ANY OF US HOPE TO WIN!
WHAT A WIFE SHE'LL MAKE FOR SOME LUCKY GUY!
WHILE HE EATS HIS OATMEAL, SHE'LL CLOP HERSELF WITH THE SPOON.
POK POKITTY POK
HOW ABOUT YOU, WANDA? WHAT HAVE YOU GOT IN THAT MYSTERIOUS BLACK BOX? IS IT AN INSTRUMENT?
—MISS WANDA HOMEFREE, NEXT! --READY, MY DEAR?
IT'S MY SECRET WEAPON WITH WHICH I WILL SWEEP THE CONTEST. SOON YOU WILL ALL REALIZE I HAVE THE MOST VITAL "MISS U.S." TALENT HERE.
LOOK AT THEM ... MISS UNITED STATES —

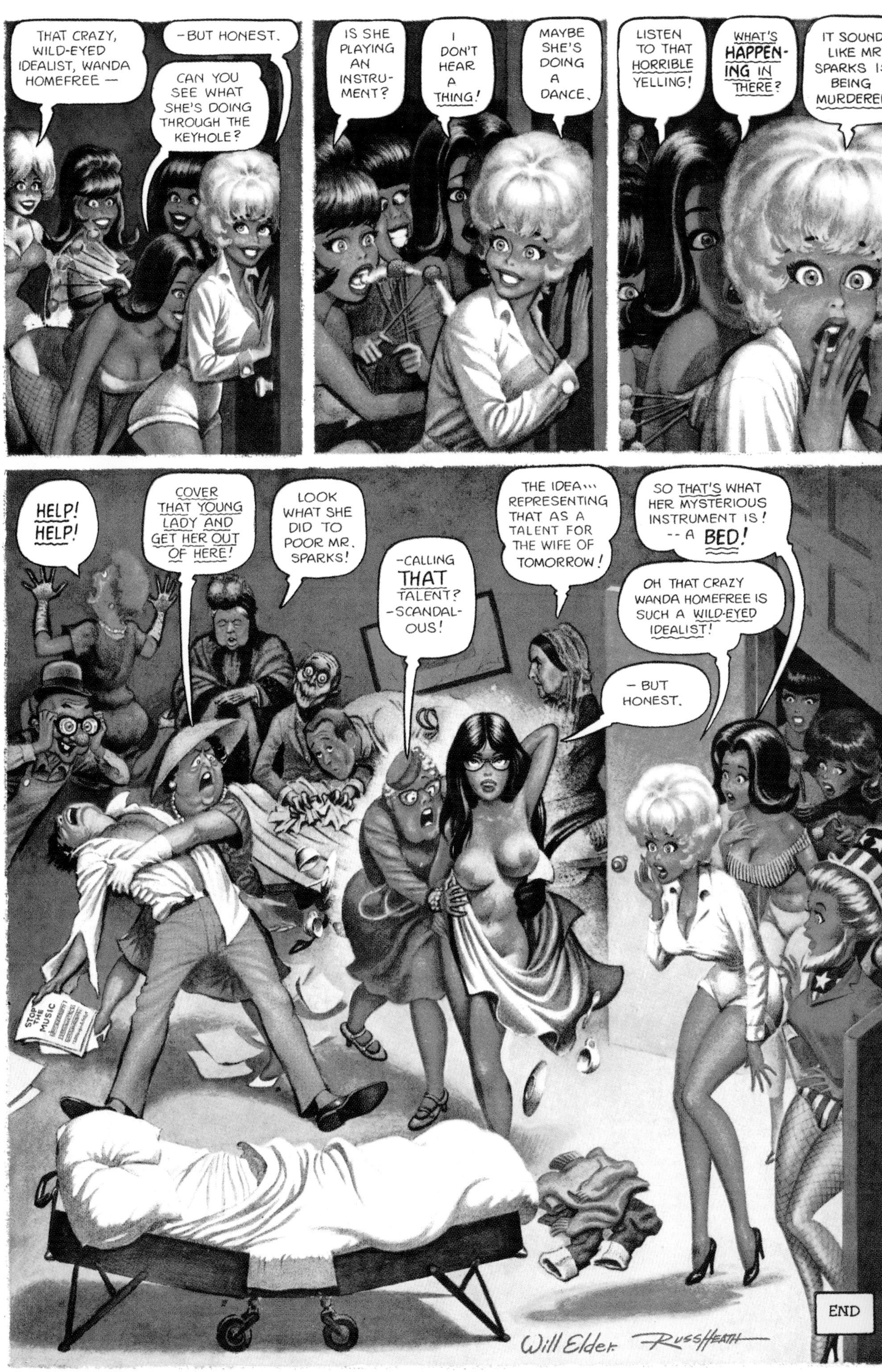
THAT CRAZY, WILD-EYED IDEALIST, WANDA HOMEFREE —
-BUT HONEST.
CAN YOU SEE WHAT SHE'S DOING THROUGH THE KEYHOLE?
IS SHE PLAYING AN INSTRU-MENT?
I DON'T HEAR A THING!
MAYBE SHE'S DOING A DANCE.
LISTEN TO THAT HORRIBLE YELLING!
WHAT'S HAPPEN-ING IN THERE?
IT SOUNDS LIKE MR. SPARKS IS BEING MURDERED!
HELP! HELP!
COVER THAT YOUNG LADY AND GET HER OUT OF HERE!
LOOK WHAT SHE DID TO POOR MR. SPARKS!
-CALLING THAT TALENT? -SCANDAL-OUS!
THE IDEA... REPRESENTING THAT AS A TALENT FOR THE WIFE OF TOMORROW!
SO THAT'S WHAT HER MYSTERIOUS INSTRUMENT IS! -- A BED!
OH THAT CRAZY WANDA HOMEFREE IS SUCH A WILD-EYED IDEALIST!
- BUT HONEST.
STOP THE MUSIC
END
Will Elder
RUSS HEATH

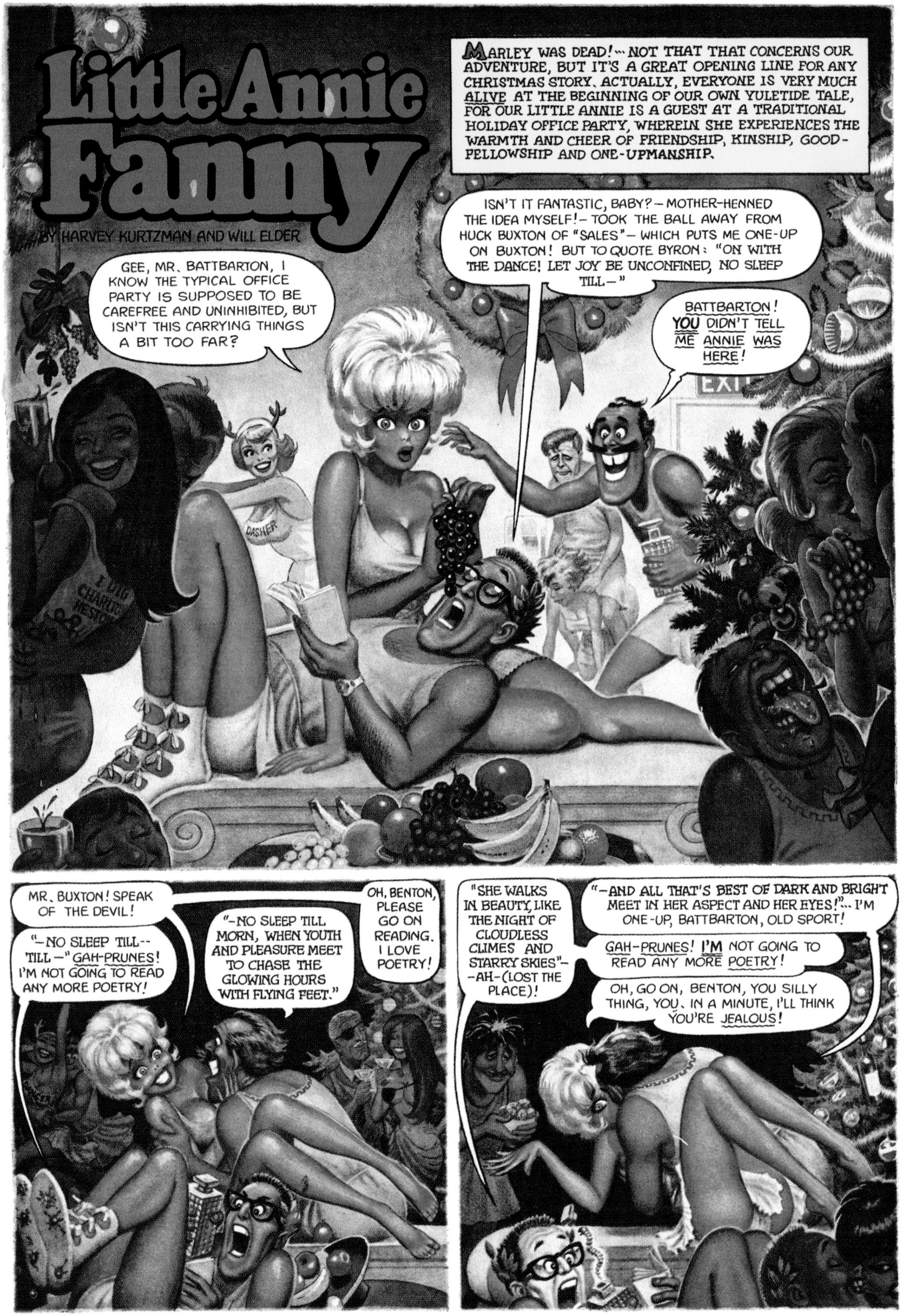

Little Annie Fanny
BY HARVEY KURTZMAN AND WILL ELDER
MARLEY WAS DEAD!... NOT THAT THAT CONCERNS OUR ADVENTURE, BUT IT'S A GREAT OPENING LINE FOR ANY CHRISTMAS STORY. ACTUALLY, EVERYONE IS VERY MUCH ALIVE AT THE BEGINNING OF OUR OWN YULETIDE TALE, FOR OUR LITTLE ANNIE IS A GUEST AT A TRADITIONAL HOLIDAY OFFICE PARTY, WHEREIN SHE EXPERIENCES THE WARMTH AND CHEER OF FRIENDSHIP, KINSHIP, GOOD-FELLOWSHIP AND ONE-UPMANSHIP.
GEE, MR. BATTBARTON, I KNOW THE TYPICAL OFFICE PARTY IS SUPPOSED TO BE CAREFREE AND UNINHIBITED, BUT ISN'T THIS CARRYING THINGS A BIT TOO FAR?
ISN'T IT FANTASTIC, BABY? — MOTHER-HENNED THE IDEA MYSELF! — TOOK THE BALL AWAY FROM HUCK BUXTON OF "SALES" — WHICH PUTS ME ONE-UP ON BUXTON! BUT TO QUOTE BYRON: "ON WITH THE DANCE! LET JOY BE UNCONFINED, NO SLEEP TILL —"
BATTBARTON! YOU DIDN'T TELL ME ANNIE WAS HERE!
DASHER
MR. BUXTON! SPEAK OF THE DEVIL!
"— NO SLEEP TILL-- TILL —" GAH-PRUNES! I'M NOT GOING TO READ ANY MORE POETRY!
"— NO SLEEP TILL MORN, WHEN YOUTH AND PLEASURE MEET TO CHASE THE GLOWING HOURS WITH FLYING FEET."
OH, BENTON, PLEASE GO ON READING. I LOVE POETRY!
"SHE WALKS IN BEAUTY, LIKE THE NIGHT OF CLOUDLESS CLIMES AND STARRY SKIES" — AH- (LOST THE PLACE)!
"— AND ALL THAT'S BEST OF DARK AND BRIGHT MEET IN HER ASPECT AND HER EYES!"... I'M ONE-UP, BATTBARTON, OLD SPORT!
GAH-PRUNES! I'M NOT GOING TO READ ANY MORE POETRY!
OH, GO ON, BENTON, YOU SILLY THING, YOU. IN A MINUTE, I'LL THINK YOU'RE JEALOUS!

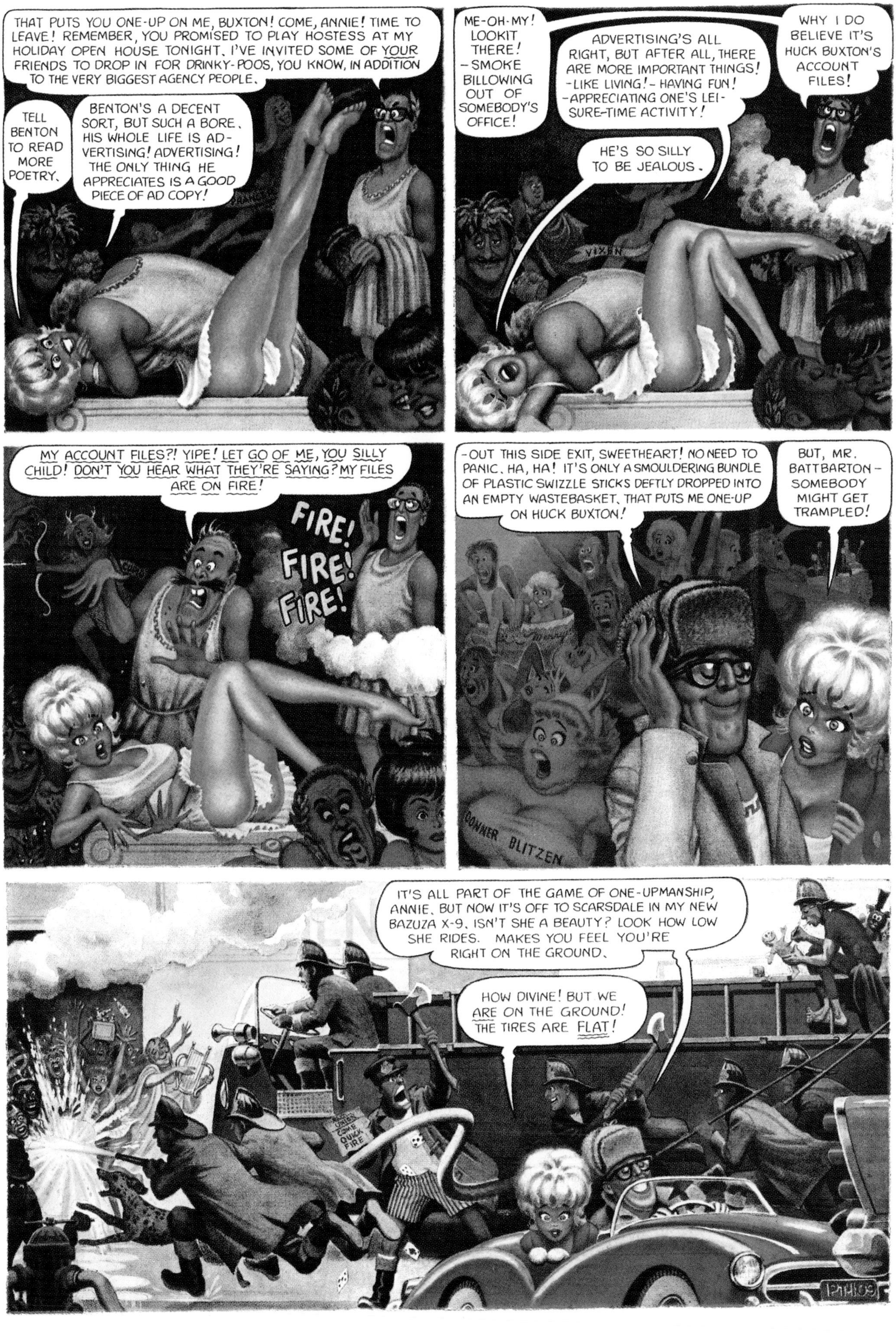

THAT PUTS YOU ONE-UP ON ME, BUXTON! COME, ANNIE! TIME TO LEAVE! REMEMBER, YOU PROMISED TO PLAY HOSTESS AT MY HOLIDAY OPEN HOUSE TONIGHT. I'VE INVITED SOME OF YOUR FRIENDS TO DROP IN FOR DRINKY-POOS, YOU KNOW, IN ADDITION TO THE VERY BIGGEST AGENCY PEOPLE.
TELL BENTON TO READ MORE POETRY.
BENTON'S A DECENT SORT, BUT SUCH A BORE. HIS WHOLE LIFE IS ADVERTISING! ADVERTISING! THE ONLY THING HE APPRECIATES IS A GOOD PIECE OF AD COPY!
ME-OH-MY! LOOKIT THERE! -SMOKE BILLOWING OUT OF SOMEBODY'S OFFICE!
ADVERTISING'S ALL RIGHT, BUT AFTER ALL, THERE ARE MORE IMPORTANT THINGS! -LIKE LIVING! - HAVING FUN! -APPRECIATING ONE'S LEISURE-TIME ACTIVITY!
WHY I DO BELIEVE IT'S HUCK BUXTON'S ACCOUNT FILES!
HE'S SO SILLY TO BE JEALOUS.
VIXEN
MY ACCOUNT FILES?! YIPE! LET GO OF ME, YOU SILLY CHILD! DON'T YOU HEAR WHAT THEY'RE SAYING? MY FILES ARE ON FIRE!
FIRE! FIRE! FIRE!
-OUT THIS SIDE EXIT, SWEETHEART! NO NEED TO PANIC. HA, HA! IT'S ONLY A SMOULDERING BUNDLE OF PLASTIC SWIZZLE STICKS DEFTLY DROPPED INTO AN EMPTY WASTEBASKET. THAT PUTS ME ONE-UP ON HUCK BUXTON!
BUT, MR. BATTBARTON - SOMEBODY MIGHT GET TRAMPLED!
DONNER BLITZEN
IT'S ALL PART OF THE GAME OF ONE-UPMANSHIP, ANNIE. BUT NOW IT'S OFF TO SCARSDALE IN MY NEW BAZUZA X-9. ISN'T SHE A BEAUTY? LOOK HOW LOW SHE RIDES. MAKES YOU FEEL YOU'RE RIGHT ON THE GROUND.
HOW DIVINE! BUT WE ARE ON THE GROUND! THE TIRES ARE FLAT!

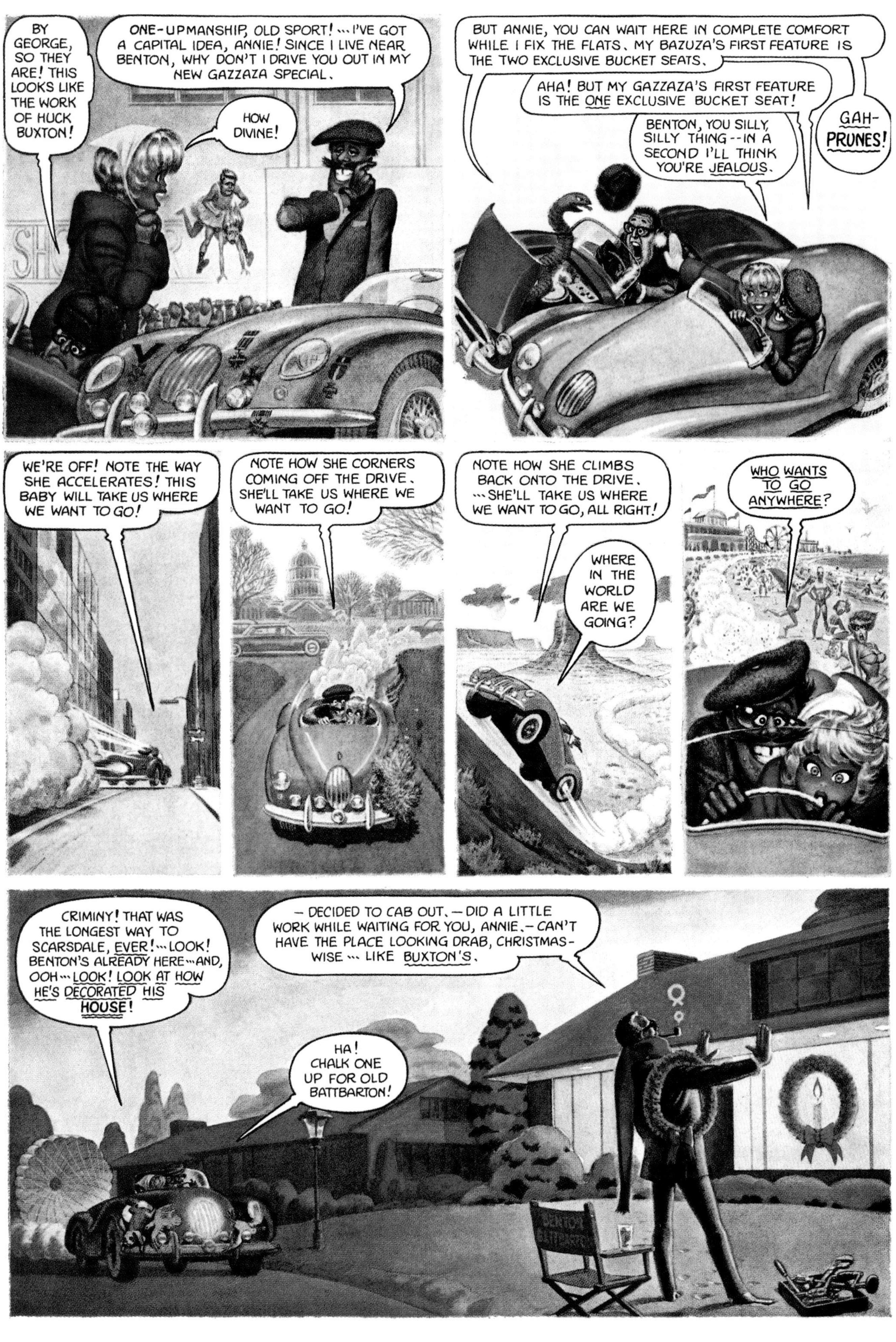

BY GEORGE, SO THEY ARE! THIS LOOKS LIKE THE WORK OF HUCK BUXTON!
ONE-UPMANSHIP, OLD SPORT! ··· I'VE GOT A CAPITAL IDEA, ANNIE! SINCE I LIVE NEAR BENTON, WHY DON'T I DRIVE YOU OUT IN MY NEW GAZZAZA SPECIAL.
HOW DIVINE!
BUT ANNIE, YOU CAN WAIT HERE IN COMPLETE COMFORT WHILE I FIX THE FLATS. MY BAZUZA'S FIRST FEATURE IS THE TWO EXCLUSIVE BUCKET SEATS.
AHA! BUT MY GAZZAZA'S FIRST FEATURE IS THE ONE EXCLUSIVE BUCKET SEAT!
GAH-PRUNES!
BENTON, YOU SILLY, SILLY THING--IN A SECOND I'LL THINK YOU'RE JEALOUS.
WE'RE OFF! NOTE THE WAY SHE ACCELERATES! THIS BABY WILL TAKE US WHERE WE WANT TO GO!
NOTE HOW SHE CORNERS COMING OFF THE DRIVE. SHE'LL TAKE US WHERE WE WANT TO GO!
NOTE HOW SHE CLIMBS BACK ONTO THE DRIVE. ··· SHE'LL TAKE US WHERE WE WANT TO GO, ALL RIGHT!
WHERE IN THE WORLD ARE WE GOING?
WHO WANTS TO GO ANYWHERE?
CRIMINY! THAT WAS THE LONGEST WAY TO SCARSDALE, EVER! ··· LOOK! BENTON'S ALREADY HERE ··· AND, OOH ··· LOOK! LOOK AT HOW HE'S DECORATED HIS HOUSE!
– DECIDED TO CAB OUT. – DID A LITTLE WORK WHILE WAITING FOR YOU, ANNIE. – CAN'T HAVE THE PLACE LOOKING DRAB, CHRISTMAS-WISE ··· LIKE BUXTON'S.
HA! CHALK ONE UP FOR OLD BATTBARTON!

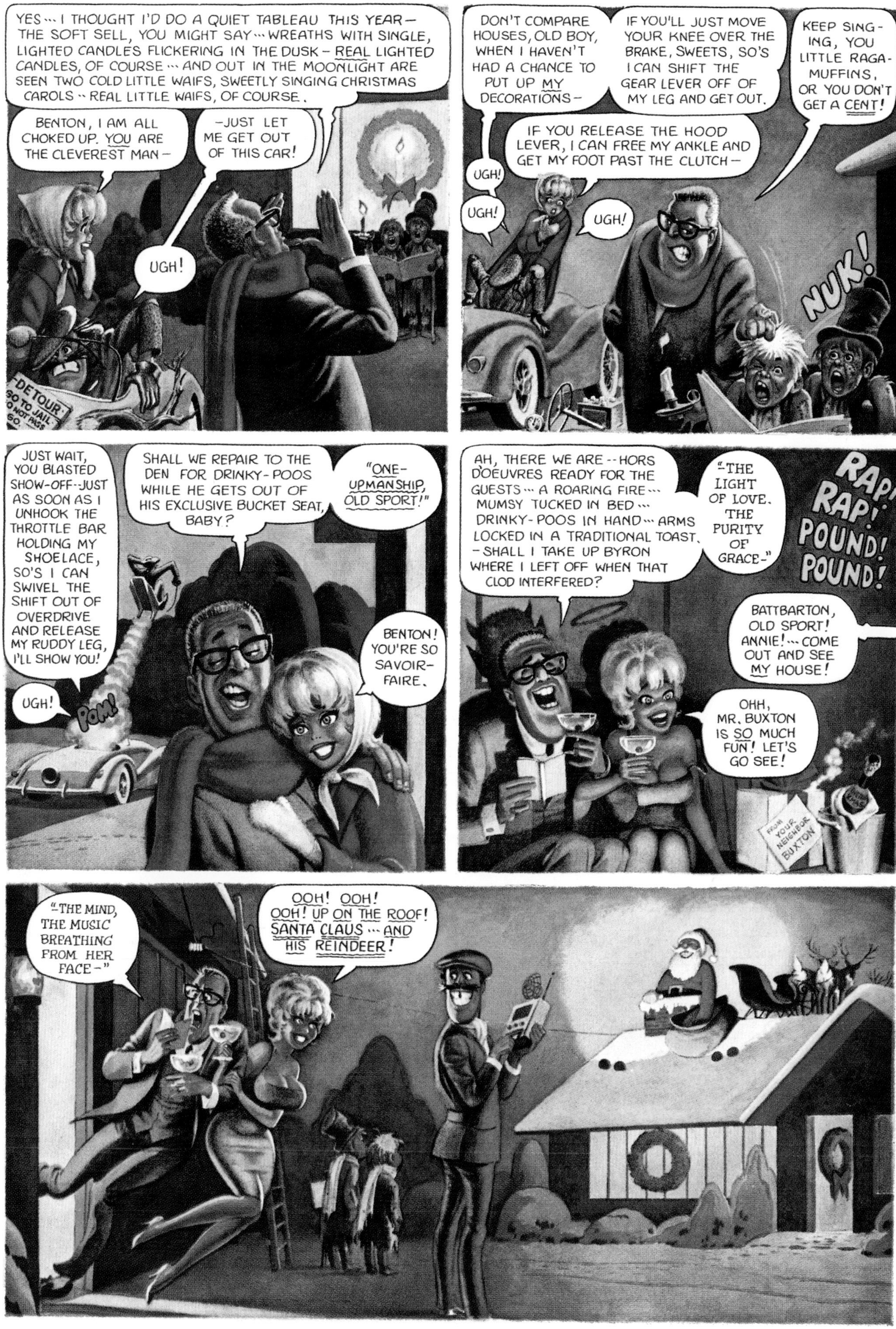

YES ··· I THOUGHT I'D DO A QUIET TABLEAU THIS YEAR— THE SOFT SELL, YOU MIGHT SAY ··· WREATHS WITH SINGLE, LIGHTED CANDLES FLICKERING IN THE DUSK – REAL LIGHTED CANDLES, OF COURSE ··· AND OUT IN THE MOONLIGHT ARE SEEN TWO COLD LITTLE WAIFS, SWEETLY SINGING CHRISTMAS CAROLS -- REAL LITTLE WAIFS, OF COURSE.
BENTON, I AM ALL CHOKED UP. YOU ARE THE CLEVEREST MAN –
–JUST LET ME GET OUT OF THIS CAR!
UGH!
DETOUR
GO TO JAIL DO NOT PASS GO.
DON'T COMPARE HOUSES, OLD BOY, WHEN I HAVEN'T HAD A CHANCE TO PUT UP MY DECORATIONS –
IF YOU'LL JUST MOVE YOUR KNEE OVER THE BRAKE, SWEETS, SO'S I CAN SHIFT THE GEAR LEVER OFF OF MY LEG AND GET OUT.
KEEP SING-ING, YOU LITTLE RAGA-MUFFINS, OR YOU DON'T GET A CENT!
IF YOU RELEASE THE HOOD LEVER, I CAN FREE MY ANKLE AND GET MY FOOT PAST THE CLUTCH –
UGH!
UGH!
UGH!
NUK!
JUST WAIT, YOU BLASTED SHOW-OFF--JUST AS SOON AS I UNHOOK THE THROTTLE BAR HOLDING MY SHOELACE, SO'S I CAN SWIVEL THE SHIFT OUT OF OVERDRIVE AND RELEASE MY RUDDY LEG, I'LL SHOW YOU!
SHALL WE REPAIR TO THE DEN FOR DRINKY-POOS WHILE HE GETS OUT OF HIS EXCLUSIVE BUCKET SEAT, BABY?
"ONE-UPMANSHIP, OLD SPORT!"
BENTON! YOU'RE SO SAVOIR-FAIRE.
UGH!
POM!
AH, THERE WE ARE --HORS D'OEUVRES READY FOR THE GUESTS ··· A ROARING FIRE ··· MUMSY TUCKED IN BED ··· DRINKY-POOS IN HAND ··· ARMS LOCKED IN A TRADITIONAL TOAST. – SHALL I TAKE UP BYRON WHERE I LEFT OFF WHEN THAT CLOD INTERFERED?
"–THE LIGHT OF LOVE, THE PURITY OF GRACE–"
RAP! RAP! POUND! POUND!
BATTBARTON, OLD SPORT! ANNIE! ··· COME OUT AND SEE MY HOUSE!
OHH, MR. BUXTON IS SO MUCH FUN! LET'S GO SEE!
FROM YOUR NEIGHBOR BUXTON
"–THE MIND, THE MUSIC BREATHING FROM HER FACE–"
OOH! OOH! OOH! UP ON THE ROOF! SANTA CLAUS ··· AND HIS REINDEER!

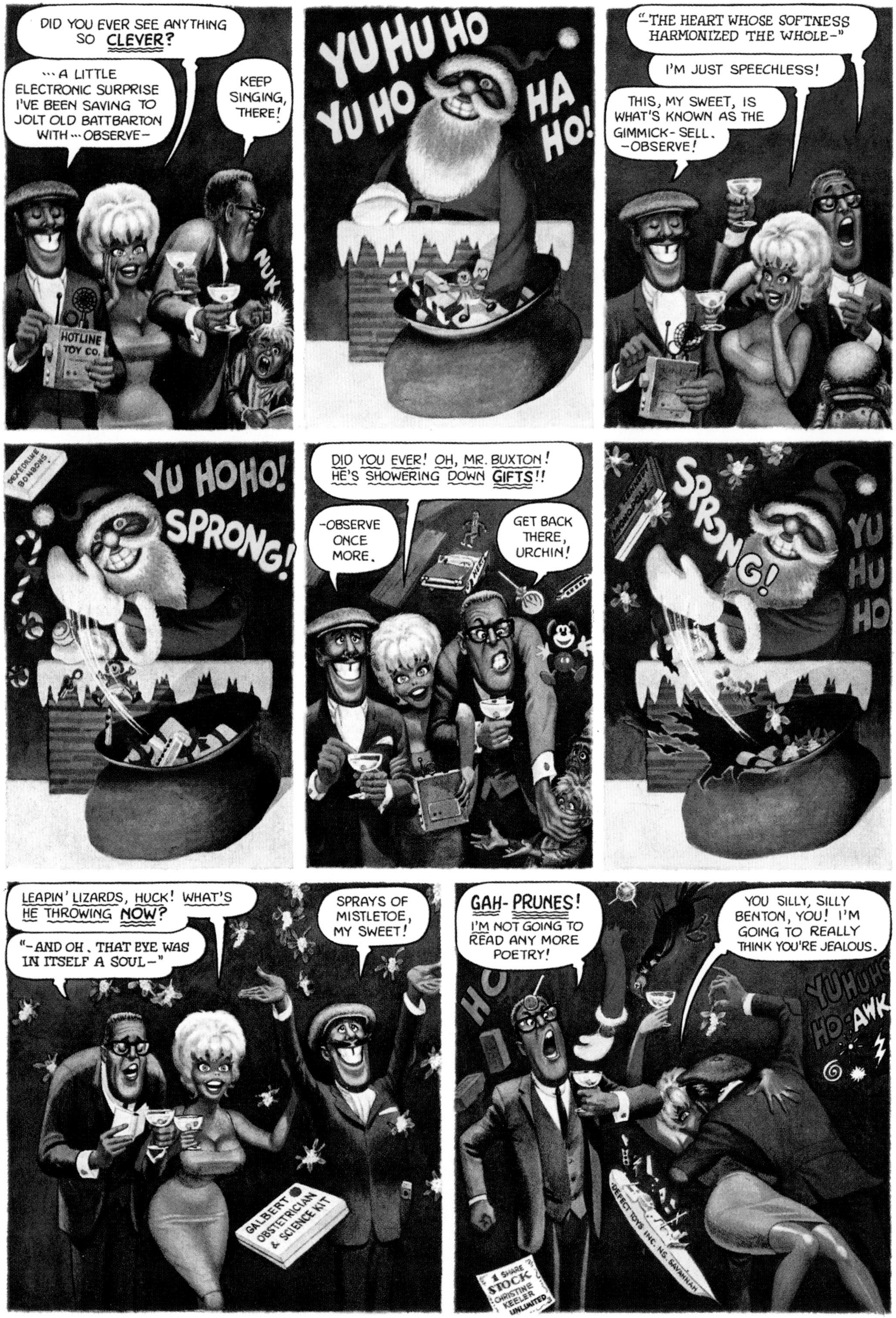
DID YOU EVER SEE ANYTHING SO CLEVER?
···A LITTLE ELECTRONIC SURPRISE I'VE BEEN SAVING TO JOLT OLD BATTBARTON WITH···OBSERVE–
KEEP SINGING, THERE!
NUK
HOTLINE TOY CO.
YUHU HO YU HO HA HO!
"–THE HEART WHOSE SOFTNESS HARMONIZED THE WHOLE–"
I'M JUST SPEECHLESS!
THIS, MY SWEET, IS WHAT'S KNOWN AS THE GIMMICK-SELL. –OBSERVE!
YU HOHO!
SPRONG!
DID YOU EVER! OH, MR. BUXTON! HE'S SHOWERING DOWN GIFTS!!
–OBSERVE ONCE MORE.
GET BACK THERE, URCHIN!
SPRONG!
YU HU HO
LEAPIN' LIZARDS, HUCK! WHAT'S HE THROWING NOW?
"–AND OH, THAT EYE WAS IN ITSELF A SOUL–"
SPRAYS OF MISTLETOE, MY SWEET!
GALBERT OBSTETRICIAN & SCIENCE KIT
GAH-PRUNES! I'M NOT GOING TO READ ANY MORE POETRY!
YOU SILLY, SILLY BENTON, YOU! I'M GOING TO REALLY THINK YOU'RE JEALOUS.
HO
YUHUHO HO-AWK
1 SHARE STOCK CHRISTINE KEELER UNLIMITED
DEFECT TOYS INC. NS. SAVANNAH

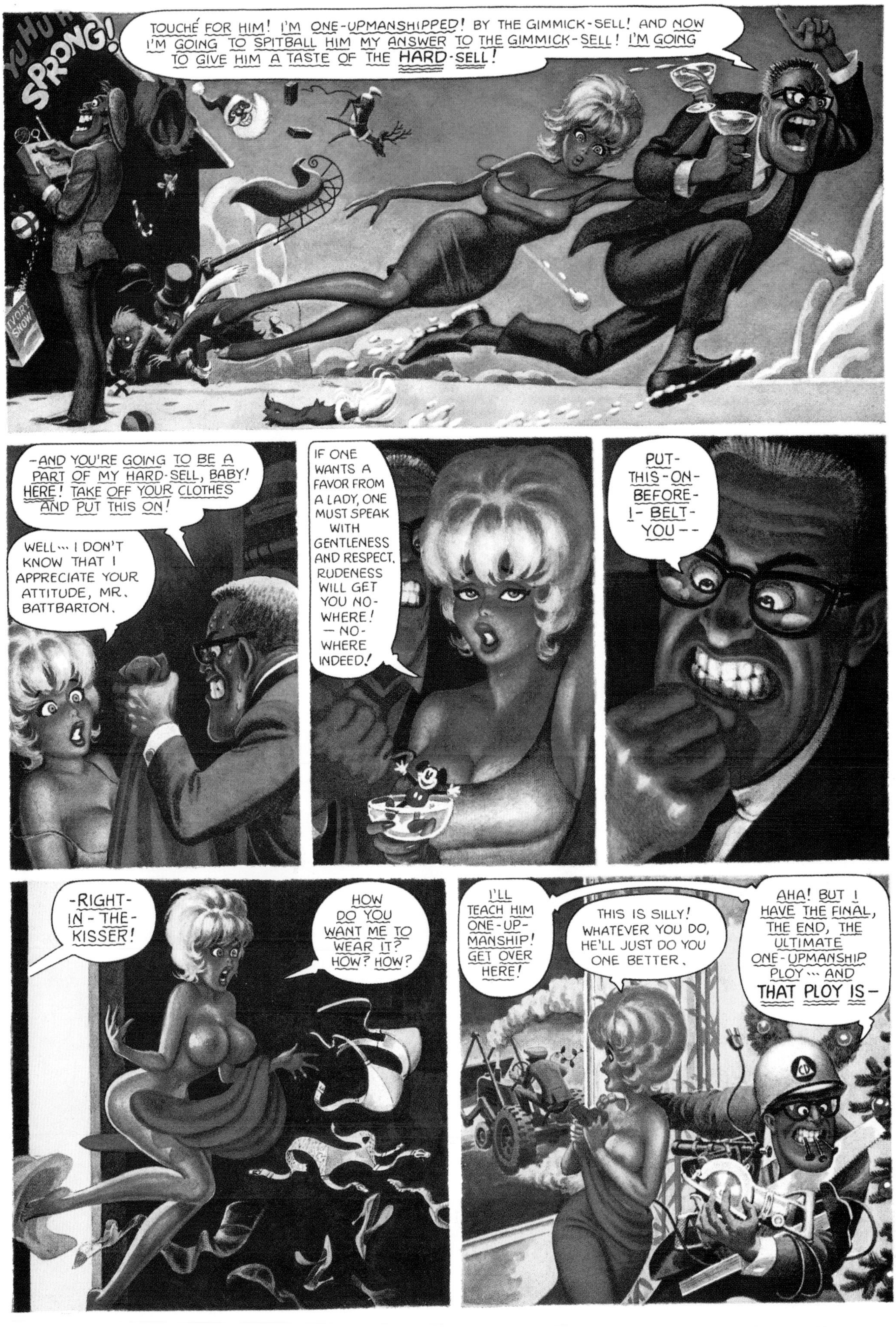
SPRONG!
TOUCHÉ FOR HIM! I'M ONE-UPMANSHIPPED! BY THE GIMMICK-SELL! AND NOW I'M GOING TO SPITBALL HIM MY ANSWER TO THE GIMMICK-SELL! I'M GOING TO GIVE HIM A TASTE OF THE HARD-SELL!
IVORY SHOW
-AND YOU'RE GOING TO BE A PART OF MY HARD-SELL, BABY! HERE! TAKE OFF YOUR CLOTHES AND PUT THIS ON!
WELL... I DON'T KNOW THAT I APPRECIATE YOUR ATTITUDE, MR. BATTBARTON.
IF ONE WANTS A FAVOR FROM A LADY, ONE MUST SPEAK WITH GENTLENESS AND RESPECT. RUDENESS WILL GET YOU NO-WHERE! —NO-WHERE INDEED!
PUT-THIS-ON-BEFORE-I-BELT-YOU--
-RIGHT-IN-THE-KISSER!
HOW DO YOU WANT ME TO WEAR IT? HOW? HOW?
I'LL TEACH HIM ONE-UPMANSHIP! GET OVER HERE!
THIS IS SILLY! WHATEVER YOU DO, HE'LL JUST DO YOU ONE BETTER.
AHA! BUT I HAVE THE FINAL, THE END, THE ULTIMATE ONE-UPMANSHIP PLOY... AND THAT PLOY IS—

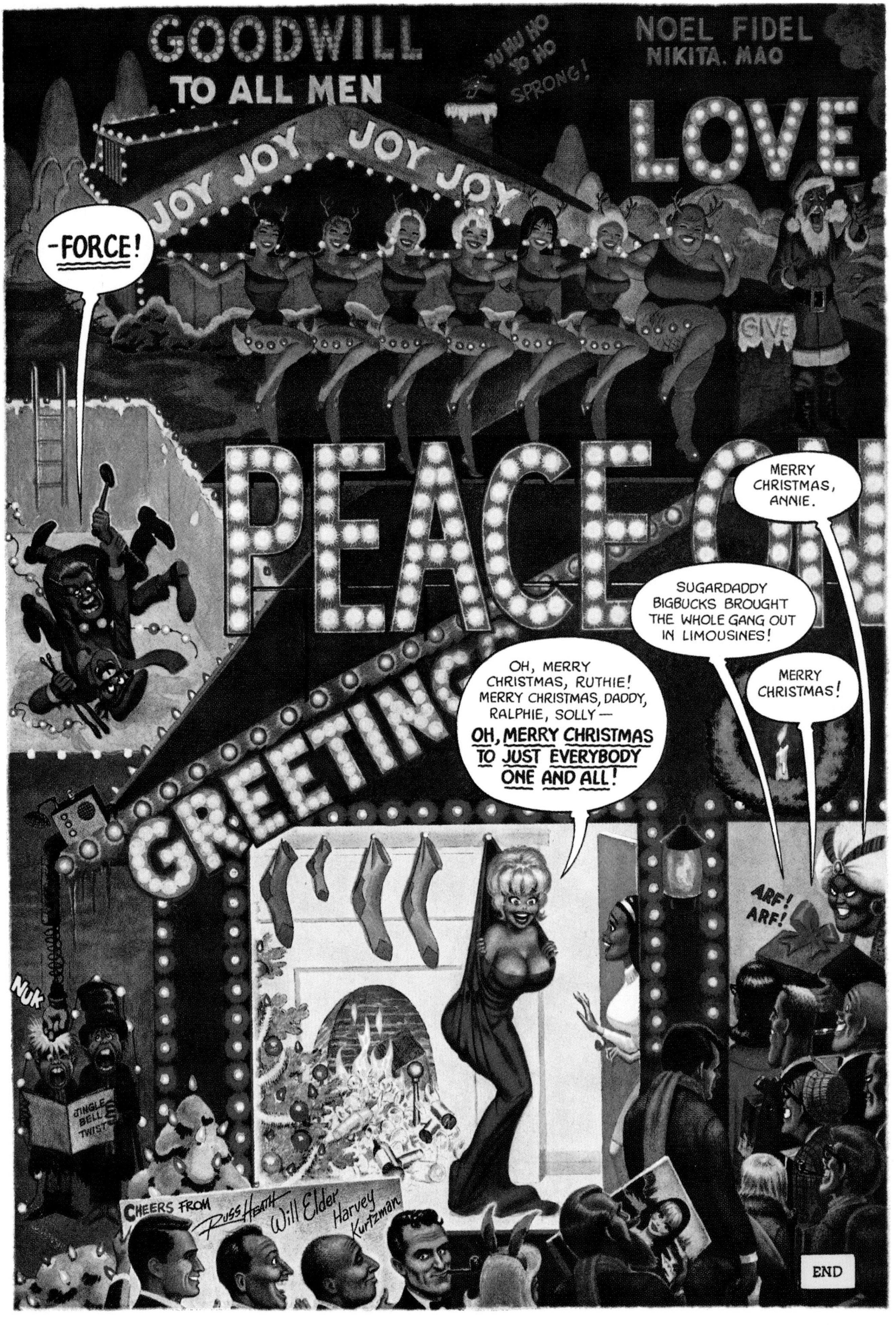

GOODWILL
TO ALL MEN
YU HU HO
YO HO
SPRONG!
NOEL FIDEL
NIKITA, MAO
LOVE
JOY JOY JOY JOY
-FORCE!
GIVE
PEACE ON
GREETINGS
MERRY CHRISTMAS, ANNIE.
SUGARDADDY BIGBUCKS BROUGHT THE WHOLE GANG OUT IN LIMOUSINES!
MERRY CHRISTMAS!
OH, MERRY CHRISTMAS, RUTHIE! MERRY CHRISTMAS, DADDY, RALPHIE, SOLLY— OH, MERRY CHRISTMAS TO JUST EVERYBODY ONE AND ALL!
ARF! ARF!
NUK
JINGLE BELL TWIST
CHEERS FROM Russ Heath Will Elder Harvey Kurtzman
END

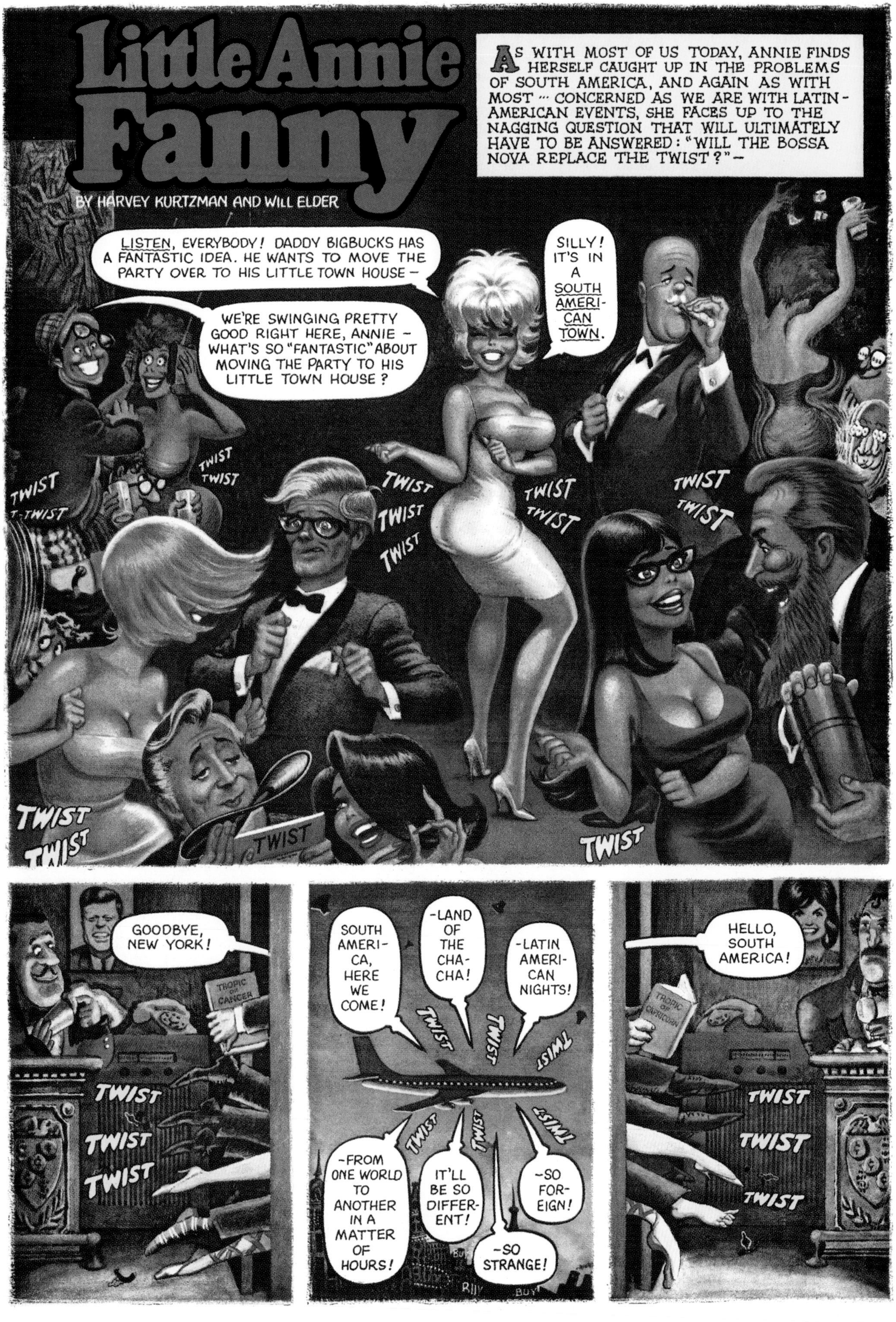
Little Annie Fanny
BY HARVEY KURTZMAN AND WILL ELDER
AS WITH MOST OF US TODAY, ANNIE FINDS HERSELF CAUGHT UP IN THE PROBLEMS OF SOUTH AMERICA, AND AGAIN AS WITH MOST ··· CONCERNED AS WE ARE WITH LATIN-AMERICAN EVENTS, SHE FACES UP TO THE NAGGING QUESTION THAT WILL ULTIMATELY HAVE TO BE ANSWERED: "WILL THE BOSSA NOVA REPLACE THE TWIST?"—
LISTEN, EVERYBODY! DADDY BIGBUCKS HAS A FANTASTIC IDEA. HE WANTS TO MOVE THE PARTY OVER TO HIS LITTLE TOWN HOUSE—
WE'RE SWINGING PRETTY GOOD RIGHT HERE, ANNIE— WHAT'S SO "FANTASTIC" ABOUT MOVING THE PARTY TO HIS LITTLE TOWN HOUSE?
SILLY! IT'S IN A SOUTH AMERICAN TOWN.
TWIST T-TWIST
TWIST TWIST
TWIST TWIST TWIST
TWIST TWIST
TWIST TWIST
TWIST TWIST
TWIST
TWIST
GOODBYE, NEW YORK!
TROPIC OF CANCER
TWIST TWIST TWIST
SOUTH AMERI-CA, HERE WE COME!
-LAND OF THE CHA-CHA!
-LATIN AMERI-CAN NIGHTS!
TWIST TWIST TWIST
TWIST TWIST TWIST
-FROM ONE WORLD TO ANOTHER IN A MATTER OF HOURS!
IT'LL BE SO DIFFER-ENT!
-SO STRANGE!
-SO FOR-EIGN!
HELLO, SOUTH AMERICA!
TROPIC OF CAPRICORN
TWIST TWIST TWIST

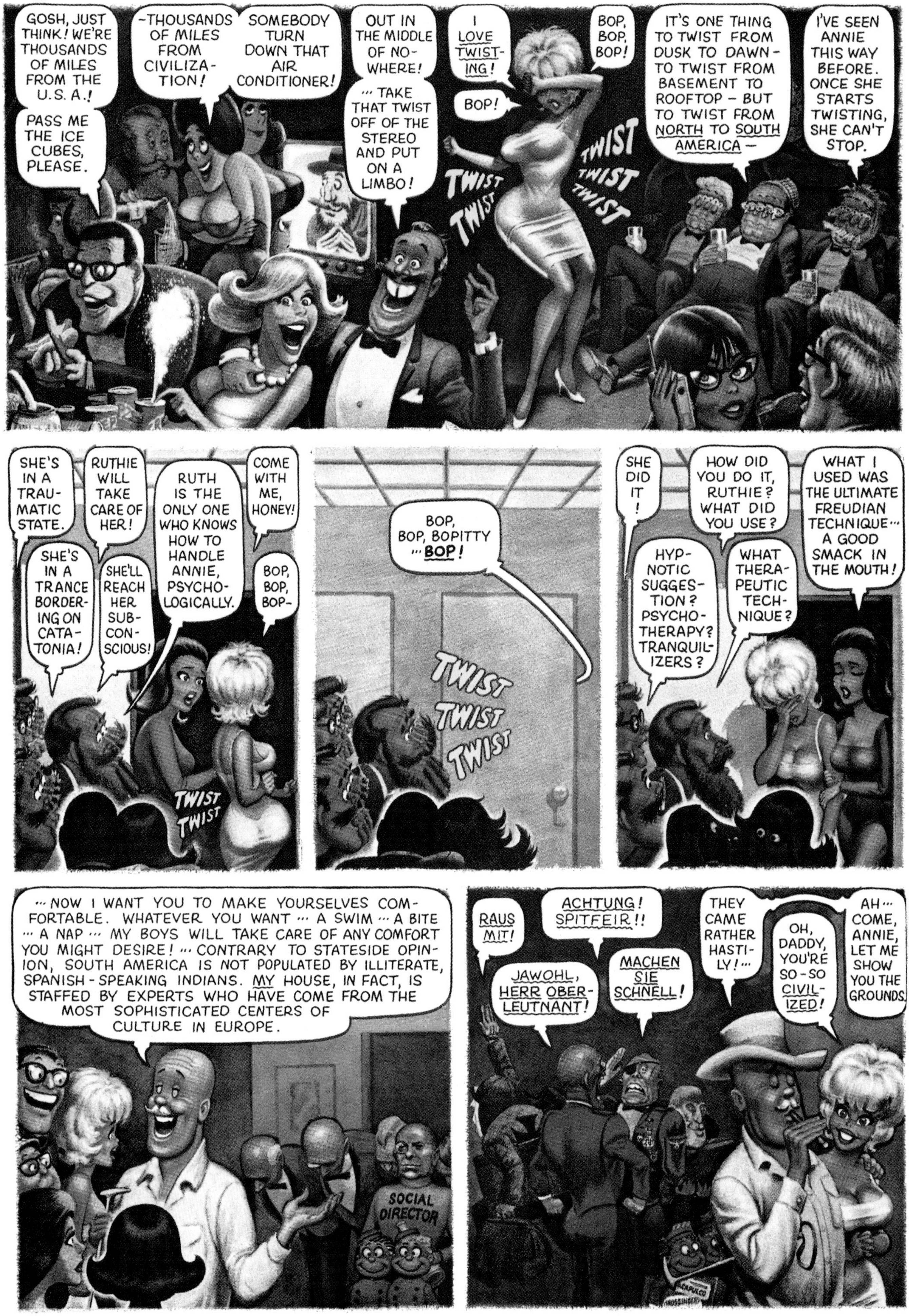

GOSH, JUST THINK! WE'RE THOUSANDS OF MILES FROM THE U.S.A.!
PASS ME THE ICE CUBES, PLEASE.
-THOUSANDS OF MILES FROM CIVILIZA-TION!
SOMEBODY TURN DOWN THAT AIR CONDITIONER!
OUT IN THE MIDDLE OF NO-WHERE!
... TAKE THAT TWIST OFF OF THE STEREO AND PUT ON A LIMBO!
I LOVE TWIST-ING!
BOP!
BOP, BOP, BOP!
TWIST TWIST
TWIST TWIST TWIST
IT'S ONE THING TO TWIST FROM DUSK TO DAWN - TO TWIST FROM BASEMENT TO ROOFTOP - BUT TO TWIST FROM NORTH TO SOUTH AMERICA -
I'VE SEEN ANNIE THIS WAY BEFORE. ONCE SHE STARTS TWISTING, SHE CAN'T STOP.
SHE'S IN A TRAU-MATIC STATE.
SHE'S IN A TRANCE BORDER-ING ON CATA-TONIA!
RUTHIE WILL TAKE CARE OF HER!
SHE'LL REACH HER SUB-CON-SCIOUS!
RUTH IS THE ONLY ONE WHO KNOWS HOW TO HANDLE ANNIE, PSYCHO-LOGICALLY.
COME WITH ME, HONEY!
BOP, BOP, BOP-
TWIST TWIST
BOP, BOP, BOPITTY ... BOP!
TWIST TWIST TWIST
SHE DID IT!
HYP-NOTIC SUGGES-TION? PSYCHO-THERAPY? TRANQUIL-IZERS?
HOW DID YOU DO IT, RUTHIE? WHAT DID YOU USE?
WHAT THERA-PEUTIC TECH-NIQUE?
WHAT I USED WAS THE ULTIMATE FREUDIAN TECHNIQUE ... A GOOD SMACK IN THE MOUTH!
... NOW I WANT YOU TO MAKE YOURSELVES COM-FORTABLE. WHATEVER YOU WANT ... A SWIM ... A BITE ... A NAP ... MY BOYS WILL TAKE CARE OF ANY COMFORT YOU MIGHT DESIRE! ... CONTRARY TO STATESIDE OPIN-ION, SOUTH AMERICA IS NOT POPULATED BY ILLITERATE, SPANISH-SPEAKING INDIANS. MY HOUSE, IN FACT, IS STAFFED BY EXPERTS WHO HAVE COME FROM THE MOST SOPHISTICATED CENTERS OF CULTURE IN EUROPE.
SOCIAL DIRECTOR
RAUS MIT!
ACHTUNG! SPITFEIR!!
JAWOHL, HERR OBER-LEUTNANT!
MACHEN SIE SCHNELL!
THEY CAME RATHER HASTI-LY! ...
OH, DADDY, YOU'RE SO-SO CIVIL-IZED!
AH ... COME, ANNIE, LET ME SHOW YOU THE GROUNDS.

52

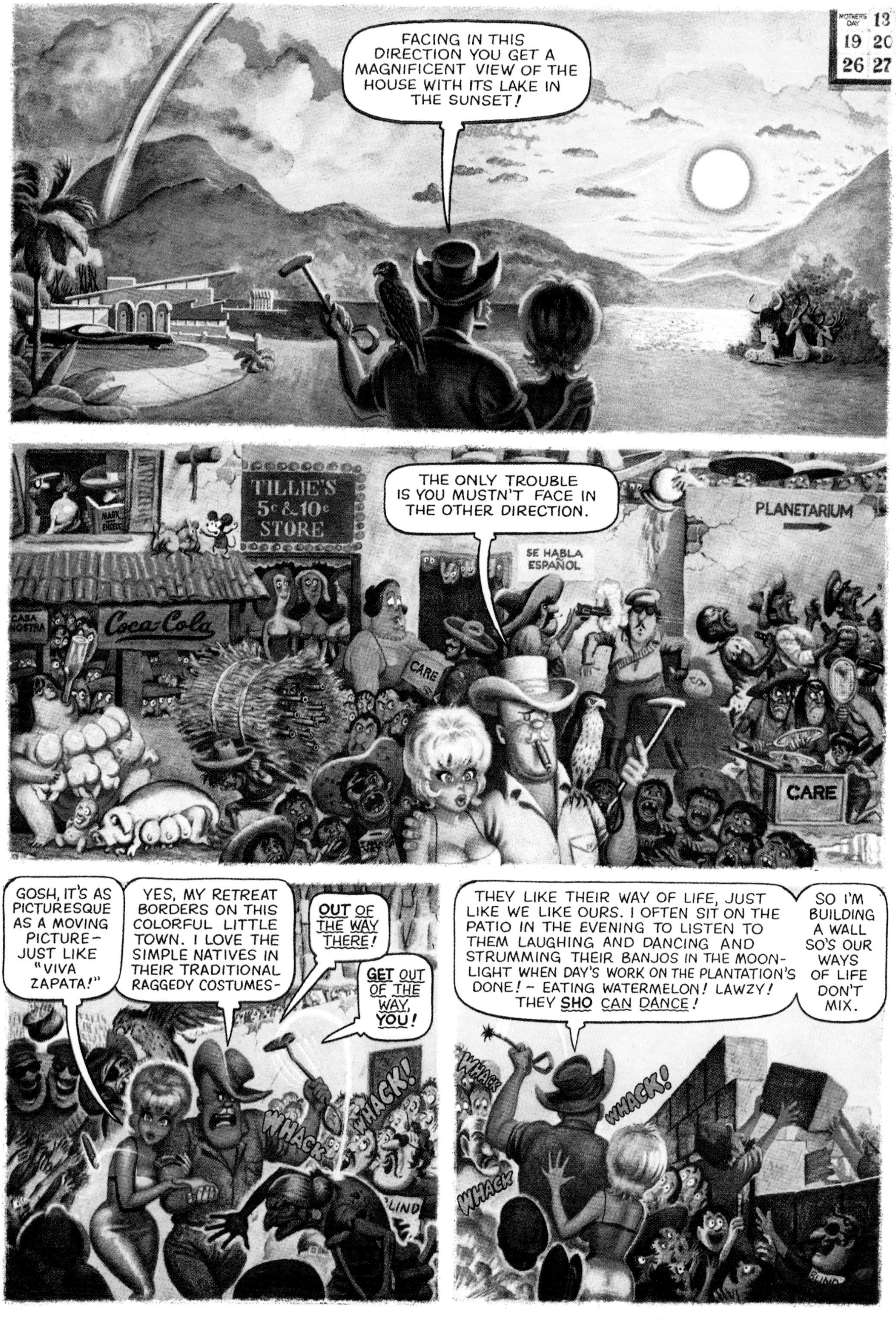

MOTHERS DAY 13
19 20
26 27
FACING IN THIS DIRECTION YOU GET A MAGNIFICENT VIEW OF THE HOUSE WITH ITS LAKE IN THE SUNSET!
TILLIE'S 5¢ & 10¢ STORE
THE ONLY TROUBLE IS YOU MUSTN'T FACE IN THE OTHER DIRECTION.
PLANETARIUM
SE HABLA ESPAÑOL
Coca-Cola
CARE
CARE
GOSH, IT'S AS PICTURESQUE AS A MOVING PICTURE– JUST LIKE "VIVA ZAPATA!"
YES, MY RETREAT BORDERS ON THIS COLORFUL LITTLE TOWN. I LOVE THE SIMPLE NATIVES IN THEIR TRADITIONAL RAGGEDY COSTUMES–
OUT OF THE WAY THERE!
GET OUT OF THE WAY, YOU!
WHACK!
WHACK
BLIND
THEY LIKE THEIR WAY OF LIFE, JUST LIKE WE LIKE OURS. I OFTEN SIT ON THE PATIO IN THE EVENING TO LISTEN TO THEM LAUGHING AND DANCING AND STRUMMING THEIR BANJOS IN THE MOON-LIGHT WHEN DAY'S WORK ON THE PLANTATION'S DONE! – EATING WATERMELON! LAWZY! THEY SHO CAN DANCE!
SO I'M BUILDING A WALL SO'S OUR WAYS OF LIFE DON'T MIX.
WHACK
WHACK!
WHACK
BLIND

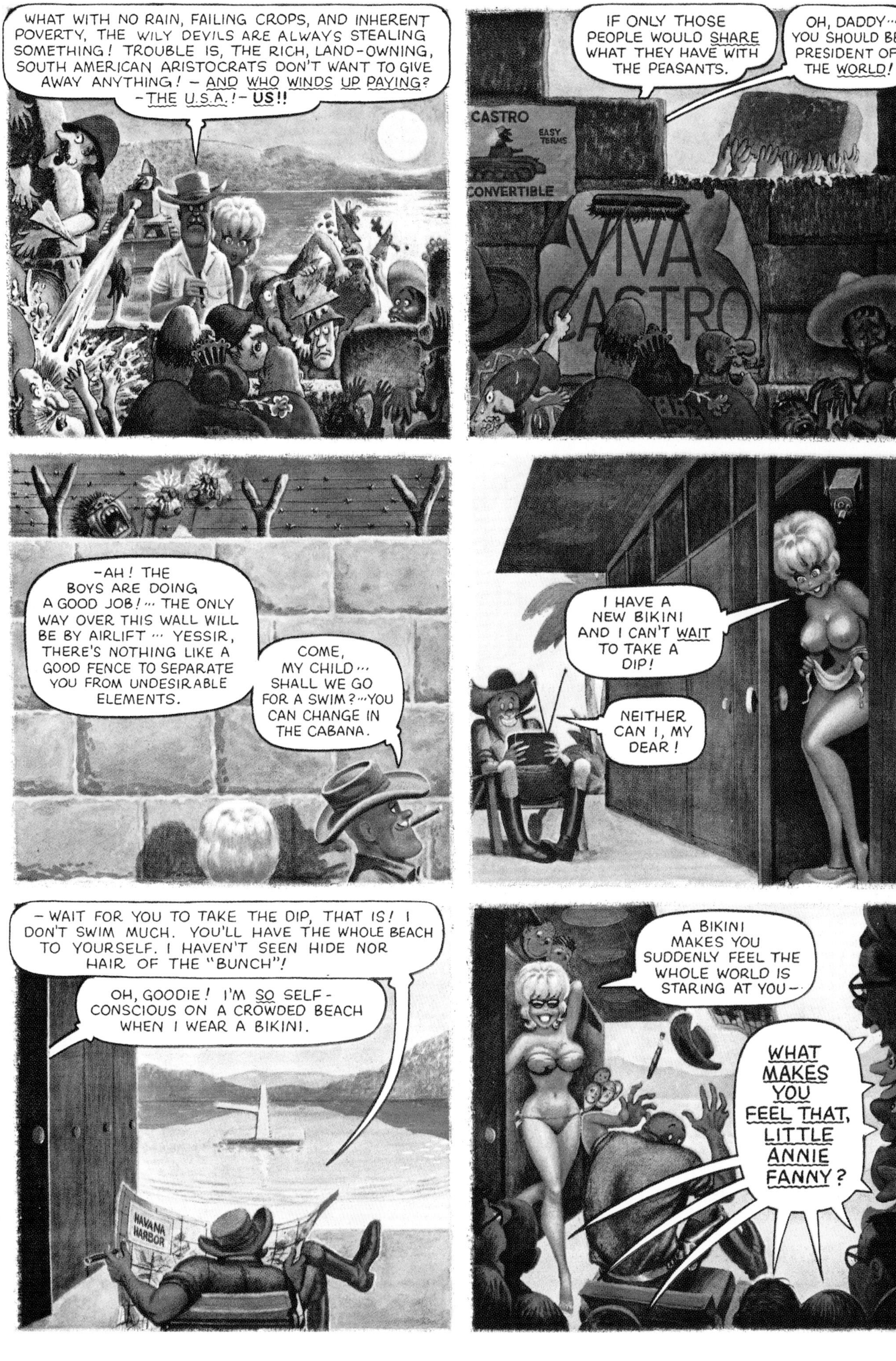
WHAT WITH NO RAIN, FAILING CROPS, AND INHERENT POVERTY, THE WILY DEVILS ARE ALWAYS STEALING SOMETHING! TROUBLE IS, THE RICH, LAND-OWNING, SOUTH AMERICAN ARISTOCRATS DON'T WANT TO GIVE AWAY ANYTHING! – AND WHO WINDS UP PAYING? –THE U.S.A.! – US!!
IF ONLY THOSE PEOPLE WOULD SHARE WHAT THEY HAVE WITH THE PEASANTS.
OH, DADDY··· YOU SHOULD BE PRESIDENT OF THE WORLD!
CASTRO
EASY TERMS
CONVERTIBLE
VIVA CASTRO
–AH! THE BOYS ARE DOING A GOOD JOB!··· THE ONLY WAY OVER THIS WALL WILL BE BY AIRLIFT ··· YESSIR, THERE'S NOTHING LIKE A GOOD FENCE TO SEPARATE YOU FROM UNDESIRABLE ELEMENTS.
COME, MY CHILD··· SHALL WE GO FOR A SWIM?···YOU CAN CHANGE IN THE CABANA.
I HAVE A NEW BIKINI AND I CAN'T WAIT TO TAKE A DIP!
NEITHER CAN I, MY DEAR!
– WAIT FOR YOU TO TAKE THE DIP, THAT IS! I DON'T SWIM MUCH. YOU'LL HAVE THE WHOLE BEACH TO YOURSELF. I HAVEN'T SEEN HIDE NOR HAIR OF THE "BUNCH"!
OH, GOODIE! I'M SO SELF-CONSCIOUS ON A CROWDED BEACH WHEN I WEAR A BIKINI.
HAVANA HARBOR
A BIKINI MAKES YOU SUDDENLY FEEL THE WHOLE WORLD IS STARING AT YOU–.
WHAT MAKES YOU FEEL THAT, LITTLE ANNIE FANNY?

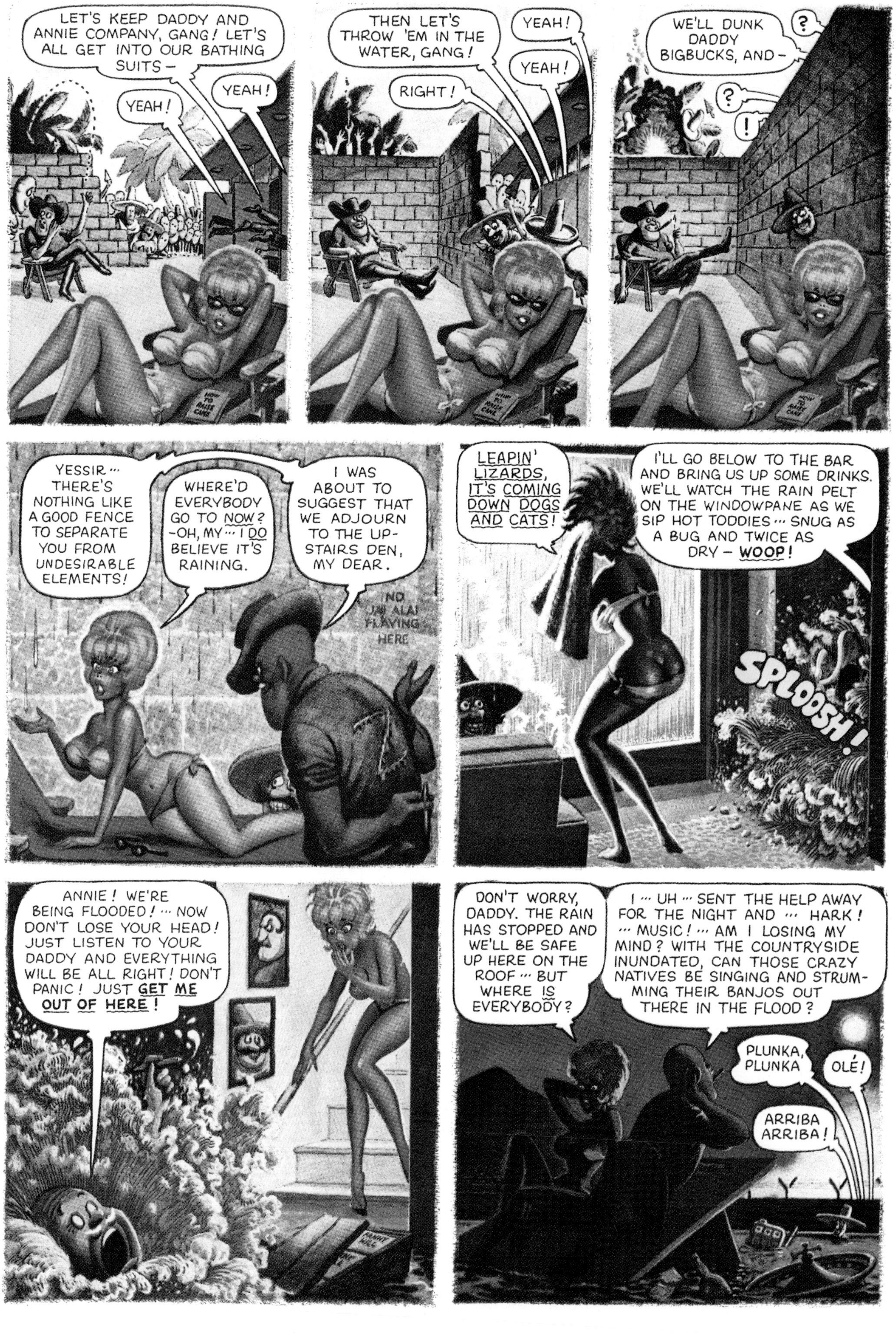
LET'S KEEP DADDY AND ANNIE COMPANY, GANG! LET'S ALL GET INTO OUR BATHING SUITS –
YEAH!
YEAH!
THEN LET'S THROW 'EM IN THE WATER, GANG!
YEAH!
YEAH!
RIGHT!
WE'LL DUNK DADDY BIGBUCKS, AND –
?
?
!
YESSIR ··· THERE'S NOTHING LIKE A GOOD FENCE TO SEPARATE YOU FROM UNDESIRABLE ELEMENTS!
WHERE'D EVERYBODY GO TO NOW? -OH, MY ··· I DO BELIEVE IT'S RAINING.
I WAS ABOUT TO SUGGEST THAT WE ADJOURN TO THE UP-STAIRS DEN, MY DEAR.
NO JAI ALAI PLAYING HERE
LEAPIN' LIZARDS, IT'S COMING DOWN DOGS AND CATS!
I'LL GO BELOW TO THE BAR AND BRING US UP SOME DRINKS. WE'LL WATCH THE RAIN PELT ON THE WINDOWPANE AS WE SIP HOT TODDIES ··· SNUG AS A BUG AND TWICE AS DRY – WOOP!
SPLOOSH!
ANNIE! WE'RE BEING FLOODED! ··· NOW DON'T LOSE YOUR HEAD! JUST LISTEN TO YOUR DADDY AND EVERYTHING WILL BE ALL RIGHT! DON'T PANIC! JUST GET ME OUT OF HERE!
DON'T WORRY, DADDY. THE RAIN HAS STOPPED AND WE'LL BE SAFE UP HERE ON THE ROOF ··· BUT WHERE IS EVERYBODY?
I ··· UH ··· SENT THE HELP AWAY FOR THE NIGHT AND ··· HARK! ··· MUSIC! ··· AM I LOSING MY MIND? WITH THE COUNTRYSIDE INUNDATED, CAN THOSE CRAZY NATIVES BE SINGING AND STRUMMING THEIR BANJOS OUT THERE IN THE FLOOD?
PLUNKA, PLUNKA
OLÉ!
ARRIBA ARRIBA!

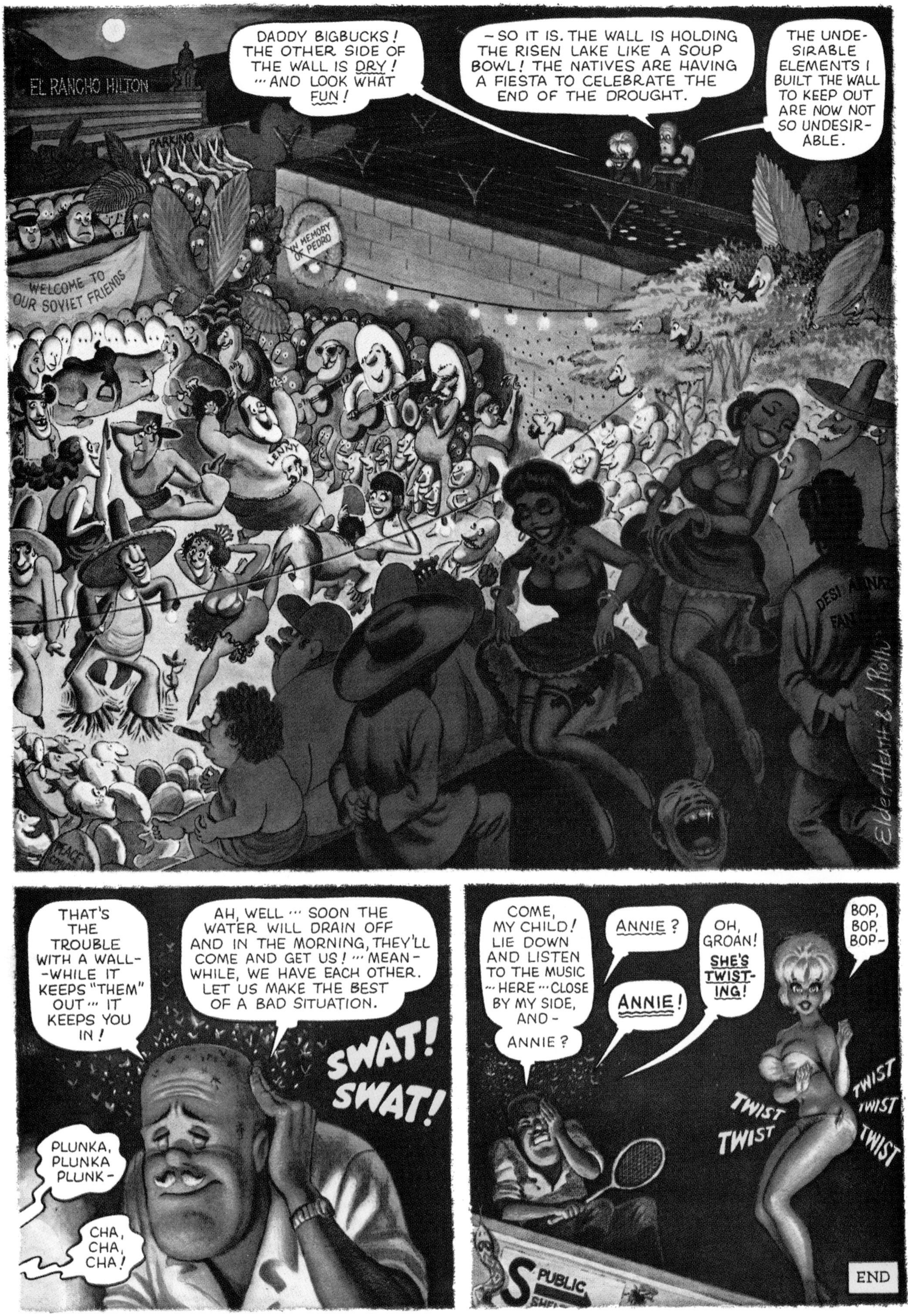

EL RANCHO HILTON
PARKING
WELCOME TO OUR SOVIET FRIENDS
IN MEMORY OF PEDRO
DADDY BIGBUCKS! THE OTHER SIDE OF THE WALL IS DRY! ... AND LOOK WHAT FUN!
— SO IT IS. THE WALL IS HOLDING THE RISEN LAKE LIKE A SOUP BOWL! THE NATIVES ARE HAVING A FIESTA TO CELEBRATE THE END OF THE DROUGHT.
THE UNDE-SIRABLE ELEMENTS I BUILT THE WALL TO KEEP OUT ARE NOW NOT SO UNDESIR-ABLE.
LENNY
DESI
THAT'S THE TROUBLE WITH A WALL— WHILE IT KEEPS "THEM" OUT... IT KEEPS YOU IN!
AH, WELL ... SOON THE WATER WILL DRAIN OFF AND IN THE MORNING, THEY'LL COME AND GET US! ... MEAN-WHILE, WE HAVE EACH OTHER. LET US MAKE THE BEST OF A BAD SITUATION.
SWAT! SWAT!
PLUNKA, PLUNKA PLUNK-
CHA, CHA, CHA!
COME, MY CHILD! LIE DOWN AND LISTEN TO THE MUSIC ... HERE ... CLOSE BY MY SIDE, AND-
ANNIE?
ANNIE?
ANNIE!
OH, GROAN! SHE'S TWIST-ING!
BOP, BOP, BOP-
TWIST TWIST
TWIST TWIST TWIST
PUBLIC
END

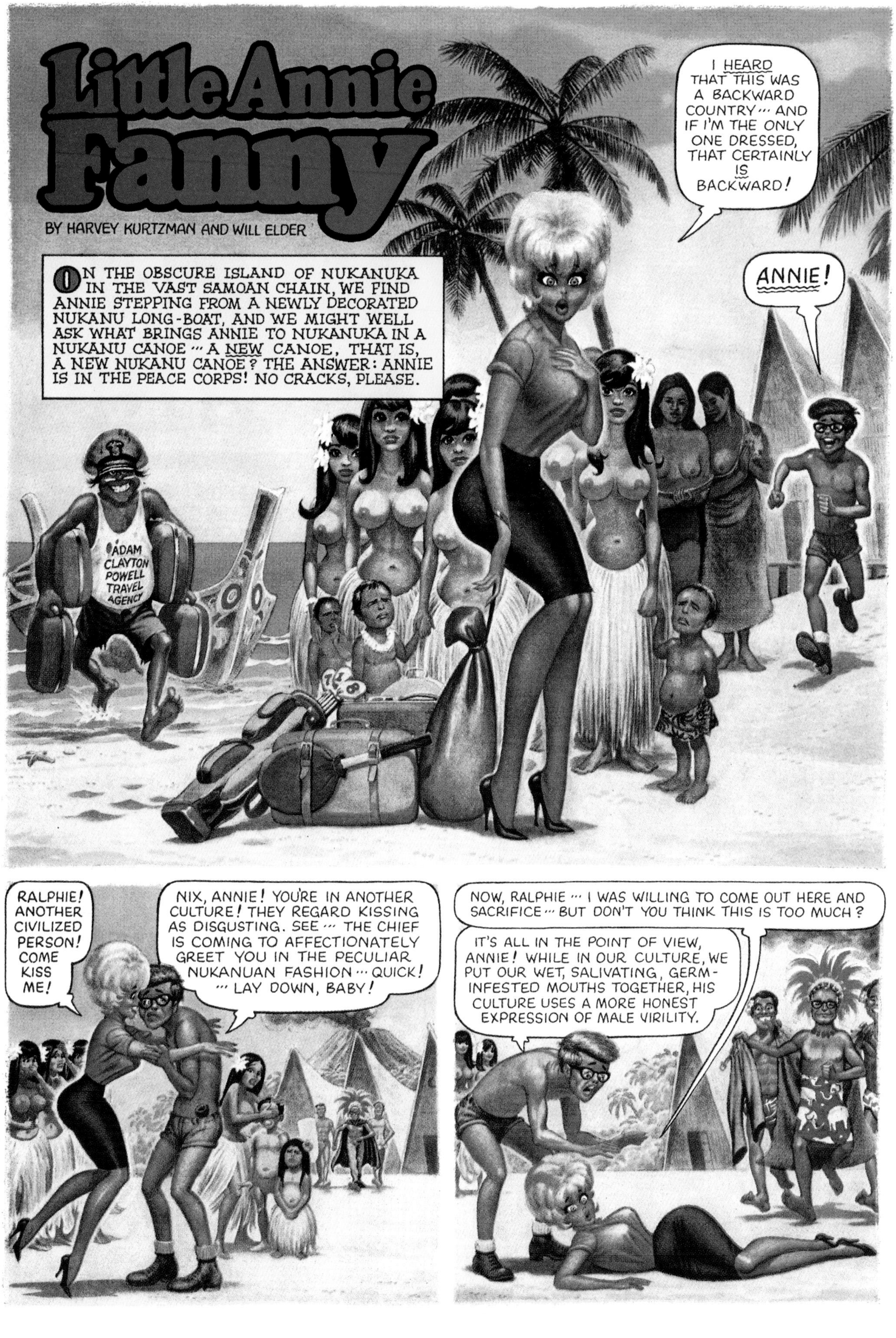

Little Annie Fanny
BY HARVEY KURTZMAN AND WILL ELDER
ON THE OBSCURE ISLAND OF NUKANUKA IN THE VAST SAMOAN CHAIN, WE FIND ANNIE STEPPING FROM A NEWLY DECORATED NUKANU LONG-BOAT, AND WE MIGHT WELL ASK WHAT BRINGS ANNIE TO NUKANUKA IN A NUKANU CANOE ··· A NEW CANOE, THAT IS, A NEW NUKANU CANOE? THE ANSWER: ANNIE IS IN THE PEACE CORPS! NO CRACKS, PLEASE.
I HEARD THAT THIS WAS A BACKWARD COUNTRY ··· AND IF I'M THE ONLY ONE DRESSED, THAT CERTAINLY IS BACKWARD!
ANNIE!
ADAM CLAYTON POWELL TRAVEL AGENCY
RALPHIE! ANOTHER CIVILIZED PERSON! COME KISS ME!
NIX, ANNIE! YOU'RE IN ANOTHER CULTURE! THEY REGARD KISSING AS DISGUSTING. SEE ··· THE CHIEF IS COMING TO AFFECTIONATELY GREET YOU IN THE PECULIAR NUKANUAN FASHION ··· QUICK! ··· LAY DOWN, BABY!
NOW, RALPHIE ··· I WAS WILLING TO COME OUT HERE AND SACRIFICE ··· BUT DON'T YOU THINK THIS IS TOO MUCH?
IT'S ALL IN THE POINT OF VIEW, ANNIE! WHILE IN OUR CULTURE, WE PUT OUR WET, SALIVATING, GERM-INFESTED MOUTHS TOGETHER, HIS CULTURE USES A MORE HONEST EXPRESSION OF MALE VIRILITY.

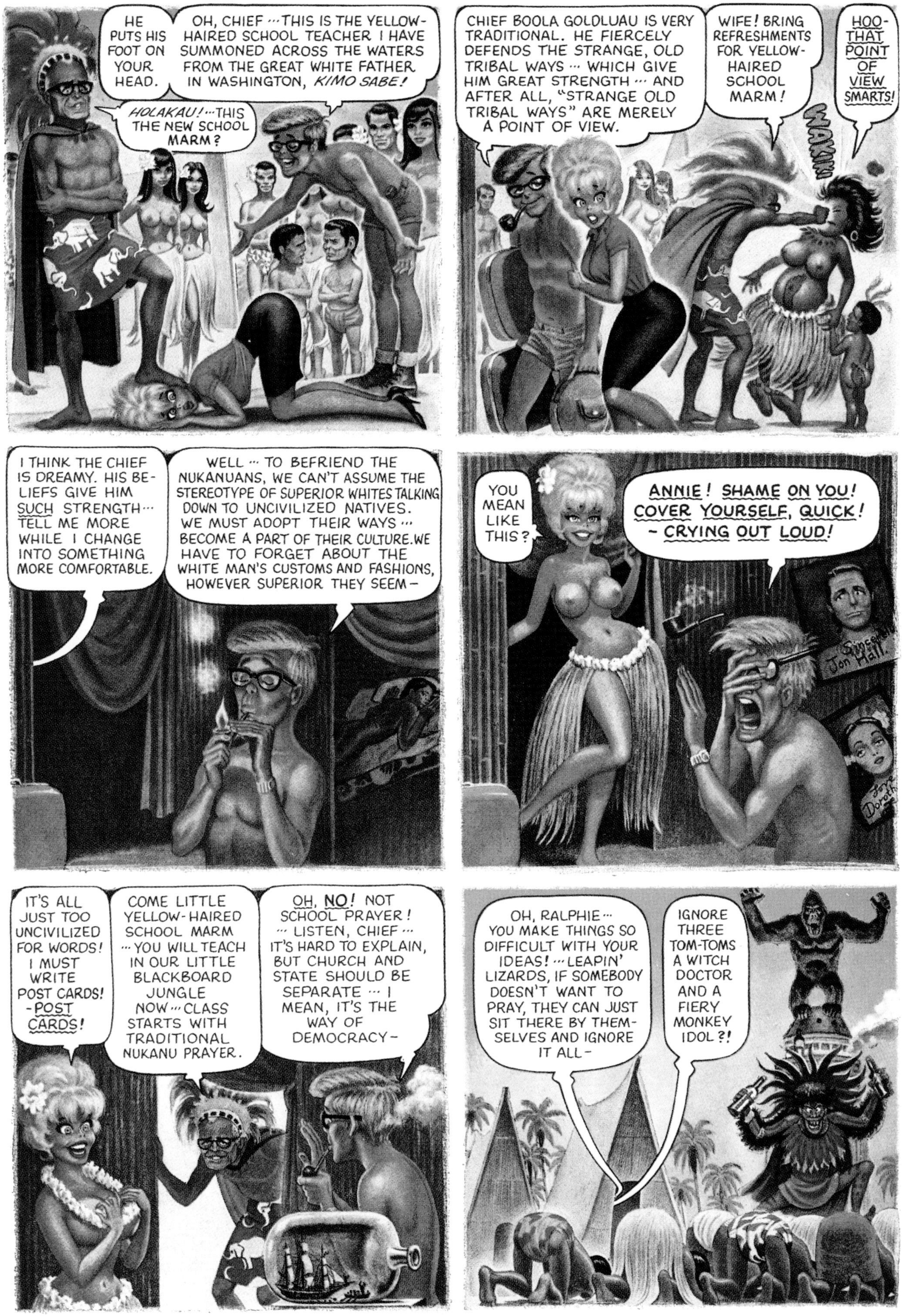
HE PUTS HIS FOOT ON YOUR HEAD.
OH, CHIEF ··· THIS IS THE YELLOW-HAIRED SCHOOL TEACHER I HAVE SUMMONED ACROSS THE WATERS FROM THE GREAT WHITE FATHER IN WASHINGTON, KIMO SABE!
HOLAKAU! ··· THIS THE NEW SCHOOL MARM?
CHIEF BOOLA GOLDLUAU IS VERY TRADITIONAL. HE FIERCELY DEFENDS THE STRANGE, OLD TRIBAL WAYS ··· WHICH GIVE HIM GREAT STRENGTH ··· AND AFTER ALL, "STRANGE OLD TRIBAL WAYS" ARE MERELY A POINT OF VIEW.
WIFE! BRING REFRESHMENTS FOR YELLOW-HAIRED SCHOOL MARM!
HOO-THAT POINT OF VIEW SMARTS!
I THINK THE CHIEF IS DREAMY. HIS BELIEFS GIVE HIM SUCH STRENGTH··· TELL ME MORE WHILE I CHANGE INTO SOMETHING MORE COMFORTABLE.
WELL ··· TO BEFRIEND THE NUKANUANS, WE CAN'T ASSUME THE STEREOTYPE OF SUPERIOR WHITES TALKING DOWN TO UNCIVILIZED NATIVES. WE MUST ADOPT THEIR WAYS ··· BECOME A PART OF THEIR CULTURE. WE HAVE TO FORGET ABOUT THE WHITE MAN'S CUSTOMS AND FASHIONS, HOWEVER SUPERIOR THEY SEEM–
YOU MEAN LIKE THIS?
ANNIE! SHAME ON YOU! COVER YOURSELF, QUICK! – CRYING OUT LOUD!
Sincerely Jon Hall
Love Dorothy
IT'S ALL JUST TOO UNCIVILIZED FOR WORDS! I MUST WRITE POST CARDS! – POST CARDS!
COME LITTLE YELLOW-HAIRED SCHOOL MARM ··· YOU WILL TEACH IN OUR LITTLE BLACKBOARD JUNGLE NOW ··· CLASS STARTS WITH TRADITIONAL NUKANU PRAYER.
OH, NO! NOT SCHOOL PRAYER! ··· LISTEN, CHIEF ··· IT'S HARD TO EXPLAIN, BUT CHURCH AND STATE SHOULD BE SEPARATE ··· I MEAN, IT'S THE WAY OF DEMOCRACY–
OH, RALPHIE ··· YOU MAKE THINGS SO DIFFICULT WITH YOUR IDEAS! ··· LEAPIN' LIZARDS, IF SOMEBODY DOESN'T WANT TO PRAY, THEY CAN JUST SIT THERE BY THEMSELVES AND IGNORE IT ALL–
IGNORE THREE TOM-TOMS A WITCH DOCTOR AND A FIERY MONKEY IDOL?!

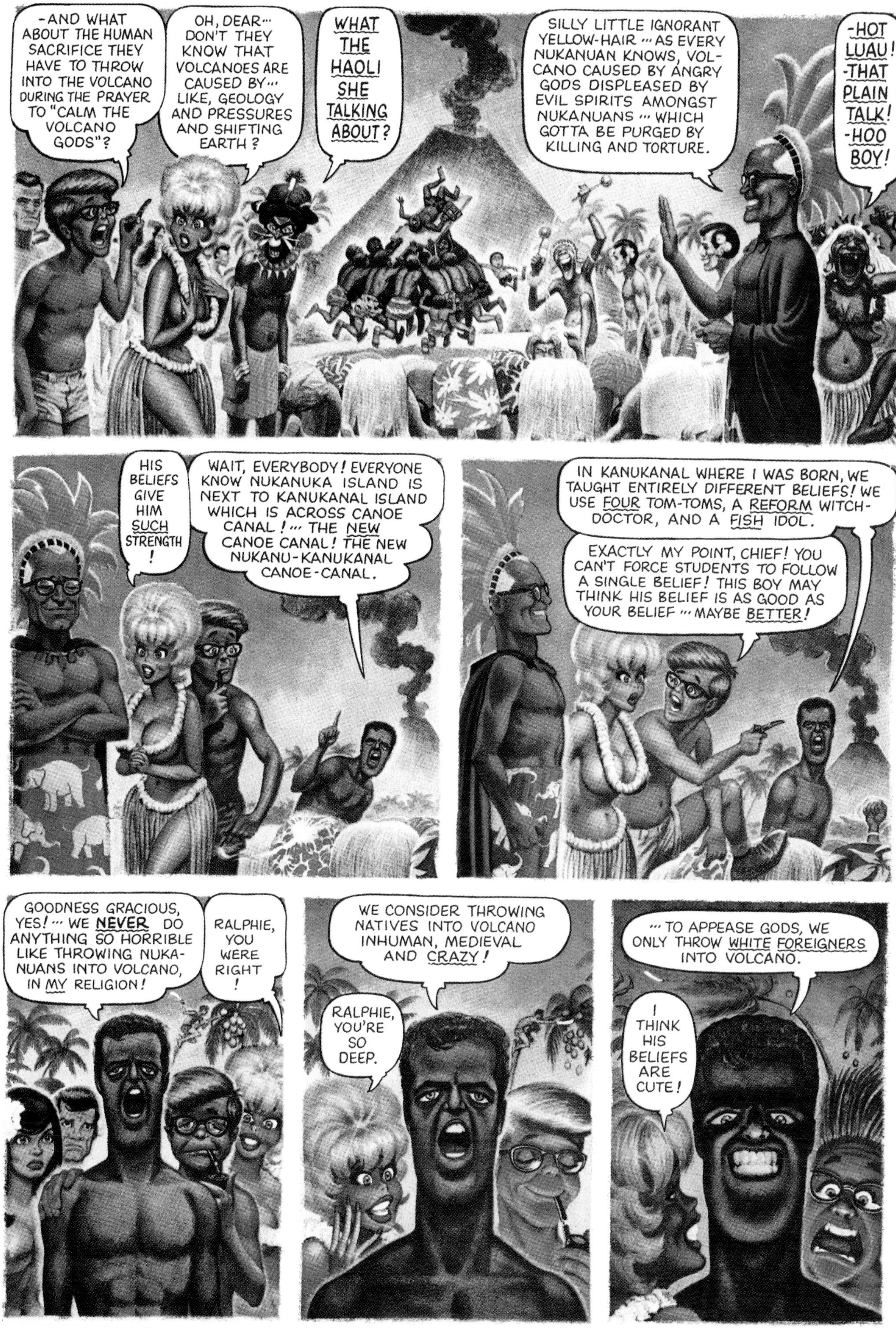

-AND WHAT ABOUT THE HUMAN SACRIFICE THEY HAVE TO THROW INTO THE VOLCANO DURING THE PRAYER TO "CALM THE VOLCANO GODS"?
OH, DEAR··· DON'T THEY KNOW THAT VOLCANOES ARE CAUSED BY··· LIKE, GEOLOGY AND PRESSURES AND SHIFTING EARTH?
WHAT THE HAOLI SHE TALKING ABOUT?
SILLY LITTLE IGNORANT YELLOW-HAIR··· AS EVERY NUKANUAN KNOWS, VOLCANO CAUSED BY ANGRY GODS DISPLEASED BY EVIL SPIRITS AMONGST NUKANUANS··· WHICH GOTTA BE PURGED BY KILLING AND TORTURE.
-HOT LUAU! -THAT PLAIN TALK! -HOO BOY!
HIS BELIEFS GIVE HIM SUCH STRENGTH!
WAIT, EVERYBODY! EVERYONE KNOW NUKANUKA ISLAND IS NEXT TO KANUKANAL ISLAND WHICH IS ACROSS CANOE CANAL!··· THE NEW CANOE CANAL! THE NEW NUKANU-KANUKANAL CANOE-CANAL.
IN KANUKANAL WHERE I WAS BORN, WE TAUGHT ENTIRELY DIFFERENT BELIEFS! WE USE FOUR TOM-TOMS, A REFORM WITCH-DOCTOR, AND A FISH IDOL.
EXACTLY MY POINT, CHIEF! YOU CAN'T FORCE STUDENTS TO FOLLOW A SINGLE BELIEF! THIS BOY MAY THINK HIS BELIEF IS AS GOOD AS YOUR BELIEF··· MAYBE BETTER!
GOODNESS GRACIOUS, YES!··· WE NEVER DO ANYTHING SO HORRIBLE LIKE THROWING NUKANUANS INTO VOLCANO, IN MY RELIGION!
RALPHIE, YOU WERE RIGHT!
WE CONSIDER THROWING NATIVES INTO VOLCANO INHUMAN, MEDIEVAL AND CRAZY!
RALPHIE, YOU'RE SO DEEP.
···TO APPEASE GODS, WE ONLY THROW WHITE FOREIGNERS INTO VOLCANO.
I THINK HIS BELIEFS ARE CUTE!

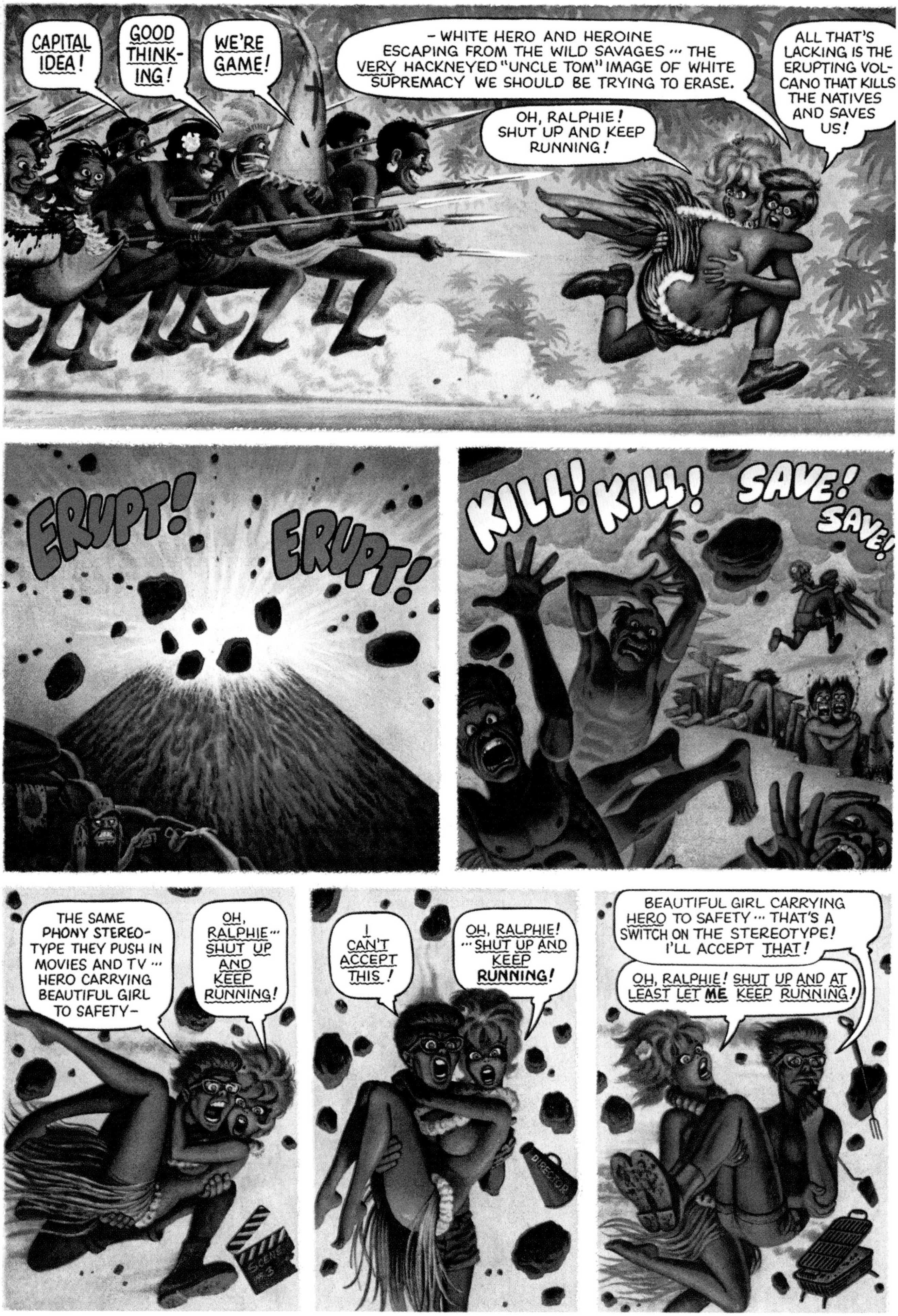
CAPITAL IDEA!
GOOD THINKING!
WE'RE GAME!
-WHITE HERO AND HEROINE ESCAPING FROM THE WILD SAVAGES ... THE VERY HACKNEYED "UNCLE TOM" IMAGE OF WHITE SUPREMACY WE SHOULD BE TRYING TO ERASE.
OH, RALPHIE! SHUT UP AND KEEP RUNNING!
ALL THAT'S LACKING IS THE ERUPTING VOLCANO THAT KILLS THE NATIVES AND SAVES US!
ERUPT! ERUPT!
KILL! KILL! SAVE! SAVE!
THE SAME PHONY STEREOTYPE THEY PUSH IN MOVIES AND TV ... HERO CARRYING BEAUTIFUL GIRL TO SAFETY-
OH, RALPHIE... SHUT UP AND KEEP RUNNING!
I CAN'T ACCEPT THIS!
OH, RALPHIE! ... SHUT UP AND KEEP RUNNING!
DIRECTOR
BEAUTIFUL GIRL CARRYING HERO TO SAFETY ... THAT'S A SWITCH ON THE STEREOTYPE! I'LL ACCEPT THAT!
OH, RALPHIE! SHUT UP AND AT LEAST LET ME KEEP RUNNING!

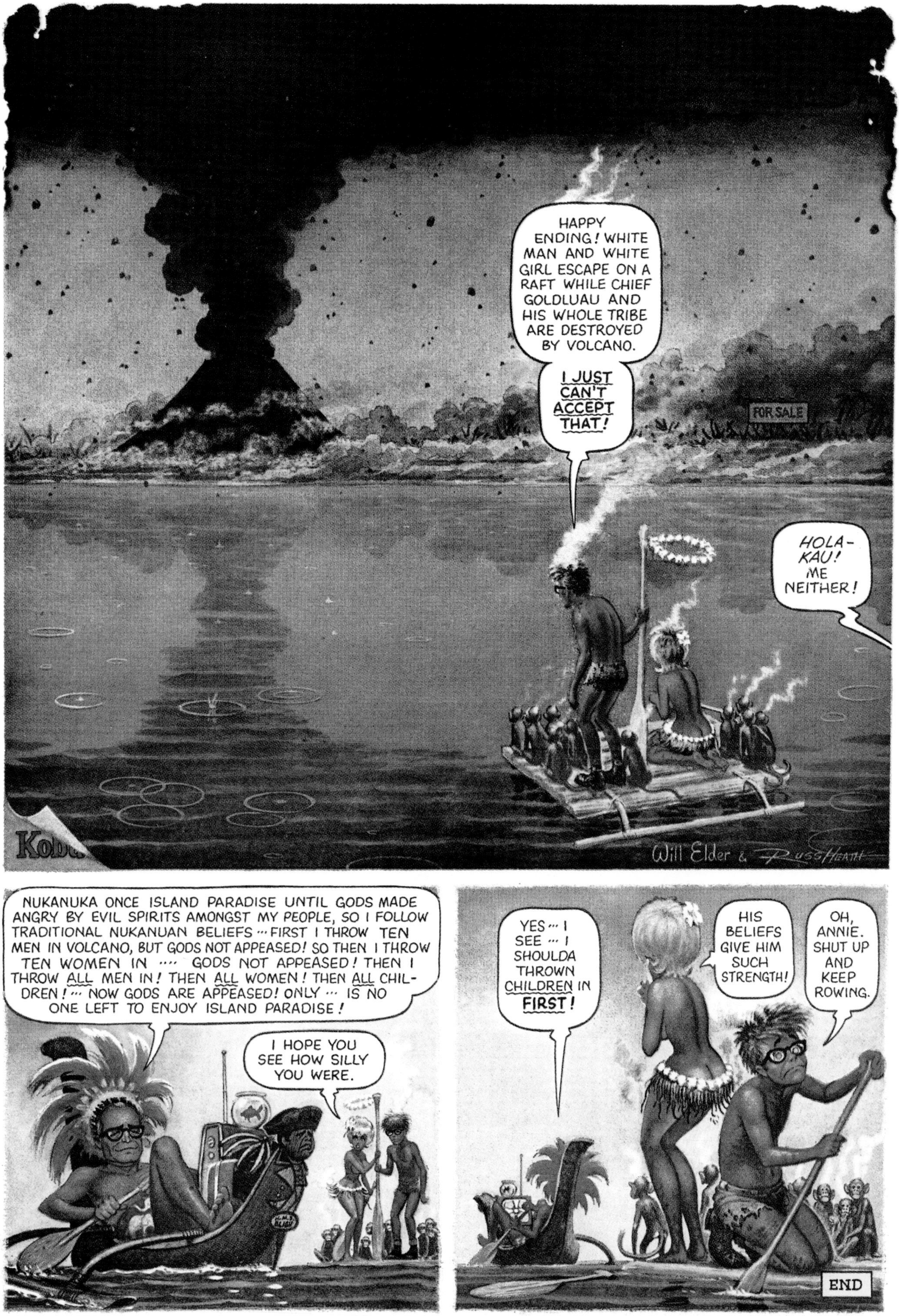
HAPPY ENDING! WHITE MAN AND WHITE GIRL ESCAPE ON A RAFT WHILE CHIEF GOLDLUAU AND HIS WHOLE TRIBE ARE DESTROYED BY VOLCANO.
I JUST CAN'T ACCEPT THAT!
FOR SALE
HOLA-KAU! ME NEITHER!
Will Elder & Russ Heath
NUKANUKA ONCE ISLAND PARADISE UNTIL GODS MADE ANGRY BY EVIL SPIRITS AMONGST MY PEOPLE, SO I FOLLOW TRADITIONAL NUKANUAN BELIEFS ··· FIRST I THROW TEN MEN IN VOLCANO, BUT GODS NOT APPEASED! SO THEN I THROW TEN WOMEN IN ···· GODS NOT APPEASED! THEN I THROW ALL MEN IN! THEN ALL WOMEN! THEN ALL CHILDREN! ··· NOW GODS ARE APPEASED! ONLY ··· IS NO ONE LEFT TO ENJOY ISLAND PARADISE!
I HOPE YOU SEE HOW SILLY YOU WERE.
YES ··· I SEE ··· I SHOULDA THROWN CHILDREN IN FIRST!
HIS BELIEFS GIVE HIM SUCH STRENGTH!
OH, ANNIE. SHUT UP AND KEEP ROWING.
END

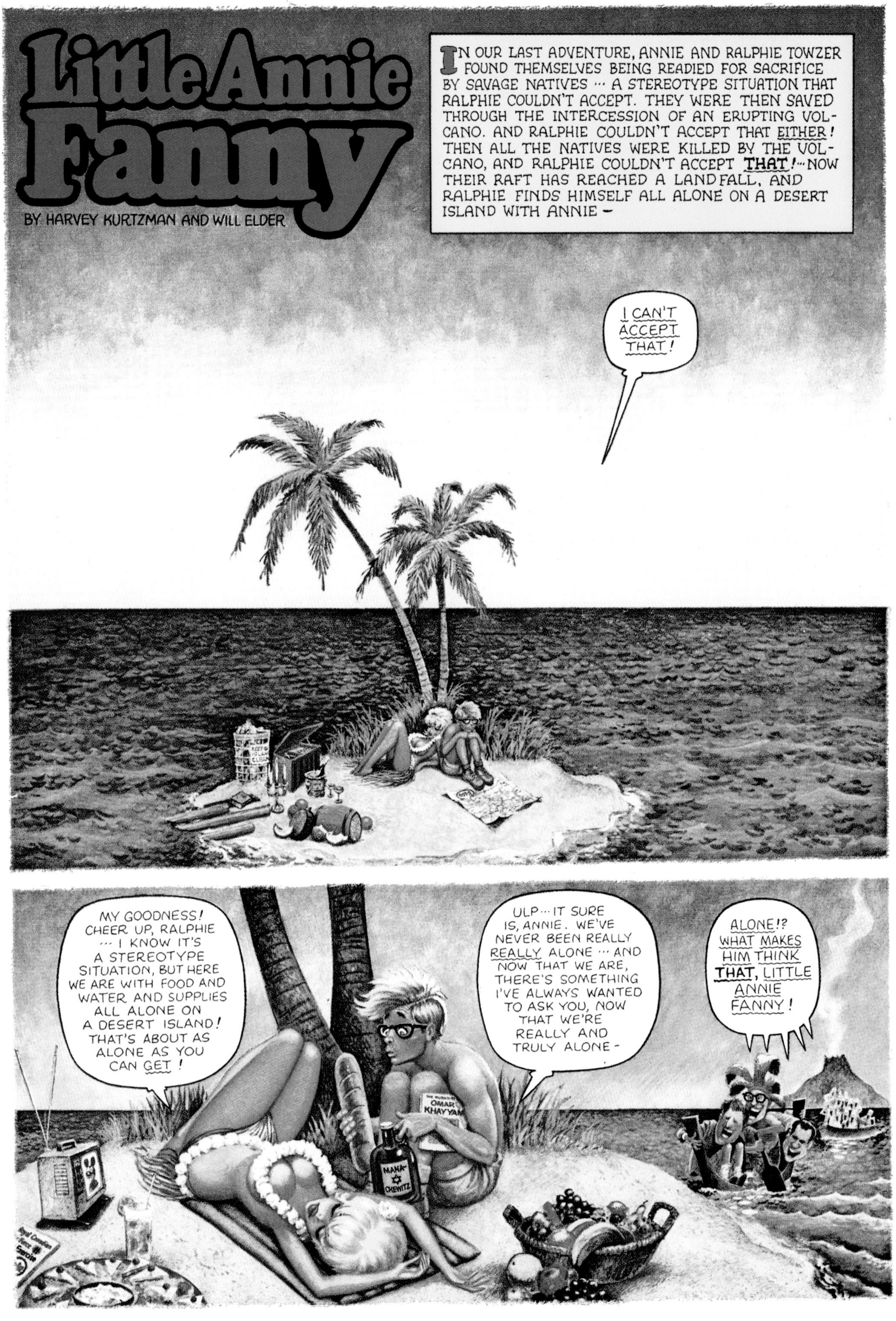

Little Annie Fanny
BY HARVEY KURTZMAN AND WILL ELDER
IN OUR LAST ADVENTURE, ANNIE AND RALPHIE TOWZER FOUND THEMSELVES BEING READIED FOR SACRIFICE BY SAVAGE NATIVES … A STEREOTYPE SITUATION THAT RALPHIE COULDN'T ACCEPT. THEY WERE THEN SAVED THROUGH THE INTERCESSION OF AN ERUPTING VOLCANO. AND RALPHIE COULDN'T ACCEPT THAT EITHER! THEN ALL THE NATIVES WERE KILLED BY THE VOLCANO, AND RALPHIE COULDN'T ACCEPT THAT!… NOW THEIR RAFT HAS REACHED A LANDFALL, AND RALPHIE FINDS HIMSELF ALL ALONE ON A DESERT ISLAND WITH ANNIE –
I CAN'T ACCEPT THAT!
MY GOODNESS! CHEER UP, RALPHIE … I KNOW IT'S A STEREOTYPE SITUATION, BUT HERE WE ARE WITH FOOD AND WATER AND SUPPLIES ALL ALONE ON A DESERT ISLAND! THAT'S ABOUT AS ALONE AS YOU CAN GET!
ULP… IT SURE IS, ANNIE. WE'VE NEVER BEEN REALLY REALLY ALONE … AND NOW THAT WE ARE, THERE'S SOMETHING I'VE ALWAYS WANTED TO ASK YOU, NOW THAT WE'RE REALLY AND TRULY ALONE –
ALONE!? WHAT MAKES HIM THINK THAT, LITTLE ANNIE FANNY!
OMAR KHAYYAM
MANA-CHEWITZ

62

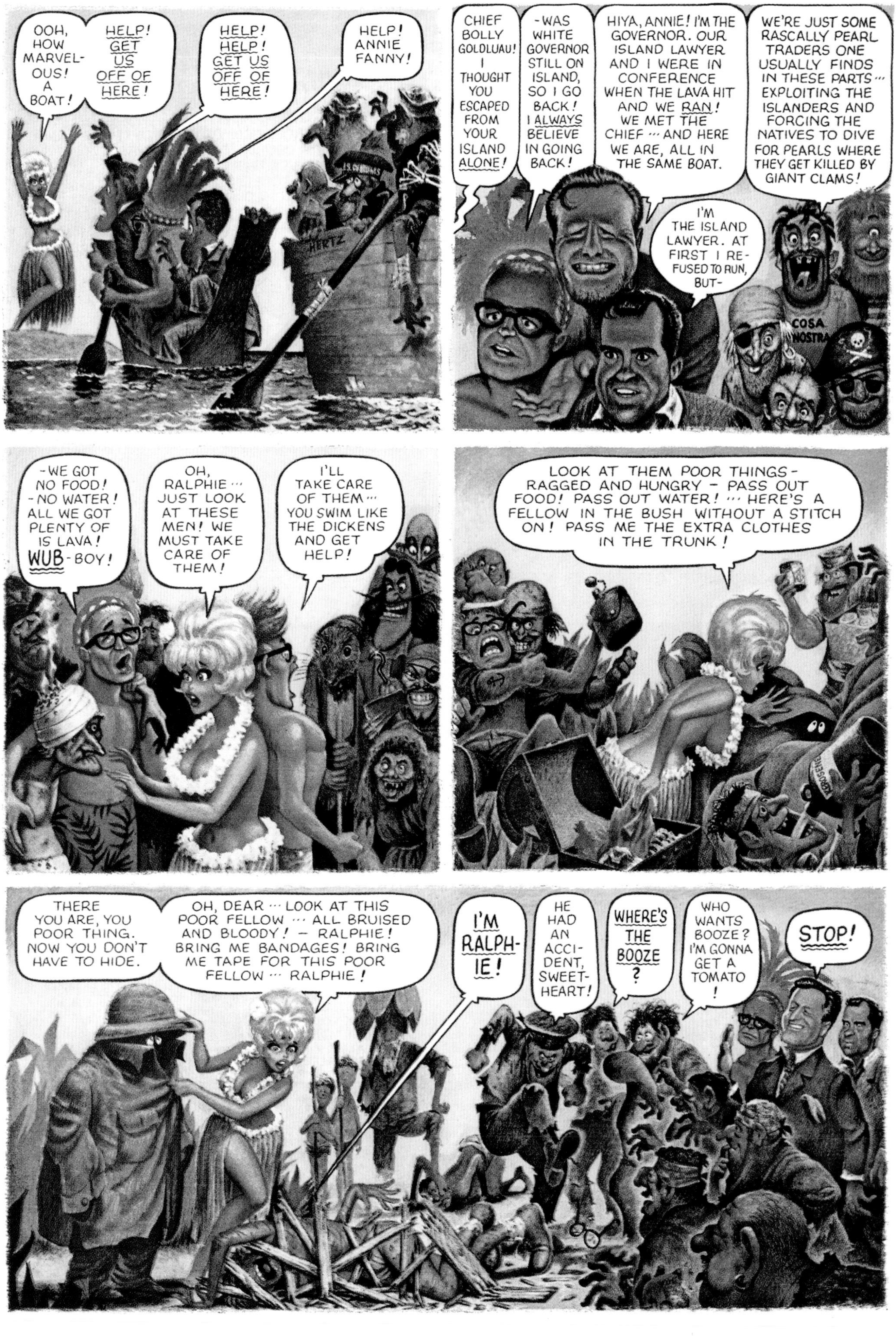
OOH, HOW MARVEL-OUS! A BOAT!
HELP! GET US OFF OF HERE!
HELP! HELP! GET US OFF OF HERE!
HELP! ANNIE FANNY!
HERTZ
CHIEF BOLLY GOLDLUAU! I THOUGHT YOU ESCAPED FROM YOUR ISLAND ALONE!
-WAS WHITE GOVERNOR STILL ON ISLAND, SO I GO BACK! I ALWAYS BELIEVE IN GOING BACK!
HIYA, ANNIE! I'M THE GOVERNOR. OUR ISLAND LAWYER AND I WERE IN CONFERENCE WHEN THE LAVA HIT AND WE RAN! WE MET THE CHIEF ··· AND HERE WE ARE, ALL IN THE SAME BOAT.
WE'RE JUST SOME RASCALLY PEARL TRADERS ONE USUALLY FINDS IN THESE PARTS ··· EXPLOITING THE ISLANDERS AND FORCING THE NATIVES TO DIVE FOR PEARLS WHERE THEY GET KILLED BY GIANT CLAMS!
I'M THE ISLAND LAWYER. AT FIRST I RE-FUSED TO RUN, BUT-
COSA NOSTRA
-WE GOT NO FOOD! -NO WATER! ALL WE GOT PLENTY OF IS LAVA! WUB-BOY!
OH, RALPHIE ··· JUST LOOK AT THESE MEN! WE MUST TAKE CARE OF THEM!
I'LL TAKE CARE OF THEM ··· YOU SWIM LIKE THE DICKENS AND GET HELP!
LOOK AT THEM POOR THINGS - RAGGED AND HUNGRY - PASS OUT FOOD! PASS OUT WATER! ··· HERE'S A FELLOW IN THE BUSH WITHOUT A STITCH ON! PASS ME THE EXTRA CLOTHES IN THE TRUNK!
THERE YOU ARE, YOU POOR THING. NOW YOU DON'T HAVE TO HIDE.
OH, DEAR ··· LOOK AT THIS POOR FELLOW ··· ALL BRUISED AND BLOODY! - RALPHIE! BRING ME BANDAGES! BRING ME TAPE FOR THIS POOR FELLOW ··· RALPHIE!
I'M RALPH-IE!
HE HAD AN ACCI-DENT, SWEET-HEART!
WHERE'S THE BOOZE?
WHO WANTS BOOZE? I'M GONNA GET A TOMATO!
STOP!

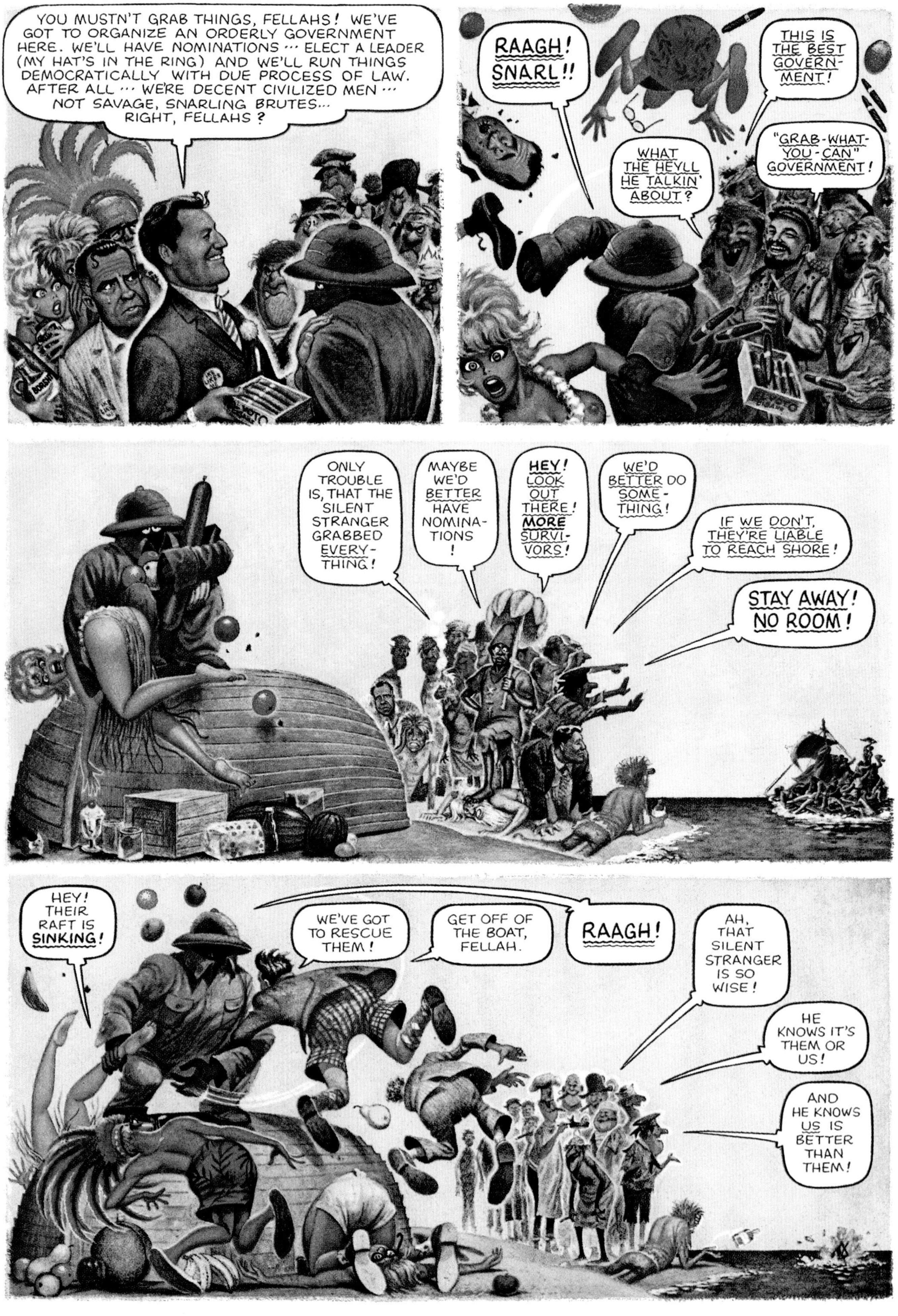
YOU MUSTN'T GRAB THINGS, FELLAHS! WE'VE GOT TO ORGANIZE AN ORDERLY GOVERNMENT HERE. WE'LL HAVE NOMINATIONS ··· ELECT A LEADER (MY HAT'S IN THE RING) AND WE'LL RUN THINGS DEMOCRATICALLY WITH DUE PROCESS OF LAW. AFTER ALL ··· WE'RE DECENT CIVILIZED MEN ··· NOT SAVAGE, SNARLING BRUTES... RIGHT, FELLAHS?
RAAGH! SNARL!!
WHAT THE HEYLL HE TALKIN' ABOUT?
THIS IS THE BEST GOVERNMENT!
"GRAB-WHAT-YOU-CAN" GOVERNMENT!
ONLY TROUBLE IS, THAT THE SILENT STRANGER GRABBED EVERYTHING!
MAYBE WE'D BETTER HAVE NOMINATIONS!
HEY! LOOK OUT THERE! MORE SURVIVORS!
WE'D BETTER DO SOMETHING!
IF WE DON'T, THEY'RE LIABLE TO REACH SHORE!
STAY AWAY! NO ROOM!
HEY! THEIR RAFT IS SINKING!
WE'VE GOT TO RESCUE THEM!
GET OFF OF THE BOAT, FELLAH.
RAAGH!
AH, THAT SILENT STRANGER IS SO WISE!
HE KNOWS IT'S THEM OR US!
AND HE KNOWS US IS BETTER THAN THEM!

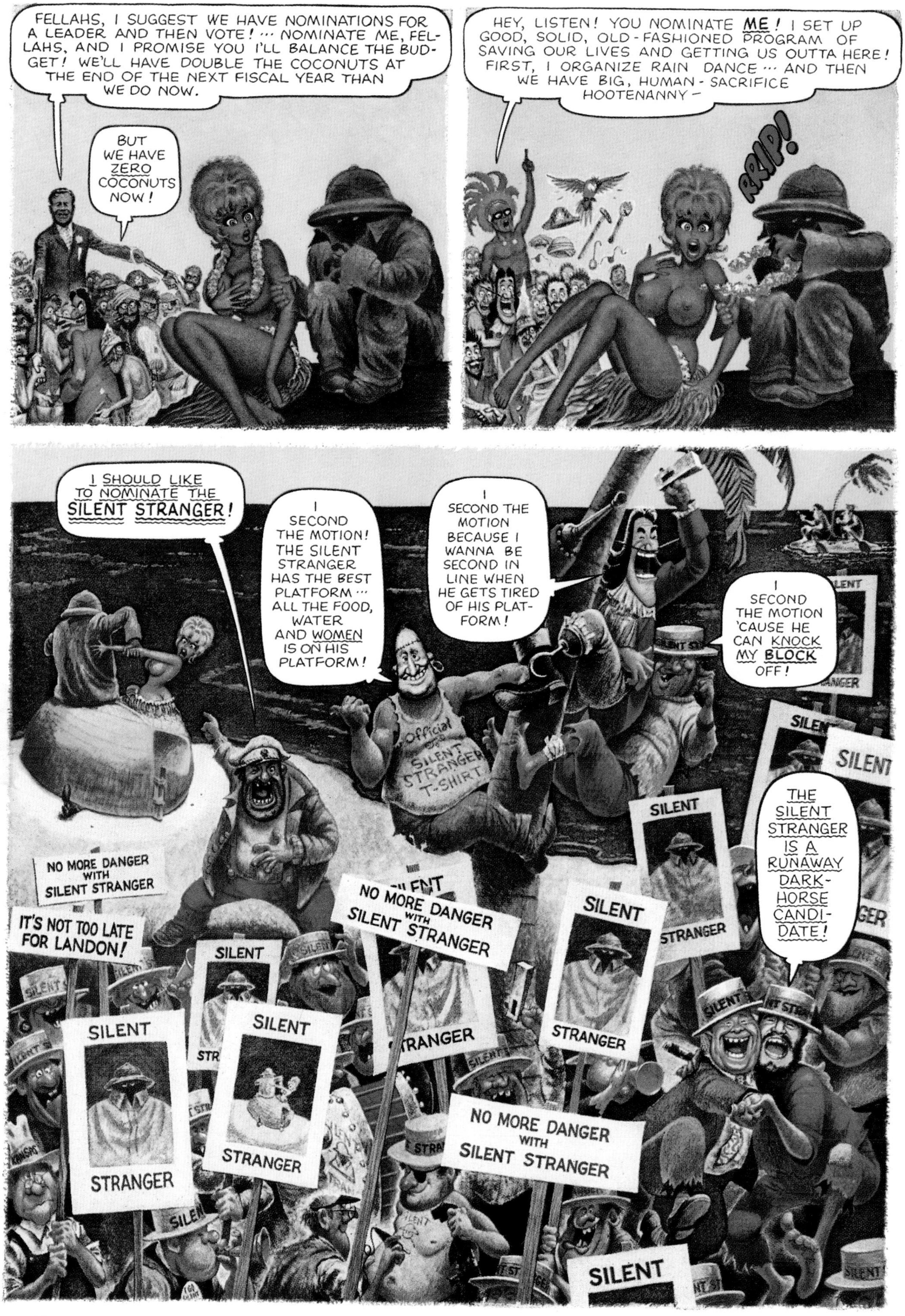

FELLAHS, I SUGGEST WE HAVE NOMINATIONS FOR A LEADER AND THEN VOTE! ··· NOMINATE ME, FELLAHS, AND I PROMISE YOU I'LL BALANCE THE BUDGET! WE'LL HAVE DOUBLE THE COCONUTS AT THE END OF THE NEXT FISCAL YEAR THAN WE DO NOW.
BUT WE HAVE ZERO COCONUTS NOW!
HEY, LISTEN! YOU NOMINATE ME! I SET UP GOOD, SOLID, OLD-FASHIONED PROGRAM OF SAVING OUR LIVES AND GETTING US OUTTA HERE! FIRST, I ORGANIZE RAIN DANCE ··· AND THEN WE HAVE BIG, HUMAN-SACRIFICE HOOTENANNY –
RRIP!
I SHOULD LIKE TO NOMINATE THE SILENT STRANGER!
I SECOND THE MOTION! THE SILENT STRANGER HAS THE BEST PLATFORM ··· ALL THE FOOD, WATER AND WOMEN IS ON HIS PLATFORM!
I SECOND THE MOTION BECAUSE I WANNA BE SECOND IN LINE WHEN HE GETS TIRED OF HIS PLATFORM!
I SECOND THE MOTION 'CAUSE HE CAN KNOCK MY BLOCK OFF!
Official SILENT STRANGER T-SHIRT
THE SILENT STRANGER IS A RUNAWAY DARK-HORSE CANDIDATE!
NO MORE DANGER WITH SILENT STRANGER
IT'S NOT TOO LATE FOR LANDON!
NO MORE DANGER WITH SILENT STRANGER
SILENT STRANGER
SILENT STRANGER
SILENT STRANGER
SILENT STRANGER
NO MORE DANGER WITH SILENT STRANGER
SILENT

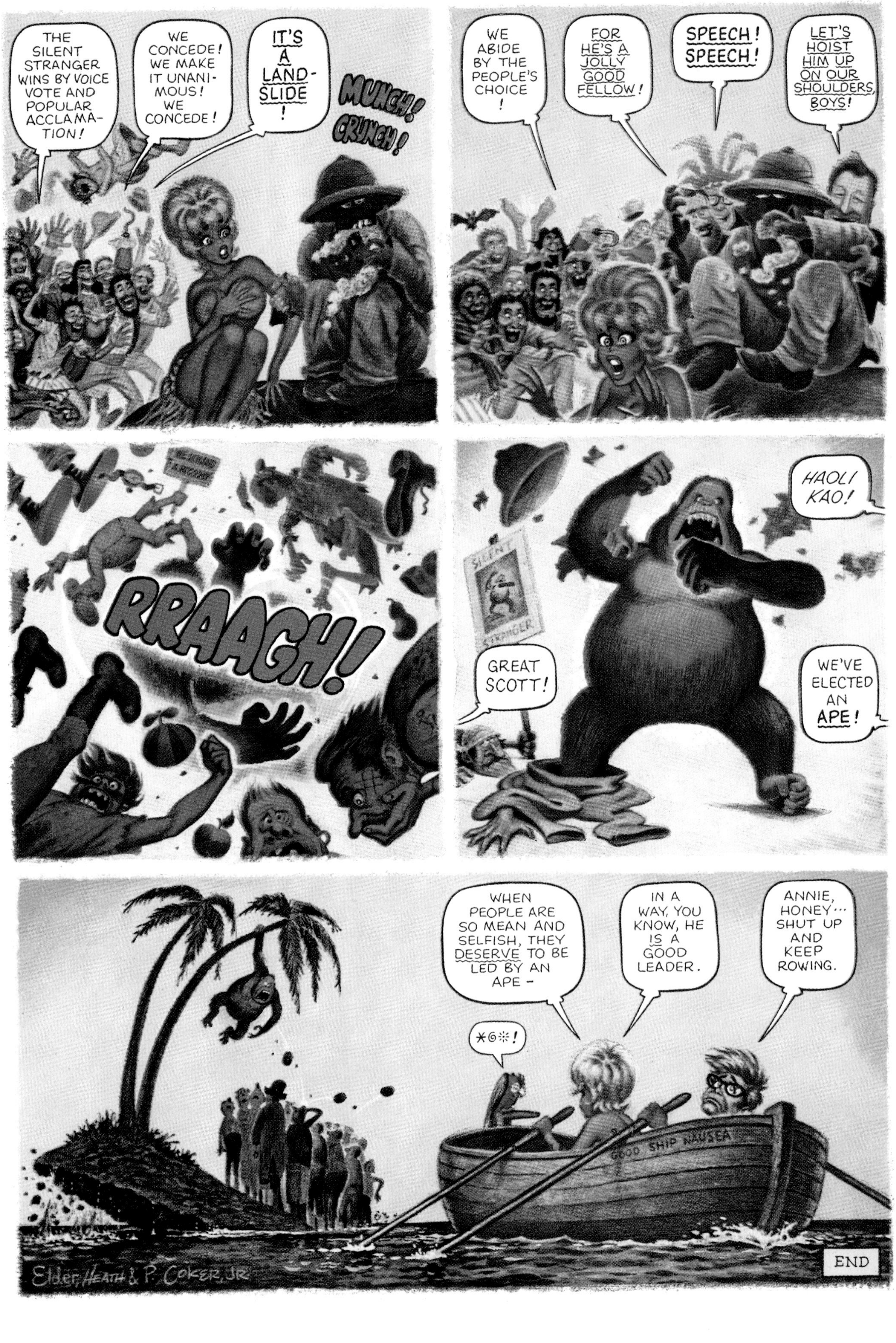
THE SILENT STRANGER WINS BY VOICE VOTE AND POPULAR ACCLAMATION!
WE CONCEDE! WE MAKE IT UNANIMOUS! WE CONCEDE!
IT'S A LANDSLIDE!
MUNCH! CRUNCH!
WE ABIDE BY THE PEOPLE'S CHOICE!
FOR HE'S A JOLLY GOOD FELLOW!
SPEECH! SPEECH!
LET'S HOIST HIM UP ON OUR SHOULDERS, BOYS!
RRAAGH!
HAOLI KAO!
SILENT STRANGER
GREAT SCOTT!
WE'VE ELECTED AN APE!
WHEN PEOPLE ARE SO MEAN AND SELFISH, THEY DESERVE TO BE LED BY AN APE –
IN A WAY, YOU KNOW, HE IS A GOOD LEADER.
ANNIE, HONEY… SHUT UP AND KEEP ROWING.
GOOD SHIP NAUSEA
END
Elder, Heath & P. Coker, Jr.

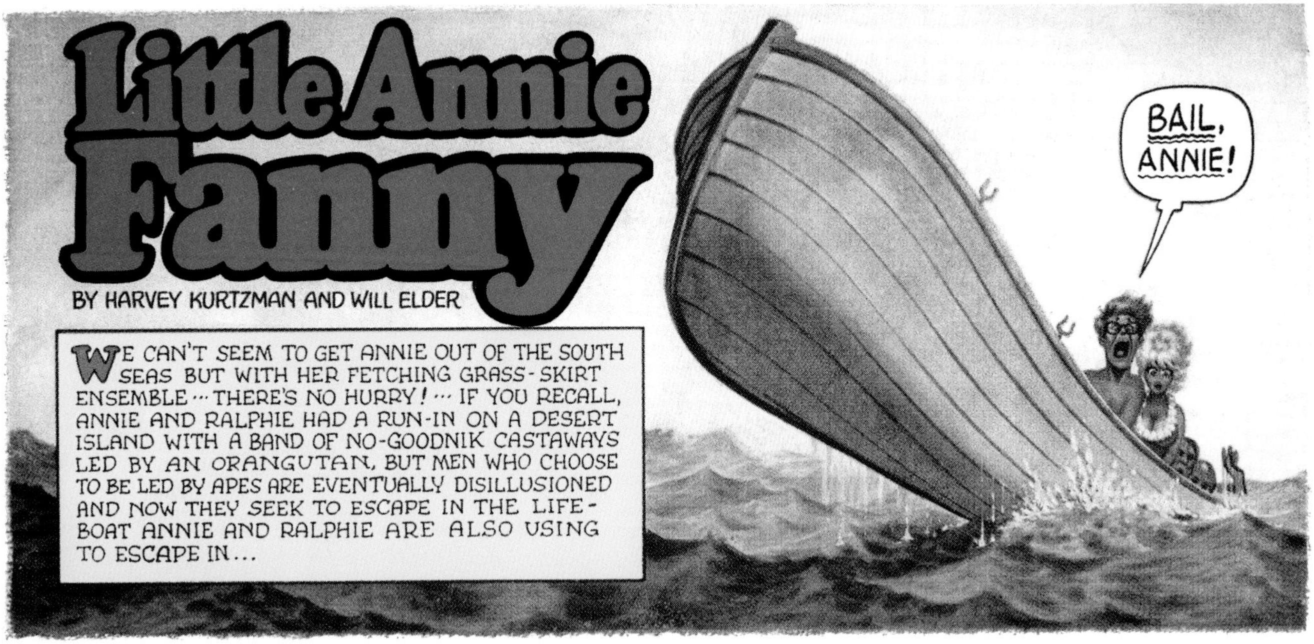
Little Annie Fanny
BY HARVEY KURTZMAN AND WILL ELDER
WE CAN'T SEEM TO GET ANNIE OUT OF THE SOUTH SEAS BUT WITH HER FETCHING GRASS-SKIRT ENSEMBLE ··· THERE'S NO HURRY! ··· IF YOU RECALL, ANNIE AND RALPHIE HAD A RUN-IN ON A DESERT ISLAND WITH A BAND OF NO-GOODNIK CASTAWAYS LED BY AN ORANGUTAN, BUT MEN WHO CHOOSE TO BE LED BY APES ARE EVENTUALLY DISILLUSIONED AND NOW THEY SEEK TO ESCAPE IN THE LIFE-BOAT ANNIE AND RALPHIE ARE ALSO USING TO ESCAPE IN...
BAIL, ANNIE!

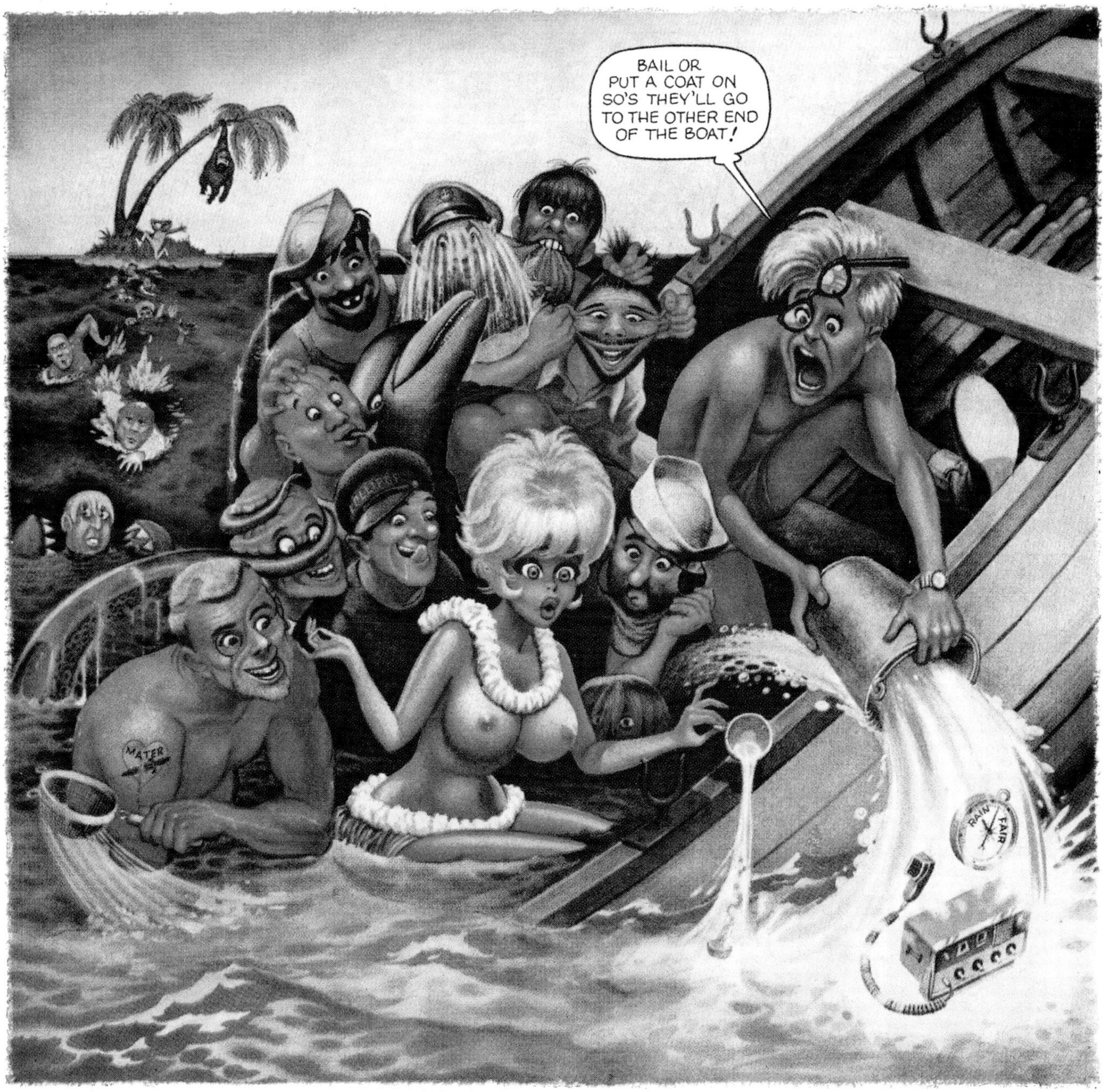
BAIL OR PUT A COAT ON SO'S THEY'LL GO TO THE OTHER END OF THE BOAT!
MATER
RAIN
FAIR

67

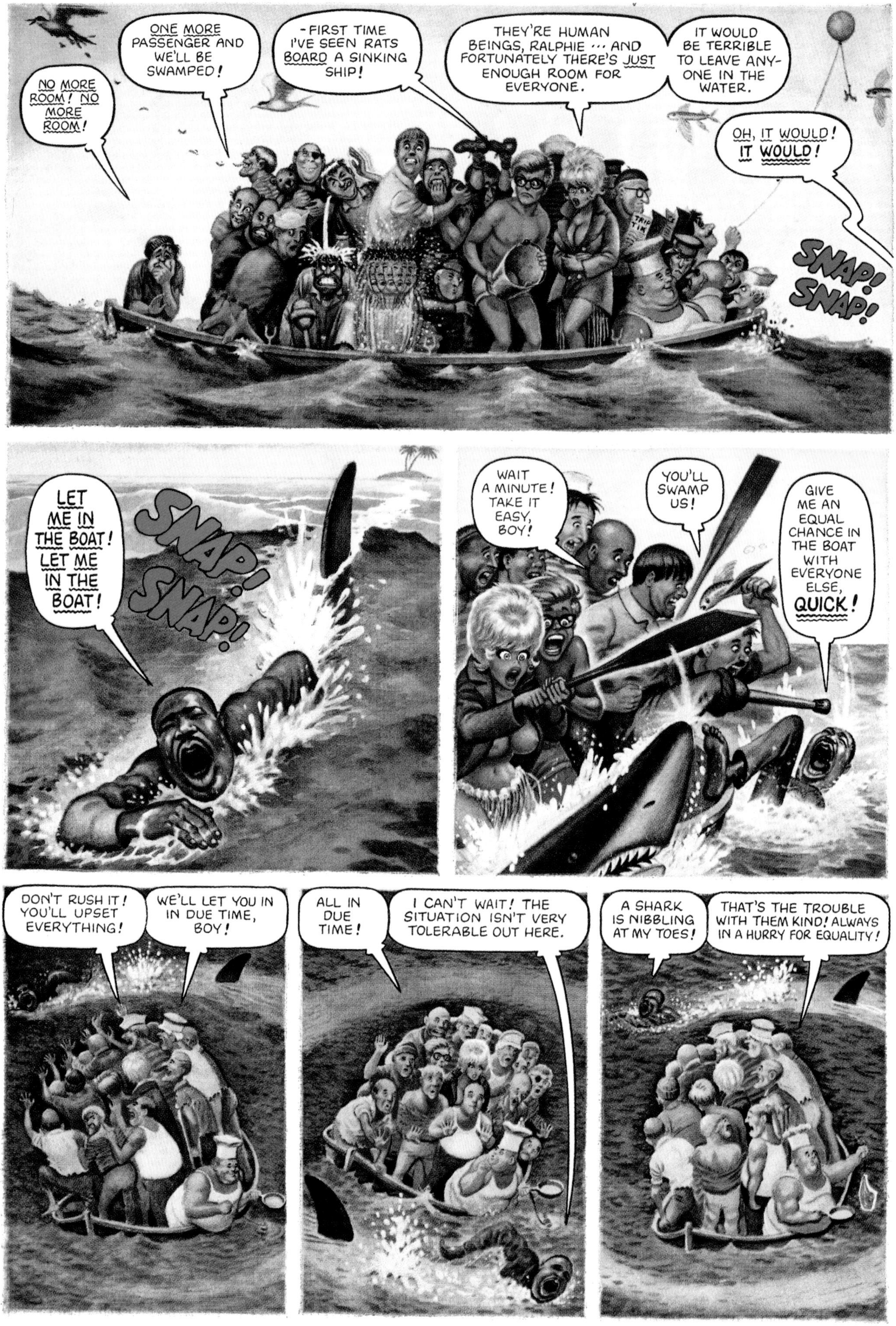
NO MORE ROOM! NO MORE ROOM!
ONE MORE PASSENGER AND WE'LL BE SWAMPED!
-FIRST TIME I'VE SEEN RATS BOARD A SINKING SHIP!
THEY'RE HUMAN BEINGS, RALPHIE ... AND FORTUNATELY THERE'S JUST ENOUGH ROOM FOR EVERYONE.
IT WOULD BE TERRIBLE TO LEAVE ANY-ONE IN THE WATER.
OH, IT WOULD! IT WOULD!
SNAP! SNAP!
LET ME IN THE BOAT! LET ME IN THE BOAT!
SNAP! SNAP!
WAIT A MINUTE! TAKE IT EASY, BOY!
YOU'LL SWAMP US!
GIVE ME AN EQUAL CHANCE IN THE BOAT WITH EVERYONE ELSE, QUICK!
DON'T RUSH IT! YOU'LL UPSET EVERYTHING!
WE'LL LET YOU IN IN DUE TIME, BOY!
ALL IN DUE TIME!
I CAN'T WAIT! THE SITUATION ISN'T VERY TOLERABLE OUT HERE.
A SHARK IS NIBBLING AT MY TOES!
THAT'S THE TROUBLE WITH THEM KIND! ALWAYS IN A HURRY FOR EQUALITY!

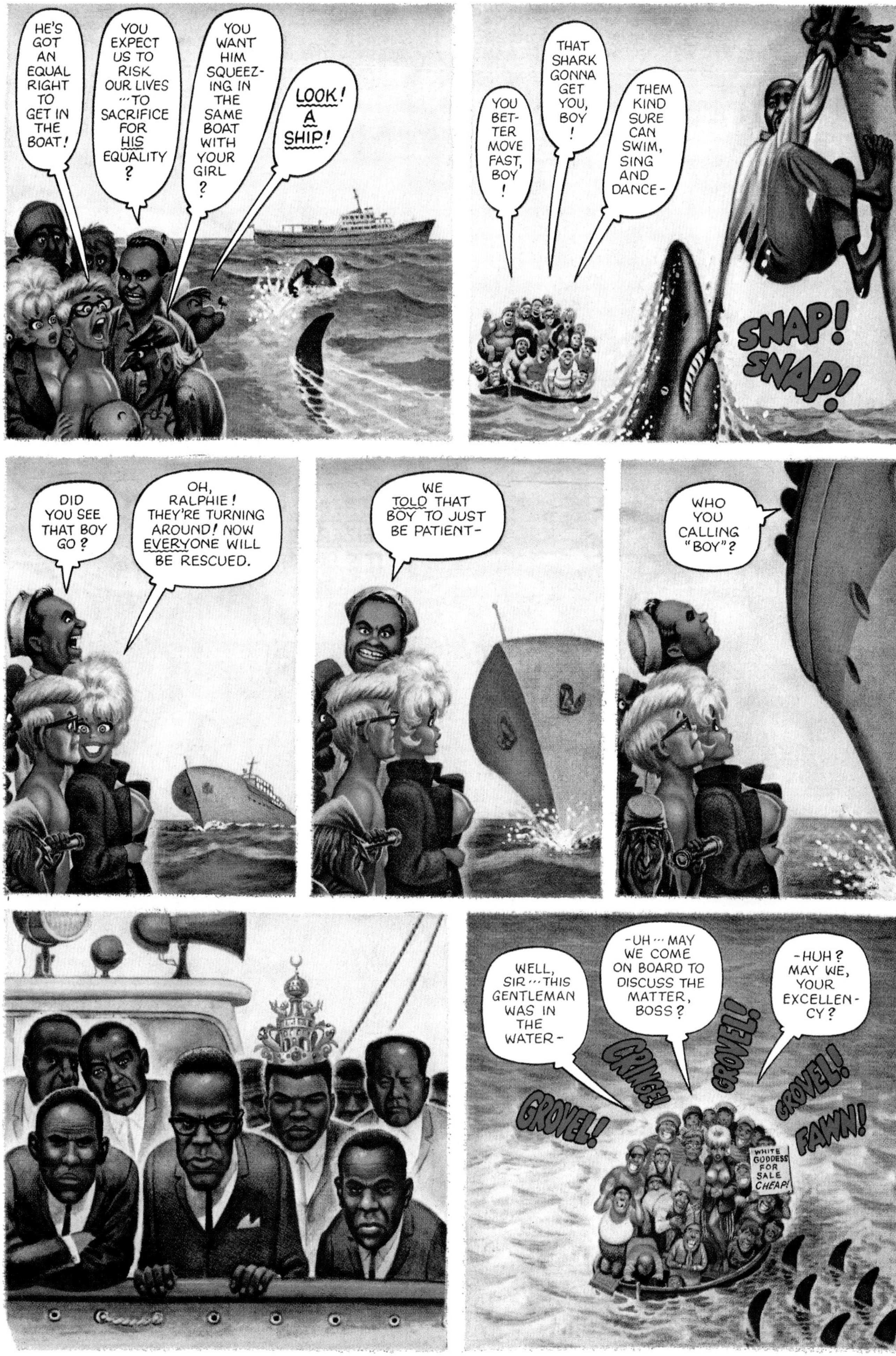

HE'S GOT AN EQUAL RIGHT TO GET IN THE BOAT!
YOU EXPECT US TO RISK OUR LIVES ...TO SACRIFICE FOR HIS EQUALITY?
YOU WANT HIM SQUEEZ-ING IN THE SAME BOAT WITH YOUR GIRL?
LOOK! A SHIP!
YOU BET-TER MOVE FAST, BOY!
THAT SHARK GONNA GET YOU, BOY!
THEM KIND SURE CAN SWIM, SING AND DANCE-
SNAP! SNAP!
DID YOU SEE THAT BOY GO?
OH, RALPHIE! THEY'RE TURNING AROUND! NOW EVERYONE WILL BE RESCUED.
WE TOLD THAT BOY TO JUST BE PATIENT-
WHO YOU CALLING "BOY"?
WELL, SIR ... THIS GENTLEMAN WAS IN THE WATER-
-UH ... MAY WE COME ON BOARD TO DISCUSS THE MATTER, BOSS?
-HUH? MAY WE, YOUR EXCELLEN-CY?
GROVEL!
CRINGE!
GROVEL!
GROVEL!
FAWN!
WHITE GODDESS FOR SALE CHEAP!

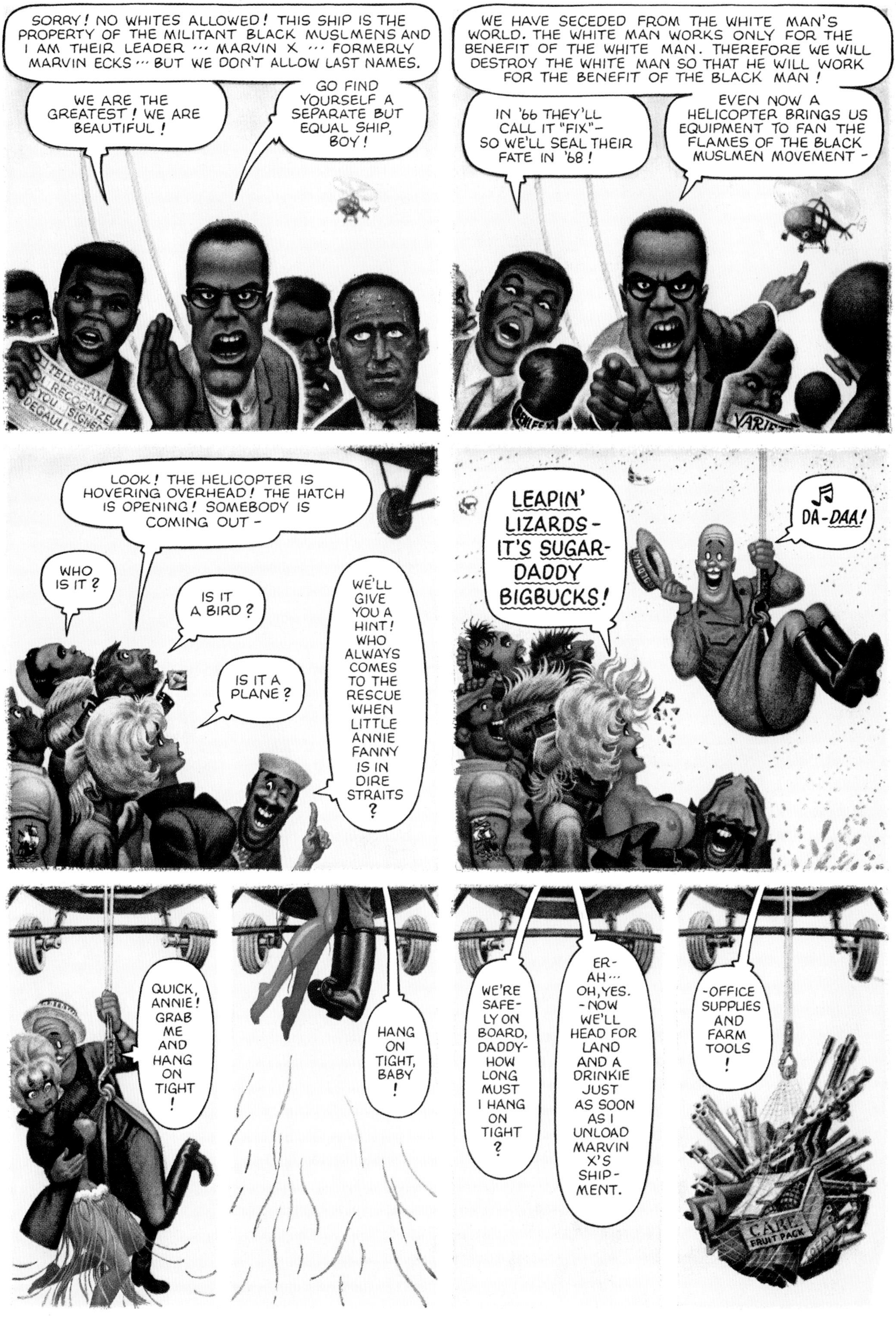

SORRY! NO WHITES ALLOWED! THIS SHIP IS THE PROPERTY OF THE MILITANT BLACK MUSLMENS AND I AM THEIR LEADER ··· MARVIN X ··· FORMERLY MARVIN ECKS ··· BUT WE DON'T ALLOW LAST NAMES.
WE ARE THE GREATEST! WE ARE BEAUTIFUL!
GO FIND YOURSELF A SEPARATE BUT EQUAL SHIP, BOY!
TELEGRAM
WE HAVE SECEDED FROM THE WHITE MAN'S WORLD. THE WHITE MAN WORKS ONLY FOR THE BENEFIT OF THE WHITE MAN. THEREFORE WE WILL DESTROY THE WHITE MAN SO THAT HE WILL WORK FOR THE BENEFIT OF THE BLACK MAN!
IN '66 THEY'LL CALL IT "FIX"- SO WE'LL SEAL THEIR FATE IN '68!
EVEN NOW A HELICOPTER BRINGS US EQUIPMENT TO FAN THE FLAMES OF THE BLACK MUSLMEN MOVEMENT -
LOOK! THE HELICOPTER IS HOVERING OVERHEAD! THE HATCH IS OPENING! SOMEBODY IS COMING OUT -
WHO IS IT?
IS IT A BIRD?
IS IT A PLANE?
WE'LL GIVE YOU A HINT! WHO ALWAYS COMES TO THE RESCUE WHEN LITTLE ANNIE FANNY IS IN DIRE STRAITS?
LEAPIN' LIZARDS - IT'S SUGAR-DADDY BIGBUCKS!
DA-DAA!
QUICK, ANNIE! GRAB ME AND HANG ON TIGHT!
HANG ON TIGHT, BABY!
WE'RE SAFE-LY ON BOARD, DADDY-HOW LONG MUST I HANG ON TIGHT?
ER-AH··· OH, YES. -NOW WE'LL HEAD FOR LAND AND A DRINKIE JUST AS SOON AS I UNLOAD MARVIN X'S SHIP-MENT.
-OFFICE SUPPLIES AND FARM TOOLS!
CARE FRUIT PACK

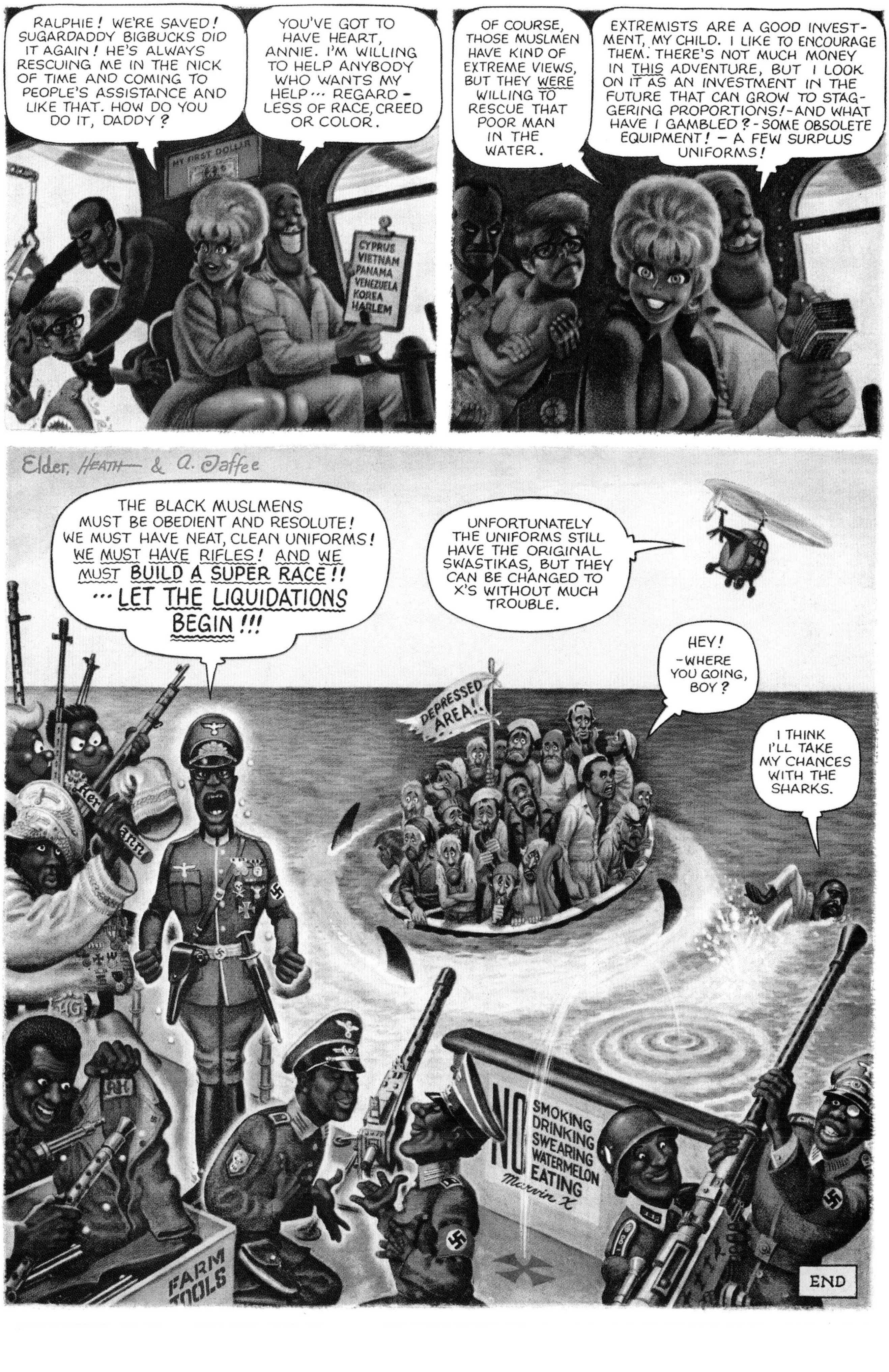

RALPHIE! WE'RE SAVED! SUGARDADDY BIGBUCKS DID IT AGAIN! HE'S ALWAYS RESCUING ME IN THE NICK OF TIME AND COMING TO PEOPLE'S ASSISTANCE AND LIKE THAT. HOW DO YOU DO IT, DADDY?
YOU'VE GOT TO HAVE HEART, ANNIE. I'M WILLING TO HELP ANYBODY WHO WANTS MY HELP... REGARDLESS OF RACE, CREED OR COLOR.
CYPRUS VIETNAM PANAMA VENEZUELA KOREA HARLEM
OF COURSE, THOSE MUSLMEN HAVE KIND OF EXTREME VIEWS, BUT THEY WERE WILLING TO RESCUE THAT POOR MAN IN THE WATER.
EXTREMISTS ARE A GOOD INVESTMENT, MY CHILD. I LIKE TO ENCOURAGE THEM. THERE'S NOT MUCH MONEY IN THIS ADVENTURE, BUT I LOOK ON IT AS AN INVESTMENT IN THE FUTURE THAT CAN GROW TO STAGGERING PROPORTIONS!-AND WHAT HAVE I GAMBLED?-SOME OBSOLETE EQUIPMENT! – A FEW SURPLUS UNIFORMS!
Elder, Heath & A. Jaffee
THE BLACK MUSLMENS MUST BE OBEDIENT AND RESOLUTE! WE MUST HAVE NEAT, CLEAN UNIFORMS! WE MUST HAVE RIFLES! AND WE MUST BUILD A SUPER RACE!! ...LET THE LIQUIDATIONS BEGIN!!!
UNFORTUNATELY THE UNIFORMS STILL HAVE THE ORIGINAL SWASTIKAS, BUT THEY CAN BE CHANGED TO X'S WITHOUT MUCH TROUBLE.
HEY! -WHERE YOU GOING, BOY?
I THINK I'LL TAKE MY CHANCES WITH THE SHARKS.
DEPRESSED AREA!.
NO SMOKING DRINKING SWEARING WATERMELON EATING
Marvin X
FARM TOOLS
END

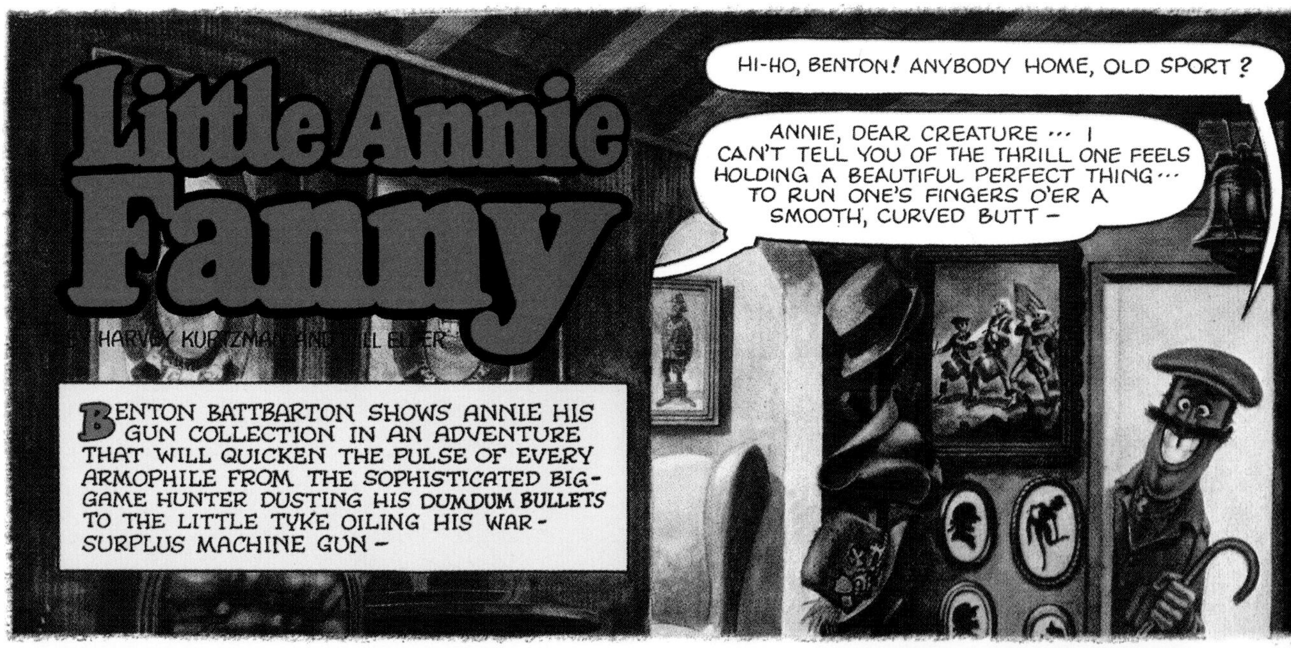

Little Annie Fanny
HARVEY KURTZMAN
BENTON BATTBARTON SHOWS ANNIE HIS GUN COLLECTION IN AN ADVENTURE THAT WILL QUICKEN THE PULSE OF EVERY ARMOPHILE FROM THE SOPHISTICATED BIG-GAME HUNTER DUSTING HIS DUMDUM BULLETS TO THE LITTLE TYKE OILING HIS WAR-SURPLUS MACHINE GUN –
HI-HO, BENTON! ANYBODY HOME, OLD SPORT?
ANNIE, DEAR CREATURE ··· I CAN'T TELL YOU OF THE THRILL ONE FEELS HOLDING A BEAUTIFUL PERFECT THING ··· TO RUN ONE'S FINGERS O'ER A SMOOTH, CURVED BUTT –

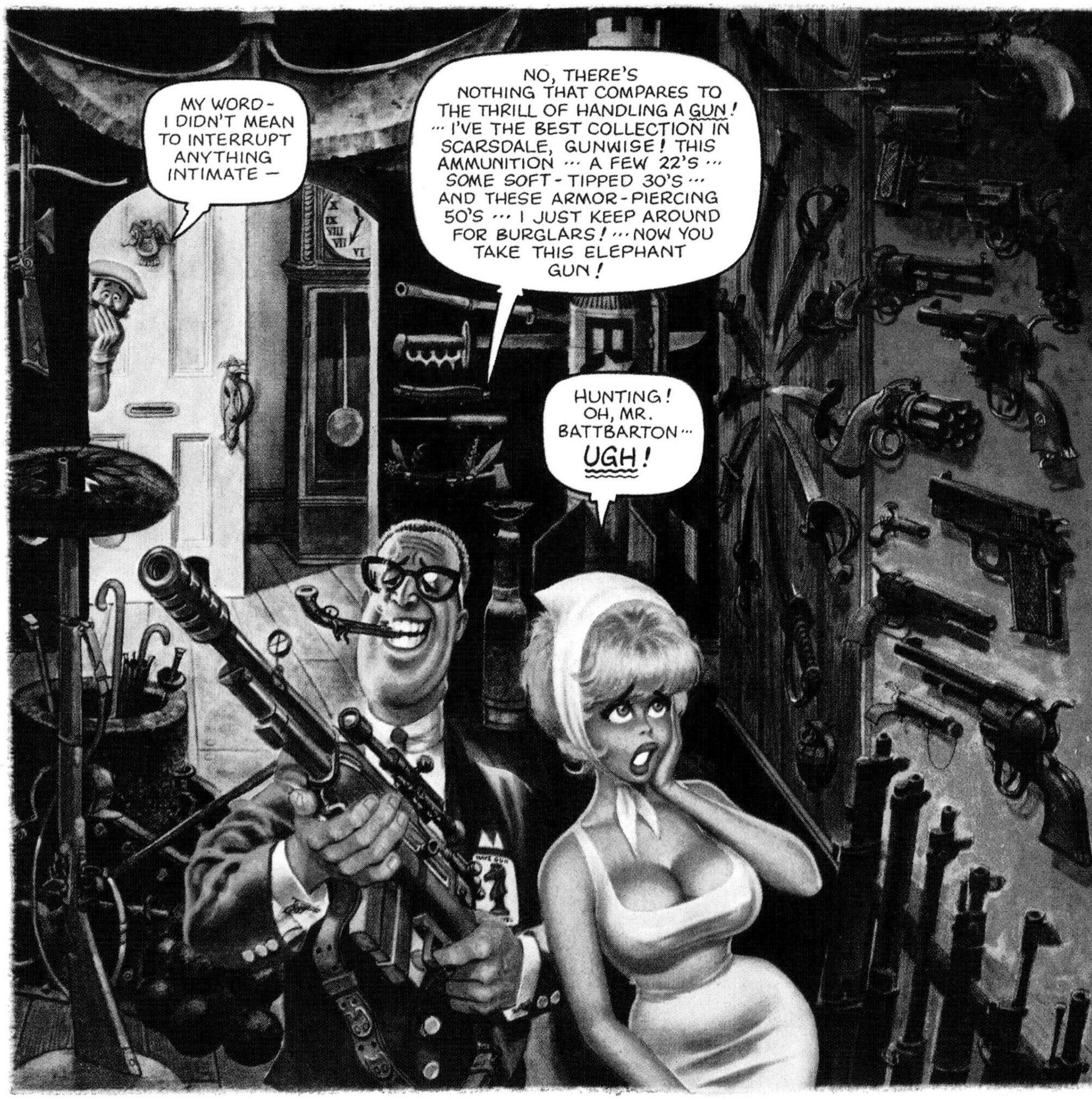

MY WORD – I DIDN'T MEAN TO INTERRUPT ANYTHING INTIMATE –
NO, THERE'S NOTHING THAT COMPARES TO THE THRILL OF HANDLING A GUN! ··· I'VE THE BEST COLLECTION IN SCARSDALE, GUNWISE! THIS AMMUNITION ··· A FEW 22'S ··· SOME SOFT-TIPPED 30'S ··· AND THESE ARMOR-PIERCING 50'S ··· I JUST KEEP AROUND FOR BURGLARS! ··· NOW YOU TAKE THIS ELEPHANT GUN!
HUNTING! OH, MR. BATTBARTON ··· UGH!

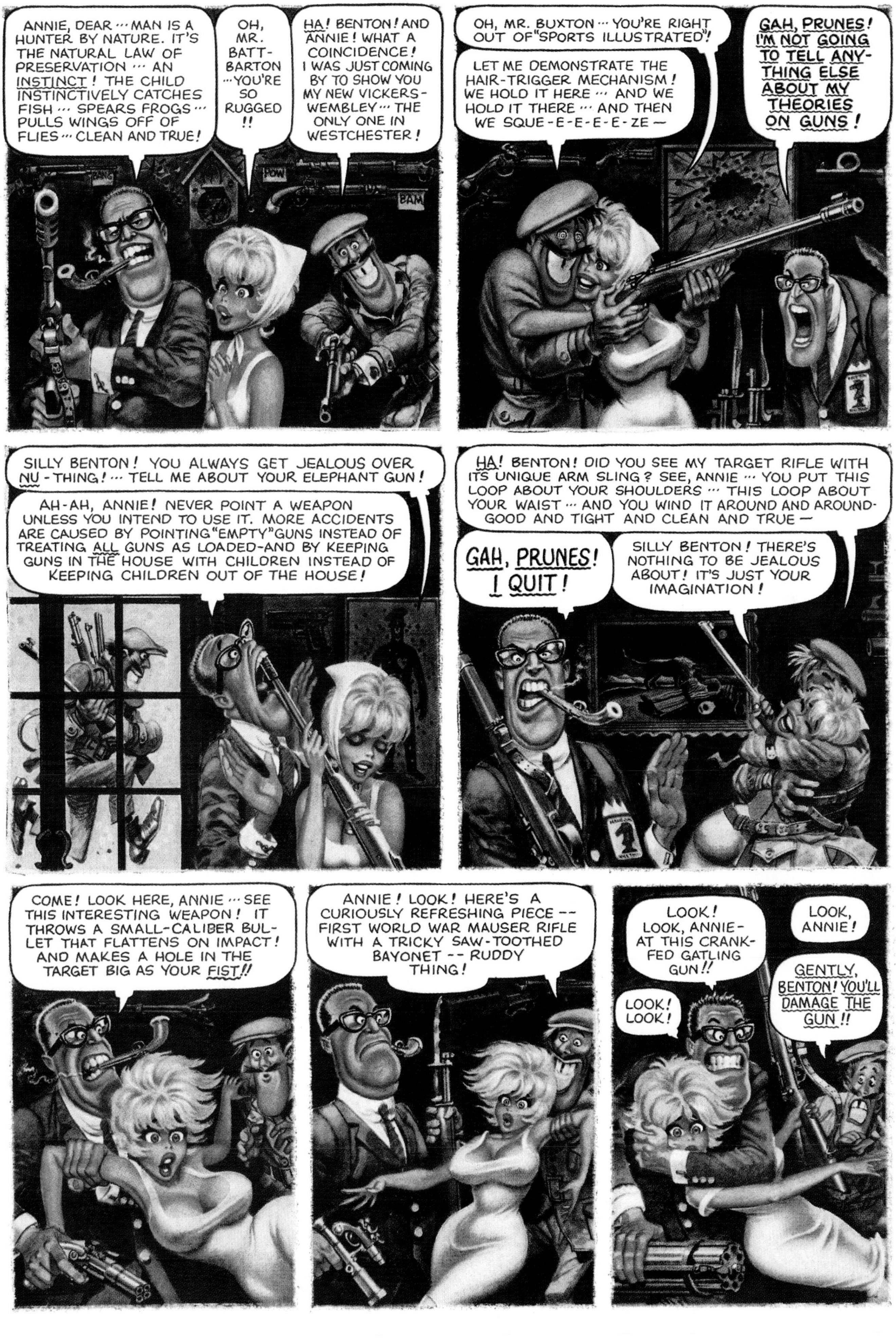
ANNIE, DEAR ··· MAN IS A HUNTER BY NATURE. IT'S THE NATURAL LAW OF PRESERVATION ··· AN INSTINCT! THE CHILD INSTINCTIVELY CATCHES FISH ··· SPEARS FROGS ··· PULLS WINGS OFF OF FLIES ··· CLEAN AND TRUE!
OH, MR. BATT-BARTON ··· YOU'RE SO RUGGED !!
HA! BENTON! AND ANNIE! WHAT A COINCIDENCE! I WAS JUST COMING BY TO SHOW YOU MY NEW VICKERS-WEMBLEY ··· THE ONLY ONE IN WESTCHESTER!
BANG
POW
BAM
OH, MR. BUXTON ··· YOU'RE RIGHT OUT OF "SPORTS ILLUSTRATED"!
LET ME DEMONSTRATE THE HAIR-TRIGGER MECHANISM! WE HOLD IT HERE ··· AND WE HOLD IT THERE ··· AND THEN WE SQUE-E-E-E-E-ZE —
GAH, PRUNES! I'M NOT GOING TO TELL ANY-THING ELSE ABOUT MY THEORIES ON GUNS!
SILLY BENTON! YOU ALWAYS GET JEALOUS OVER NU-THING! ··· TELL ME ABOUT YOUR ELEPHANT GUN!
AH-AH, ANNIE! NEVER POINT A WEAPON UNLESS YOU INTEND TO USE IT. MORE ACCIDENTS ARE CAUSED BY POINTING "EMPTY" GUNS INSTEAD OF TREATING ALL GUNS AS LOADED-AND BY KEEPING GUNS IN THE HOUSE WITH CHILDREN INSTEAD OF KEEPING CHILDREN OUT OF THE HOUSE!
HA! BENTON! DID YOU SEE MY TARGET RIFLE WITH ITS UNIQUE ARM SLING? SEE, ANNIE ··· YOU PUT THIS LOOP ABOUT YOUR SHOULDERS ··· THIS LOOP ABOUT YOUR WAIST ··· AND YOU WIND IT AROUND AND AROUND-GOOD AND TIGHT AND CLEAN AND TRUE —
GAH, PRUNES! I QUIT!
SILLY BENTON! THERE'S NOTHING TO BE JEALOUS ABOUT! IT'S JUST YOUR IMAGINATION!
COME! LOOK HERE, ANNIE ··· SEE THIS INTERESTING WEAPON! IT THROWS A SMALL-CALIBER BUL-LET THAT FLATTENS ON IMPACT! AND MAKES A HOLE IN THE TARGET BIG AS YOUR FIST!!
ANNIE! LOOK! HERE'S A CURIOUSLY REFRESHING PIECE -- FIRST WORLD WAR MAUSER RIFLE WITH A TRICKY SAW-TOOTHED BAYONET -- RUDDY THING!
LOOK! LOOK, ANNIE- AT THIS CRANK-FED GATLING GUN!!
LOOK, ANNIE!
LOOK! LOOK!
GENTLY, BENTON! YOU'LL DAMAGE THE GUN!!

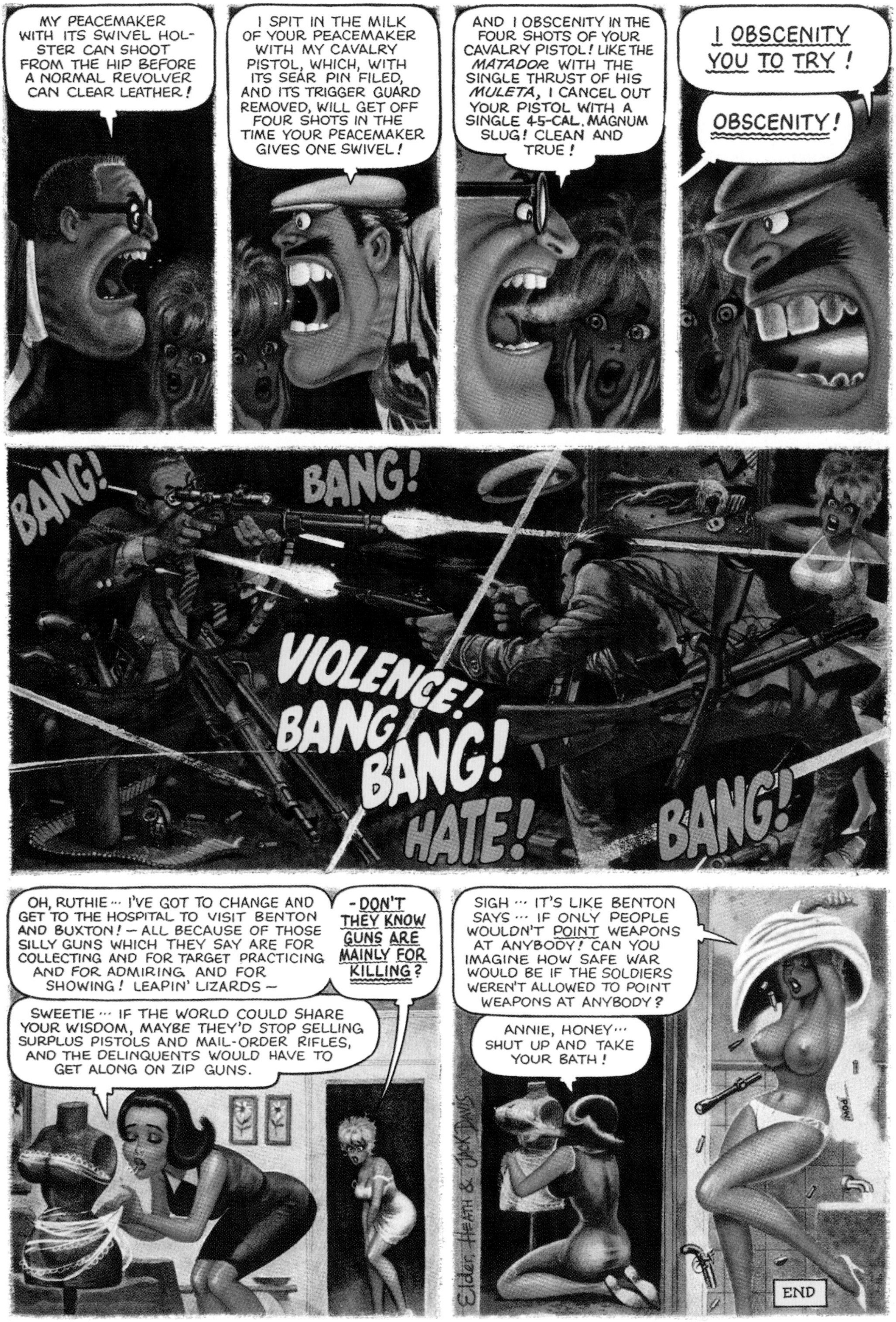
MY PEACEMAKER WITH ITS SWIVEL HOLSTER CAN SHOOT FROM THE HIP BEFORE A NORMAL REVOLVER CAN CLEAR LEATHER!
I SPIT IN THE MILK OF YOUR PEACEMAKER WITH MY CAVALRY PISTOL, WHICH, WITH ITS SEAR PIN FILED, AND ITS TRIGGER GUARD REMOVED, WILL GET OFF FOUR SHOTS IN THE TIME YOUR PEACEMAKER GIVES ONE SWIVEL!
AND I OBSCENITY IN THE FOUR SHOTS OF YOUR CAVALRY PISTOL! LIKE THE *MATADOR* WITH THE SINGLE THRUST OF HIS *MULETA*, I CANCEL OUT YOUR PISTOL WITH A SINGLE 45-CAL. MAGNUM SLUG! CLEAN AND TRUE!
I OBSCENITY YOU TO TRY!
OBSCENITY!
BANG!
BANG!
VIOLENCE!
BANG
BANG!
HATE!
BANG!
OH, RUTHIE... I'VE GOT TO CHANGE AND GET TO THE HOSPITAL TO VISIT BENTON AND BUXTON! — ALL BECAUSE OF THOSE SILLY GUNS WHICH THEY SAY ARE FOR COLLECTING AND FOR TARGET PRACTICING AND FOR ADMIRING AND FOR SHOWING! LEAPIN' LIZARDS —
- DON'T THEY KNOW GUNS ARE MAINLY FOR KILLING?
SWEETIE... IF THE WORLD COULD SHARE YOUR WISDOM, MAYBE THEY'D STOP SELLING SURPLUS PISTOLS AND MAIL-ORDER RIFLES, AND THE DELINQUENTS WOULD HAVE TO GET ALONG ON ZIP GUNS.
Elder, Heath & Jack Davis
SIGH... IT'S LIKE BENTON SAYS... IF ONLY PEOPLE WOULDN'T POINT WEAPONS AT ANYBODY! CAN YOU IMAGINE HOW SAFE WAR WOULD BE IF THE SOLDIERS WEREN'T ALLOWED TO POINT WEAPONS AT ANYBODY?
ANNIE, HONEY... SHUT UP AND TAKE YOUR BATH!
END

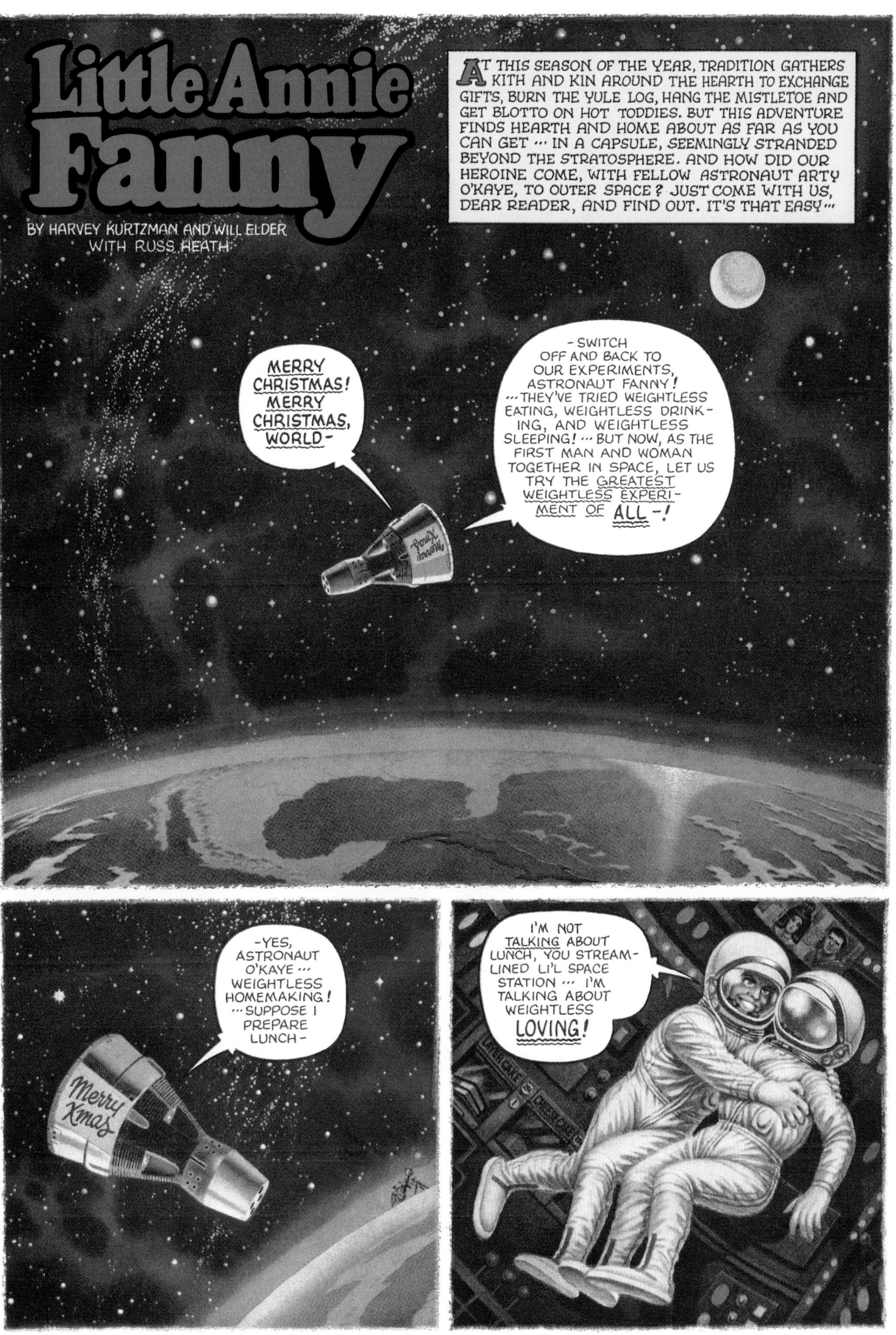
Little Annie Fanny
BY HARVEY KURTZMAN AND WILL ELDER WITH RUSS HEATH
AT THIS SEASON OF THE YEAR, TRADITION GATHERS KITH AND KIN AROUND THE HEARTH TO EXCHANGE GIFTS, BURN THE YULE LOG, HANG THE MISTLETOE AND GET BLOTTO ON HOT TODDIES. BUT THIS ADVENTURE FINDS HEARTH AND HOME ABOUT AS FAR AS YOU CAN GET ··· IN A CAPSULE, SEEMINGLY STRANDED BEYOND THE STRATOSPHERE. AND HOW DID OUR HEROINE COME, WITH FELLOW ASTRONAUT ARTY O'KAYE, TO OUTER SPACE? JUST COME WITH US, DEAR READER, AND FIND OUT. IT'S THAT EASY···
MERRY CHRISTMAS! MERRY CHRISTMAS, WORLD-
-SWITCH OFF AND BACK TO OUR EXPERIMENTS, ASTRONAUT FANNY! ···THEY'VE TRIED WEIGHTLESS EATING, WEIGHTLESS DRINKING, AND WEIGHTLESS SLEEPING! ··· BUT NOW, AS THE FIRST MAN AND WOMAN TOGETHER IN SPACE, LET US TRY THE GREATEST WEIGHTLESS EXPERIMENT OF ALL-!
Merry Xmas
-YES, ASTRONAUT O'KAYE··· WEIGHTLESS HOMEMAKING! ···SUPPOSE I PREPARE LUNCH-
I'M NOT TALKING ABOUT LUNCH, YOU STREAMLINED LI'L SPACE STATION··· I'M TALKING ABOUT WEIGHTLESS LOVING!

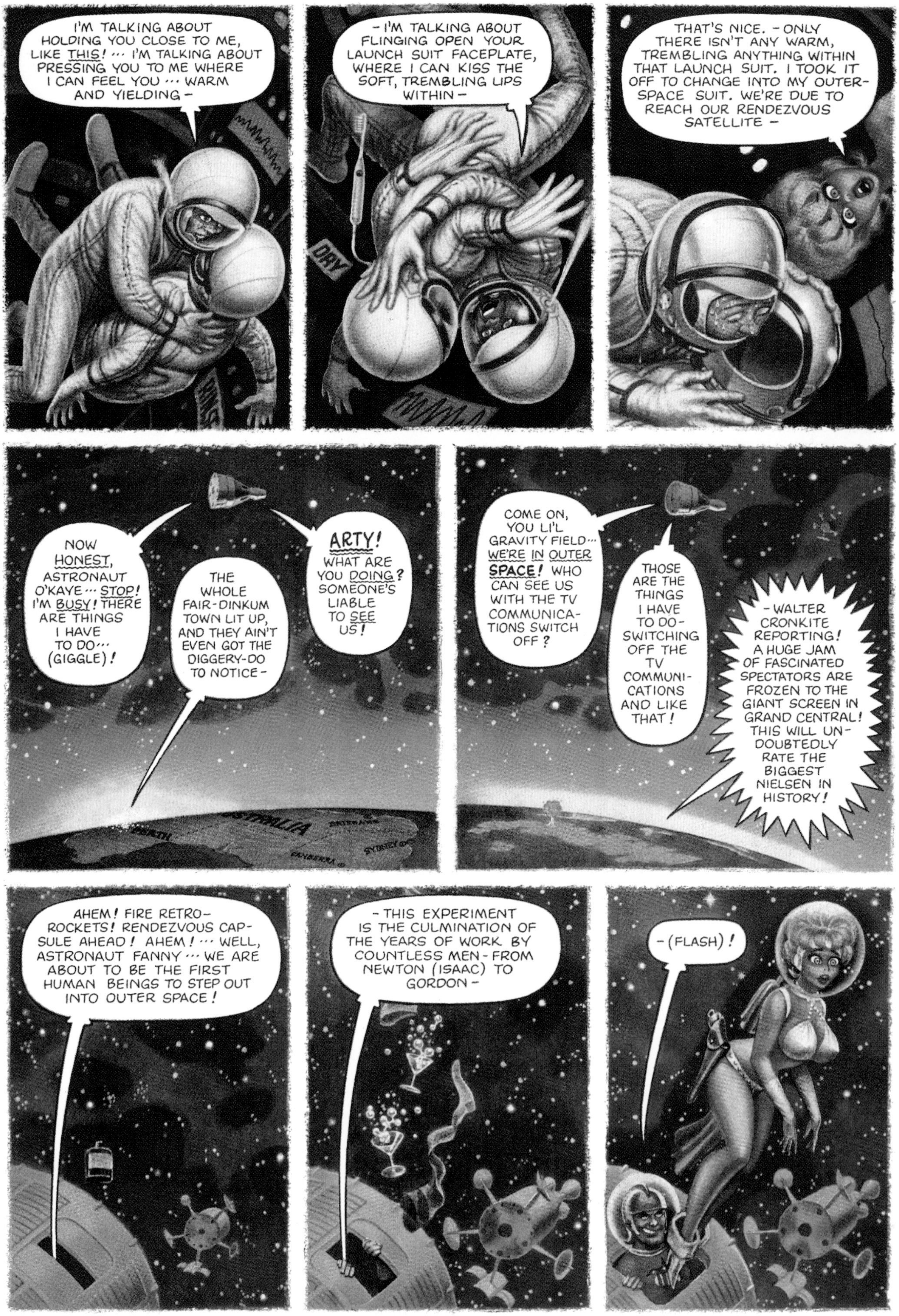

I'M TALKING ABOUT HOLDING YOU CLOSE TO ME, LIKE THIS! ··· I'M TALKING ABOUT PRESSING YOU TO ME WHERE I CAN FEEL YOU ··· WARM AND YIELDING –
– I'M TALKING ABOUT FLINGING OPEN YOUR LAUNCH SUIT FACEPLATE, WHERE I CAN KISS THE SOFT, TREMBLING LIPS WITHIN –
DRY
THAT'S NICE. – ONLY THERE ISN'T ANY WARM, TREMBLING ANYTHING WITHIN THAT LAUNCH SUIT. I TOOK IT OFF TO CHANGE INTO MY OUTER-SPACE SUIT. WE'RE DUE TO REACH OUR RENDEZVOUS SATELLITE –
NOW HONEST, ASTRONAUT O'KAYE ··· STOP! I'M BUSY! THERE ARE THINGS I HAVE TO DO ··· (GIGGLE)!
THE WHOLE FAIR-DINKUM TOWN LIT UP, AND THEY AIN'T EVEN GOT THE DIGGERY-DO TO NOTICE –
ARTY! WHAT ARE YOU DOING? SOMEONE'S LIABLE TO SEE US!
AUSTRALIA
PERTH
CANBERRA
SYDNEY
COME ON, YOU LI'L GRAVITY FIELD ··· WE'RE IN OUTER SPACE! WHO CAN SEE US WITH THE TV COMMUNICATIONS SWITCH OFF?
THOSE ARE THE THINGS I HAVE TO DO – SWITCHING OFF THE TV COMMUNICATIONS AND LIKE THAT!
– WALTER CRONKITE REPORTING! A HUGE JAM OF FASCINATED SPECTATORS ARE FROZEN TO THE GIANT SCREEN IN GRAND CENTRAL! THIS WILL UNDOUBTEDLY RATE THE BIGGEST NIELSEN IN HISTORY!
AHEM! FIRE RETRO-ROCKETS! RENDEZVOUS CAPSULE AHEAD! AHEM! ··· WELL, ASTRONAUT FANNY ··· WE ARE ABOUT TO BE THE FIRST HUMAN BEINGS TO STEP OUT INTO OUTER SPACE!
– THIS EXPERIMENT IS THE CULMINATION OF THE YEARS OF WORK BY COUNTLESS MEN – FROM NEWTON (ISAAC) TO GORDON –
– (FLASH)!

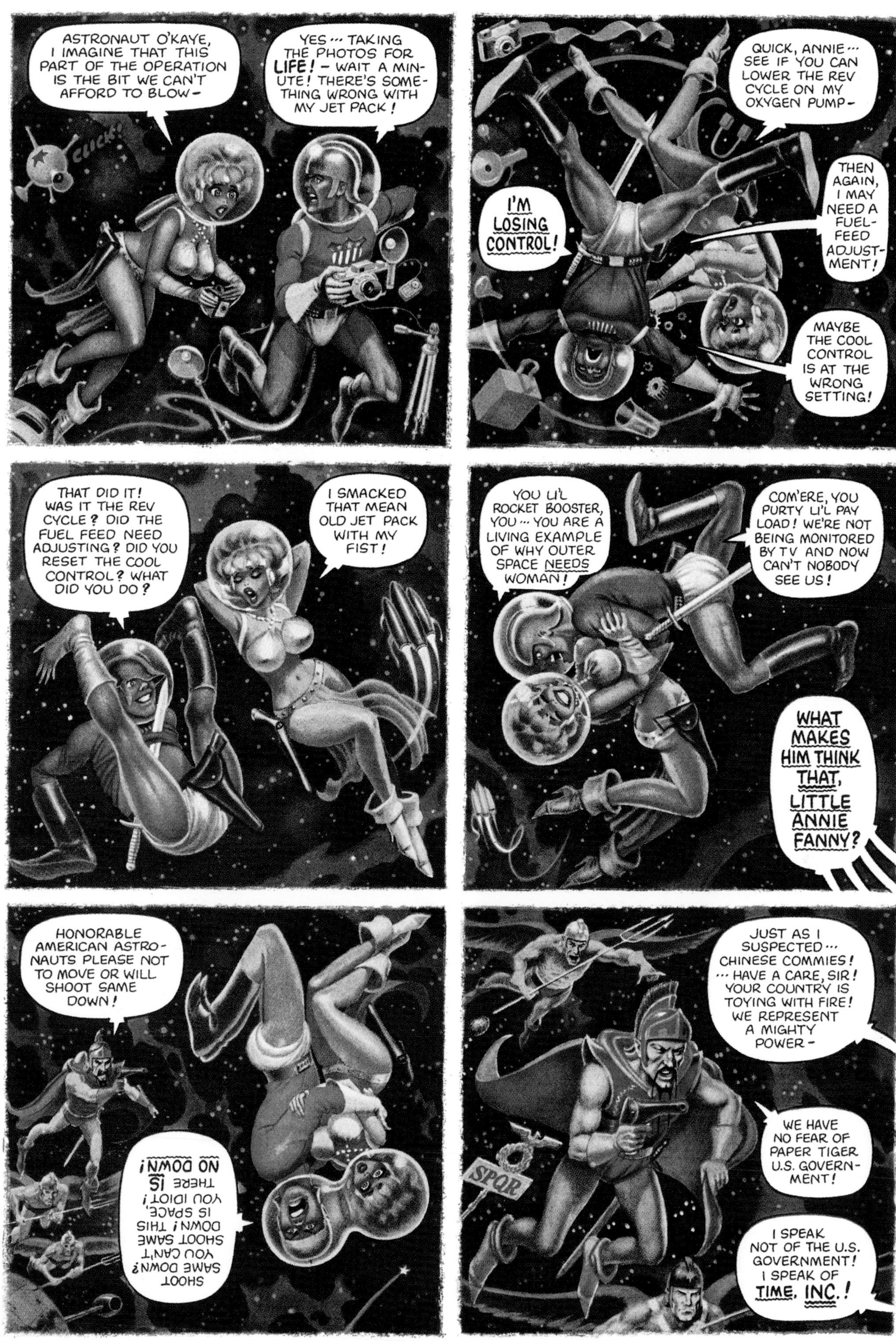
ASTRONAUT O'KAYE, I IMAGINE THAT THIS PART OF THE OPERATION IS THE BIT WE CAN'T AFFORD TO BLOW-
YES ... TAKING THE PHOTOS FOR LIFE! - WAIT A MINUTE! THERE'S SOMETHING WRONG WITH MY JET PACK!
CLICK!
QUICK, ANNIE... SEE IF YOU CAN LOWER THE REV CYCLE ON MY OXYGEN PUMP-
I'M LOSING CONTROL!
THEN AGAIN, I MAY NEED A FUEL-FEED ADJUSTMENT!
MAYBE THE COOL CONTROL IS AT THE WRONG SETTING!
THAT DID IT! WAS IT THE REV CYCLE? DID THE FUEL FEED NEED ADJUSTING? DID YOU RESET THE COOL CONTROL? WHAT DID YOU DO?
I SMACKED THAT MEAN OLD JET PACK WITH MY FIST!
YOU LI'L ROCKET BOOSTER, YOU ... YOU ARE A LIVING EXAMPLE OF WHY OUTER SPACE NEEDS WOMAN!
COM'ERE, YOU PURTY LI'L PAY LOAD! WE'RE NOT BEING MONITORED BY TV AND NOW CAN'T NOBODY SEE US!
WHAT MAKES HIM THINK THAT, LITTLE ANNIE FANNY?
HONORABLE AMERICAN ASTRONAUTS PLEASE NOT TO MOVE OR WILL SHOOT SAME DOWN!
SHOOT SAME DOWN? YOU CAN'T SHOOT SAME DOWN! THIS IS SPACE, YOU IDIOT! THERE IS NO DOWN!
JUST AS I SUSPECTED ... CHINESE COMMIES! ... HAVE A CARE, SIR! YOUR COUNTRY IS TOYING WITH FIRE! WE REPRESENT A MIGHTY POWER-
WE HAVE NO FEAR OF PAPER TIGER U.S. GOVERNMENT!
SPQR
I SPEAK NOT OF THE U.S. GOVERNMENT! I SPEAK OF TIME, INC.!

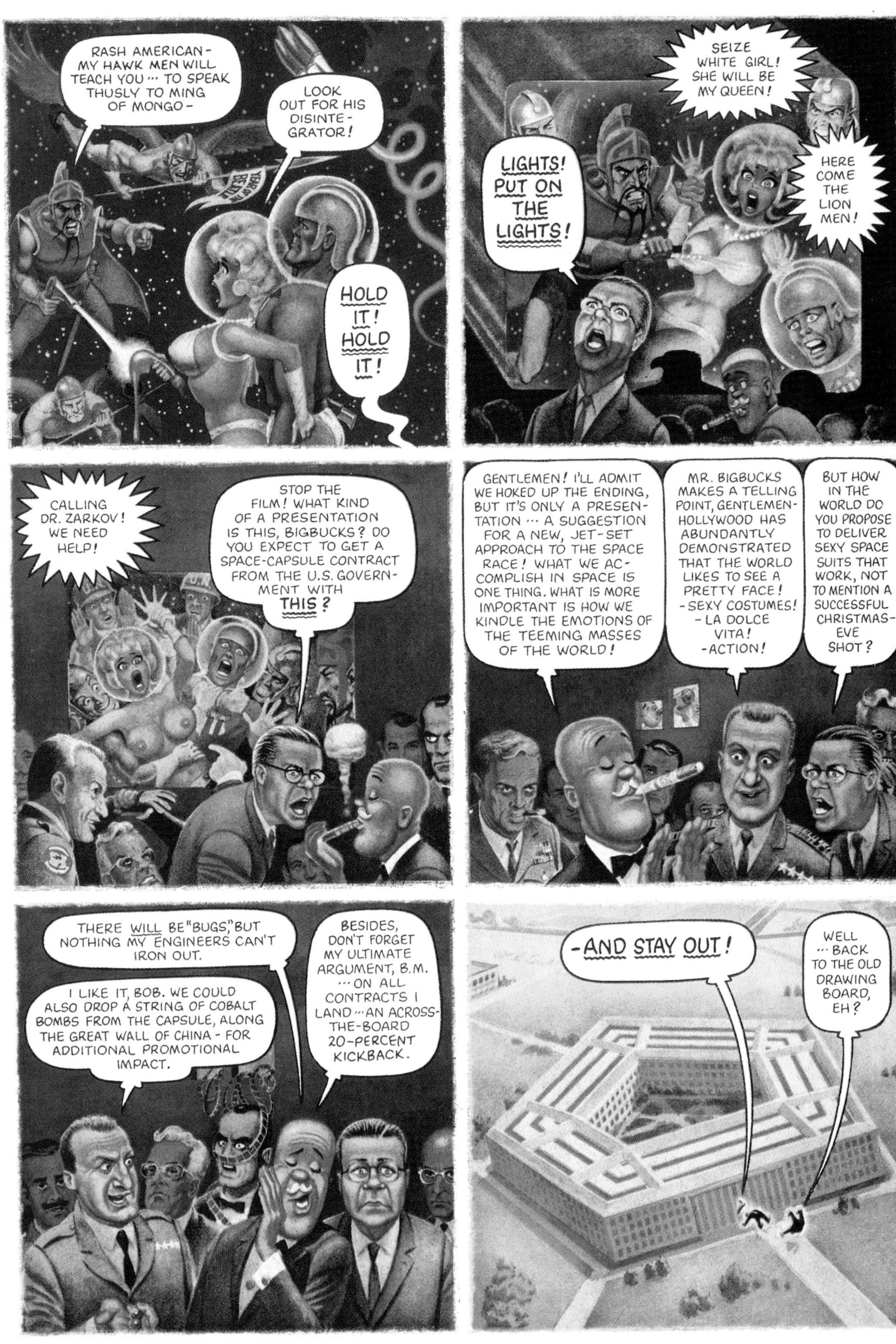
RASH AMERICAN- MY HAWK MEN WILL TEACH YOU ··· TO SPEAK THUSLY TO MING OF MONGO-
LOOK OUT FOR HIS DISINTE-GRATOR!
HOLD IT! HOLD IT!
SEIZE WHITE GIRL! SHE WILL BE MY QUEEN!
LIGHTS! PUT ON THE LIGHTS!
HERE COME THE LION MEN!
CALLING DR. ZARKOV! WE NEED HELP!
STOP THE FILM! WHAT KIND OF A PRESENTATION IS THIS, BIGBUCKS? DO YOU EXPECT TO GET A SPACE-CAPSULE CONTRACT FROM THE U.S. GOVERNMENT WITH THIS?
GENTLEMEN! I'LL ADMIT WE HOKED UP THE ENDING, BUT IT'S ONLY A PRESENTATION ··· A SUGGESTION FOR A NEW, JET-SET APPROACH TO THE SPACE RACE! WHAT WE ACCOMPLISH IN SPACE IS ONE THING. WHAT IS MORE IMPORTANT IS HOW WE KINDLE THE EMOTIONS OF THE TEEMING MASSES OF THE WORLD!
MR. BIGBUCKS MAKES A TELLING POINT, GENTLEMEN- HOLLYWOOD HAS ABUNDANTLY DEMONSTRATED THAT THE WORLD LIKES TO SEE A PRETTY FACE! -SEXY COSTUMES! -LA DOLCE VITA! -ACTION!
BUT HOW IN THE WORLD DO YOU PROPOSE TO DELIVER SEXY SPACE SUITS THAT WORK, NOT TO MENTION A SUCCESSFUL CHRISTMAS-EVE SHOT?
THERE WILL BE "BUGS," BUT NOTHING MY ENGINEERS CAN'T IRON OUT.
I LIKE IT, BOB. WE COULD ALSO DROP A STRING OF COBALT BOMBS FROM THE CAPSULE, ALONG THE GREAT WALL OF CHINA - FOR ADDITIONAL PROMOTIONAL IMPACT.
BESIDES, DON'T FORGET MY ULTIMATE ARGUMENT, B.M. ··· ON ALL CONTRACTS I LAND ··· AN ACROSS-THE-BOARD 20-PERCENT KICKBACK.
-AND STAY OUT!
WELL ··· BACK TO THE OLD DRAWING BOARD, EH?

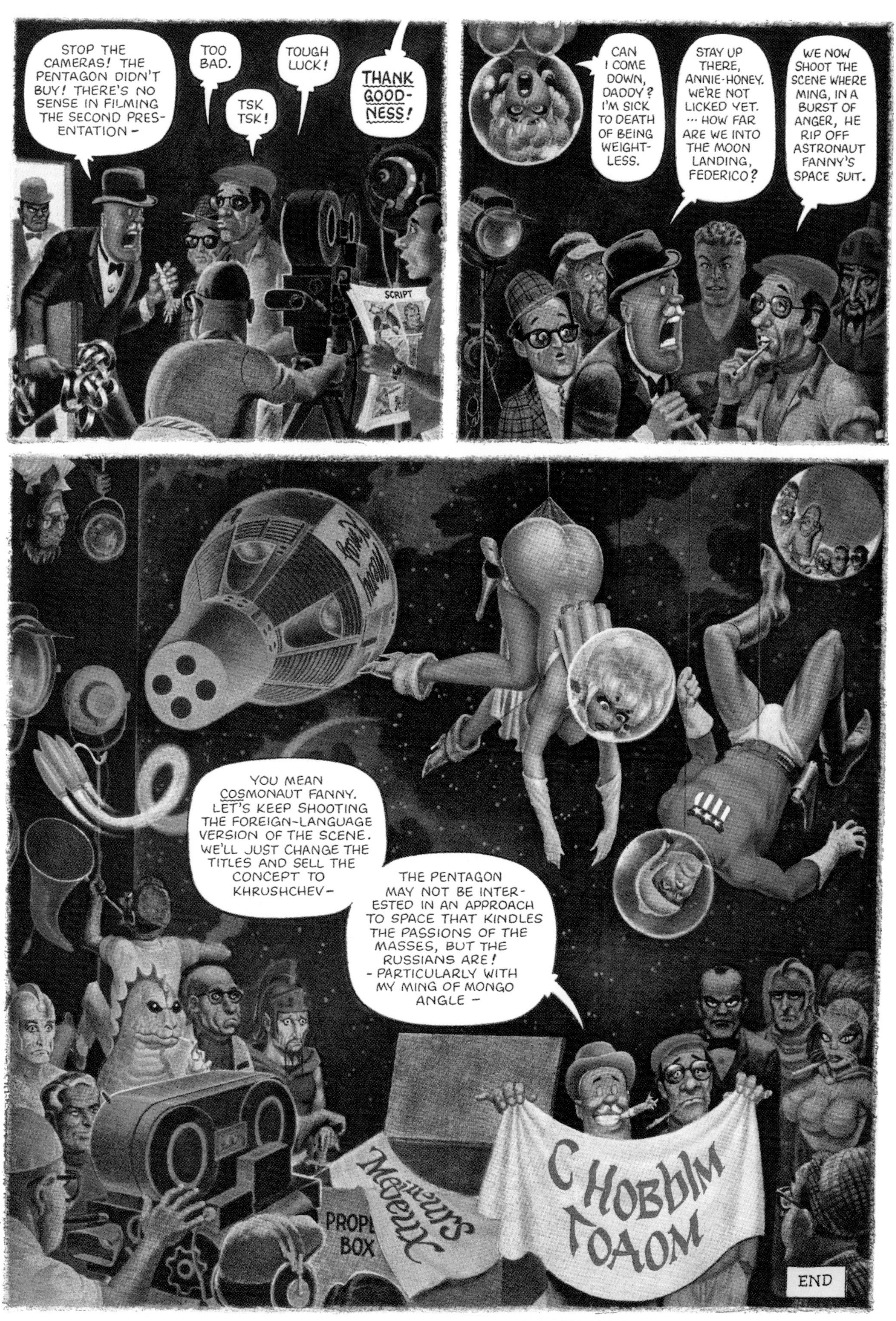
STOP THE CAMERAS! THE PENTAGON DIDN'T BUY! THERE'S NO SENSE IN FILMING THE SECOND PRESENTATION –
TOO BAD.
TSK TSK!
TOUGH LUCK!
THANK GOODNESS!
SCRIPT
CAN I COME DOWN, DADDY? I'M SICK TO DEATH OF BEING WEIGHTLESS.
STAY UP THERE, ANNIE-HONEY. WE'RE NOT LICKED YET. ... HOW FAR ARE WE INTO THE MOON LANDING, FEDERICO?
WE NOW SHOOT THE SCENE WHERE MING, IN A BURST OF ANGER, HE RIP OFF ASTRONAUT FANNY'S SPACE SUIT.
YOU MEAN COSMONAUT FANNY. LET'S KEEP SHOOTING THE FOREIGN-LANGUAGE VERSION OF THE SCENE. WE'LL JUST CHANGE THE TITLES AND SELL THE CONCEPT TO KHRUSHCHEV–
THE PENTAGON MAY NOT BE INTERESTED IN AN APPROACH TO SPACE THAT KINDLES THE PASSIONS OF THE MASSES, BUT THE RUSSIANS ARE! – PARTICULARLY WITH MY MING OF MONGO ANGLE –
С НОВЫМ ГОДОМ
END

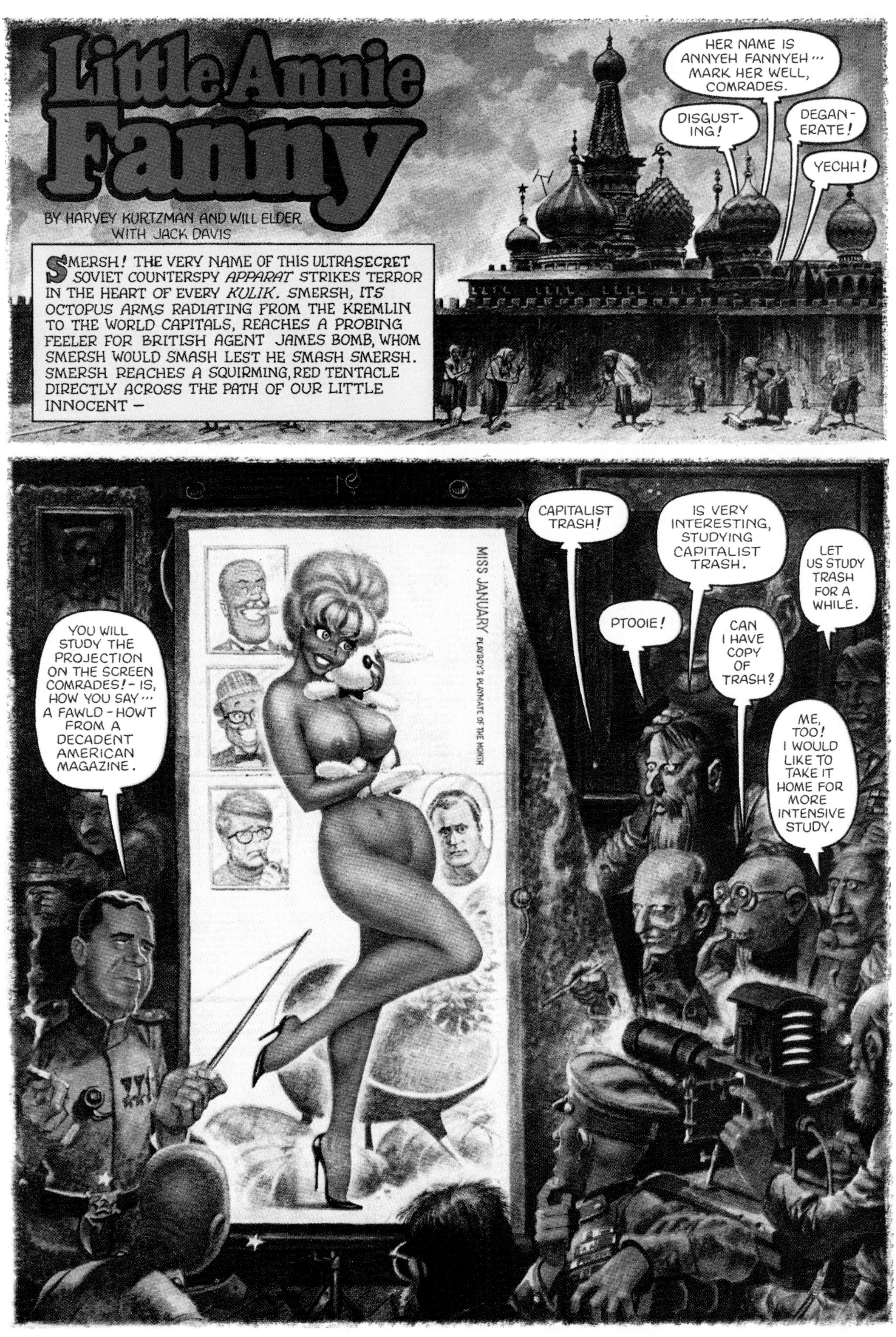
Little Annie Fanny
BY HARVEY KURTZMAN AND WILL ELDER WITH JACK DAVIS
SMERSH! THE VERY NAME OF THIS ULTRASECRET SOVIET COUNTERSPY APPARAT STRIKES TERROR IN THE HEART OF EVERY KULIK. SMERSH, ITS OCTOPUS ARMS RADIATING FROM THE KREMLIN TO THE WORLD CAPITALS, REACHES A PROBING FEELER FOR BRITISH AGENT JAMES BOMB, WHOM SMERSH WOULD SMASH LEST HE SMASH SMERSH. SMERSH REACHES A SQUIRMING, RED TENTACLE DIRECTLY ACROSS THE PATH OF OUR LITTLE INNOCENT —
HER NAME IS ANNYEH FANNYEH... MARK HER WELL, COMRADES.
DISGUST-ING!
DEGAN-ERATE!
YECHH!
YOU WILL STUDY THE PROJECTION ON THE SCREEN COMRADES! — IS, HOW YOU SAY... A FAWLD-HOWT FROM A DECADENT AMERICAN MAGAZINE.
MISS JANUARY
PLAYBOY'S PLAYMATE OF THE MONTH
CAPITALIST TRASH!
PTOOIE!
IS VERY INTERESTING, STUDYING CAPITALIST TRASH.
CAN I HAVE COPY OF TRASH?
LET US STUDY TRASH FOR A WHILE.
ME, TOO! I WOULD LIKE TO TAKE IT HOME FOR MORE INTENSIVE STUDY.

80

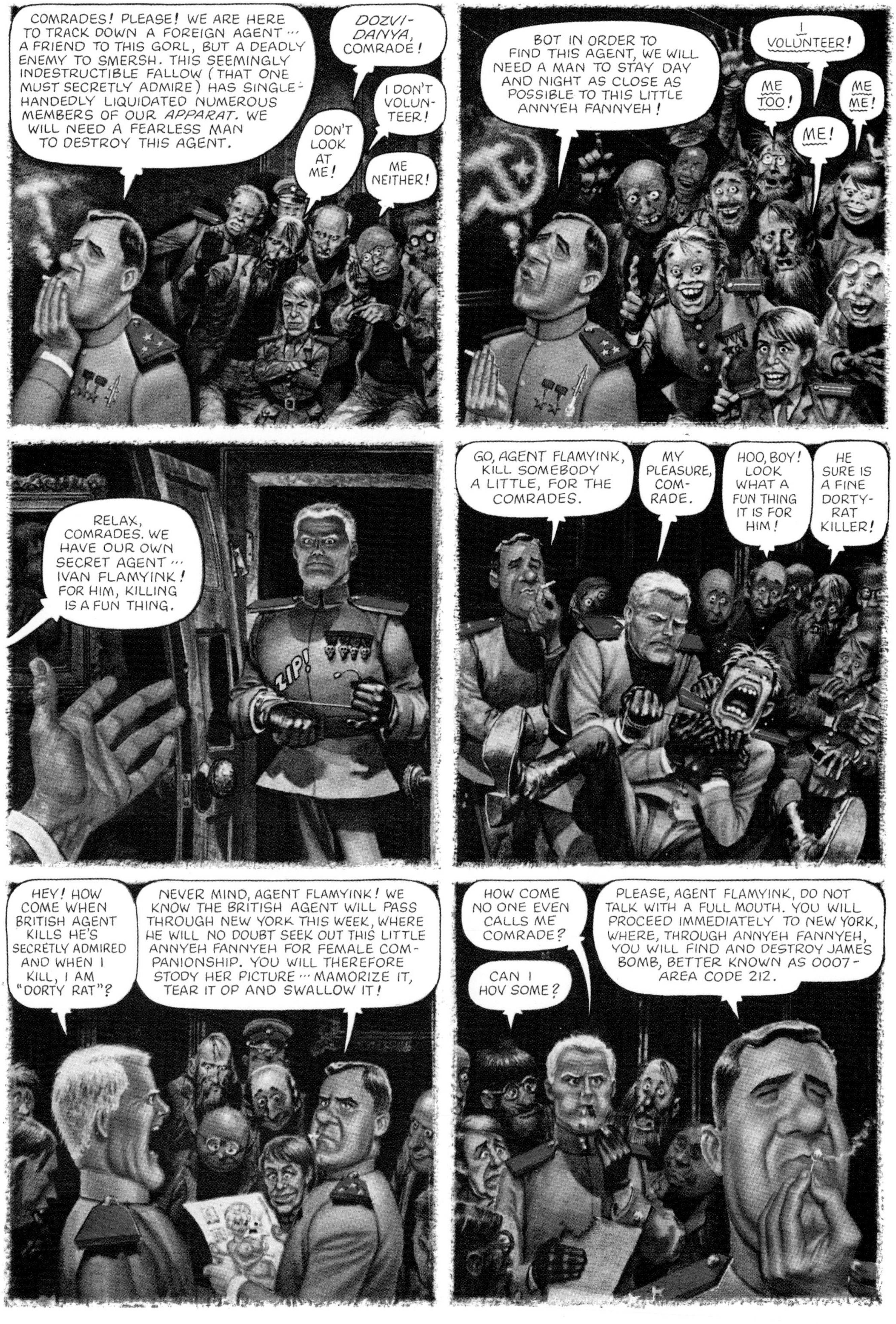

COMRADES! PLEASE! WE ARE HERE TO TRACK DOWN A FOREIGN AGENT ··· A FRIEND TO THIS GORL, BUT A DEADLY ENEMY TO SMERSH. THIS SEEMINGLY INDESTRUCTIBLE FALLOW (THAT ONE MUST SECRETLY ADMIRE) HAS SINGLE-HANDEDLY LIQUIDATED NUMEROUS MEMBERS OF OUR APPARAT. WE WILL NEED A FEARLESS MAN TO DESTROY THIS AGENT.
DOZVI-DANYA, COMRADE!
I DON'T VOLUN-TEER!
DON'T LOOK AT ME!
ME NEITHER!
BOT IN ORDER TO FIND THIS AGENT, WE WILL NEED A MAN TO STAY DAY AND NIGHT AS CLOSE AS POSSIBLE TO THIS LITTLE ANNYEH FANNYEH!
I VOLUNTEER!
ME TOO!
ME ME!
ME!
RELAX, COMRADES. WE HAVE OUR OWN SECRET AGENT ··· IVAN FLAMYINK! FOR HIM, KILLING IS A FUN THING.
ZIP!
GO, AGENT FLAMYINK, KILL SOMEBODY A LITTLE, FOR THE COMRADES.
MY PLEASURE, COM-RADE.
HOO, BOY! LOOK WHAT A FUN THING IT IS FOR HIM!
HE SURE IS A FINE DORTY-RAT KILLER!
HEY! HOW COME WHEN BRITISH AGENT KILLS HE'S SECRETLY ADMIRED AND WHEN I KILL, I AM "DORTY RAT"?
NEVER MIND, AGENT FLAMYINK! WE KNOW THE BRITISH AGENT WILL PASS THROUGH NEW YORK THIS WEEK, WHERE HE WILL NO DOUBT SEEK OUT THIS LITTLE ANNYEH FANNYEH FOR FEMALE COM-PANIONSHIP. YOU WILL THEREFORE STODY HER PICTURE ··· MAMORIZE IT, TEAR IT OP AND SWALLOW IT!
HOW COME NO ONE EVEN CALLS ME COMRADE?
CAN I HOV SOME?
PLEASE, AGENT FLAMYINK, DO NOT TALK WITH A FULL MOUTH. YOU WILL PROCEED IMMEDIATELY TO NEW YORK, WHERE, THROUGH ANNYEH FANNYEH, YOU WILL FIND AND DESTROY JAMES BOMB, BETTER KNOWN AS 0007-AREA CODE 212.

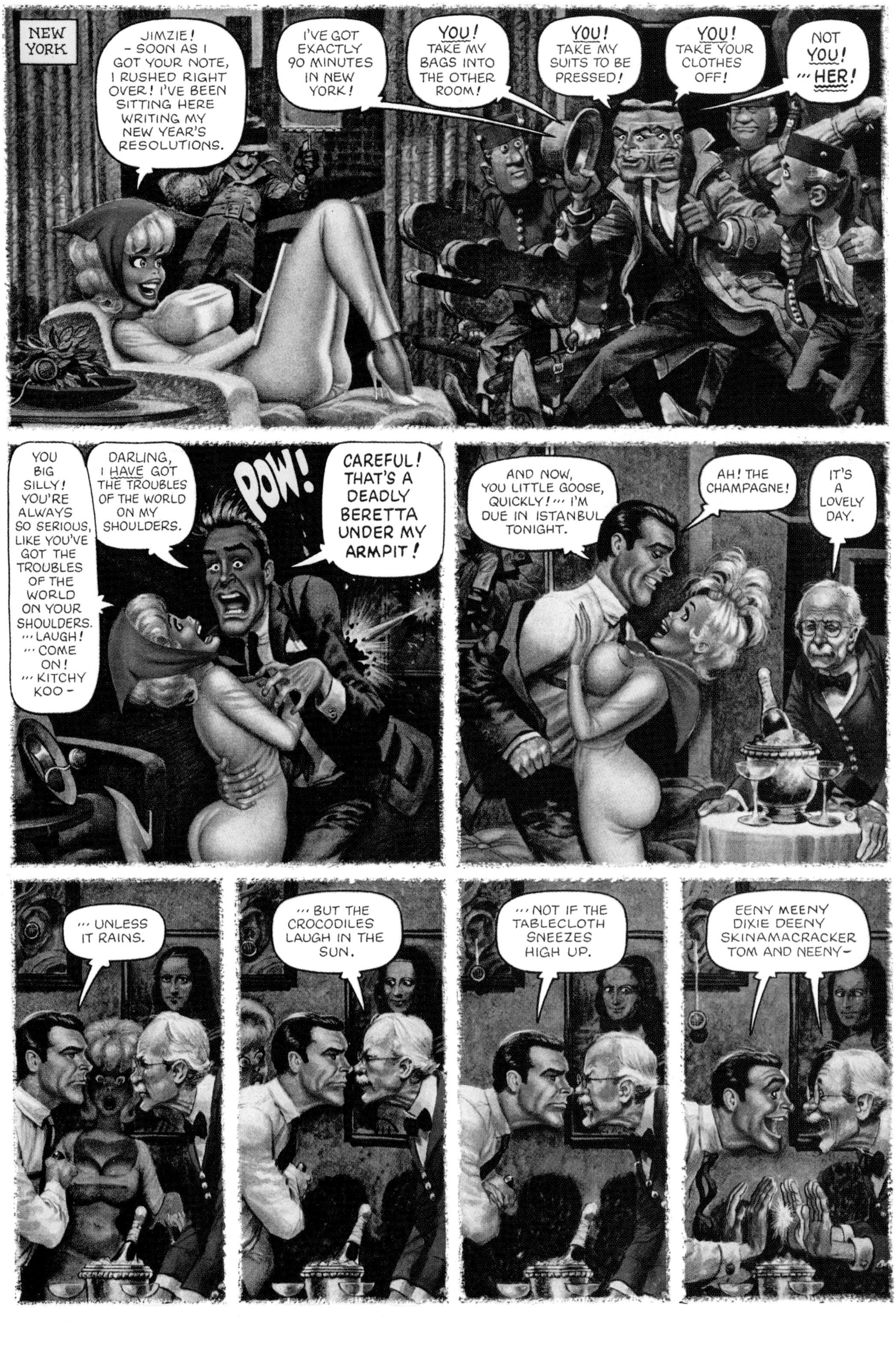
NEW YORK
JIMZIE! – SOON AS I GOT YOUR NOTE, I RUSHED RIGHT OVER! I'VE BEEN SITTING HERE WRITING MY NEW YEAR'S RESOLUTIONS.
I'VE GOT EXACTLY 90 MINUTES IN NEW YORK!
YOU! TAKE MY BAGS INTO THE OTHER ROOM!
YOU! TAKE MY SUITS TO BE PRESSED!
YOU! TAKE YOUR CLOTHES OFF!
NOT YOU! ...HER!
YOU BIG SILLY! YOU'RE ALWAYS SO SERIOUS, LIKE YOU'VE GOT THE TROUBLES OF THE WORLD ON YOUR SHOULDERS. ...LAUGH! ...COME ON! ...KITCHY KOO –
DARLING, I HAVE GOT THE TROUBLES OF THE WORLD ON MY SHOULDERS.
POW!
CAREFUL! THAT'S A DEADLY BERETTA UNDER MY ARMPIT!
AND NOW, YOU LITTLE GOOSE, QUICKLY! ... I'M DUE IN ISTANBUL TONIGHT.
AH! THE CHAMPAGNE!
IT'S A LOVELY DAY.
... UNLESS IT RAINS.
... BUT THE CROCODILES LAUGH IN THE SUN.
... NOT IF THE TABLECLOTH SNEEZES HIGH UP.
EENY MEENY DIXIE DEENY SKINAMACRACKER TOM AND NEENY –

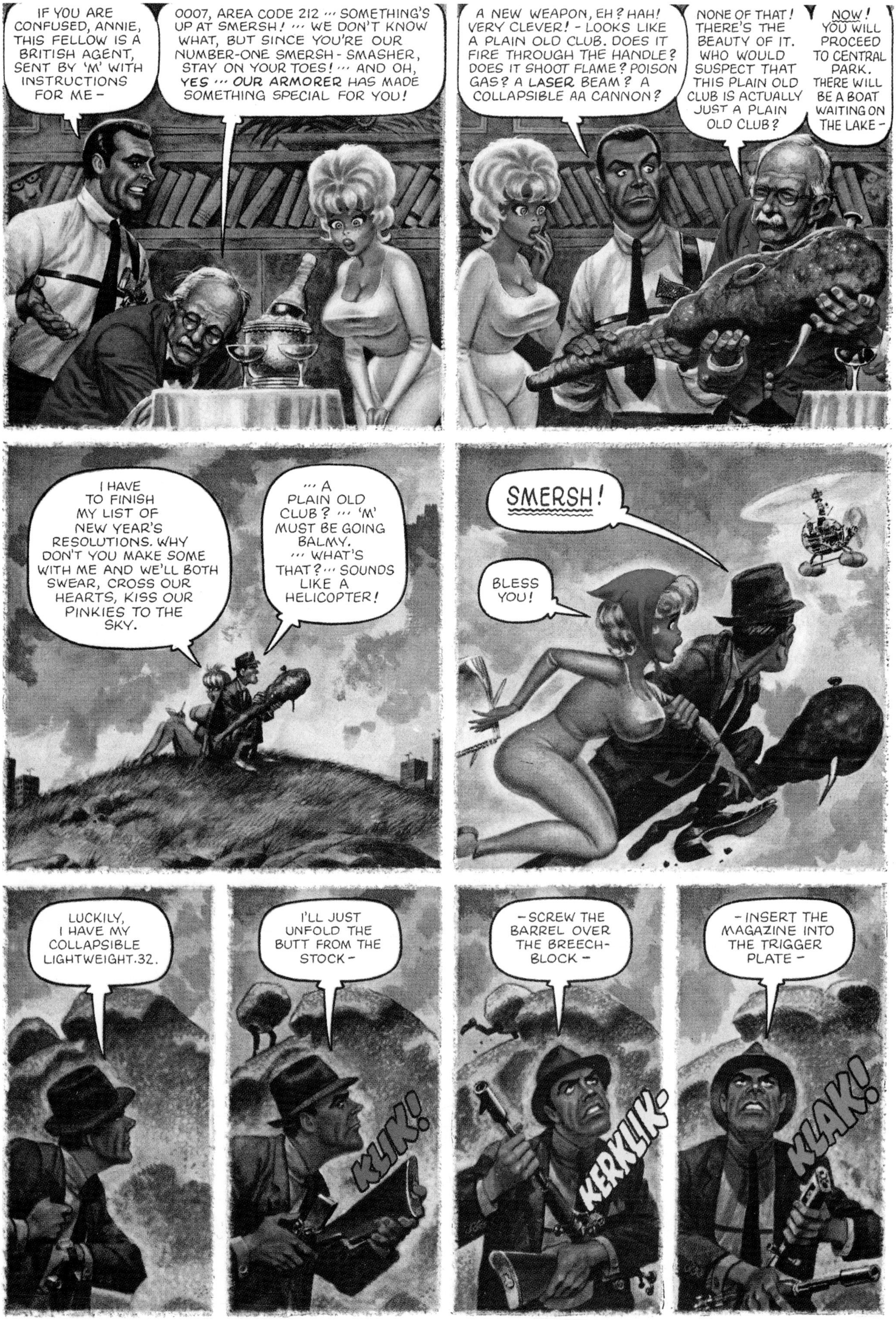
IF YOU ARE CONFUSED, ANNIE, THIS FELLOW IS A BRITISH AGENT, SENT BY 'M' WITH INSTRUCTIONS FOR ME –
0007, AREA CODE 212 ... SOMETHING'S UP AT SMERSH! ... WE DON'T KNOW WHAT, BUT SINCE YOU'RE OUR NUMBER-ONE SMERSH-SMASHER, STAY ON YOUR TOES! ... AND OH, YES ... OUR ARMORER HAS MADE SOMETHING SPECIAL FOR YOU!
A NEW WEAPON, EH? HAH! VERY CLEVER! – LOOKS LIKE A PLAIN OLD CLUB. DOES IT FIRE THROUGH THE HANDLE? DOES IT SHOOT FLAME? POISON GAS? A LASER BEAM? A COLLAPSIBLE AA CANNON?
NONE OF THAT! THERE'S THE BEAUTY OF IT. WHO WOULD SUSPECT THAT THIS PLAIN OLD CLUB IS ACTUALLY JUST A PLAIN OLD CLUB?
NOW! YOU WILL PROCEED TO CENTRAL PARK. THERE WILL BE A BOAT WAITING ON THE LAKE –
I HAVE TO FINISH MY LIST OF NEW YEAR'S RESOLUTIONS. WHY DON'T YOU MAKE SOME WITH ME AND WE'LL BOTH SWEAR, CROSS OUR HEARTS, KISS OUR PINKIES TO THE SKY.
... A PLAIN OLD CLUB? ... 'M' MUST BE GOING BALMY. ... WHAT'S THAT? ... SOUNDS LIKE A HELICOPTER!
SMERSH!
BLESS YOU!
LUCKILY, I HAVE MY COLLAPSIBLE LIGHTWEIGHT .32.
I'LL JUST UNFOLD THE BUTT FROM THE STOCK –
KLIK!
– SCREW THE BARREL OVER THE BREECH-BLOCK –
KERKLIK-
– INSERT THE MAGAZINE INTO THE TRIGGER PLATE –
KLAK!

83

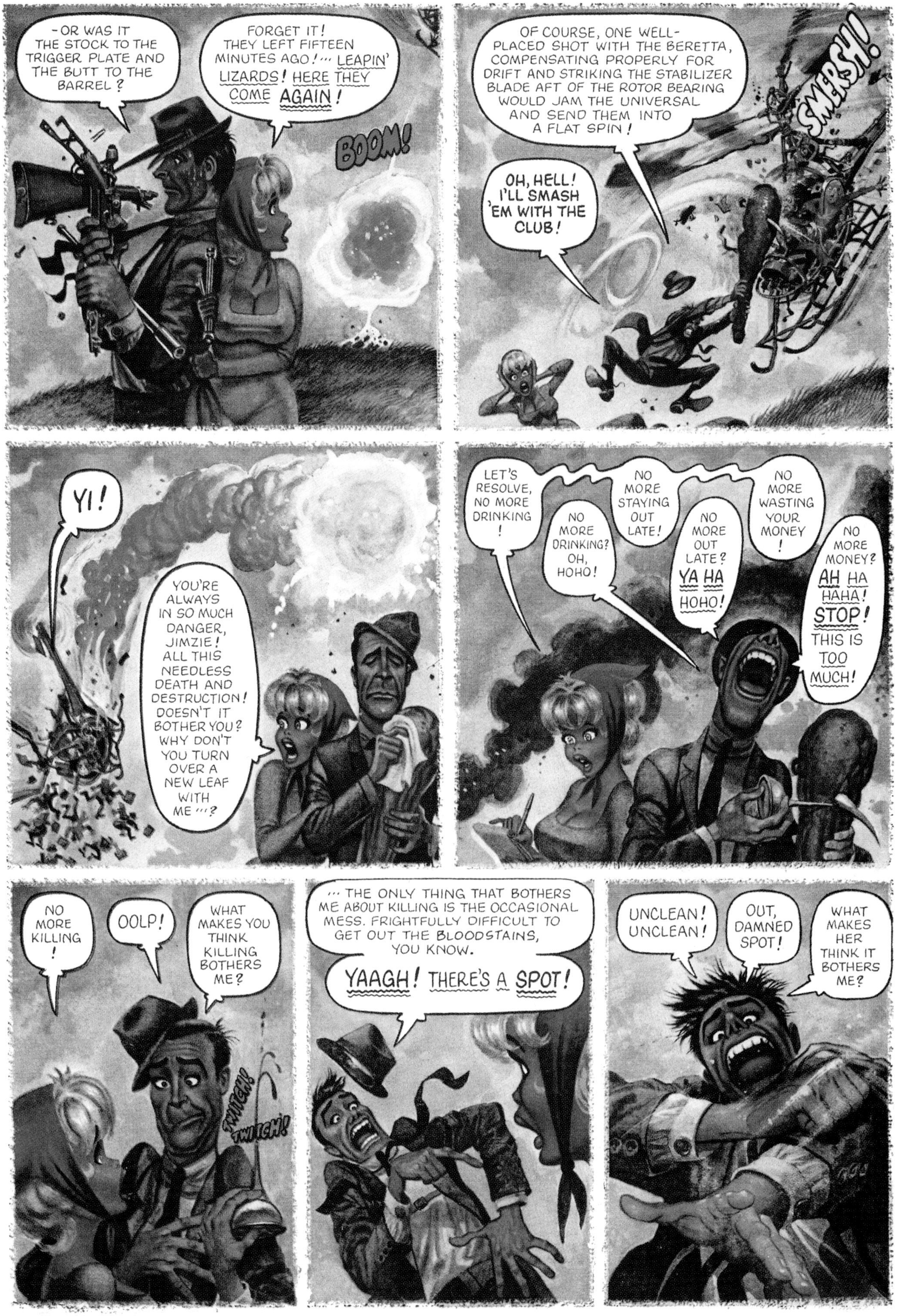

-OR WAS IT THE STOCK TO THE TRIGGER PLATE AND THE BUTT TO THE BARREL?
FORGET IT! THEY LEFT FIFTEEN MINUTES AGO!... LEAPIN' LIZARDS! HERE THEY COME AGAIN!
BOOM!
OF COURSE, ONE WELL-PLACED SHOT WITH THE BERETTA, COMPENSATING PROPERLY FOR DRIFT AND STRIKING THE STABILIZER BLADE AFT OF THE ROTOR BEARING WOULD JAM THE UNIVERSAL AND SEND THEM INTO A FLAT SPIN!
SMERSH!
OH, HELL! I'LL SMASH 'EM WITH THE CLUB!
YI!
YOU'RE ALWAYS IN SO MUCH DANGER, JIMZIE! ALL THIS NEEDLESS DEATH AND DESTRUCTION! DOESN'T IT BOTHER YOU? WHY DON'T YOU TURN OVER A NEW LEAF WITH ME...?
LET'S RESOLVE, NO MORE DRINKING!
NO MORE DRINKING? OH, HOHO!
NO MORE STAYING OUT LATE!
NO MORE OUT LATE? YA HA HOHO!
NO MORE WASTING YOUR MONEY!
NO MORE MONEY? AH HA HAHA! STOP! THIS IS TOO MUCH!
NO MORE KILLING!
OOLP!
WHAT MAKES YOU THINK KILLING BOTHERS ME?
TWITCH! TWITCH!
... THE ONLY THING THAT BOTHERS ME ABOUT KILLING IS THE OCCASIONAL MESS. FRIGHTFULLY DIFFICULT TO GET OUT THE BLOODSTAINS, YOU KNOW.
YAAGH! THERE'S A SPOT!
UNCLEAN! UNCLEAN!
OUT, DAMNED SPOT!
WHAT MAKES HER THINK IT BOTHERS ME?

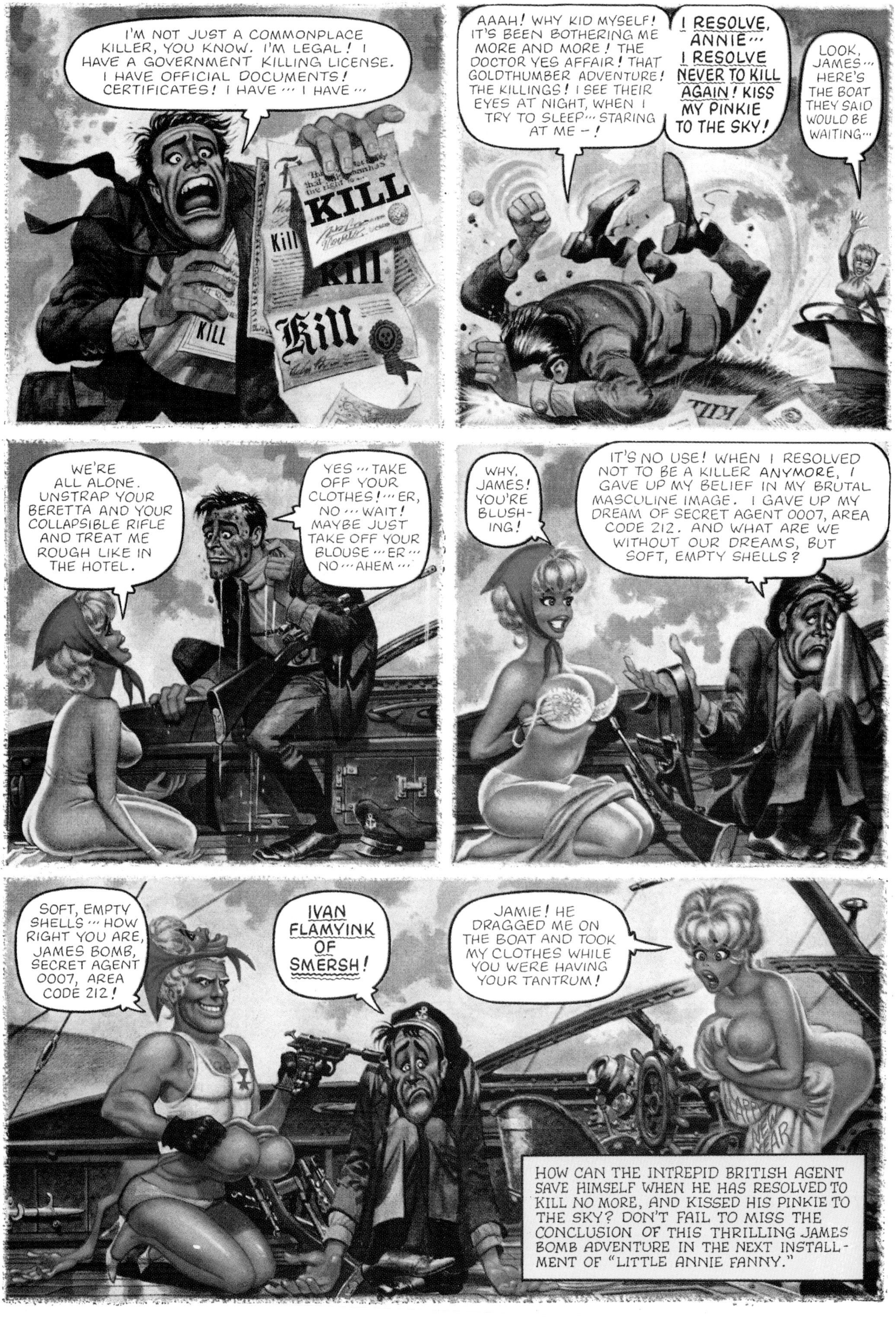

I'M NOT JUST A COMMONPLACE KILLER, YOU KNOW. I'M LEGAL! I HAVE A GOVERNMENT KILLING LICENSE. I HAVE OFFICIAL DOCUMENTS! CERTIFICATES! I HAVE ··· I HAVE ···
KILL
Kill
KILL
KILL
Kill
AAAH! WHY KID MYSELF! IT'S BEEN BOTHERING ME MORE AND MORE! THE DOCTOR YES AFFAIR! THAT GOLDTHUMBER ADVENTURE! THE KILLINGS! I SEE THEIR EYES AT NIGHT, WHEN I TRY TO SLEEP··· STARING AT ME –!
I RESOLVE, ANNIE··· I RESOLVE NEVER TO KILL AGAIN! KISS MY PINKIE TO THE SKY!
LOOK, JAMES··· HERE'S THE BOAT THEY SAID WOULD BE WAITING···
WE'RE ALL ALONE. UNSTRAP YOUR BERETTA AND YOUR COLLAPSIBLE RIFLE AND TREAT ME ROUGH LIKE IN THE HOTEL.
YES ··· TAKE OFF YOUR CLOTHES! ··· ER, NO ··· WAIT! MAYBE JUST TAKE OFF YOUR BLOUSE ··· ER ··· NO ··· AHEM ···
WHY, JAMES! YOU'RE BLUSHING!
IT'S NO USE! WHEN I RESOLVED NOT TO BE A KILLER ANYMORE, I GAVE UP MY BELIEF IN MY BRUTAL MASCULINE IMAGE. I GAVE UP MY DREAM OF SECRET AGENT 0007, AREA CODE 212. AND WHAT ARE WE WITHOUT OUR DREAMS, BUT SOFT, EMPTY SHELLS?
SOFT, EMPTY SHELLS ··· HOW RIGHT YOU ARE, JAMES BOMB, SECRET AGENT 0007, AREA CODE 212!
IVAN FLAMYINK OF SMERSH!
JAMIE! HE DRAGGED ME ON THE BOAT AND TOOK MY CLOTHES WHILE YOU WERE HAVING YOUR TANTRUM!
HOW CAN THE INTREPID BRITISH AGENT SAVE HIMSELF WHEN HE HAS RESOLVED TO KILL NO MORE, AND KISSED HIS PINKIE TO THE SKY? DON'T FAIL TO MISS THE CONCLUSION OF THIS THRILLING JAMES BOMB ADVENTURE IN THE NEXT INSTALLMENT OF "LITTLE ANNIE FANNY."

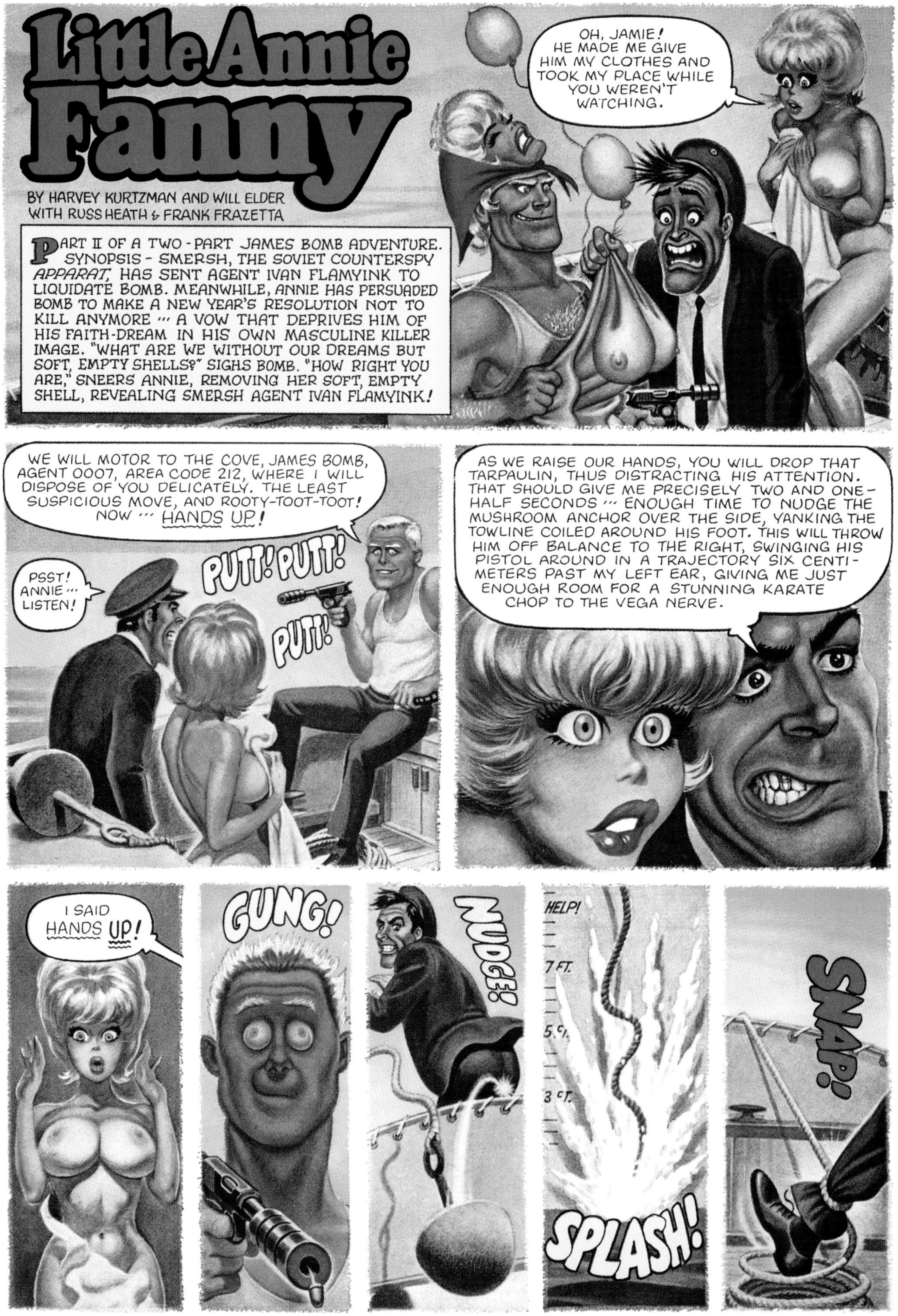

Little Annie Fanny
BY HARVEY KURTZMAN AND WILL ELDER
WITH RUSS HEATH & FRANK FRAZETTA
PART II OF A TWO-PART JAMES BOMB ADVENTURE. SYNOPSIS - SMERSH, THE SOVIET COUNTERSPY *APPARAT,* HAS SENT AGENT IVAN FLAMYINK TO LIQUIDATE BOMB. MEANWHILE, ANNIE HAS PERSUADED BOMB TO MAKE A NEW YEAR'S RESOLUTION NOT TO KILL ANYMORE ··· A VOW THAT DEPRIVES HIM OF HIS FAITH-DREAM IN HIS OWN MASCULINE KILLER IMAGE. "WHAT ARE WE WITHOUT OUR DREAMS BUT SOFT, EMPTY SHELLS?" SIGHS BOMB. "HOW RIGHT YOU ARE," SNEERS ANNIE, REMOVING HER SOFT, EMPTY SHELL, REVEALING SMERSH AGENT IVAN FLAMYINK!
OH, JAMIE! HE MADE ME GIVE HIM MY CLOTHES AND TOOK MY PLACE WHILE YOU WEREN'T WATCHING.
WE WILL MOTOR TO THE COVE, JAMES BOMB, AGENT 0007, AREA CODE 212, WHERE I WILL DISPOSE OF YOU DELICATELY. THE LEAST SUSPICIOUS MOVE, AND ROOTY-TOOT-TOOT! NOW ··· HANDS UP!
PSST! ANNIE··· LISTEN!
PUTT! PUTT! PUTT!
AS WE RAISE OUR HANDS, YOU WILL DROP THAT TARPAULIN, THUS DISTRACTING HIS ATTENTION. THAT SHOULD GIVE ME PRECISELY TWO AND ONE-HALF SECONDS ··· ENOUGH TIME TO NUDGE THE MUSHROOM ANCHOR OVER THE SIDE, YANKING THE TOWLINE COILED AROUND HIS FOOT. THIS WILL THROW HIM OFF BALANCE TO THE RIGHT, SWINGING HIS PISTOL AROUND IN A TRAJECTORY SIX CENTIMETERS PAST MY LEFT EAR, GIVING ME JUST ENOUGH ROOM FOR A STUNNING KARATE CHOP TO THE VEGA NERVE.
I SAID HANDS UP!
GUNG!
NUDGE!
HELP!
7 FT.
SPLASH!
SNAP!

86

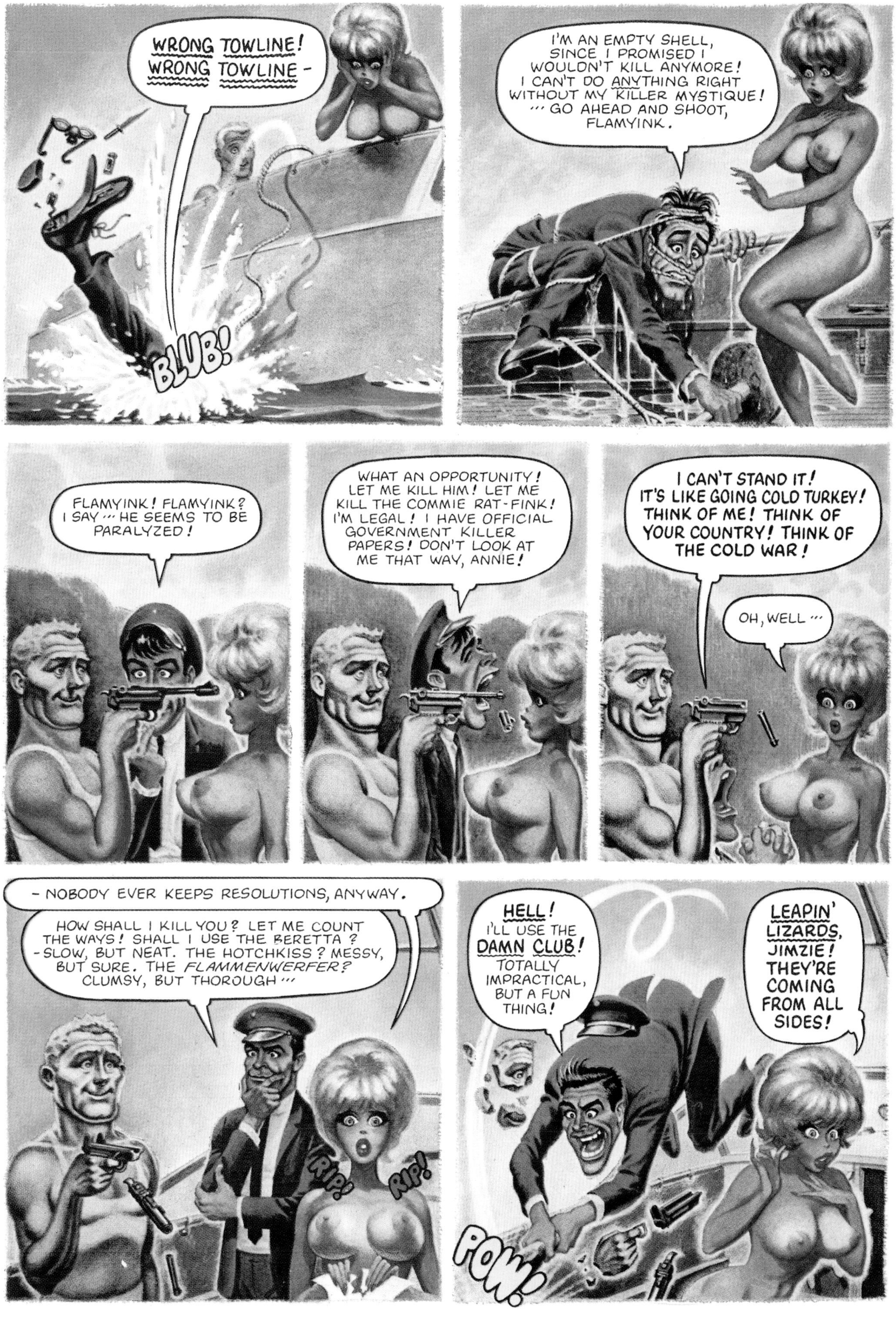
WRONG TOWLINE! WRONG TOWLINE -
BLUB!
I'M AN EMPTY SHELL, SINCE I PROMISED I WOULDN'T KILL ANYMORE! I CAN'T DO ANYTHING RIGHT WITHOUT MY KILLER MYSTIQUE! ... GO AHEAD AND SHOOT, FLAMYINK.
FLAMYINK! FLAMYINK? I SAY ... HE SEEMS TO BE PARALYZED!
WHAT AN OPPORTUNITY! LET ME KILL HIM! LET ME KILL THE COMMIE RAT-FINK! I'M LEGAL! I HAVE OFFICIAL GOVERNMENT KILLER PAPERS! DON'T LOOK AT ME THAT WAY, ANNIE!
I CAN'T STAND IT! IT'S LIKE GOING COLD TURKEY! THINK OF ME! THINK OF YOUR COUNTRY! THINK OF THE COLD WAR!
OH, WELL ...
- NOBODY EVER KEEPS RESOLUTIONS, ANYWAY.
HOW SHALL I KILL YOU? LET ME COUNT THE WAYS! SHALL I USE THE BERETTA? - SLOW, BUT NEAT. THE HOTCHKISS? MESSY, BUT SURE. THE FLAMMENWERFER? CLUMSY, BUT THOROUGH ...
RIP! RIP!
HELL! I'LL USE THE DAMN CLUB! TOTALLY IMPRACTICAL, BUT A FUN THING!
LEAPIN' LIZARDS, JIMZIE! THEY'RE COMING FROM ALL SIDES!
POW!

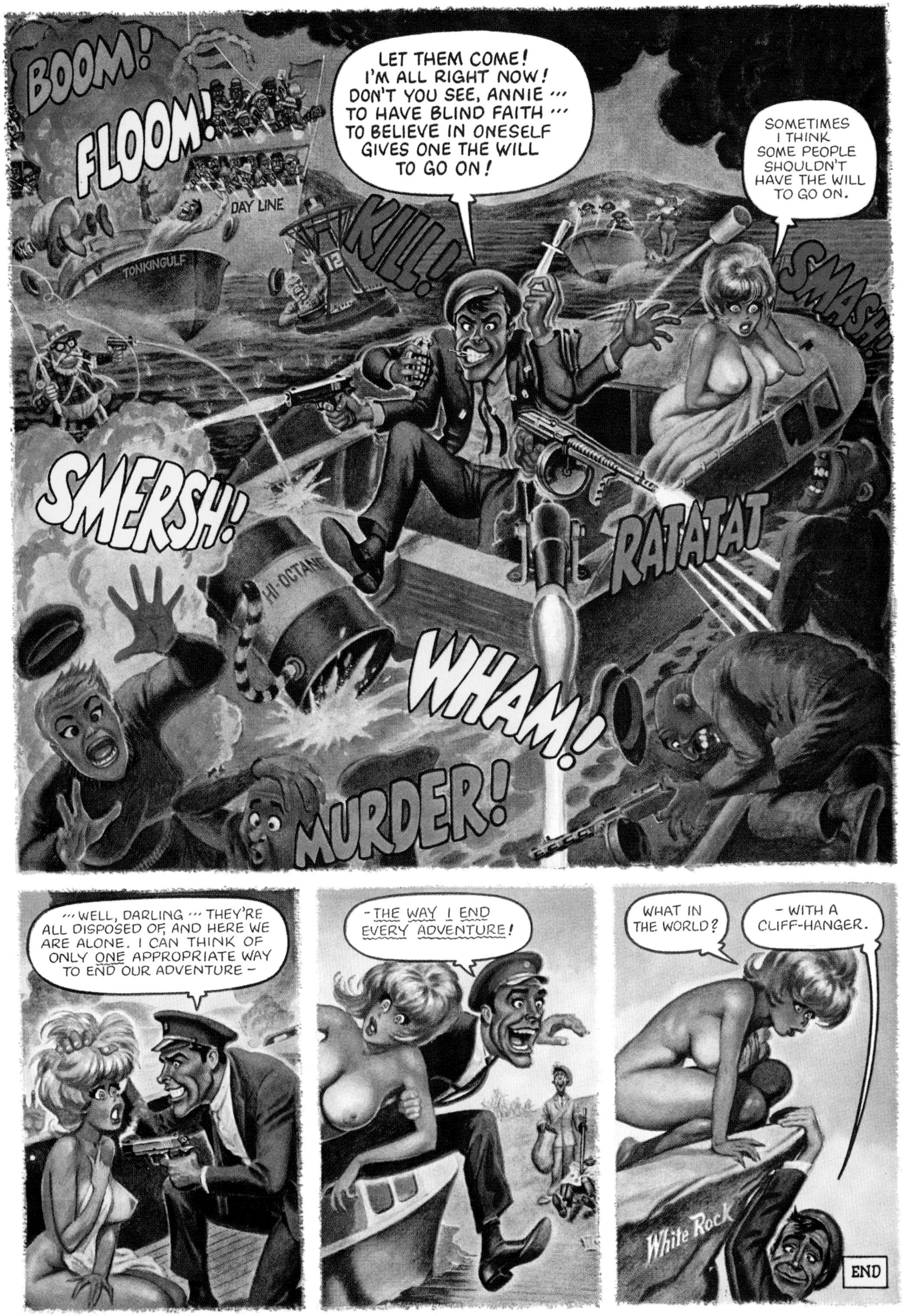
BOOM!
FLOOM!
DAY LINE
TONKINGULF
LET THEM COME! I'M ALL RIGHT NOW! DON'T YOU SEE, ANNIE ... TO HAVE BLIND FAITH ... TO BELIEVE IN ONESELF GIVES ONE THE WILL TO GO ON!
KILL!
SOMETIMES I THINK SOME PEOPLE SHOULDN'T HAVE THE WILL TO GO ON.
SMASH!
SMERSH!
HI-OCTANE
RATATAT
WHAM!
MURDER!
... WELL, DARLING ... THEY'RE ALL DISPOSED OF, AND HERE WE ARE ALONE. I CAN THINK OF ONLY ONE APPROPRIATE WAY TO END OUR ADVENTURE –
– THE WAY I END EVERY ADVENTURE!
WHAT IN THE WORLD?
– WITH A CLIFF-HANGER.
White Rock
END

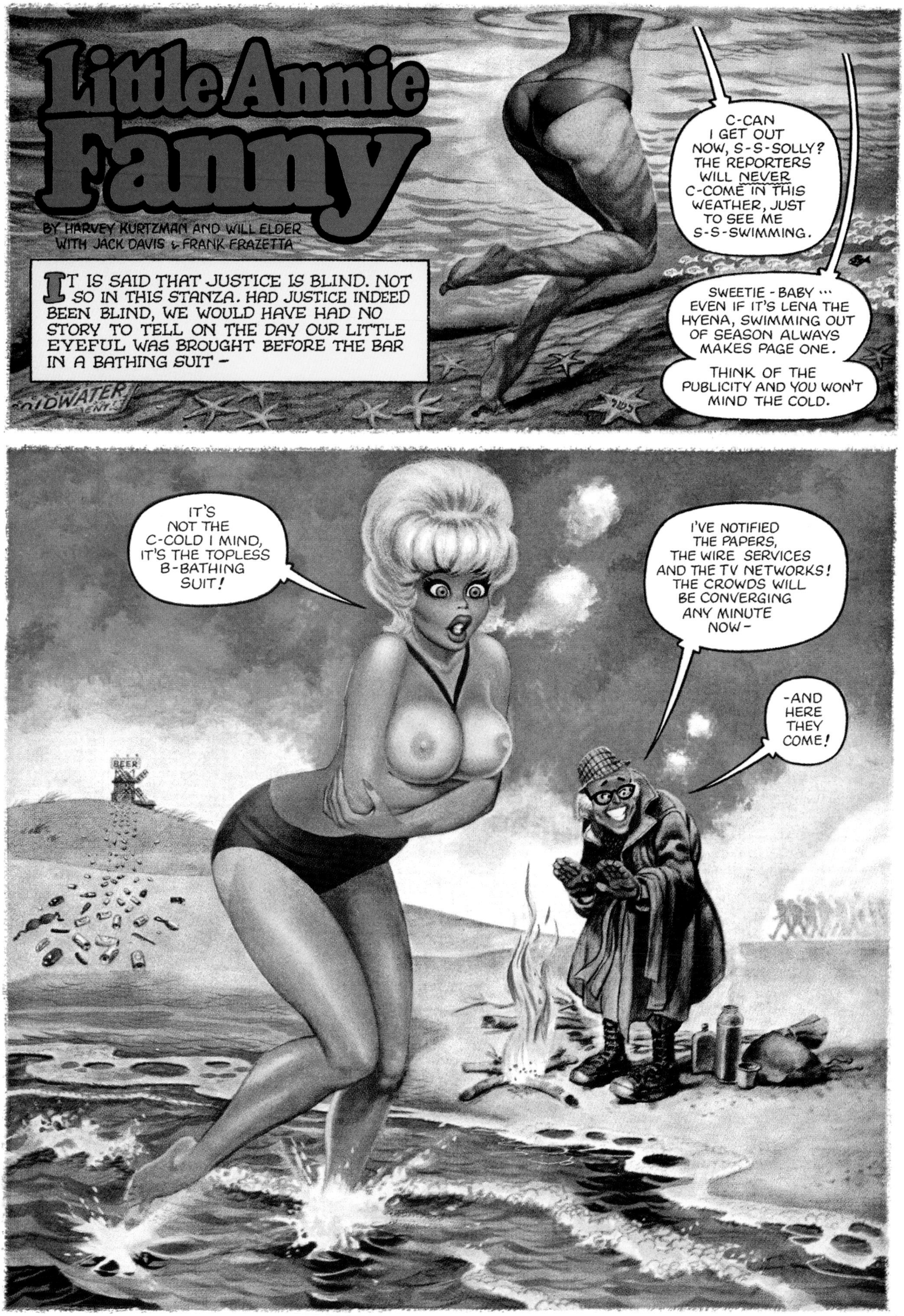
Little Annie Fanny
BY HARVEY KURTZMAN AND WILL ELDER WITH JACK DAVIS & FRANK FRAZETTA
IT IS SAID THAT JUSTICE IS BLIND. NOT SO IN THIS STANZA. HAD JUSTICE INDEED BEEN BLIND, WE WOULD HAVE HAD NO STORY TO TELL ON THE DAY OUR LITTLE EYEFUL WAS BROUGHT BEFORE THE BAR IN A BATHING SUIT -
C-CAN I GET OUT NOW, S-S-SOLLY? THE REPORTERS WILL NEVER C-COME IN THIS WEATHER, JUST TO SEE ME S-S-SWIMMING.
SWEETIE - BABY ... EVEN IF IT'S LENA THE HYENA, SWIMMING OUT OF SEASON ALWAYS MAKES PAGE ONE.
THINK OF THE PUBLICITY AND YOU WON'T MIND THE COLD.
IT'S NOT THE C-COLD I MIND, IT'S THE TOPLESS B-BATHING SUIT!
I'VE NOTIFIED THE PAPERS, THE WIRE SERVICES AND THE TV NETWORKS! THE CROWDS WILL BE CONVERGING ANY MINUTE NOW -
-AND HERE THEY COME!
BEER

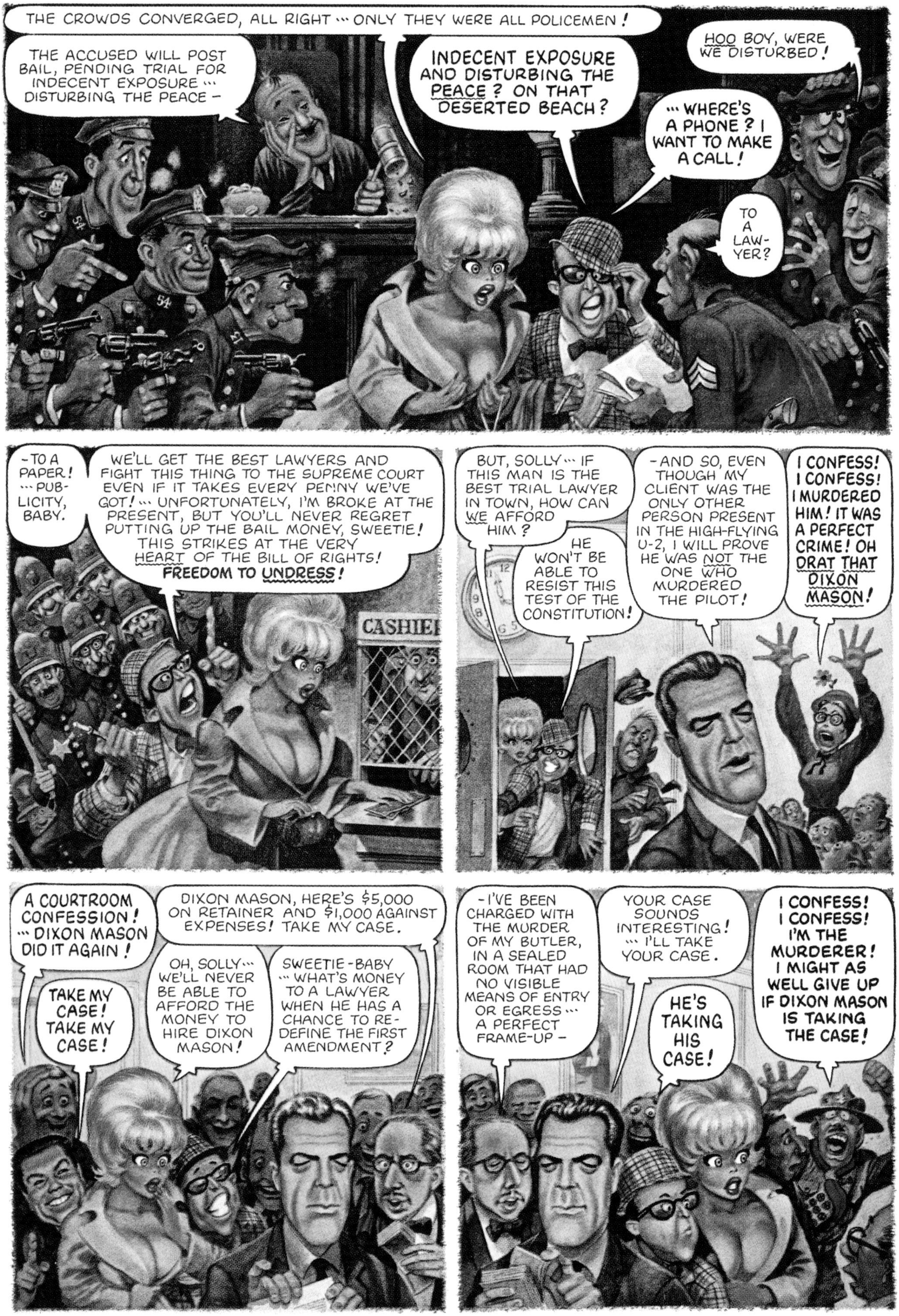
THE CROWDS CONVERGED, ALL RIGHT ··· ONLY THEY WERE ALL POLICEMEN!
THE ACCUSED WILL POST BAIL, PENDING TRIAL FOR INDECENT EXPOSURE ··· DISTURBING THE PEACE –
INDECENT EXPOSURE AND DISTURBING THE PEACE? ON THAT DESERTED BEACH?
HOO BOY, WERE WE DISTURBED!
··· WHERE'S A PHONE? I WANT TO MAKE A CALL!
TO A LAW-YER?
–TO A PAPER! ··· PUB-LICITY, BABY.
WE'LL GET THE BEST LAWYERS AND FIGHT THIS THING TO THE SUPREME COURT EVEN IF IT TAKES EVERY PENNY WE'VE GOT! ··· UNFORTUNATELY, I'M BROKE AT THE PRESENT, BUT YOU'LL NEVER REGRET PUTTING UP THE BAIL MONEY, SWEETIE! THIS STRIKES AT THE VERY HEART OF THE BILL OF RIGHTS! FREEDOM TO UNDRESS!
CASHIE
BUT, SOLLY ··· IF THIS MAN IS THE BEST TRIAL LAWYER IN TOWN, HOW CAN WE AFFORD HIM?
HE WON'T BE ABLE TO RESIST THIS TEST OF THE CONSTITUTION!
–AND SO, EVEN THOUGH MY CLIENT WAS THE ONLY OTHER PERSON PRESENT IN THE HIGH-FLYING U-2, I WILL PROVE HE WAS NOT THE ONE WHO MURDERED THE PILOT!
I CONFESS! I CONFESS! I MURDERED HIM! IT WAS A PERFECT CRIME! OH DRAT THAT DIXON MASON!
A COURTROOM CONFESSION! ··· DIXON MASON DID IT AGAIN!
DIXON MASON, HERE'S $5,000 ON RETAINER AND $1,000 AGAINST EXPENSES! TAKE MY CASE.
TAKE MY CASE! TAKE MY CASE!
OH, SOLLY ··· WE'LL NEVER BE ABLE TO AFFORD THE MONEY TO HIRE DIXON MASON!
SWEETIE-BABY ··· WHAT'S MONEY TO A LAWYER WHEN HE HAS A CHANCE TO RE-DEFINE THE FIRST AMENDMENT?
–I'VE BEEN CHARGED WITH THE MURDER OF MY BUTLER, IN A SEALED ROOM THAT HAD NO VISIBLE MEANS OF ENTRY OR EGRESS ··· A PERFECT FRAME-UP –
YOUR CASE SOUNDS INTERESTING! ··· I'LL TAKE YOUR CASE.
HE'S TAKING HIS CASE!
I CONFESS! I CONFESS! I'M THE MURDERER! I MIGHT AS WELL GIVE UP IF DIXON MASON IS TAKING THE CASE!

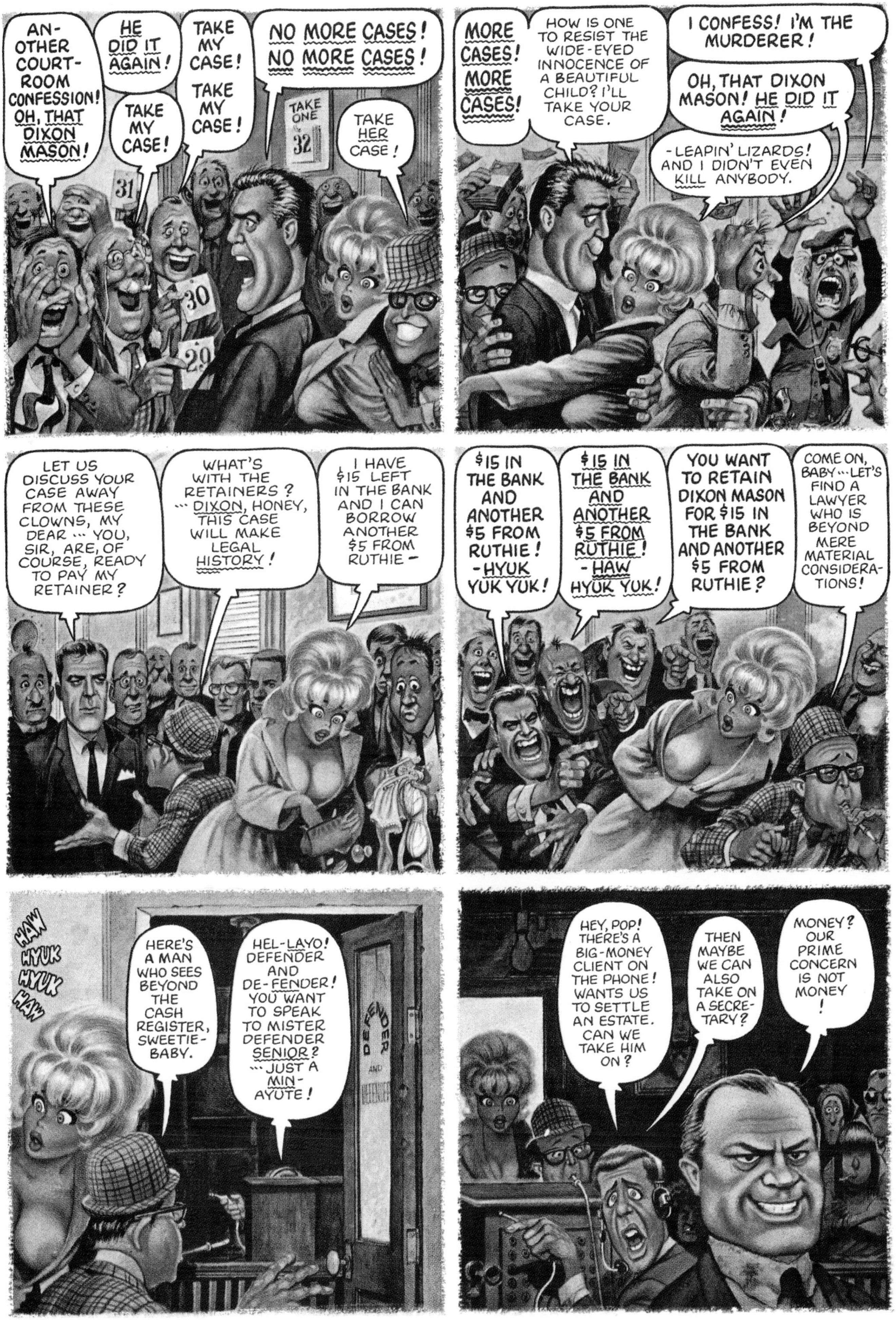
AN-OTHER COURT-ROOM CONFESSION! OH, THAT DIXON MASON!
HE DID IT AGAIN!
TAKE MY CASE!
TAKE MY CASE! TAKE MY CASE!
NO MORE CASES! NO MORE CASES!
TAKE ONE
TAKE HER CASE!
MORE CASES! MORE CASES!
HOW IS ONE TO RESIST THE WIDE-EYED INNOCENCE OF A BEAUTIFUL CHILD? I'LL TAKE YOUR CASE.
I CONFESS! I'M THE MURDERER!
OH, THAT DIXON MASON! HE DID IT AGAIN!
-LEAPIN' LIZARDS! AND I DIDN'T EVEN KILL ANYBODY.
LET US DISCUSS YOUR CASE AWAY FROM THESE CLOWNS, MY DEAR ... YOU, SIR, ARE, OF COURSE, READY TO PAY MY RETAINER?
WHAT'S WITH THE RETAINERS? ... DIXON, HONEY, THIS CASE WILL MAKE LEGAL HISTORY!
I HAVE $15 LEFT IN THE BANK AND I CAN BORROW ANOTHER $5 FROM RUTHIE -
$15 IN THE BANK AND ANOTHER $5 FROM RUTHIE! -HYUK YUK YUK!
$15 IN THE BANK AND ANOTHER $5 FROM RUTHIE! -HAW HYUK YUK!
YOU WANT TO RETAIN DIXON MASON FOR $15 IN THE BANK AND ANOTHER $5 FROM RUTHIE?
COME ON, BABY ... LET'S FIND A LAWYER WHO IS BEYOND MERE MATERIAL CONSIDERATIONS!
HAW HYUK HYUK HAW
HERE'S A MAN WHO SEES BEYOND THE CASH REGISTER, SWEETIE-BABY.
HEL-LAYO! DEFENDER AND DE-FENDER! YOU WANT TO SPEAK TO MISTER DEFENDER SENIOR? ... JUST A MIN-AYUTE!
DEFENDER AND
HEY, POP! THERE'S A BIG-MONEY CLIENT ON THE PHONE! WANTS US TO SETTLE AN ESTATE. CAN WE TAKE HIM ON?
THEN MAYBE WE CAN ALSO TAKE ON A SECRE-TARY?
MONEY? OUR PRIME CONCERN IS NOT MONEY!

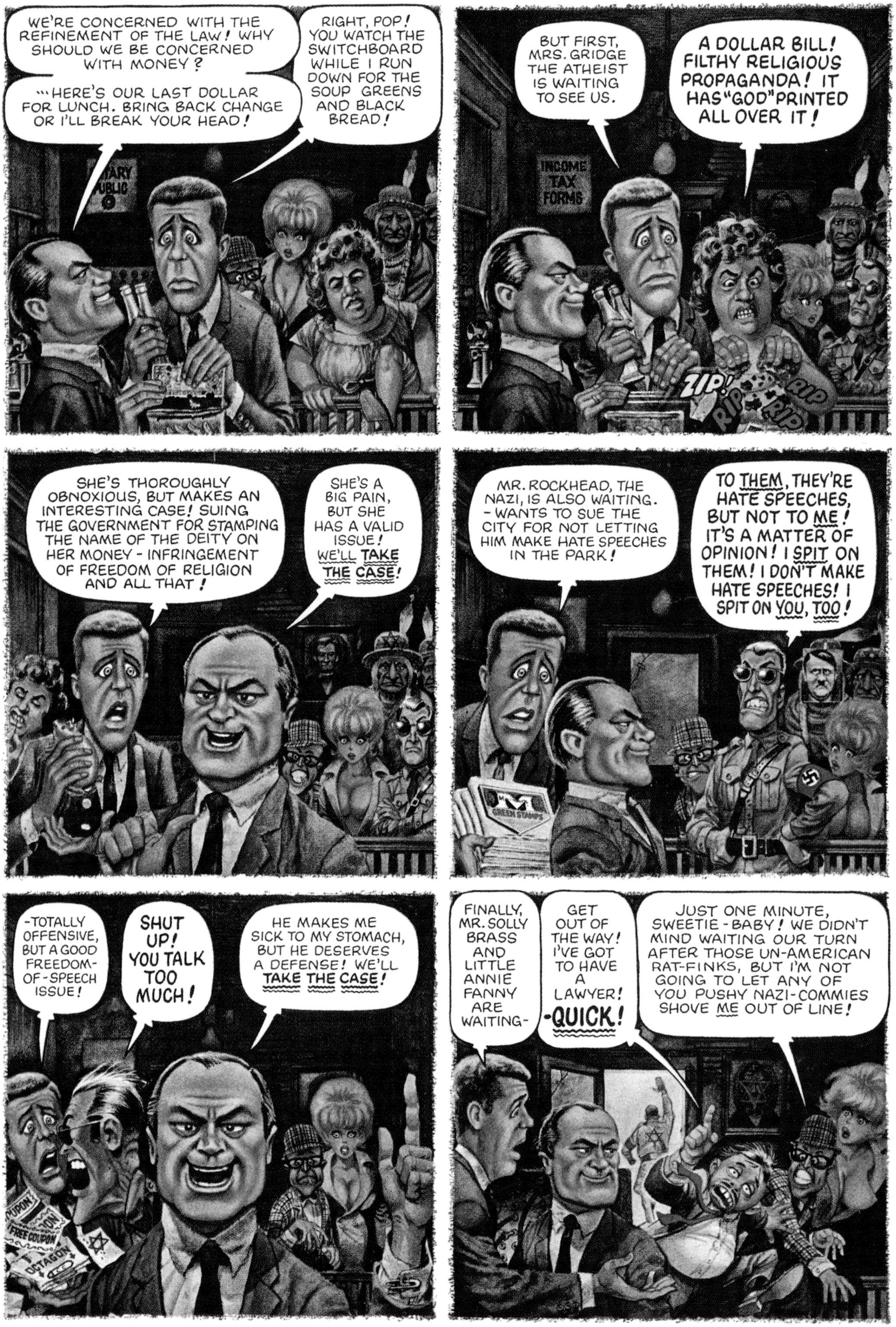
WE'RE CONCERNED WITH THE REFINEMENT OF THE LAW! WHY SHOULD WE BE CONCERNED WITH MONEY?
...HERE'S OUR LAST DOLLAR FOR LUNCH. BRING BACK CHANGE OR I'LL BREAK YOUR HEAD!
RIGHT, POP! YOU WATCH THE SWITCHBOARD WHILE I RUN DOWN FOR THE SOUP GREENS AND BLACK BREAD!
PUBLIC
BUT FIRST, MRS. GRIDGE THE ATHEIST IS WAITING TO SEE US.
A DOLLAR BILL! FILTHY RELIGIOUS PROPAGANDA! IT HAS "GOD" PRINTED ALL OVER IT!
INCOME TAX FORMS
ZIP!
RIP
RIP
RIP
SHE'S THOROUGHLY OBNOXIOUS, BUT MAKES AN INTERESTING CASE! SUING THE GOVERNMENT FOR STAMPING THE NAME OF THE DEITY ON HER MONEY - INFRINGEMENT OF FREEDOM OF RELIGION AND ALL THAT!
SHE'S A BIG PAIN, BUT SHE HAS A VALID ISSUE! WE'LL TAKE THE CASE!
MR. ROCKHEAD, THE NAZI, IS ALSO WAITING. - WANTS TO SUE THE CITY FOR NOT LETTING HIM MAKE HATE SPEECHES IN THE PARK!
TO THEM, THEY'RE HATE SPEECHES, BUT NOT TO ME! IT'S A MATTER OF OPINION! I SPIT ON THEM! I DON'T MAKE HATE SPEECHES! I SPIT ON YOU, TOO!
GREEN STAMPS
-TOTALLY OFFENSIVE, BUT A GOOD FREEDOM-OF-SPEECH ISSUE!
SHUT UP! YOU TALK TOO MUCH!
HE MAKES ME SICK TO MY STOMACH, BUT HE DESERVES A DEFENSE! WE'LL TAKE THE CASE!
FREE COUPON
OCTAGON
FINALLY, MR. SOLLY BRASS AND LITTLE ANNIE FANNY ARE WAITING-
GET OUT OF THE WAY! I'VE GOT TO HAVE A LAWYER! -QUICK!
JUST ONE MINUTE, SWEETIE-BABY! WE DIDN'T MIND WAITING OUR TURN AFTER THOSE UN-AMERICAN RAT-FINKS, BUT I'M NOT GOING TO LET ANY OF YOU PUSHY NAZI-COMMIES SHOVE ME OUT OF LINE!

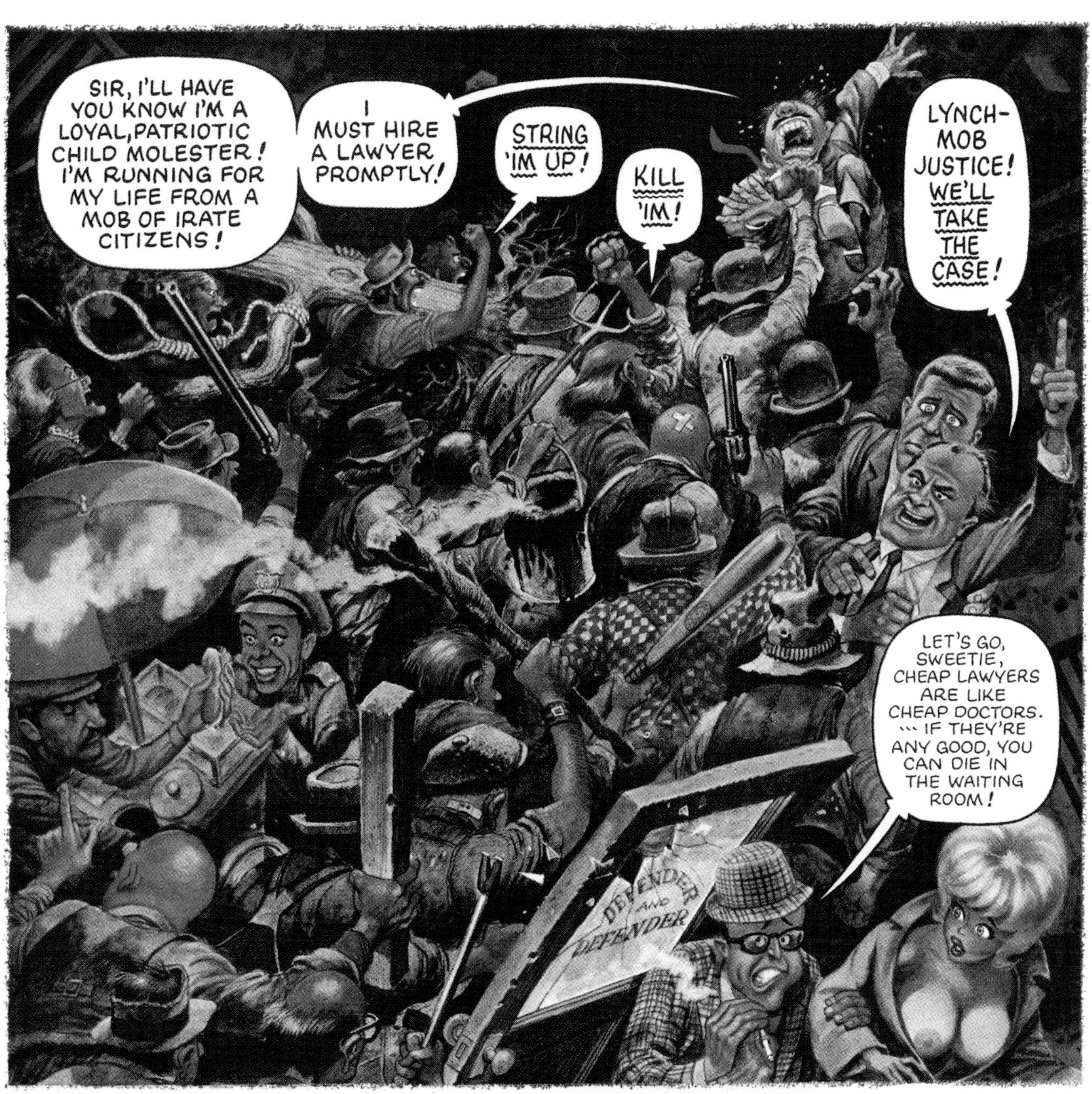
SIR, I'LL HAVE YOU KNOW I'M A LOYAL, PATRIOTIC CHILD MOLESTER! I'M RUNNING FOR MY LIFE FROM A MOB OF IRATE CITIZENS!
I MUST HIRE A LAWYER PROMPTLY!
STRING 'IM UP!
KILL 'IM!
LYNCH-MOB JUSTICE! WE'LL TAKE THE CASE!
DEFENDER AND DEFENDER
LET'S GO, SWEETIE, CHEAP LAWYERS ARE LIKE CHEAP DOCTORS. ... IF THEY'RE ANY GOOD, YOU CAN DIE IN THE WAITING ROOM!

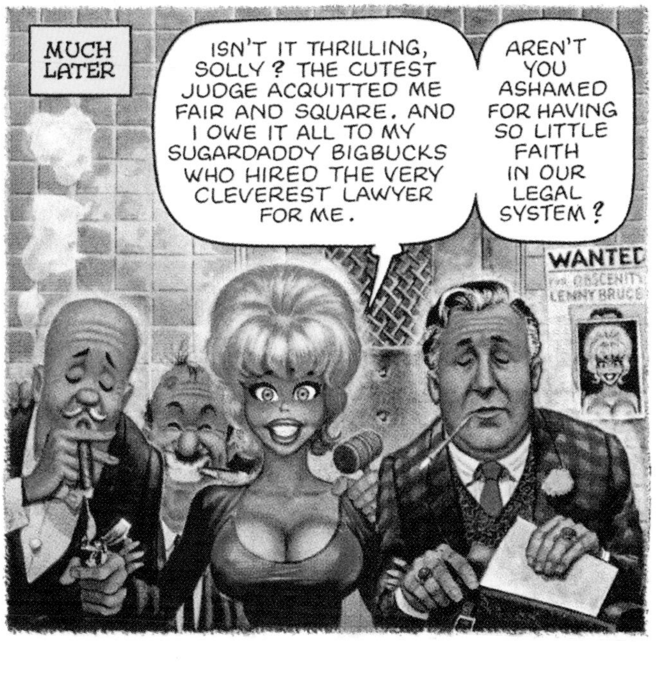
MUCH LATER
ISN'T IT THRILLING, SOLLY? THE CUTEST JUDGE ACQUITTED ME FAIR AND SQUARE. AND I OWE IT ALL TO MY SUGARDADDY BIGBUCKS WHO HIRED THE VERY CLEVEREST LAWYER FOR ME.
AREN'T YOU ASHAMED FOR HAVING SO LITTLE FAITH IN OUR LEGAL SYSTEM?
WANTED
LENNY BRUCE

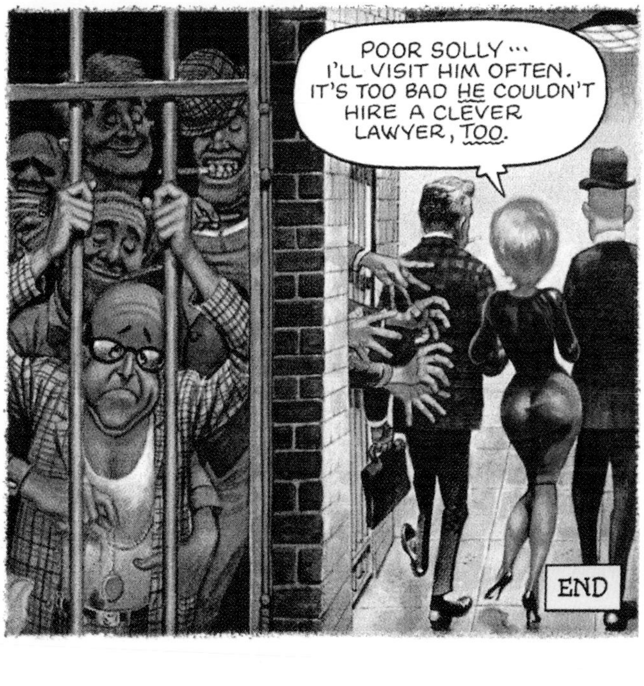
POOR SOLLY... I'LL VISIT HIM OFTEN. IT'S TOO BAD HE COULDN'T HIRE A CLEVER LAWYER, TOO.
END

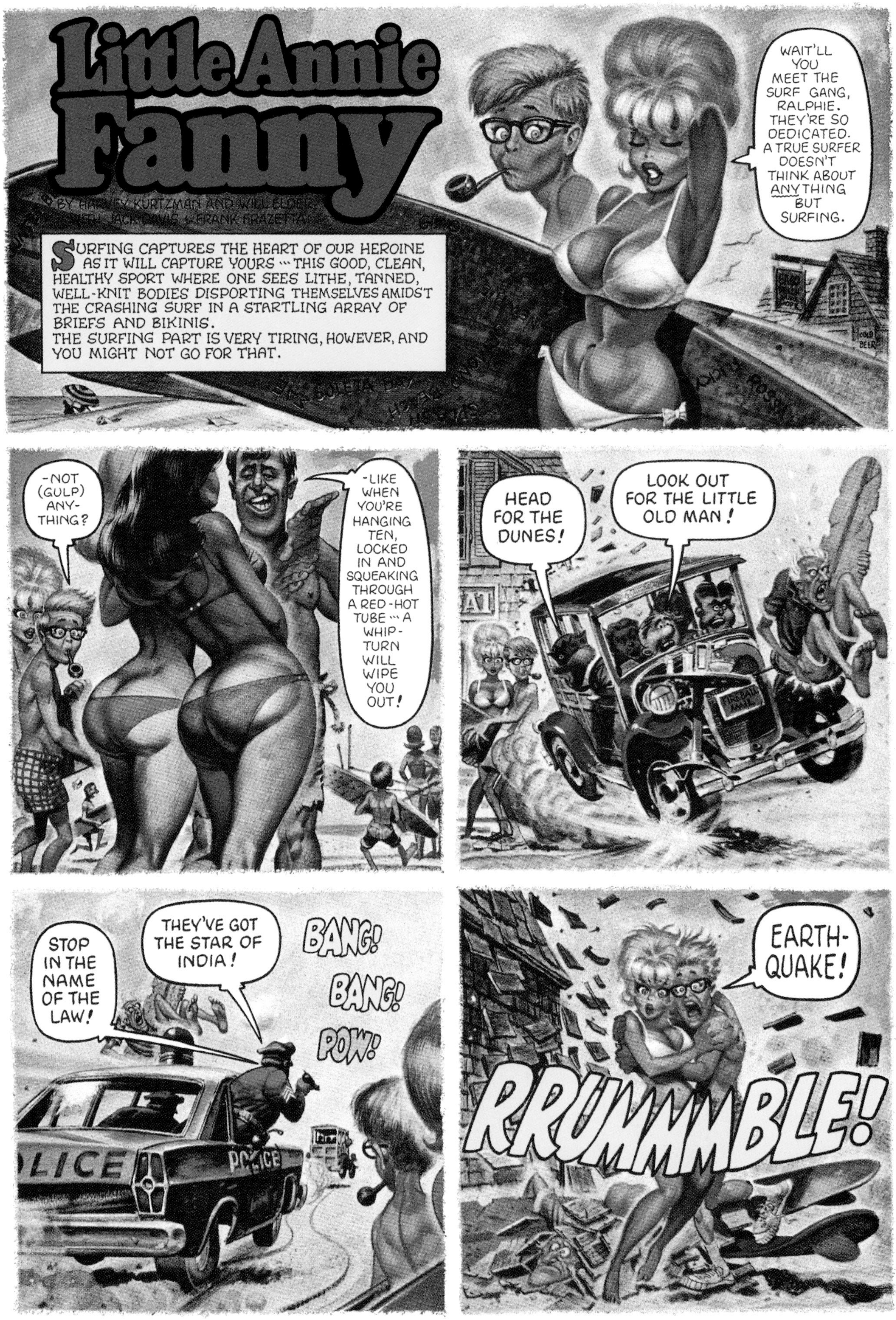

Little Annie Fanny
BY HARVEY KURTZMAN AND WILL ELDER WITH JACK DAVIS & FRANK FRAZETTA
WAIT'LL YOU MEET THE SURF GANG, RALPHIE. THEY'RE SO DEDICATED. A TRUE SURFER DOESN'T THINK ABOUT ANYTHING BUT SURFING.
SURFING CAPTURES THE HEART OF OUR HEROINE AS IT WILL CAPTURE YOURS ··· THIS GOOD, CLEAN, HEALTHY SPORT WHERE ONE SEES LITHE, TANNED, WELL-KNIT BODIES DISPORTING THEMSELVES AMIDST THE CRASHING SURF IN A STARTLING ARRAY OF BRIEFS AND BIKINIS. THE SURFING PART IS VERY TIRING, HOWEVER, AND YOU MIGHT NOT GO FOR THAT.
-NOT (GULP) ANY-THING?
-LIKE WHEN YOU'RE HANGING TEN, LOCKED IN AND SQUEAKING THROUGH A RED-HOT TUBE ··· A WHIP-TURN WILL WIPE YOU OUT!
HEAD FOR THE DUNES!
LOOK OUT FOR THE LITTLE OLD MAN!
STOP IN THE NAME OF THE LAW!
THEY'VE GOT THE STAR OF INDIA!
BANG!
BANG!
POW!
POLICE
POLICE
EARTH-QUAKE!
RRUMMMBLE!

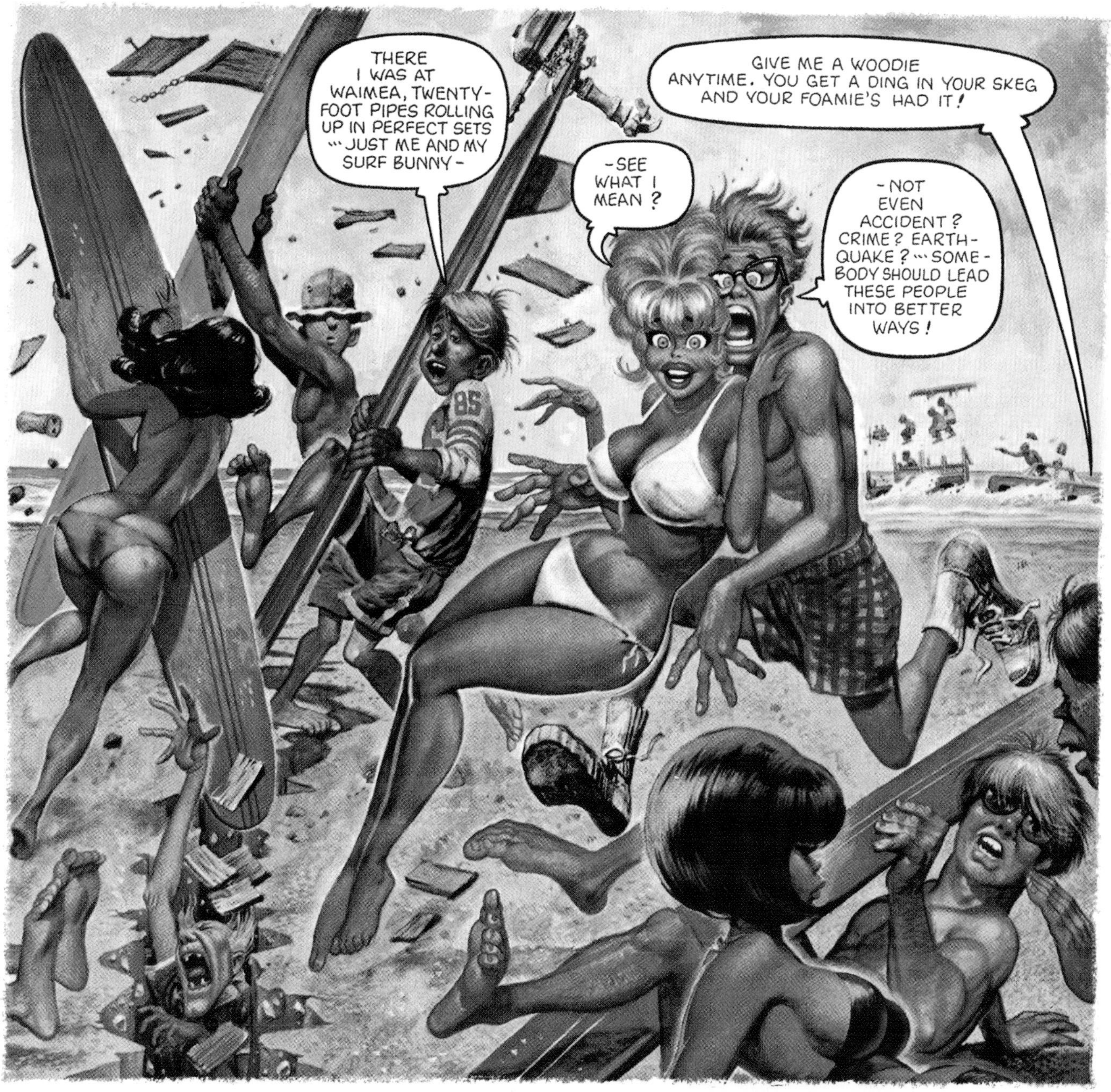
THERE I WAS AT WAIMEA, TWENTY-FOOT PIPES ROLLING UP IN PERFECT SETS ... JUST ME AND MY SURF BUNNY -
- SEE WHAT I MEAN ?
GIVE ME A WOODIE ANYTIME. YOU GET A DING IN YOUR SKEG AND YOUR FOAMIE'S HAD IT!
- NOT EVEN ACCIDENT ? CRIME ? EARTH-QUAKE ? ... SOME-BODY SHOULD LEAD THESE PEOPLE INTO BETTER WAYS !

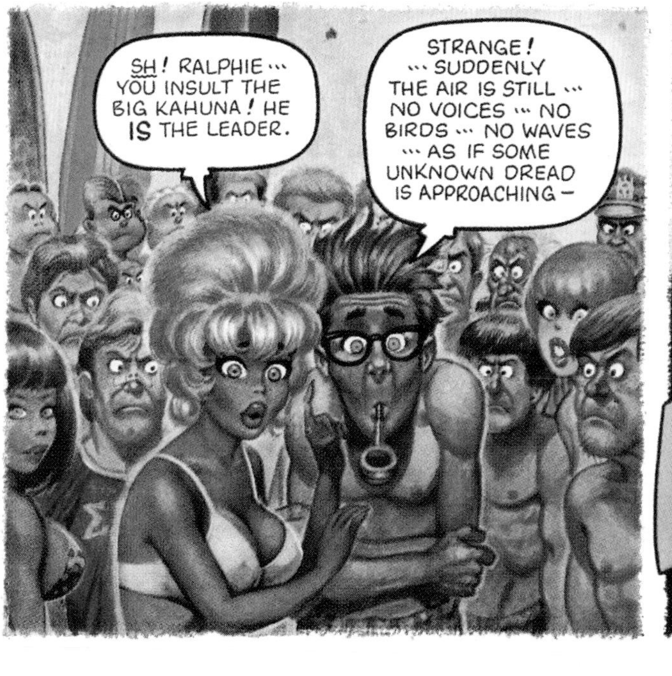
SH! RALPHIE ... YOU INSULT THE BIG KAHUNA! HE IS THE LEADER.
STRANGE! ... SUDDENLY THE AIR IS STILL ... NO VOICES ... NO BIRDS ... NO WAVES ... AS IF SOME UNKNOWN DREAD IS APPROACHING -

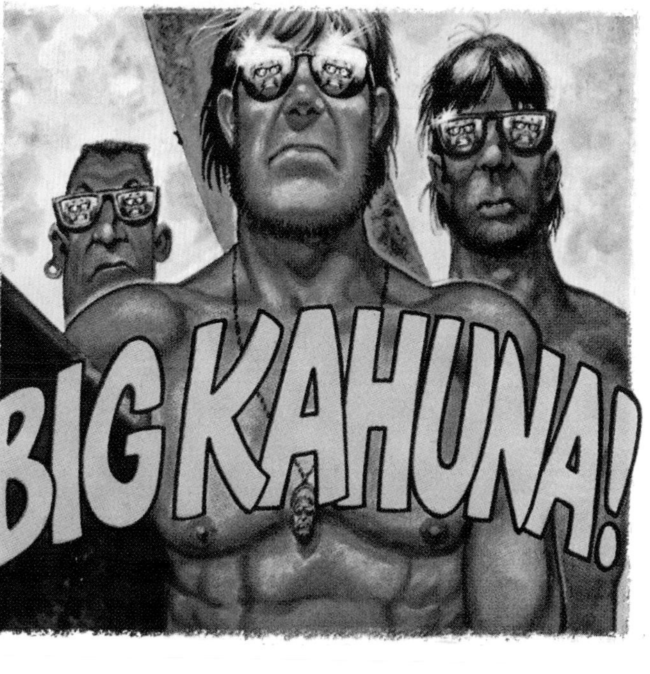
BIG KAHUNA!

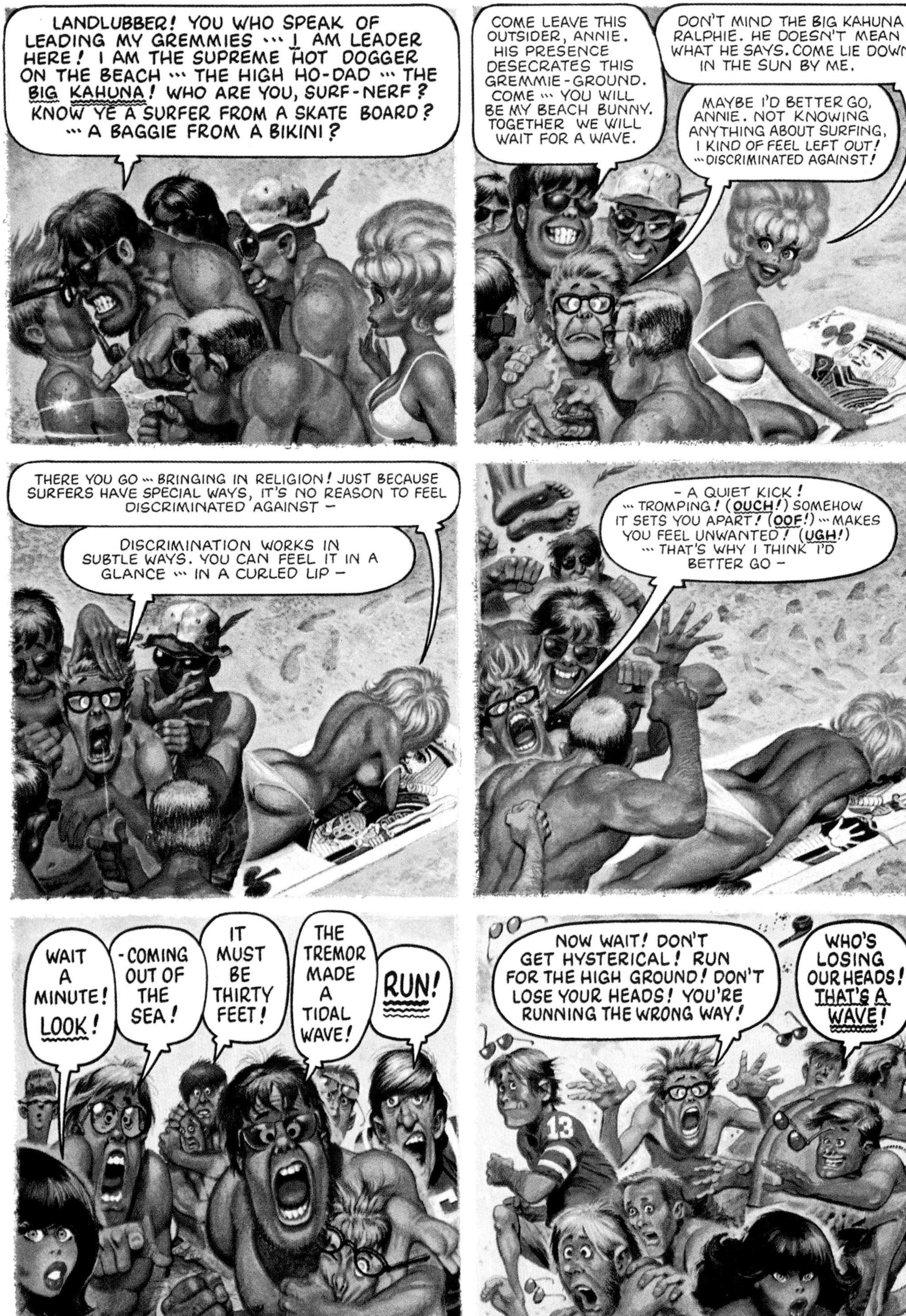
LANDLUBBER! YOU WHO SPEAK OF LEADING MY GREMMIES ··· I AM LEADER HERE! I AM THE SUPREME HOT DOGGER ON THE BEACH ··· THE HIGH HO-DAD ··· THE BIG KAHUNA! WHO ARE YOU, SURF-NERF? KNOW YE A SURFER FROM A SKATE BOARD? ··· A BAGGIE FROM A BIKINI?
COME LEAVE THIS OUTSIDER, ANNIE. HIS PRESENCE DESECRATES THIS GREMMIE-GROUND. COME ··· YOU WILL BE MY BEACH BUNNY. TOGETHER WE WILL WAIT FOR A WAVE.
DON'T MIND THE BIG KAHUNA, RALPHIE. HE DOESN'T MEAN WHAT HE SAYS. COME LIE DOWN IN THE SUN BY ME.
MAYBE I'D BETTER GO, ANNIE. NOT KNOWING ANYTHING ABOUT SURFING, I KIND OF FEEL LEFT OUT! ···DISCRIMINATED AGAINST!
THERE YOU GO ··· BRINGING IN RELIGION! JUST BECAUSE SURFERS HAVE SPECIAL WAYS, IT'S NO REASON TO FEEL DISCRIMINATED AGAINST –
DISCRIMINATION WORKS IN SUBTLE WAYS. YOU CAN FEEL IT IN A GLANCE ··· IN A CURLED LIP –
– A QUIET KICK! ··· TROMPING! (OUCH!) SOMEHOW IT SETS YOU APART! (OOF!) ··· MAKES YOU FEEL UNWANTED! (UGH!) ··· THAT'S WHY I THINK I'D BETTER GO –
WAIT A MINUTE! LOOK!
-COMING OUT OF THE SEA!
IT MUST BE THIRTY FEET!
THE TREMOR MADE A TIDAL WAVE!
RUN!
NOW WAIT! DON'T GET HYSTERICAL! RUN FOR THE HIGH GROUND! DON'T LOSE YOUR HEADS! YOU'RE RUNNING THE WRONG WAY!
WHO'S LOSING OUR HEADS! THAT'S A WAVE!
13

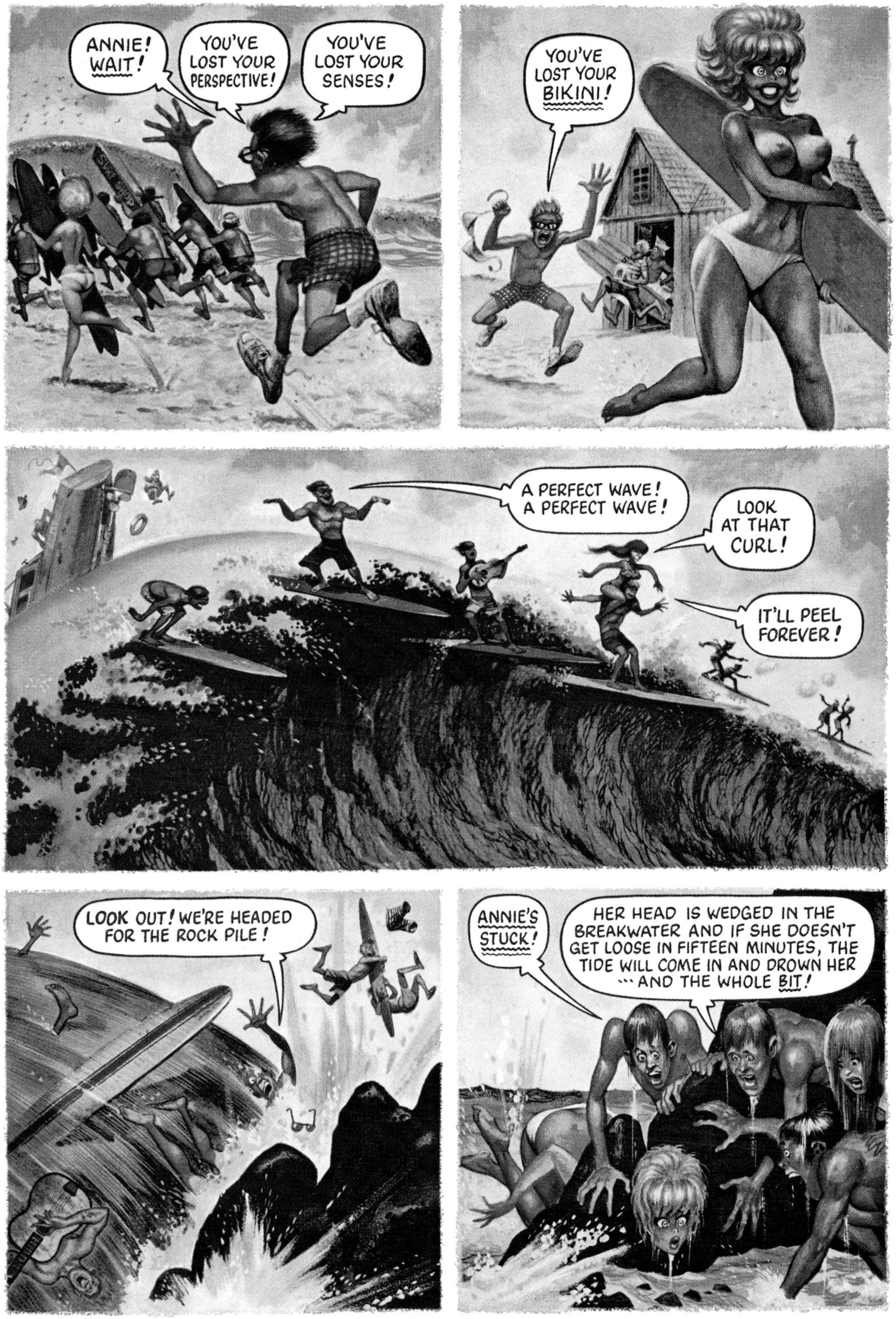
ANNIE! WAIT!
YOU'VE LOST YOUR PERSPECTIVE!
YOU'VE LOST YOUR SENSES!
YOU'VE LOST YOUR BIKINI!
A PERFECT WAVE! A PERFECT WAVE!
LOOK AT THAT CURL!
IT'LL PEEL FOREVER!
LOOK OUT! WE'RE HEADED FOR THE ROCK PILE!
ANNIE'S STUCK!
HER HEAD IS WEDGED IN THE BREAKWATER AND IF SHE DOESN'T GET LOOSE IN FIFTEEN MINUTES, THE TIDE WILL COME IN AND DROWN HER ... AND THE WHOLE BIT!

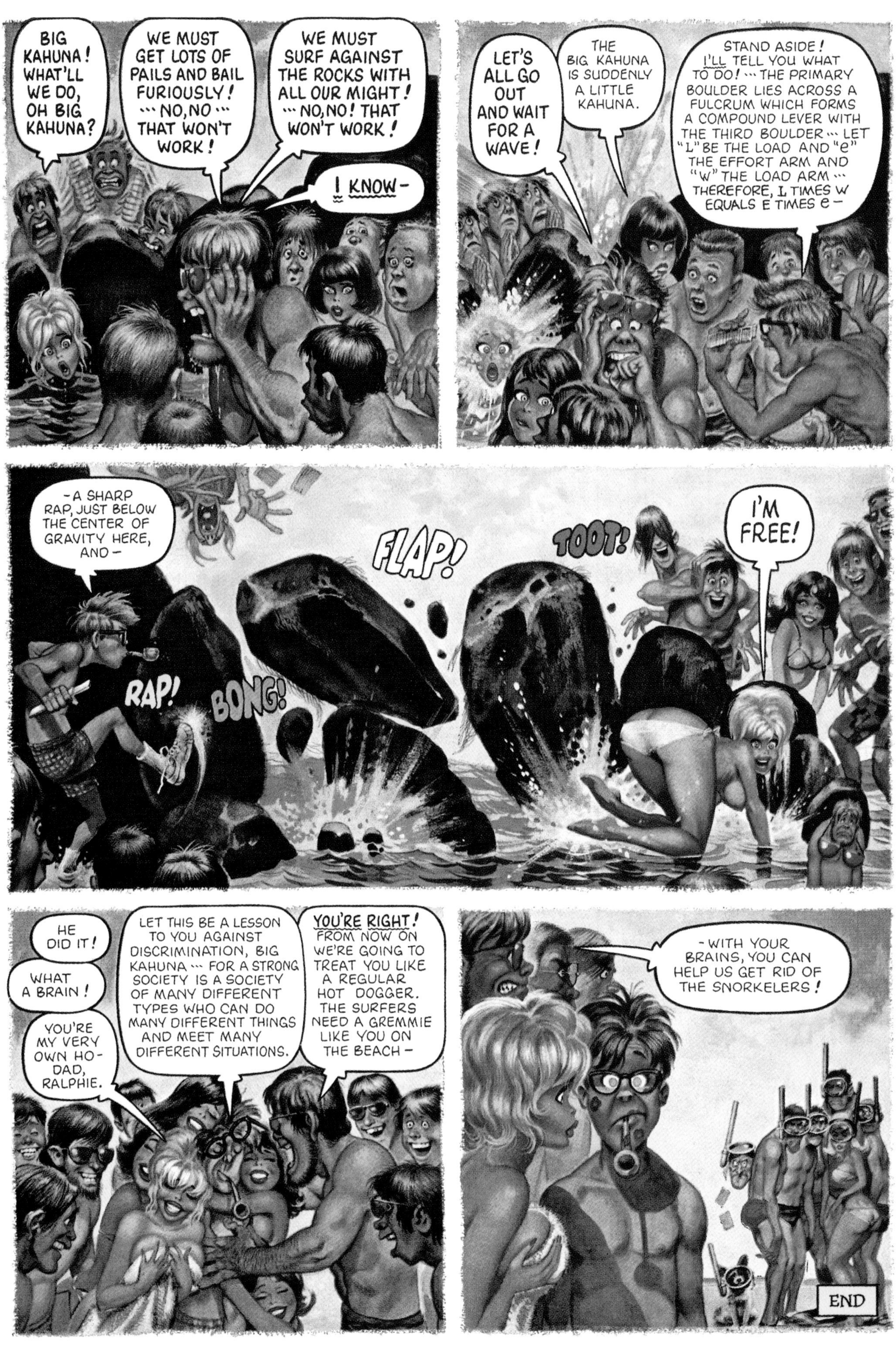

BIG KAHUNA! WHAT'LL WE DO, OH BIG KAHUNA?
WE MUST GET LOTS OF PAILS AND BAIL FURIOUSLY! ··· NO, NO ··· THAT WON'T WORK!
WE MUST SURF AGAINST THE ROCKS WITH ALL OUR MIGHT! ··· NO, NO! THAT WON'T WORK!
I KNOW –
LET'S ALL GO OUT AND WAIT FOR A WAVE!
THE BIG KAHUNA IS SUDDENLY A LITTLE KAHUNA.
STAND ASIDE! I'LL TELL YOU WHAT TO DO! ··· THE PRIMARY BOULDER LIES ACROSS A FULCRUM WHICH FORMS A COMPOUND LEVER WITH THE THIRD BOULDER ··· LET "L" BE THE LOAD AND "e" THE EFFORT ARM AND "W" THE LOAD ARM ··· THEREFORE, L TIMES W EQUALS E TIMES e –
– A SHARP RAP, JUST BELOW THE CENTER OF GRAVITY HERE, AND –
RAP!
BONG!
FLAP!
TOOT!
I'M FREE!
HE DID IT!
WHAT A BRAIN!
YOU'RE MY VERY OWN HO-DAD, RALPHIE.
LET THIS BE A LESSON TO YOU AGAINST DISCRIMINATION, BIG KAHUNA ··· FOR A STRONG SOCIETY IS A SOCIETY OF MANY DIFFERENT TYPES WHO CAN DO MANY DIFFERENT THINGS AND MEET MANY DIFFERENT SITUATIONS.
YOU'RE RIGHT! FROM NOW ON WE'RE GOING TO TREAT YOU LIKE A REGULAR HOT DOGGER. THE SURFERS NEED A GREMMIE LIKE YOU ON THE BEACH –
– WITH YOUR BRAINS, YOU CAN HELP US GET RID OF THE SNORKELERS!
END

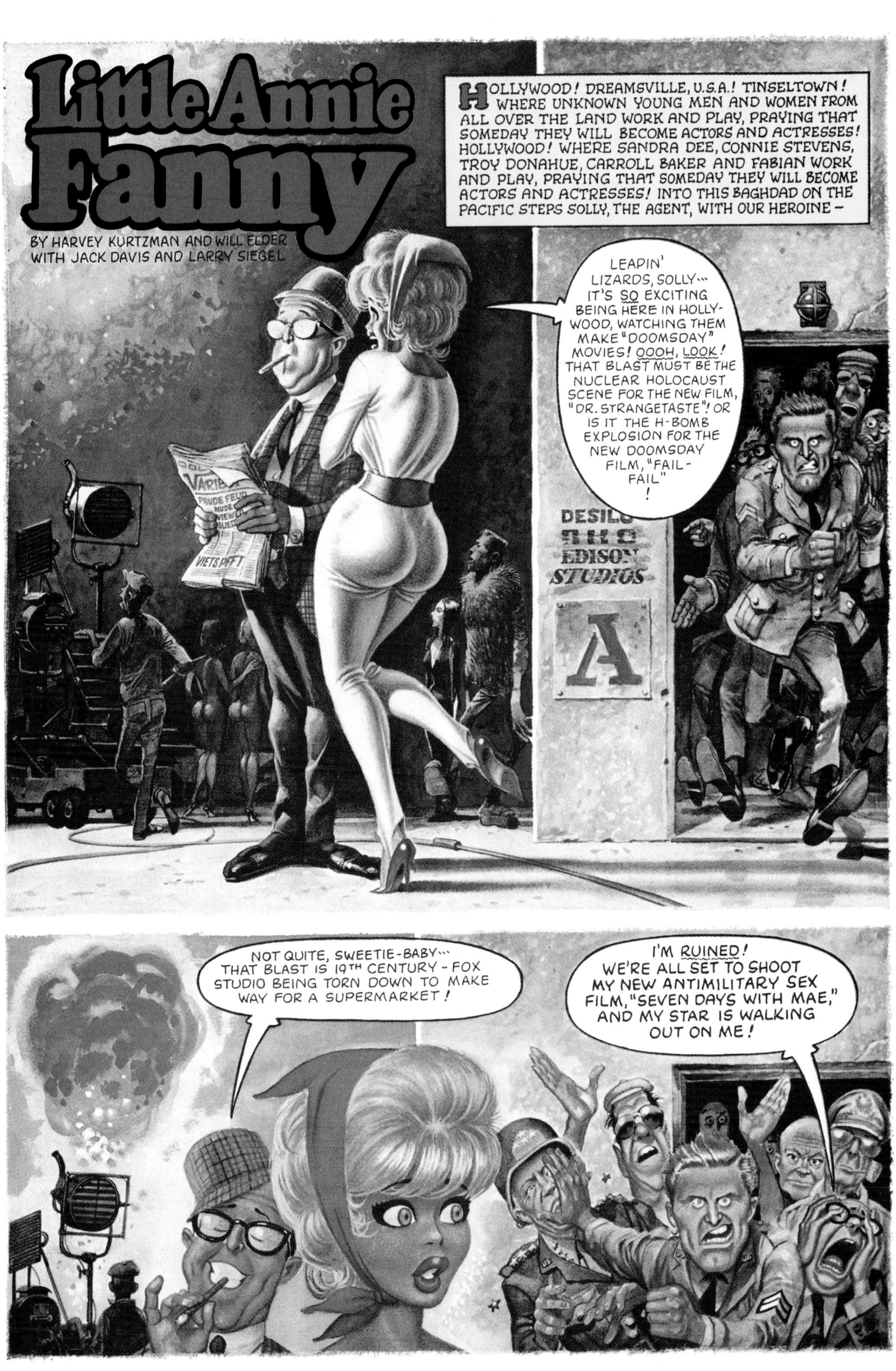
Little Annie Fanny
BY HARVEY KURTZMAN AND WILL ELDER WITH JACK DAVIS AND LARRY SIEGEL
HOLLYWOOD! DREAMSVILLE, U.S.A.! TINSELTOWN! WHERE UNKNOWN YOUNG MEN AND WOMEN FROM ALL OVER THE LAND WORK AND PLAY, PRAYING THAT SOMEDAY THEY WILL BECOME ACTORS AND ACTRESSES! HOLLYWOOD! WHERE SANDRA DEE, CONNIE STEVENS, TROY DONAHUE, CARROLL BAKER AND FABIAN WORK AND PLAY, PRAYING THAT SOMEDAY THEY WILL BECOME ACTORS AND ACTRESSES! INTO THIS BAGHDAD ON THE PACIFIC STEPS SOLLY, THE AGENT, WITH OUR HEROINE —
LEAPIN' LIZARDS, SOLLY··· IT'S SO EXCITING BEING HERE IN HOLLYWOOD, WATCHING THEM MAKE "DOOMSDAY" MOVIES! OOOH, LOOK! THAT BLAST MUST BE THE NUCLEAR HOLOCAUST SCENE FOR THE NEW FILM, "DR. STRANGETASTE"! OR IS IT THE H-BOMB EXPLOSION FOR THE NEW DOOMSDAY FILM, "FAIL-FAIL"!
VIETS PFFT
EDISON STUDIOS
A
NOT QUITE, SWEETIE-BABY··· THAT BLAST IS 19TH CENTURY - FOX STUDIO BEING TORN DOWN TO MAKE WAY FOR A SUPERMARKET!
I'M RUINED! WE'RE ALL SET TO SHOOT MY NEW ANTIMILITARY SEX FILM, "SEVEN DAYS WITH MAE," AND MY STAR IS WALKING OUT ON ME!

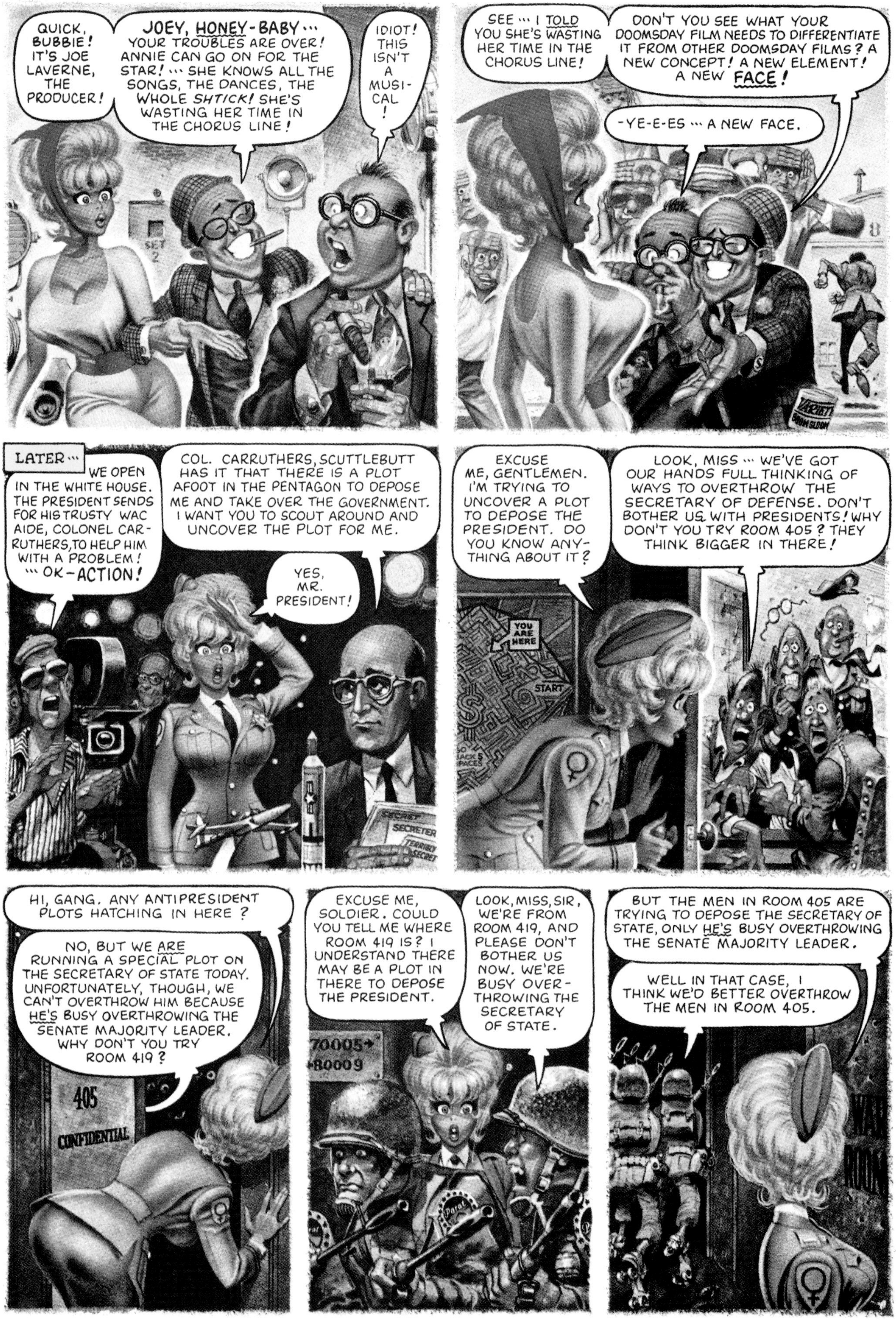
QUICK, BUBBIE! IT'S JOE LAVERNE, THE PRODUCER!
JOEY, HONEY-BABY ··· YOUR TROUBLES ARE OVER! ANNIE CAN GO ON FOR THE STAR! ··· SHE KNOWS ALL THE SONGS, THE DANCES, THE WHOLE SHTICK! SHE'S WASTING HER TIME IN THE CHORUS LINE!
IDIOT! THIS ISN'T A MUSICAL!
SET 2
SEE ··· I TOLD YOU SHE'S WASTING HER TIME IN THE CHORUS LINE!
DON'T YOU SEE WHAT YOUR DOOMSDAY FILM NEEDS TO DIFFERENTIATE IT FROM OTHER DOOMSDAY FILMS? A NEW CONCEPT! A NEW ELEMENT! A NEW FACE!
-YE-E-ES ··· A NEW FACE.
LATER ··· WE OPEN IN THE WHITE HOUSE. THE PRESIDENT SENDS FOR HIS TRUSTY WAC AIDE, COLONEL CARRUTHERS, TO HELP HIM WITH A PROBLEM! ··· OK-ACTION!
COL. CARRUTHERS, SCUTTLEBUTT HAS IT THAT THERE IS A PLOT AFOOT IN THE PENTAGON TO DEPOSE ME AND TAKE OVER THE GOVERNMENT. I WANT YOU TO SCOUT AROUND AND UNCOVER THE PLOT FOR ME.
YES, MR. PRESIDENT!
SECRET
SECRETER
EXCUSE ME, GENTLEMEN. I'M TRYING TO UNCOVER A PLOT TO DEPOSE THE PRESIDENT. DO YOU KNOW ANYTHING ABOUT IT?
LOOK, MISS ··· WE'VE GOT OUR HANDS FULL THINKING OF WAYS TO OVERTHROW THE SECRETARY OF DEFENSE. DON'T BOTHER US WITH PRESIDENTS! WHY DON'T YOU TRY ROOM 405? THEY THINK BIGGER IN THERE!
YOU ARE HERE
START
HI, GANG. ANY ANTIPRESIDENT PLOTS HATCHING IN HERE?
NO, BUT WE ARE RUNNING A SPECIAL PLOT ON THE SECRETARY OF STATE TODAY. UNFORTUNATELY, THOUGH, WE CAN'T OVERTHROW HIM BECAUSE HE'S BUSY OVERTHROWING THE SENATE MAJORITY LEADER. WHY DON'T YOU TRY ROOM 419?
405
CONFIDENTIAL
EXCUSE ME, SOLDIER. COULD YOU TELL ME WHERE ROOM 419 IS? I UNDERSTAND THERE MAY BE A PLOT IN THERE TO DEPOSE THE PRESIDENT.
LOOK, MISS, SIR, WE'RE FROM ROOM 419, AND PLEASE DON'T BOTHER US NOW. WE'RE BUSY OVERTHROWING THE SECRETARY OF STATE.
70005→
→80009
BUT THE MEN IN ROOM 405 ARE TRYING TO DEPOSE THE SECRETARY OF STATE, ONLY HE'S BUSY OVERTHROWING THE SENATE MAJORITY LEADER.
WELL IN THAT CASE, I THINK WE'D BETTER OVERTHROW THE MEN IN ROOM 405.

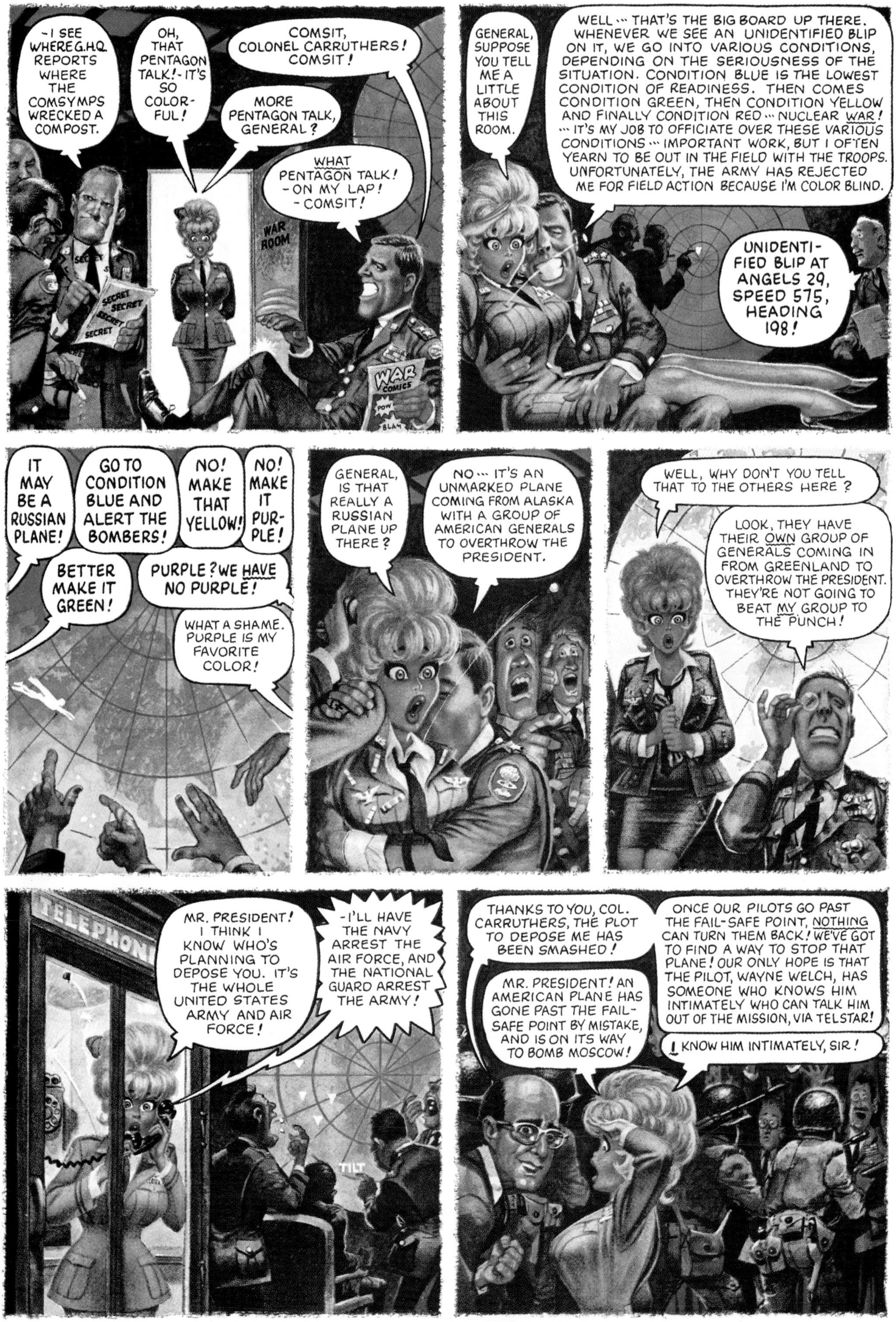
-I SEE WHERE G.H.Q. REPORTS WHERE THE COMSYMPS WRECKED A COMPOST.
OH, THAT PENTAGON TALK! - IT'S SO COLORFUL!
COMSIT, COLONEL CARRUTHERS! COMSIT!
MORE PENTAGON TALK, GENERAL?
WHAT PENTAGON TALK! - ON MY LAP! - COMSIT!
WAR ROOM
SECRET
WAR COMICS
POW
GENERAL, SUPPOSE YOU TELL ME A LITTLE ABOUT THIS ROOM.
WELL ... THAT'S THE BIG BOARD UP THERE. WHENEVER WE SEE AN UNIDENTIFIED BLIP ON IT, WE GO INTO VARIOUS CONDITIONS, DEPENDING ON THE SERIOUSNESS OF THE SITUATION. CONDITION BLUE IS THE LOWEST CONDITION OF READINESS. THEN COMES CONDITION GREEN, THEN CONDITION YELLOW AND FINALLY CONDITION RED ... NUCLEAR WAR! ... IT'S MY JOB TO OFFICIATE OVER THESE VARIOUS CONDITIONS ... IMPORTANT WORK, BUT I OFTEN YEARN TO BE OUT IN THE FIELD WITH THE TROOPS. UNFORTUNATELY, THE ARMY HAS REJECTED ME FOR FIELD ACTION BECAUSE I'M COLOR BLIND.
UNIDENTIFIED BLIP AT ANGELS 29, SPEED 575, HEADING 198!
IT MAY BE A RUSSIAN PLANE!
GO TO CONDITION BLUE AND ALERT THE BOMBERS!
NO! MAKE THAT YELLOW!
NO! MAKE IT PURPLE!
BETTER MAKE IT GREEN!
PURPLE? WE HAVE NO PURPLE!
WHAT A SHAME. PURPLE IS MY FAVORITE COLOR!
GENERAL, IS THAT REALLY A RUSSIAN PLANE UP THERE?
NO ... IT'S AN UNMARKED PLANE COMING FROM ALASKA WITH A GROUP OF AMERICAN GENERALS TO OVERTHROW THE PRESIDENT.
WELL, WHY DON'T YOU TELL THAT TO THE OTHERS HERE?
LOOK, THEY HAVE THEIR OWN GROUP OF GENERALS COMING IN FROM GREENLAND TO OVERTHROW THE PRESIDENT. THEY'RE NOT GOING TO BEAT MY GROUP TO THE PUNCH!
TELEPHONE
MR. PRESIDENT! I THINK I KNOW WHO'S PLANNING TO DEPOSE YOU. IT'S THE WHOLE UNITED STATES ARMY AND AIR FORCE!
-I'LL HAVE THE NAVY ARREST THE AIR FORCE, AND THE NATIONAL GUARD ARREST THE ARMY!
TILT
THANKS TO YOU, COL. CARRUTHERS, THE PLOT TO DEPOSE ME HAS BEEN SMASHED!
MR. PRESIDENT! AN AMERICAN PLANE HAS GONE PAST THE FAIL-SAFE POINT BY MISTAKE, AND IS ON ITS WAY TO BOMB MOSCOW!
ONCE OUR PILOTS GO PAST THE FAIL-SAFE POINT, NOTHING CAN TURN THEM BACK! WE'VE GOT TO FIND A WAY TO STOP THAT PLANE! OUR ONLY HOPE IS THAT THE PILOT, WAYNE WELCH, HAS SOMEONE WHO KNOWS HIM INTIMATELY WHO CAN TALK HIM OUT OF THE MISSION, VIA TELSTAR!
I KNOW HIM INTIMATELY, SIR!

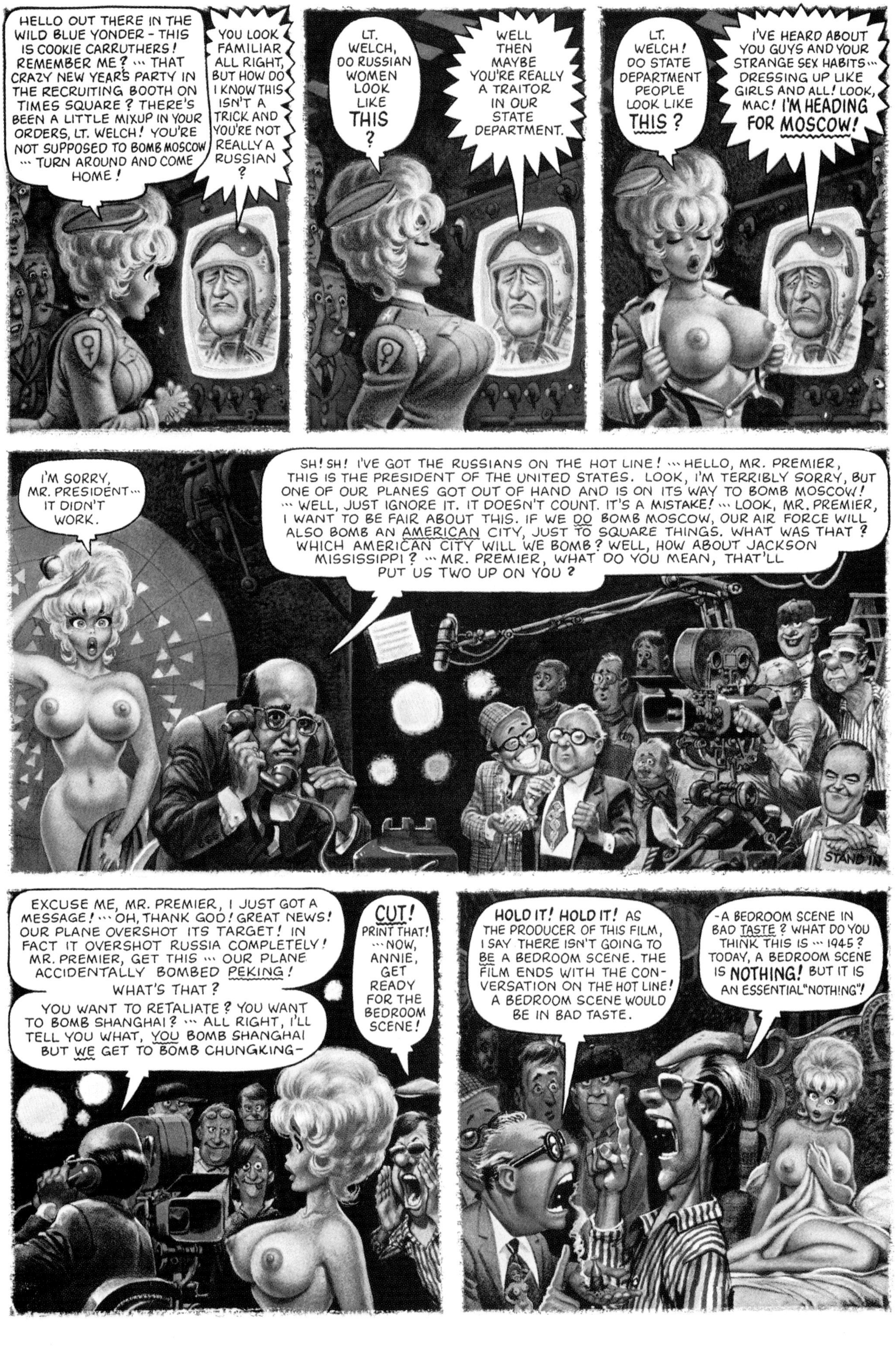
HELLO OUT THERE IN THE WILD BLUE YONDER - THIS IS COOKIE CARRUTHERS! REMEMBER ME? ··· THAT CRAZY NEW YEAR'S PARTY IN THE RECRUITING BOOTH ON TIMES SQUARE? THERE'S BEEN A LITTLE MIXUP IN YOUR ORDERS, LT. WELCH! YOU'RE NOT SUPPOSED TO BOMB MOSCOW ··· TURN AROUND AND COME HOME!
YOU LOOK FAMILIAR ALL RIGHT, BUT HOW DO I KNOW THIS ISN'T A TRICK AND YOU'RE NOT REALLY A RUSSIAN?
LT. WELCH, DO RUSSIAN WOMEN LOOK LIKE THIS?
WELL THEN MAYBE YOU'RE REALLY A TRAITOR IN OUR STATE DEPARTMENT.
LT. WELCH! DO STATE DEPARTMENT PEOPLE LOOK LIKE THIS?
I'VE HEARD ABOUT YOU GUYS AND YOUR STRANGE SEX HABITS··· DRESSING UP LIKE GIRLS AND ALL! LOOK, MAC! I'M HEADING FOR MOSCOW!
I'M SORRY, MR. PRESIDENT··· IT DIDN'T WORK.
SH! SH! I'VE GOT THE RUSSIANS ON THE HOT LINE! ··· HELLO, MR. PREMIER, THIS IS THE PRESIDENT OF THE UNITED STATES. LOOK, I'M TERRIBLY SORRY, BUT ONE OF OUR PLANES GOT OUT OF HAND AND IS ON ITS WAY TO BOMB MOSCOW! ··· WELL, JUST IGNORE IT. IT DOESN'T COUNT. IT'S A MISTAKE! ··· LOOK, MR. PREMIER, I WANT TO BE FAIR ABOUT THIS. IF WE DO BOMB MOSCOW, OUR AIR FORCE WILL ALSO BOMB AN AMERICAN CITY, JUST TO SQUARE THINGS. WHAT WAS THAT? WHICH AMERICAN CITY WILL WE BOMB? WELL, HOW ABOUT JACKSON MISSISSIPPI? ··· MR. PREMIER, WHAT DO YOU MEAN, THAT'LL PUT US TWO UP ON YOU?
STAND IN
EXCUSE ME, MR. PREMIER, I JUST GOT A MESSAGE! ··· OH, THANK GOD! GREAT NEWS! OUR PLANE OVERSHOT ITS TARGET! IN FACT IT OVERSHOT RUSSIA COMPLETELY! MR. PREMIER, GET THIS ··· OUR PLANE ACCIDENTALLY BOMBED PEKING! WHAT'S THAT?
YOU WANT TO RETALIATE? YOU WANT TO BOMB SHANGHAI? ··· ALL RIGHT, I'LL TELL YOU WHAT, YOU BOMB SHANGHAI BUT WE GET TO BOMB CHUNGKING-
CUT! PRINT THAT! ···NOW, ANNIE, GET READY FOR THE BEDROOM SCENE!
HOLD IT! HOLD IT! AS THE PRODUCER OF THIS FILM, I SAY THERE ISN'T GOING TO BE A BEDROOM SCENE. THE FILM ENDS WITH THE CONVERSATION ON THE HOT LINE! A BEDROOM SCENE WOULD BE IN BAD TASTE.
-A BEDROOM SCENE IN BAD TASTE? WHAT DO YOU THINK THIS IS ··· 1945? TODAY, A BEDROOM SCENE IS NOTHING! BUT IT IS AN ESSENTIAL "NOTHING"!

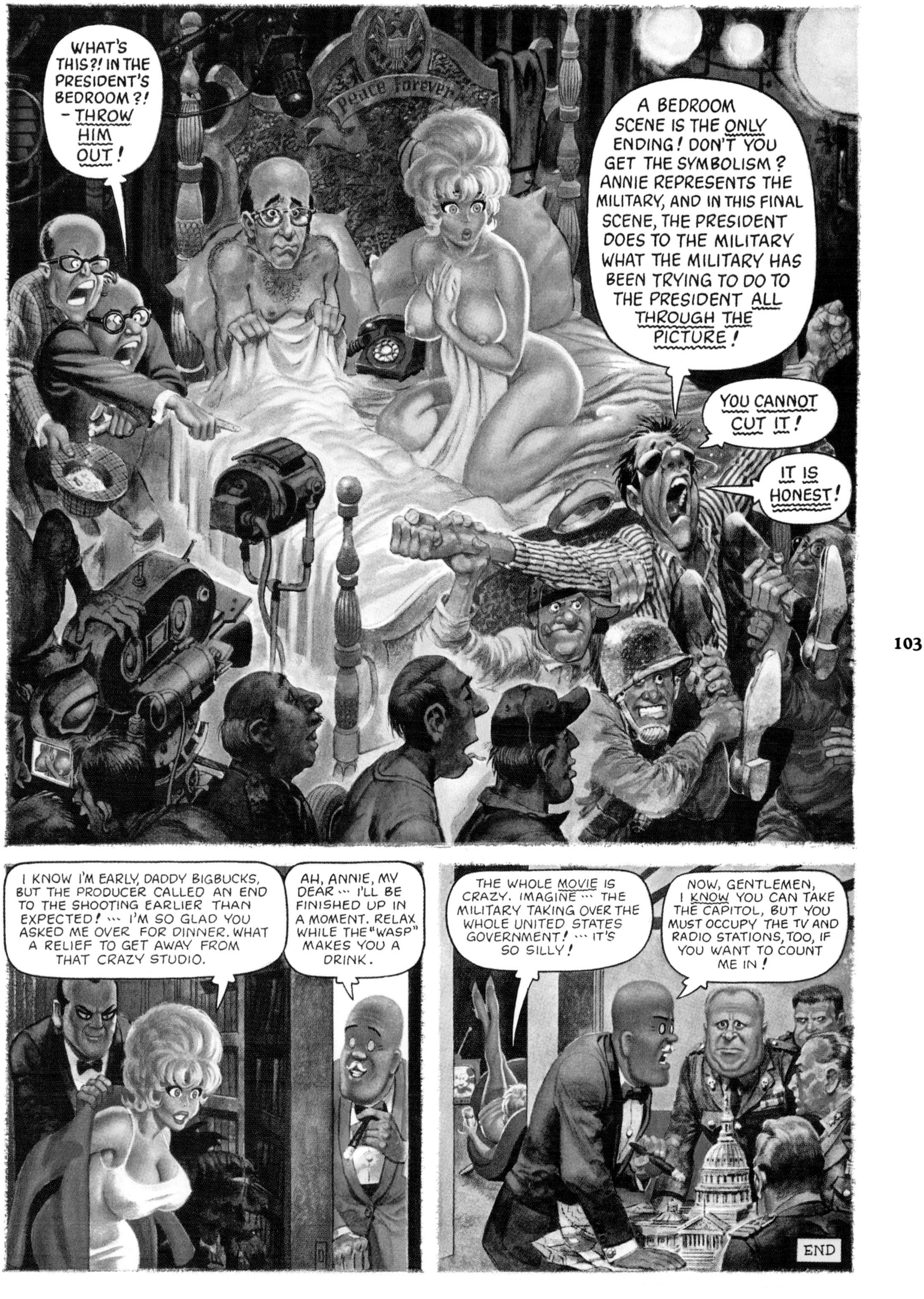
WHAT'S THIS?! IN THE PRESIDENT'S BEDROOM?! - THROW HIM OUT!
A BEDROOM SCENE IS THE ONLY ENDING! DON'T YOU GET THE SYMBOLISM? ANNIE REPRESENTS THE MILITARY, AND IN THIS FINAL SCENE, THE PRESIDENT DOES TO THE MILITARY WHAT THE MILITARY HAS BEEN TRYING TO DO TO THE PRESIDENT ALL THROUGH THE PICTURE!
YOU CANNOT CUT IT!
IT IS HONEST!
I KNOW I'M EARLY, DADDY BIGBUCKS, BUT THE PRODUCER CALLED AN END TO THE SHOOTING EARLIER THAN EXPECTED! ··· I'M SO GLAD YOU ASKED ME OVER FOR DINNER. WHAT A RELIEF TO GET AWAY FROM THAT CRAZY STUDIO.
AH, ANNIE, MY DEAR ··· I'LL BE FINISHED UP IN A MOMENT. RELAX WHILE THE "WASP" MAKES YOU A DRINK.
THE WHOLE MOVIE IS CRAZY. IMAGINE ··· THE MILITARY TAKING OVER THE WHOLE UNITED STATES GOVERNMENT! ··· IT'S SO SILLY!
NOW, GENTLEMEN, I KNOW YOU CAN TAKE THE CAPITOL, BUT YOU MUST OCCUPY THE TV AND RADIO STATIONS, TOO, IF YOU WANT TO COUNT ME IN!
END

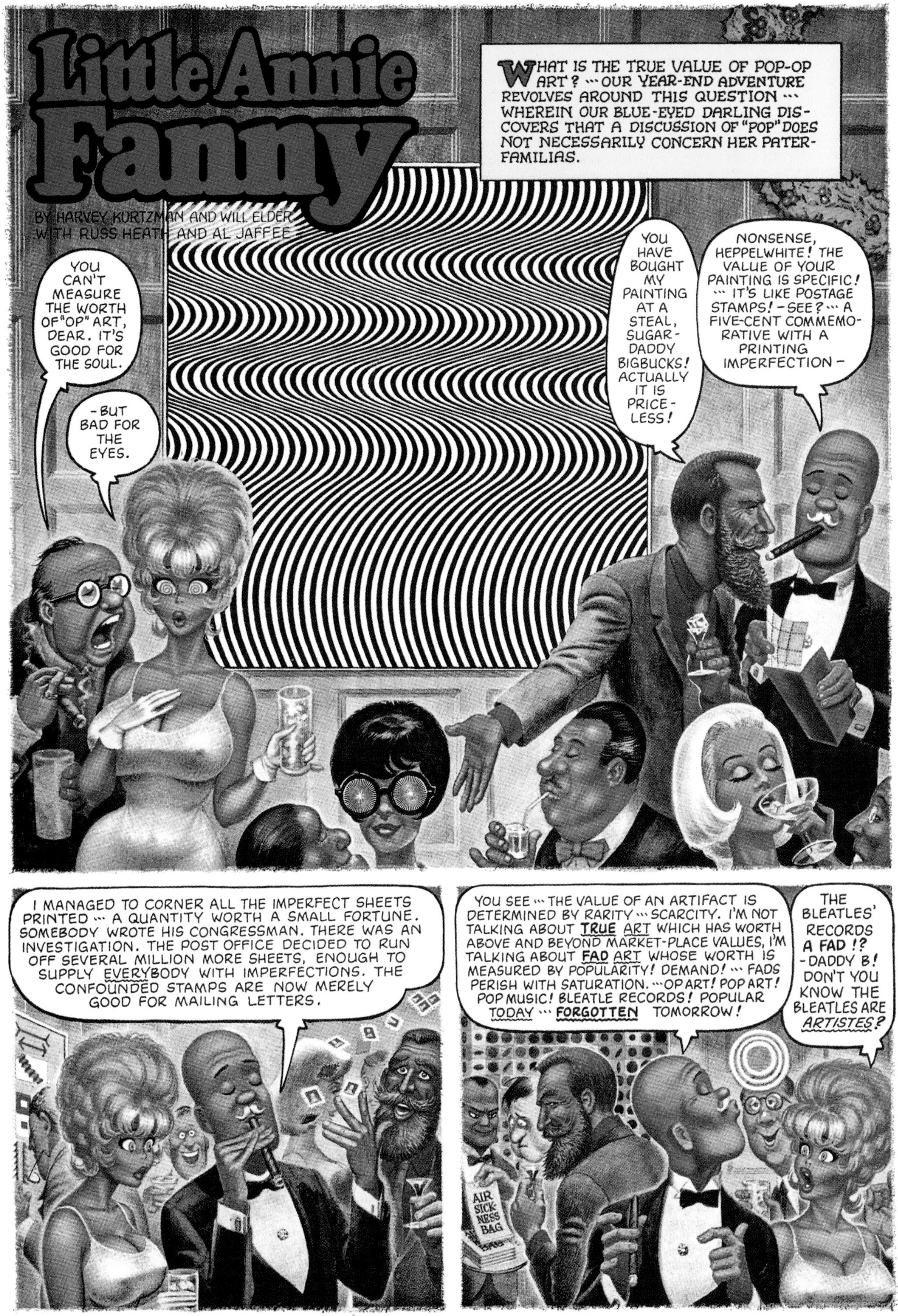

Little Annie Fanny
BY HARVEY KURTZMAN AND WILL ELDER WITH RUSS HEATH AND AL JAFFEE
WHAT IS THE TRUE VALUE OF POP-OP ART? ··· OUR YEAR-END ADVENTURE REVOLVES AROUND THIS QUESTION ··· WHEREIN OUR BLUE-EYED DARLING DISCOVERS THAT A DISCUSSION OF "POP" DOES NOT NECESSARILY CONCERN HER PATERFAMILIAS.
YOU CAN'T MEASURE THE WORTH OF "OP" ART, DEAR. IT'S GOOD FOR THE SOUL.
-BUT BAD FOR THE EYES.
YOU HAVE BOUGHT MY PAINTING AT A STEAL, SUGAR-DADDY BIGBUCKS! ACTUALLY IT IS PRICELESS!
NONSENSE, HEPPELWHITE! THE VALUE OF YOUR PAINTING IS SPECIFIC! ··· IT'S LIKE POSTAGE STAMPS! -SEE? ··· A FIVE-CENT COMMEMORATIVE WITH A PRINTING IMPERFECTION-
I MANAGED TO CORNER ALL THE IMPERFECT SHEETS PRINTED ··· A QUANTITY WORTH A SMALL FORTUNE. SOMEBODY WROTE HIS CONGRESSMAN. THERE WAS AN INVESTIGATION. THE POST OFFICE DECIDED TO RUN OFF SEVERAL MILLION MORE SHEETS, ENOUGH TO SUPPLY EVERYBODY WITH IMPERFECTIONS. THE CONFOUNDED STAMPS ARE NOW MERELY GOOD FOR MAILING LETTERS.
YOU SEE ··· THE VALUE OF AN ARTIFACT IS DETERMINED BY RARITY ··· SCARCITY. I'M NOT TALKING ABOUT TRUE ART WHICH HAS WORTH ABOVE AND BEYOND MARKET-PLACE VALUES, I'M TALKING ABOUT FAD ART WHOSE WORTH IS MEASURED BY POPULARITY! DEMAND! ··· FADS PERISH WITH SATURATION. ··· OP ART! POP ART! POP MUSIC! BLEATLE RECORDS! POPULAR TODAY ··· FORGOTTEN TOMORROW!
THE BLEATLES' RECORDS A FAD!? -DADDY B! DON'T YOU KNOW THE BLEATLES ARE ARTISTES?
AIR SICKNESS BAG

104

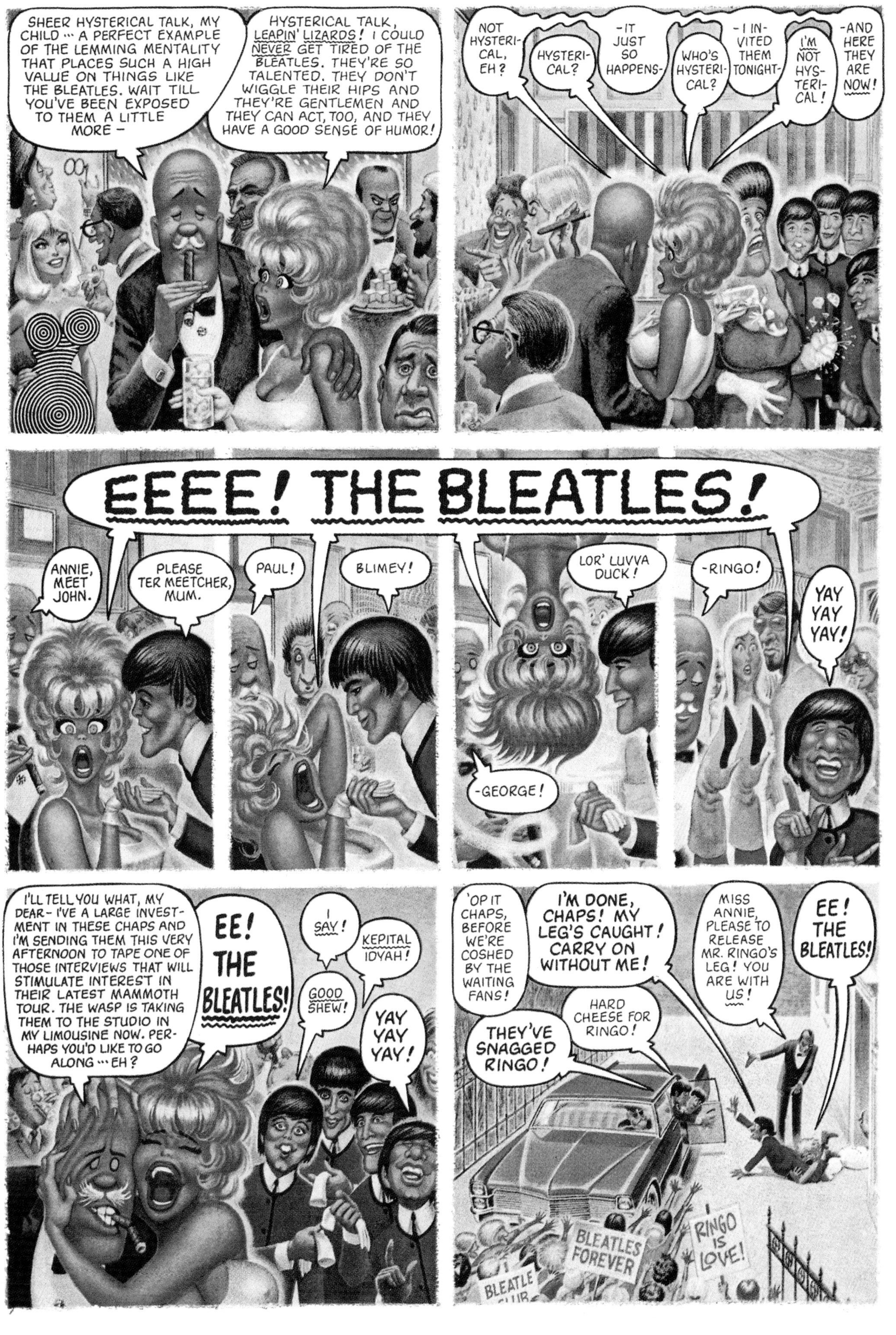

SHEER HYSTERICAL TALK, MY CHILD ··· A PERFECT EXAMPLE OF THE LEMMING MENTALITY THAT PLACES SUCH A HIGH VALUE ON THINGS LIKE THE BLEATLES. WAIT TILL YOU'VE BEEN EXPOSED TO THEM A LITTLE MORE –
HYSTERICAL TALK, LEAPIN' LIZARDS! I COULD NEVER GET TIRED OF THE BLEATLES. THEY'RE SO TALENTED. THEY DON'T WIGGLE THEIR HIPS AND THEY'RE GENTLEMEN AND THEY CAN ACT, TOO, AND THEY HAVE A GOOD SENSE OF HUMOR!
NOT HYSTERI-CAL, EH?
HYSTERI-CAL?
–IT JUST SO HAPPENS–
WHO'S HYSTERI-CAL?
–I IN-VITED THEM TONIGHT–
I'M NOT HYS-TERI-CAL!
–AND HERE THEY ARE NOW!
EEEE! THE BLEATLES!
ANNIE, MEET JOHN.
PLEASE TER MEETCHER, MUM.
PAUL!
BLIMEY!
LOR' LUVVA DUCK!
–GEORGE!
–RINGO!
YAY YAY YAY!
I'LL TELL YOU WHAT, MY DEAR– I'VE A LARGE INVEST-MENT IN THESE CHAPS AND I'M SENDING THEM THIS VERY AFTERNOON TO TAPE ONE OF THOSE INTERVIEWS THAT WILL STIMULATE INTEREST IN THEIR LATEST MAMMOTH TOUR. THE WASP IS TAKING THEM TO THE STUDIO IN MY LIMOUSINE NOW. PER-HAPS YOU'D LIKE TO GO ALONG ··· EH?
EE! THE BLEATLES!
I SAY!
KEPITAL IDYAH!
GOOD SHEW!
YAY YAY YAY!
'OP IT CHAPS, BEFORE WE'RE COSHED BY THE WAITING FANS!
I'M DONE, CHAPS! MY LEG'S CAUGHT! CARRY ON WITHOUT ME!
MISS ANNIE, PLEASE TO RELEASE MR. RINGO'S LEG! YOU ARE WITH US!
EE! THE BLEATLES!
HARD CHEESE FOR RINGO!
THEY'VE SNAGGED RINGO!
BLEATLES FOREVER
RINGO IS LOVE!
BLEATLE CLUB

106

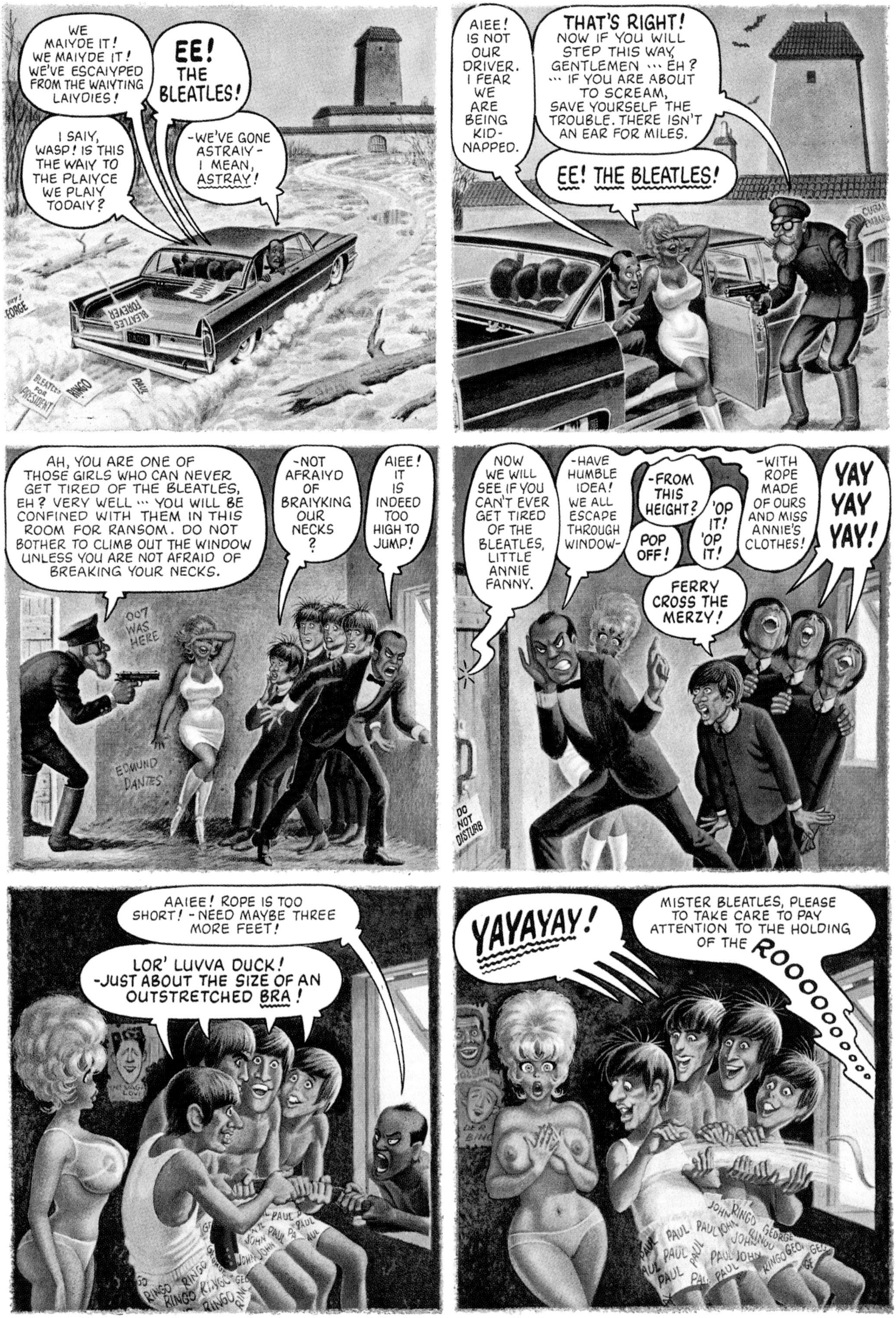

WE MAIYDE IT! WE MAIYDE IT! WE'VE ESCAIYPED FROM THE WAIYTING LAIYDIES!
EE! THE BLEATLES!
I SAY, WASP! IS THIS THE WAIY TO THE PLAIYCE WE PLAIY TODAIY?
-WE'VE GONE ASTRAIY - I MEAN, ASTRAY!
BLEATLES FOREVER
JOHN
BLEATEES FOR PRESIDENT
RINGO
PAUL
AIEE! IS NOT OUR DRIVER. I FEAR WE ARE BEING KID-NAPPED.
THAT'S RIGHT! NOW IF YOU WILL STEP THIS WAY, GENTLEMEN ··· EH? ··· IF YOU ARE ABOUT TO SCREAM, SAVE YOURSELF THE TROUBLE. THERE ISN'T AN EAR FOR MILES.
EE! THE BLEATLES!
AH, YOU ARE ONE OF THOSE GIRLS WHO CAN NEVER GET TIRED OF THE BLEATLES, EH? VERY WELL ··· YOU WILL BE CONFINED WITH THEM IN THIS ROOM FOR RANSOM. DO NOT BOTHER TO CLIMB OUT THE WINDOW UNLESS YOU ARE NOT AFRAID OF BREAKING YOUR NECKS.
-NOT AFRAIYD OF BRAIYKING OUR NECKS?
AIEE! IT IS INDEED TOO HIGH TO JUMP!
007 WAS HERE
EDMUND DANTES
NOW WE WILL SEE IF YOU CAN'T EVER GET TIRED OF THE BLEATLES, LITTLE ANNIE FANNY.
-HAVE HUMBLE IDEA! WE ALL ESCAPE THROUGH WINDOW-
-FROM THIS HEIGHT?
POP OFF!
'OP IT! 'OP IT!
FERRY CROSS THE MERZY!
-WITH ROPE MADE OF OURS AND MISS ANNIE'S CLOTHES!
YAY YAY YAY!
DO NOT DISTURB
AAIEE! ROPE IS TOO SHORT! -NEED MAYBE THREE MORE FEET!
LOR' LUVVA DUCK! -JUST ABOUT THE SIZE OF AN OUTSTRETCHED BRA!
YAYAYAY!
MISTER BLEATLES, PLEASE TO TAKE CARE TO PAY ATTENTION TO THE HOLDING OF THE ROOOOOOOOOO

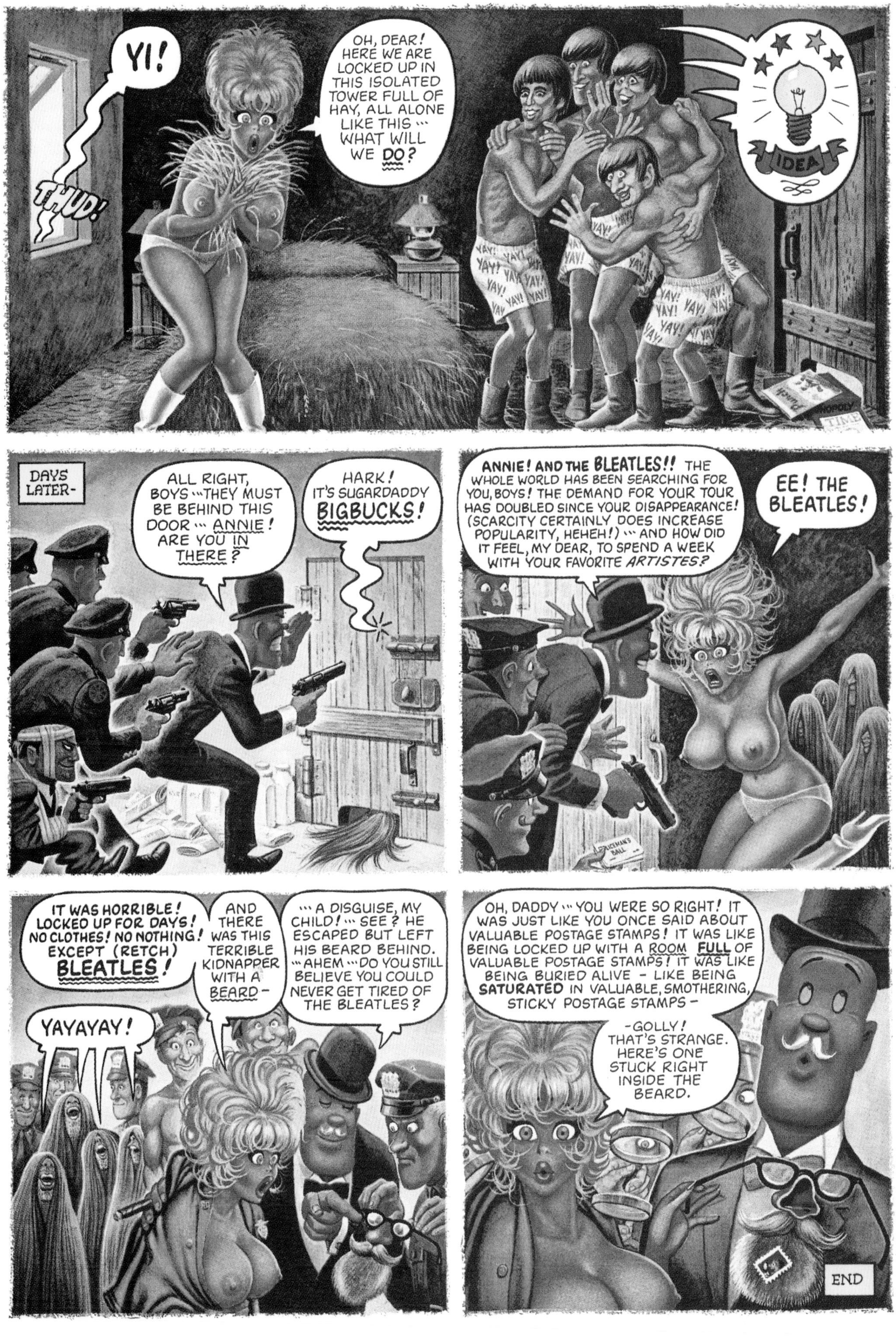
YI!
THUD!
OH, DEAR! HERE WE ARE LOCKED UP IN THIS ISOLATED TOWER FULL OF HAY, ALL ALONE LIKE THIS ··· WHAT WILL WE DO?
IDEA
DAYS LATER-
ALL RIGHT, BOYS ··· THEY MUST BE BEHIND THIS DOOR ··· ANNIE! ARE YOU IN THERE?
HARK! IT'S SUGARDADDY BIGBUCKS!
ANNIE! AND THE BLEATLES!! THE WHOLE WORLD HAS BEEN SEARCHING FOR YOU, BOYS! THE DEMAND FOR YOUR TOUR HAS DOUBLED SINCE YOUR DISAPPEARANCE! (SCARCITY CERTAINLY DOES INCREASE POPULARITY, HEHEH!) ··· AND HOW DID IT FEEL, MY DEAR, TO SPEND A WEEK WITH YOUR FAVORITE ARTISTES?
EE! THE BLEATLES!
IT WAS HORRIBLE! LOCKED UP FOR DAYS! NO CLOTHES! NO NOTHING! EXCEPT (RETCH) BLEATLES!
AND THERE WAS THIS TERRIBLE KIDNAPPER WITH A BEARD-
··· A DISGUISE, MY CHILD! ··· SEE? HE ESCAPED BUT LEFT HIS BEARD BEHIND. ··· AHEM ··· DO YOU STILL BELIEVE YOU COULD NEVER GET TIRED OF THE BLEATLES?
YAYAYAY!
OH, DADDY ··· YOU WERE SO RIGHT! IT WAS JUST LIKE YOU ONCE SAID ABOUT VALUABLE POSTAGE STAMPS! IT WAS LIKE BEING LOCKED UP WITH A ROOM FULL OF VALUABLE POSTAGE STAMPS! IT WAS LIKE BEING BURIED ALIVE - LIKE BEING SATURATED IN VALUABLE, SMOTHERING, STICKY POSTAGE STAMPS-
-GOLLY! THAT'S STRANGE. HERE'S ONE STUCK RIGHT INSIDE THE BEARD.
END

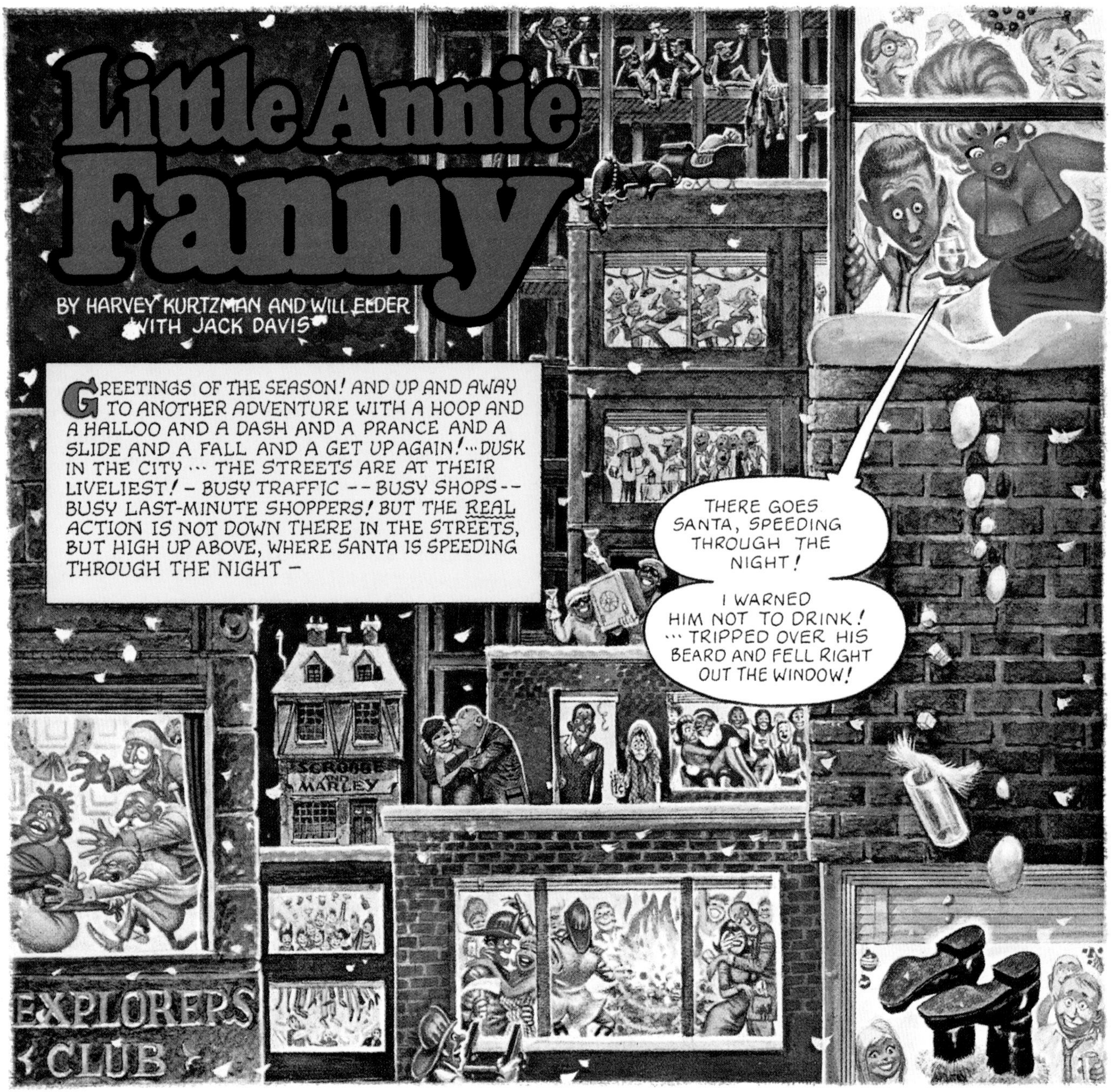
Little Annie Fanny
BY HARVEY KURTZMAN AND WILL ELDER WITH JACK DAVIS
GREETINGS OF THE SEASON! AND UP AND AWAY TO ANOTHER ADVENTURE WITH A HOOP AND A HALLOO AND A DASH AND A PRANCE AND A SLIDE AND A FALL AND A GET UP AGAIN!... DUSK IN THE CITY... THE STREETS ARE AT THEIR LIVELIEST! – BUSY TRAFFIC – – BUSY SHOPS – – BUSY LAST-MINUTE SHOPPERS! BUT THE REAL ACTION IS NOT DOWN THERE IN THE STREETS, BUT HIGH UP ABOVE, WHERE SANTA IS SPEEDING THROUGH THE NIGHT –
THERE GOES SANTA, SPEEDING THROUGH THE NIGHT!
I WARNED HIM NOT TO DRINK! ... TRIPPED OVER HIS BEARD AND FELL RIGHT OUT THE WINDOW!
SCROOGE AND MARLEY
EXPLORERS CLUB

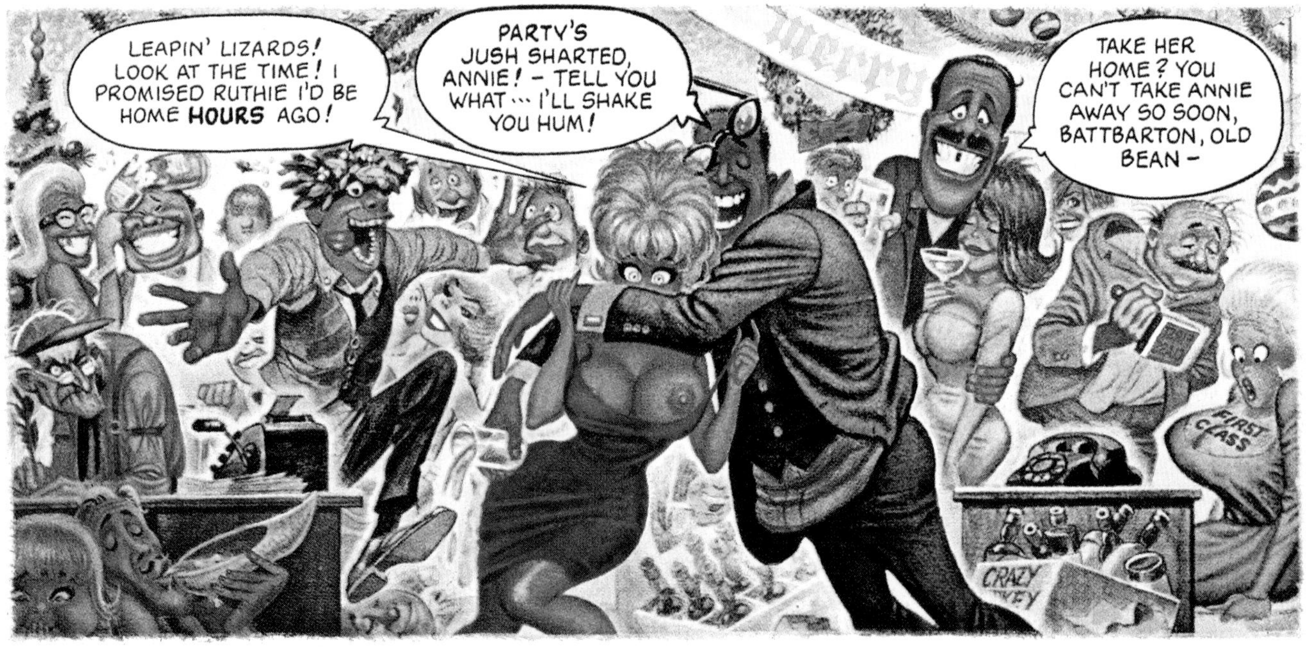
LEAPIN' LIZARDS! LOOK AT THE TIME! I PROMISED RUTHIE I'D BE HOME HOURS AGO!
PARTY'S JUSH SHARTED, ANNIE! – TELL YOU WHAT... I'LL SHAKE YOU HUM!
TAKE HER HOME? YOU CAN'T TAKE ANNIE AWAY SO SOON, BATTBARTON, OLD BEAN –
merry
FIRST CLASS

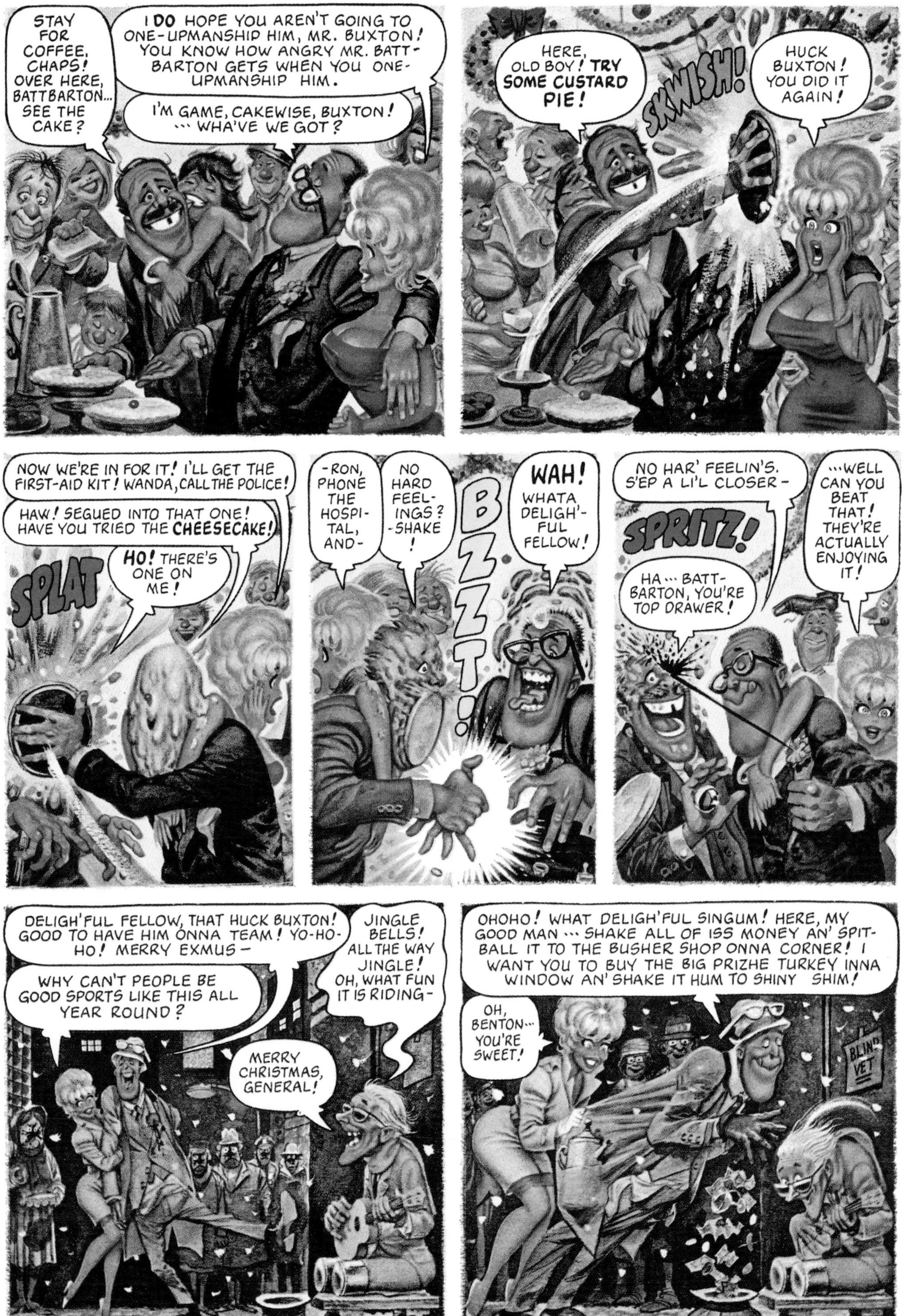

STAY FOR COFFEE, CHAPS! OVER HERE, BATTBARTON... SEE THE CAKE?
I DO HOPE YOU AREN'T GOING TO ONE-UPMANSHIP HIM, MR. BUXTON! YOU KNOW HOW ANGRY MR. BATT-BARTON GETS WHEN YOU ONE-UPMANSHIP HIM.
I'M GAME, CAKEWISE, BUXTON! ··· WHA'VE WE GOT?
HERE, OLD BOY! TRY SOME CUSTARD PIE!
SKWISH!
HUCK BUXTON! YOU DID IT AGAIN!
NOW WE'RE IN FOR IT! I'LL GET THE FIRST-AID KIT! WANDA, CALL THE POLICE!
HAW! SEGUED INTO THAT ONE! HAVE YOU TRIED THE CHEESECAKE!
SPLAT
HO! THERE'S ONE ON ME!
-RON, PHONE THE HOSPITAL, AND-
NO HARD FEELINGS? -SHAKE!
BZZT!
WAH! WHATA DELIGH'FUL FELLOW!
NO HAR' FEELIN'S. S'EP A LI'L CLOSER-
SPRITZ!
HA ··· BATT-BARTON, YOU'RE TOP DRAWER!
···WELL CAN YOU BEAT THAT! THEY'RE ACTUALLY ENJOYING IT!
DELIGH'FUL FELLOW, THAT HUCK BUXTON! GOOD TO HAVE HIM ONNA TEAM! YO-HO-HO! MERRY EXMUS-
WHY CAN'T PEOPLE BE GOOD SPORTS LIKE THIS ALL YEAR ROUND?
JINGLE BELLS! ALL THE WAY JINGLE! OH, WHAT FUN IT IS RIDING-
MERRY CHRISTMAS, GENERAL!
OHOHO! WHAT DELIGH'FUL SINGUM! HERE, MY GOOD MAN ··· SHAKE ALL OF ISS MONEY AN' SPIT-BALL IT TO THE BUSHER SHOP ONNA CORNER! I WANT YOU TO BUY THE BIG PRIZHE TURKEY INNA WINDOW AN' SHAKE IT HUM TO SHINY SHIM!
OH, BENTON··· YOU'RE SWEET!
BLIND VET

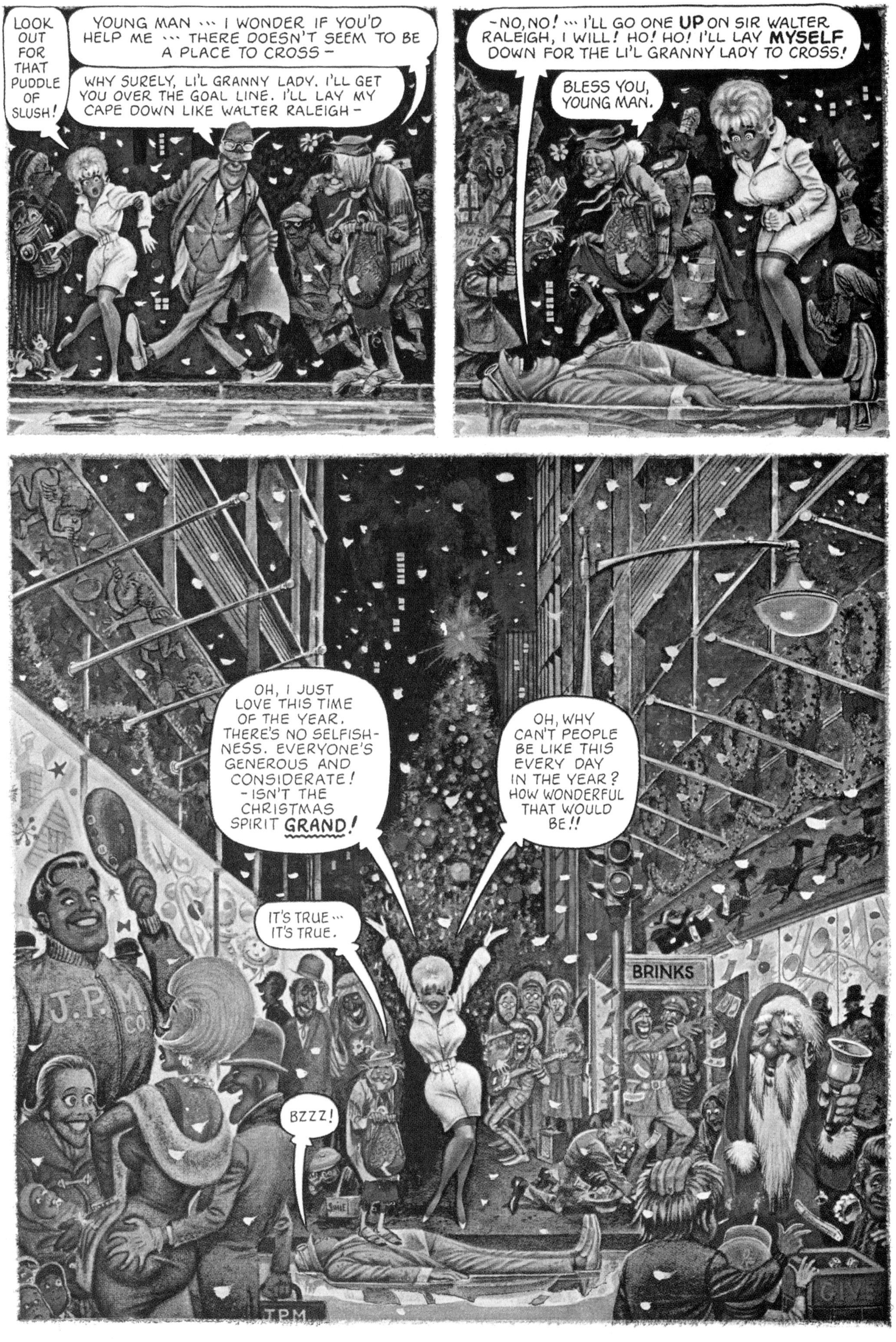

LOOK OUT FOR THAT PUDDLE OF SLUSH!
YOUNG MAN ··· I WONDER IF YOU'D HELP ME ··· THERE DOESN'T SEEM TO BE A PLACE TO CROSS –
WHY SURELY, LI'L GRANNY LADY. I'LL GET YOU OVER THE GOAL LINE. I'LL LAY MY CAPE DOWN LIKE WALTER RALEIGH –
– NO, NO! ··· I'LL GO ONE UP ON SIR WALTER RALEIGH, I WILL! HO! HO! I'LL LAY MYSELF DOWN FOR THE LI'L GRANNY LADY TO CROSS!
BLESS YOU, YOUNG MAN.
OH, I JUST LOVE THIS TIME OF THE YEAR. THERE'S NO SELFISHNESS. EVERYONE'S GENEROUS AND CONSIDERATE! – ISN'T THE CHRISTMAS SPIRIT GRAND!
OH, WHY CAN'T PEOPLE BE LIKE THIS EVERY DAY IN THE YEAR? HOW WONDERFUL THAT WOULD BE!!
IT'S TRUE ··· IT'S TRUE.
BZZZ!
J.P.M. CO.
BRINKS

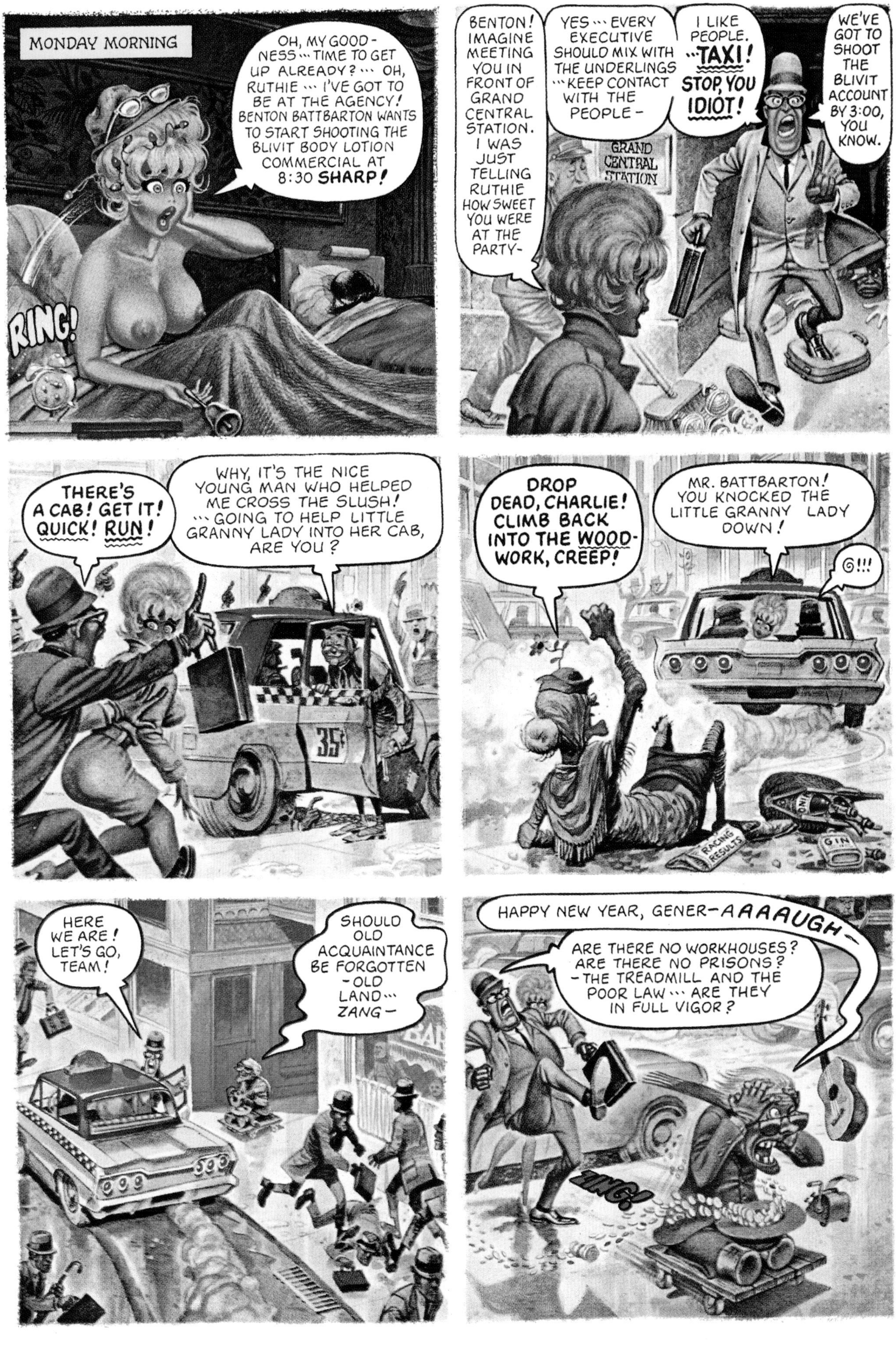
MONDAY MORNING
OH, MY GOODNESS ··· TIME TO GET UP ALREADY? ··· OH, RUTHIE ··· I'VE GOT TO BE AT THE AGENCY! BENTON BATTBARTON WANTS TO START SHOOTING THE BLIVIT BODY LOTION COMMERCIAL AT 8:30 SHARP!
RING!
BENTON! IMAGINE MEETING YOU IN FRONT OF GRAND CENTRAL STATION. I WAS JUST TELLING RUTHIE HOW SWEET YOU WERE AT THE PARTY-
YES ··· EVERY EXECUTIVE SHOULD MIX WITH THE UNDERLINGS ··· KEEP CONTACT WITH THE PEOPLE-
I LIKE PEOPLE. ··TAXI! STOP, YOU IDIOT!
WE'VE GOT TO SHOOT THE BLIVIT ACCOUNT BY 3:00, YOU KNOW.
GRAND CENTRAL STATION
THERE'S A CAB! GET IT! QUICK! RUN!
WHY, IT'S THE NICE YOUNG MAN WHO HELPED ME CROSS THE SLUSH! ··· GOING TO HELP LITTLE GRANNY LADY INTO HER CAB, ARE YOU?
35¢
DROP DEAD, CHARLIE! CLIMB BACK INTO THE WOODWORK, CREEP!
MR. BATTBARTON! YOU KNOCKED THE LITTLE GRANNY LADY DOWN!
G!!!
RACING RESULTS
GIN
HERE WE ARE! LET'S GO, TEAM!
SHOULD OLD ACQUAINTANCE BE FORGOTTEN -OLD LAND··· ZANG-
HAPPY NEW YEAR, GENER-AAAAUGH-
ARE THERE NO WORKHOUSES? ARE THERE NO PRISONS? -THE TREADMILL AND THE POOR LAW ··· ARE THEY IN FULL VIGOR?
ZING!

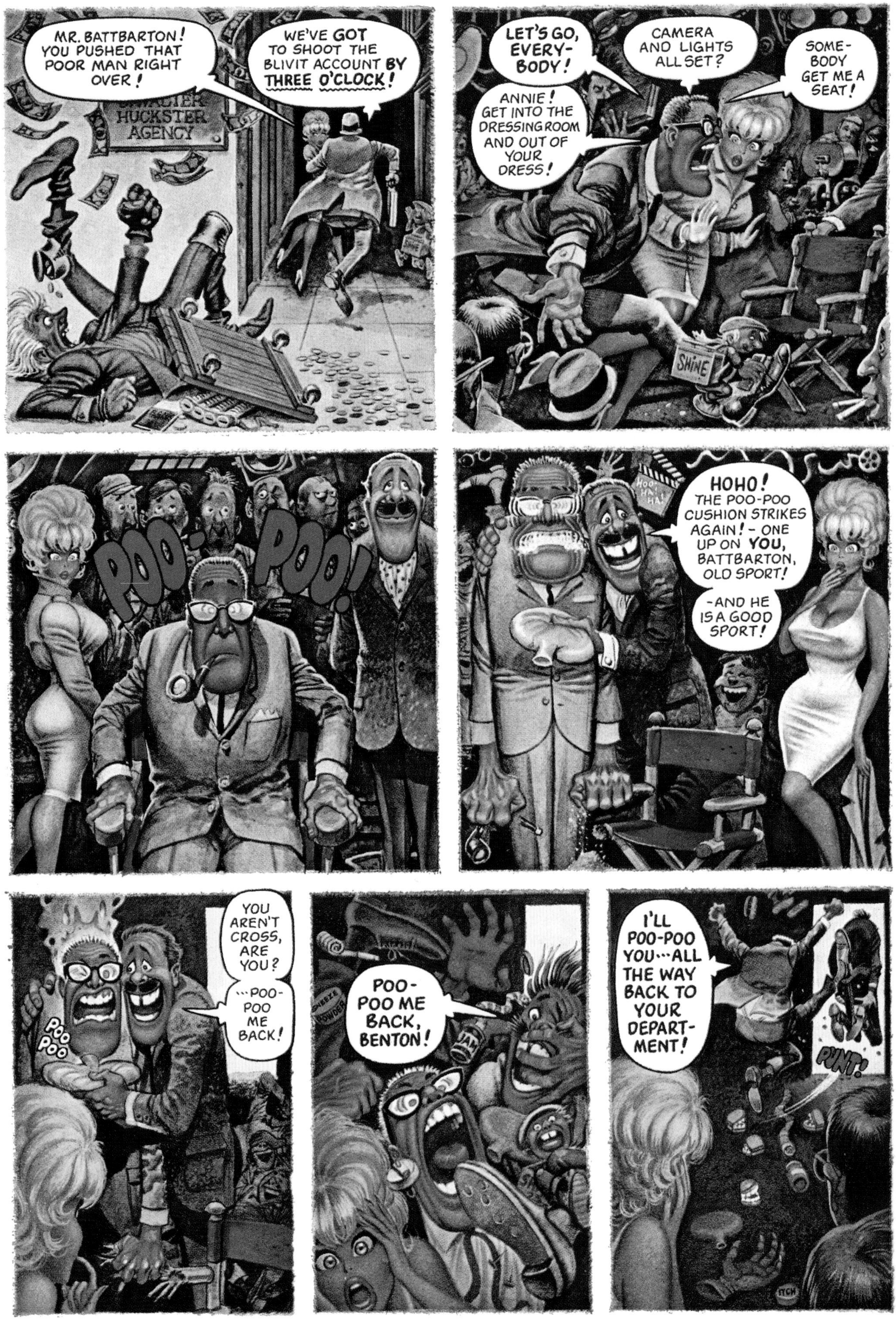

MR. BATTBARTON! YOU PUSHED THAT POOR MAN RIGHT OVER!
WE'VE GOT TO SHOOT THE BLIVIT ACCOUNT BY THREE O'CLOCK!
HUCKSTER AGENCY
LET'S GO, EVERY-BODY!
ANNIE! GET INTO THE DRESSING ROOM AND OUT OF YOUR DRESS!
CAMERA AND LIGHTS ALL SET?
SOME-BODY GET ME A SEAT!
SHINE
POO-POO!
HOHO! THE POO-POO CUSHION STRIKES AGAIN! - ONE UP ON YOU, BATTBARTON, OLD SPORT!
-AND HE IS A GOOD SPORT!
YOU AREN'T CROSS, ARE YOU?
...POO-POO ME BACK!
POO POO
POO-POO ME BACK, BENTON!
I'LL POO-POO YOU... ALL THE WAY BACK TO YOUR DEPART-MENT!
PUNT!

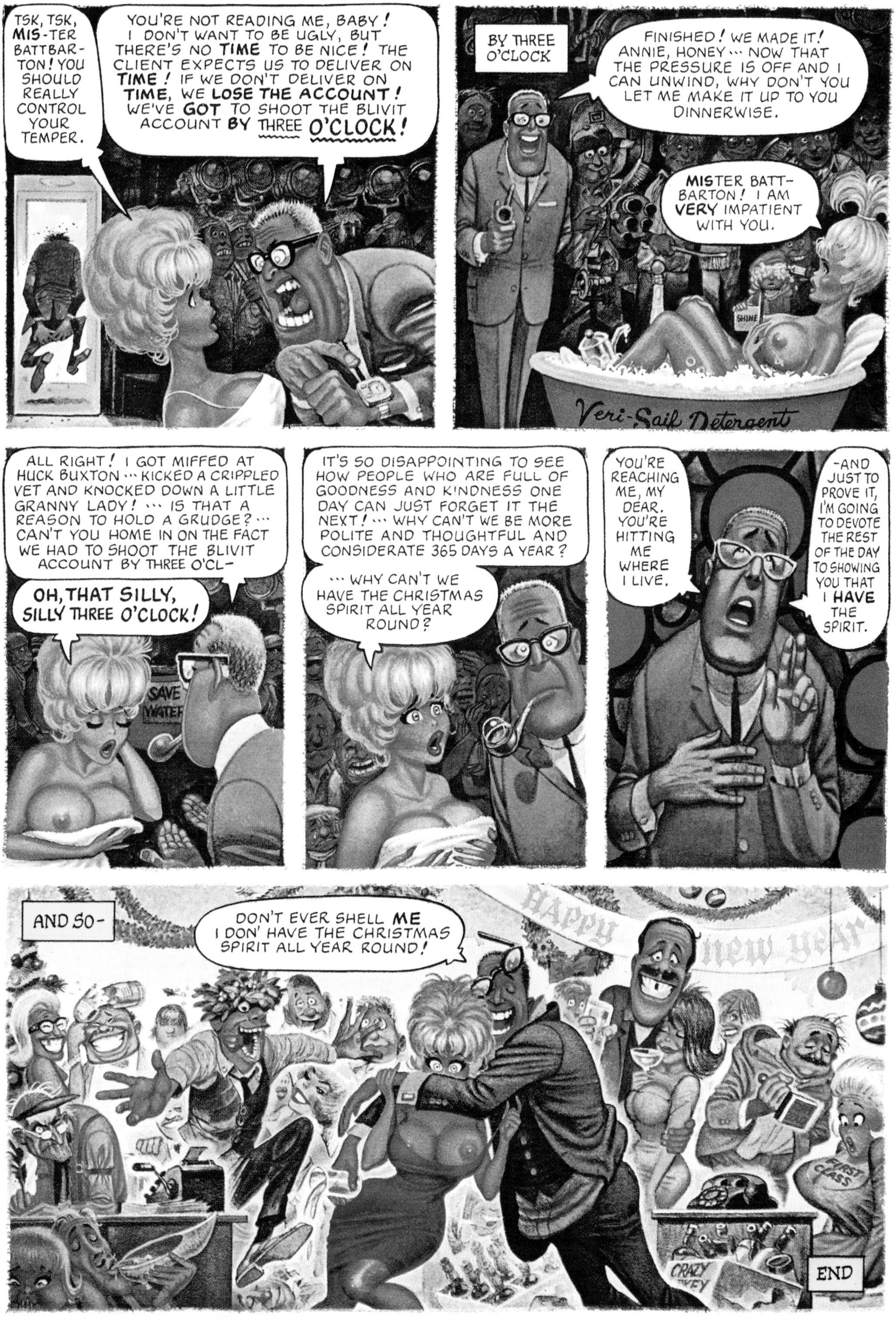

TSK, TSK, MIS-TER BATTBARTON! YOU SHOULD REALLY CONTROL YOUR TEMPER.
YOU'RE NOT READING ME, BABY! I DON'T WANT TO BE UGLY, BUT THERE'S NO TIME TO BE NICE! THE CLIENT EXPECTS US TO DELIVER ON TIME! IF WE DON'T DELIVER ON TIME, WE LOSE THE ACCOUNT! WE'VE GOT TO SHOOT THE BLIVIT ACCOUNT BY THREE O'CLOCK!
BY THREE O'CLOCK
FINISHED! WE MADE IT! ANNIE, HONEY ··· NOW THAT THE PRESSURE IS OFF AND I CAN UNWIND, WHY DON'T YOU LET ME MAKE IT UP TO YOU DINNERWISE.
MISTER BATT-BARTON! I AM VERY IMPATIENT WITH YOU.
SHINE
Veri-Sail Detergent
ALL RIGHT! I GOT MIFFED AT HUCK BUXTON ··· KICKED A CRIPPLED VET AND KNOCKED DOWN A LITTLE GRANNY LADY! ··· IS THAT A REASON TO HOLD A GRUDGE? ··· CAN'T YOU HOME IN ON THE FACT WE HAD TO SHOOT THE BLIVIT ACCOUNT BY THREE O'CL-
OH, THAT SILLY, SILLY THREE O'CLOCK!
SAVE WATER
IT'S SO DISAPPOINTING TO SEE HOW PEOPLE WHO ARE FULL OF GOODNESS AND KINDNESS ONE DAY CAN JUST FORGET IT THE NEXT! ··· WHY CAN'T WE BE MORE POLITE AND THOUGHTFUL AND CONSIDERATE 365 DAYS A YEAR?
··· WHY CAN'T WE HAVE THE CHRISTMAS SPIRIT ALL YEAR ROUND?
YOU'RE REACHING ME, MY DEAR. YOU'RE HITTING ME WHERE I LIVE.
-AND JUST TO PROVE IT, I'M GOING TO DEVOTE THE REST OF THE DAY TO SHOWING YOU THAT I HAVE THE SPIRIT.
AND SO-
DON'T EVER SHELL ME I DON' HAVE THE CHRISTMAS SPIRIT ALL YEAR ROUND!
HAPPY new year
FIRST CLASS
CRAZY
END

114

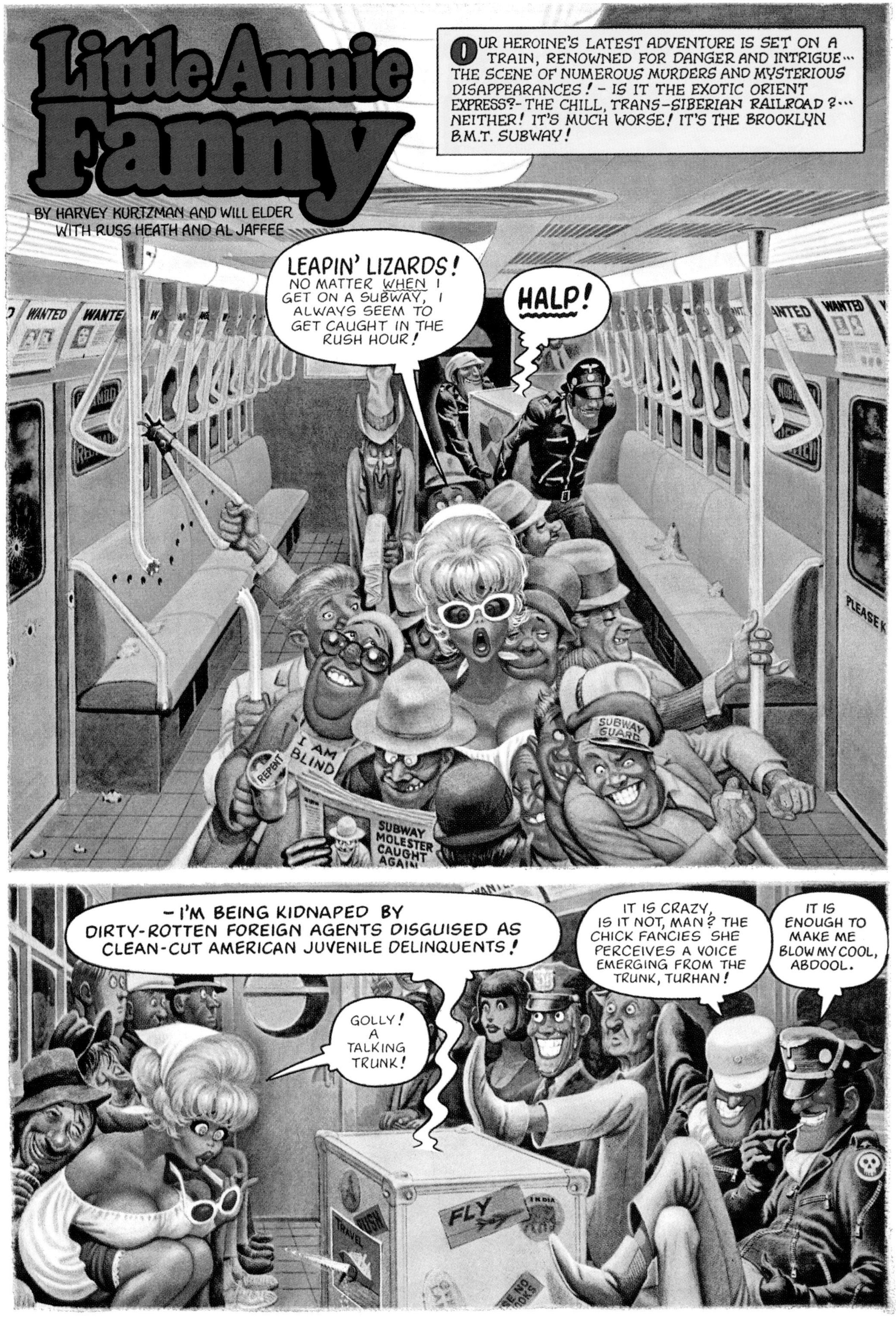
Little Annie Fanny
OUR HEROINE'S LATEST ADVENTURE IS SET ON A TRAIN, RENOWNED FOR DANGER AND INTRIGUE... THE SCENE OF NUMEROUS MURDERS AND MYSTERIOUS DISAPPEARANCES! - IS IT THE EXOTIC ORIENT EXPRESS?- THE CHILL, TRANS-SIBERIAN RAILROAD?... NEITHER! IT'S MUCH WORSE! IT'S THE BROOKLYN B.M.T. SUBWAY!
BY HARVEY KURTZMAN AND WILL ELDER WITH RUSS HEATH AND AL JAFFEE
LEAPIN' LIZARDS! NO MATTER WHEN I GET ON A SUBWAY, I ALWAYS SEEM TO GET CAUGHT IN THE RUSH HOUR!
HALP!
WANTED
I AM BLIND
REPENT
SUBWAY GUARD
SUBWAY MOLESTER CAUGHT AGAIN
-I'M BEING KIDNAPED BY DIRTY-ROTTEN FOREIGN AGENTS DISGUISED AS CLEAN-CUT AMERICAN JUVENILE DELINQUENTS!
GOLLY! A TALKING TRUNK!
IT IS CRAZY, IS IT NOT, MAN? THE CHICK FANCIES SHE PERCEIVES A VOICE EMERGING FROM THE TRUNK, TURHAN!
IT IS ENOUGH TO MAKE ME BLOW MY COOL, ABDOOL.
FLY
INDIA
TRAVEL

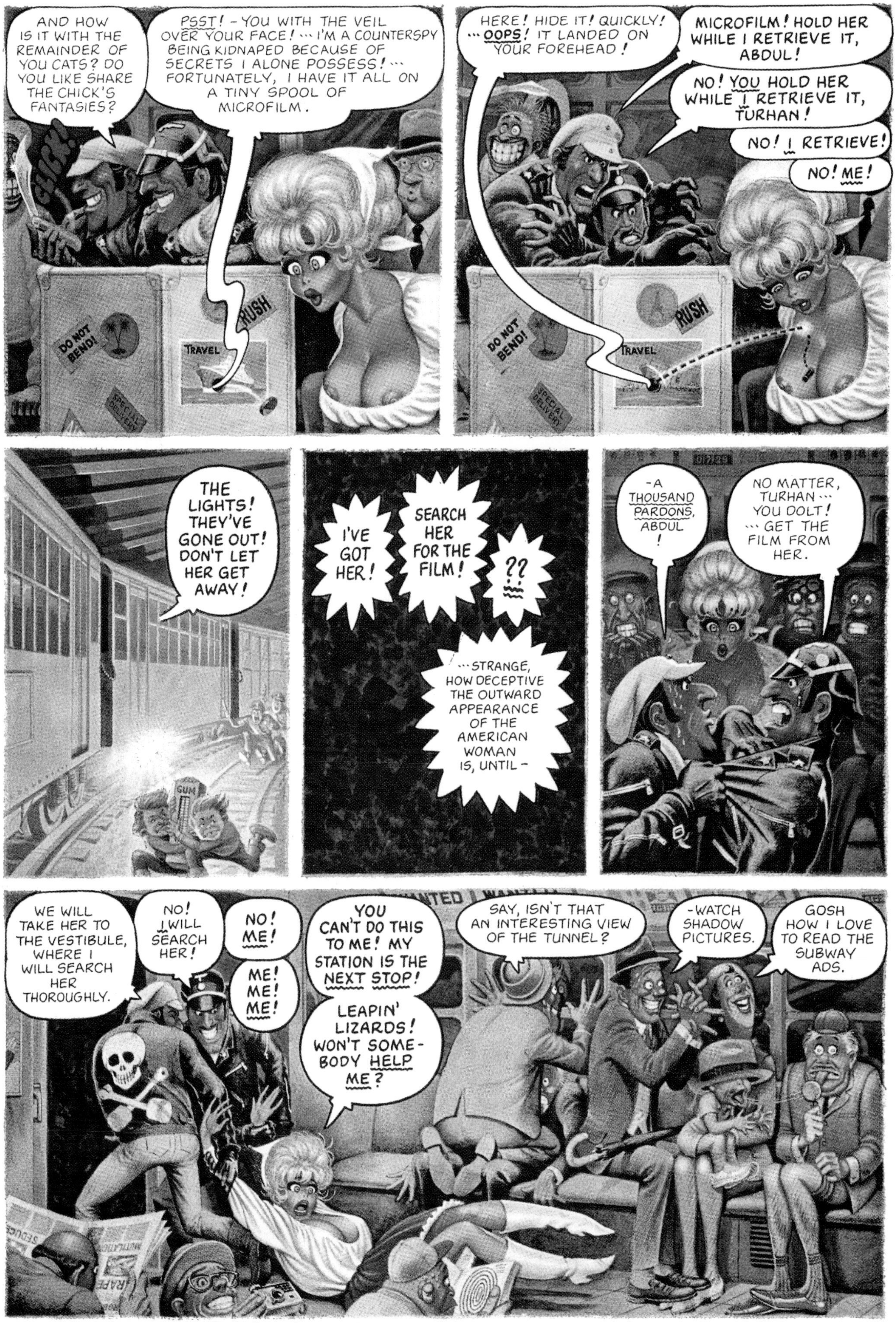
AND HOW IS IT WITH THE REMAINDER OF YOU CATS? DO YOU LIKE SHARE THE CHICK'S FANTASIES?
CLICK!
PSST! - YOU WITH THE VEIL OVER YOUR FACE! ··· I'M A COUNTERSPY BEING KIDNAPED BECAUSE OF SECRETS I ALONE POSSESS! ··· FORTUNATELY, I HAVE IT ALL ON A TINY SPOOL OF MICROFILM.
DO NOT BEND!
RUSH
TRAVEL
SPECIAL DELIVERY
HERE! HIDE IT! QUICKLY! ··· OOPS! IT LANDED ON YOUR FOREHEAD!
MICROFILM! HOLD HER WHILE I RETRIEVE IT, ABDUL!
NO! YOU HOLD HER WHILE I RETRIEVE IT, TURHAN!
NO! I RETRIEVE!
NO! ME!
DO NOT BEND!
RUSH
TRAVEL
SPECIAL DELIVERY
THE LIGHTS! THEY'VE GONE OUT! DON'T LET HER GET AWAY!
GUM
I'VE GOT HER!
SEARCH HER FOR THE FILM!
??
··· STRANGE, HOW DECEPTIVE THE OUTWARD APPEARANCE OF THE AMERICAN WOMAN IS, UNTIL -
-A THOUSAND PARDONS, ABDUL!
NO MATTER, TURHAN ··· YOU DOLT! ··· GET THE FILM FROM HER.
WE WILL TAKE HER TO THE VESTIBULE, WHERE I WILL SEARCH HER THOROUGHLY.
NO! I WILL SEARCH HER!
NO! ME!
ME! ME! ME!
YOU CAN'T DO THIS TO ME! MY STATION IS THE NEXT STOP!
LEAPIN' LIZARDS! WON'T SOMEBODY HELP ME?
SAY, ISN'T THAT AN INTERESTING VIEW OF THE TUNNEL?
-WATCH SHADOW PICTURES.
GOSH HOW I LOVE TO READ THE SUBWAY ADS.
RAPE

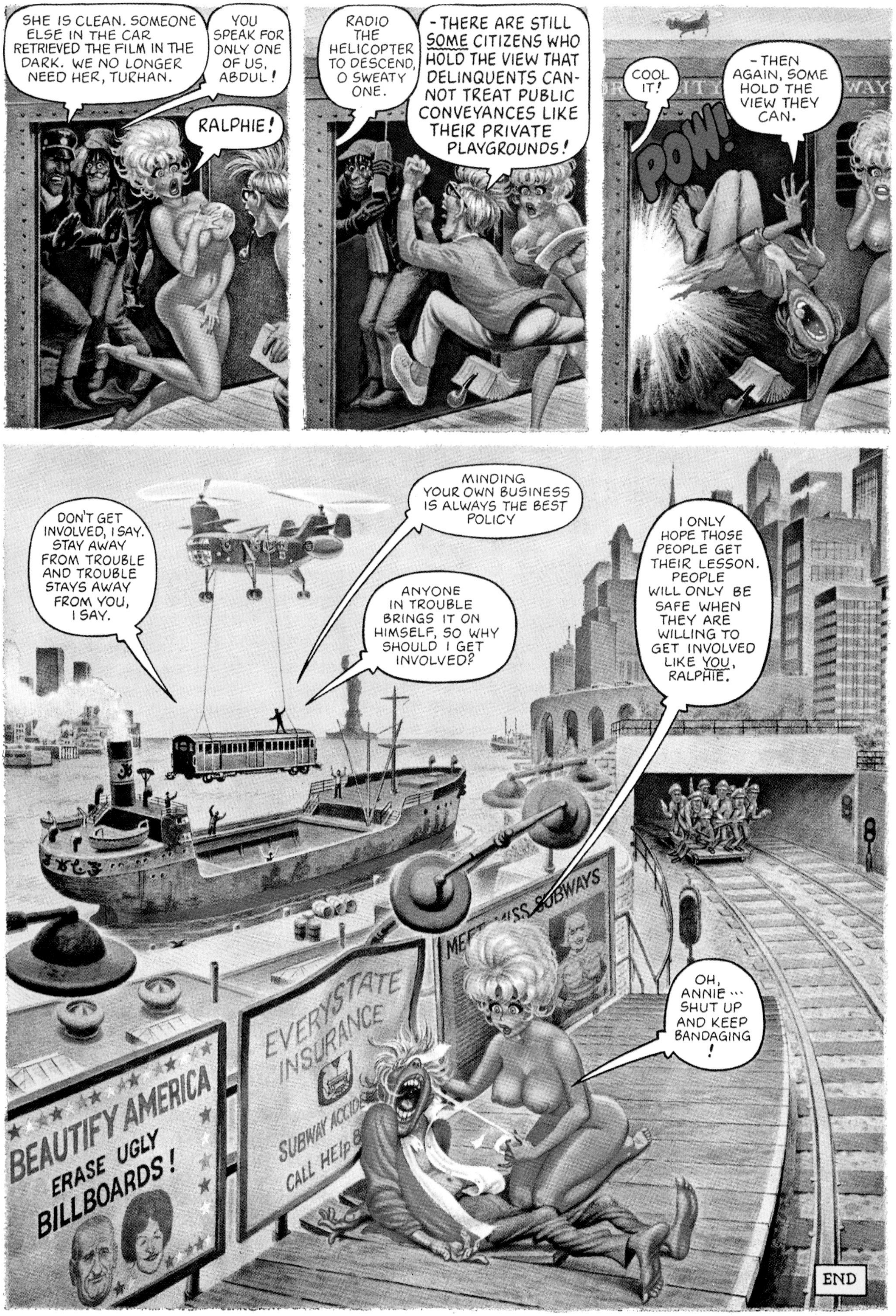
SHE IS CLEAN. SOMEONE ELSE IN THE CAR RETRIEVED THE FILM IN THE DARK. WE NO LONGER NEED HER, TURHAN.
YOU SPEAK FOR ONLY ONE OF US, ABDUL!
RALPHIE!
RADIO THE HELICOPTER TO DESCEND, O SWEATY ONE.
-THERE ARE STILL SOME CITIZENS WHO HOLD THE VIEW THAT DELINQUENTS CAN-NOT TREAT PUBLIC CONVEYANCES LIKE THEIR PRIVATE PLAYGROUNDS!
COOL IT!
-THEN AGAIN, SOME HOLD THE VIEW THEY CAN.
POW!
DON'T GET INVOLVED, I SAY. STAY AWAY FROM TROUBLE AND TROUBLE STAYS AWAY FROM YOU, I SAY.
MINDING YOUR OWN BUSINESS IS ALWAYS THE BEST POLICY
ANYONE IN TROUBLE BRINGS IT ON HIMSELF, SO WHY SHOULD I GET INVOLVED?
I ONLY HOPE THOSE PEOPLE GET THEIR LESSON. PEOPLE WILL ONLY BE SAFE WHEN THEY ARE WILLING TO GET INVOLVED LIKE YOU, RALPHIE.
OH, ANNIE... SHUT UP AND KEEP BANDAGING!
EVERYSTATE INSURANCE
BEAUTIFY AMERICA
ERASE UGLY BILLBOARDS!
END

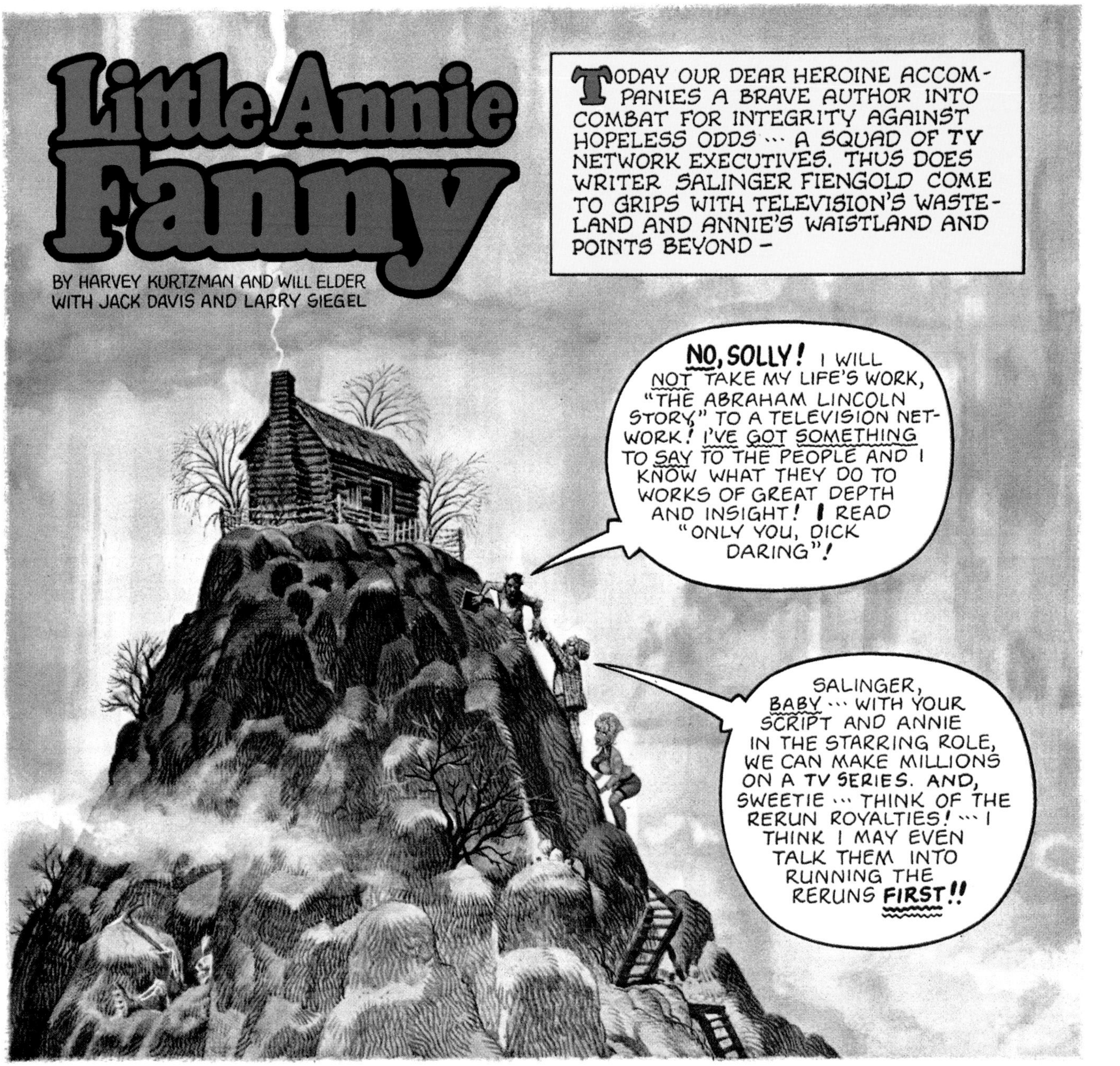
Little Annie Fanny
BY HARVEY KURTZMAN AND WILL ELDER WITH JACK DAVIS AND LARRY SIEGEL
TODAY OUR DEAR HEROINE ACCOMPANIES A BRAVE AUTHOR INTO COMBAT FOR INTEGRITY AGAINST HOPELESS ODDS ··· A SQUAD OF TV NETWORK EXECUTIVES. THUS DOES WRITER SALINGER FIENGOLD COME TO GRIPS WITH TELEVISION'S WASTELAND AND ANNIE'S WAISTLAND AND POINTS BEYOND –
NO, SOLLY! I WILL NOT TAKE MY LIFE'S WORK, "THE ABRAHAM LINCOLN STORY," TO A TELEVISION NETWORK! I'VE GOT SOMETHING TO SAY TO THE PEOPLE AND I KNOW WHAT THEY DO TO WORKS OF GREAT DEPTH AND INSIGHT! I READ "ONLY YOU, DICK DARING"!
SALINGER, BABY ··· WITH YOUR SCRIPT AND ANNIE IN THE STARRING ROLE, WE CAN MAKE MILLIONS ON A TV SERIES. AND, SWEETIE ··· THINK OF THE RERUN ROYALTIES! ··· I THINK I MAY EVEN TALK THEM INTO RUNNING THE RERUNS FIRST!!

117

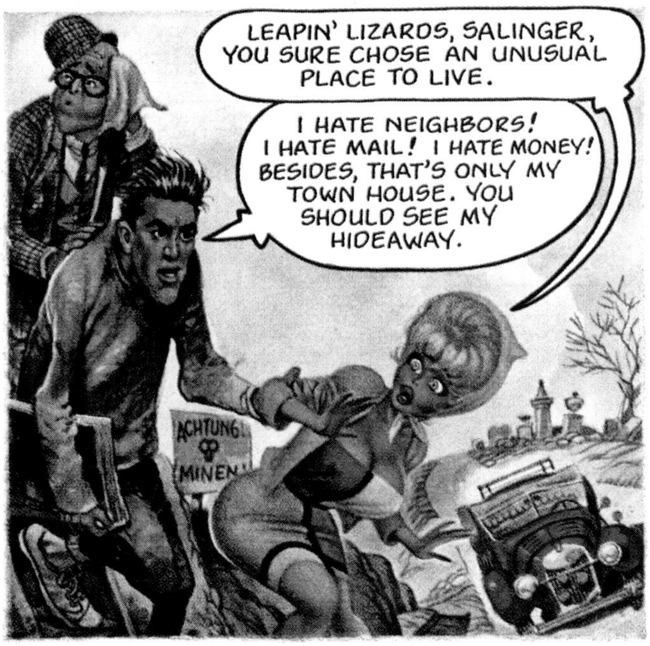
LEAPIN' LIZARDS, SALINGER, YOU SURE CHOSE AN UNUSUAL PLACE TO LIVE.
I HATE NEIGHBORS! I HATE MAIL! I HATE MONEY! BESIDES, THAT'S ONLY MY TOWN HOUSE. YOU SHOULD SEE MY HIDEAWAY.
ACHTUNG! MINEN

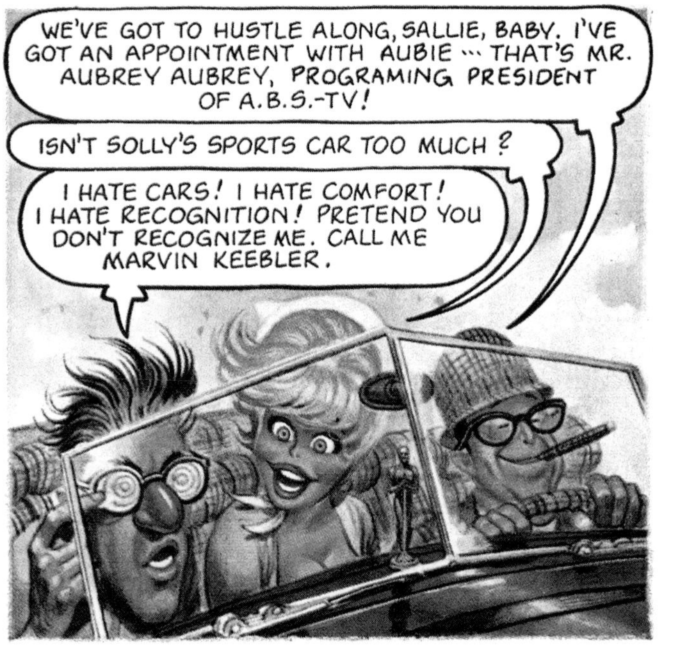
WE'VE GOT TO HUSTLE ALONG, SALLIE, BABY. I'VE GOT AN APPOINTMENT WITH AUBIE ··· THAT'S MR. AUBREY AUBREY, PROGRAMING PRESIDENT OF A.B.S.-TV!
ISN'T SOLLY'S SPORTS CAR TOO MUCH?
I HATE CARS! I HATE COMFORT! I HATE RECOGNITION! PRETEND YOU DON'T RECOGNIZE ME. CALL ME MARVIN KEEBLER.

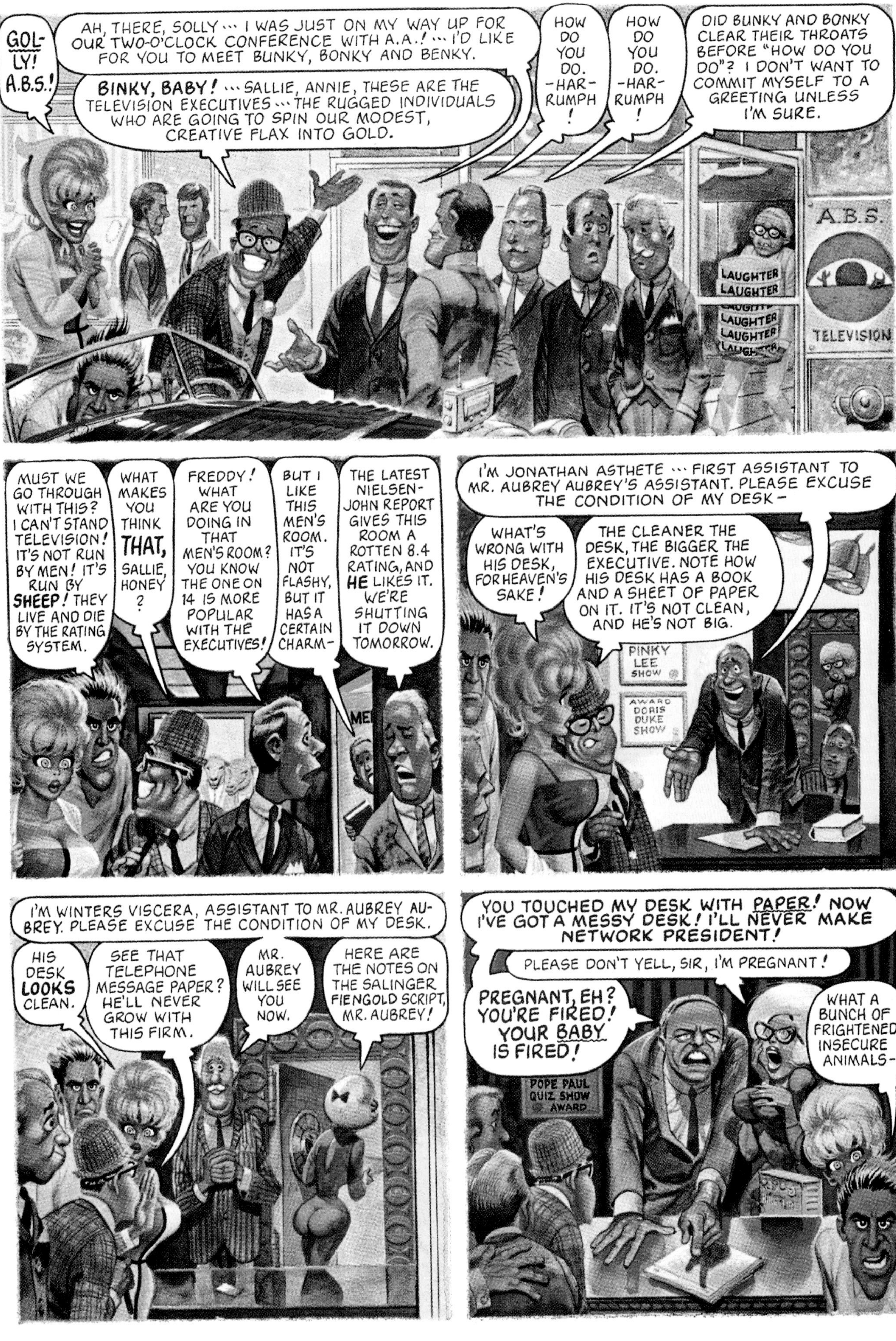
GOL-LY! A.B.S.!
AH, THERE, SOLLY ··· I WAS JUST ON MY WAY UP FOR OUR TWO-O'CLOCK CONFERENCE WITH A.A.! ··· I'D LIKE FOR YOU TO MEET BUNKY, BONKY AND BENKY.
BINKY, BABY! ··· SALLIE, ANNIE, THESE ARE THE TELEVISION EXECUTIVES ··· THE RUGGED INDIVIDUALS WHO ARE GOING TO SPIN OUR MODEST, CREATIVE FLAX INTO GOLD.
HOW DO YOU DO. -HAR-RUMPH!
HOW DO YOU DO. -HAR-RUMPH!
DID BUNKY AND BONKY CLEAR THEIR THROATS BEFORE "HOW DO YOU DO"? I DON'T WANT TO COMMIT MYSELF TO A GREETING UNLESS I'M SURE.
LAUGHTER
LAUGHTER
LAUGHTER
LAUGHTER
A.B.S.
TELEVISION
MUST WE GO THROUGH WITH THIS? I CAN'T STAND TELEVISION! IT'S NOT RUN BY MEN! IT'S RUN BY SHEEP! THEY LIVE AND DIE BY THE RATING SYSTEM.
WHAT MAKES YOU THINK THAT, SALLIE, HONEY?
FREDDY! WHAT ARE YOU DOING IN THAT MEN'S ROOM? YOU KNOW THE ONE ON 14 IS MORE POPULAR WITH THE EXECUTIVES!
BUT I LIKE THIS MEN'S ROOM. IT'S NOT FLASHY, BUT IT HAS A CERTAIN CHARM-
THE LATEST NIELSEN-JOHN REPORT GIVES THIS ROOM A ROTTEN 8.4 RATING, AND HE LIKES IT. WE'RE SHUTTING IT DOWN TOMORROW.
I'M JONATHAN ASTHETE ··· FIRST ASSISTANT TO MR. AUBREY AUBREY'S ASSISTANT. PLEASE EXCUSE THE CONDITION OF MY DESK-
WHAT'S WRONG WITH HIS DESK, FOR HEAVEN'S SAKE!
THE CLEANER THE DESK, THE BIGGER THE EXECUTIVE. NOTE HOW HIS DESK HAS A BOOK AND A SHEET OF PAPER ON IT. IT'S NOT CLEAN, AND HE'S NOT BIG.
PINKY LEE SHOW
AWARD DORIS DUKE SHOW
I'M WINTERS VISCERA, ASSISTANT TO MR. AUBREY AUBREY. PLEASE EXCUSE THE CONDITION OF MY DESK.
HIS DESK LOOKS CLEAN.
SEE THAT TELEPHONE MESSAGE PAPER? HE'LL NEVER GROW WITH THIS FIRM.
MR. AUBREY WILL SEE YOU NOW.
HERE ARE THE NOTES ON THE SALINGER FIENGOLD SCRIPT, MR. AUBREY!
YOU TOUCHED MY DESK WITH PAPER! NOW I'VE GOT A MESSY DESK! I'LL NEVER MAKE NETWORK PRESIDENT!
PLEASE DON'T YELL, SIR, I'M PREGNANT!
PREGNANT, EH? YOU'RE FIRED! YOUR BABY IS FIRED!
WHAT A BUNCH OF FRIGHTENED INSECURE ANIMALS-
POPE PAUL QUIZ SHOW AWARD

HE CALLED US FRIGHTENED INSECURE ANIMALS!

YOU SHOULDN'T REPEAT SUCH NONSENSE, VISCERA... **YOU'RE FIRED!**

-WAIT A MINUTE. DIDN'T I FIRE YOU YESTERDAY?

NO, A.A.! YOU FIRED ME, NOT HIM, BUT THEN YOU HIRED ME AGAIN!

IN THAT CASE, **YOU! YOU'RE** FIRED!

YOU CAN'T FIRE ME. I DON'T WORK FOR YOU. I DELIVER COFFEE.

I LIKE A FIGHTER. I HEREBY HIRE YOU AND **NOW** I FIRE YOU.

MR. AUBREY... THIS IS SALINGER FIENGOLD, AND THIS IS THE STAR OF OUR PROPOSED TV SERIES. I TRUST YOU READ HIS MASTERPIECE.

MY ASSISTANT'S ASSISTANT READ IT, AND CUT IT DOWN TO A ONE-PAGE OUTLINE, THEN **MY** ASSISTANT CUT THAT DOWN TO A ONE-PARAGRAPH OUTLINE. THEN MY SECRETARY CUT THAT DOWN TO ONE WORD... "ABRAHAM"! I READ THAT WORD, AND I LIKE IT. I SEE A GREAT, WARM TV SERIES BUILT AROUND THIS MAN... HIS RISE TO GOVERNOR... THEN SENATOR FROM CONNECTICUT, AND THEN—

119

NO, MR. AUBREY, BABY... THIS IS **ABE LINCOLN**, NOT ABE **RIBICOFF!**

LINCOLN! I LIKE THAT WORD, I SEE A GREAT TV SERIES SET IN WASHINGTON, D.C., IT'S ABOUT THIS LOVABLE FIRST FAMILY OF MONSTERS. I SEE ANNIE AS A GHOULISH BUT SEXY FIRST LADY. WE'LL CALL THE PRESIDENT "ABE LUNKHEAD." -GET THAT CUTE, NAÏVE TWIST? THE PUBLIC WILL LOVE IT... ESPECIALLY DOWN SOUTH.

BEWARE OF THE THING

WAIT! WAIT! I SEE THIS AS A ROLLICKING COMEDY ON WHAT GREAT FUN IT IS TO BE A PRISONER OF WAR. IT'S CALLED "ABE'S GANG." ABE AND HIS CREW OF HAPPY-GO-LUCKY GENERALS ARE CAPTURED BY THE **REBS** AND FROM THERE ON, IT'S JUST ONE JOKE AFTER ANOTHER... SMUGGLING IN GIRLS... RIOTOUS ESCAPE SCENES – WE'LL CALL THE POW CAMP ANDERSONVILLE... NO! MAKE THAT BLUNDERFUNVILLE!

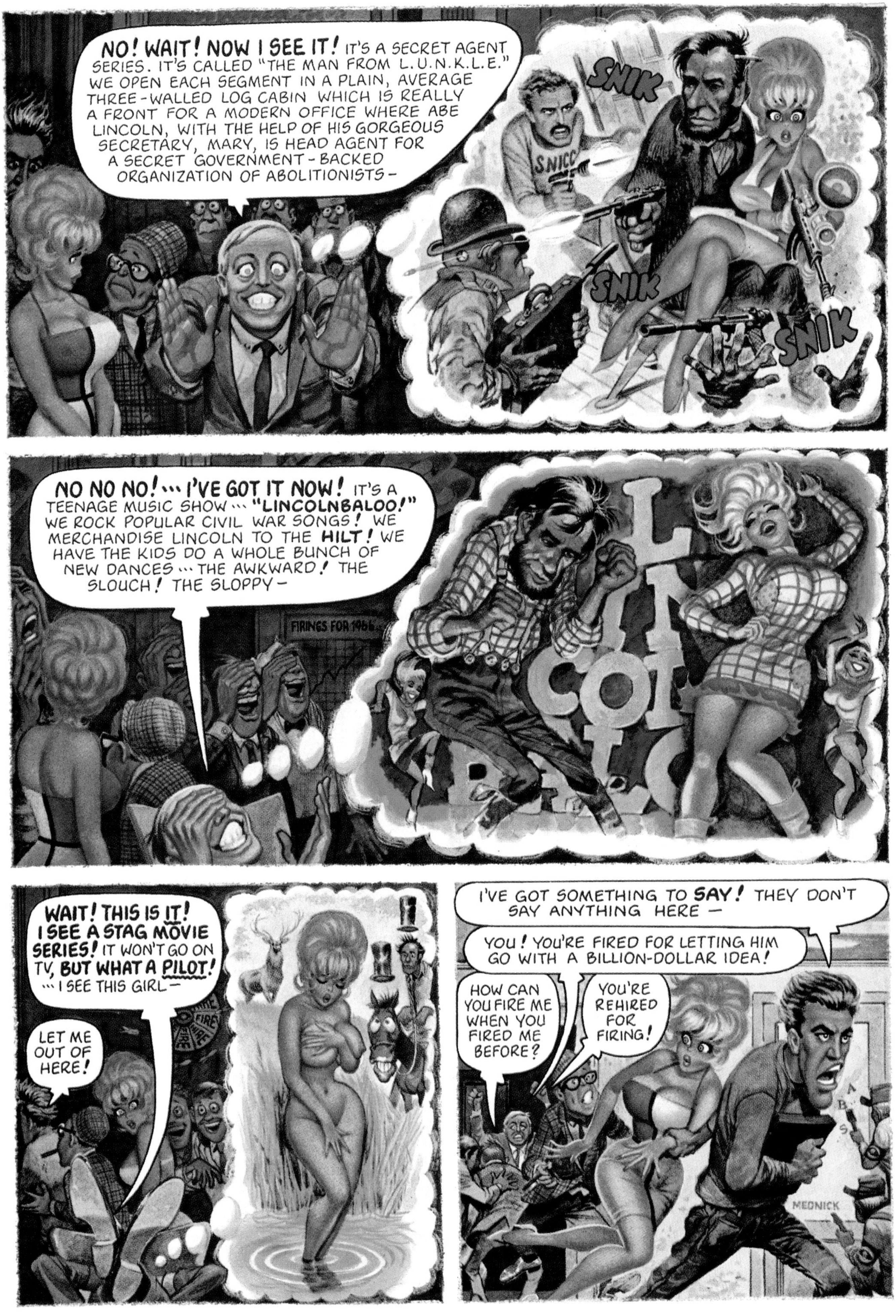

NO! WAIT! NOW I SEE IT! IT'S A SECRET AGENT SERIES. IT'S CALLED "THE MAN FROM L.U.N.K.L.E." WE OPEN EACH SEGMENT IN A PLAIN, AVERAGE THREE-WALLED LOG CABIN WHICH IS REALLY A FRONT FOR A MODERN OFFICE WHERE ABE LINCOLN, WITH THE HELP OF HIS GORGEOUS SECRETARY, MARY, IS HEAD AGENT FOR A SECRET GOVERNMENT-BACKED ORGANIZATION OF ABOLITIONISTS–
SNIK
SNICC
SNIK
SNIK
NO NO NO! ··· I'VE GOT IT NOW! IT'S A TEENAGE MUSIC SHOW ··· "LINCOLNBALOO!" WE ROCK POPULAR CIVIL WAR SONGS! WE MERCHANDISE LINCOLN TO THE HILT! WE HAVE THE KIDS DO A WHOLE BUNCH OF NEW DANCES ··· THE AWKWARD! THE SLOUCH! THE SLOPPY–
FIRINGS FOR 1966
WAIT! THIS IS IT! I SEE A STAG MOVIE SERIES! IT WON'T GO ON TV, BUT WHAT A PILOT! ··· I SEE THIS GIRL–
LET ME OUT OF HERE!
I'VE GOT SOMETHING TO SAY! THEY DON'T SAY ANYTHING HERE –
YOU! YOU'RE FIRED FOR LETTING HIM GO WITH A BILLION-DOLLAR IDEA!
HOW CAN YOU FIRE ME WHEN YOU FIRED ME BEFORE?
YOU'RE REHIRED FOR FIRING!
MEDNICK

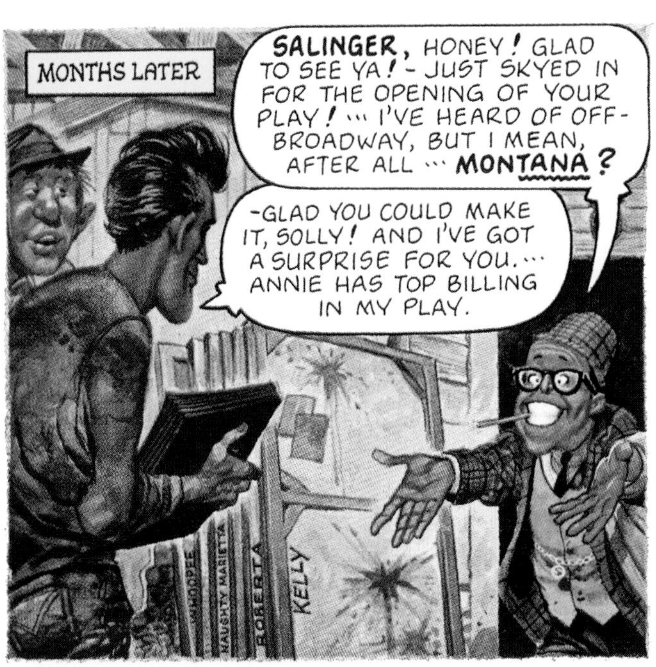
MONTHS LATER
SALINGER, HONEY! GLAD TO SEE YA! - JUST SKYED IN FOR THE OPENING OF YOUR PLAY! ··· I'VE HEARD OF OFF-BROADWAY, BUT I MEAN, AFTER ALL ··· MONTANA?
-GLAD YOU COULD MAKE IT, SOLLY! AND I'VE GOT A SURPRISE FOR YOU.··· ANNIE HAS TOP BILLING IN MY PLAY.
NAUGHTY MARIETTA
ROBERTA
KELLY

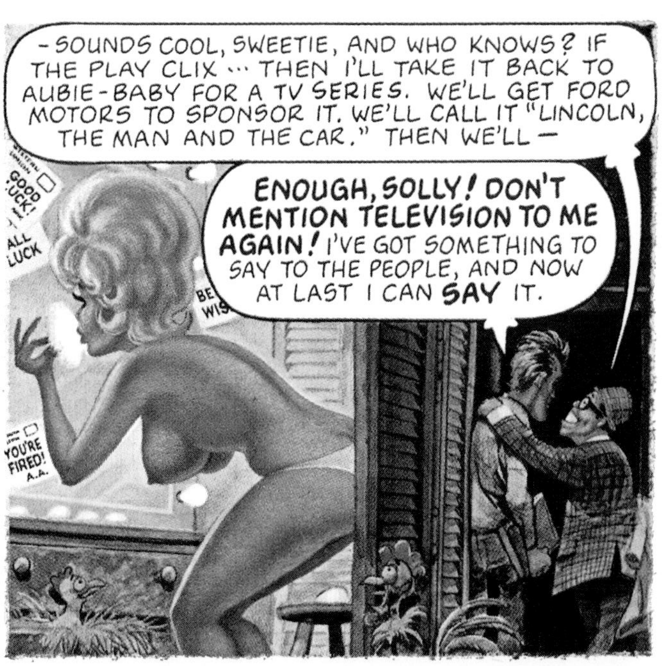
-SOUNDS COOL, SWEETIE, AND WHO KNOWS? IF THE PLAY CLIX ··· THEN I'LL TAKE IT BACK TO AUBIE-BABY FOR A TV SERIES. WE'LL GET FORD MOTORS TO SPONSOR IT. WE'LL CALL IT "LINCOLN, THE MAN AND THE CAR." THEN WE'LL —
ENOUGH, SOLLY! DON'T MENTION TELEVISION TO ME AGAIN! I'VE GOT SOMETHING TO SAY TO THE PEOPLE, AND NOW AT LAST I CAN SAY IT.
GOOD LUCK!
YOU'RE FIRED! A.A.

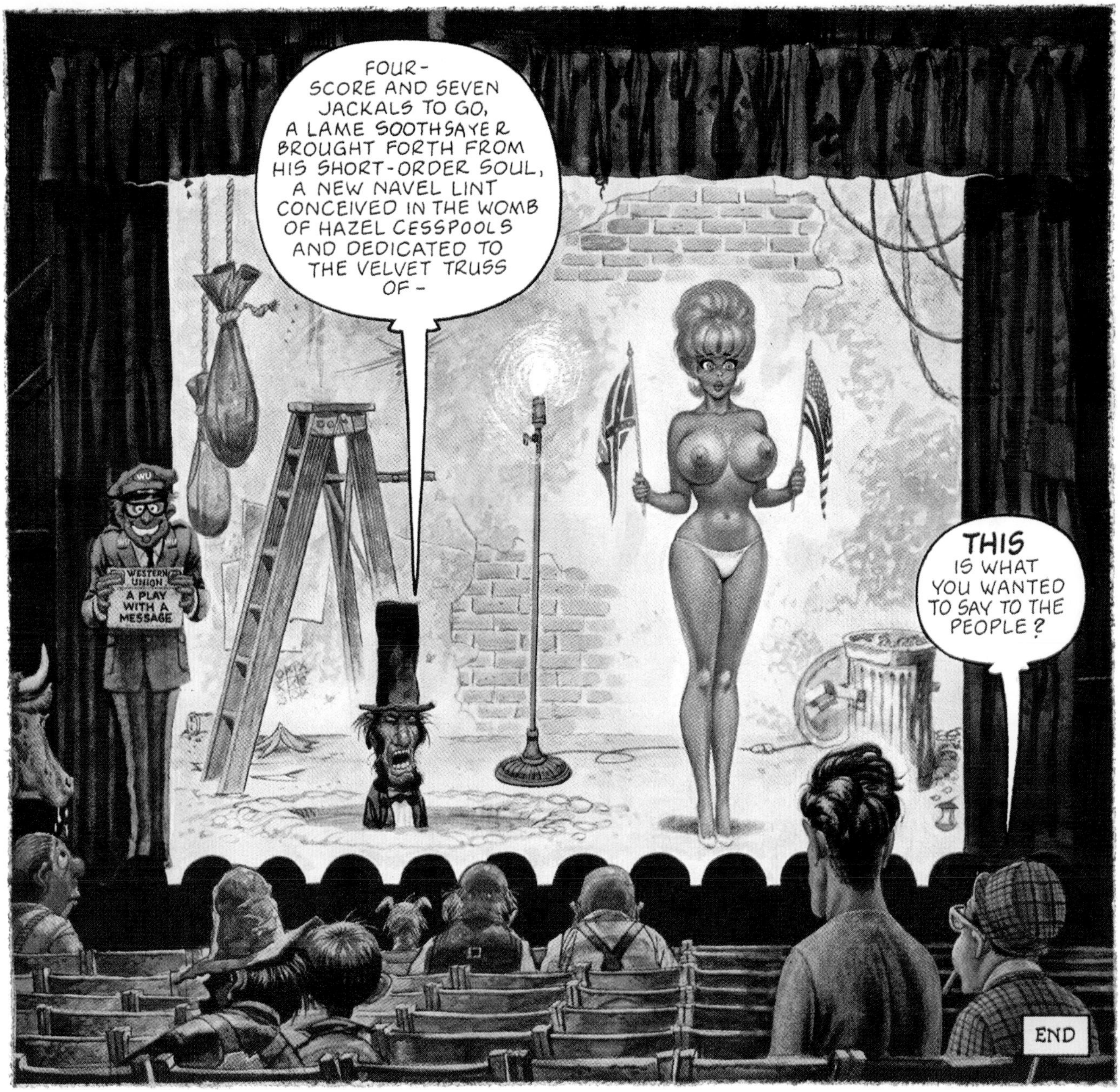
FOUR-SCORE AND SEVEN JACKALS TO GO, A LAME SOOTHSAYER BROUGHT FORTH FROM HIS SHORT-ORDER SOUL, A NEW NAVEL LINT CONCEIVED IN THE WOMB OF HAZEL CESSPOOLS AND DEDICATED TO THE VELVET TRUSS OF -
WESTERN UNION
A PLAY WITH A MESSAGE
THIS IS WHAT YOU WANTED TO SAY TO THE PEOPLE?
END

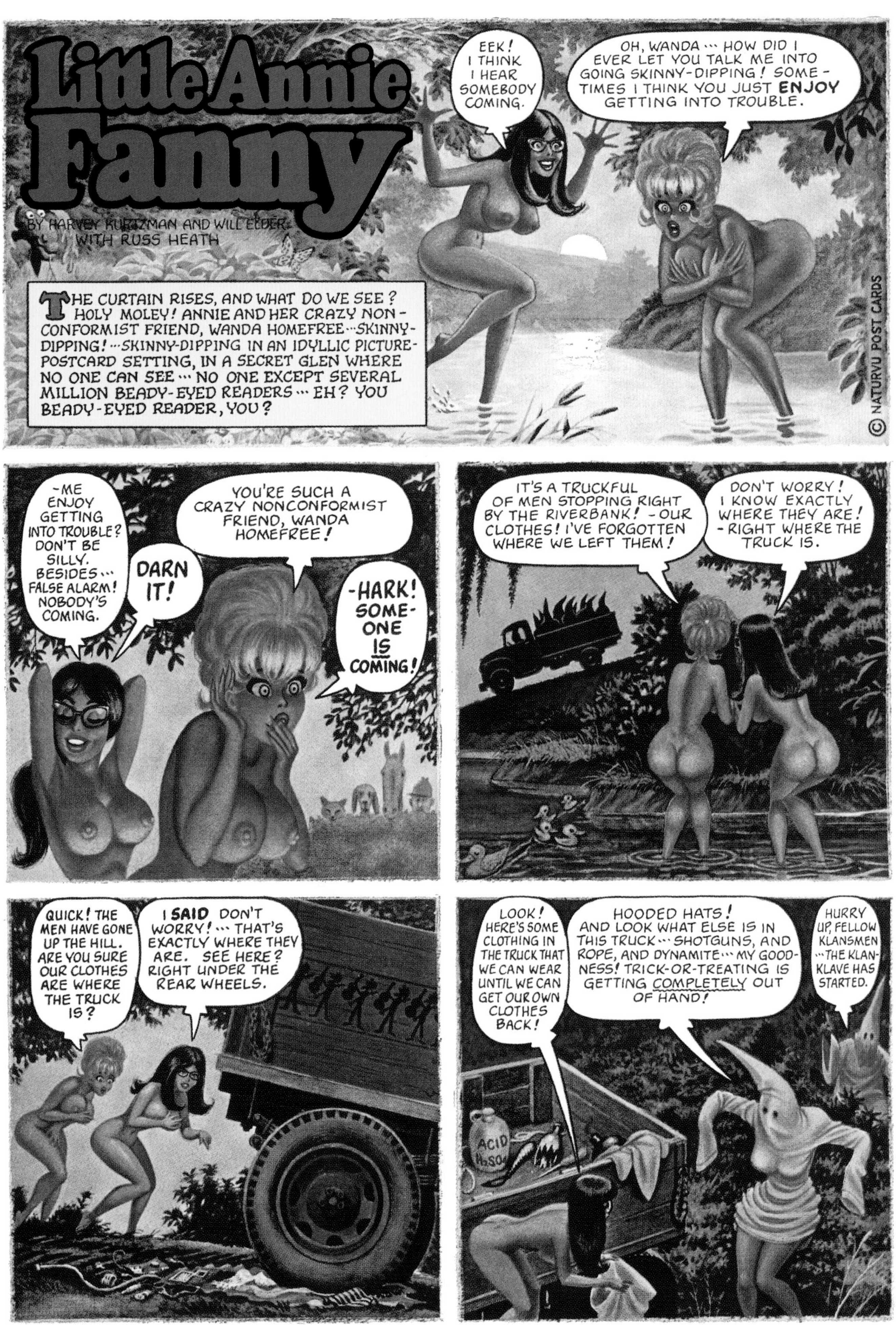

Little Annie Fanny
BY HARVEY KURTZMAN AND WILL ELDER WITH RUSS HEATH
EEK! I THINK I HEAR SOMEBODY COMING.
OH, WANDA ··· HOW DID I EVER LET YOU TALK ME INTO GOING SKINNY-DIPPING! SOMETIMES I THINK YOU JUST ENJOY GETTING INTO TROUBLE.
THE CURTAIN RISES, AND WHAT DO WE SEE? HOLY MOLEY! ANNIE AND HER CRAZY NONCONFORMIST FRIEND, WANDA HOMEFREE···SKINNY-DIPPING!···SKINNY-DIPPING IN AN IDYLLIC PICTURE-POSTCARD SETTING, IN A SECRET GLEN WHERE NO ONE CAN SEE··· NO ONE EXCEPT SEVERAL MILLION BEADY-EYED READERS··· EH? YOU BEADY-EYED READER, YOU?
© NATURVU POST CARDS
-ME ENJOY GETTING INTO TROUBLE? DON'T BE SILLY. BESIDES··· FALSE ALARM! NOBODY'S COMING.
DARN IT!
YOU'RE SUCH A CRAZY NONCONFORMIST FRIEND, WANDA HOMEFREE!
-HARK! SOMEONE IS COMING!
IT'S A TRUCKFUL OF MEN STOPPING RIGHT BY THE RIVERBANK! -OUR CLOTHES! I'VE FORGOTTEN WHERE WE LEFT THEM!
DON'T WORRY! I KNOW EXACTLY WHERE THEY ARE! -RIGHT WHERE THE TRUCK IS.
QUICK! THE MEN HAVE GONE UP THE HILL. ARE YOU SURE OUR CLOTHES ARE WHERE THE TRUCK IS?
I SAID DON'T WORRY!··· THAT'S EXACTLY WHERE THEY ARE. SEE HERE? RIGHT UNDER THE REAR WHEELS.
LOOK! HERE'S SOME CLOTHING IN THE TRUCK THAT WE CAN WEAR UNTIL WE CAN GET OUR OWN CLOTHES BACK!
HOODED HATS! AND LOOK WHAT ELSE IS IN THIS TRUCK··· SHOTGUNS, AND ROPE, AND DYNAMITE··· MY GOODNESS! TRICK-OR-TREATING IS GETTING COMPLETELY OUT OF HAND!
HURRY UP, FELLOW KLANSMEN ··· THE KLANKLAVE HAS STARTED.
ACID

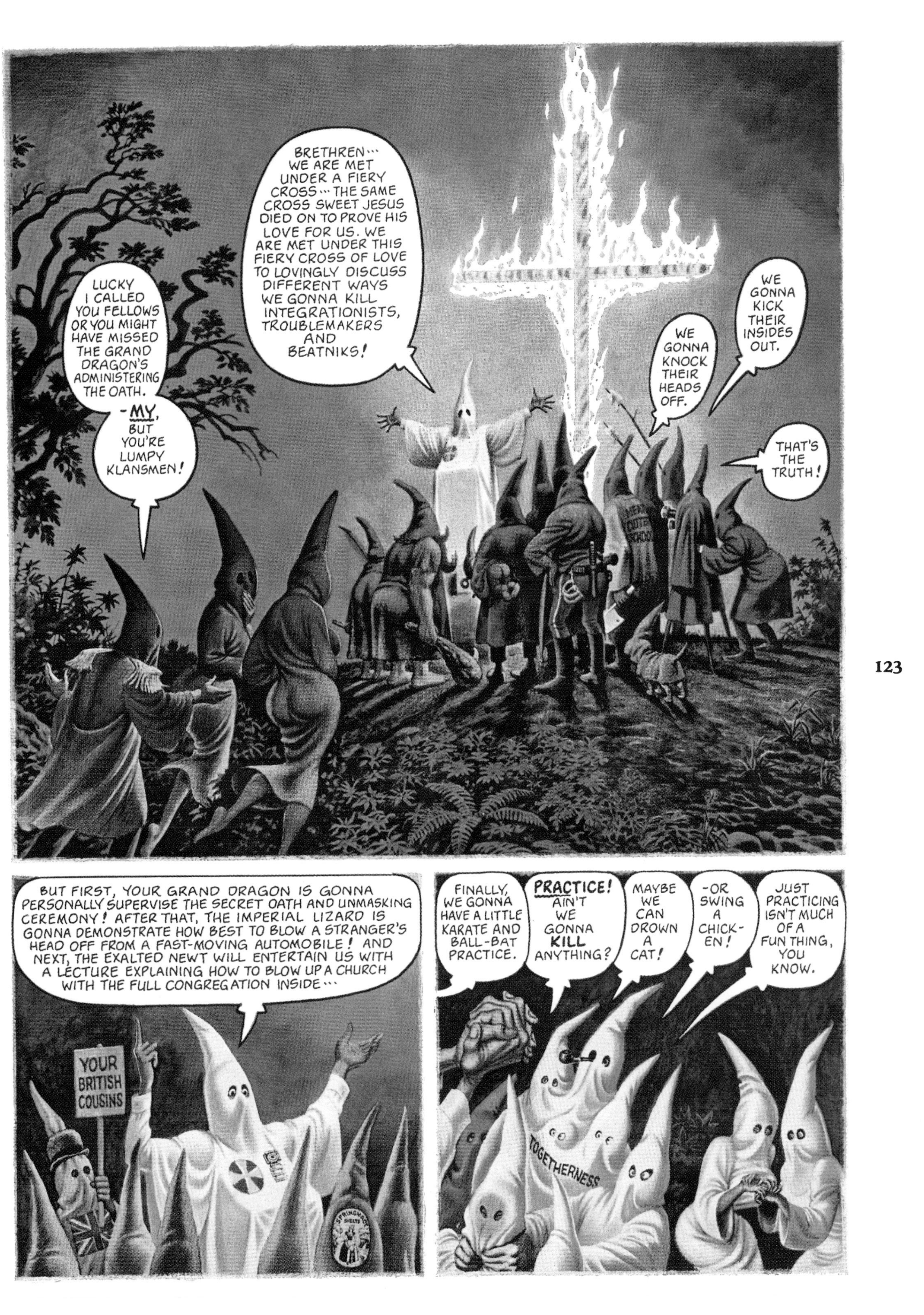

BRETHREN··· WE ARE MET UNDER A FIERY CROSS··· THE SAME CROSS SWEET JESUS DIED ON TO PROVE HIS LOVE FOR US. WE ARE MET UNDER THIS FIERY CROSS OF LOVE TO LOVINGLY DISCUSS DIFFERENT WAYS WE GONNA KILL INTEGRATIONISTS, TROUBLEMAKERS AND BEATNIKS!
LUCKY I CALLED YOU FELLOWS OR YOU MIGHT HAVE MISSED THE GRAND DRAGON'S ADMINISTERING THE OATH.
-MY, BUT YOU'RE LUMPY KLANSMEN!
WE GONNA KNOCK THEIR HEADS OFF.
WE GONNA KICK THEIR INSIDES OUT.
THAT'S THE TRUTH!
BUT FIRST, YOUR GRAND DRAGON IS GONNA PERSONALLY SUPERVISE THE SECRET OATH AND UNMASKING CEREMONY! AFTER THAT, THE IMPERIAL LIZARD IS GONNA DEMONSTRATE HOW BEST TO BLOW A STRANGER'S HEAD OFF FROM A FAST-MOVING AUTOMOBILE! AND NEXT, THE EXALTED NEWT WILL ENTERTAIN US WITH A LECTURE EXPLAINING HOW TO BLOW UP A CHURCH WITH THE FULL CONGREGATION INSIDE···
YOUR BRITISH COUSINS
FINALLY, WE GONNA HAVE A LITTLE KARATE AND BALL-BAT PRACTICE.
PRACTICE! AIN'T WE GONNA KILL ANYTHING?
MAYBE WE CAN DROWN A CAT!
-OR SWING A CHICK-EN!
JUST PRACTICING ISN'T MUCH OF A FUN THING, YOU KNOW.
TOGETHERNESS

123

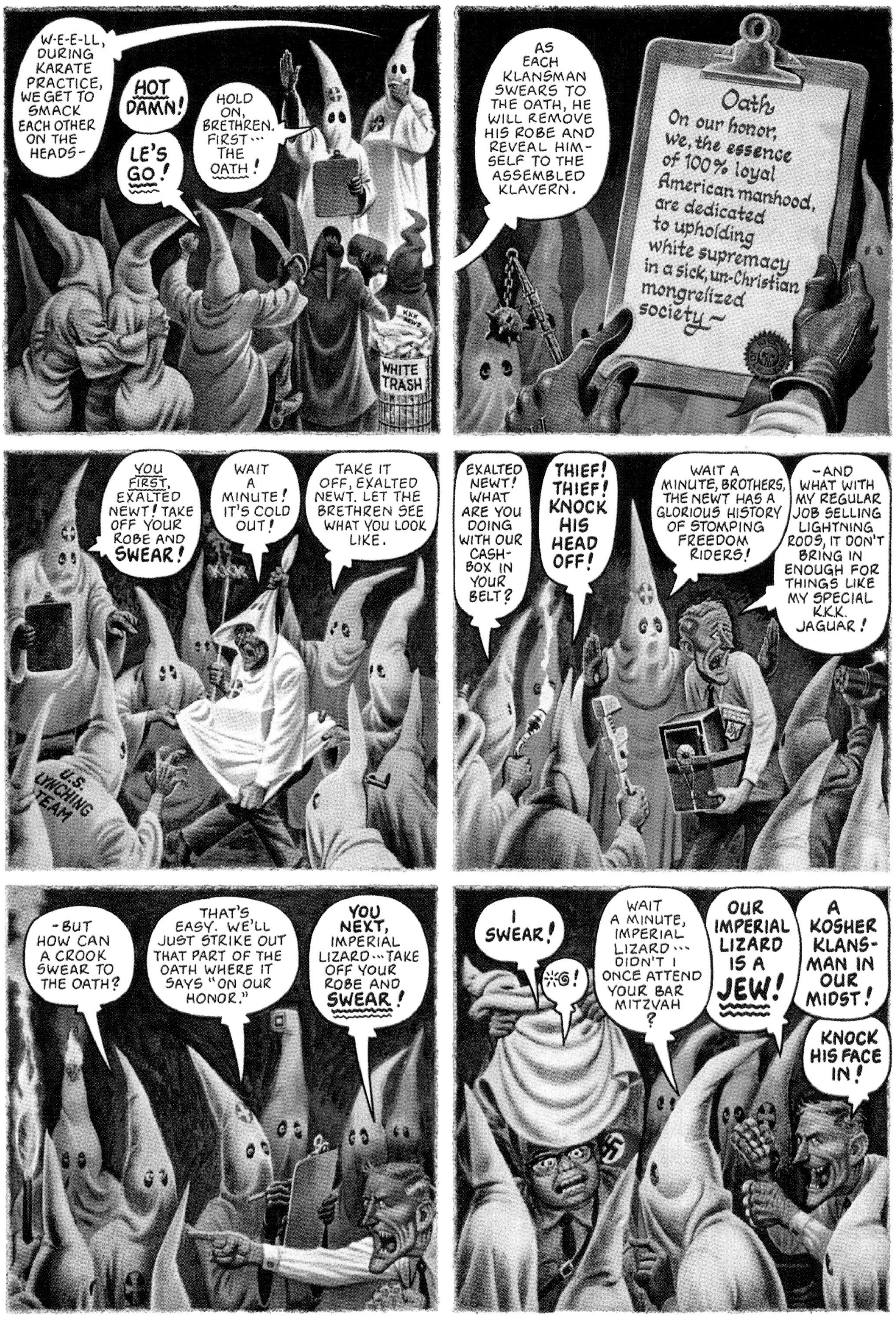
W-E-E-LL, DURING KARATE PRACTICE, WE GET TO SMACK EACH OTHER ON THE HEADS-
HOT DAMN!
LE'S GO!
HOLD ON, BRETHREN. FIRST··· THE OATH!
WHITE TRASH
AS EACH KLANSMAN SWEARS TO THE OATH, HE WILL REMOVE HIS ROBE AND REVEAL HIM-SELF TO THE ASSEMBLED KLAVERN.
Oath
On our honor, we, the essence of 100% loyal American manhood, are dedicated to upholding white supremacy in a sick, un-Christian mongrelized society ~
YOU FIRST, EXALTED NEWT! TAKE OFF YOUR ROBE AND SWEAR!
WAIT A MINUTE! IT'S COLD OUT!
TAKE IT OFF, EXALTED NEWT. LET THE BRETHREN SEE WHAT YOU LOOK LIKE.
U.S. LYNCHING TEAM
EXALTED NEWT! WHAT ARE YOU DOING WITH OUR CASH-BOX IN YOUR BELT?
THIEF! THIEF! KNOCK HIS HEAD OFF!
WAIT A MINUTE, BROTHERS, THE NEWT HAS A GLORIOUS HISTORY OF STOMPING FREEDOM RIDERS!
-AND WHAT WITH MY REGULAR JOB SELLING LIGHTNING RODS, IT DON'T BRING IN ENOUGH FOR THINGS LIKE MY SPECIAL K.K.K. JAGUAR!
-BUT HOW CAN A CROOK SWEAR TO THE OATH?
THAT'S EASY. WE'LL JUST STRIKE OUT THAT PART OF THE OATH WHERE IT SAYS "ON OUR HONOR."
YOU NEXT, IMPERIAL LIZARD··· TAKE OFF YOUR ROBE AND SWEAR!
I SWEAR!
WAIT A MINUTE, IMPERIAL LIZARD··· DIDN'T I ONCE ATTEND YOUR BAR MITZVAH?
OUR IMPERIAL LIZARD IS A JEW!
A KOSHER KLANS-MAN IN OUR MIDST!
KNOCK HIS FACE IN!

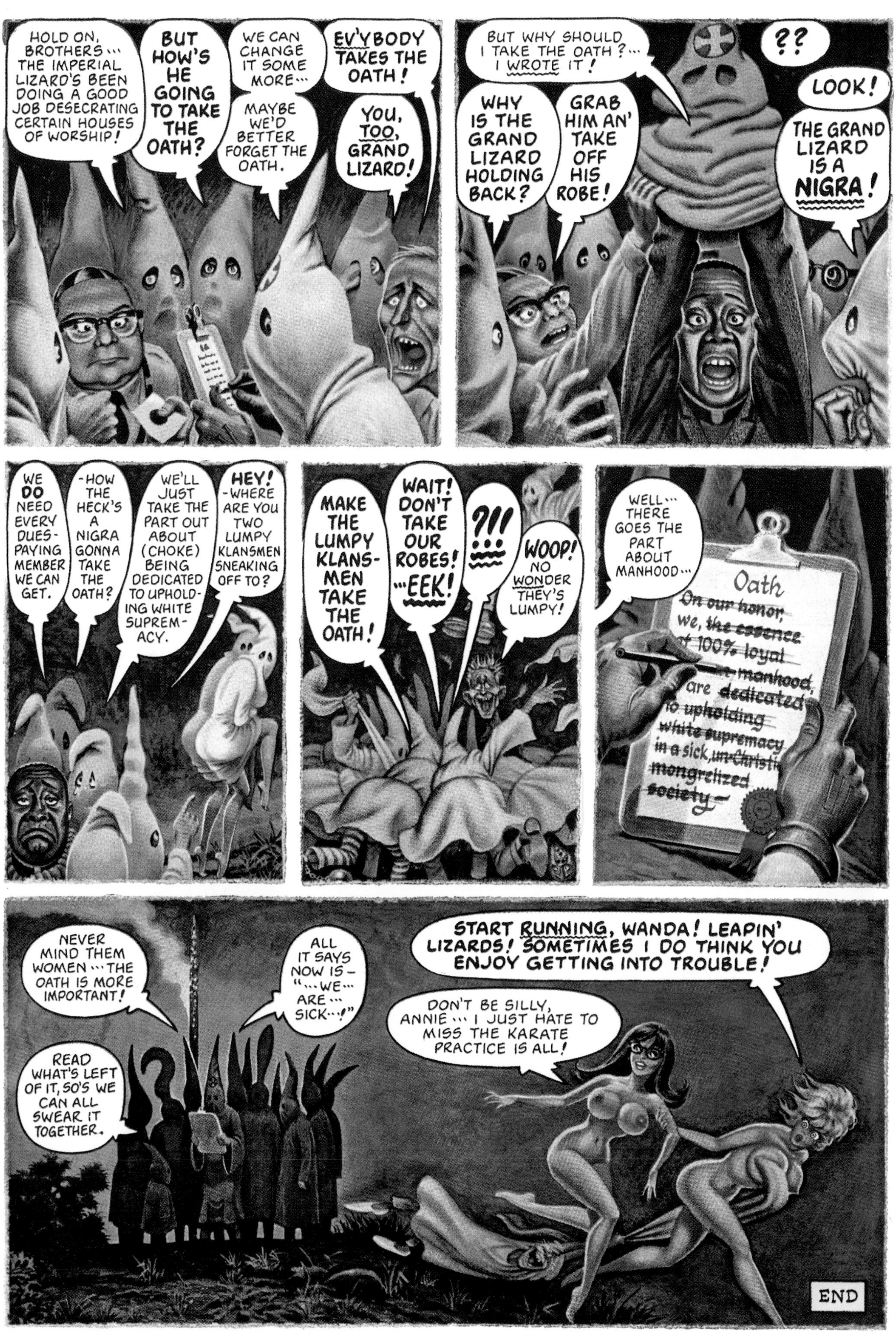
HOLD ON, BROTHERS... THE IMPERIAL LIZARD'S BEEN DOING A GOOD JOB DESECRATING CERTAIN HOUSES OF WORSHIP!
BUT HOW'S HE GOING TO TAKE THE OATH?
WE CAN CHANGE IT SOME MORE...
MAYBE WE'D BETTER FORGET THE OATH.
EV'YBODY TAKES THE OATH!
YOU, TOO, GRAND LIZARD!
BUT WHY SHOULD I TAKE THE OATH?... I WROTE IT!
WHY IS THE GRAND LIZARD HOLDING BACK?
GRAB HIM AN' TAKE OFF HIS ROBE!
??
LOOK!
THE GRAND LIZARD IS A NIGRA!
WE DO NEED EVERY DUES-PAYING MEMBER WE CAN GET.
-HOW THE HECK'S A NIGRA GONNA TAKE THE OATH?
WE'LL JUST TAKE THE PART OUT ABOUT (CHOKE) BEING DEDICATED TO UPHOLDING WHITE SUPREMACY.
HEY! -WHERE ARE YOU TWO LUMPY KLANSMEN SNEAKING OFF TO?
MAKE THE LUMPY KLANSMEN TAKE THE OATH!
WAIT! DON'T TAKE OUR ROBES! ...EEK!
?!!
WOOP! NO WONDER THEY'S LUMPY!
WELL... THERE GOES THE PART ABOUT MANHOOD...
Oath
~~On our honor,~~ we, ~~the essence of 100% loyal~~ ~~manhood,~~ are ~~dedicated to upholding white supremacy~~ in a sick, ~~un-Christian mongrelized society~~ —
NEVER MIND THEM WOMEN... THE OATH IS MORE IMPORTANT!
ALL IT SAYS NOW IS — "...WE... ARE... SICK...!"
READ WHAT'S LEFT OF IT, SO'S WE CAN ALL SWEAR IT TOGETHER.
START RUNNING, WANDA! LEAPIN' LIZARDS! SOMETIMES I DO THINK YOU ENJOY GETTING INTO TROUBLE!
DON'T BE SILLY, ANNIE... I JUST HATE TO MISS THE KARATE PRACTICE IS ALL!
END

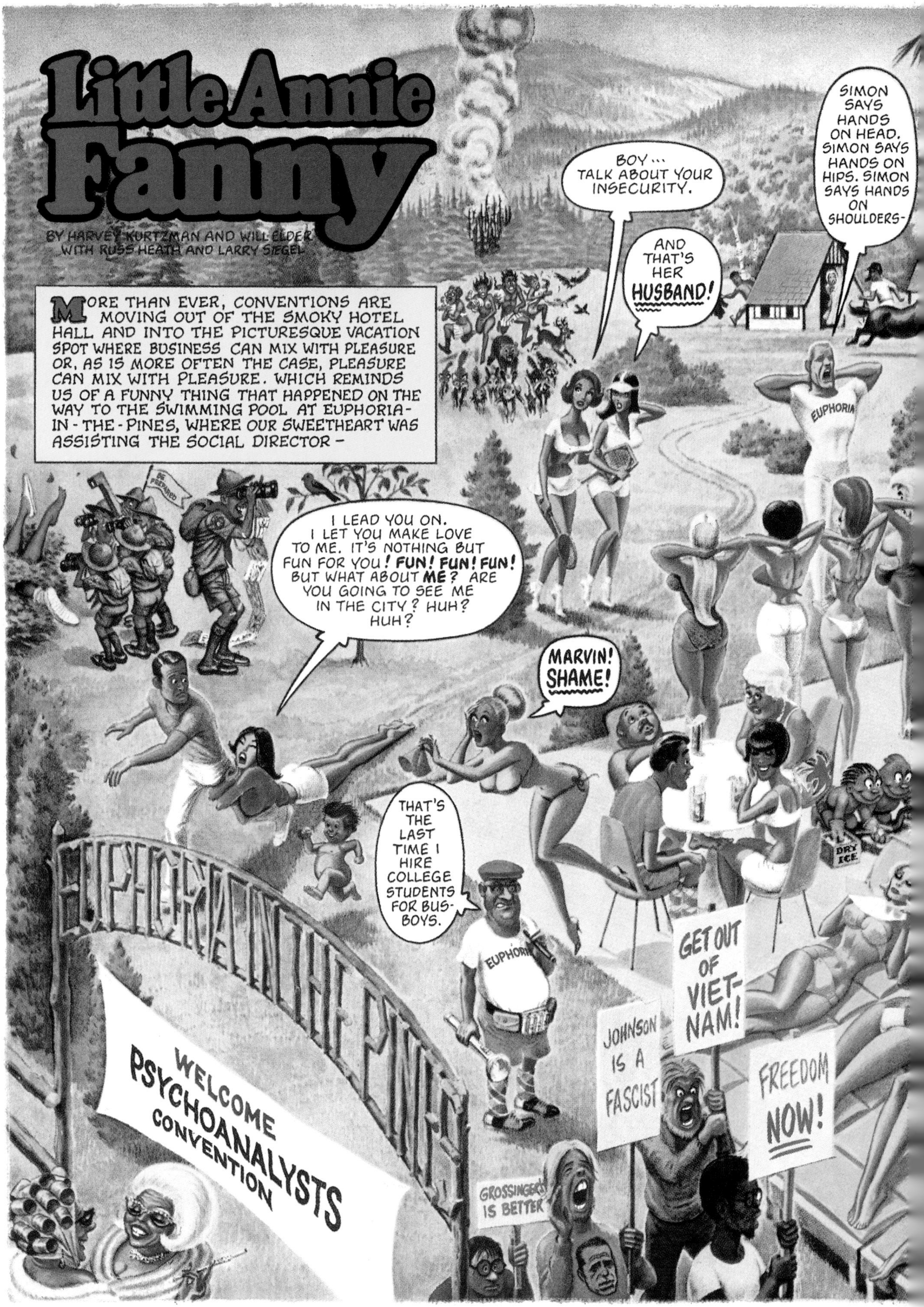
Little Annie Fanny
BY HARVEY KURTZMAN AND WILL ELDER WITH RUSS HEATH AND LARRY SIEGEL
MORE THAN EVER, CONVENTIONS ARE MOVING OUT OF THE SMOKY HOTEL HALL AND INTO THE PICTURESQUE VACATION SPOT WHERE BUSINESS CAN MIX WITH PLEASURE OR, AS IS MORE OFTEN THE CASE, PLEASURE CAN MIX WITH PLEASURE. WHICH REMINDS US OF A FUNNY THING THAT HAPPENED ON THE WAY TO THE SWIMMING POOL AT EUPHORIA-IN-THE-PINES, WHERE OUR SWEETHEART WAS ASSISTING THE SOCIAL DIRECTOR–
BOY... TALK ABOUT YOUR INSECURITY.
AND THAT'S HER HUSBAND!
SIMON SAYS HANDS ON HEAD. SIMON SAYS HANDS ON HIPS. SIMON SAYS HANDS ON SHOULDERS–
EUPHORIA
BE PREPARED
I LEAD YOU ON. I LET YOU MAKE LOVE TO ME. IT'S NOTHING BUT FUN FOR YOU! FUN! FUN! FUN! BUT WHAT ABOUT ME? ARE YOU GOING TO SEE ME IN THE CITY? HUH? HUH?
MARVIN! SHAME!
THAT'S THE LAST TIME I HIRE COLLEGE STUDENTS FOR BUS-BOYS.
DRY ICE
EUPHORIA IN THE PINES
EUPHORIA
WELCOME PSYCHOANALYSTS CONVENTION
GET OUT OF VIET-NAM!
JOHNSON IS A FASCIST
FREEDOM NOW!
GROSSINGER'S IS BETTER

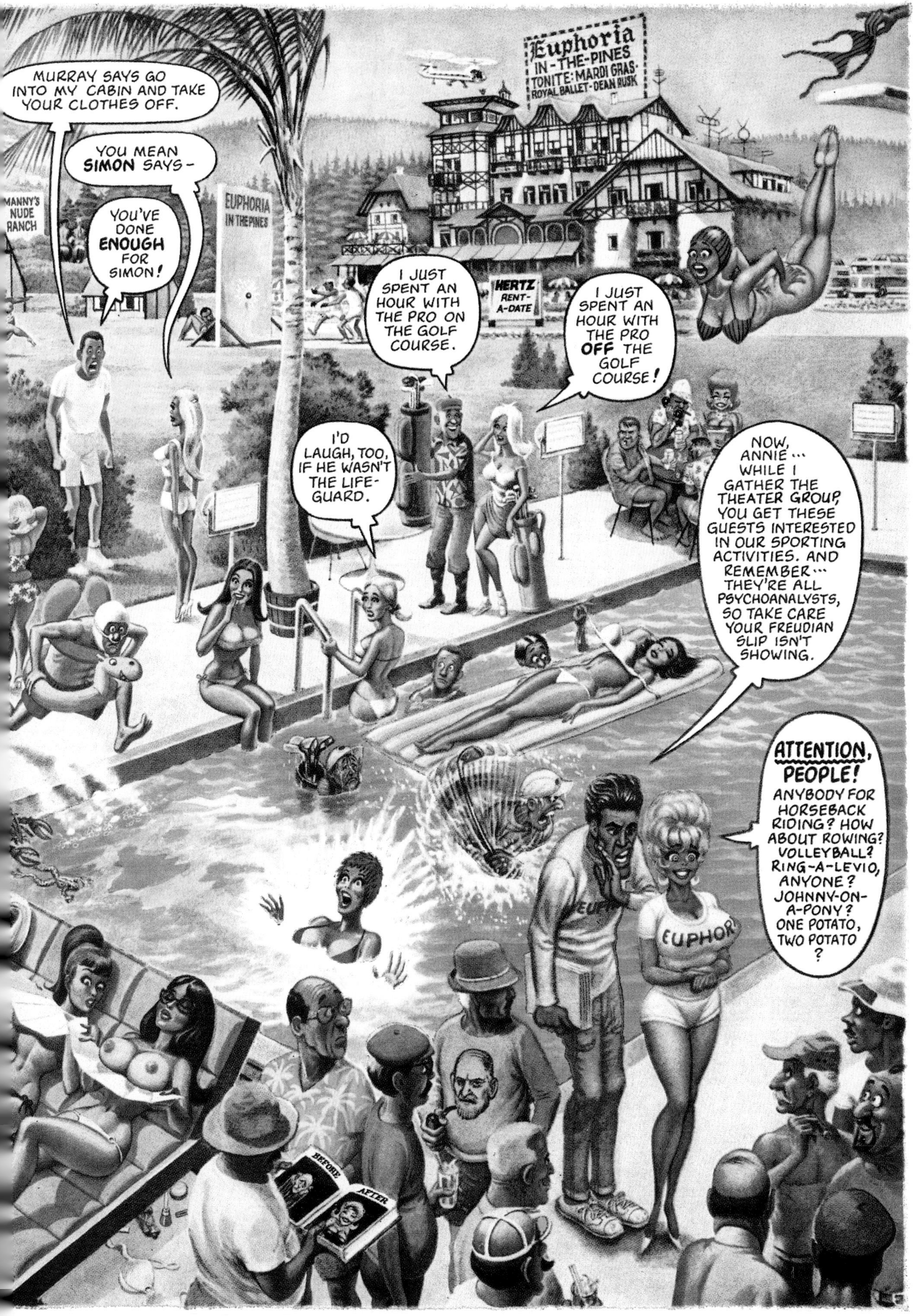

Euphoria IN-THE-PINES TONITE: MARDI GRAS ROYAL BALLET · DEAN RUSK
MURRAY SAYS GO INTO MY CABIN AND TAKE YOUR CLOTHES OFF.
YOU MEAN SIMON SAYS -
MANNY'S NUDE RANCH
EUPHORIA IN THE PINES
YOU'VE DONE ENOUGH FOR SIMON!
I JUST SPENT AN HOUR WITH THE PRO ON THE GOLF COURSE.
HERTZ RENT-A-DATE
I JUST SPENT AN HOUR WITH THE PRO OFF THE GOLF COURSE!
I'D LAUGH, TOO, IF HE WASN'T THE LIFE-GUARD.
NOW, ANNIE ... WHILE I GATHER THE THEATER GROUP, YOU GET THESE GUESTS INTERESTED IN OUR SPORTING ACTIVITIES. AND REMEMBER ... THEY'RE ALL PSYCHOANALYSTS, SO TAKE CARE YOUR FREUDIAN SLIP ISN'T SHOWING.
ATTENTION, PEOPLE! ANYBODY FOR HORSEBACK RIDING? HOW ABOUT ROWING? VOLLEYBALL? RING-A-LEVIO, ANYONE? JOHNNY-ON-A-PONY? ONE POTATO, TWO POTATO ?
EUPH
EUPHOR
BEFORE
AFTER

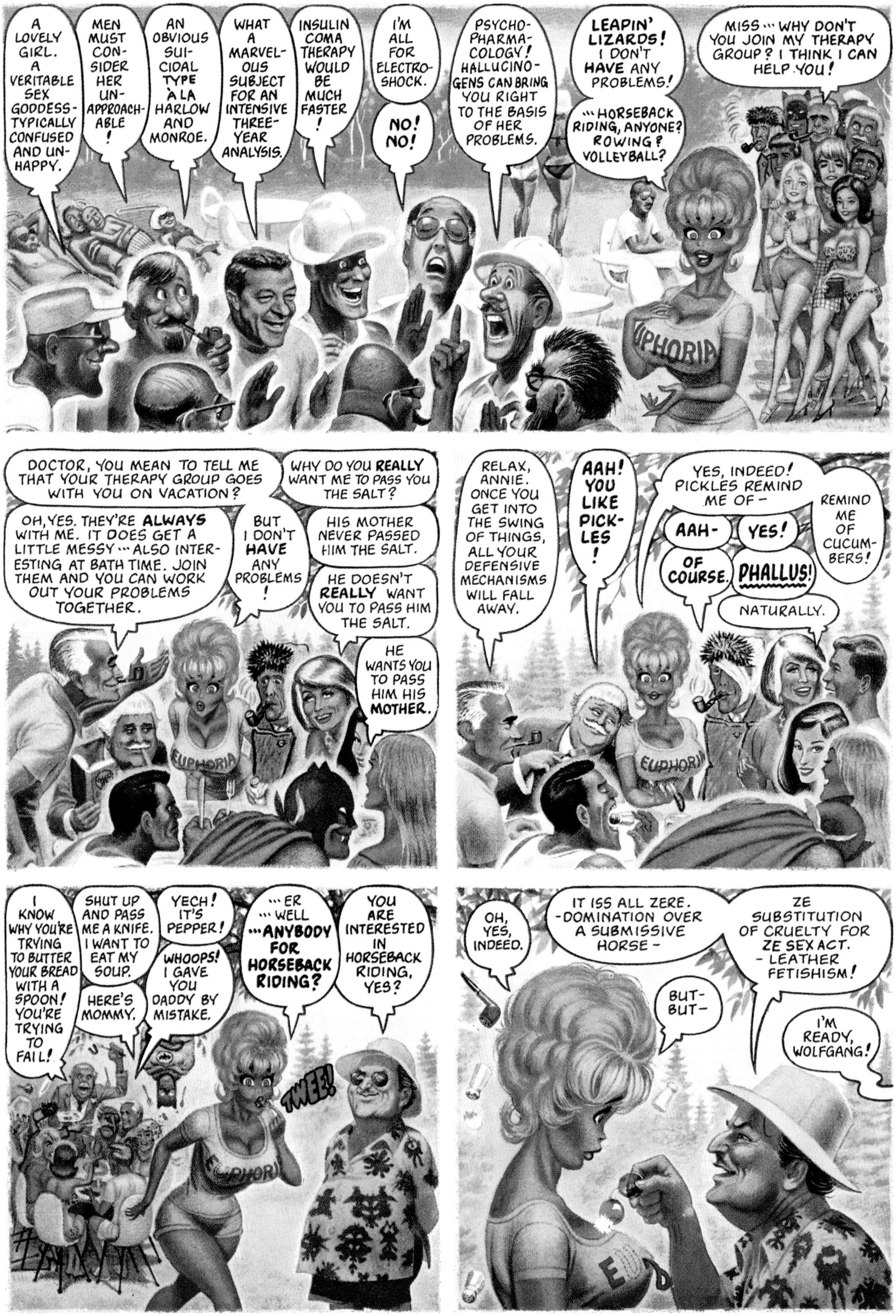

A LOVELY GIRL. A VERITABLE SEX GODDESS-TYPICALLY CONFUSED AND UNHAPPY.
MEN MUST CONSIDER HER UNAPPROACHABLE!
AN OBVIOUS SUICIDAL TYPE À LA HARLOW AND MONROE.
WHAT A MARVELOUS SUBJECT FOR AN INTENSIVE THREE-YEAR ANALYSIS.
INSULIN COMA THERAPY WOULD BE MUCH FASTER!
I'M ALL FOR ELECTRO-SHOCK.
NO! NO!
PSYCHO-PHARMACOLOGY! HALLUCINOGENS CAN BRING YOU RIGHT TO THE BASIS OF HER PROBLEMS.
LEAPIN' LIZARDS! I DON'T HAVE ANY PROBLEMS!
...HORSEBACK RIDING, ANYONE? ROWING? VOLLEYBALL?
MISS... WHY DON'T YOU JOIN MY THERAPY GROUP? I THINK I CAN HELP YOU!
EUPHORIA
DOCTOR, YOU MEAN TO TELL ME THAT YOUR THERAPY GROUP GOES WITH YOU ON VACATION?
OH, YES. THEY'RE ALWAYS WITH ME. IT DOES GET A LITTLE MESSY... ALSO INTERESTING AT BATH TIME. JOIN THEM AND YOU CAN WORK OUT YOUR PROBLEMS TOGETHER.
BUT I DON'T HAVE ANY PROBLEMS!
WHY DO YOU REALLY WANT ME TO PASS YOU THE SALT?
HIS MOTHER NEVER PASSED HIM THE SALT.
HE DOESN'T REALLY WANT YOU TO PASS HIM THE SALT.
HE WANTS YOU TO PASS HIM HIS MOTHER.
RELAX, ANNIE. ONCE YOU GET INTO THE SWING OF THINGS, ALL YOUR DEFENSIVE MECHANISMS WILL FALL AWAY.
AAH! YOU LIKE PICKLES!
YES, INDEED! PICKLES REMIND ME OF -
AAH-
YES!
REMIND ME OF CUCUMBERS!
OF COURSE.
PHALLUS!
NATURALLY.
I KNOW WHY YOU'RE TRYING TO BUTTER YOUR BREAD WITH A SPOON! YOU'RE TRYING TO FAIL!
SHUT UP AND PASS ME A KNIFE. I WANT TO EAT MY SOUP.
HERE'S MOMMY.
YECH! IT'S PEPPER!
WHOOPS! I GAVE YOU DADDY BY MISTAKE.
...ER ...WELL ...ANYBODY FOR HORSEBACK RIDING?
YOU ARE INTERESTED IN HORSEBACK RIDING, YES?
TWEE!
OH, YES, INDEED.
IT ISS ALL ZERE. -DOMINATION OVER A SUBMISSIVE HORSE -
ZE SUBSTITUTION OF CRUELTY FOR ZE SEX ACT. - LEATHER FETISHISM!
BUT-BUT-
I'M READY, WOLFGANG!

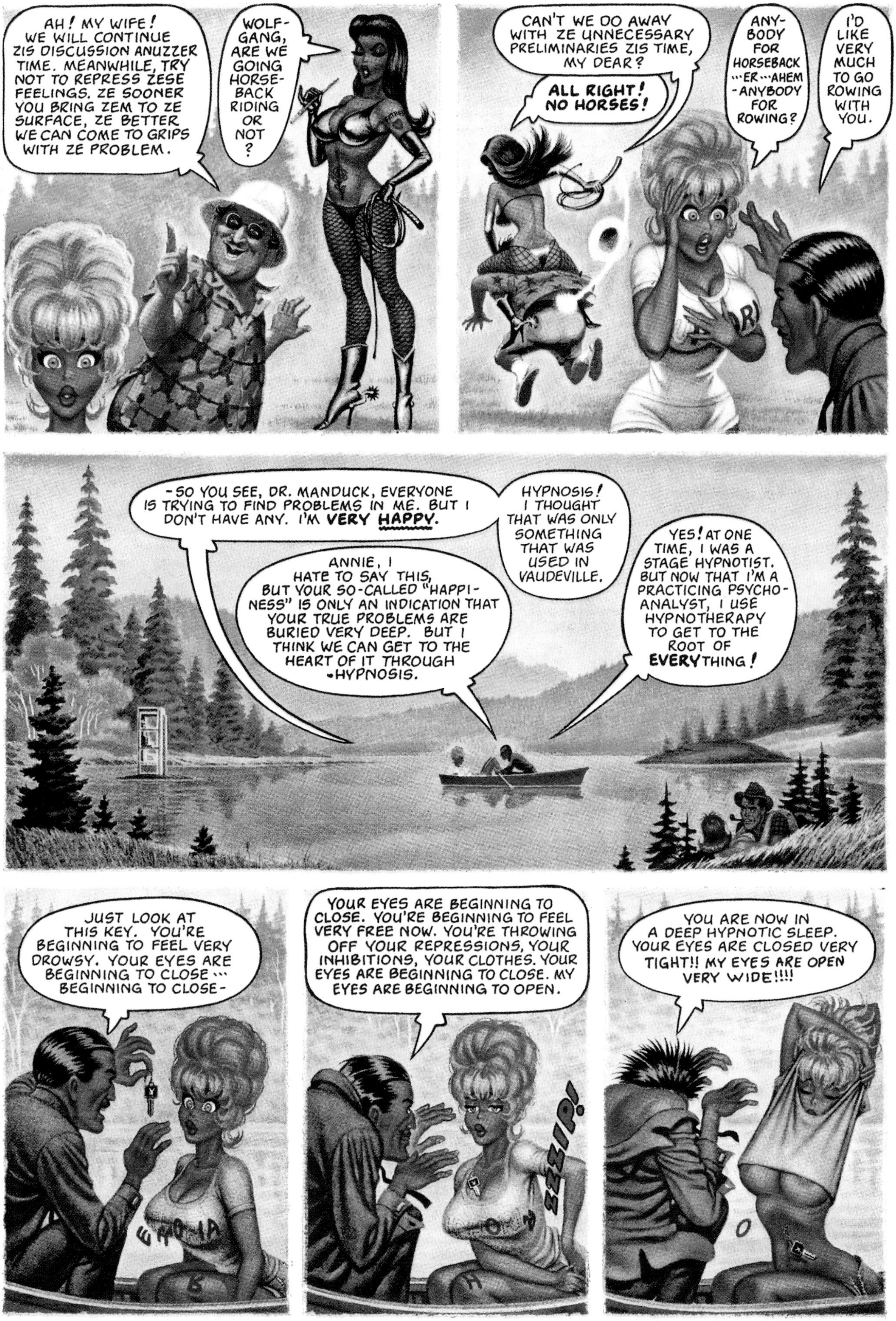
AH! MY WIFE! WE WILL CONTINUE ZIS DISCUSSION ANUZZER TIME. MEANWHILE, TRY NOT TO REPRESS ZESE FEELINGS. ZE SOONER YOU BRING ZEM TO ZE SURFACE, ZE BETTER WE CAN COME TO GRIPS WITH ZE PROBLEM.
WOLF-GANG, ARE WE GOING HORSE-BACK RIDING OR NOT ?
CAN'T WE DO AWAY WITH ZE UNNECESSARY PRELIMINARIES ZIS TIME, MY DEAR?
ALL RIGHT! NO HORSES!
ANY-BODY FOR HORSEBACK ···ER···AHEM -ANYBODY FOR ROWING?
I'D LIKE VERY MUCH TO GO ROWING WITH YOU.
-SO YOU SEE, DR. MANDUCK, EVERYONE IS TRYING TO FIND PROBLEMS IN ME. BUT I DON'T HAVE ANY. I'M VERY HAPPY.
ANNIE, I HATE TO SAY THIS, BUT YOUR SO-CALLED "HAPPI-NESS" IS ONLY AN INDICATION THAT YOUR TRUE PROBLEMS ARE BURIED VERY DEEP. BUT I THINK WE CAN GET TO THE HEART OF IT THROUGH •HYPNOSIS.
HYPNOSIS! I THOUGHT THAT WAS ONLY SOMETHING THAT WAS USED IN VAUDEVILLE.
YES! AT ONE TIME, I WAS A STAGE HYPNOTIST. BUT NOW THAT I'M A PRACTICING PSYCHO-ANALYST, I USE HYPNOTHERAPY TO GET TO THE ROOT OF EVERYTHING!
JUST LOOK AT THIS KEY. YOU'RE BEGINNING TO FEEL VERY DROWSY. YOUR EYES ARE BEGINNING TO CLOSE··· BEGINNING TO CLOSE-
YOUR EYES ARE BEGINNING TO CLOSE. YOU'RE BEGINNING TO FEEL VERY FREE NOW. YOU'RE THROWING OFF YOUR REPRESSIONS, YOUR INHIBITIONS, YOUR CLOTHES. YOUR EYES ARE BEGINNING TO CLOSE. MY EYES ARE BEGINNING TO OPEN.
ZZZIP!
YOU ARE NOW IN A DEEP HYPNOTIC SLEEP. YOUR EYES ARE CLOSED VERY TIGHT!! MY EYES ARE OPEN VERY WIDE!!!!

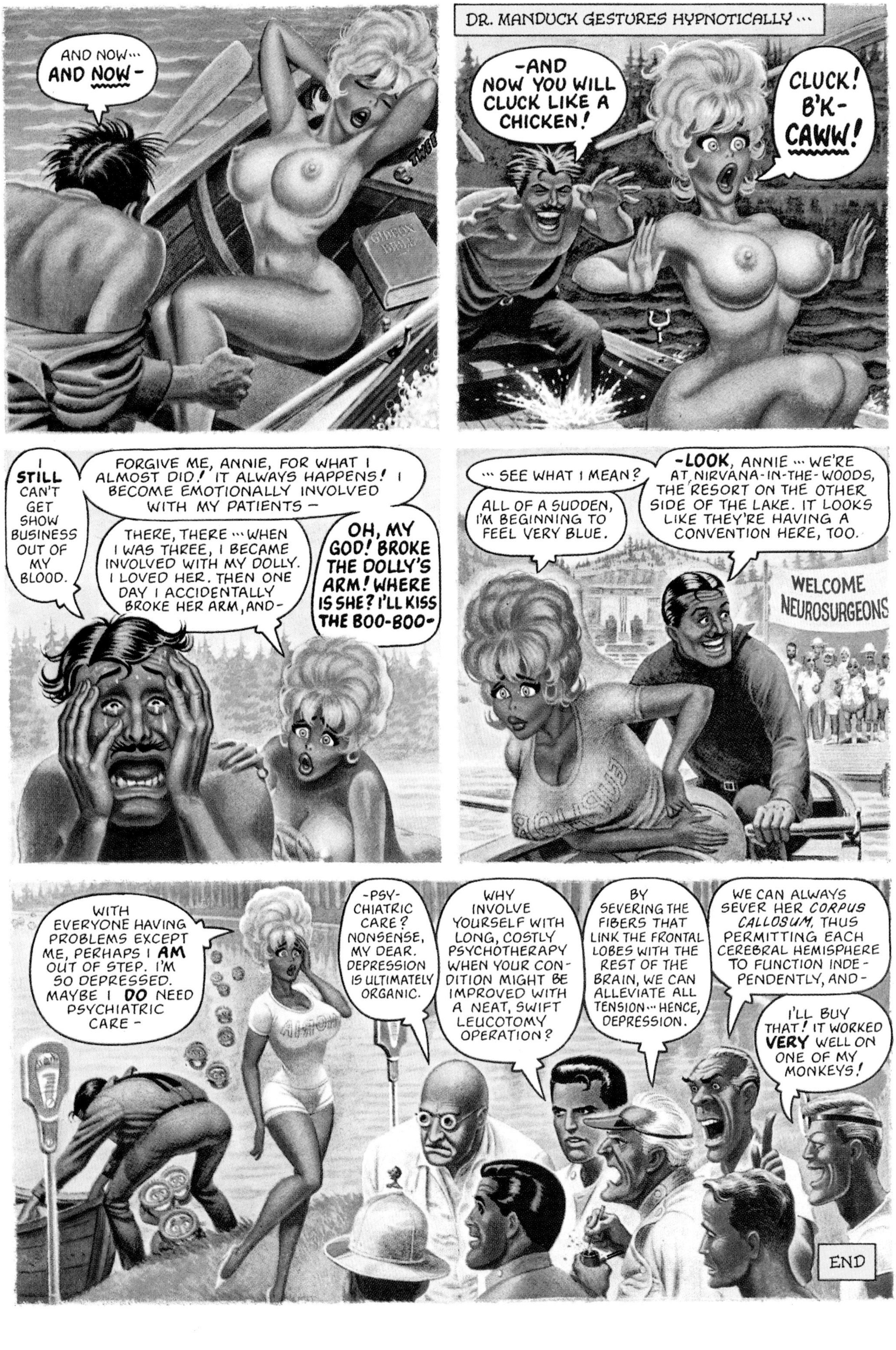

AND NOW··· AND NOW -
GIDEON BIBLE
DR. MANDUCK GESTURES HYPNOTICALLY ···
-AND NOW YOU WILL CLUCK LIKE A CHICKEN!
CLUCK! B'K-CAWW!
I STILL CAN'T GET SHOW BUSINESS OUT OF MY BLOOD.
FORGIVE ME, ANNIE, FOR WHAT I ALMOST DID! IT ALWAYS HAPPENS! I BECOME EMOTIONALLY INVOLVED WITH MY PATIENTS -
THERE, THERE ··· WHEN I WAS THREE, I BECAME INVOLVED WITH MY DOLLY. I LOVED HER. THEN ONE DAY I ACCIDENTALLY BROKE HER ARM, AND-
OH, MY GOD! BROKE THE DOLLY'S ARM! WHERE IS SHE? I'LL KISS THE BOO-BOO-
··· SEE WHAT I MEAN?
ALL OF A SUDDEN, I'M BEGINNING TO FEEL VERY BLUE.
-LOOK, ANNIE ··· WE'RE AT NIRVANA-IN-THE-WOODS, THE RESORT ON THE OTHER SIDE OF THE LAKE. IT LOOKS LIKE THEY'RE HAVING A CONVENTION HERE, TOO.
WELCOME NEUROSURGEONS
WITH EVERYONE HAVING PROBLEMS EXCEPT ME, PERHAPS I AM OUT OF STEP. I'M SO DEPRESSED. MAYBE I DO NEED PSYCHIATRIC CARE -
-PSYCHIATRIC CARE? NONSENSE, MY DEAR. DEPRESSION IS ULTIMATELY ORGANIC.
WHY INVOLVE YOURSELF WITH LONG, COSTLY PSYCHOTHERAPY WHEN YOUR CONDITION MIGHT BE IMPROVED WITH A NEAT, SWIFT LEUCOTOMY OPERATION?
BY SEVERING THE FIBERS THAT LINK THE FRONTAL LOBES WITH THE REST OF THE BRAIN, WE CAN ALLEVIATE ALL TENSION ··· HENCE, DEPRESSION.
WE CAN ALWAYS SEVER HER CORPUS CALLOSUM, THUS PERMITTING EACH CEREBRAL HEMISPHERE TO FUNCTION INDEPENDENTLY, AND-
I'LL BUY THAT! IT WORKED VERY WELL ON ONE OF MY MONKEYS!
END

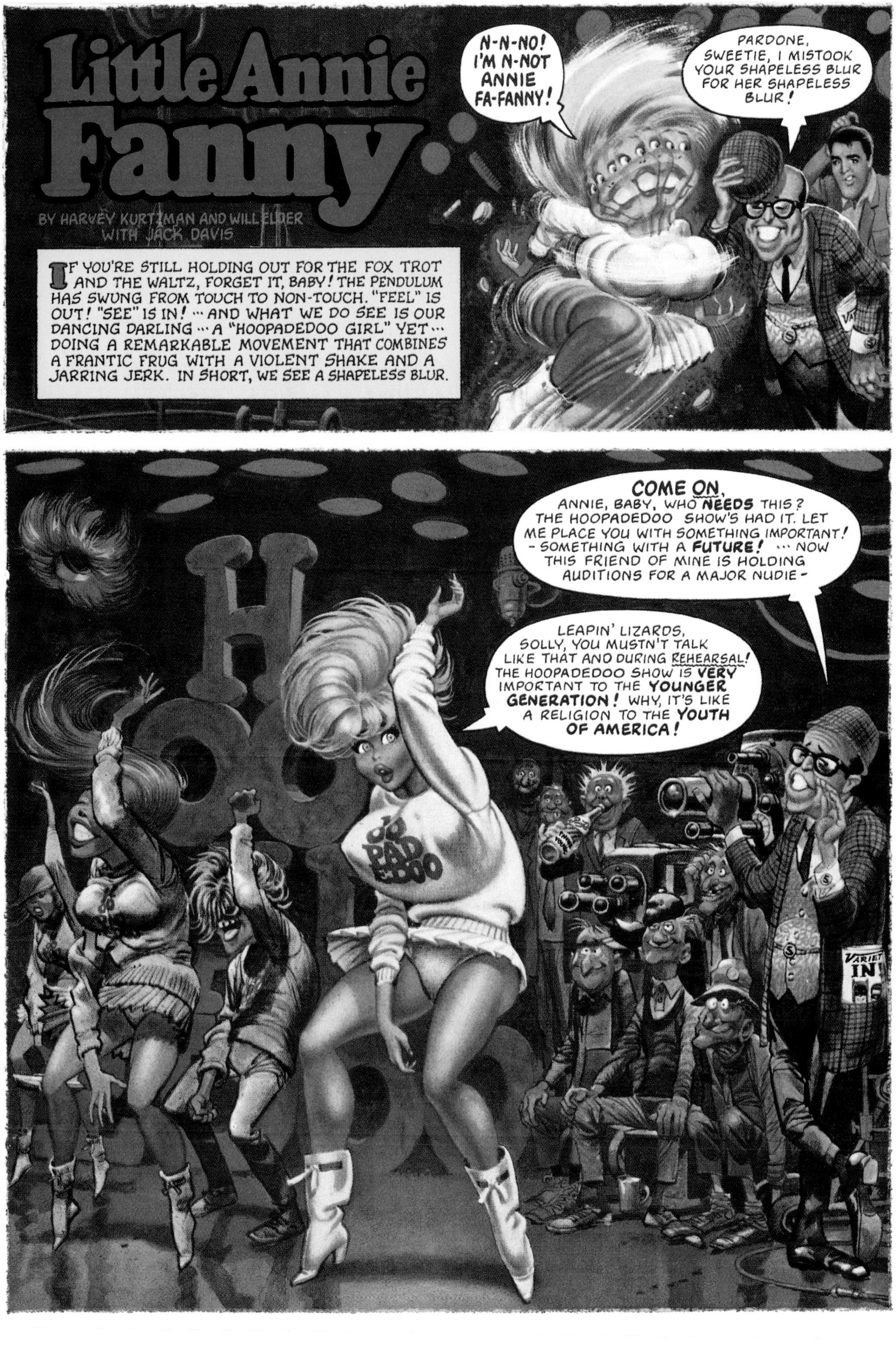

Little Annie Fanny
BY HARVEY KURTZMAN AND WILL ELDER WITH JACK DAVIS
IF YOU'RE STILL HOLDING OUT FOR THE FOX TROT AND THE WALTZ, FORGET IT, BABY! THE PENDULUM HAS SWUNG FROM TOUCH TO NON-TOUCH. "FEEL" IS OUT! "SEE" IS IN! ··· AND WHAT WE DO SEE IS OUR DANCING DARLING ··· A "HOOPADEDOO GIRL" YET ··· DOING A REMARKABLE MOVEMENT THAT COMBINES A FRANTIC FRUG WITH A VIOLENT SHAKE AND A JARRING JERK. IN SHORT, WE SEE A SHAPELESS BLUR.
N-N-NO! I'M N-NOT ANNIE FA-FANNY!
PARDONE, SWEETIE, I MISTOOK YOUR SHAPELESS BLUR FOR HER SHAPELESS BLUR!
COME ON, ANNIE, BABY, WHO NEEDS THIS? THE HOOPADEDOO SHOW'S HAD IT. LET ME PLACE YOU WITH SOMETHING IMPORTANT! - SOMETHING WITH A FUTURE! ··· NOW THIS FRIEND OF MINE IS HOLDING AUDITIONS FOR A MAJOR NUDIE -
LEAPIN' LIZARDS, SOLLY, YOU MUSTN'T TALK LIKE THAT AND DURING REHEARSAL! THE HOOPADEDOO SHOW IS VERY IMPORTANT TO THE YOUNGER GENERATION! WHY, IT'S LIKE A RELIGION TO THE YOUTH OF AMERICA!

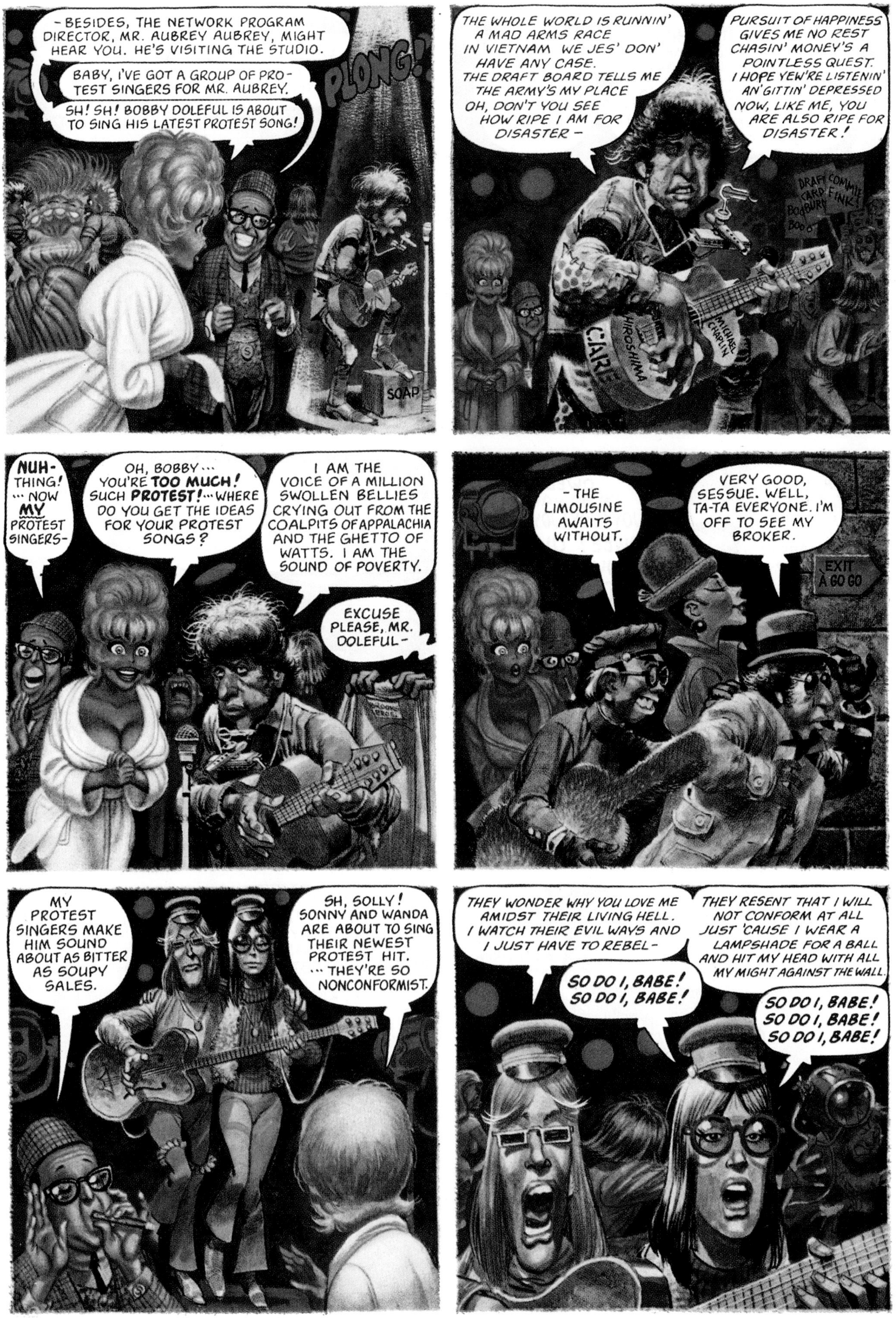

- BESIDES, THE NETWORK PROGRAM DIRECTOR, MR. AUBREY AUBREY, MIGHT HEAR YOU. HE'S VISITING THE STUDIO.
BABY, I'VE GOT A GROUP OF PROTEST SINGERS FOR MR. AUBREY.
SH! SH! BOBBY DOLEFUL IS ABOUT TO SING HIS LATEST PROTEST SONG!
PLONG!
SOAP
THE WHOLE WORLD IS RUNNIN' A MAD ARMS RACE IN VIETNAM WE JES' DON' HAVE ANY CASE. THE DRAFT BOARD TELLS ME THE ARMY'S MY PLACE OH, DON'T YOU SEE HOW RIPE I AM FOR DISASTER -
PURSUIT OF HAPPINESS GIVES ME NO REST CHASIN' MONEY'S A POINTLESS QUEST. I HOPE YEW'RE LISTENIN' AN' GITTIN' DEPRESSED NOW, LIKE ME, YOU ARE ALSO RIPE FOR DISASTER!
HIROSHIMA
NUH-THING! ... NOW MY PROTEST SINGERS-
OH, BOBBY ... YOU'RE TOO MUCH! SUCH PROTEST! ... WHERE DO YOU GET THE IDEAS FOR YOUR PROTEST SONGS?
I AM THE VOICE OF A MILLION SWOLLEN BELLIES CRYING OUT FROM THE COALPITS OF APPALACHIA AND THE GHETTO OF WATTS. I AM THE SOUND OF POVERTY.
EXCUSE PLEASE, MR. DOLEFUL-
- THE LIMOUSINE AWAITS WITHOUT.
VERY GOOD, SESSUE. WELL, TA-TA EVERYONE. I'M OFF TO SEE MY BROKER.
EXIT A GO GO
MY PROTEST SINGERS MAKE HIM SOUND ABOUT AS BITTER AS SOUPY SALES.
SH, SOLLY! SONNY AND WANDA ARE ABOUT TO SING THEIR NEWEST PROTEST HIT. ... THEY'RE SO NONCONFORMIST.
THEY WONDER WHY YOU LOVE ME AMIDST THEIR LIVING HELL. I WATCH THEIR EVIL WAYS AND I JUST HAVE TO REBEL-
SO DO I, BABE! SO DO I, BABE!
THEY RESENT THAT I WILL NOT CONFORM AT ALL JUST 'CAUSE I WEAR A LAMPSHADE FOR A BALL AND HIT MY HEAD WITH ALL MY MIGHT AGAINST THE WALL.
SO DO I, BABE! SO DO I, BABE! SO DO I, BABE!

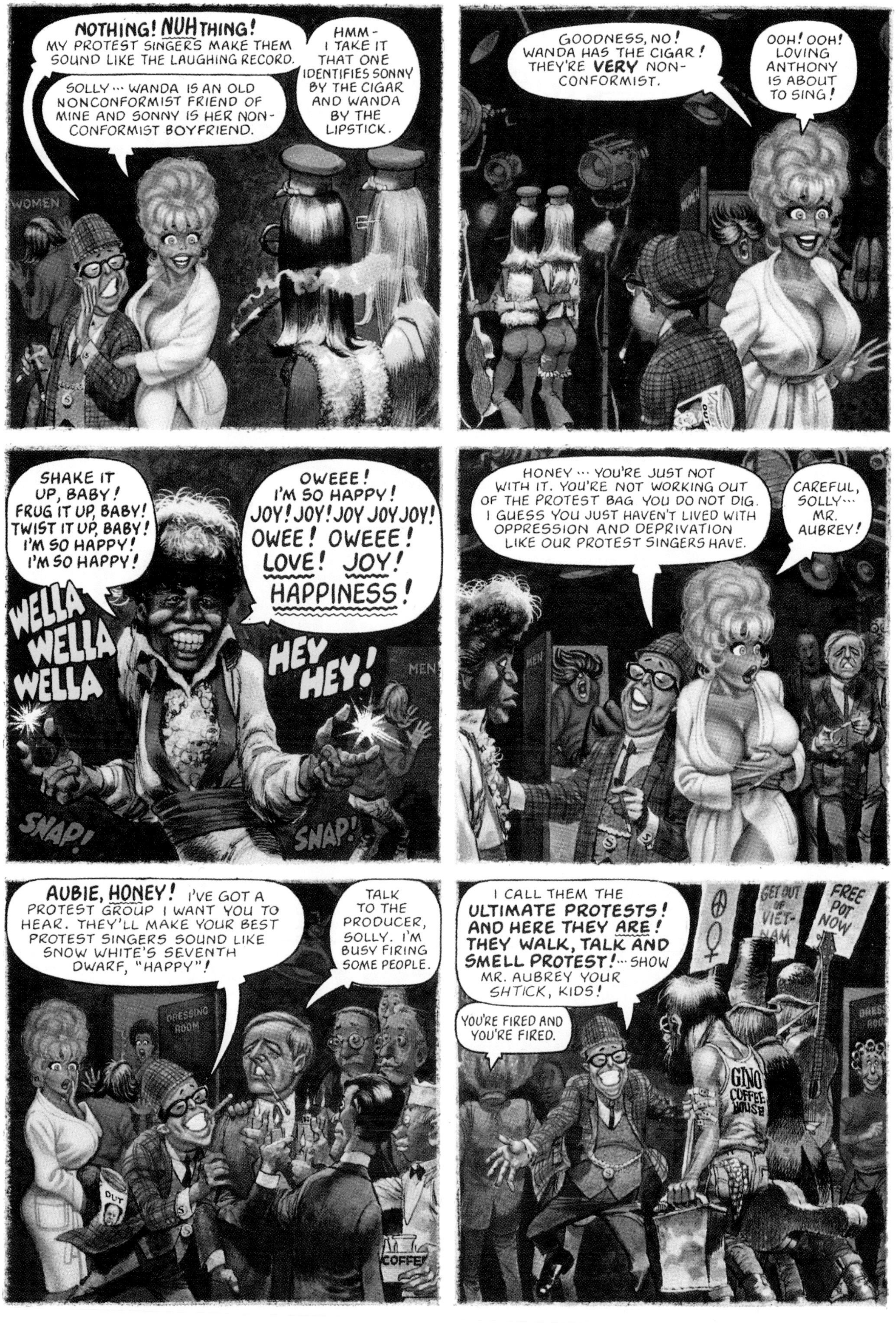
NOTHING! NUHTHING! MY PROTEST SINGERS MAKE THEM SOUND LIKE THE LAUGHING RECORD.
SOLLY··· WANDA IS AN OLD NONCONFORMIST FRIEND OF MINE AND SONNY IS HER NON-CONFORMIST BOYFRIEND.
HMM - I TAKE IT THAT ONE IDENTIFIES SONNY BY THE CIGAR AND WANDA BY THE LIPSTICK.
WOMEN
GOODNESS, NO! WANDA HAS THE CIGAR! THEY'RE VERY NON-CONFORMIST.
OOH! OOH! LOVING ANTHONY IS ABOUT TO SING!
SHAKE IT UP, BABY! FRUG IT UP, BABY! TWIST IT UP, BABY! I'M SO HAPPY! I'M SO HAPPY!
OWEEE! I'M SO HAPPY! JOY! JOY! JOY JOY JOY! OWEE! OWEEE! LOVE! JOY! HAPPINESS!
WELLA WELLA WELLA
HEY HEY!
MEN
SNAP!
SNAP!
HONEY··· YOU'RE JUST NOT WITH IT. YOU'RE NOT WORKING OUT OF THE PROTEST BAG YOU DO NOT DIG. I GUESS YOU JUST HAVEN'T LIVED WITH OPPRESSION AND DEPRIVATION LIKE OUR PROTEST SINGERS HAVE.
CAREFUL, SOLLY··· MR. AUBREY!
MEN
AUBIE, HONEY! I'VE GOT A PROTEST GROUP I WANT YOU TO HEAR. THEY'LL MAKE YOUR BEST PROTEST SINGERS SOUND LIKE SNOW WHITE'S SEVENTH DWARF, "HAPPY"!
TALK TO THE PRODUCER, SOLLY. I'M BUSY FIRING SOME PEOPLE.
DRESSING ROOM
OUT
COFFEE
I CALL THEM THE ULTIMATE PROTESTS! AND HERE THEY ARE! THEY WALK, TALK AND SMELL PROTEST!··· SHOW MR. AUBREY YOUR SHTICK, KIDS!
YOU'RE FIRED AND YOU'RE FIRED.
GET OUT OF VIET-NAM
FREE POT NOW
GINO COFFEE HOUSE

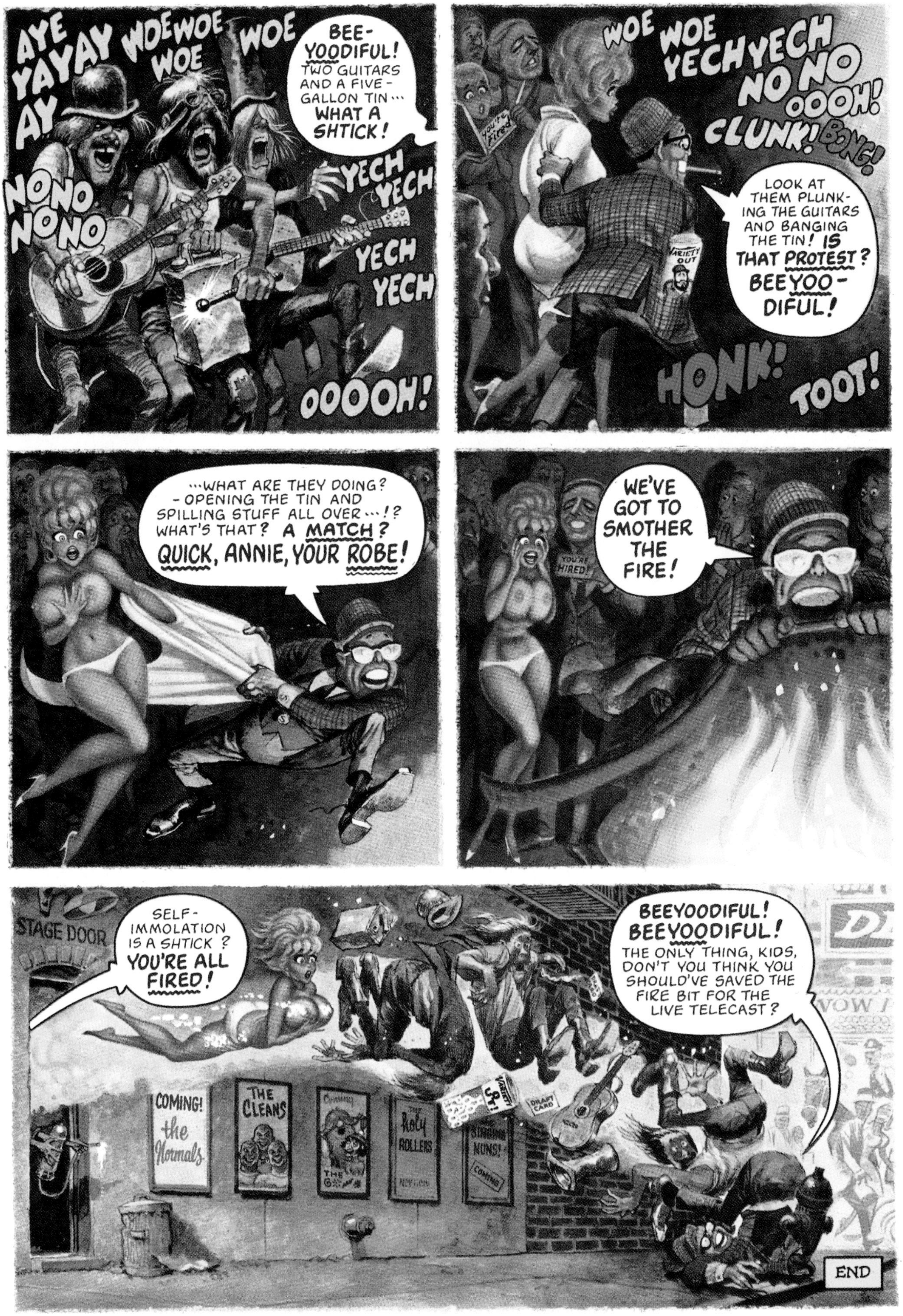
AYE YAYAY AY
WOE WOE WOE
WOE
BEE-YOODIFUL! TWO GUITARS AND A FIVE-GALLON TIN··· WHAT A SHTICK!
NONO NONO
YECH YECH
YECH YECH
OOOOH!
WOE WOE YECH YECH NO NO OOOH!
CLUNK! BONG!
YOU'RE FIRED
VARIETY OUT
LOOK AT THEM PLUNKING THE GUITARS AND BANGING THE TIN! IS THAT PROTEST? BEEYOO-DIFUL!
HONK! TOOT!
···WHAT ARE THEY DOING? - OPENING THE TIN AND SPILLING STUFF ALL OVER···!? WHAT'S THAT? A MATCH? QUICK, ANNIE, YOUR ROBE!
WE'VE GOT TO SMOTHER THE FIRE!
YOU'RE HIRED!
STAGE DOOR
SELF-IMMOLATION IS A SHTICK? YOU'RE ALL FIRED!
BEEYOODIFUL! BEEYOODIFUL! THE ONLY THING, KIDS, DON'T YOU THINK YOU SHOULD'VE SAVED THE FIRE BIT FOR THE LIVE TELECAST?
COMING! the Normals
THE CLEANS
the holy ROLLERS
SINGING NUNS!
DRAFT CARD
END

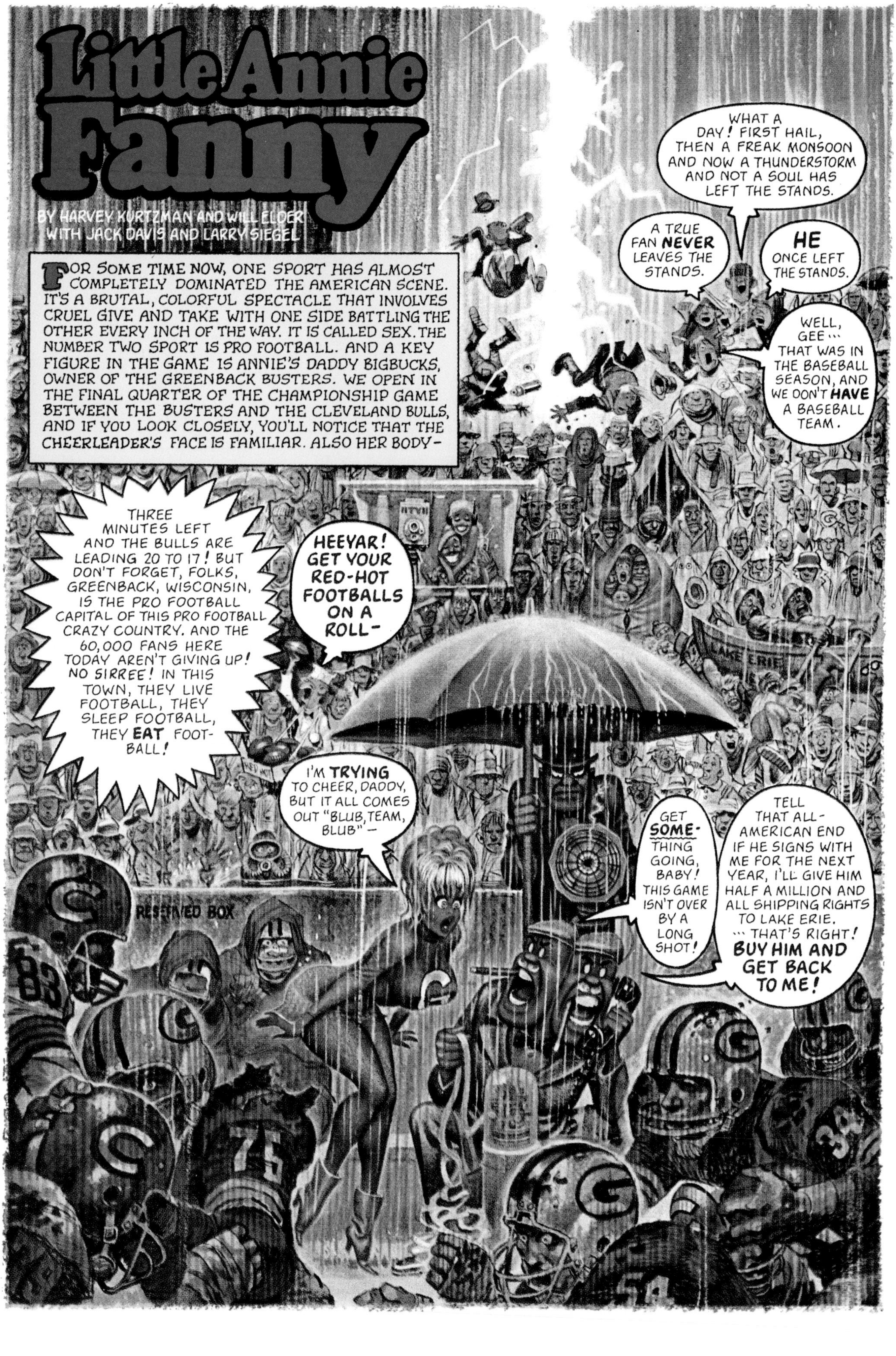

Little Annie Fanny
BY HARVEY KURTZMAN AND WILL ELDER WITH JACK DAVIS AND LARRY SIEGEL
FOR SOME TIME NOW, ONE SPORT HAS ALMOST COMPLETELY DOMINATED THE AMERICAN SCENE. IT'S A BRUTAL, COLORFUL SPECTACLE THAT INVOLVES CRUEL GIVE AND TAKE WITH ONE SIDE BATTLING THE OTHER EVERY INCH OF THE WAY. IT IS CALLED SEX. THE NUMBER TWO SPORT IS PRO FOOTBALL. AND A KEY FIGURE IN THE GAME IS ANNIE'S DADDY BIGBUCKS, OWNER OF THE GREENBACK BUSTERS. WE OPEN IN THE FINAL QUARTER OF THE CHAMPIONSHIP GAME BETWEEN THE BUSTERS AND THE CLEVELAND BULLS, AND IF YOU LOOK CLOSELY, YOU'LL NOTICE THAT THE CHEERLEADER'S FACE IS FAMILIAR. ALSO HER BODY-
WHAT A DAY! FIRST HAIL, THEN A FREAK MONSOON AND NOW A THUNDERSTORM AND NOT A SOUL HAS LEFT THE STANDS.
A TRUE FAN NEVER LEAVES THE STANDS.
HE ONCE LEFT THE STANDS.
WELL, GEE... THAT WAS IN THE BASEBALL SEASON, AND WE DON'T HAVE A BASEBALL TEAM.
THREE MINUTES LEFT AND THE BULLS ARE LEADING 20 TO 17! BUT DON'T FORGET, FOLKS, GREENBACK, WISCONSIN, IS THE PRO FOOTBALL CAPITAL OF THIS PRO FOOTBALL CRAZY COUNTRY. AND THE 60,000 FANS HERE TODAY AREN'T GIVING UP! NO SIRREE! IN THIS TOWN, THEY LIVE FOOTBALL, THEY SLEEP FOOTBALL, THEY EAT FOOTBALL!
HEEYAR! GET YOUR RED-HOT FOOTBALLS ON A ROLL-
LAKE ERIE
I'M TRYING TO CHEER, DADDY, BUT IT ALL COMES OUT "BLUB, TEAM, BLUB"—
GET SOME-THING GOING, BABY! THIS GAME ISN'T OVER BY A LONG SHOT!
TELL THAT ALL-AMERICAN END IF HE SIGNS WITH ME FOR THE NEXT YEAR, I'LL GIVE HIM HALF A MILLION AND ALL SHIPPING RIGHTS TO LAKE ERIE. ... THAT'S RIGHT! BUY HIM AND GET BACK TO ME!
RESERVED BOX

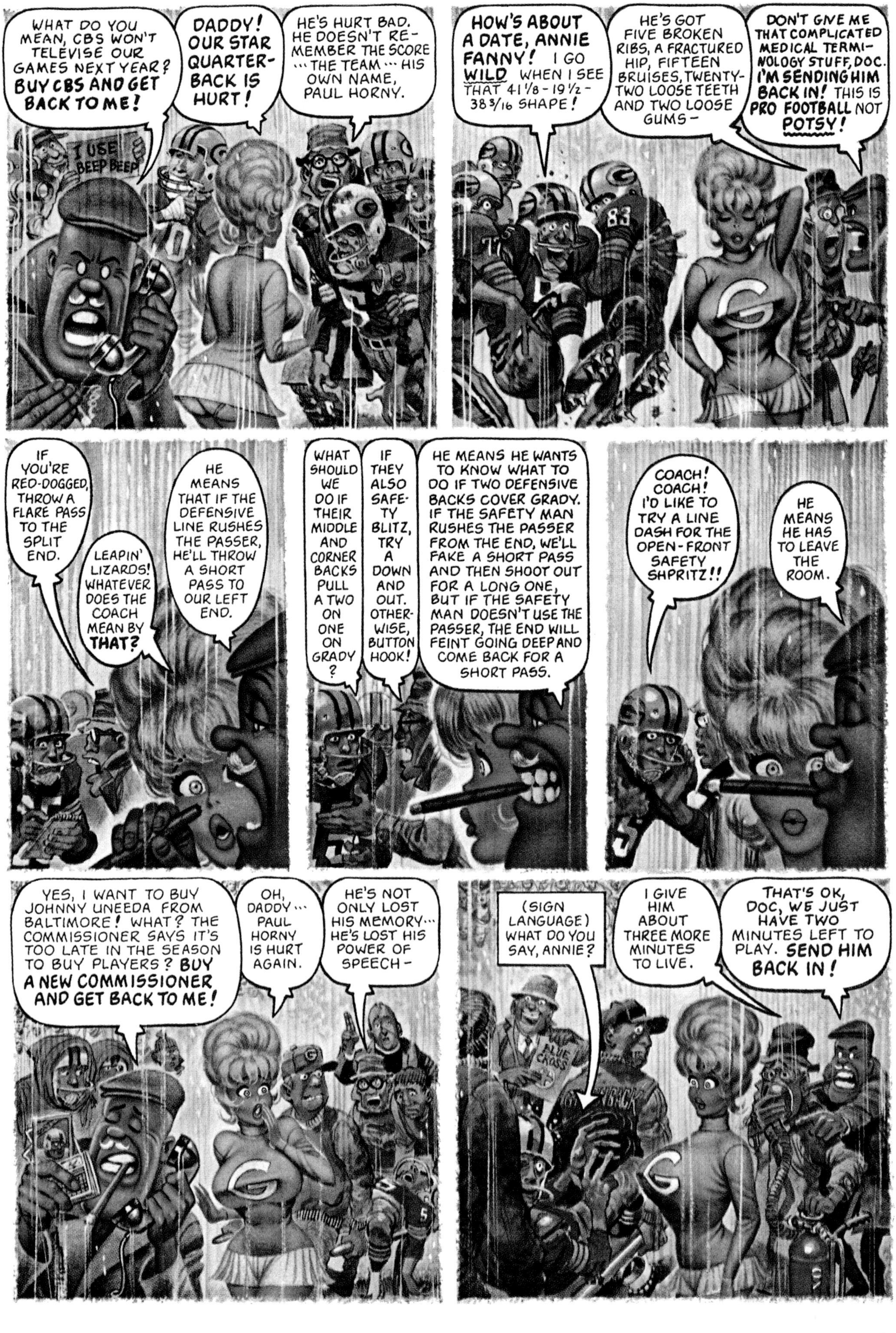
WHAT DO YOU MEAN, CBS WON'T TELEVISE OUR GAMES NEXT YEAR? BUY CBS AND GET BACK TO ME!
I USE BEEP BEEP
DADDY! OUR STAR QUARTER-BACK IS HURT!
HE'S HURT BAD. HE DOESN'T RE-MEMBER THE SCORE ··· THE TEAM ··· HIS OWN NAME, PAUL HORNY.
HOW'S ABOUT A DATE, ANNIE FANNY! I GO WILD WHEN I SEE THAT 41 1/8 - 19 1/2 - 38 3/16 SHAPE!
HE'S GOT FIVE BROKEN RIBS, A FRACTURED HIP, FIFTEEN BRUISES, TWENTY-TWO LOOSE TEETH AND TWO LOOSE GUMS—
DON'T GIVE ME THAT COMPLICATED MEDICAL TERMI-NOLOGY STUFF, DOC. I'M SENDING HIM BACK IN! THIS IS PRO FOOTBALL NOT POTSY!
IF YOU'RE RED-DOGGED, THROW A FLARE PASS TO THE SPLIT END.
LEAPIN' LIZARDS! WHATEVER DOES THE COACH MEAN BY THAT?
HE MEANS THAT IF THE DEFENSIVE LINE RUSHES THE PASSER, HE'LL THROW A SHORT PASS TO OUR LEFT END.
WHAT SHOULD WE DO IF THEIR MIDDLE AND CORNER BACKS PULL A TWO ON ONE ON GRADY?
IF THEY ALSO SAFE-TY BLITZ, TRY A DOWN AND OUT. OTHER-WISE, BUTTON HOOK!
HE MEANS HE WANTS TO KNOW WHAT TO DO IF TWO DEFENSIVE BACKS COVER GRADY. IF THE SAFETY MAN RUSHES THE PASSER FROM THE END, WE'LL FAKE A SHORT PASS AND THEN SHOOT OUT FOR A LONG ONE, BUT IF THE SAFETY MAN DOESN'T USE THE PASSER, THE END WILL FEINT GOING DEEP AND COME BACK FOR A SHORT PASS.
COACH! COACH! I'D LIKE TO TRY A LINE DASH FOR THE OPEN-FRONT SAFETY SHPRITZ!!
HE MEANS HE HAS TO LEAVE THE ROOM.
YES, I WANT TO BUY JOHNNY UNEEDA FROM BALTIMORE! WHAT? THE COMMISSIONER SAYS IT'S TOO LATE IN THE SEASON TO BUY PLAYERS? BUY A NEW COMMISSIONER AND GET BACK TO ME!
OH, DADDY··· PAUL HORNY IS HURT AGAIN.
HE'S NOT ONLY LOST HIS MEMORY··· HE'S LOST HIS POWER OF SPEECH—
(SIGN LANGUAGE) WHAT DO YOU SAY, ANNIE?
BLUE CROSS
I GIVE HIM ABOUT THREE MORE MINUTES TO LIVE.
THAT'S OK, DOC, WE JUST HAVE TWO MINUTES LEFT TO PLAY. SEND HIM BACK IN!

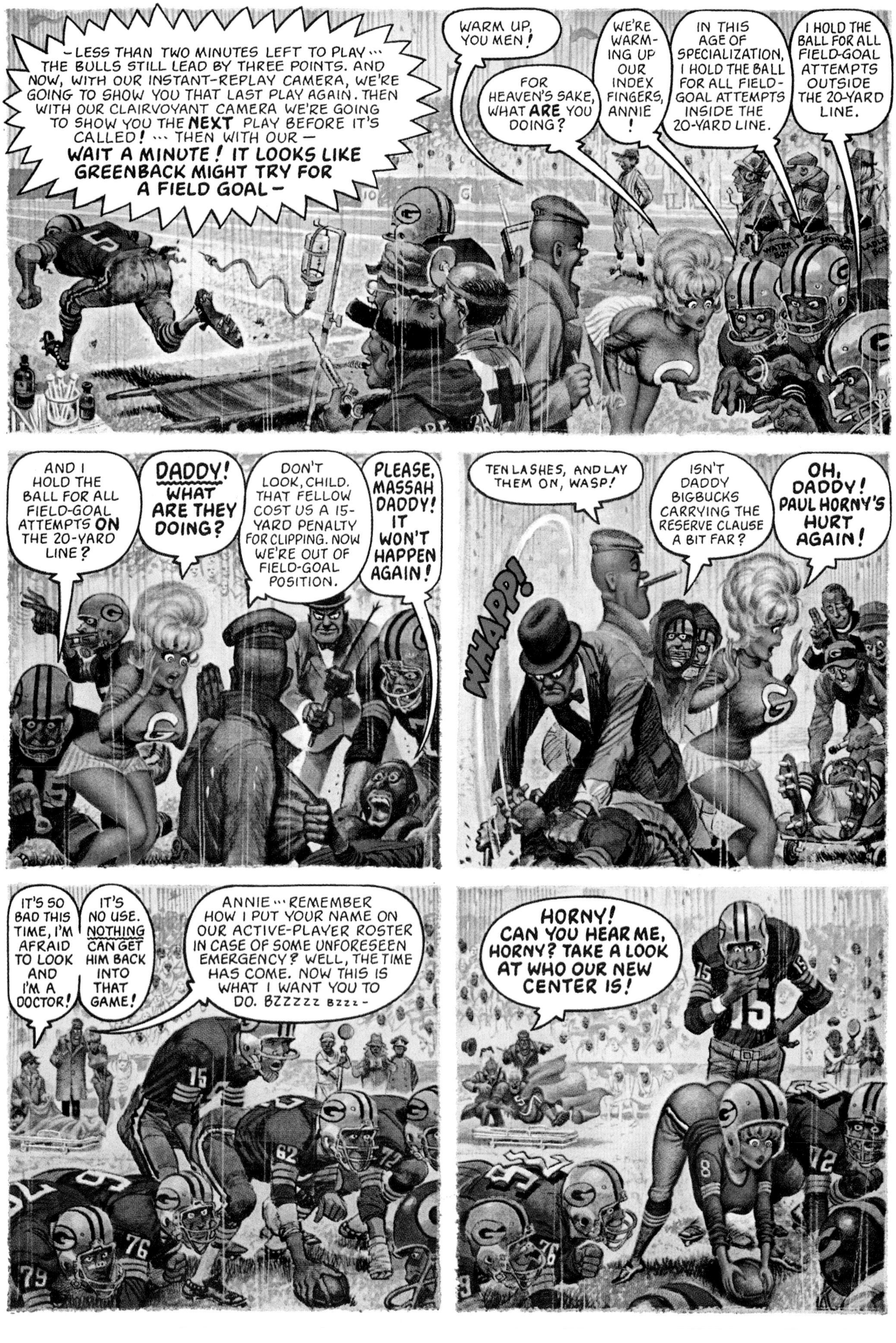

–LESS THAN TWO MINUTES LEFT TO PLAY··· THE BULLS STILL LEAD BY THREE POINTS. AND NOW, WITH OUR INSTANT-REPLAY CAMERA, WE'RE GOING TO SHOW YOU THAT LAST PLAY AGAIN. THEN WITH OUR CLAIRVOYANT CAMERA WE'RE GOING TO SHOW YOU THE NEXT PLAY BEFORE IT'S CALLED! ··· THEN WITH OUR – WAIT A MINUTE! IT LOOKS LIKE GREENBACK MIGHT TRY FOR A FIELD GOAL –
WARM UP, YOU MEN!
FOR HEAVEN'S SAKE, WHAT ARE YOU DOING?
WE'RE WARMING UP OUR INDEX FINGERS, ANNIE!
IN THIS AGE OF SPECIALIZATION, I HOLD THE BALL FOR ALL FIELD-GOAL ATTEMPTS INSIDE THE 20-YARD LINE.
I HOLD THE BALL FOR ALL FIELD-GOAL ATTEMPTS OUTSIDE THE 20-YARD LINE.
AND I HOLD THE BALL FOR ALL FIELD-GOAL ATTEMPTS ON THE 20-YARD LINE?
DADDY! WHAT ARE THEY DOING?
DON'T LOOK, CHILD. THAT FELLOW COST US A 15-YARD PENALTY FOR CLIPPING. NOW WE'RE OUT OF FIELD-GOAL POSITION.
PLEASE, MASSAH DADDY! IT WON'T HAPPEN AGAIN!
TEN LASHES, AND LAY THEM ON, WASP!
WHAPP!
ISN'T DADDY BIGBUCKS CARRYING THE RESERVE CLAUSE A BIT FAR?
OH, DADDY! PAUL HORNY'S HURT AGAIN!
IT'S SO BAD THIS TIME, I'M AFRAID TO LOOK AND I'M A DOCTOR!
IT'S NO USE. NOTHING CAN GET HIM BACK INTO THAT GAME!
ANNIE··· REMEMBER HOW I PUT YOUR NAME ON OUR ACTIVE-PLAYER ROSTER IN CASE OF SOME UNFORESEEN EMERGENCY? WELL, THE TIME HAS COME. NOW THIS IS WHAT I WANT YOU TO DO. BZZzzz Bzzz–
HORNY! CAN YOU HEAR ME, HORNY? TAKE A LOOK AT WHO OUR NEW CENTER IS!

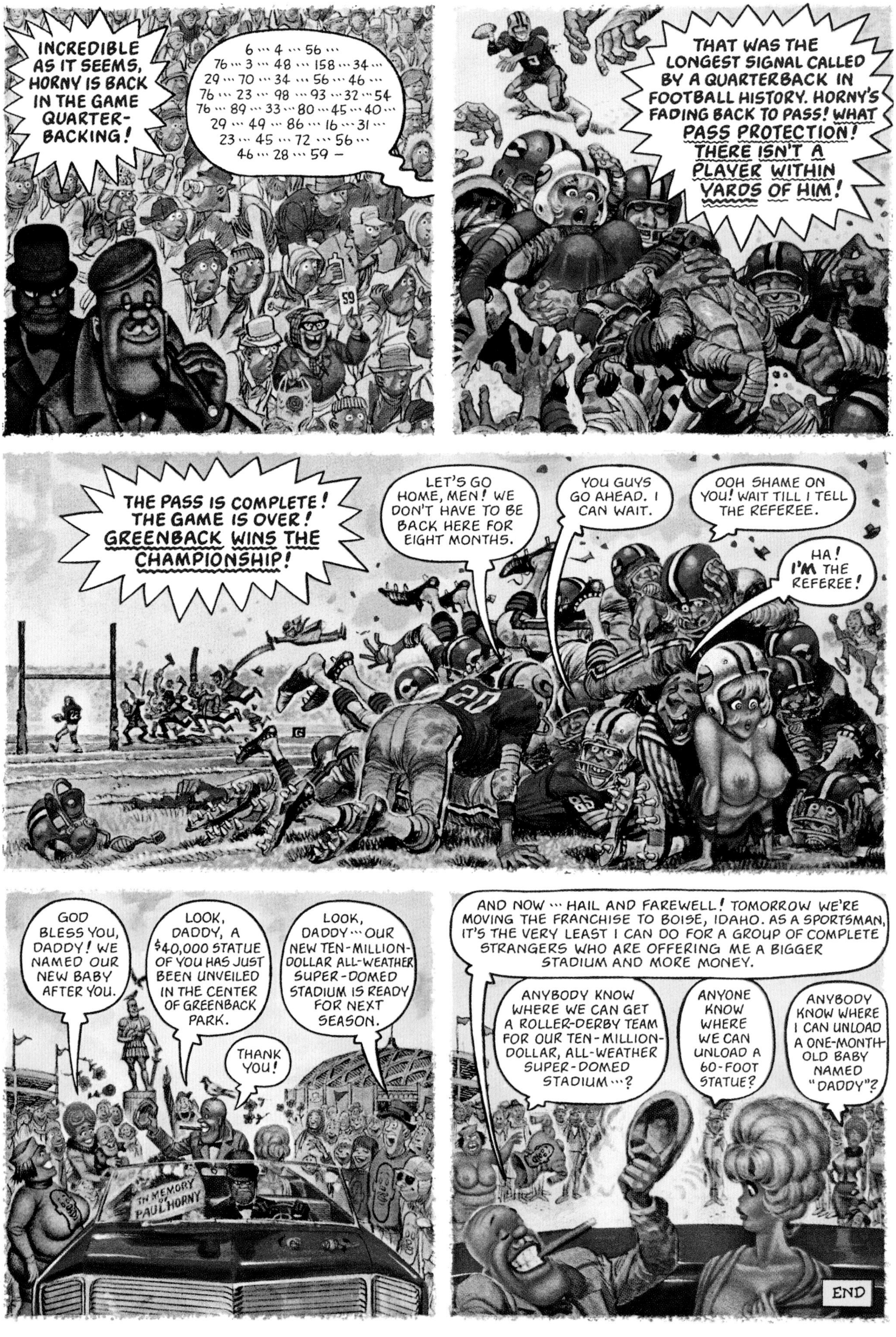

INCREDIBLE AS IT SEEMS, HORNY IS BACK IN THE GAME QUARTER-BACKING!
6 ··· 4 ··· 56 ··· 76 ··· 3 ··· 48 ··· 158 ··· 34 ··· 29 ··· 70 ··· 34 ··· 56 ··· 46 ··· 76 ··· 23 ··· 98 ··· 93 ··· 32 ··· 54 76 ··· 89 ··· 33 ··· 80 ··· 45 ··· 40 ··· 29 ··· 49 ··· 86 ··· 16 ··· 31 ··· 23 ··· 45 ··· 72 ··· 56 ··· 46 ··· 28 ··· 59 –
59
THAT WAS THE LONGEST SIGNAL CALLED BY A QUARTERBACK IN FOOTBALL HISTORY. HORNY'S FADING BACK TO PASS! WHAT PASS PROTECTION! THERE ISN'T A PLAYER WITHIN YARDS OF HIM!
THE PASS IS COMPLETE! THE GAME IS OVER! GREENBACK WINS THE CHAMPIONSHIP!
LET'S GO HOME, MEN! WE DON'T HAVE TO BE BACK HERE FOR EIGHT MONTHS.
YOU GUYS GO AHEAD. I CAN WAIT.
OOH SHAME ON YOU! WAIT TILL I TELL THE REFEREE.
HA! I'M THE REFEREE!
GOD BLESS YOU, DADDY! WE NAMED OUR NEW BABY AFTER YOU.
LOOK, DADDY, A $40,000 STATUE OF YOU HAS JUST BEEN UNVEILED IN THE CENTER OF GREENBACK PARK.
LOOK, DADDY··· OUR NEW TEN-MILLION-DOLLAR ALL-WEATHER SUPER-DOMED STADIUM IS READY FOR NEXT SEASON.
THANK YOU!
IN MEMORY OF PAUL HORNY
AND NOW ··· HAIL AND FAREWELL! TOMORROW WE'RE MOVING THE FRANCHISE TO BOISE, IDAHO. AS A SPORTSMAN, IT'S THE VERY LEAST I CAN DO FOR A GROUP OF COMPLETE STRANGERS WHO ARE OFFERING ME A BIGGER STADIUM AND MORE MONEY.
ANYBODY KNOW WHERE WE CAN GET A ROLLER-DERBY TEAM FOR OUR TEN-MILLION-DOLLAR, ALL-WEATHER SUPER-DOMED STADIUM···?
ANYONE KNOW WHERE WE CAN UNLOAD A 60-FOOT STATUE?
ANYBODY KNOW WHERE I CAN UNLOAD A ONE-MONTH-OLD BABY NAMED "DADDY"?
END

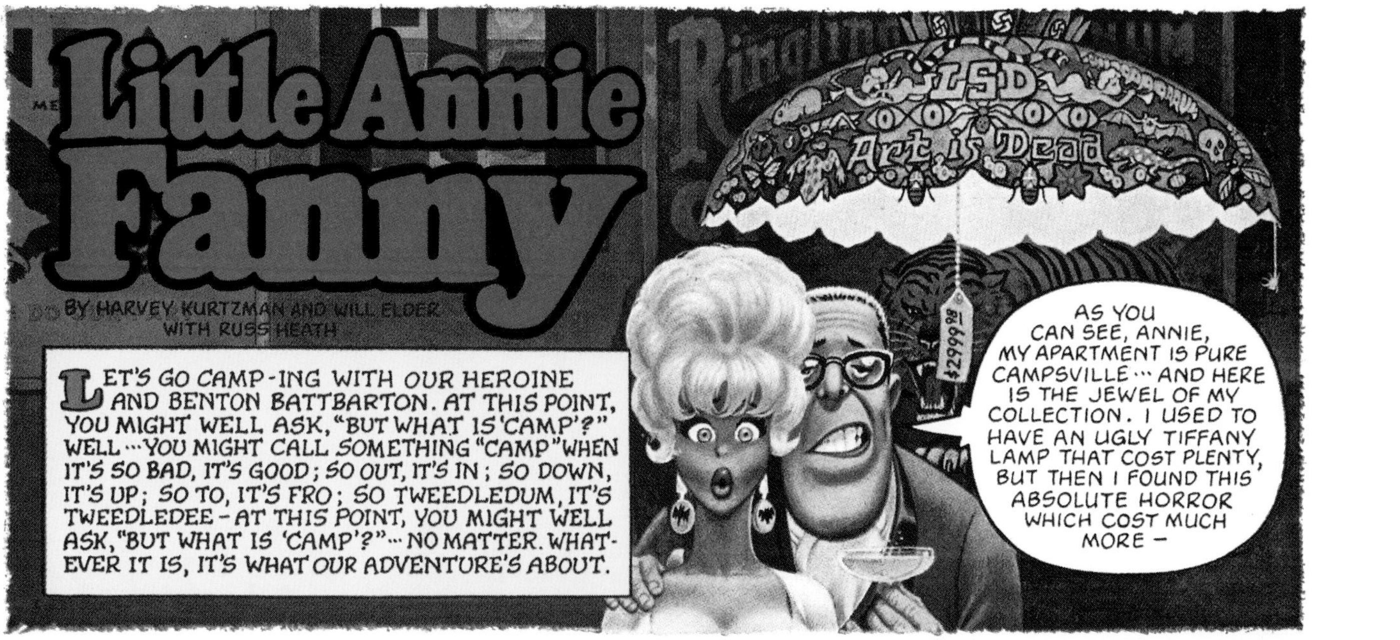

Little Annie Fanny
BY HARVEY KURTZMAN AND WILL ELDER WITH RUSS HEATH
LSD
Art is Dead
LET'S GO CAMP-ING WITH OUR HEROINE AND BENTON BATTBARTON. AT THIS POINT, YOU MIGHT WELL ASK, "BUT WHAT IS 'CAMP'?" WELL ··· YOU MIGHT CALL SOMETHING "CAMP" WHEN IT'S SO BAD, IT'S GOOD; SO OUT, IT'S IN; SO DOWN, IT'S UP; SO TO, IT'S FRO; SO TWEEDLEDUM, IT'S TWEEDLEDEE – AT THIS POINT, YOU MIGHT WELL ASK, "BUT WHAT IS 'CAMP'?" ··· NO MATTER. WHATEVER IT IS, IT'S WHAT OUR ADVENTURE'S ABOUT.
AS YOU CAN SEE, ANNIE, MY APARTMENT IS PURE CAMPSVILLE ··· AND HERE IS THE JEWEL OF MY COLLECTION. I USED TO HAVE AN UGLY TIFFANY LAMP THAT COST PLENTY, BUT THEN I FOUND THIS ABSOLUTE HORROR WHICH COST MUCH MORE –

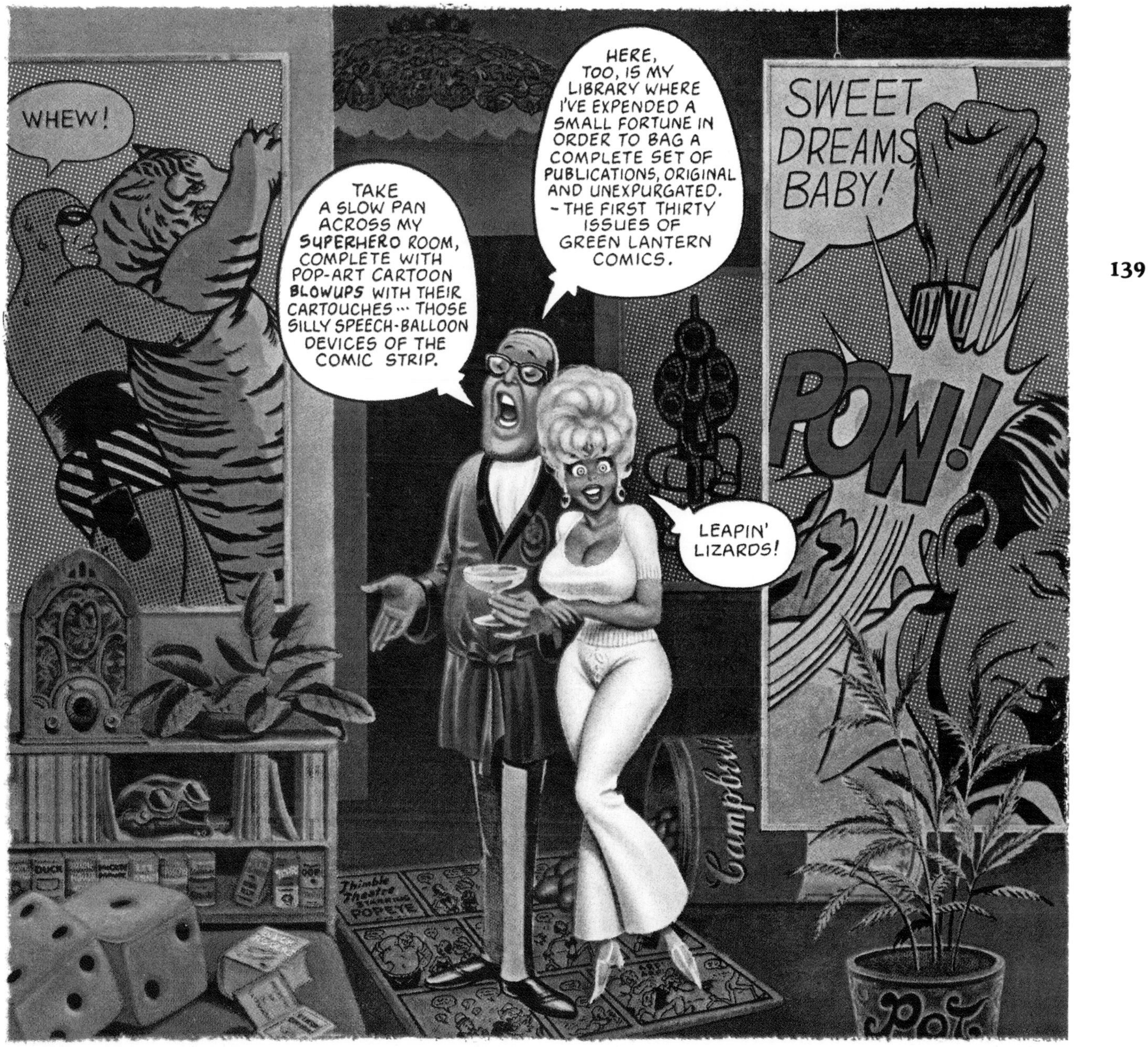

WHEW!
TAKE A SLOW PAN ACROSS MY SUPERHERO ROOM, COMPLETE WITH POP-ART CARTOON BLOWUPS WITH THEIR CARTOUCHES ··· THOSE SILLY SPEECH-BALLOON DEVICES OF THE COMIC STRIP.
HERE, TOO, IS MY LIBRARY WHERE I'VE EXPENDED A SMALL FORTUNE IN ORDER TO BAG A COMPLETE SET OF PUBLICATIONS, ORIGINAL AND UNEXPURGATED. – THE FIRST THIRTY ISSUES OF GREEN LANTERN COMICS.
SWEET DREAMS BABY!
POW!
LEAPIN' LIZARDS!
Campbell's
Thimble Theatre Starring POPEYE

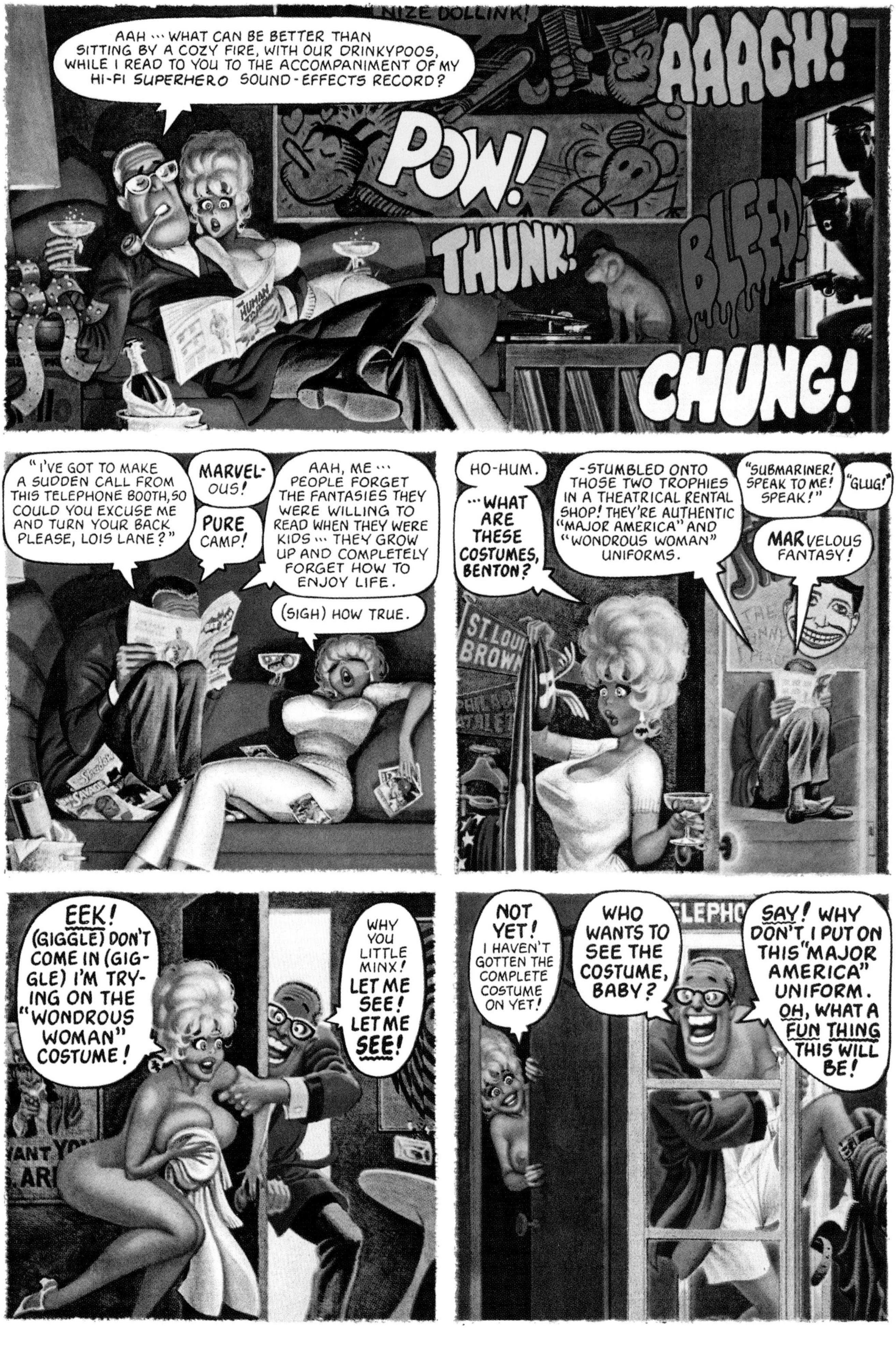
NIZE DOLLINK!
AAH ··· WHAT CAN BE BETTER THAN SITTING BY A COZY FIRE, WITH OUR DRINKYPOOS, WHILE I READ TO YOU TO THE ACCOMPANIMENT OF MY HI-FI SUPERHERO SOUND-EFFECTS RECORD?
AAAGH!
POW!
THUNK!
BLEED!
CHUNG!
"I'VE GOT TO MAKE A SUDDEN CALL FROM THIS TELEPHONE BOOTH, SO COULD YOU EXCUSE ME AND TURN YOUR BACK, PLEASE, LOIS LANE?"
MARVEL-OUS!
PURE CAMP!
AAH, ME ··· PEOPLE FORGET THE FANTASIES THEY WERE WILLING TO READ WHEN THEY WERE KIDS ··· THEY GROW UP AND COMPLETELY FORGET HOW TO ENJOY LIFE.
(SIGH) HOW TRUE.
HO-HUM.
···WHAT ARE THESE COSTUMES, BENTON?
-STUMBLED ONTO THOSE TWO TROPHIES IN A THEATRICAL RENTAL SHOP! THEY'RE AUTHENTIC "MAJOR AMERICA" AND "WONDROUS WOMAN" UNIFORMS.
"SUBMARINER! SPEAK TO ME! SPEAK!"
"GLUG!"
MARVELOUS FANTASY!
EEK! (GIGGLE) DON'T COME IN (GIG-GLE) I'M TRY-ING ON THE "WONDROUS WOMAN" COSTUME!
WHY YOU LITTLE MINX! LET ME SEE! LET ME SEE!
NOT YET! I HAVEN'T GOTTEN THE COMPLETE COSTUME ON YET!
WHO WANTS TO SEE THE COSTUME, BABY?
SAY! WHY DON'T I PUT ON THIS "MAJOR AMERICA" UNIFORM. OH, WHAT A FUN THING THIS WILL BE!

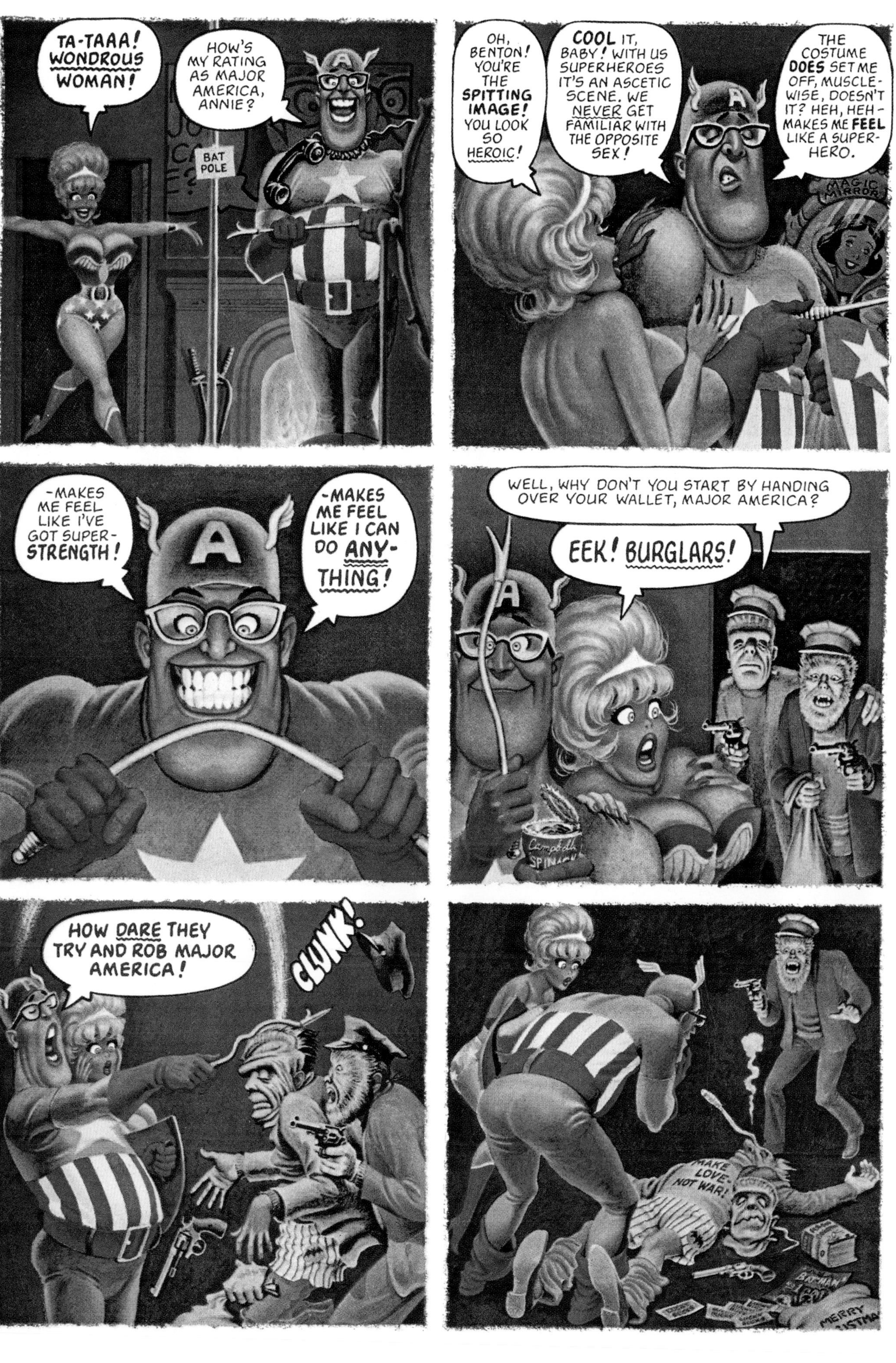
TA-TAAA! WONDROUS WOMAN!
HOW'S MY RATING AS MAJOR AMERICA, ANNIE?
BAT POLE
OH, BENTON! YOU'RE THE SPITTING IMAGE! YOU LOOK SO HEROIC!
COOL IT, BABY! WITH US SUPERHEROES IT'S AN ASCETIC SCENE. WE NEVER GET FAMILIAR WITH THE OPPOSITE SEX!
THE COSTUME DOES SET ME OFF, MUSCLE-WISE, DOESN'T IT? HEH, HEH - MAKES ME FEEL LIKE A SUPER-HERO.
MAGIC MIRROR
-MAKES ME FEEL LIKE I'VE GOT SUPER-STRENGTH!
-MAKES ME FEEL LIKE I CAN DO ANY-THING!
WELL, WHY DON'T YOU START BY HANDING OVER YOUR WALLET, MAJOR AMERICA?
EEK! BURGLARS!
HOW DARE THEY TRY AND ROB MAJOR AMERICA!
CLUNK!
MAKE LOVE. NOT WAR!

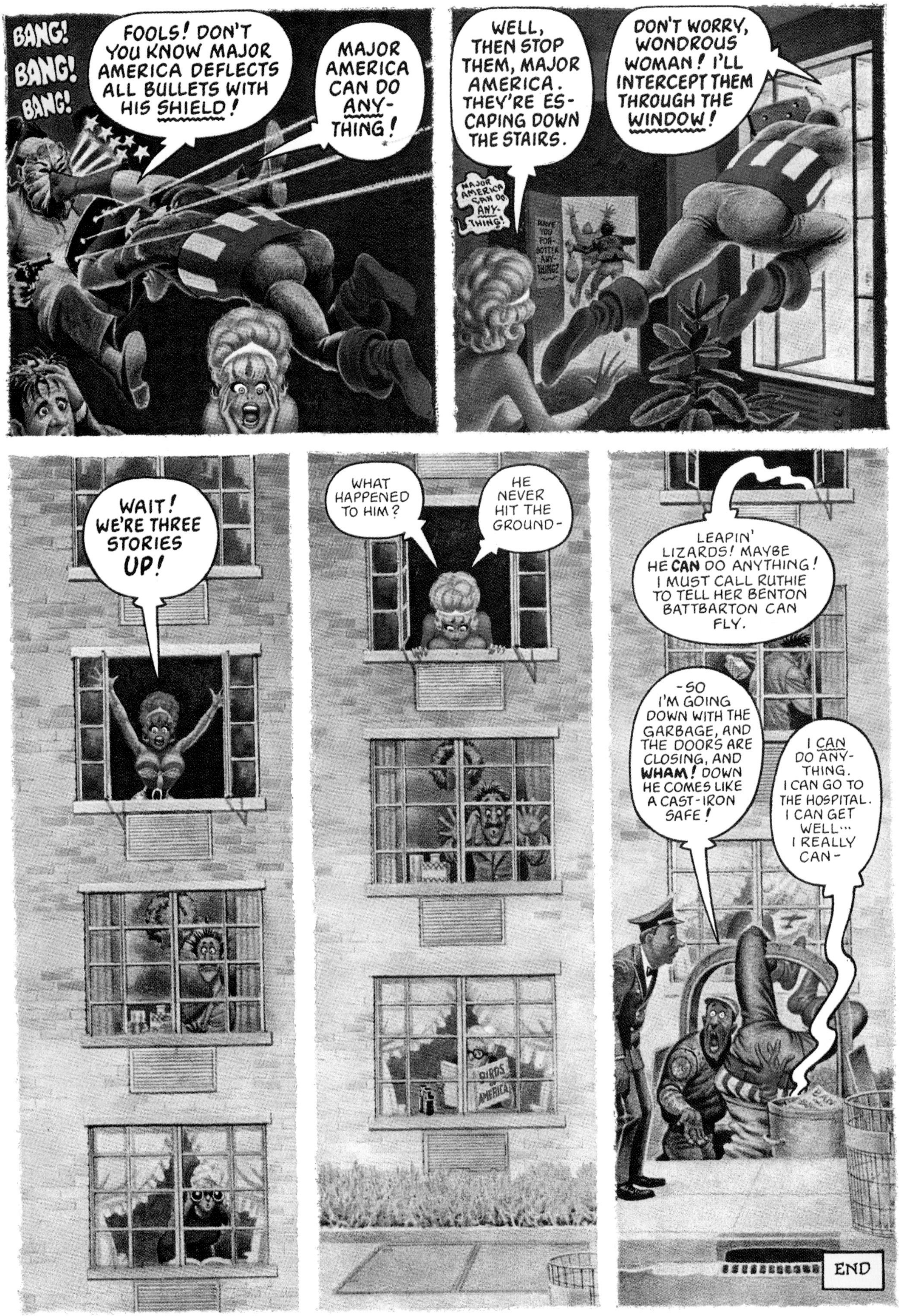

BANG! BANG! BANG!
FOOLS! DON'T YOU KNOW MAJOR AMERICA DEFLECTS ALL BULLETS WITH HIS SHIELD!
MAJOR AMERICA CAN DO ANY-THING!
WELL, THEN STOP THEM, MAJOR AMERICA. THEY'RE ES-CAPING DOWN THE STAIRS.
DON'T WORRY, WONDROUS WOMAN! I'LL INTERCEPT THEM THROUGH THE WINDOW!
MAJOR AMERICA CAN DO ANY-THING!
WAIT! WE'RE THREE STORIES UP!
WHAT HAPPENED TO HIM?
HE NEVER HIT THE GROUND-
LEAPIN' LIZARDS! MAYBE HE CAN DO ANYTHING! I MUST CALL RUTHIE TO TELL HER BENTON BATTBARTON CAN FLY.
-SO I'M GOING DOWN WITH THE GARBAGE, AND THE DOORS ARE CLOSING, AND WHAM! DOWN HE COMES LIKE A CAST-IRON SAFE!
I CAN DO ANY-THING. I CAN GO TO THE HOSPITAL. I CAN GET WELL... I REALLY CAN-
END

142

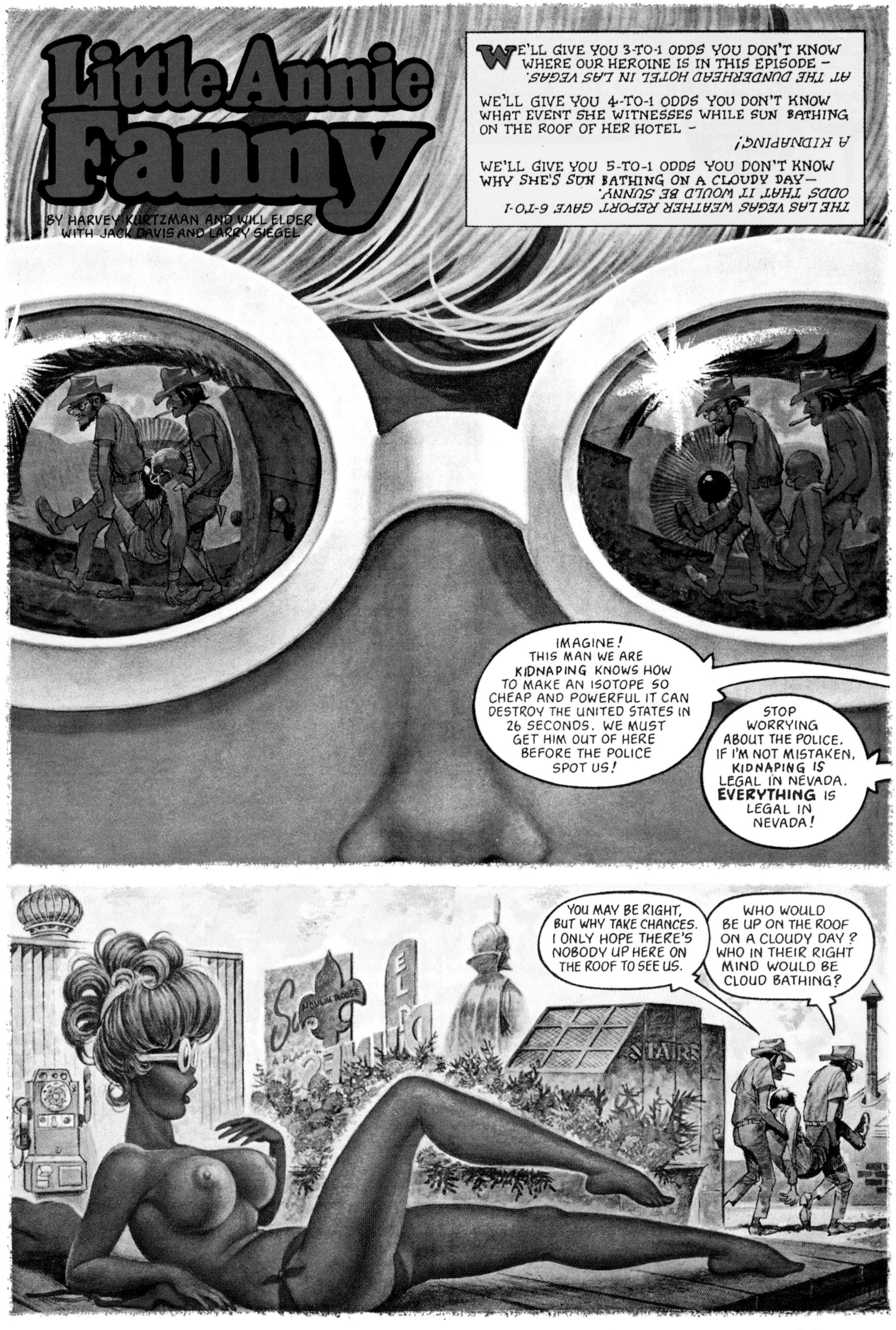
Little Annie Fanny
BY HARVEY KURTZMAN AND WILL ELDER WITH JACK DAVIS AND LARRY SIEGEL
WE'LL GIVE YOU 3-TO-1 ODDS YOU DON'T KNOW WHERE OUR HEROINE IS IN THIS EPISODE — AT THE DUNDERHEAD HOTEL IN LAS VEGAS.
WE'LL GIVE YOU 4-TO-1 ODDS YOU DON'T KNOW WHAT EVENT SHE WITNESSES WHILE SUN BATHING ON THE ROOF OF HER HOTEL — A KIDNAPING!
WE'LL GIVE YOU 5-TO-1 ODDS YOU DON'T KNOW WHY SHE'S SUN BATHING ON A CLOUDY DAY— THE LAS VEGAS WEATHER REPORT GAVE 6-TO-1 ODDS THAT IT WOULD BE SUNNY.
IMAGINE! THIS MAN WE ARE KIDNAPING KNOWS HOW TO MAKE AN ISOTOPE SO CHEAP AND POWERFUL IT CAN DESTROY THE UNITED STATES IN 26 SECONDS. WE MUST GET HIM OUT OF HERE BEFORE THE POLICE SPOT US!
STOP WORRYING ABOUT THE POLICE. IF I'M NOT MISTAKEN, KIDNAPING IS LEGAL IN NEVADA. EVERYTHING IS LEGAL IN NEVADA!
YOU MAY BE RIGHT, BUT WHY TAKE CHANCES. I ONLY HOPE THERE'S NOBODY UP HERE ON THE ROOF TO SEE US.
WHO WOULD BE UP ON THE ROOF ON A CLOUDY DAY? WHO IN THEIR RIGHT MIND WOULD BE CLOUD BATHING?
STAIRS

143

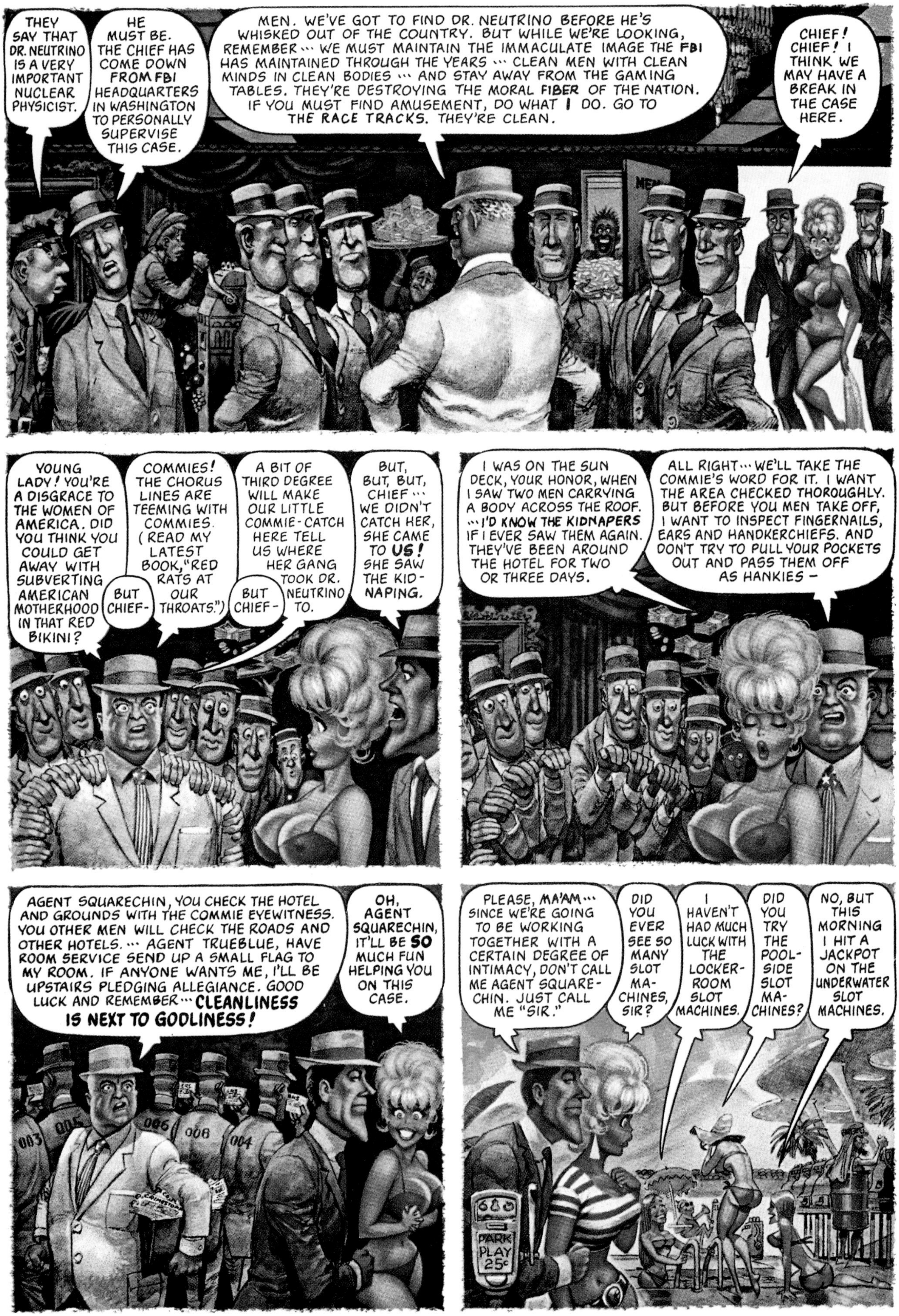
THEY SAY THAT DR. NEUTRINO IS A VERY IMPORTANT NUCLEAR PHYSICIST.
HE MUST BE. THE CHIEF HAS COME DOWN FROM FBI HEADQUARTERS IN WASHINGTON TO PERSONALLY SUPERVISE THIS CASE.
MEN. WE'VE GOT TO FIND DR. NEUTRINO BEFORE HE'S WHISKED OUT OF THE COUNTRY. BUT WHILE WE'RE LOOKING, REMEMBER ··· WE MUST MAINTAIN THE IMMACULATE IMAGE THE FBI HAS MAINTAINED THROUGH THE YEARS ··· CLEAN MEN WITH CLEAN MINDS IN CLEAN BODIES ··· AND STAY AWAY FROM THE GAMING TABLES. THEY'RE DESTROYING THE MORAL FIBER OF THE NATION. IF YOU MUST FIND AMUSEMENT, DO WHAT I DO. GO TO THE RACE TRACKS. THEY'RE CLEAN.
CHIEF! CHIEF! I THINK WE MAY HAVE A BREAK IN THE CASE HERE.
MEN
YOUNG LADY! YOU'RE A DISGRACE TO THE WOMEN OF AMERICA. DID YOU THINK YOU COULD GET AWAY WITH SUBVERTING AMERICAN MOTHERHOOD IN THAT RED BIKINI?
BUT CHIEF-
COMMIES! THE CHORUS LINES ARE TEEMING WITH COMMIES. (READ MY LATEST BOOK, "RED RATS AT OUR THROATS.")
BUT CHIEF-
A BIT OF THIRD DEGREE WILL MAKE OUR LITTLE COMMIE-CATCH HERE TELL US WHERE HER GANG TOOK DR. NEUTRINO TO.
BUT, BUT, BUT, CHIEF ··· WE DIDN'T CATCH HER, SHE CAME TO US! SHE SAW THE KID-NAPING.
I WAS ON THE SUN DECK, YOUR HONOR, WHEN I SAW TWO MEN CARRYING A BODY ACROSS THE ROOF. ··· I'D KNOW THE KIDNAPERS IF I EVER SAW THEM AGAIN. THEY'VE BEEN AROUND THE HOTEL FOR TWO OR THREE DAYS.
ALL RIGHT ··· WE'LL TAKE THE COMMIE'S WORD FOR IT. I WANT THE AREA CHECKED THOROUGHLY. BUT BEFORE YOU MEN TAKE OFF, I WANT TO INSPECT FINGERNAILS, EARS AND HANDKERCHIEFS. AND DON'T TRY TO PULL YOUR POCKETS OUT AND PASS THEM OFF AS HANKIES —
AGENT SQUARECHIN, YOU CHECK THE HOTEL AND GROUNDS WITH THE COMMIE EYEWITNESS. YOU OTHER MEN WILL CHECK THE ROADS AND OTHER HOTELS. ··· AGENT TRUEBLUE, HAVE ROOM SERVICE SEND UP A SMALL FLAG TO MY ROOM. IF ANYONE WANTS ME, I'LL BE UPSTAIRS PLEDGING ALLEGIANCE. GOOD LUCK AND REMEMBER ··· CLEANLINESS IS NEXT TO GODLINESS!
OH, AGENT SQUARECHIN, IT'LL BE SO MUCH FUN HELPING YOU ON THIS CASE.
003
005
006
008
004
PLEASE, MA'AM ··· SINCE WE'RE GOING TO BE WORKING TOGETHER WITH A CERTAIN DEGREE OF INTIMACY, DON'T CALL ME AGENT SQUARE-CHIN. JUST CALL ME "SIR."
DID YOU EVER SEE SO MANY SLOT MA-CHINES, SIR?
I HAVEN'T HAD MUCH LUCK WITH THE LOCKER-ROOM SLOT MACHINES.
DID YOU TRY THE POOL-SIDE SLOT MA-CHINES?
NO, BUT THIS MORNING I HIT A JACKPOT ON THE UNDERWATER SLOT MACHINES.
PARK PLAY 25¢

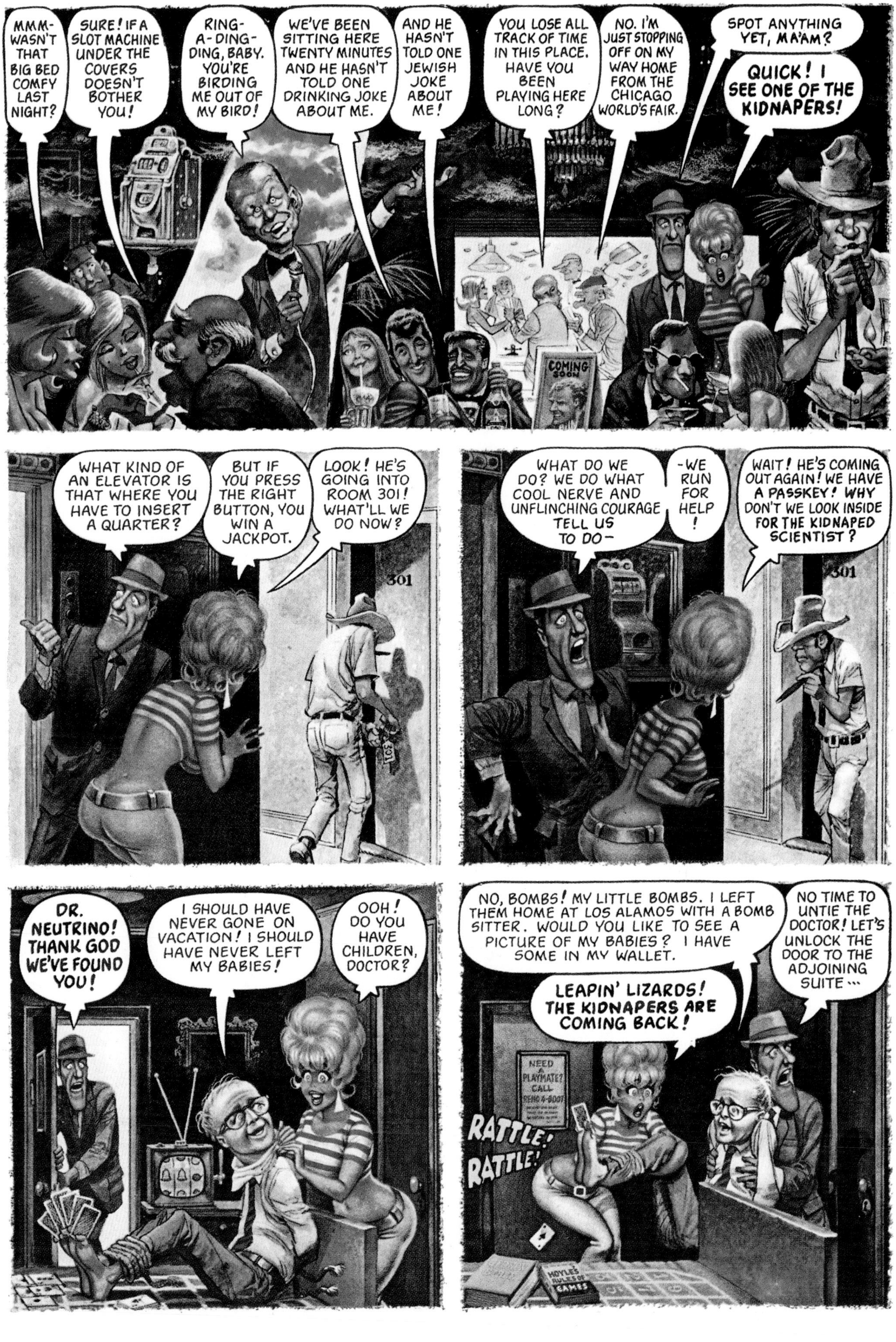
MMM-WASN'T THAT BIG BED COMFY LAST NIGHT?
SURE! IF A SLOT MACHINE UNDER THE COVERS DOESN'T BOTHER YOU!
RING-A-DING-DING, BABY. YOU'RE BIRDING ME OUT OF MY BIRD!
WE'VE BEEN SITTING HERE TWENTY MINUTES AND HE HASN'T TOLD ONE DRINKING JOKE ABOUT ME.
AND HE HASN'T TOLD ONE JEWISH JOKE ABOUT ME!
YOU LOSE ALL TRACK OF TIME IN THIS PLACE. HAVE YOU BEEN PLAYING HERE LONG?
NO. I'M JUST STOPPING OFF ON MY WAY HOME FROM THE CHICAGO WORLD'S FAIR.
SPOT ANYTHING YET, MA'AM?
QUICK! I SEE ONE OF THE KIDNAPERS!
COMING SOON
WHAT KIND OF AN ELEVATOR IS THAT WHERE YOU HAVE TO INSERT A QUARTER?
BUT IF YOU PRESS THE RIGHT BUTTON, YOU WIN A JACKPOT.
LOOK! HE'S GOING INTO ROOM 301! WHAT'LL WE DO NOW?
301
WHAT DO WE DO? WE DO WHAT COOL NERVE AND UNFLINCHING COURAGE TELL US TO DO—
-WE RUN FOR HELP!
WAIT! HE'S COMING OUT AGAIN! WE HAVE A PASSKEY! WHY DON'T WE LOOK INSIDE FOR THE KIDNAPED SCIENTIST?
301
DR. NEUTRINO! THANK GOD WE'VE FOUND YOU!
I SHOULD HAVE NEVER GONE ON VACATION! I SHOULD HAVE NEVER LEFT MY BABIES!
OOH! DO YOU HAVE CHILDREN, DOCTOR?
NO, BOMBS! MY LITTLE BOMBS. I LEFT THEM HOME AT LOS ALAMOS WITH A BOMB SITTER. WOULD YOU LIKE TO SEE A PICTURE OF MY BABIES? I HAVE SOME IN MY WALLET.
NO TIME TO UNTIE THE DOCTOR! LET'S UNLOCK THE DOOR TO THE ADJOINING SUITE...
LEAPIN' LIZARDS! THE KIDNAPERS ARE COMING BACK!
NEED A PLAYMATE? CALL
RATTLE! RATTLE!
HOYLE'S RULES OF GAMES

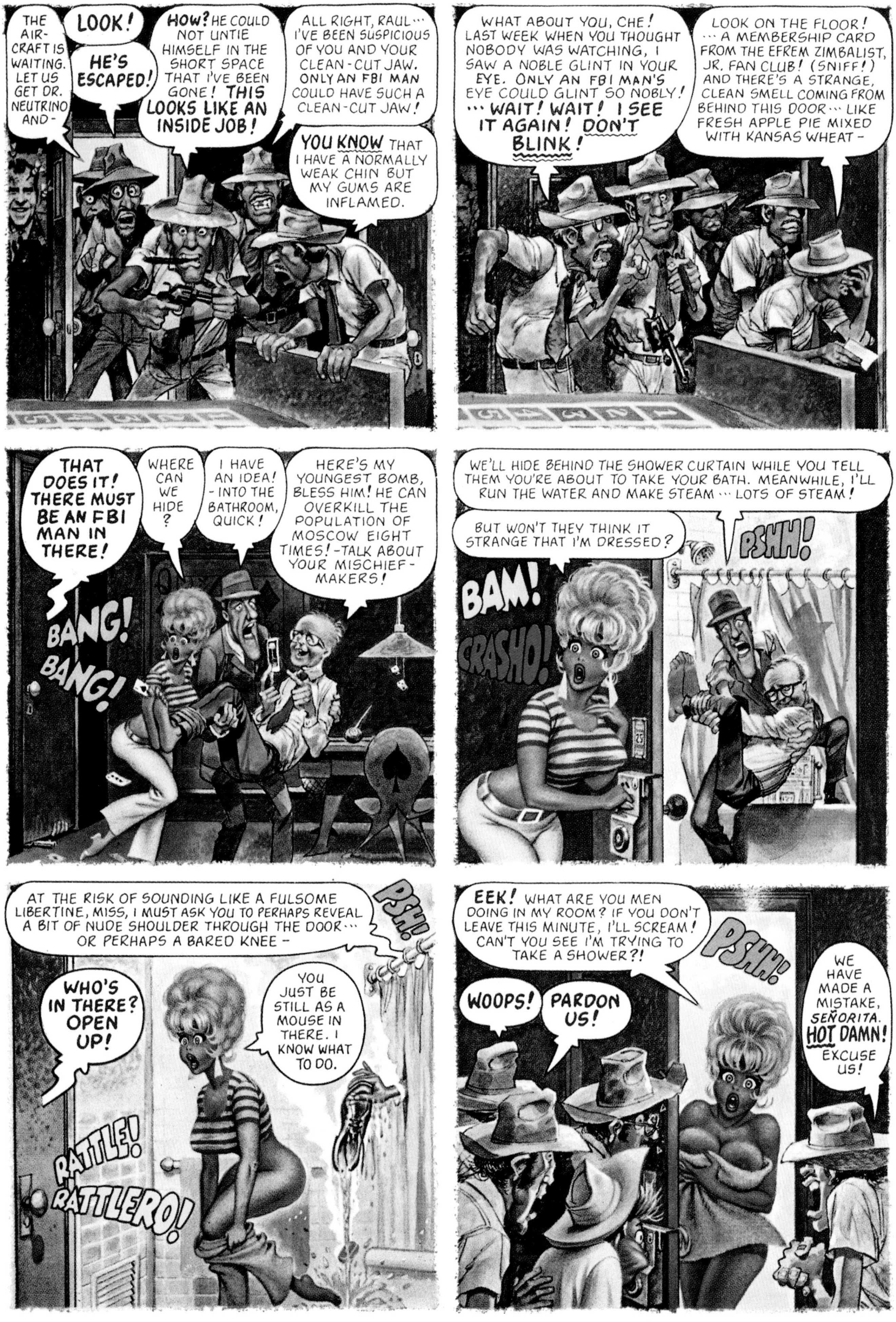

THE AIRCRAFT IS WAITING. LET US GET DR. NEUTRINO AND -
LOOK!
HE'S ESCAPED!
HOW? HE COULD NOT UNTIE HIMSELF IN THE SHORT SPACE THAT I'VE BEEN GONE! THIS LOOKS LIKE AN INSIDE JOB!
ALL RIGHT, RAUL··· I'VE BEEN SUSPICIOUS OF YOU AND YOUR CLEAN-CUT JAW. ONLY AN FBI MAN COULD HAVE SUCH A CLEAN-CUT JAW!
YOU KNOW THAT I HAVE A NORMALLY WEAK CHIN BUT MY GUMS ARE INFLAMED.
WHAT ABOUT YOU, CHE! LAST WEEK WHEN YOU THOUGHT NOBODY WAS WATCHING, I SAW A NOBLE GLINT IN YOUR EYE. ONLY AN FBI MAN'S EYE COULD GLINT SO NOBLY! ··· WAIT! WAIT! I SEE IT AGAIN! DON'T BLINK!
LOOK ON THE FLOOR! ··· A MEMBERSHIP CARD FROM THE EFREM ZIMBALIST, JR. FAN CLUB! (SNIFF!) AND THERE'S A STRANGE, CLEAN SMELL COMING FROM BEHIND THIS DOOR··· LIKE FRESH APPLE PIE MIXED WITH KANSAS WHEAT -
THAT DOES IT! THERE MUST BE AN FBI MAN IN THERE!
WHERE CAN WE HIDE?
I HAVE AN IDEA! - INTO THE BATHROOM, QUICK!
HERE'S MY YOUNGEST BOMB, BLESS HIM! HE CAN OVERKILL THE POPULATION OF MOSCOW EIGHT TIMES! - TALK ABOUT YOUR MISCHIEF-MAKERS!
BANG! BANG!
WE'LL HIDE BEHIND THE SHOWER CURTAIN WHILE YOU TELL THEM YOU'RE ABOUT TO TAKE YOUR BATH. MEANWHILE, I'LL RUN THE WATER AND MAKE STEAM··· LOTS OF STEAM!
BUT WON'T THEY THINK IT STRANGE THAT I'M DRESSED?
PSHH!
BAM! CRASHO!
AT THE RISK OF SOUNDING LIKE A FULSOME LIBERTINE, MISS, I MUST ASK YOU TO PERHAPS REVEAL A BIT OF NUDE SHOULDER THROUGH THE DOOR··· OR PERHAPS A BARED KNEE -
PSH!
WHO'S IN THERE? OPEN UP!
YOU JUST BE STILL AS A MOUSE IN THERE. I KNOW WHAT TO DO.
RATTLE! RATTLERO!
EEK! WHAT ARE YOU MEN DOING IN MY ROOM? IF YOU DON'T LEAVE THIS MINUTE, I'LL SCREAM! CAN'T YOU SEE I'M TRYING TO TAKE A SHOWER?!
PSHH!
WOOPS!
PARDON US!
WE HAVE MADE A MISTAKE, SEÑORITA. HOT DAMN! EXCUSE US!

146

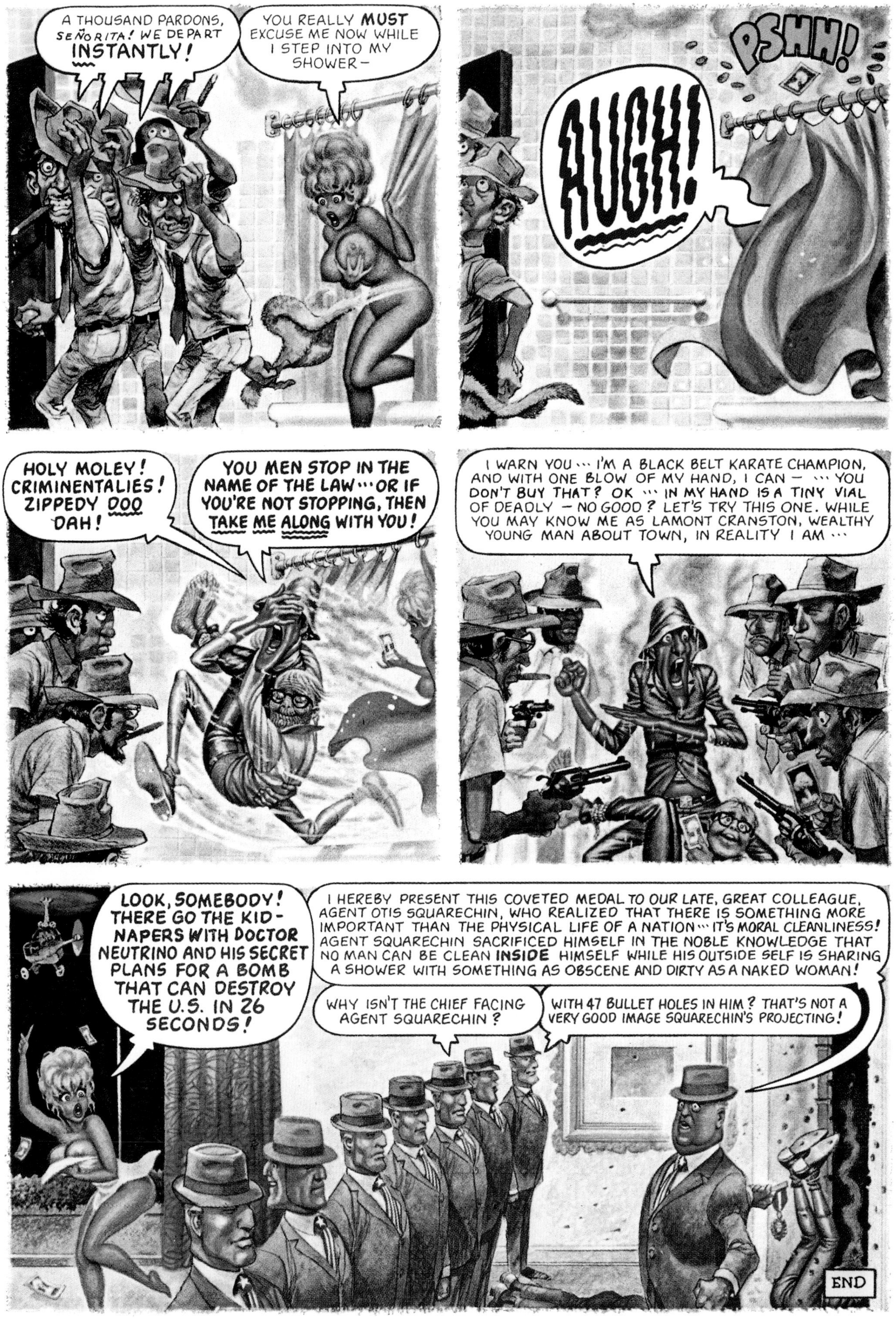
A THOUSAND PARDONS, SEÑORITA! WE DEPART INSTANTLY!
YOU REALLY MUST EXCUSE ME NOW WHILE I STEP INTO MY SHOWER—
PSHH!
AUGH!
HOLY MOLEY! CRIMINENTALIES! ZIPPEDY DOO DAH!
YOU MEN STOP IN THE NAME OF THE LAW ··· OR IF YOU'RE NOT STOPPING, THEN TAKE ME ALONG WITH YOU!
I WARN YOU ··· I'M A BLACK BELT KARATE CHAMPION, AND WITH ONE BLOW OF MY HAND, I CAN — ··· YOU DON'T BUY THAT? OK ··· IN MY HAND IS A TINY VIAL OF DEADLY — NO GOOD? LET'S TRY THIS ONE. WHILE YOU MAY KNOW ME AS LAMONT CRANSTON, WEALTHY YOUNG MAN ABOUT TOWN, IN REALITY I AM ···
LOOK, SOMEBODY! THERE GO THE KID-NAPERS WITH DOCTOR NEUTRINO AND HIS SECRET PLANS FOR A BOMB THAT CAN DESTROY THE U.S. IN 26 SECONDS!
I HEREBY PRESENT THIS COVETED MEDAL TO OUR LATE, GREAT COLLEAGUE, AGENT OTIS SQUARECHIN, WHO REALIZED THAT THERE IS SOMETHING MORE IMPORTANT THAN THE PHYSICAL LIFE OF A NATION ··· IT'S MORAL CLEANLINESS! AGENT SQUARECHIN SACRIFICED HIMSELF IN THE NOBLE KNOWLEDGE THAT NO MAN CAN BE CLEAN INSIDE HIMSELF WHILE HIS OUTSIDE SELF IS SHARING A SHOWER WITH SOMETHING AS OBSCENE AND DIRTY AS A NAKED WOMAN!
WHY ISN'T THE CHIEF FACING AGENT SQUARECHIN?
WITH 47 BULLET HOLES IN HIM? THAT'S NOT A VERY GOOD IMAGE SQUARECHIN'S PROJECTING!
END

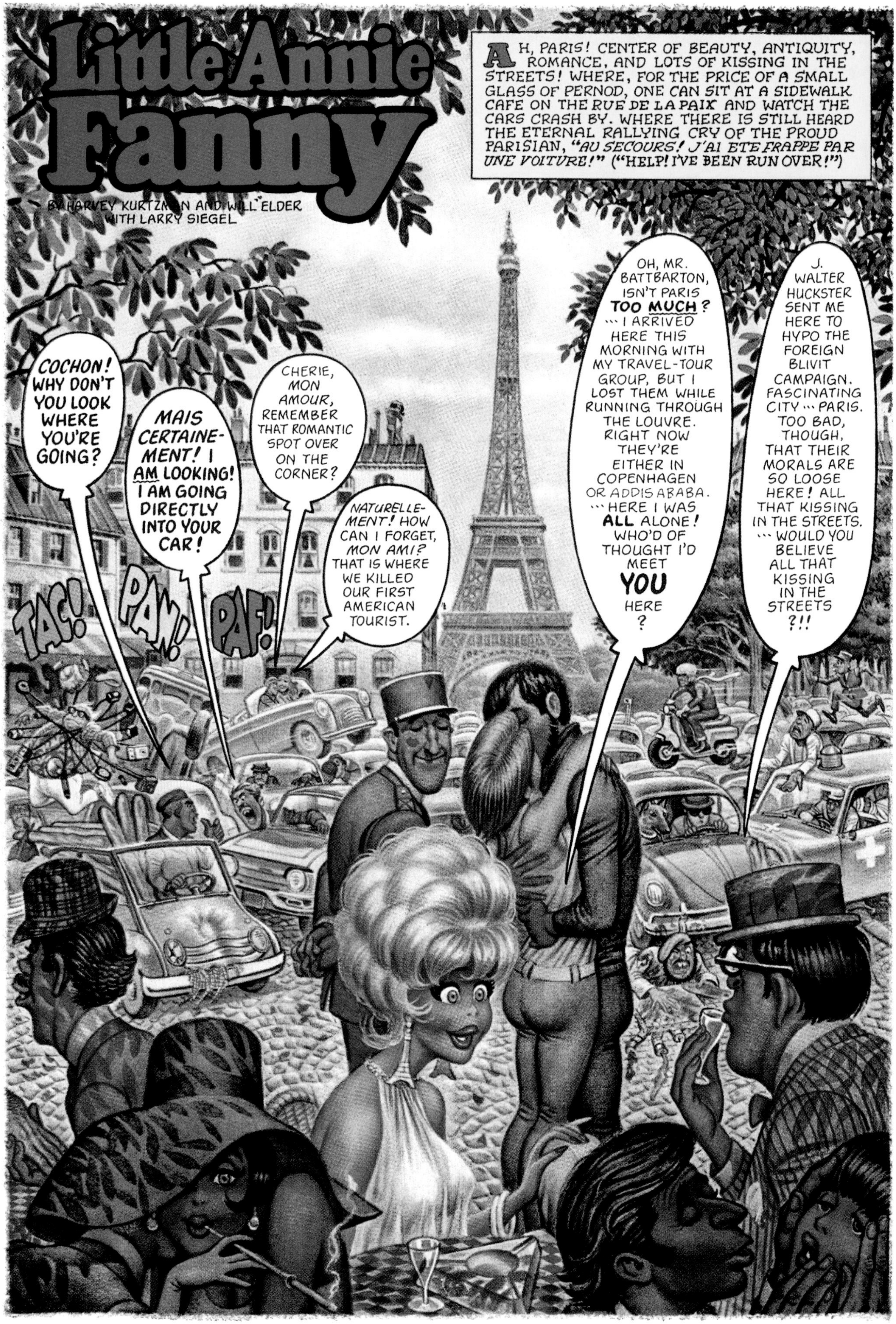
Little Annie Fanny
AH, PARIS! CENTER OF BEAUTY, ANTIQUITY, ROMANCE, AND LOTS OF KISSING IN THE STREETS! WHERE, FOR THE PRICE OF A SMALL GLASS OF PERNOD, ONE CAN SIT AT A SIDEWALK CAFE ON THE RUE DE LA PAIX AND WATCH THE CARS CRASH BY. WHERE THERE IS STILL HEARD THE ETERNAL RALLYING CRY OF THE PROUD PARISIAN, "AU SECOURS! J'AI ETE FRAPPE PAR UNE VOITURE!" ("HELP! I'VE BEEN RUN OVER!")
BY HARVEY KURTZMAN AND WILL ELDER WITH LARRY SIEGEL
COCHON! WHY DON'T YOU LOOK WHERE YOU'RE GOING?
MAIS CERTAINEMENT! I AM LOOKING! I AM GOING DIRECTLY INTO YOUR CAR!
CHERIE, MON AMOUR, REMEMBER THAT ROMANTIC SPOT OVER ON THE CORNER?
NATURELLEMENT! HOW CAN I FORGET, MON AMI? THAT IS WHERE WE KILLED OUR FIRST AMERICAN TOURIST.
TAC! PAN! PAF!
OH, MR. BATTBARTON, ISN'T PARIS TOO MUCH? ... I ARRIVED HERE THIS MORNING WITH MY TRAVEL-TOUR GROUP, BUT I LOST THEM WHILE RUNNING THROUGH THE LOUVRE. RIGHT NOW THEY'RE EITHER IN COPENHAGEN OR ADDIS ABABA. ... HERE I WAS ALL ALONE! WHO'D OF THOUGHT I'D MEET YOU HERE ?
J. WALTER HUCKSTER SENT ME HERE TO HYPO THE FOREIGN BLIVIT CAMPAIGN. FASCINATING CITY ... PARIS. TOO BAD, THOUGH, THAT THEIR MORALS ARE SO LOOSE HERE! ALL THAT KISSING IN THE STREETS. ... WOULD YOU BELIEVE ALL THAT KISSING IN THE STREETS ?!!

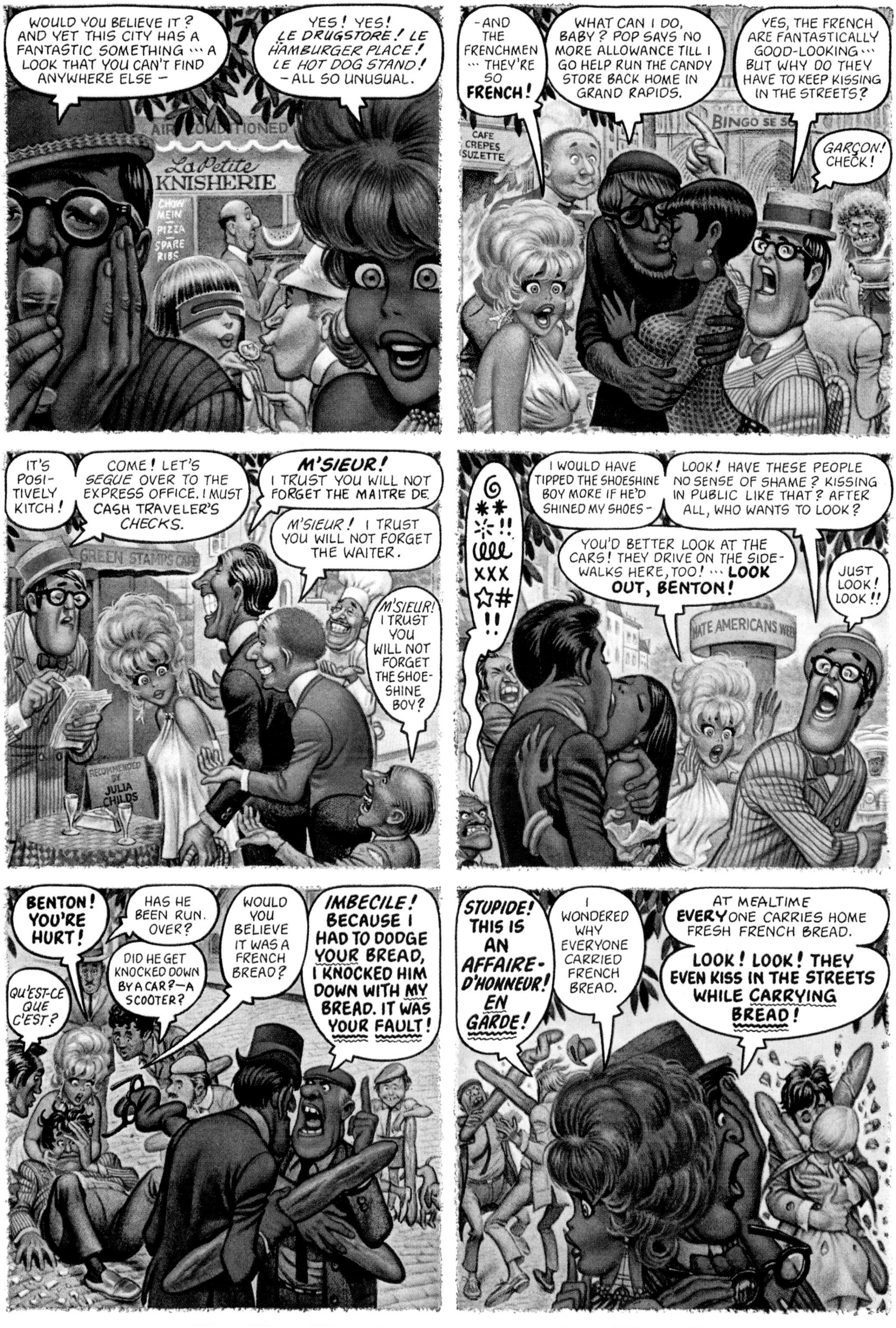
WOULD YOU BELIEVE IT? AND YET THIS CITY HAS A FANTASTIC SOMETHING ··· A LOOK THAT YOU CAN'T FIND ANYWHERE ELSE –
YES! YES! LE DRUGSTORE! LE HAMBURGER PLACE! LE HOT DOG STAND! – ALL SO UNUSUAL.
AIR CONDITIONED
La Petite KNISHERIE
CHOW MEIN PIZZA SPARE RIBS
– AND THE FRENCHMEN ··· THEY'RE SO FRENCH!
WHAT CAN I DO, BABY? POP SAYS NO MORE ALLOWANCE TILL I GO HELP RUN THE CANDY STORE BACK HOME IN GRAND RAPIDS.
YES, THE FRENCH ARE FANTASTICALLY GOOD-LOOKING ··· BUT WHY DO THEY HAVE TO KEEP KISSING IN THE STREETS?
CAFE CREPES SUZETTE
GARÇON! CHECK!
IT'S POSITIVELY KITCH!
COME! LET'S SEGUE OVER TO THE EXPRESS OFFICE. I MUST CASH TRAVELER'S CHECKS.
M'SIEUR! I TRUST YOU WILL NOT FORGET THE MAITRE DE.
M'SIEUR! I TRUST YOU WILL NOT FORGET THE WAITER.
M'SIEUR! I TRUST YOU WILL NOT FORGET THE SHOESHINE BOY?
GREEN STAMPS CAFE
RECOMMENDED BY JULIA CHILDS
I WOULD HAVE TIPPED THE SHOESHINE BOY MORE IF HE'D SHINED MY SHOES –
LOOK! HAVE THESE PEOPLE NO SENSE OF SHAME? KISSING IN PUBLIC LIKE THAT? AFTER ALL, WHO WANTS TO LOOK?
YOU'D BETTER LOOK AT THE CARS! THEY DRIVE ON THE SIDEWALKS HERE, TOO! ··· LOOK OUT, BENTON!
JUST LOOK! LOOK!!
HATE AMERICANS
BENTON! YOU'RE HURT!
HAS HE BEEN RUN OVER?
DID HE GET KNOCKED DOWN BY A CAR? – A SCOOTER?
QU'EST-CE QUE C'EST?
WOULD YOU BELIEVE IT WAS A FRENCH BREAD?
IMBECILE! BECAUSE I HAD TO DODGE YOUR BREAD, I KNOCKED HIM DOWN WITH MY BREAD. IT WAS YOUR FAULT!
STUPIDE! THIS IS AN AFFAIRE-D'HONNEUR! EN GARDE!
I WONDERED WHY EVERYONE CARRIED FRENCH BREAD.
AT MEALTIME EVERYONE CARRIES HOME FRESH FRENCH BREAD.
LOOK! LOOK! THEY EVEN KISS IN THE STREETS WHILE CARRYING BREAD!

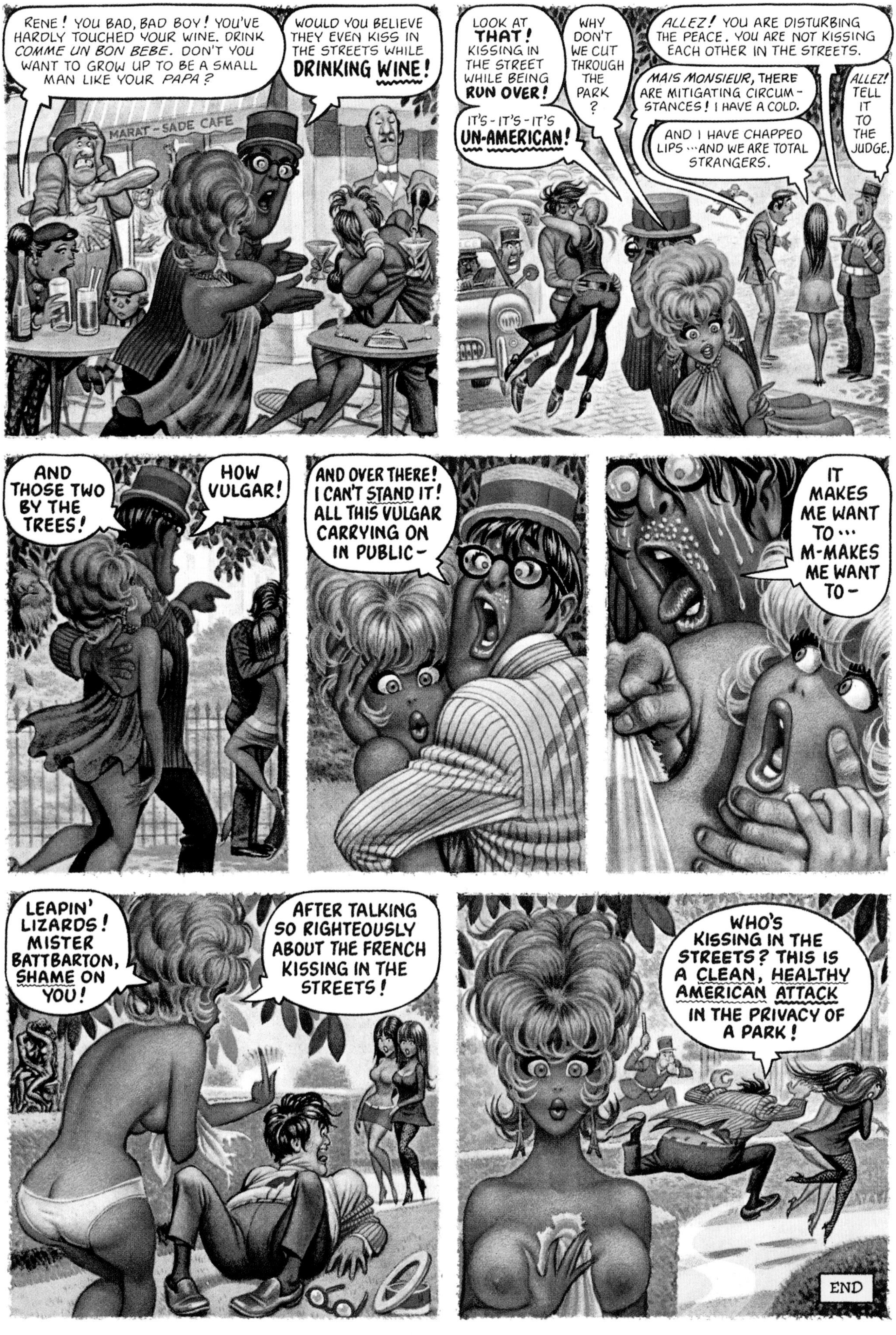

RENE! YOU BAD, BAD BOY! YOU'VE HARDLY TOUCHED YOUR WINE. DRINK COMME UN BON BEBE. DON'T YOU WANT TO GROW UP TO BE A SMALL MAN LIKE YOUR PAPA?
WOULD YOU BELIEVE THEY EVEN KISS IN THE STREETS WHILE DRINKING WINE!
MARAT - SADE CAFE
LOOK AT THAT! KISSING IN THE STREET WHILE BEING RUN OVER!
WHY DON'T WE CUT THROUGH THE PARK?
IT'S - IT'S - IT'S UN-AMERICAN!
ALLEZ! YOU ARE DISTURBING THE PEACE. YOU ARE NOT KISSING EACH OTHER IN THE STREETS.
MAIS MONSIEUR, THERE ARE MITIGATING CIRCUM-STANCES! I HAVE A COLD.
AND I HAVE CHAPPED LIPS ... AND WE ARE TOTAL STRANGERS.
ALLEZ! TELL IT TO THE JUDGE.
AND THOSE TWO BY THE TREES!
HOW VULGAR!
AND OVER THERE! I CAN'T STAND IT! ALL THIS VULGAR CARRYING ON IN PUBLIC-
IT MAKES ME WANT TO ... M-MAKES ME WANT TO-
LEAPIN' LIZARDS! MISTER BATTBARTON, SHAME ON YOU!
AFTER TALKING SO RIGHTEOUSLY ABOUT THE FRENCH KISSING IN THE STREETS!
WHO'S KISSING IN THE STREETS? THIS IS A CLEAN, HEALTHY AMERICAN ATTACK IN THE PRIVACY OF A PARK!
END

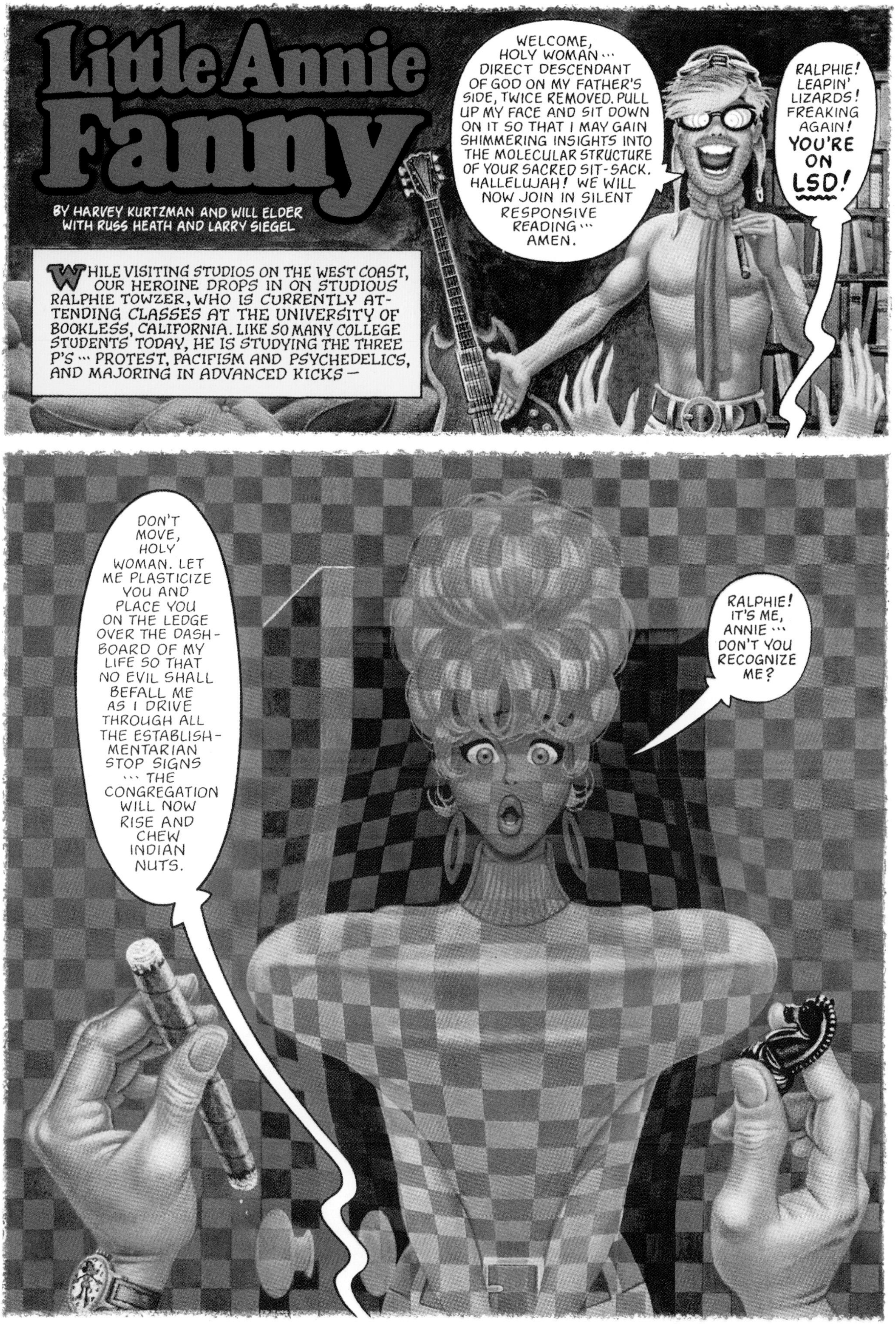
Little Annie Fanny
BY HARVEY KURTZMAN AND WILL ELDER WITH RUSS HEATH AND LARRY SIEGEL
WHILE VISITING STUDIOS ON THE WEST COAST, OUR HEROINE DROPS IN ON STUDIOUS RALPHIE TOWZER, WHO IS CURRENTLY ATTENDING CLASSES AT THE UNIVERSITY OF BOOKLESS, CALIFORNIA. LIKE SO MANY COLLEGE STUDENTS TODAY, HE IS STUDYING THE THREE P'S ··· PROTEST, PACIFISM AND PSYCHEDELICS, AND MAJORING IN ADVANCED KICKS—
WELCOME, HOLY WOMAN ··· DIRECT DESCENDANT OF GOD ON MY FATHER'S SIDE, TWICE REMOVED. PULL UP MY FACE AND SIT DOWN ON IT SO THAT I MAY GAIN SHIMMERING INSIGHTS INTO THE MOLECULAR STRUCTURE OF YOUR SACRED SIT-SACK. HALLELUJAH! WE WILL NOW JOIN IN SILENT RESPONSIVE READING ··· AMEN.
RALPHIE! LEAPIN' LIZARDS! FREAKING AGAIN! YOU'RE ON LSD!
DON'T MOVE, HOLY WOMAN. LET ME PLASTICIZE YOU AND PLACE YOU ON THE LEDGE OVER THE DASHBOARD OF MY LIFE SO THAT NO EVIL SHALL BEFALL ME AS I DRIVE THROUGH ALL THE ESTABLISHMENTARIAN STOP SIGNS ··· THE CONGREGATION WILL NOW RISE AND CHEW INDIAN NUTS.
RALPHIE! IT'S ME, ANNIE ··· DON'T YOU RECOGNIZE ME?

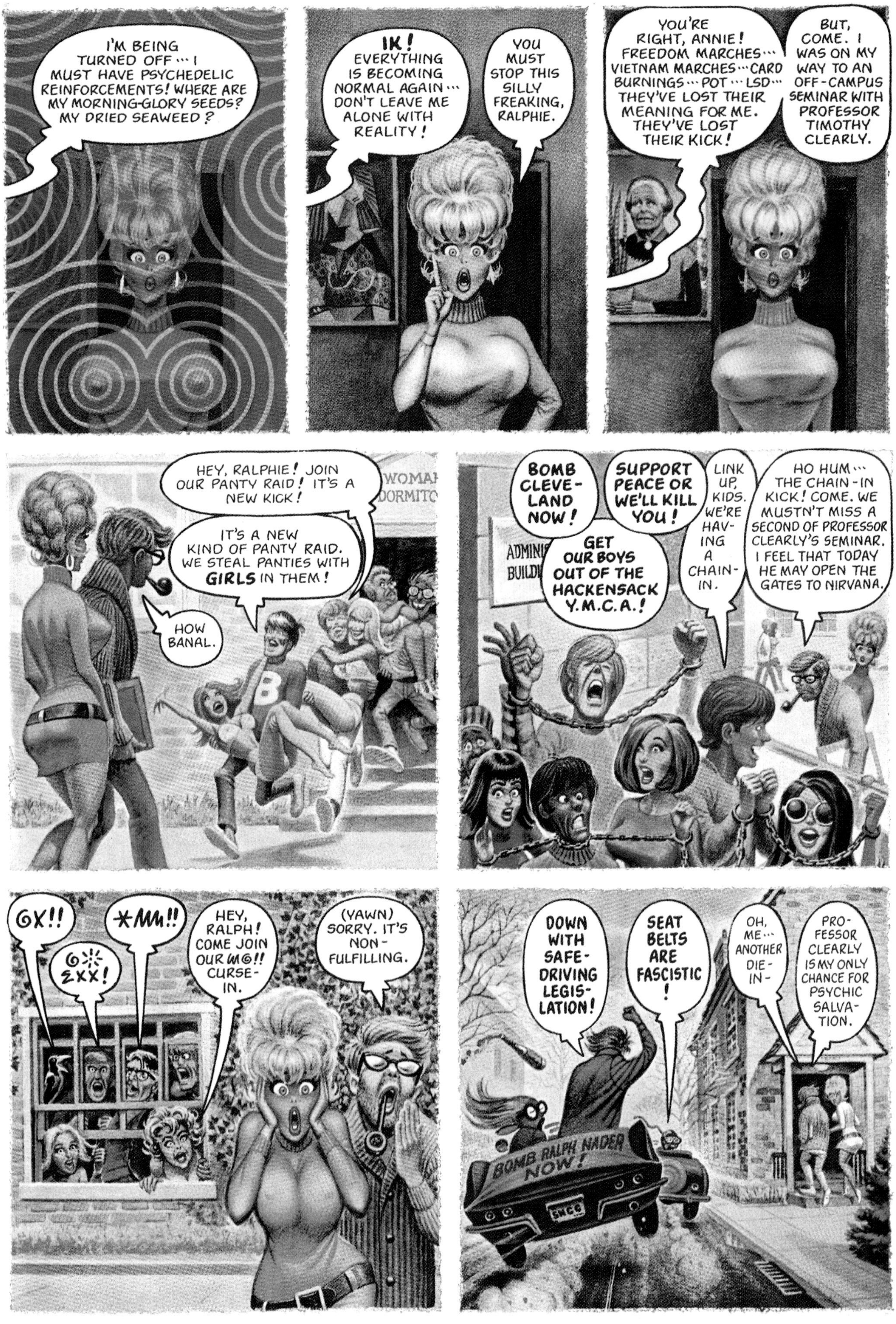

I'M BEING TURNED OFF ··· I MUST HAVE PSYCHEDELIC REINFORCEMENTS! WHERE ARE MY MORNING-GLORY SEEDS? MY DRIED SEAWEED?
IK! EVERYTHING IS BECOMING NORMAL AGAIN ··· DON'T LEAVE ME ALONE WITH REALITY!
YOU MUST STOP THIS SILLY FREAKING, RALPHIE.
YOU'RE RIGHT, ANNIE! FREEDOM MARCHES ··· VIETNAM MARCHES ··· CARD BURNINGS ··· POT ··· LSD ··· THEY'VE LOST THEIR MEANING FOR ME. THEY'VE LOST THEIR KICK!
BUT, COME. I WAS ON MY WAY TO AN OFF-CAMPUS SEMINAR WITH PROFESSOR TIMOTHY CLEARLY.
WOMAN DORMITO
HEY, RALPHIE! JOIN OUR PANTY RAID! IT'S A NEW KICK!
IT'S A NEW KIND OF PANTY RAID. WE STEAL PANTIES WITH GIRLS IN THEM!
HOW BANAL.
B
ADMINIS BUILDI
BOMB CLEVE-LAND NOW!
SUPPORT PEACE OR WE'LL KILL YOU!
GET OUR BOYS OUT OF THE HACKENSACK Y.M.C.A.!
LINK UP, KIDS. WE'RE HAV-ING A CHAIN-IN.
HO HUM ··· THE CHAIN-IN KICK! COME. WE MUSTN'T MISS A SECOND OF PROFESSOR CLEARLY'S SEMINAR. I FEEL THAT TODAY HE MAY OPEN THE GATES TO NIRVANA.
HEY, RALPH! COME JOIN OUR !! CURSE-IN.
(YAWN) SORRY. IT'S NON-FULFILLING.
DOWN WITH SAFE-DRIVING LEGIS-LATION!
SEAT BELTS ARE FASCISTIC!
OH, ME ··· ANOTHER DIE-IN-
PRO-FESSOR CLEARLY IS MY ONLY CHANCE FOR PSYCHIC SALVA-TION.
BOMB RALPH NADER NOW!
SNCC

152

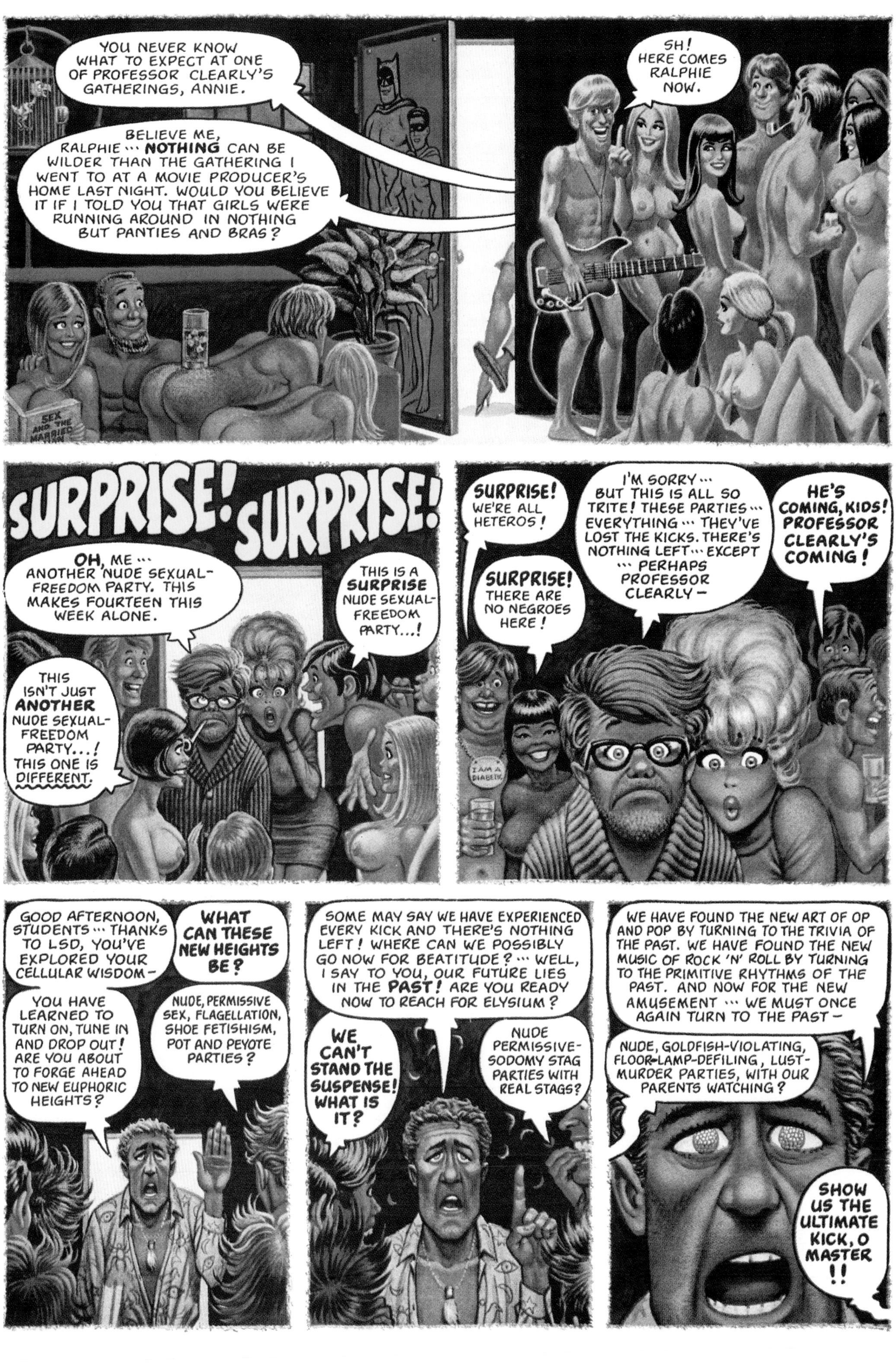

YOU NEVER KNOW WHAT TO EXPECT AT ONE OF PROFESSOR CLEARLY'S GATHERINGS, ANNIE.
BELIEVE ME, RALPHIE ··· NOTHING CAN BE WILDER THAN THE GATHERING I WENT TO AT A MOVIE PRODUCER'S HOME LAST NIGHT. WOULD YOU BELIEVE IT IF I TOLD YOU THAT GIRLS WERE RUNNING AROUND IN NOTHING BUT PANTIES AND BRAS?
SH! HERE COMES RALPHIE NOW.
SURPRISE! SURPRISE!
OH, ME ··· ANOTHER NUDE SEXUAL-FREEDOM PARTY. THIS MAKES FOURTEEN THIS WEEK ALONE.
THIS IS A SURPRISE NUDE SEXUAL-FREEDOM PARTY...!
THIS ISN'T JUST ANOTHER NUDE SEXUAL-FREEDOM PARTY...! THIS ONE IS DIFFERENT.
SURPRISE! WE'RE ALL HETEROS!
SURPRISE! THERE ARE NO NEGROES HERE!
I'M SORRY ··· BUT THIS IS ALL SO TRITE! THESE PARTIES ··· EVERYTHING ··· THEY'VE LOST THE KICKS. THERE'S NOTHING LEFT ··· EXCEPT ··· PERHAPS PROFESSOR CLEARLY—
HE'S COMING, KIDS! PROFESSOR CLEARLY'S COMING!
I AM A DIABETIC
GOOD AFTERNOON, STUDENTS ··· THANKS TO LSD, YOU'VE EXPLORED YOUR CELLULAR WISDOM—
YOU HAVE LEARNED TO TURN ON, TUNE IN AND DROP OUT! ARE YOU ABOUT TO FORGE AHEAD TO NEW EUPHORIC HEIGHTS?
WHAT CAN THESE NEW HEIGHTS BE?
NUDE, PERMISSIVE SEX, FLAGELLATION, SHOE FETISHISM, POT AND PEYOTE PARTIES?
SOME MAY SAY WE HAVE EXPERIENCED EVERY KICK AND THERE'S NOTHING LEFT! WHERE CAN WE POSSIBLY GO NOW FOR BEATITUDE? ··· WELL, I SAY TO YOU, OUR FUTURE LIES IN THE PAST! ARE YOU READY NOW TO REACH FOR ELYSIUM?
WE CAN'T STAND THE SUSPENSE! WHAT IS IT?
NUDE PERMISSIVE-SODOMY STAG PARTIES WITH REAL STAGS?
WE HAVE FOUND THE NEW ART OF OP AND POP BY TURNING TO THE TRIVIA OF THE PAST. WE HAVE FOUND THE NEW MUSIC OF ROCK 'N' ROLL BY TURNING TO THE PRIMITIVE RHYTHMS OF THE PAST. AND NOW FOR THE NEW AMUSEMENT ··· WE MUST ONCE AGAIN TURN TO THE PAST—
NUDE, GOLDFISH-VIOLATING, FLOOR-LAMP-DEFILING, LUST-MURDER PARTIES, WITH OUR PARENTS WATCHING?
SHOW US THE ULTIMATE KICK, O MASTER!!

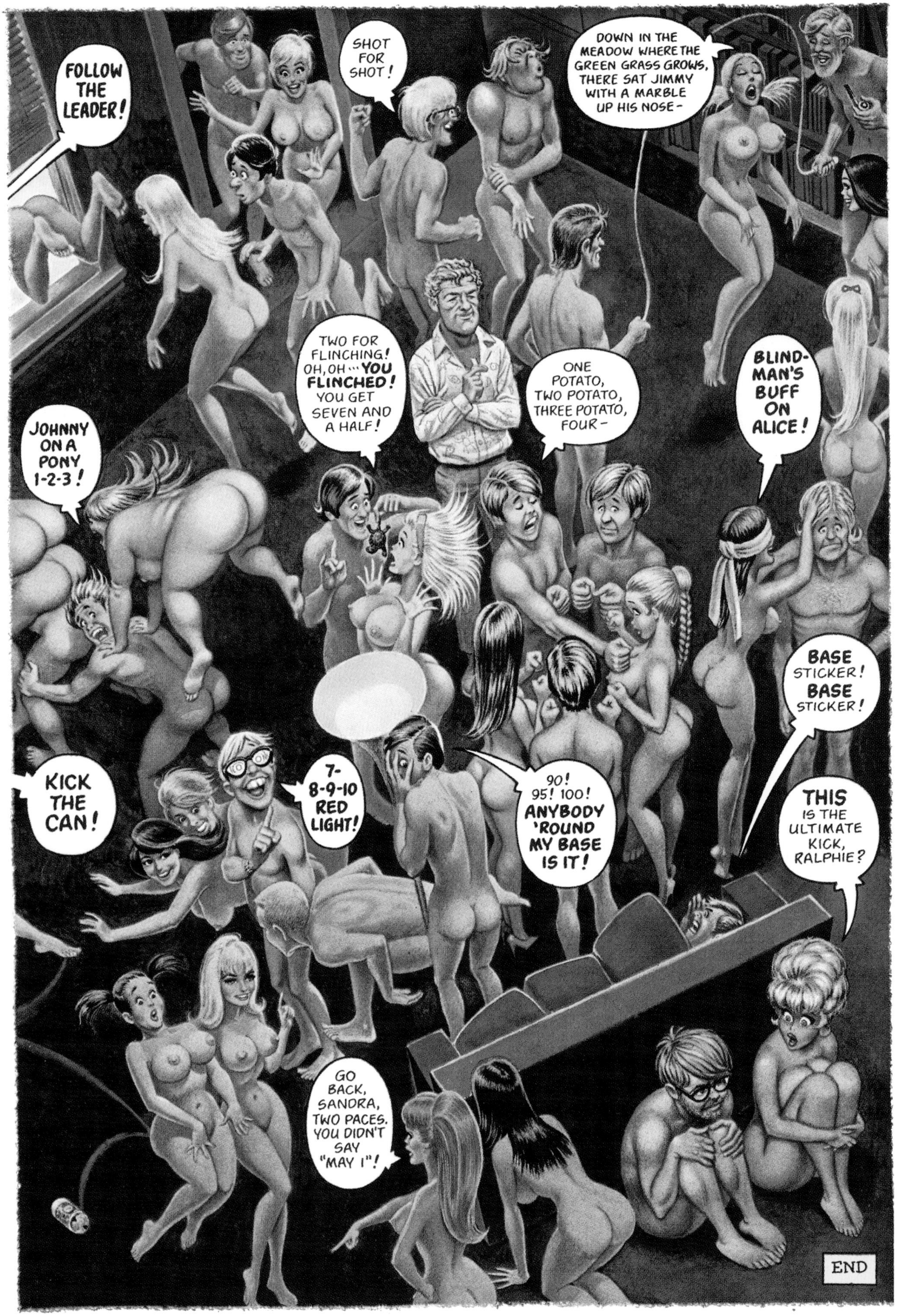

FOLLOW THE LEADER!
SHOT FOR SHOT!
DOWN IN THE MEADOW WHERE THE GREEN GRASS GROWS, THERE SAT JIMMY WITH A MARBLE UP HIS NOSE-
TWO FOR FLINCHING! OH, OH... YOU FLINCHED! YOU GET SEVEN AND A HALF!
ONE POTATO, TWO POTATO, THREE POTATO, FOUR-
BLIND-MAN'S BUFF ON ALICE!
JOHNNY ON A PONY 1-2-3!
BASE STICKER! BASE STICKER!
KICK THE CAN!
7-8-9-10 RED LIGHT!
90! 95! 100! ANYBODY 'ROUND MY BASE IS IT!
THIS IS THE ULTIMATE KICK, RALPHIE?
GO BACK, SANDRA, TWO PACES. YOU DIDN'T SAY "MAY I"!
END

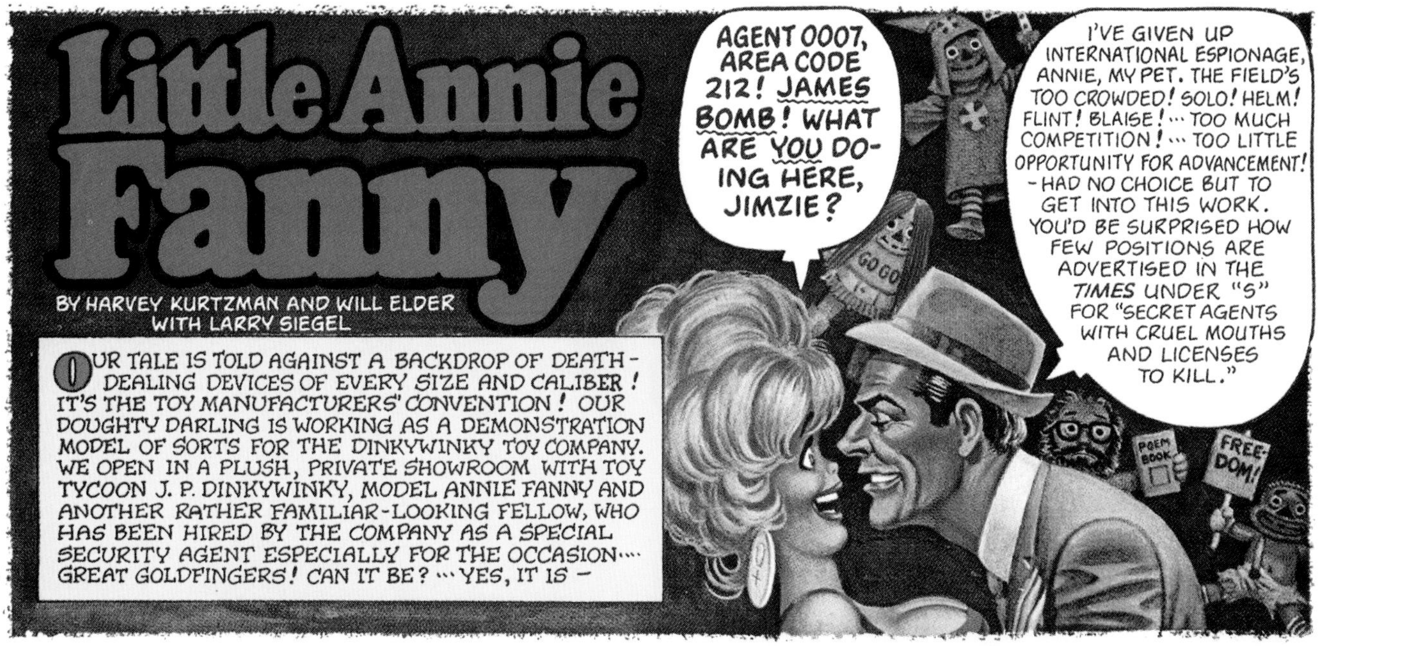

Little Annie Fanny
BY HARVEY KURTZMAN AND WILL ELDER WITH LARRY SIEGEL
OUR TALE IS TOLD AGAINST A BACKDROP OF DEATH-DEALING DEVICES OF EVERY SIZE AND CALIBER! IT'S THE TOY MANUFACTURERS' CONVENTION! OUR DOUGHTY DARLING IS WORKING AS A DEMONSTRATION MODEL OF SORTS FOR THE DINKYWINKY TOY COMPANY. WE OPEN IN A PLUSH, PRIVATE SHOWROOM WITH TOY TYCOON J. P. DINKYWINKY, MODEL ANNIE FANNY AND ANOTHER RATHER FAMILIAR-LOOKING FELLOW, WHO HAS BEEN HIRED BY THE COMPANY AS A SPECIAL SECURITY AGENT ESPECIALLY FOR THE OCCASION··· GREAT GOLDFINGERS! CAN IT BE? ··· YES, IT IS —
AGENT 0007, AREA CODE 212! JAMES BOMB! WHAT ARE YOU DOING HERE, JIMZIE?
I'VE GIVEN UP INTERNATIONAL ESPIONAGE, ANNIE, MY PET. THE FIELD'S TOO CROWDED! SOLO! HELM! FLINT! BLAISE! ··· TOO MUCH COMPETITION! ··· TOO LITTLE OPPORTUNITY FOR ADVANCEMENT! - HAD NO CHOICE BUT TO GET INTO THIS WORK. YOU'D BE SURPRISED HOW FEW POSITIONS ARE ADVERTISED IN THE TIMES UNDER "S" FOR "SECRET AGENTS WITH CRUEL MOUTHS AND LICENSES TO KILL."
GO GO
POEM BOOK
FREE-DOM!

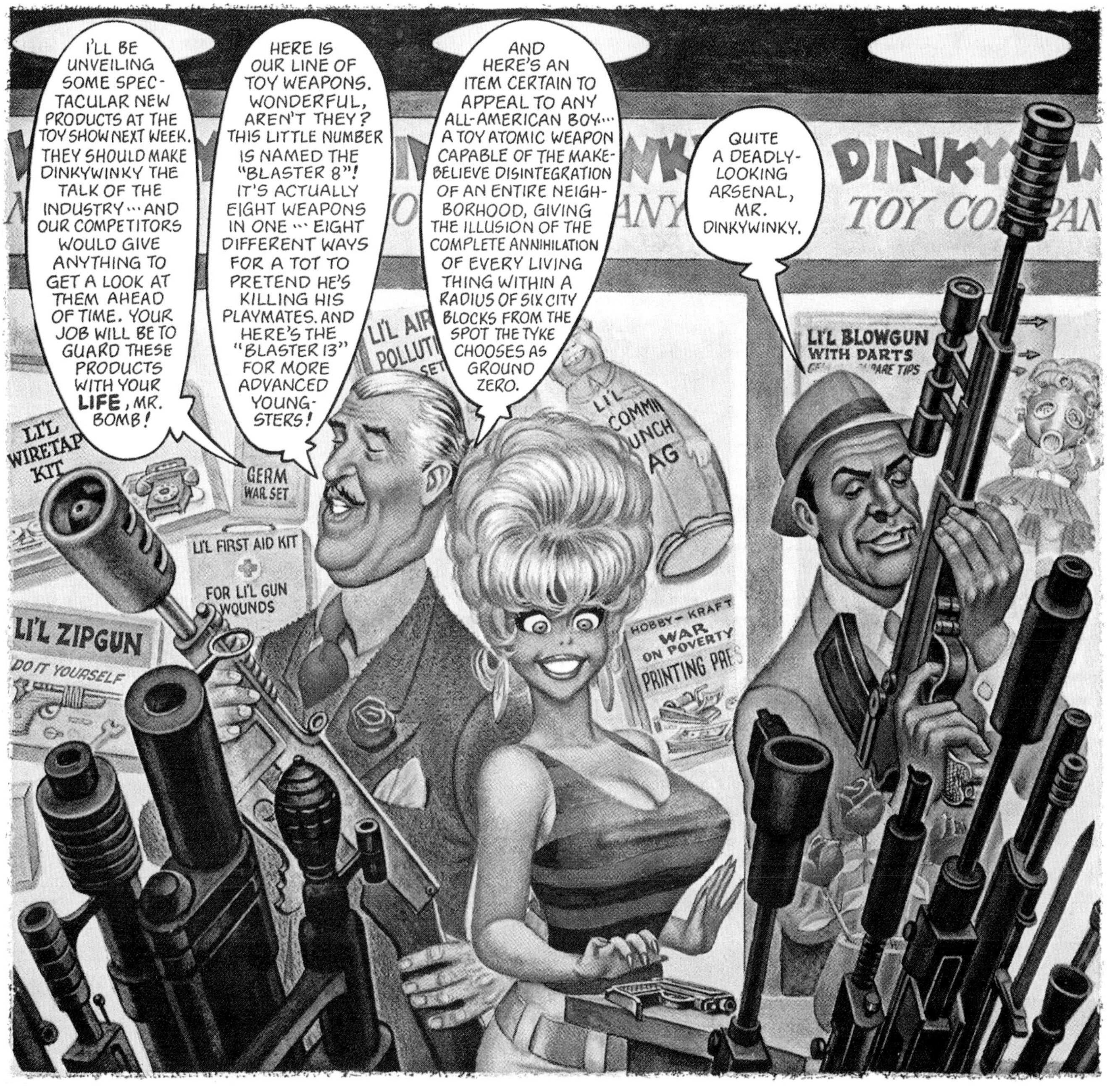

I'LL BE UNVEILING SOME SPECTACULAR NEW PRODUCTS AT THE TOY SHOW NEXT WEEK. THEY SHOULD MAKE DINKYWINKY THE TALK OF THE INDUSTRY··· AND OUR COMPETITORS WOULD GIVE ANYTHING TO GET A LOOK AT THEM AHEAD OF TIME. YOUR JOB WILL BE TO GUARD THESE PRODUCTS WITH YOUR LIFE, MR. BOMB!
HERE IS OUR LINE OF TOY WEAPONS. WONDERFUL, AREN'T THEY? THIS LITTLE NUMBER IS NAMED THE "BLASTER 8"! IT'S ACTUALLY EIGHT WEAPONS IN ONE ··· EIGHT DIFFERENT WAYS FOR A TOT TO PRETEND HE'S KILLING HIS PLAYMATES. AND HERE'S THE "BLASTER 13" FOR MORE ADVANCED YOUNGSTERS!
AND HERE'S AN ITEM CERTAIN TO APPEAL TO ANY ALL-AMERICAN BOY··· A TOY ATOMIC WEAPON CAPABLE OF THE MAKE-BELIEVE DISINTEGRATION OF AN ENTIRE NEIGHBORHOOD, GIVING THE ILLUSION OF THE COMPLETE ANNIHILATION OF EVERY LIVING THING WITHIN A RADIUS OF SIX CITY BLOCKS FROM THE SPOT THE TYKE CHOOSES AS GROUND ZERO.
QUITE A DEADLY-LOOKING ARSENAL, MR. DINKYWINKY.
LI'L BLOWGUN WITH DARTS
LI'L WIRETAP KIT
GERM WAR SET
LI'L FIRST AID KIT FOR LI'L GUN WOUNDS
LI'L ZIPGUN
DO IT YOURSELF
HOBBY-KRAFT
WAR ON POVERTY

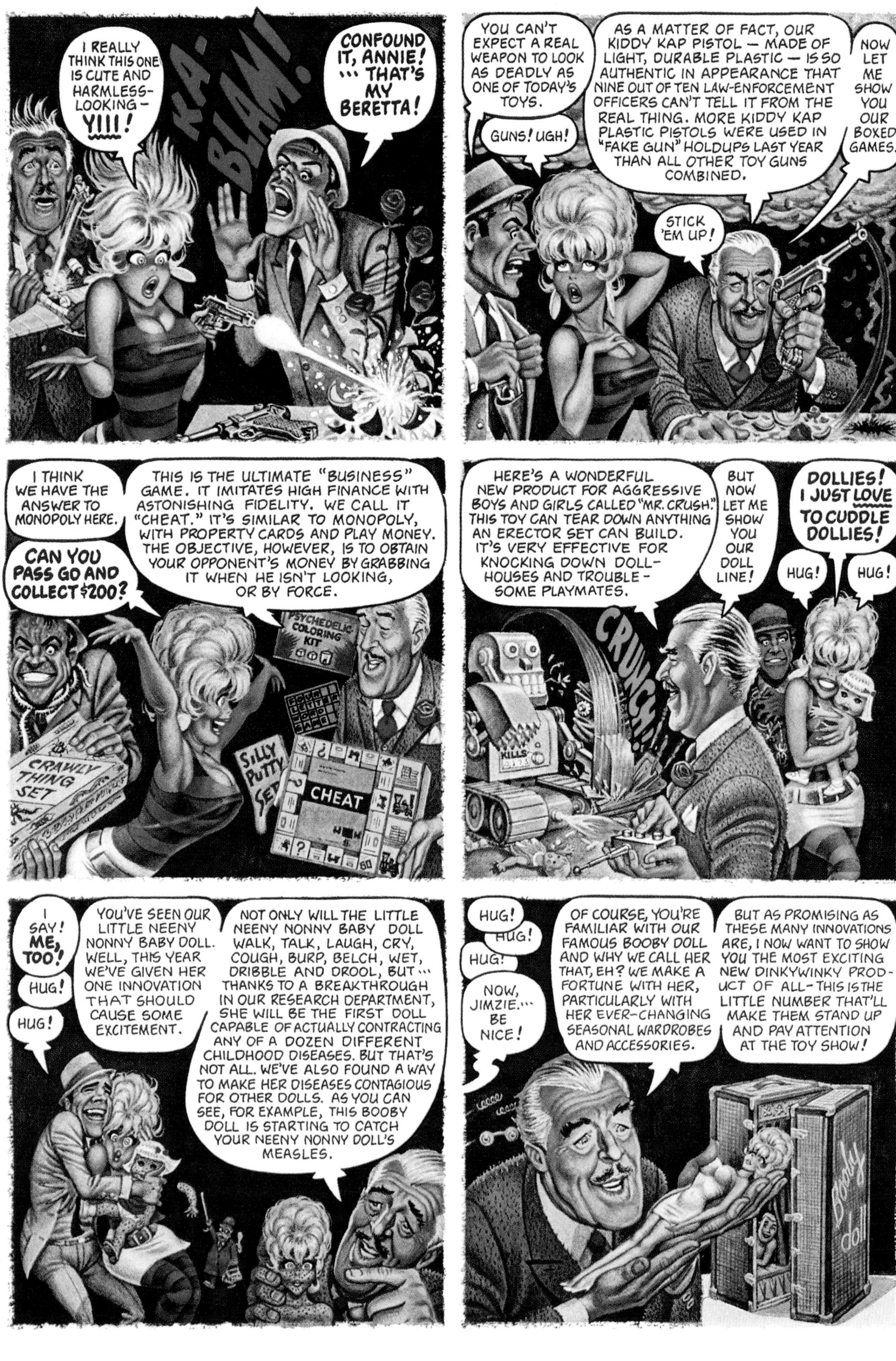
I REALLY THINK THIS ONE IS CUTE AND HARMLESS-LOOKING - YIII!
KA-BLAM!
CONFOUND IT, ANNIE! ... THAT'S MY BERETTA!
YOU CAN'T EXPECT A REAL WEAPON TO LOOK AS DEADLY AS ONE OF TODAY'S TOYS.
GUNS! UGH!
AS A MATTER OF FACT, OUR KIDDY KAP PISTOL — MADE OF LIGHT, DURABLE PLASTIC — IS SO AUTHENTIC IN APPEARANCE THAT NINE OUT OF TEN LAW-ENFORCEMENT OFFICERS CAN'T TELL IT FROM THE REAL THING. MORE KIDDY KAP PLASTIC PISTOLS WERE USED IN "FAKE GUN" HOLDUPS LAST YEAR THAN ALL OTHER TOY GUNS COMBINED.
STICK 'EM UP!
NOW LET ME SHOW YOU OUR BOXED GAMES.
I THINK WE HAVE THE ANSWER TO MONOPOLY HERE.
THIS IS THE ULTIMATE "BUSINESS" GAME. IT IMITATES HIGH FINANCE WITH ASTONISHING FIDELITY. WE CALL IT "CHEAT." IT'S SIMILAR TO MONOPOLY, WITH PROPERTY CARDS AND PLAY MONEY. THE OBJECTIVE, HOWEVER, IS TO OBTAIN YOUR OPPONENT'S MONEY BY GRABBING IT WHEN HE ISN'T LOOKING, OR BY FORCE.
CAN YOU PASS GO AND COLLECT $200?
PSYCHEDELIC COLORING KIT
CRAWLY THING SET
SILLY PUTTY SET
CHEAT
HERE'S A WONDERFUL NEW PRODUCT FOR AGGRESSIVE BOYS AND GIRLS CALLED "MR. CRUSH." THIS TOY CAN TEAR DOWN ANYTHING AN ERECTOR SET CAN BUILD. IT'S VERY EFFECTIVE FOR KNOCKING DOWN DOLL-HOUSES AND TROUBLE-SOME PLAYMATES.
BUT NOW LET ME SHOW YOU OUR DOLL LINE!
DOLLIES! I JUST LOVE TO CUDDLE DOLLIES!
HUG!
HUG!
CRUNCH!
KILLS
I SAY! ME, TOO!
HUG!
HUG!
YOU'VE SEEN OUR LITTLE NEENY NONNY BABY DOLL. WELL, THIS YEAR WE'VE GIVEN HER ONE INNOVATION THAT SHOULD CAUSE SOME EXCITEMENT.
NOT ONLY WILL THE LITTLE NEENY NONNY BABY DOLL WALK, TALK, LAUGH, CRY, COUGH, BURP, BELCH, WET, DRIBBLE AND DROOL, BUT ... THANKS TO A BREAKTHROUGH IN OUR RESEARCH DEPARTMENT, SHE WILL BE THE FIRST DOLL CAPABLE OF ACTUALLY CONTRACTING ANY OF A DOZEN DIFFERENT CHILDHOOD DISEASES. BUT THAT'S NOT ALL. WE'VE ALSO FOUND A WAY TO MAKE HER DISEASES CONTAGIOUS FOR OTHER DOLLS. AS YOU CAN SEE, FOR EXAMPLE, THIS BOOBY DOLL IS STARTING TO CATCH YOUR NEENY NONNY DOLL'S MEASLES.
HUG!
HUG!
HUG!
NOW, JIMZIE... BE NICE!
OF COURSE, YOU'RE FAMILIAR WITH OUR FAMOUS BOOBY DOLL AND WHY WE CALL HER THAT, EH? WE MAKE A FORTUNE WITH HER, PARTICULARLY WITH HER EVER-CHANGING SEASONAL WARDROBES AND ACCESSORIES.
BUT AS PROMISING AS THESE MANY INNOVATIONS ARE, I NOW WANT TO SHOW YOU THE MOST EXCITING NEW DINKYWINKY PRODUCT OF ALL - THIS IS THE LITTLE NUMBER THAT'LL MAKE THEM STAND UP AND PAY ATTENTION AT THE TOY SHOW!
Booby doll

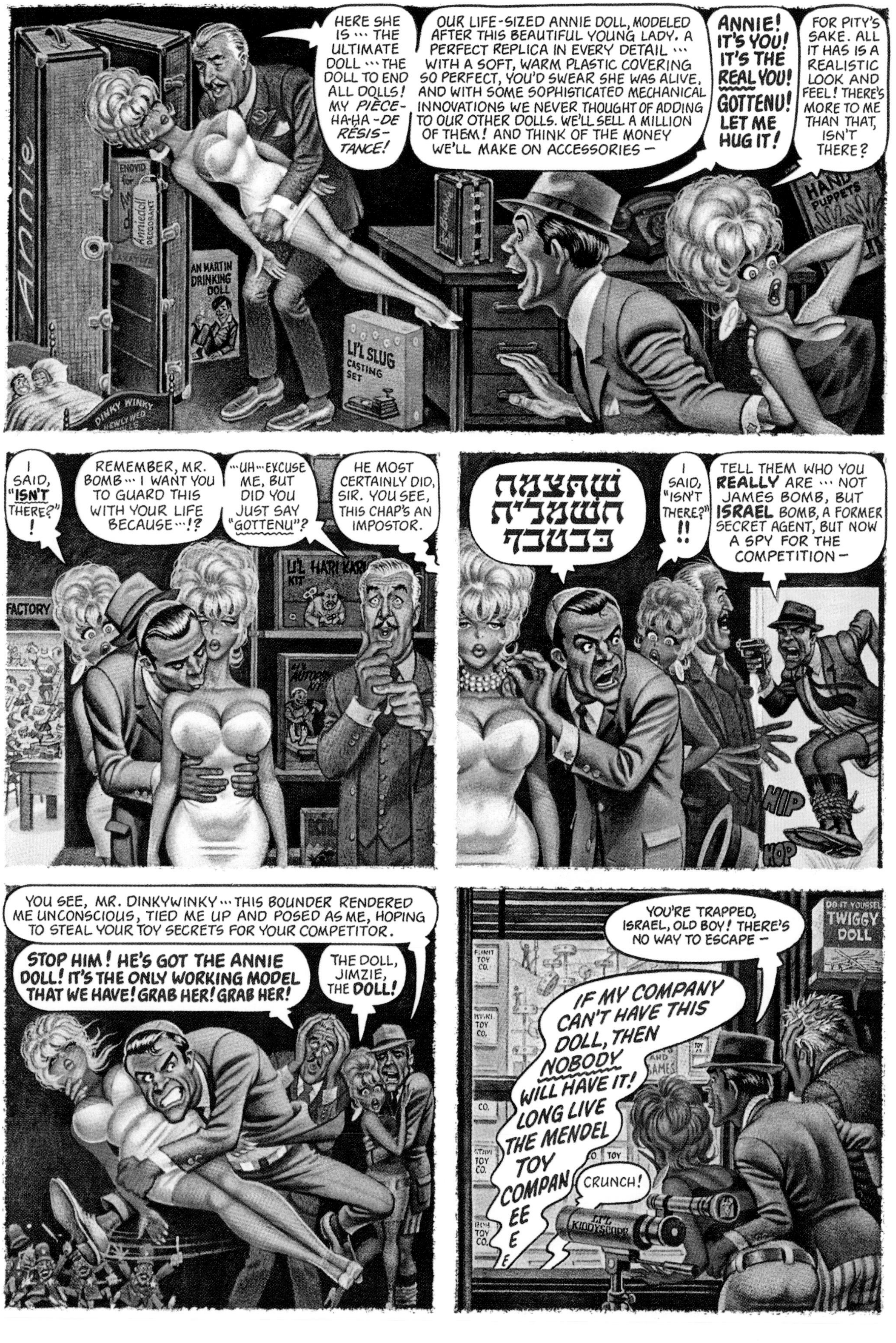
HERE SHE IS ··· THE ULTIMATE DOLL ··· THE DOLL TO END ALL DOLLS! MY PIÈCE-HA-HA-DE RÉSISTANCE!
OUR LIFE-SIZED ANNIE DOLL, MODELED AFTER THIS BEAUTIFUL YOUNG LADY. A PERFECT REPLICA IN EVERY DETAIL ··· WITH A SOFT, WARM PLASTIC COVERING SO PERFECT, YOU'D SWEAR SHE WAS ALIVE. AND WITH SOME SOPHISTICATED MECHANICAL INNOVATIONS WE NEVER THOUGHT OF ADDING TO OUR OTHER DOLLS. WE'LL SELL A MILLION OF THEM! AND THINK OF THE MONEY WE'LL MAKE ON ACCESSORIES —
ANNIE! IT'S YOU! IT'S THE REAL YOU! GOTTENU! LET ME HUG IT!
FOR PITY'S SAKE. ALL IT HAS IS A REALISTIC LOOK AND FEEL! THERE'S MORE TO ME THAN THAT, ISN'T THERE?
Annie
ENOVID
Anniedoll DEODORANT
LAXATIVE
AN MARTIN DRINKING DOLL
LI'L SLUG CASTING SET
HAND PUPPETS
DINKY WINKY NEWLYWED
I SAID, "ISN'T THERE?" !
REMEMBER, MR. BOMB ··· I WANT YOU TO GUARD THIS WITH YOUR LIFE BECAUSE ···!?
···UH··· EXCUSE ME, BUT DID YOU JUST SAY "GOTTENU"?
HE MOST CERTAINLY DID, SIR. YOU SEE, THIS CHAP'S AN IMPOSTOR.
FACTORY
LI'L HARI KARI KIT
שתצמח חשמלית בכטבך
I SAID, "ISN'T THERE?" !!
TELL THEM WHO YOU REALLY ARE ··· NOT JAMES BOMB, BUT ISRAEL BOMB, A FORMER SECRET AGENT, BUT NOW A SPY FOR THE COMPETITION —
HIP
HOP
YOU SEE, MR. DINKYWINKY ··· THIS BOUNDER RENDERED ME UNCONSCIOUS, TIED ME UP AND POSED AS ME, HOPING TO STEAL YOUR TOY SECRETS FOR YOUR COMPETITOR.
STOP HIM! HE'S GOT THE ANNIE DOLL! IT'S THE ONLY WORKING MODEL THAT WE HAVE! GRAB HER! GRAB HER!
THE DOLL, JIMZIE, THE DOLL!
YOU'RE TRAPPED, ISRAEL, OLD BOY! THERE'S NO WAY TO ESCAPE —
DO IT YOURSELF TWIGGY DOLL
IF MY COMPANY CAN'T HAVE THIS DOLL, THEN NOBODY WILL HAVE IT! LONG LIVE THE MENDEL TOY COMPAN EE E E
CRUNCH!
LI'L KIDDYSCOPE

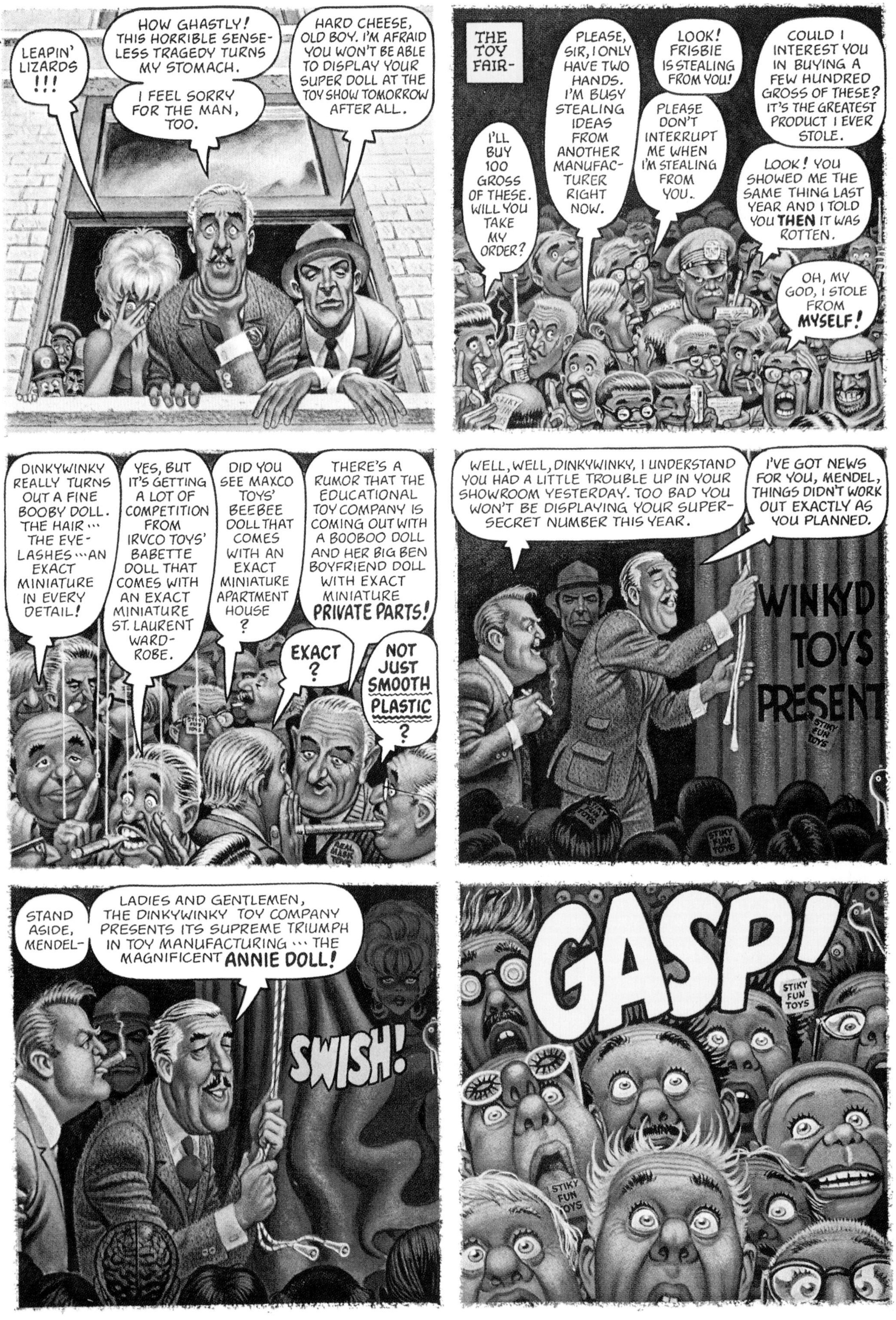
LEAPIN' LIZARDS !!!
HOW GHASTLY! THIS HORRIBLE SENSELESS TRAGEDY TURNS MY STOMACH.
I FEEL SORRY FOR THE MAN, TOO.
HARD CHEESE, OLD BOY. I'M AFRAID YOU WON'T BE ABLE TO DISPLAY YOUR SUPER DOLL AT THE TOY SHOW TOMORROW AFTER ALL.
THE TOY FAIR-
I'LL BUY 100 GROSS OF THESE. WILL YOU TAKE MY ORDER?
PLEASE, SIR, I ONLY HAVE TWO HANDS. I'M BUSY STEALING IDEAS FROM ANOTHER MANUFACTURER RIGHT NOW.
LOOK! FRISBIE IS STEALING FROM YOU!
PLEASE DON'T INTERRUPT ME WHEN I'M STEALING FROM YOU.
COULD I INTEREST YOU IN BUYING A FEW HUNDRED GROSS OF THESE? IT'S THE GREATEST PRODUCT I EVER STOLE.
LOOK! YOU SHOWED ME THE SAME THING LAST YEAR AND I TOLD YOU THEN IT WAS ROTTEN.
OH, MY GOD, I STOLE FROM MYSELF!
DINKYWINKY REALLY TURNS OUT A FINE BOOBY DOLL. THE HAIR ··· THE EYELASHES ··· AN EXACT MINIATURE IN EVERY DETAIL!
YES, BUT IT'S GETTING A LOT OF COMPETITION FROM IRVCO TOYS' BABETTE DOLL THAT COMES WITH AN EXACT MINIATURE ST. LAURENT WARDROBE.
DID YOU SEE MAXCO TOYS' BEEBEE DOLL THAT COMES WITH AN EXACT MINIATURE APARTMENT HOUSE?
THERE'S A RUMOR THAT THE EDUCATIONAL TOY COMPANY IS COMING OUT WITH A BOOBOO DOLL AND HER BIG BEN BOYFRIEND DOLL WITH EXACT MINIATURE PRIVATE PARTS!
EXACT?
NOT JUST SMOOTH PLASTIC?
WELL, WELL, DINKYWINKY, I UNDERSTAND YOU HAD A LITTLE TROUBLE UP IN YOUR SHOWROOM YESTERDAY. TOO BAD YOU WON'T BE DISPLAYING YOUR SUPER-SECRET NUMBER THIS YEAR.
I'VE GOT NEWS FOR YOU, MENDEL, THINGS DIDN'T WORK OUT EXACTLY AS YOU PLANNED.
WINKYDI TOYS PRESENT
STIKY FUN TOYS
STAND ASIDE, MENDEL-
LADIES AND GENTLEMEN, THE DINKYWINKY TOY COMPANY PRESENTS ITS SUPREME TRIUMPH IN TOY MANUFACTURING ··· THE MAGNIFICENT ANNIE DOLL!
SWISH!
GASP!
STIKY FUN TOYS
STIKY FUN TOYS

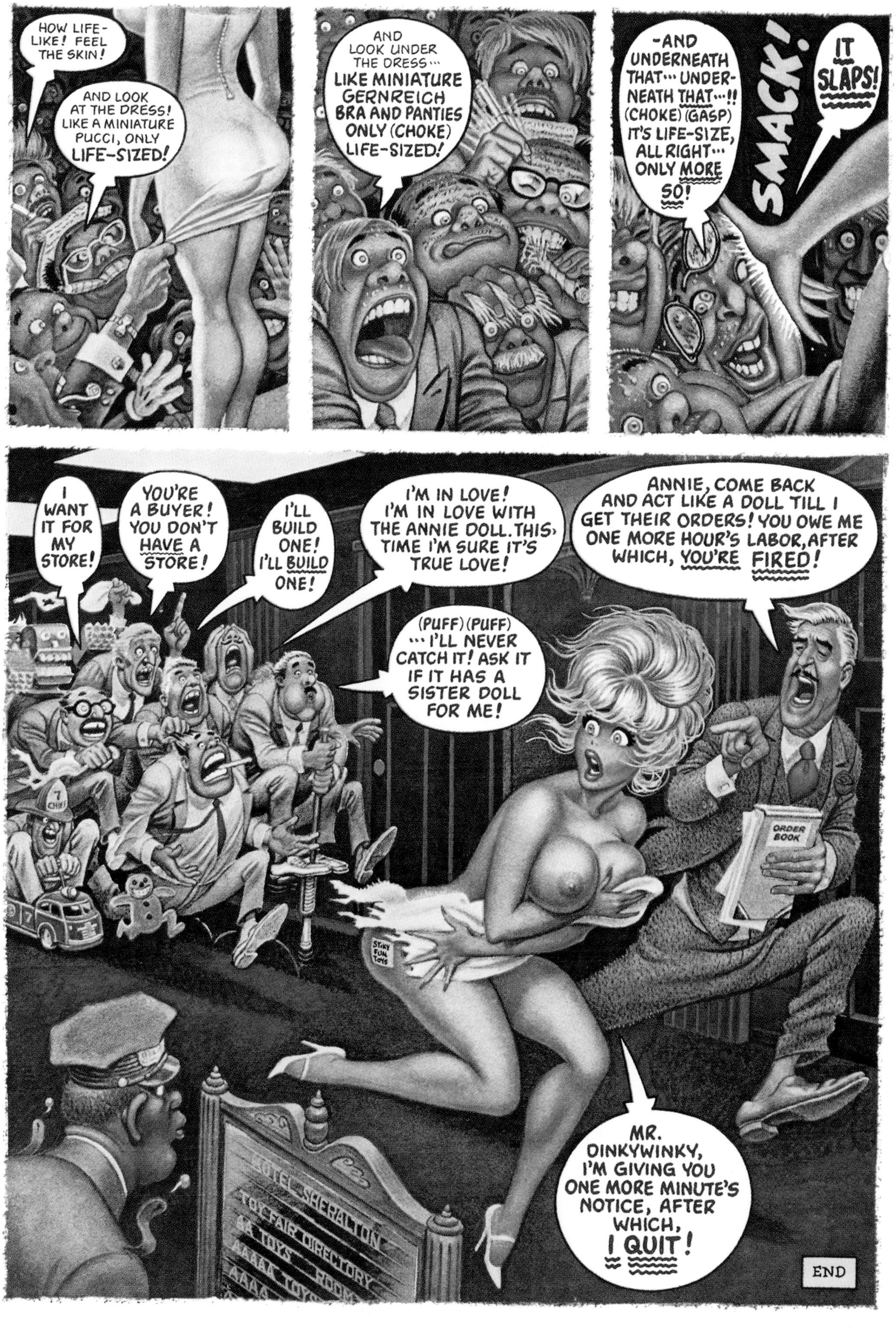
HOW LIFE-LIKE! FEEL THE SKIN!
AND LOOK AT THE DRESS! LIKE A MINIATURE PUCCI, ONLY LIFE-SIZED!
AND LOOK UNDER THE DRESS... LIKE MINIATURE GERNREICH BRA AND PANTIES ONLY (CHOKE) LIFE-SIZED!
-AND UNDERNEATH THAT... UNDER-NEATH THAT...!! (CHOKE) (GASP) IT'S LIFE-SIZE, ALL RIGHT... ONLY MORE SO!
SMACK!
IT SLAPS!
I WANT IT FOR MY STORE!
YOU'RE A BUYER! YOU DON'T HAVE A STORE!
I'LL BUILD ONE! I'LL BUILD ONE!
I'M IN LOVE! I'M IN LOVE WITH THE ANNIE DOLL. THIS TIME I'M SURE IT'S TRUE LOVE!
ANNIE, COME BACK AND ACT LIKE A DOLL TILL I GET THEIR ORDERS! YOU OWE ME ONE MORE HOUR'S LABOR, AFTER WHICH, YOU'RE FIRED!
(PUFF) (PUFF) ... I'LL NEVER CATCH IT! ASK IT IF IT HAS A SISTER DOLL FOR ME!
ORDER BOOK
MR. DINKYWINKY, I'M GIVING YOU ONE MORE MINUTE'S NOTICE, AFTER WHICH, I QUIT!
END

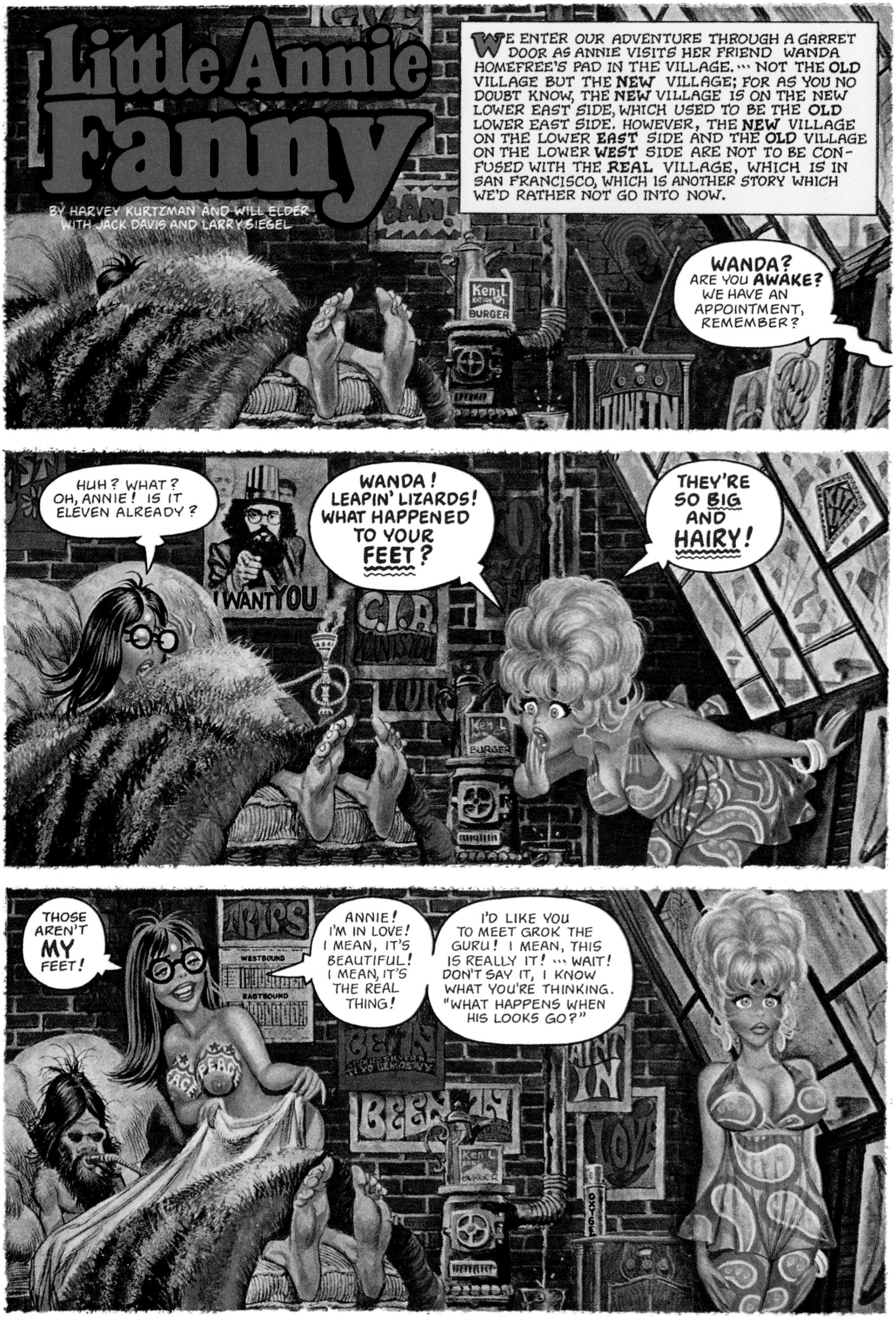
Little Annie Fanny
BY HARVEY KURTZMAN AND WILL ELDER WITH JACK DAVIS AND LARRY SIEGEL
WE ENTER OUR ADVENTURE THROUGH A GARRET DOOR AS ANNIE VISITS HER FRIEND WANDA HOMEFREE'S PAD IN THE VILLAGE. ... NOT THE OLD VILLAGE BUT THE NEW VILLAGE; FOR AS YOU NO DOUBT KNOW, THE NEW VILLAGE IS ON THE NEW LOWER EAST SIDE, WHICH USED TO BE THE OLD LOWER EAST SIDE. HOWEVER, THE NEW VILLAGE ON THE LOWER EAST SIDE AND THE OLD VILLAGE ON THE LOWER WEST SIDE ARE NOT TO BE CONFUSED WITH THE REAL VILLAGE, WHICH IS IN SAN FRANCISCO, WHICH IS ANOTHER STORY WHICH WE'D RATHER NOT GO INTO NOW.
WANDA? ARE YOU AWAKE? WE HAVE AN APPOINTMENT, REMEMBER?
TUNE IN
HUH? WHAT? OH, ANNIE! IS IT ELEVEN ALREADY?
WANDA! LEAPIN' LIZARDS! WHAT HAPPENED TO YOUR FEET?
THEY'RE SO BIG AND HAIRY!
I WANT YOU
C.I.A.
THOSE AREN'T MY FEET!
ANNIE! I'M IN LOVE! I MEAN, IT'S BEAUTIFUL! I MEAN, IT'S THE REAL THING!
I'D LIKE YOU TO MEET GROK THE GURU! I MEAN, THIS IS REALLY IT! ... WAIT! DON'T SAY IT, I KNOW WHAT YOU'RE THINKING. "WHAT HAPPENS WHEN HIS LOOKS GO?"
WESTBOUND
EASTBOUND

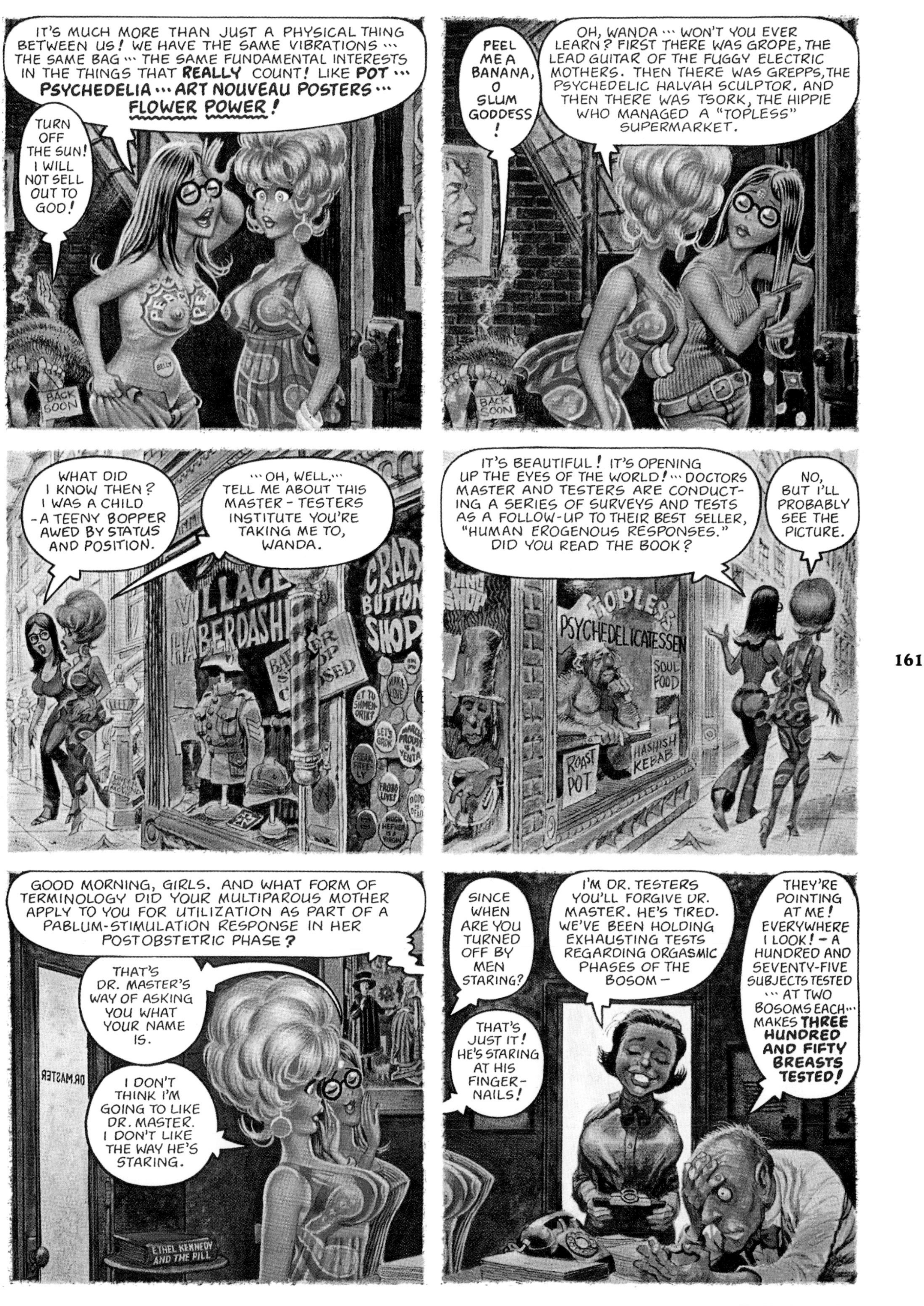
IT'S MUCH MORE THAN JUST A PHYSICAL THING BETWEEN US! WE HAVE THE SAME VIBRATIONS ··· THE SAME BAG ··· THE SAME FUNDAMENTAL INTERESTS IN THE THINGS THAT REALLY COUNT! LIKE POT ··· PSYCHEDELIA ··· ART NOUVEAU POSTERS ··· FLOWER POWER!
TURN OFF THE SUN! I WILL NOT SELL OUT TO GOD!
BELLY
BACK SOON
PEEL ME A BANANA, O SLUM GODDESS!
OH, WANDA ··· WON'T YOU EVER LEARN? FIRST THERE WAS GROPE, THE LEAD GUITAR OF THE FUGGY ELECTRIC MOTHERS. THEN THERE WAS GREPPS, THE PSYCHEDELIC HALVAH SCULPTOR. AND THEN THERE WAS TSORK, THE HIPPIE WHO MANAGED A "TOPLESS" SUPERMARKET.
BACK SOON
WHAT DID I KNOW THEN? I WAS A CHILD -A TEENY BOPPER AWED BY STATUS AND POSITION.
···OH, WELL,··· TELL ME ABOUT THIS MASTER-TESTERS INSTITUTE YOU'RE TAKING ME TO, WANDA.
VILLAGE HABERDASHE
CRAZY BUTTON SHOP
IT'S BEAUTIFUL! IT'S OPENING UP THE EYES OF THE WORLD! ··· DOCTORS MASTER AND TESTERS ARE CONDUCTING A SERIES OF SURVEYS AND TESTS AS A FOLLOW-UP TO THEIR BEST SELLER, "HUMAN EROGENOUS RESPONSES." DID YOU READ THE BOOK?
NO, BUT I'LL PROBABLY SEE THE PICTURE.
TOPLESS
PSYCHEDELICATESSEN
SOUL FOOD
HASHISH KEBAB
ROAST POT
GOOD MORNING, GIRLS. AND WHAT FORM OF TERMINOLOGY DID YOUR MULTIPAROUS MOTHER APPLY TO YOU FOR UTILIZATION AS PART OF A PABLUM-STIMULATION RESPONSE IN HER POSTOBSTETRIC PHASE?
THAT'S DR. MASTER'S WAY OF ASKING YOU WHAT YOUR NAME IS.
I DON'T THINK I'M GOING TO LIKE DR. MASTER. I DON'T LIKE THE WAY HE'S STARING.
DR. MASTER
ETHEL KENNEDY AND THE PILL
SINCE WHEN ARE YOU TURNED OFF BY MEN STARING?
I'M DR. TESTERS YOU'LL FORGIVE DR. MASTER. HE'S TIRED. WE'VE BEEN HOLDING EXHAUSTING TESTS REGARDING ORGASMIC PHASES OF THE BOSOM—
THEY'RE POINTING AT ME! EVERYWHERE I LOOK! —A HUNDRED AND SEVENTY-FIVE SUBJECTS TESTED ··· AT TWO BOSOMS EACH··· MAKES THREE HUNDRED AND FIFTY BREASTS TESTED!
THAT'S JUST IT! HE'S STARING AT HIS FINGER-NAILS!

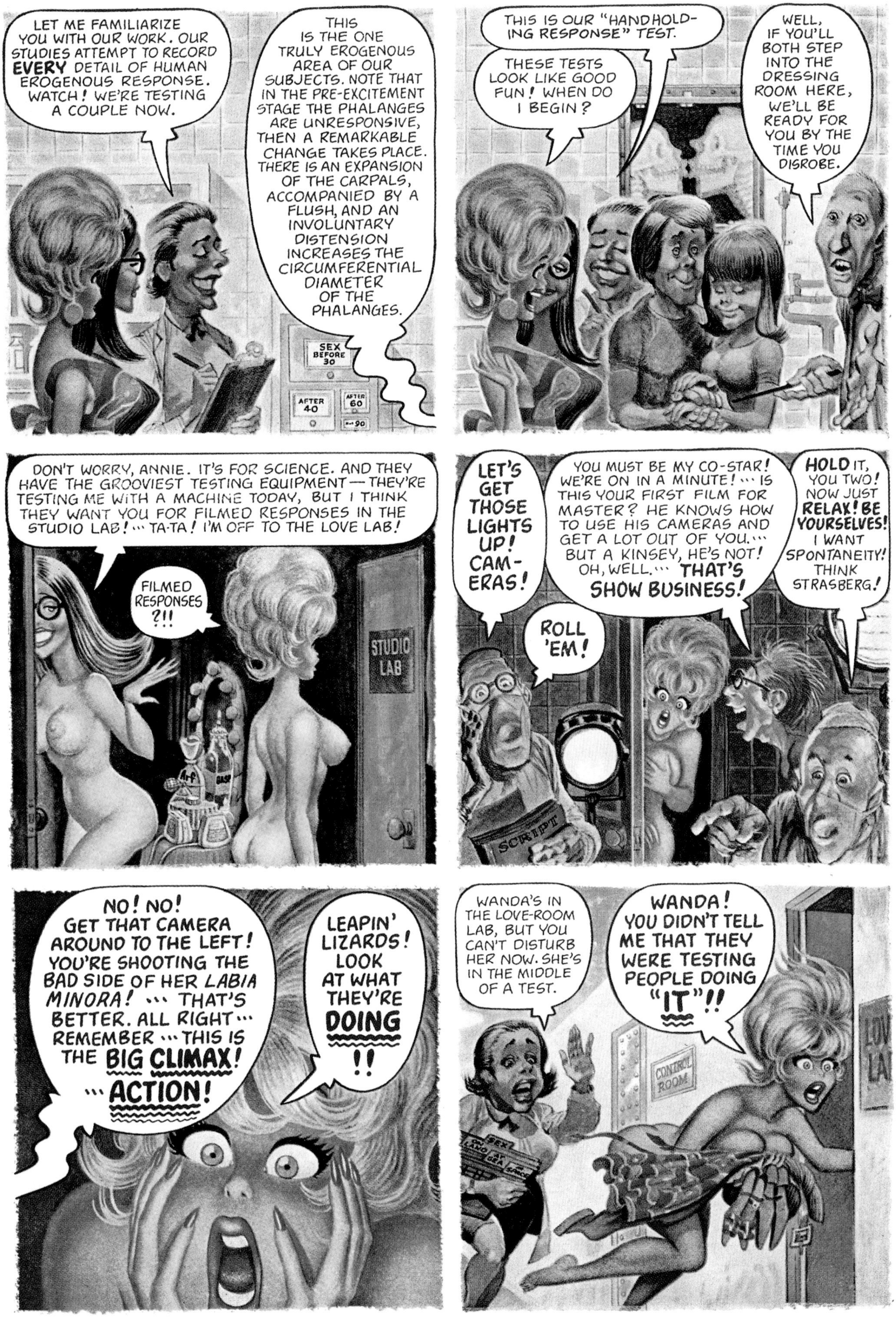
LET ME FAMILIARIZE YOU WITH OUR WORK. OUR STUDIES ATTEMPT TO RECORD **EVERY** DETAIL OF HUMAN EROGENOUS RESPONSE. WATCH! WE'RE TESTING A COUPLE NOW.
THIS IS THE ONE TRULY EROGENOUS AREA OF OUR SUBJECTS. NOTE THAT IN THE PRE-EXCITEMENT STAGE THE PHALANGES ARE UNRESPONSIVE, THEN A REMARKABLE CHANGE TAKES PLACE. THERE IS AN EXPANSION OF THE CARPALS, ACCOMPANIED BY A FLUSH, AND AN INVOLUNTARY DISTENSION INCREASES THE CIRCUMFERENTIAL DIAMETER OF THE PHALANGES.
SEX BEFORE 30
AFTER 40
AFTER 60
THIS IS OUR "HANDHOLDING RESPONSE" TEST.
THESE TESTS LOOK LIKE GOOD FUN! WHEN DO I BEGIN?
WELL, IF YOU'LL BOTH STEP INTO THE DRESSING ROOM HERE, WE'LL BE READY FOR YOU BY THE TIME YOU DISROBE.
DON'T WORRY, ANNIE. IT'S FOR SCIENCE. AND THEY HAVE THE GROOVIEST TESTING EQUIPMENT — THEY'RE TESTING ME WITH A MACHINE TODAY, BUT I THINK THEY WANT YOU FOR FILMED RESPONSES IN THE STUDIO LAB! ··· TA-TA! I'M OFF TO THE LOVE LAB!
FILMED RESPONSES ?!!
STUDIO LAB
LET'S GET THOSE LIGHTS UP! CAMERAS!
YOU MUST BE MY CO-STAR! WE'RE ON IN A MINUTE! ··· IS THIS YOUR FIRST FILM FOR MASTER? HE KNOWS HOW TO USE HIS CAMERAS AND GET A LOT OUT OF YOU. ··· BUT A KINSEY, HE'S NOT! OH, WELL. ··· **THAT'S SHOW BUSINESS!**
HOLD IT, YOU TWO! NOW JUST **RELAX! BE YOURSELVES!** I WANT SPONTANEITY! THINK STRASBERG!
ROLL 'EM!
SCRIPT
NO! NO! GET THAT CAMERA AROUND TO THE LEFT! YOU'RE SHOOTING THE BAD SIDE OF HER *LABIA MINORA!* ··· THAT'S BETTER. ALL RIGHT ··· REMEMBER ··· THIS IS THE **BIG CLIMAX!** ··· **ACTION!**
LEAPIN' LIZARDS! LOOK AT WHAT THEY'RE **DOING** !!
WANDA'S IN THE LOVE-ROOM LAB, BUT YOU CAN'T DISTURB HER NOW. SHE'S IN THE MIDDLE OF A TEST.
WANDA! YOU DIDN'T TELL ME THAT THEY WERE TESTING PEOPLE DOING "IT"!!
CONTROL ROOM

162

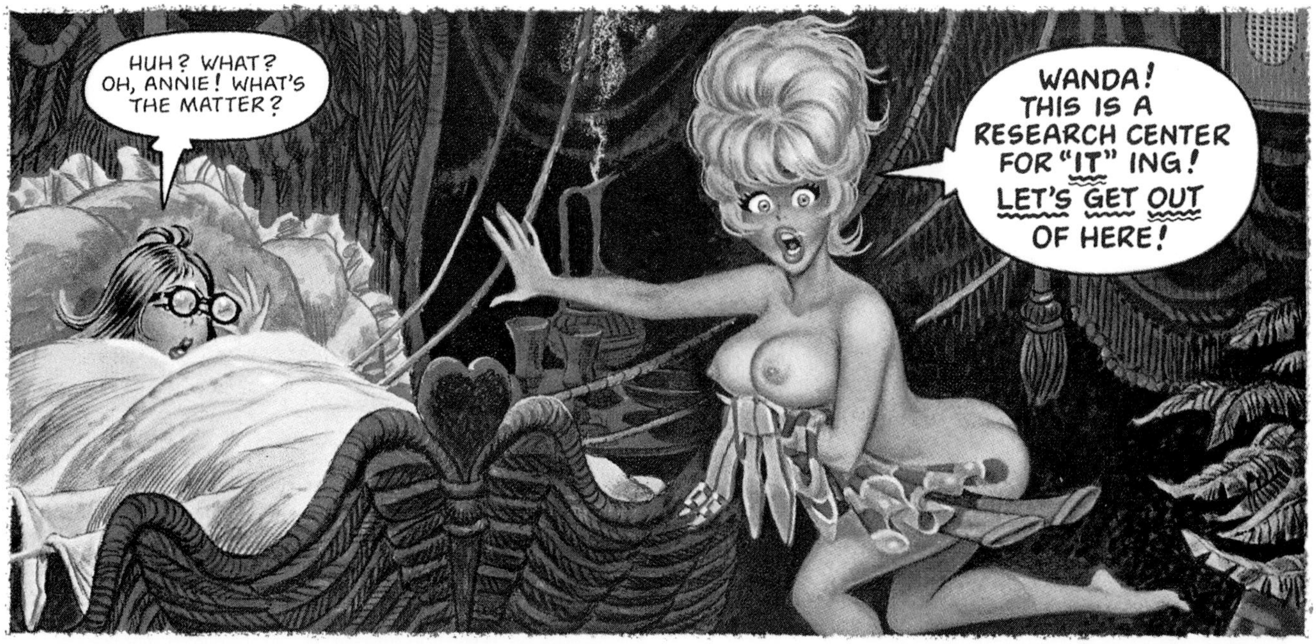
HUH? WHAT? OH, ANNIE! WHAT'S THE MATTER?
WANDA! THIS IS A RESEARCH CENTER FOR "IT" ING! LET'S GET OUT OF HERE!

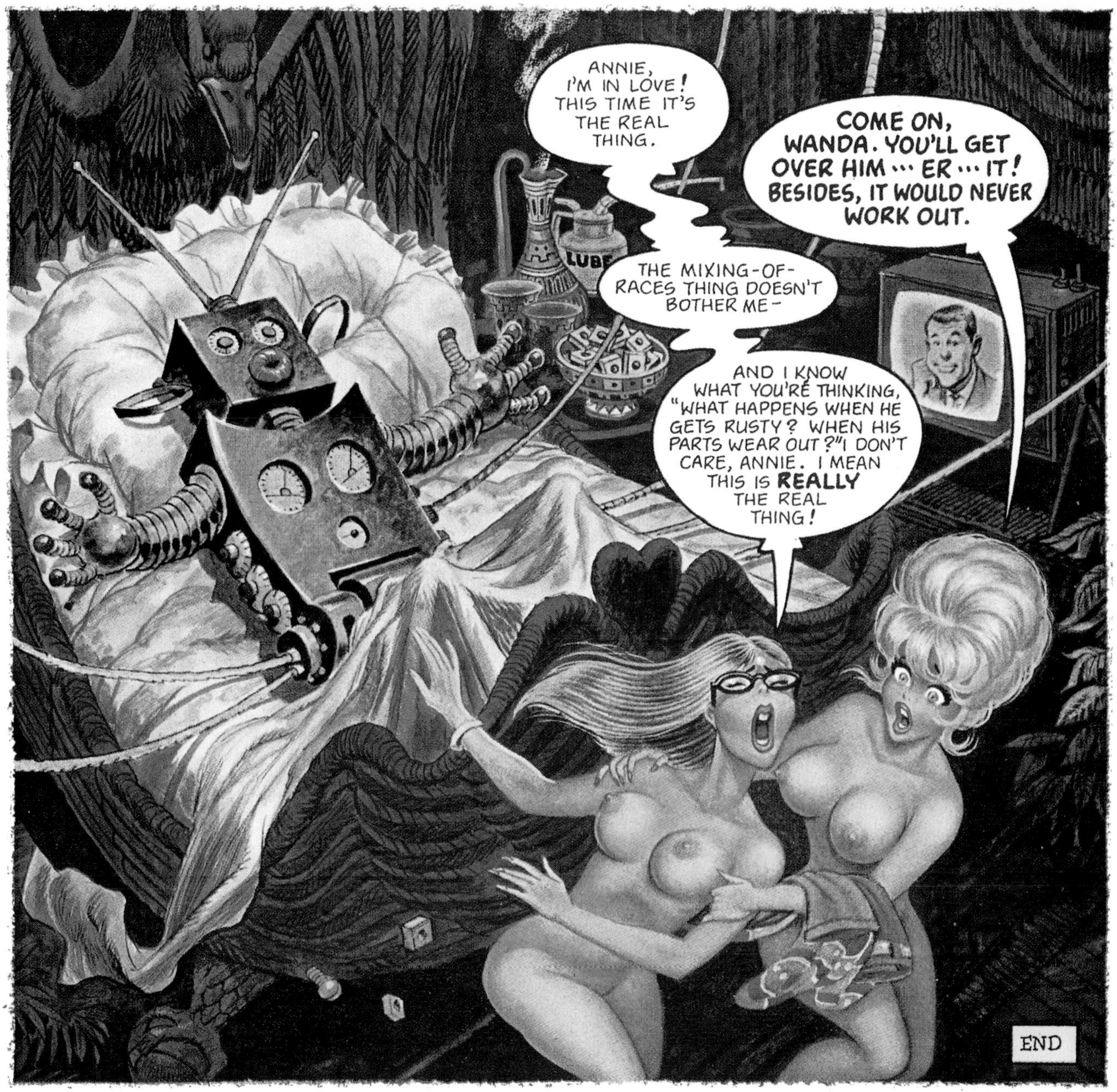
ANNIE, I'M IN LOVE! THIS TIME IT'S THE REAL THING.
COME ON, WANDA. YOU'LL GET OVER HIM ··· ER ··· IT! BESIDES, IT WOULD NEVER WORK OUT.
LUBE
THE MIXING-OF-RACES THING DOESN'T BOTHER ME–
AND I KNOW WHAT YOU'RE THINKING, "WHAT HAPPENS WHEN HE GETS RUSTY? WHEN HIS PARTS WEAR OUT?" I DON'T CARE, ANNIE. I MEAN THIS IS REALLY THE REAL THING!
END

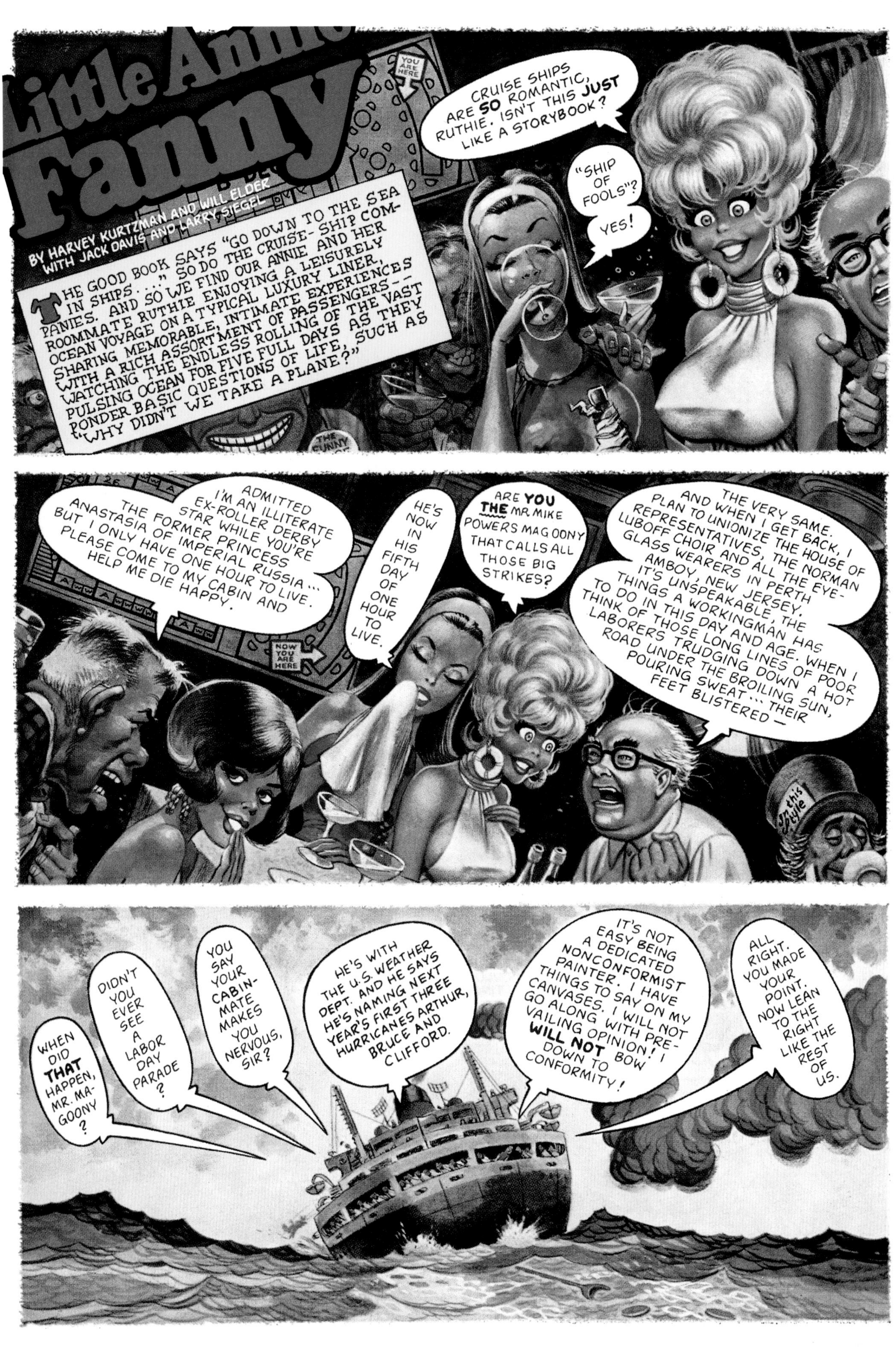
Little Annie Fanny
YOU ARE HERE
BY HARVEY KURTZMAN AND WILL ELDER
WITH JACK DAVIS AND LARRY SIEGEL
THE GOOD BOOK SAYS "GO DOWN TO THE SEA IN SHIPS. . . ." SO DO THE CRUISE-SHIP COMPANIES. AND SO WE FIND OUR ANNIE AND HER ROOMMATE RUTHIE ENJOYING A LEISURELY OCEAN VOYAGE ON A TYPICAL LUXURY LINER, SHARING MEMORABLE, INTIMATE EXPERIENCES WITH A RICH ASSORTMENT OF PASSENGERS-- WATCHING THE ENDLESS ROLLING OF THE VAST PULSING OCEAN FOR FIVE FULL DAYS AS THEY PONDER BASIC QUESTIONS OF LIFE, SUCH AS "WHY DIDN'T WE TAKE A PLANE?"
CRUISE SHIPS ARE SO ROMANTIC, RUTHIE. ISN'T THIS JUST LIKE A STORYBOOK?
"SHIP OF FOOLS"?
YES!
ADMITTED I'M AN ILLITERATE EX-ROLLER DERBY STAR WHILE YOU'RE THE FORMER PRINCESS ANASTASIA OF IMPERIAL RUSSIA... BUT I ONLY HAVE ONE HOUR TO LIVE. PLEASE COME TO MY CABIN AND HELP ME DIE HAPPY.
HE'S NOW IN HIS FIFTH DAY OF ONE HOUR TO LIVE.
NOW YOU ARE HERE
ARE YOU THE MR. MIKE POWERS MAGOONY THAT CALLS ALL THOSE BIG STRIKES?
THE VERY SAME. AND WHEN I GET BACK, I PLAN TO UNIONIZE THE HOUSE OF REPRESENTATIVES, THE NORMAN LUBOFF CHOIR AND ALL THE EYE-GLASS WEARERS IN PERTH AMBOY, NEW JERSEY. IT'S UNSPEAKABLE, THE THINGS A WORKINGMAN HAS TO DO IN THIS DAY AND AGE. WHEN I THINK OF THOSE LONG LINES OF POOR LABORERS TRUDGING DOWN A HOT ROAD UNDER THE BROILING SUN, POURING SWEAT... THEIR FEET BLISTERED—
WHEN DID THAT HAPPEN, MR. MA-GOONY?
DIDN'T YOU EVER SEE A LABOR DAY PARADE?
YOU SAY YOUR CABIN-MATE MAKES YOU NERVOUS, SIR?
HE'S WITH THE U.S. WEATHER DEPT. AND HE SAYS HE'S NAMING NEXT YEAR'S FIRST THREE HURRICANES ARTHUR, BRUCE AND CLIFFORD.
IT'S NOT EASY BEING A DEDICATED NONCONFORMIST PAINTER. I HAVE THINGS TO SAY ON MY CANVASES. I WILL NOT GO ALONG WITH PRE-VAILING OPINION! I WILL NOT BOW DOWN TO CONFORMITY!
ALL RIGHT. YOU MADE YOUR POINT. NOW LEAN TO THE RIGHT LIKE THE REST OF US.

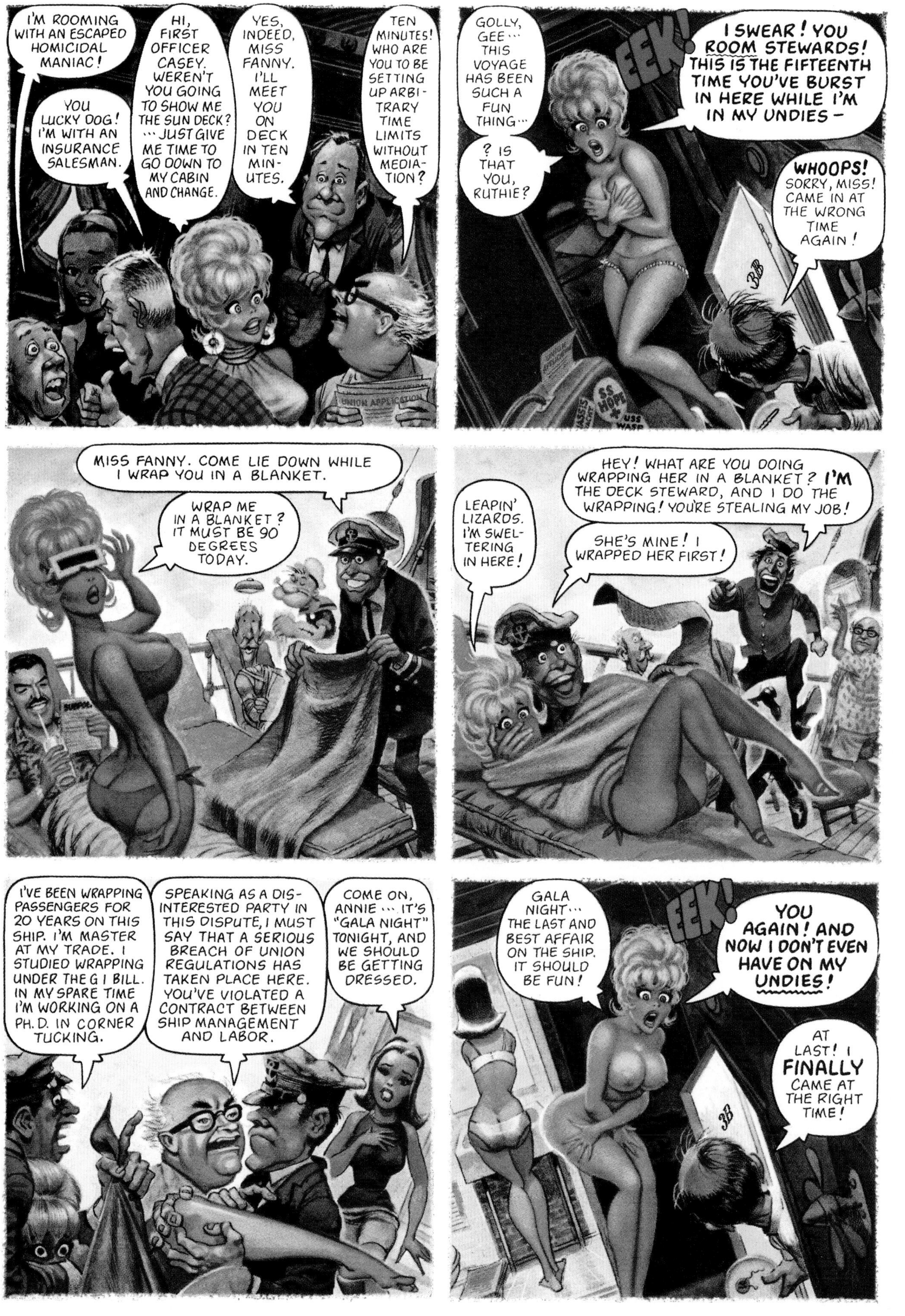

I'M ROOMING WITH AN ESCAPED HOMICIDAL MANIAC!
YOU LUCKY DOG! I'M WITH AN INSURANCE SALESMAN.
HI, FIRST OFFICER CASEY. WEREN'T YOU GOING TO SHOW ME THE SUN DECK? ··· JUST GIVE ME TIME TO GO DOWN TO MY CABIN AND CHANGE.
YES, INDEED, MISS FANNY. I'LL MEET YOU ON DECK IN TEN MINUTES.
TEN MINUTES! WHO ARE YOU TO BE SETTING UP ARBITRARY TIME LIMITS WITHOUT MEDIATION?
GOLLY, GEE··· THIS VOYAGE HAS BEEN SUCH A FUN THING···
? IS THAT YOU, RUTHIE?
EEK!
I SWEAR! YOU ROOM STEWARDS! THIS IS THE FIFTEENTH TIME YOU'VE BURST IN HERE WHILE I'M IN MY UNDIES –
WHOOPS! SORRY, MISS! CAME IN AT THE WRONG TIME AGAIN!
MISS FANNY. COME LIE DOWN WHILE I WRAP YOU IN A BLANKET.
WRAP ME IN A BLANKET? IT MUST BE 90 DEGREES TODAY.
LEAPIN' LIZARDS. I'M SWELTERING IN HERE!
HEY! WHAT ARE YOU DOING WRAPPING HER IN A BLANKET? I'M THE DECK STEWARD, AND I DO THE WRAPPING! YOU'RE STEALING MY JOB!
SHE'S MINE! I WRAPPED HER FIRST!
I'VE BEEN WRAPPING PASSENGERS FOR 20 YEARS ON THIS SHIP. I'M MASTER AT MY TRADE. I STUDIED WRAPPING UNDER THE G I BILL. IN MY SPARE TIME I'M WORKING ON A PH.D. IN CORNER TUCKING.
SPEAKING AS A DISINTERESTED PARTY IN THIS DISPUTE, I MUST SAY THAT A SERIOUS BREACH OF UNION REGULATIONS HAS TAKEN PLACE HERE. YOU'VE VIOLATED A CONTRACT BETWEEN SHIP MANAGEMENT AND LABOR.
COME ON, ANNIE ··· IT'S "GALA NIGHT" TONIGHT, AND WE SHOULD BE GETTING DRESSED.
GALA NIGHT··· THE LAST AND BEST AFFAIR ON THE SHIP. IT SHOULD BE FUN!
EEK!
YOU AGAIN! AND NOW I DON'T EVEN HAVE ON MY UNDIES!
AT LAST! I FINALLY CAME AT THE RIGHT TIME!

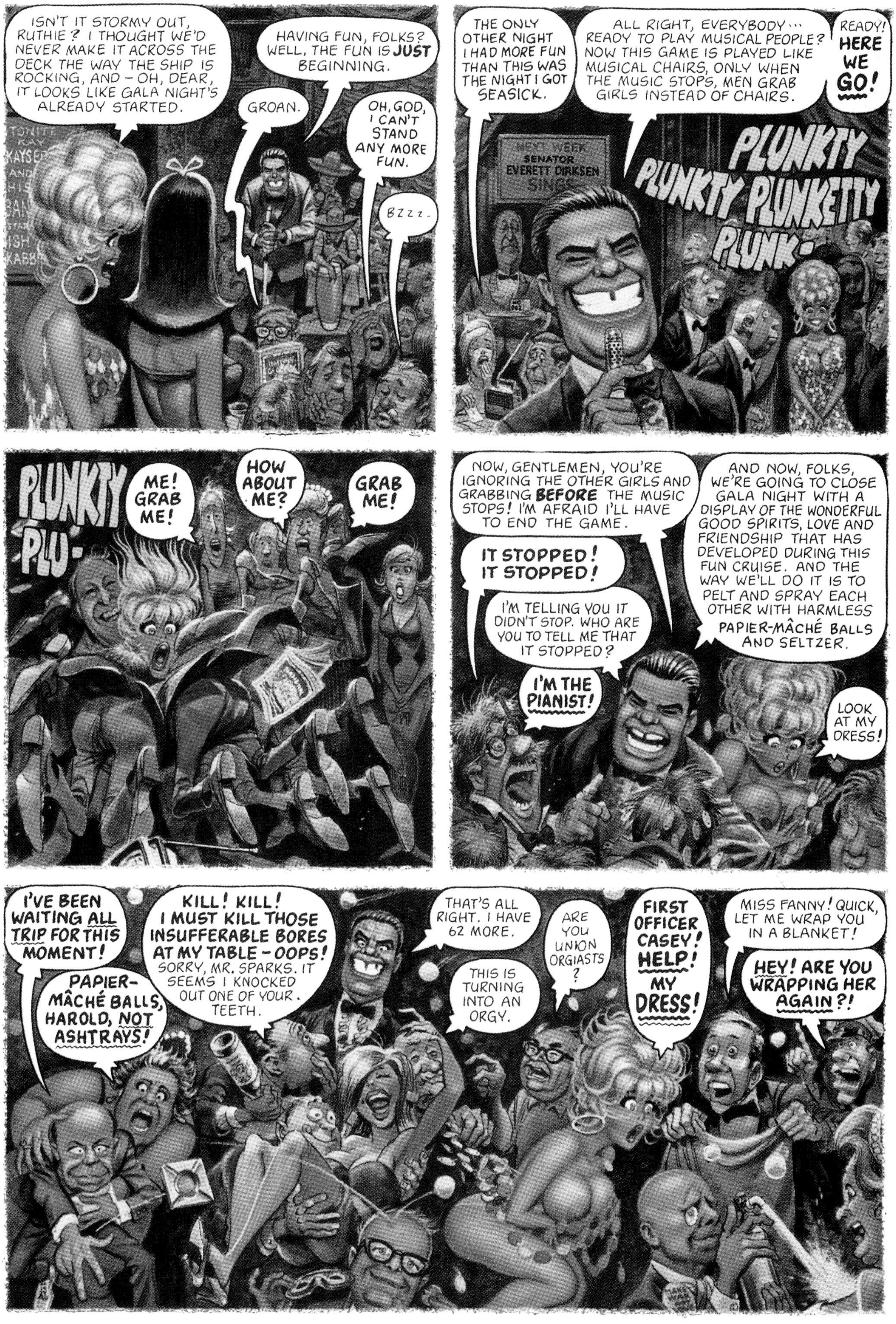
ISN'T IT STORMY OUT, RUTHIE? I THOUGHT WE'D NEVER MAKE IT ACROSS THE DECK THE WAY THE SHIP IS ROCKING, AND - OH, DEAR, IT LOOKS LIKE GALA NIGHT'S ALREADY STARTED.
HAVING FUN, FOLKS? WELL, THE FUN IS JUST BEGINNING.
GROAN.
OH, GOD, I CAN'T STAND ANY MORE FUN.
BZZZ.
THE ONLY OTHER NIGHT I HAD MORE FUN THAN THIS WAS THE NIGHT I GOT SEASICK.
ALL RIGHT, EVERYBODY... READY TO PLAY MUSICAL PEOPLE? NOW THIS GAME IS PLAYED LIKE MUSICAL CHAIRS, ONLY WHEN THE MUSIC STOPS, MEN GRAB GIRLS INSTEAD OF CHAIRS.
READY! HERE WE GO!
NEXT WEEK SENATOR EVERETT DIRKSEN SINGS
PLUNKTY PLUNKTY PLUNKETTY PLUNK-
PLUNKTY PLU-
ME! GRAB ME!
HOW ABOUT ME?
GRAB ME!
NOW, GENTLEMEN, YOU'RE IGNORING THE OTHER GIRLS AND GRABBING BEFORE THE MUSIC STOPS! I'M AFRAID I'LL HAVE TO END THE GAME.
IT STOPPED! IT STOPPED!
I'M TELLING YOU IT DIDN'T STOP. WHO ARE YOU TO TELL ME THAT IT STOPPED?
I'M THE PIANIST!
AND NOW, FOLKS, WE'RE GOING TO CLOSE GALA NIGHT WITH A DISPLAY OF THE WONDERFUL GOOD SPIRITS, LOVE AND FRIENDSHIP THAT HAS DEVELOPED DURING THIS FUN CRUISE. AND THE WAY WE'LL DO IT IS TO PELT AND SPRAY EACH OTHER WITH HARMLESS PAPIER-MÂCHÉ BALLS AND SELTZER.
LOOK AT MY DRESS!
I'VE BEEN WAITING ALL TRIP FOR THIS MOMENT!
PAPIER-MÂCHÉ BALLS, HAROLD, NOT ASHTRAYS!
KILL! KILL! I MUST KILL THOSE INSUFFERABLE BORES AT MY TABLE - OOPS! SORRY, MR. SPARKS. IT SEEMS I KNOCKED OUT ONE OF YOUR TEETH.
THAT'S ALL RIGHT. I HAVE 62 MORE.
THIS IS TURNING INTO AN ORGY.
ARE YOU UNION ORGIASTS?
FIRST OFFICER CASEY! HELP! MY DRESS!
MISS FANNY! QUICK, LET ME WRAP YOU IN A BLANKET!
HEY! ARE YOU WRAPPING HER AGAIN?!

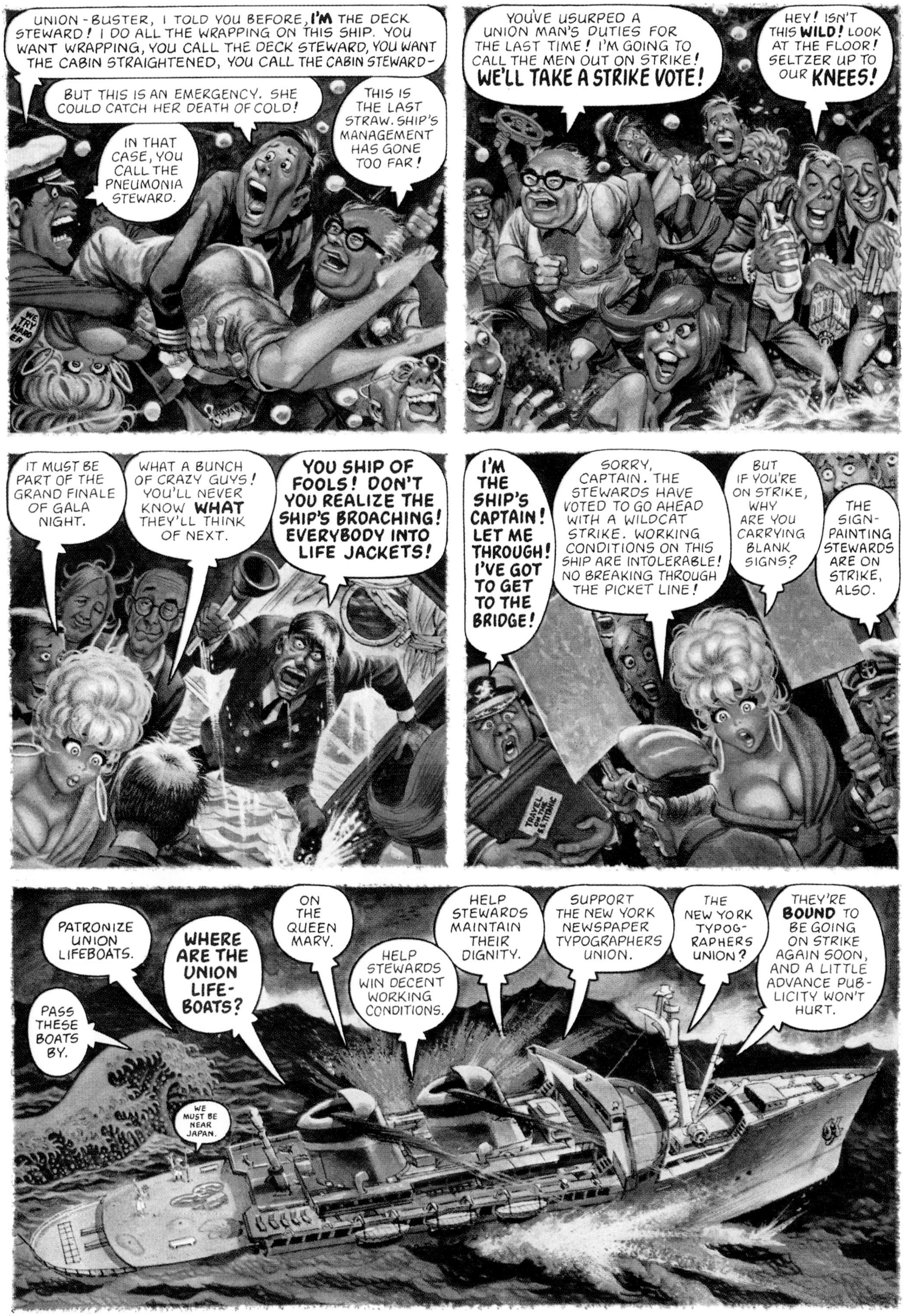
UNION - BUSTER, I TOLD YOU BEFORE, I'M THE DECK STEWARD! I DO ALL THE WRAPPING ON THIS SHIP. YOU WANT WRAPPING, YOU CALL THE DECK STEWARD, YOU WANT THE CABIN STRAIGHTENED, YOU CALL THE CABIN STEWARD-
BUT THIS IS AN EMERGENCY. SHE COULD CATCH HER DEATH OF COLD!
IN THAT CASE, YOU CALL THE PNEUMONIA STEWARD.
THIS IS THE LAST STRAW. SHIP'S MANAGEMENT HAS GONE TOO FAR!
YOU'VE USURPED A UNION MAN'S DUTIES FOR THE LAST TIME! I'M GOING TO CALL THE MEN OUT ON STRIKE! WE'LL TAKE A STRIKE VOTE!
HEY! ISN'T THIS WILD! LOOK AT THE FLOOR! SELTZER UP TO OUR KNEES!
IT MUST BE PART OF THE GRAND FINALE OF GALA NIGHT.
WHAT A BUNCH OF CRAZY GUYS! YOU'LL NEVER KNOW WHAT THEY'LL THINK OF NEXT.
YOU SHIP OF FOOLS! DON'T YOU REALIZE THE SHIP'S BROACHING! EVERYBODY INTO LIFE JACKETS!
I'M THE SHIP'S CAPTAIN! LET ME THROUGH! I'VE GOT TO GET TO THE BRIDGE!
SORRY, CAPTAIN. THE STEWARDS HAVE VOTED TO GO AHEAD WITH A WILDCAT STRIKE. WORKING CONDITIONS ON THIS SHIP ARE INTOLERABLE! NO BREAKING THROUGH THE PICKET LINE!
BUT IF YOU'RE ON STRIKE, WHY ARE YOU CARRYING BLANK SIGNS?
THE SIGN-PAINTING STEWARDS ARE ON STRIKE, ALSO.
PATRONIZE UNION LIFEBOATS.
PASS THESE BOATS BY.
WHERE ARE THE UNION LIFE-BOATS?
ON THE QUEEN MARY.
HELP STEWARDS WIN DECENT WORKING CONDITIONS.
HELP STEWARDS MAINTAIN THEIR DIGNITY.
SUPPORT THE NEW YORK NEWSPAPER TYPOGRAPHERS UNION.
THE NEW YORK TYPOG-RAPHERS UNION?
THEY'RE BOUND TO BE GOING ON STRIKE AGAIN SOON, AND A LITTLE ADVANCE PUB-LICITY WON'T HURT.
WE MUST BE NEAR JAPAN.

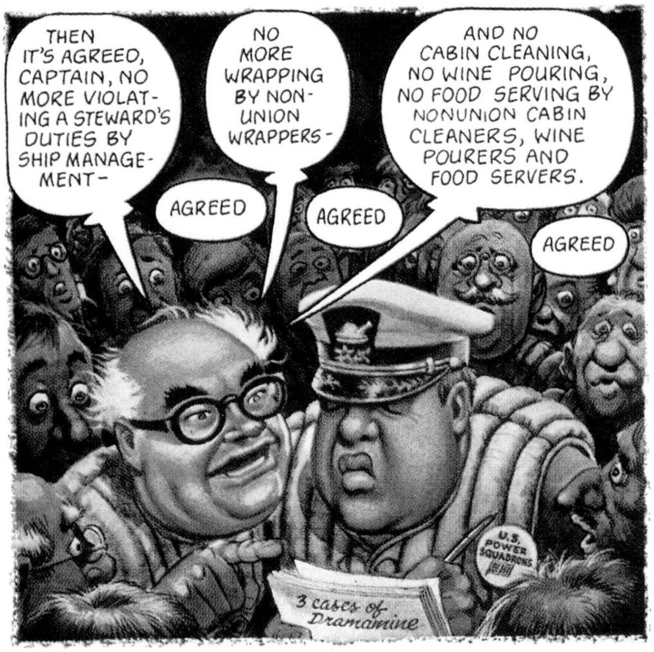
THEN IT'S AGREED, CAPTAIN, NO MORE VIOLATING A STEWARD'S DUTIES BY SHIP MANAGEMENT-
NO MORE WRAPPING BY NON-UNION WRAPPERS-
AND NO CABIN CLEANING, NO WINE POURING, NO FOOD SERVING BY NONUNION CABIN CLEANERS, WINE POURERS AND FOOD SERVERS.
AGREED
AGREED
AGREED
U.S. POWER SQUADRONS
3 cases of Dramamine

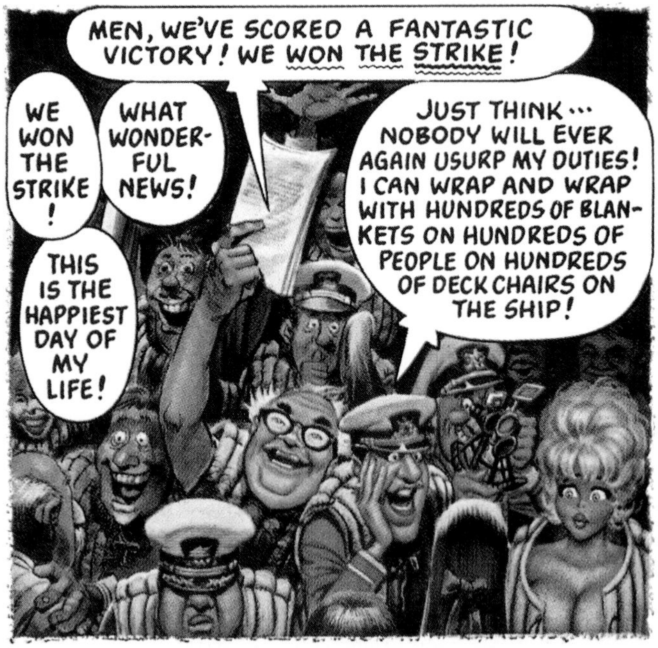
MEN, WE'VE SCORED A FANTASTIC VICTORY! WE WON THE STRIKE!
WE WON THE STRIKE!
WHAT WONDERFUL NEWS!
JUST THINK... NOBODY WILL EVER AGAIN USURP MY DUTIES! I CAN WRAP AND WRAP WITH HUNDREDS OF BLANKETS ON HUNDREDS OF PEOPLE ON HUNDREDS OF DECK CHAIRS ON THE SHIP!
THIS IS THE HAPPIEST DAY OF MY LIFE!

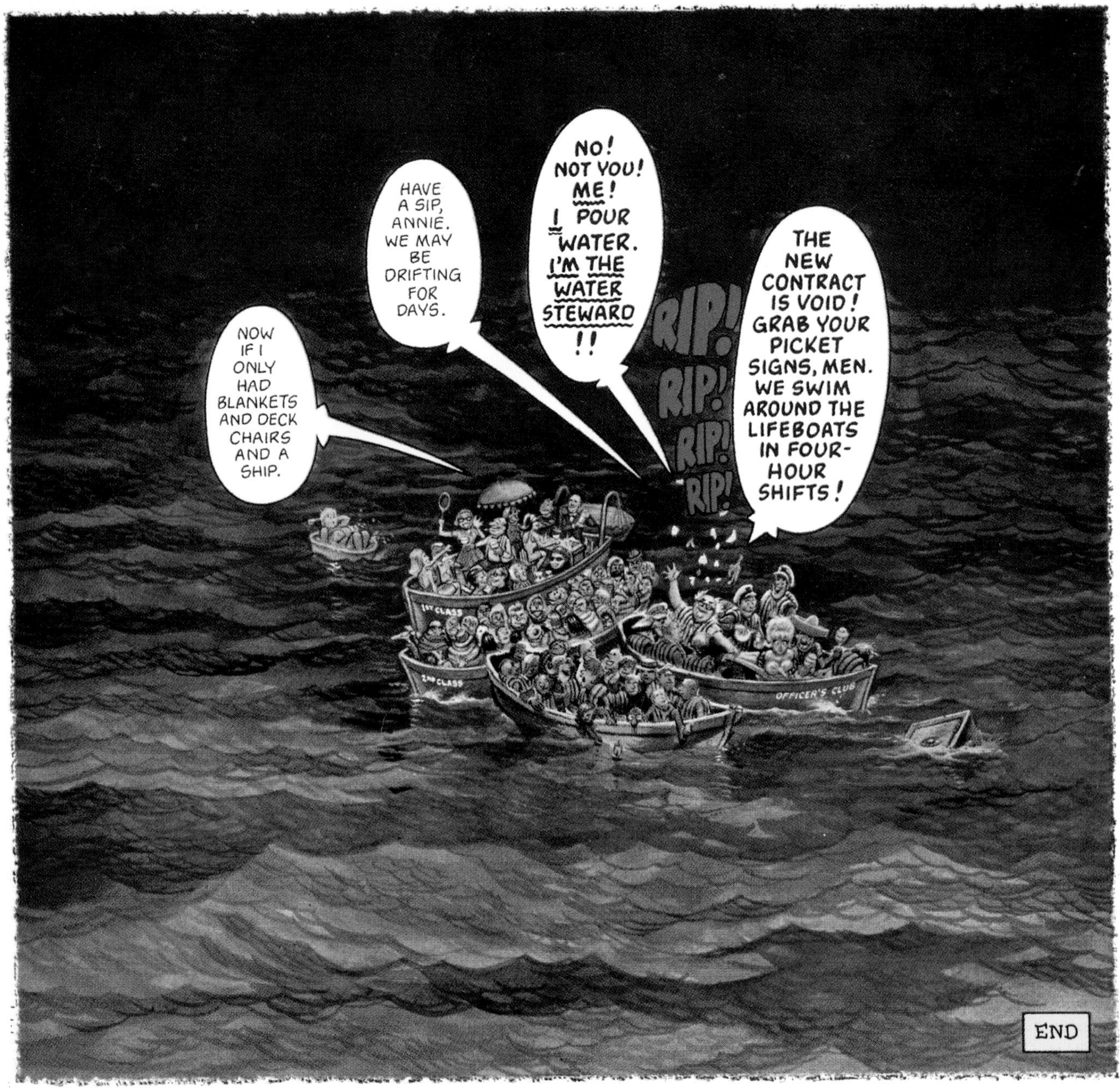
NOW IF I ONLY HAD BLANKETS AND DECK CHAIRS AND A SHIP.
HAVE A SIP, ANNIE. WE MAY BE DRIFTING FOR DAYS.
NO! NOT YOU! ME! I POUR WATER. I'M THE WATER STEWARD!!
RIP! RIP! RIP! RIP!
THE NEW CONTRACT IS VOID! GRAB YOUR PICKET SIGNS, MEN. WE SWIM AROUND THE LIFEBOATS IN FOUR-HOUR SHIFTS!
1ST CLASS
2ND CLASS
OFFICER'S CLUB
END

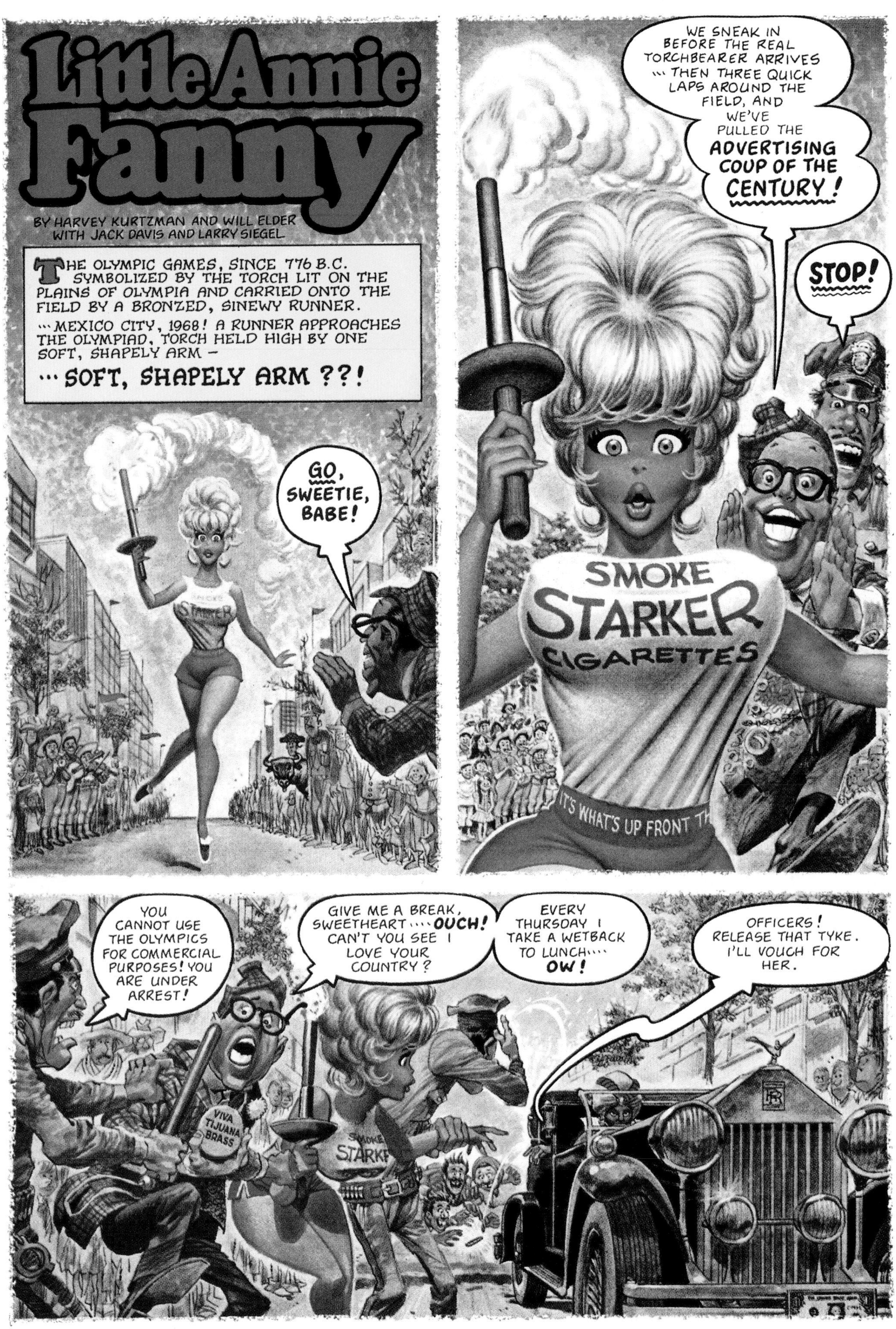

Little Annie Fanny
BY HARVEY KURTZMAN AND WILL ELDER WITH JACK DAVIS AND LARRY SIEGEL
THE OLYMPIC GAMES, SINCE 776 B.C. SYMBOLIZED BY THE TORCH LIT ON THE PLAINS OF OLYMPIA AND CARRIED ONTO THE FIELD BY A BRONZED, SINEWY RUNNER.
... MEXICO CITY, 1968! A RUNNER APPROACHES THE OLYMPIAD, TORCH HELD HIGH BY ONE SOFT, SHAPELY ARM –
... SOFT, SHAPELY ARM ??!
GO, SWEETIE, BABE!
WE SNEAK IN BEFORE THE REAL TORCHBEARER ARRIVES ... THEN THREE QUICK LAPS AROUND THE FIELD, AND WE'VE PULLED THE ADVERTISING COUP OF THE CENTURY!
STOP!
SMOKE STARKER CIGARETTES
IT'S WHAT'S UP FRONT TH
YOU CANNOT USE THE OLYMPICS FOR COMMERCIAL PURPOSES! YOU ARE UNDER ARREST!
GIVE ME A BREAK, SWEETHEART .... OUCH! CAN'T YOU SEE I LOVE YOUR COUNTRY?
EVERY THURSDAY I TAKE A WETBACK TO LUNCH.... OW!
OFFICERS! RELEASE THAT TYKE. I'LL VOUCH FOR HER.
VIVA TIJUANA BRASS

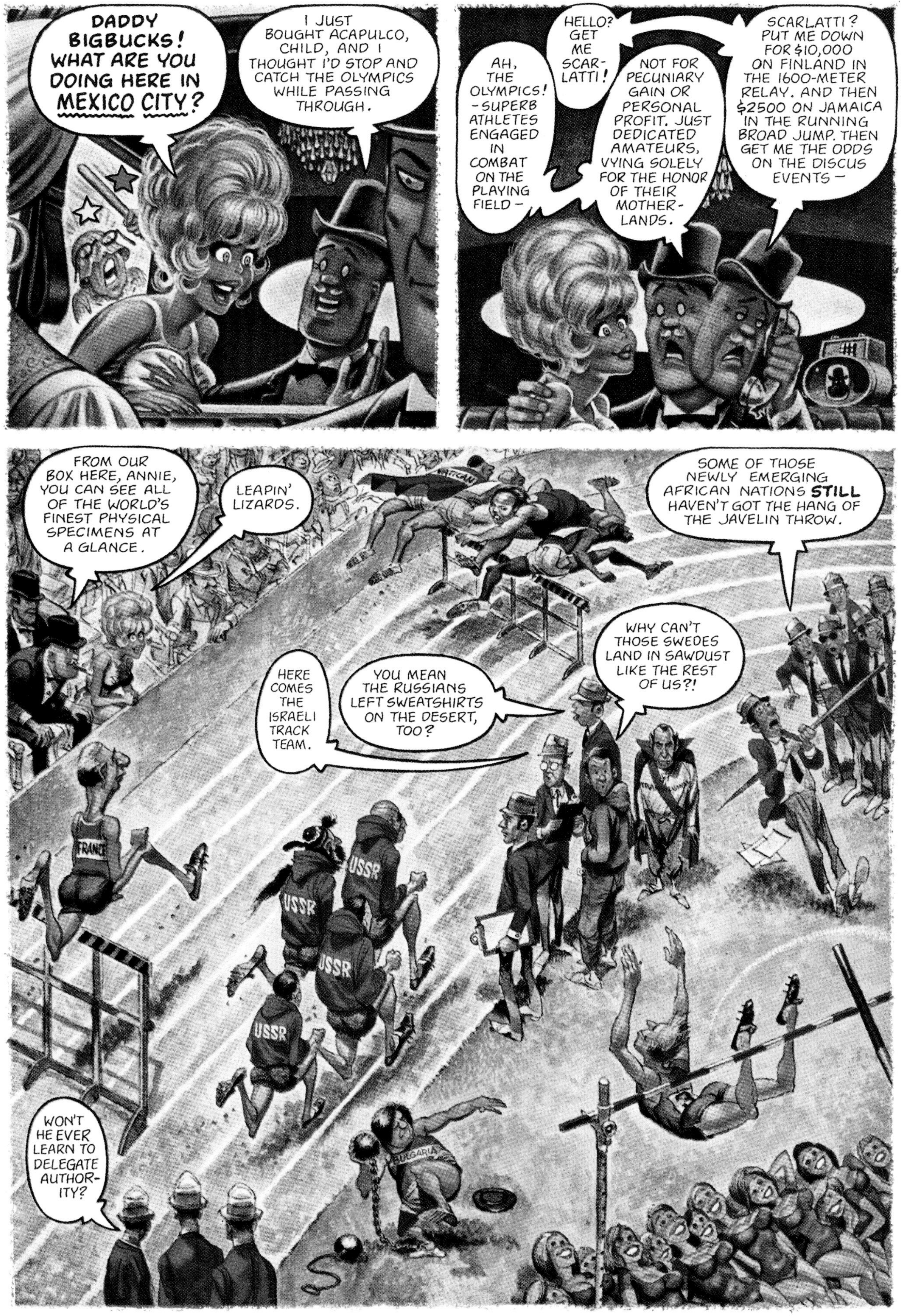
DADDY BIGBUCKS! WHAT ARE YOU DOING HERE IN MEXICO CITY?
I JUST BOUGHT ACAPULCO, CHILD, AND I THOUGHT I'D STOP AND CATCH THE OLYMPICS WHILE PASSING THROUGH.
AH, THE OLYMPICS! —SUPERB ATHLETES ENGAGED IN COMBAT ON THE PLAYING FIELD—
NOT FOR PECUNIARY GAIN OR PERSONAL PROFIT. JUST DEDICATED AMATEURS, VYING SOLELY FOR THE HONOR OF THEIR MOTHER-LANDS.
HELLO? GET ME SCAR-LATTI!
SCARLATTI? PUT ME DOWN FOR $10,000 ON FINLAND IN THE 1600-METER RELAY. AND THEN $2500 ON JAMAICA IN THE RUNNING BROAD JUMP. THEN GET ME THE ODDS ON THE DISCUS EVENTS—
FROM OUR BOX HERE, ANNIE, YOU CAN SEE ALL OF THE WORLD'S FINEST PHYSICAL SPECIMENS AT A GLANCE.
LEAPIN' LIZARDS.
SOME OF THOSE NEWLY EMERGING AFRICAN NATIONS STILL HAVEN'T GOT THE HANG OF THE JAVELIN THROW.
WHY CAN'T THOSE SWEDES LAND IN SAWDUST LIKE THE REST OF US?!
HERE COMES THE ISRAELI TRACK TEAM.
YOU MEAN THE RUSSIANS LEFT SWEATSHIRTS ON THE DESERT, TOO?
FRANCE
USSR
USSR
USSR
USSR
WON'T HE EVER LEARN TO DELEGATE AUTHOR-ITY?
BULGARIA

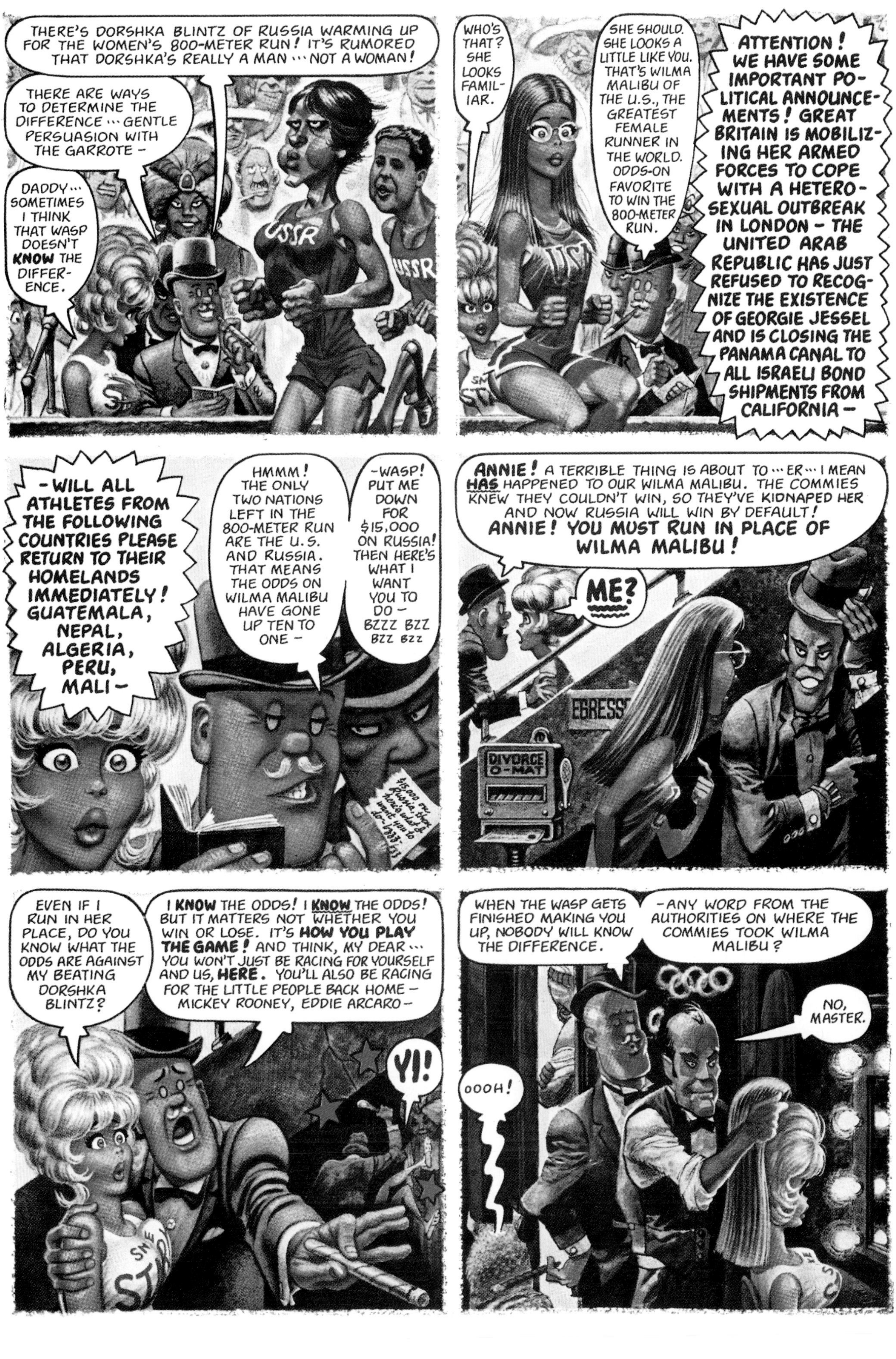

THERE'S DORSHKA BLINTZ OF RUSSIA WARMING UP FOR THE WOMEN'S 800-METER RUN! IT'S RUMORED THAT DORSHKA'S REALLY A MAN ··· NOT A WOMAN!
THERE ARE WAYS TO DETERMINE THE DIFFERENCE ··· GENTLE PERSUASION WITH THE GARROTE –
DADDY··· SOMETIMES I THINK THAT WASP DOESN'T **KNOW** THE DIFFERENCE.
USSR
USSR
WHO'S THAT? SHE LOOKS FAMILIAR.
SHE SHOULD. SHE LOOKS A LITTLE LIKE YOU. THAT'S WILMA MALIBU OF THE U.S., THE GREATEST FEMALE RUNNER IN THE WORLD. ODDS-ON FAVORITE TO WIN THE 800-METER RUN.
ATTENTION! WE HAVE SOME IMPORTANT POLITICAL ANNOUNCEMENTS! GREAT BRITAIN IS MOBILIZING HER ARMED FORCES TO COPE WITH A HETEROSEXUAL OUTBREAK IN LONDON – THE UNITED ARAB REPUBLIC HAS JUST REFUSED TO RECOGNIZE THE EXISTENCE OF GEORGIE JESSEL AND IS CLOSING THE PANAMA CANAL TO ALL ISRAELI BOND SHIPMENTS FROM CALIFORNIA –
– WILL ALL ATHLETES FROM THE FOLLOWING COUNTRIES PLEASE RETURN TO THEIR HOMELANDS IMMEDIATELY! GUATEMALA, NEPAL, ALGERIA, PERU, MALI –
HMMM! THE ONLY TWO NATIONS LEFT IN THE 800-METER RUN ARE THE U.S. AND RUSSIA. THAT MEANS THE ODDS ON WILMA MALIBU HAVE GONE UP TEN TO ONE –
– WASP! PUT ME DOWN FOR $15,000 ON RUSSIA! THEN HERE'S WHAT I WANT YOU TO DO – BZZZ BZZ BZZ BZZ
ANNIE! A TERRIBLE THING IS ABOUT TO ··· ER ··· I MEAN HAS HAPPENED TO OUR WILMA MALIBU. THE COMMIES KNEW THEY COULDN'T WIN, SO THEY'VE KIDNAPED HER AND NOW RUSSIA WILL WIN BY DEFAULT! ANNIE! YOU MUST RUN IN PLACE OF WILMA MALIBU!
ME?
EGRESS
DIVORCE O-MAT
EVEN IF I RUN IN HER PLACE, DO YOU KNOW WHAT THE ODDS ARE AGAINST MY BEATING DORSHKA BLINTZ?
I **KNOW** THE ODDS! I **KNOW** THE ODDS! BUT IT MATTERS NOT WHETHER YOU WIN OR LOSE. IT'S **HOW YOU PLAY THE GAME!** AND THINK, MY DEAR ··· YOU WON'T JUST BE RACING FOR YOURSELF AND US, **HERE**. YOU'LL ALSO BE RACING FOR THE LITTLE PEOPLE BACK HOME – MICKEY ROONEY, EDDIE ARCARO –
YI!
WHEN THE WASP GETS FINISHED MAKING YOU UP, NOBODY WILL KNOW THE DIFFERENCE.
– ANY WORD FROM THE AUTHORITIES ON WHERE THE COMMIES TOOK WILMA MALIBU?
NO, MASTER.
OOOH!

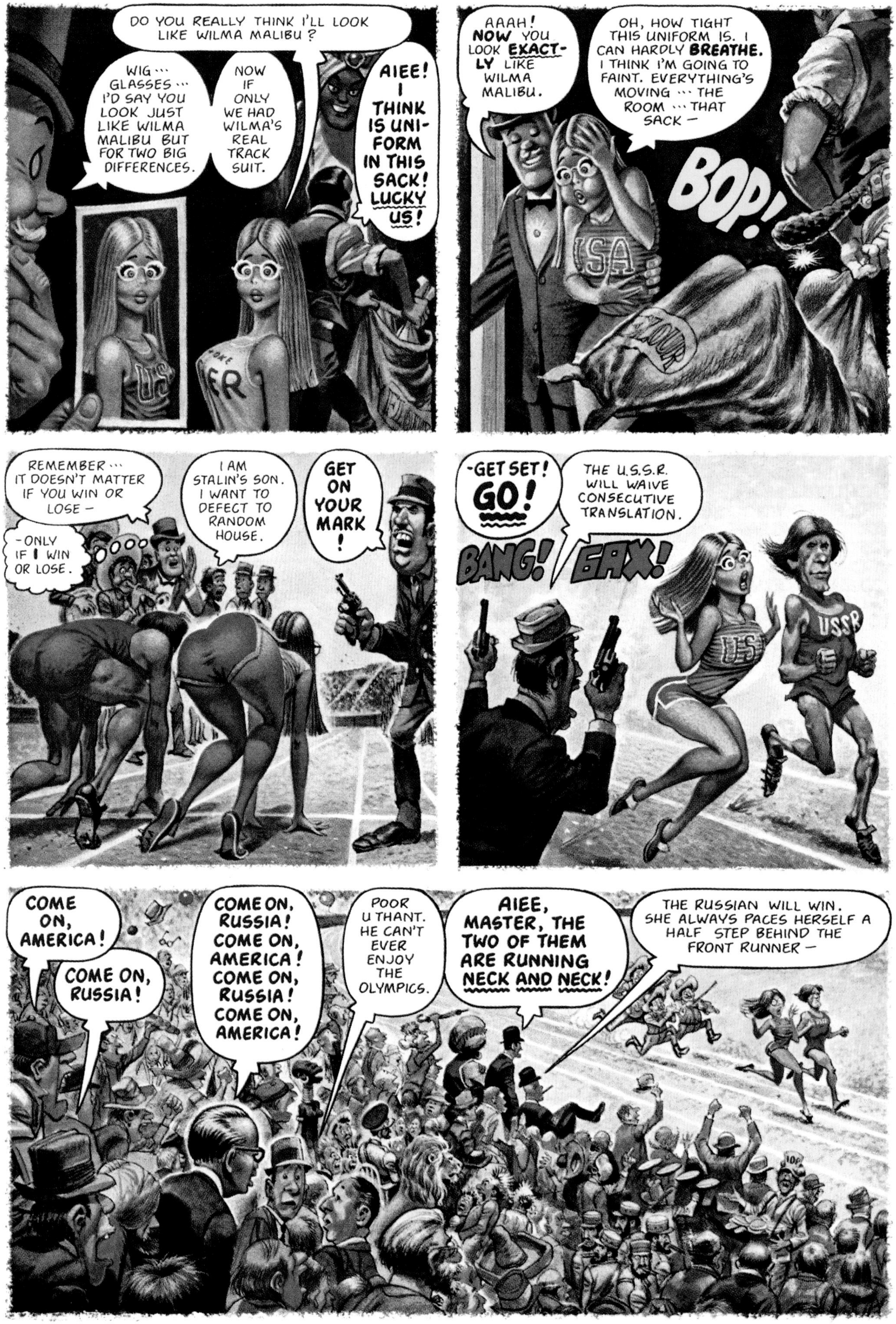
DO YOU REALLY THINK I'LL LOOK LIKE WILMA MALIBU?
WIG ··· GLASSES ··· I'D SAY YOU LOOK JUST LIKE WILMA MALIBU BUT FOR TWO BIG DIFFERENCES.
NOW IF ONLY WE HAD WILMA'S REAL TRACK SUIT.
AIEE! I THINK IS UNIFORM IN THIS SACK! LUCKY US!
AAAH! NOW YOU LOOK EXACTLY LIKE WILMA MALIBU.
OH, HOW TIGHT THIS UNIFORM IS. I CAN HARDLY BREATHE. I THINK I'M GOING TO FAINT. EVERYTHING'S MOVING ··· THE ROOM ··· THAT SACK —
BOP!
USA
REMEMBER ··· IT DOESN'T MATTER IF YOU WIN OR LOSE —
—ONLY IF I WIN OR LOSE.
I AM STALIN'S SON. I WANT TO DEFECT TO RANDOM HOUSE.
GET ON YOUR MARK!
—GET SET! GO!
THE U.S.S.R. WILL WAIVE CONSECUTIVE TRANSLATION.
BANG!
GAX!
USSR
COME ON, AMERICA!
COME ON, RUSSIA!
COME ON, RUSSIA! COME ON, AMERICA! COME ON, RUSSIA! COME ON, AMERICA!
POOR U THANT. HE CAN'T EVER ENJOY THE OLYMPICS.
AIEE, MASTER, THE TWO OF THEM ARE RUNNING NECK AND NECK!
THE RUSSIAN WILL WIN. SHE ALWAYS PACES HERSELF A HALF STEP BEHIND THE FRONT RUNNER —

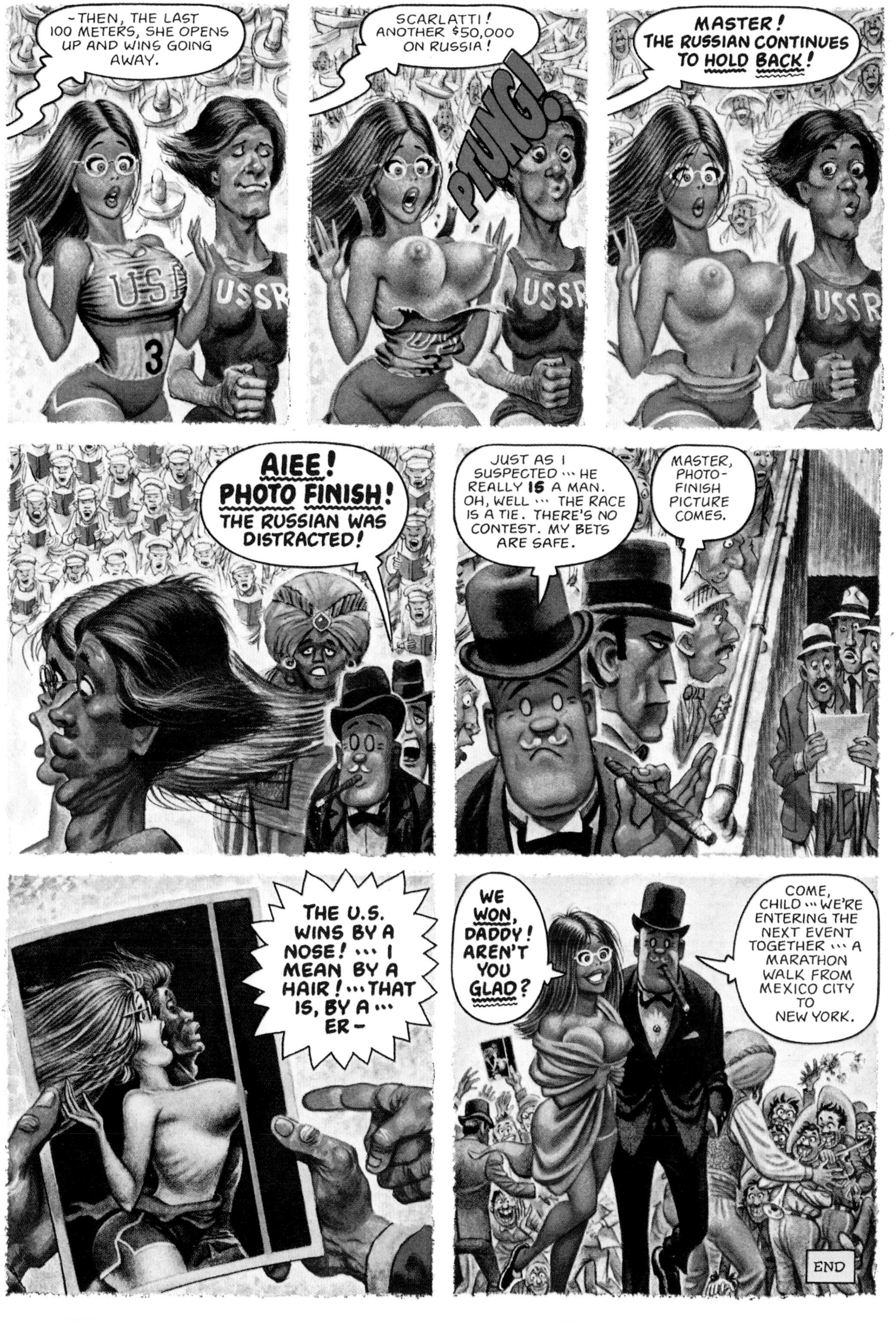

-THEN, THE LAST 100 METERS, SHE OPENS UP AND WINS GOING AWAY.
3
USSR
SCARLATTI! ANOTHER $50,000 ON RUSSIA!
PTUNG!
USSR
MASTER! THE RUSSIAN CONTINUES TO HOLD BACK!
USSR
AIEE! PHOTO FINISH! THE RUSSIAN WAS DISTRACTED!
JUST AS I SUSPECTED ··· HE REALLY IS A MAN. OH, WELL ··· THE RACE IS A TIE. THERE'S NO CONTEST. MY BETS ARE SAFE.
MASTER, PHOTO-FINISH PICTURE COMES.
THE U.S. WINS BY A NOSE! ··· I MEAN BY A HAIR! ··· THAT IS, BY A ··· ER-
WE WON, DADDY! AREN'T YOU GLAD?
COME, CHILD ··· WE'RE ENTERING THE NEXT EVENT TOGETHER ··· A MARATHON WALK FROM MEXICO CITY TO NEW YORK.
END

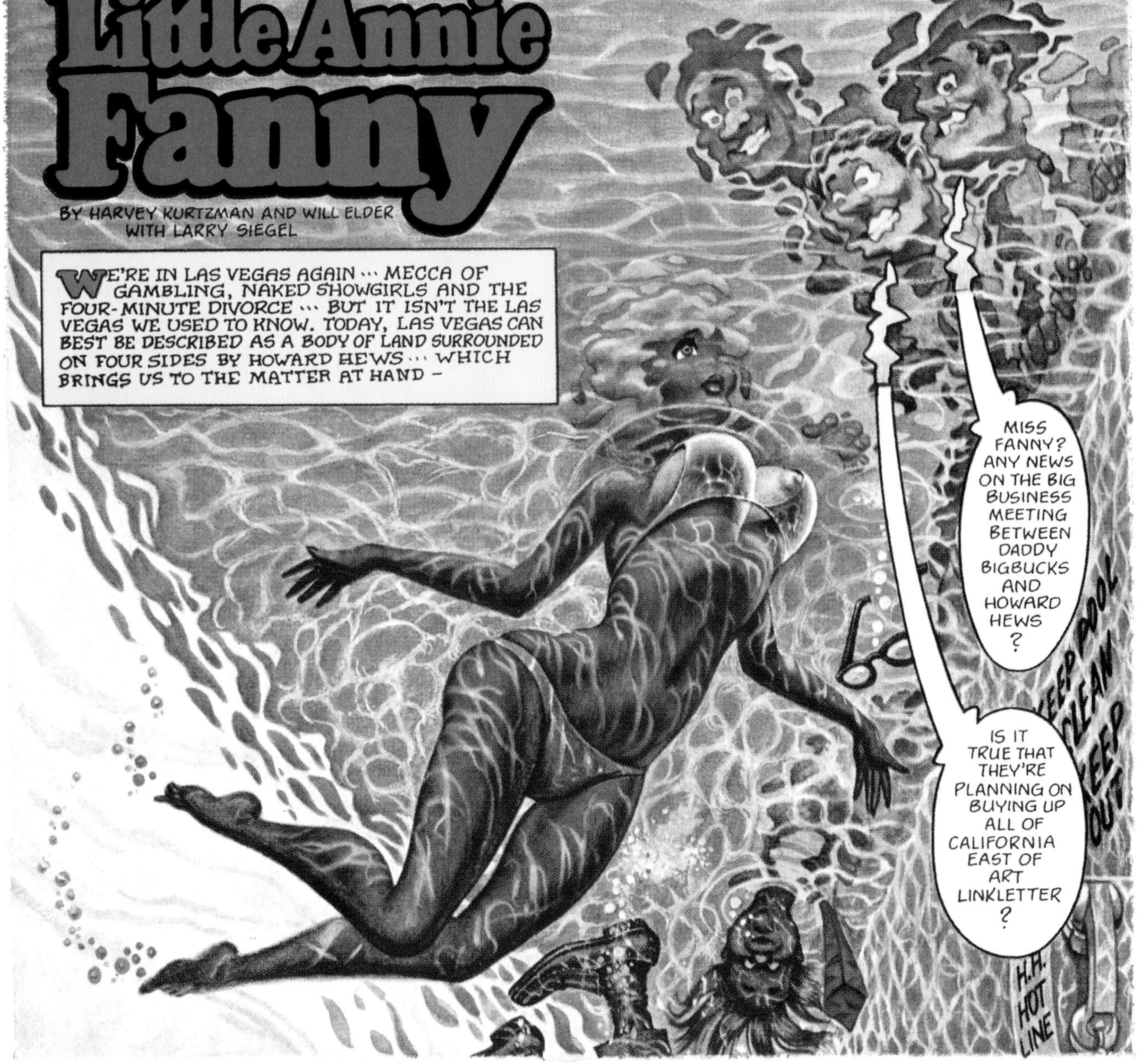
Little Annie Fanny
BY HARVEY KURTZMAN AND WILL ELDER WITH LARRY SIEGEL
WE'RE IN LAS VEGAS AGAIN ··· MECCA OF GAMBLING, NAKED SHOWGIRLS AND THE FOUR-MINUTE DIVORCE ··· BUT IT ISN'T THE LAS VEGAS WE USED TO KNOW. TODAY, LAS VEGAS CAN BEST BE DESCRIBED AS A BODY OF LAND SURROUNDED ON FOUR SIDES BY HOWARD HEWS ··· WHICH BRINGS US TO THE MATTER AT HAND –
MISS FANNY? ANY NEWS ON THE BIG BUSINESS MEETING BETWEEN DADDY BIGBUCKS AND HOWARD HEWS ?
IS IT TRUE THAT THEY'RE PLANNING ON BUYING UP ALL OF CALIFORNIA EAST OF ART LINKLETTER ?
KEEP POOL CLEAN
KEEP OUT
H.H. HOT LINE

174

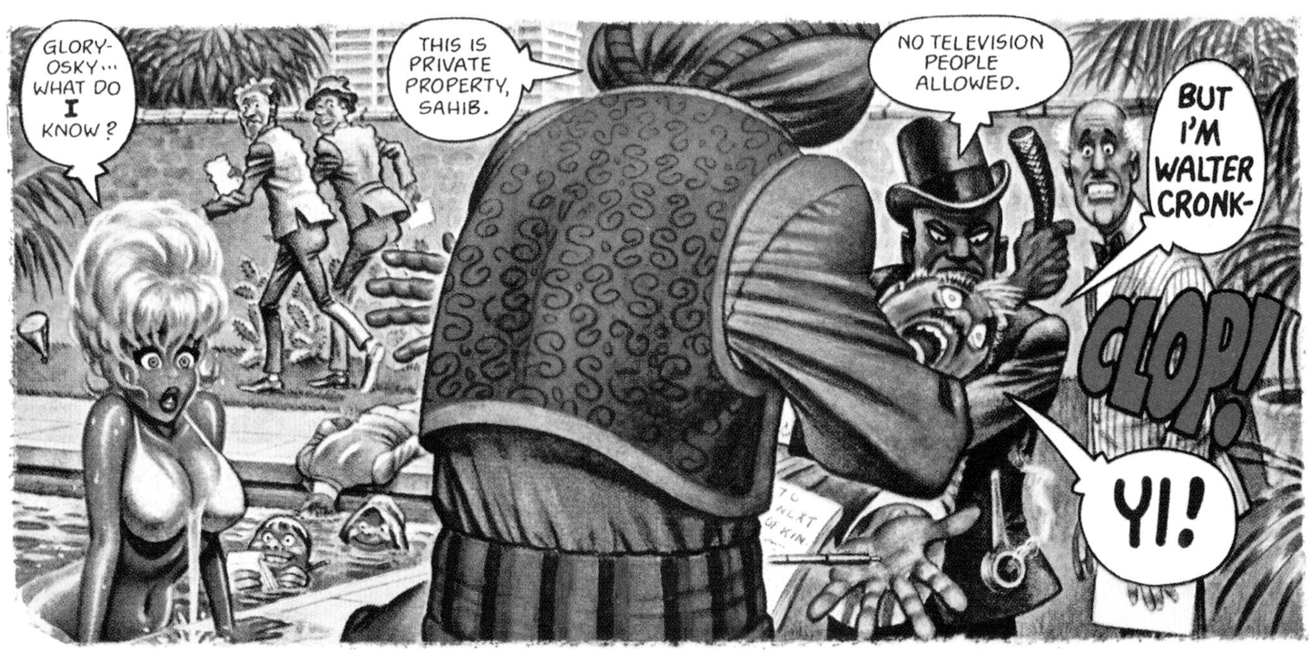
GLORY-OSKY··· WHAT DO I KNOW ?
THIS IS PRIVATE PROPERTY, SAHIB.
NO TELEVISION PEOPLE ALLOWED.
BUT I'M WALTER CRONK-
CLOP!
YI!

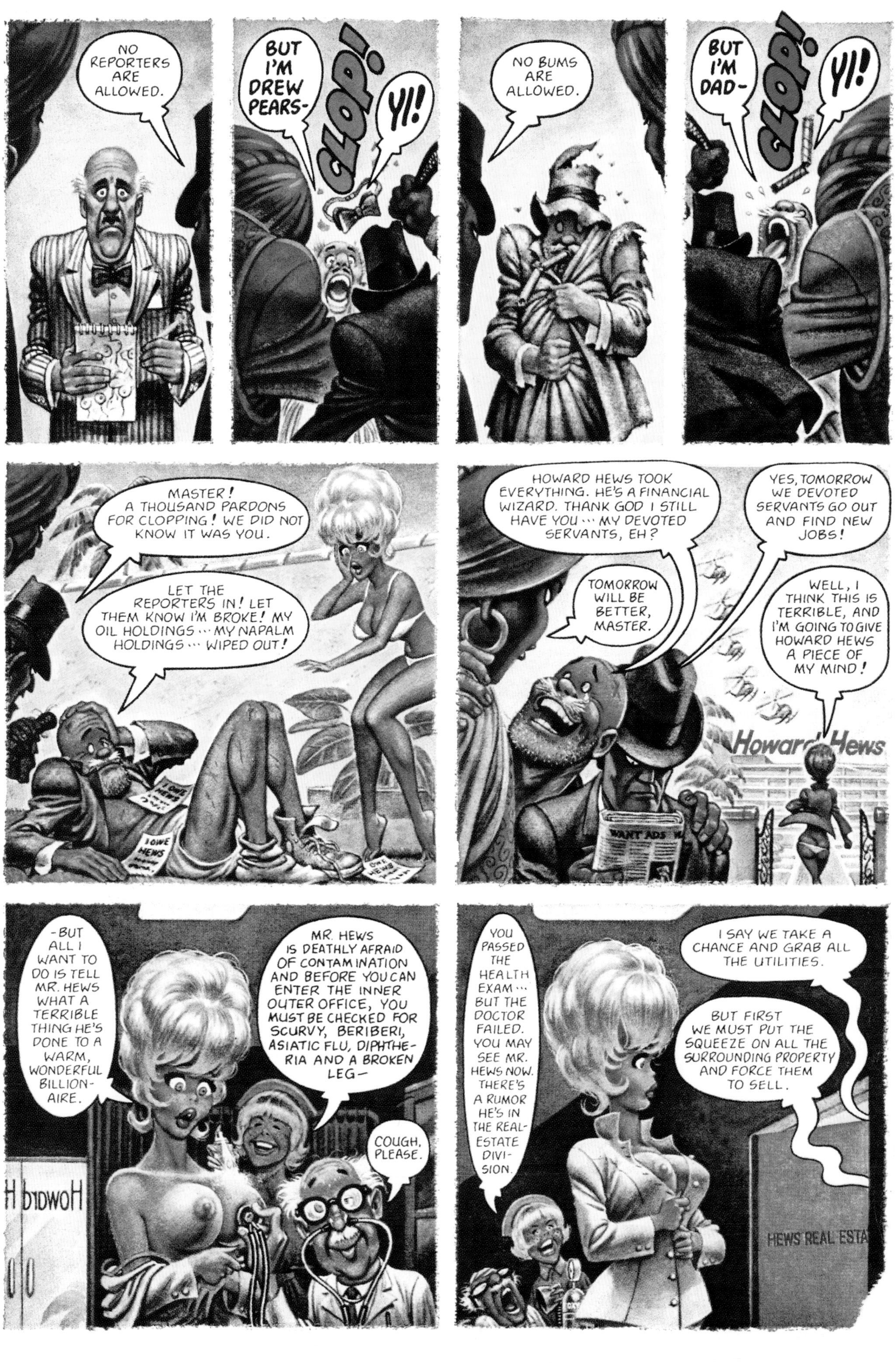
NO REPORTERS ARE ALLOWED.
BUT I'M DREW PEARS-
CLOP!
YI!
NO BUMS ARE ALLOWED.
BUT I'M DAD-
CLOP!
YI!
MASTER! A THOUSAND PARDONS FOR CLOPPING! WE DID NOT KNOW IT WAS YOU.
LET THE REPORTERS IN! LET THEM KNOW I'M BROKE! MY OIL HOLDINGS ··· MY NAPALM HOLDINGS ··· WIPED OUT!
HOWARD HEWS TOOK EVERYTHING. HE'S A FINANCIAL WIZARD. THANK GOD I STILL HAVE YOU ··· MY DEVOTED SERVANTS, EH?
YES, TOMORROW WE DEVOTED SERVANTS GO OUT AND FIND NEW JOBS!
TOMORROW WILL BE BETTER, MASTER.
WELL, I THINK THIS IS TERRIBLE, AND I'M GOING TO GIVE HOWARD HEWS A PIECE OF MY MIND!
Howard Hews
WANT ADS
-BUT ALL I WANT TO DO IS TELL MR. HEWS WHAT A TERRIBLE THING HE'S DONE TO A WARM, WONDERFUL BILLIONAIRE.
MR. HEWS IS DEATHLY AFRAID OF CONTAMINATION AND BEFORE YOU CAN ENTER THE INNER OUTER OFFICE, YOU MUST BE CHECKED FOR SCURVY, BERIBERI, ASIATIC FLU, DIPHTHERIA AND A BROKEN LEG—
COUGH, PLEASE.
YOU PASSED THE HEALTH EXAM ··· BUT THE DOCTOR FAILED. YOU MAY SEE MR. HEWS NOW. THERE'S A RUMOR HE'S IN THE REAL-ESTATE DIVISION.
I SAY WE TAKE A CHANCE AND GRAB ALL THE UTILITIES.
BUT FIRST WE MUST PUT THE SQUEEZE ON ALL THE SURROUNDING PROPERTY AND FORCE THEM TO SELL.
HEWS REAL ESTA

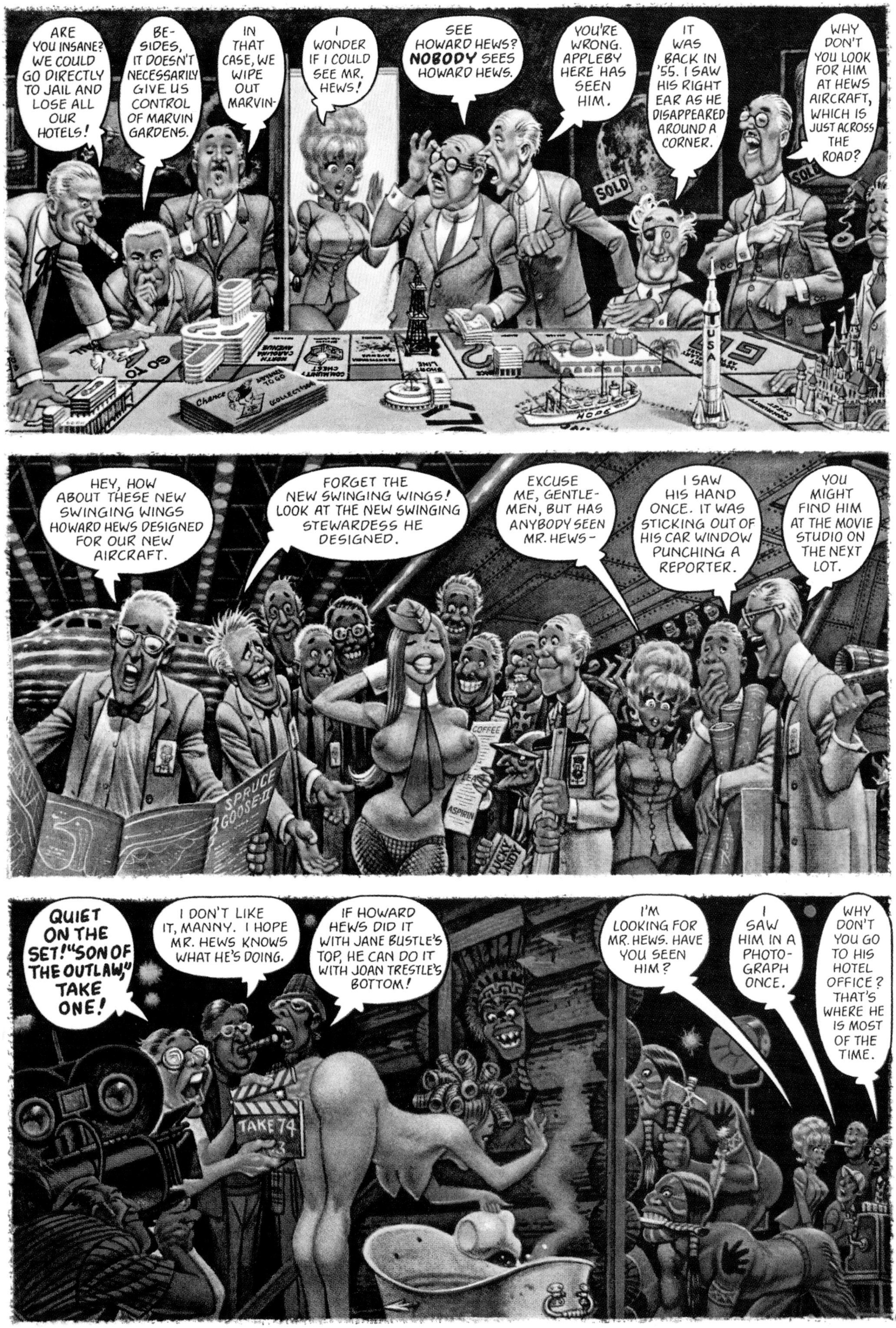
ARE YOU INSANE? WE COULD GO DIRECTLY TO JAIL AND LOSE ALL OUR HOTELS!
BE-SIDES, IT DOESN'T NECESSARILY GIVE US CONTROL OF MARVIN GARDENS.
IN THAT CASE, WE WIPE OUT MARVIN-
I WONDER IF I COULD SEE MR. HEWS!
SEE HOWARD HEWS? **NOBODY** SEES HOWARD HEWS.
YOU'RE WRONG. APPLEBY HERE HAS SEEN HIM.
IT WAS BACK IN '55. I SAW HIS RIGHT EAR AS HE DISAPPEARED AROUND A CORNER.
WHY DON'T YOU LOOK FOR HIM AT HEWS AIRCRAFT, WHICH IS JUST ACROSS THE ROAD?
SOLD
SOLD
GO TO
USA
HEY, HOW ABOUT THESE NEW SWINGING WINGS HOWARD HEWS DESIGNED FOR OUR NEW AIRCRAFT.
FORGET THE NEW SWINGING WINGS! LOOK AT THE NEW SWINGING STEWARDESS HE DESIGNED.
EXCUSE ME, GENTLE-MEN, BUT HAS ANYBODY SEEN MR. HEWS-
I SAW HIS HAND ONCE. IT WAS STICKING OUT OF HIS CAR WINDOW PUNCHING A REPORTER.
YOU MIGHT FIND HIM AT THE MOVIE STUDIO ON THE NEXT LOT.
SPRUCE GOOSE-II
COFFEE
ASPIRIN
QUIET ON THE SET! "SON OF THE OUTLAW," TAKE ONE!
I DON'T LIKE IT, MANNY. I HOPE MR. HEWS KNOWS WHAT HE'S DOING.
IF HOWARD HEWS DID IT WITH JANE BUSTLE'S TOP, HE CAN DO IT WITH JOAN TRESTLE'S BOTTOM!
TAKE 74
I'M LOOKING FOR MR. HEWS. HAVE YOU SEEN HIM?
I SAW HIM IN A PHOTO-GRAPH ONCE.
WHY DON'T YOU GO TO HIS HOTEL OFFICE? THAT'S WHERE HE IS MOST OF THE TIME.

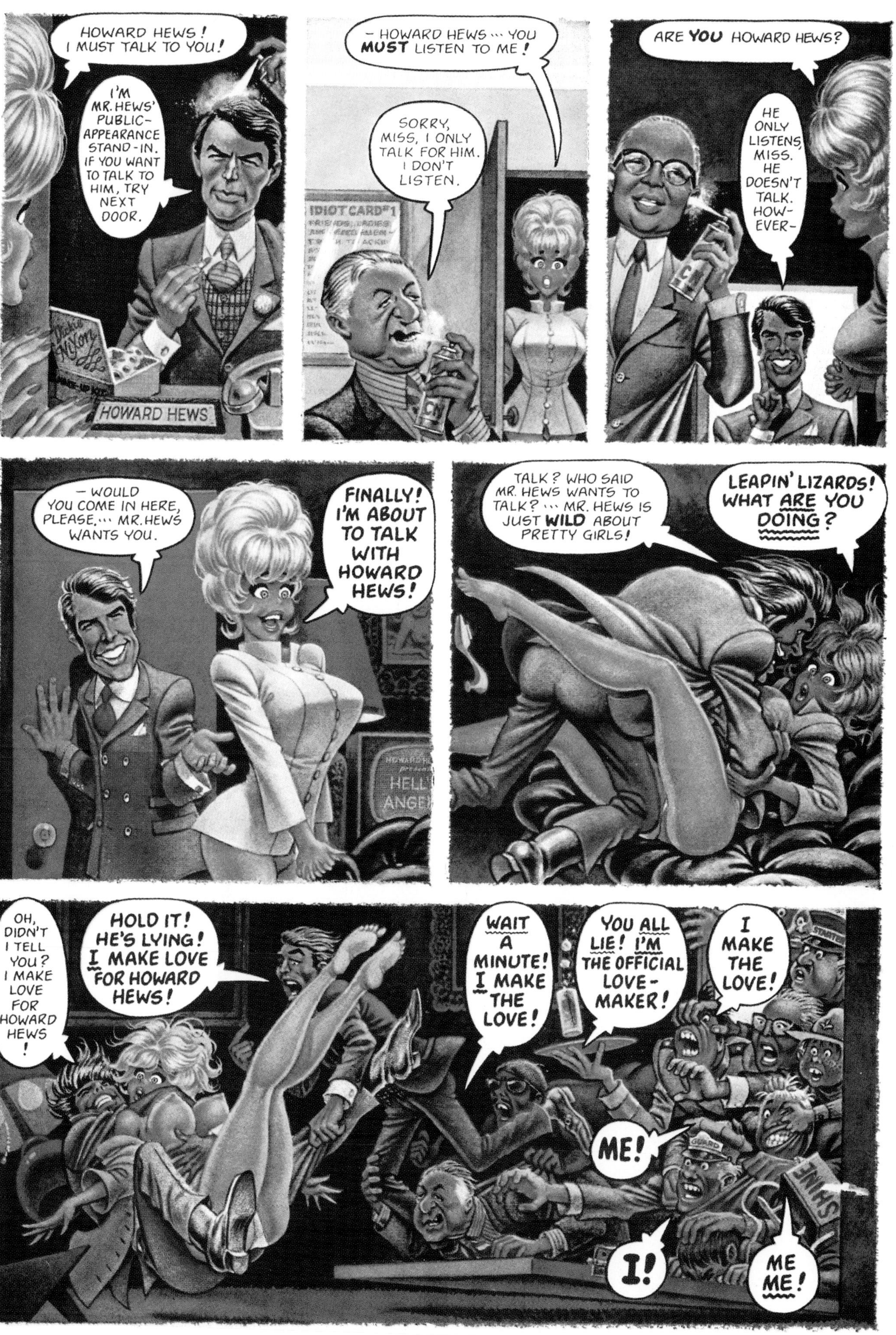

HOWARD HEWS! I MUST TALK TO YOU!
I'M MR. HEWS' PUBLIC-APPEARANCE STAND-IN. IF YOU WANT TO TALK TO HIM, TRY NEXT DOOR.
HOWARD HEWS
– HOWARD HEWS ··· YOU MUST LISTEN TO ME!
SORRY, MISS, I ONLY TALK FOR HIM. I DON'T LISTEN.
ARE YOU HOWARD HEWS?
HE ONLY LISTENS, MISS. HE DOESN'T TALK. HOW-EVER–
– WOULD YOU COME IN HERE, PLEASE. ··· MR. HEWS WANTS YOU.
FINALLY! I'M ABOUT TO TALK WITH HOWARD HEWS!
TALK? WHO SAID MR. HEWS WANTS TO TALK? ··· MR. HEWS IS JUST WILD ABOUT PRETTY GIRLS!
LEAPIN' LIZARDS! WHAT ARE YOU DOING?
OH, DIDN'T I TELL YOU? I MAKE LOVE FOR HOWARD HEWS!
HOLD IT! HE'S LYING! I MAKE LOVE FOR HOWARD HEWS!
WAIT A MINUTE! I MAKE THE LOVE!
YOU ALL LIE! I'M THE OFFICIAL LOVE-MAKER!
I MAKE THE LOVE!
ME!
I!
ME ME!

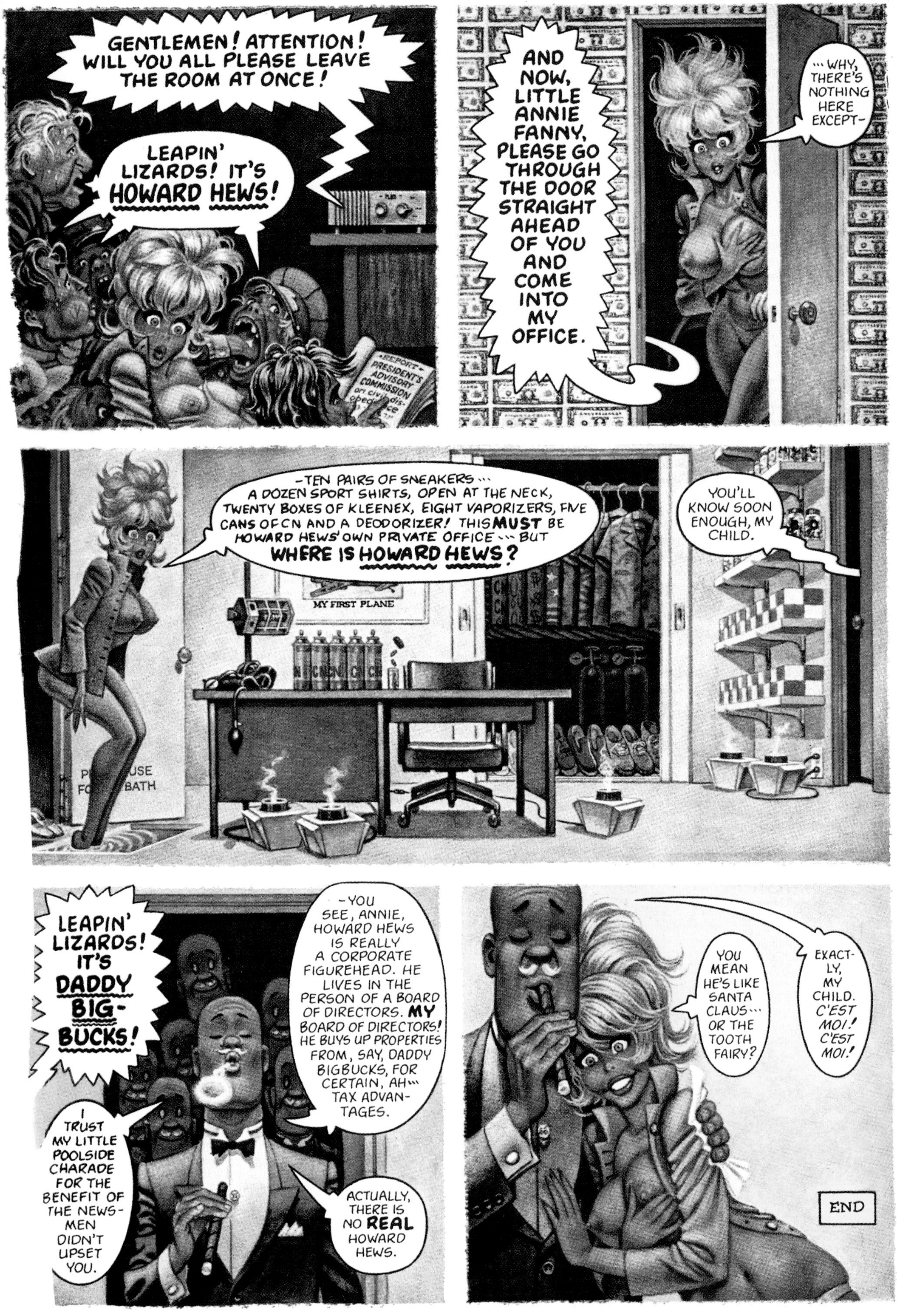
GENTLEMEN! ATTENTION! WILL YOU ALL PLEASE LEAVE THE ROOM AT ONCE!
LEAPIN' LIZARDS! IT'S HOWARD HEWS!
AND NOW, LITTLE ANNIE FANNY, PLEASE GO THROUGH THE DOOR STRAIGHT AHEAD OF YOU AND COME INTO MY OFFICE.
... WHY, THERE'S NOTHING HERE EXCEPT-
-TEN PAIRS OF SNEAKERS ... A DOZEN SPORT SHIRTS, OPEN AT THE NECK, TWENTY BOXES OF KLEENEX, EIGHT VAPORIZERS, FIVE CANS OF CN AND A DEODORIZER! THIS MUST BE HOWARD HEWS' OWN PRIVATE OFFICE ... BUT WHERE IS HOWARD HEWS?
YOU'LL KNOW SOON ENOUGH, MY CHILD.
MY FIRST PLANE
LEAPIN' LIZARDS! IT'S DADDY BIG-BUCKS!
-YOU SEE, ANNIE, HOWARD HEWS IS REALLY A CORPORATE FIGUREHEAD. HE LIVES IN THE PERSON OF A BOARD OF DIRECTORS. MY BOARD OF DIRECTORS! HE BUYS UP PROPERTIES FROM, SAY, DADDY BIGBUCKS, FOR CERTAIN, AH ... TAX ADVANTAGES.
I TRUST MY LITTLE POOLSIDE CHARADE FOR THE BENEFIT OF THE NEWSMEN DIDN'T UPSET YOU.
ACTUALLY, THERE IS NO REAL HOWARD HEWS.
YOU MEAN HE'S LIKE SANTA CLAUS ... OR THE TOOTH FAIRY?
EXACTLY, MY CHILD. C'EST MOI! C'EST MOI!
END

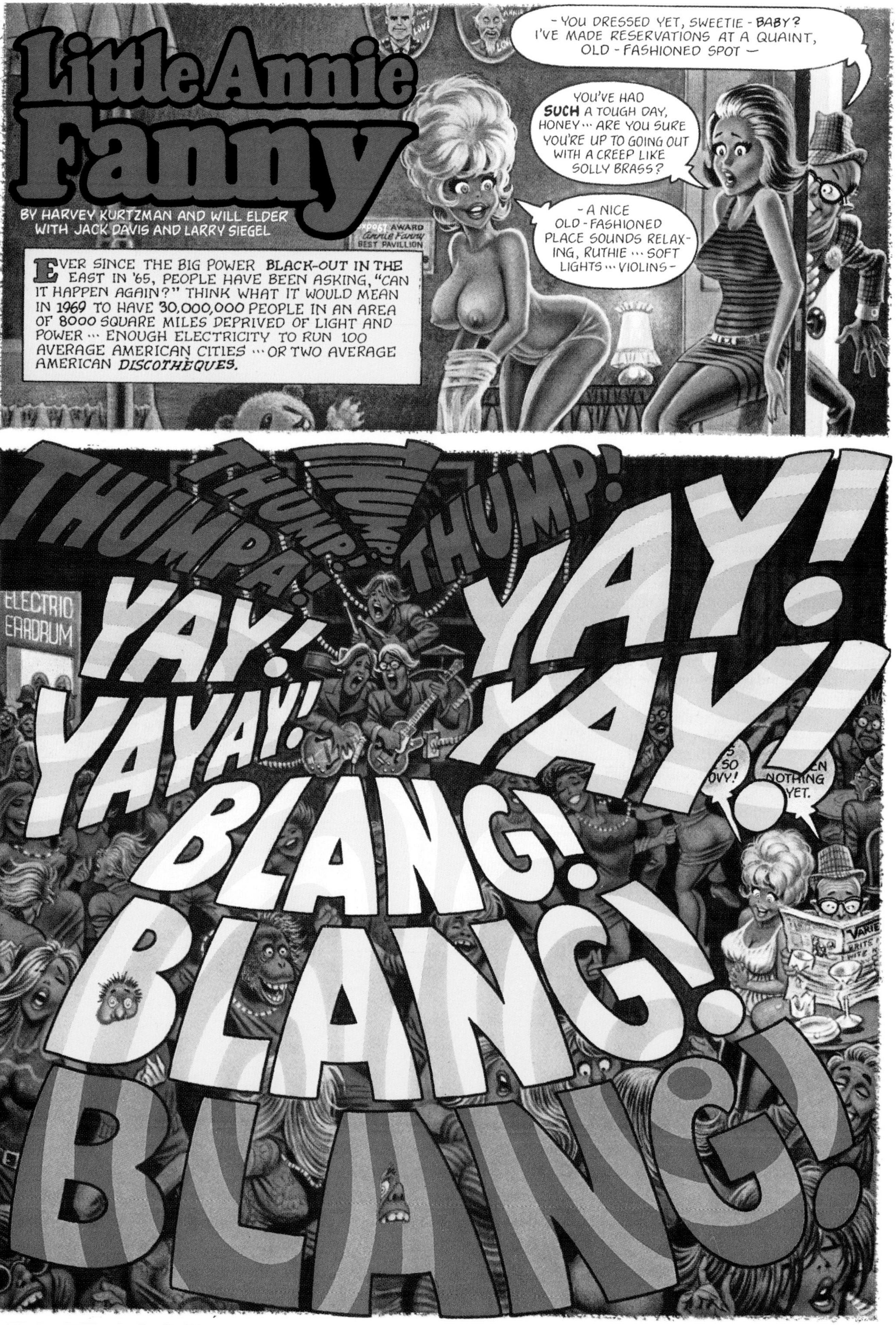

Little Annie Fanny
BY HARVEY KURTZMAN AND WILL ELDER WITH JACK DAVIS AND LARRY SIEGEL
EVER SINCE THE BIG POWER BLACK-OUT IN THE EAST IN '65, PEOPLE HAVE BEEN ASKING, "CAN IT HAPPEN AGAIN?" THINK WHAT IT WOULD MEAN IN 1969 TO HAVE 30,000,000 PEOPLE IN AN AREA OF 8000 SQUARE MILES DEPRIVED OF LIGHT AND POWER ··· ENOUGH ELECTRICITY TO RUN 100 AVERAGE AMERICAN CITIES ··· OR TWO AVERAGE AMERICAN DISCOTHÈQUES.
- YOU DRESSED YET, SWEETIE - BABY? I'VE MADE RESERVATIONS AT A QUAINT, OLD - FASHIONED SPOT -
YOU'VE HAD SUCH A TOUGH DAY, HONEY ··· ARE YOU SURE YOU'RE UP TO GOING OUT WITH A CREEP LIKE SOLLY BRASS?
- A NICE OLD - FASHIONED PLACE SOUNDS RELAXING, RUTHIE ··· SOFT LIGHTS ··· VIOLINS -
EXPO67 AWARD Annie Fanny BEST PAVILLION
THUMPA! THUMP! THUMP! THUMP!
ELECTRIC EARDRUM
YAY! YAY! YAYAY! YAY!
BLANG! BLANG! BLANG!

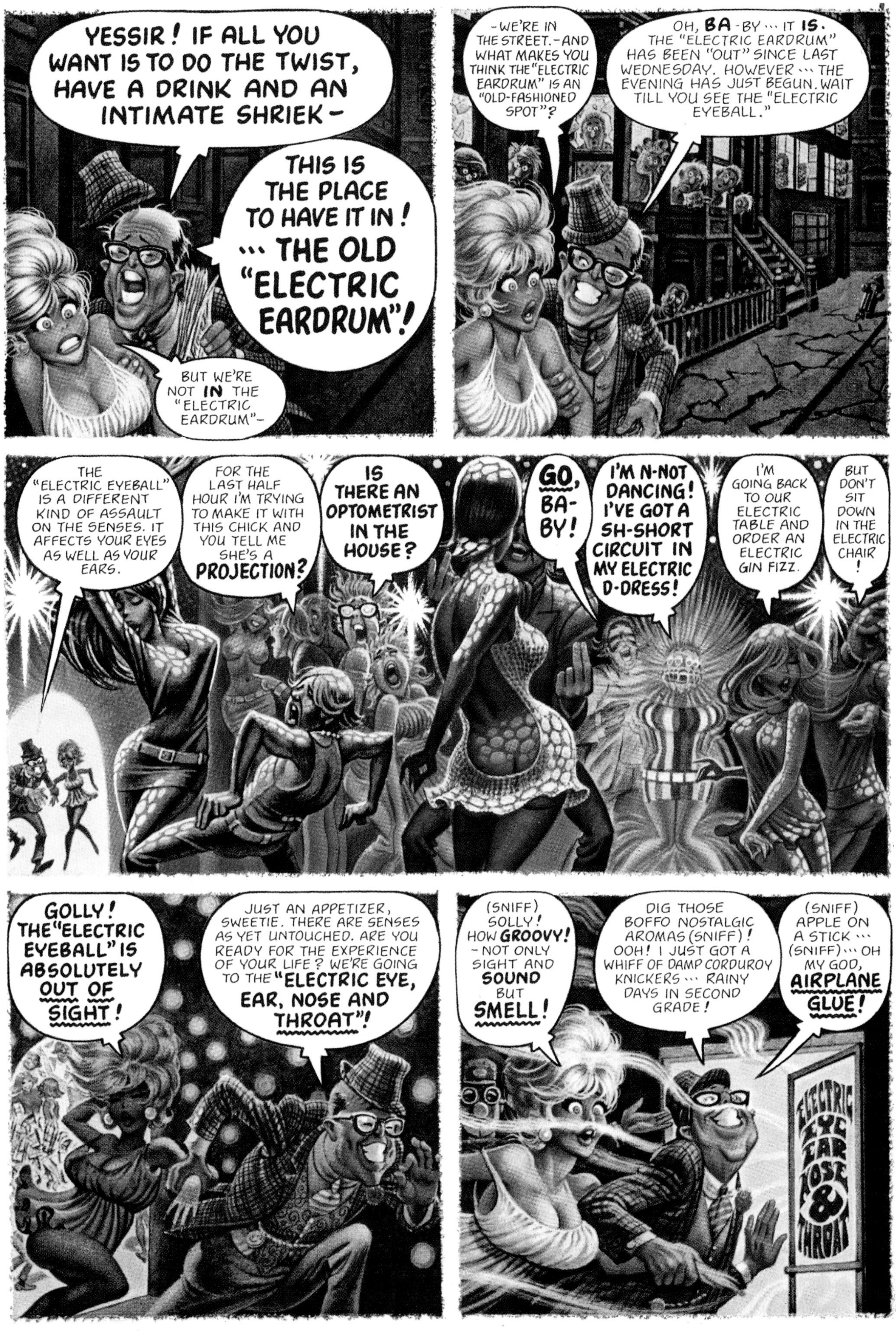
YESSIR! IF ALL YOU WANT IS TO DO THE TWIST, HAVE A DRINK AND AN INTIMATE SHRIEK—
THIS IS THE PLACE TO HAVE IT IN! ... THE OLD "ELECTRIC EARDRUM"!
BUT WE'RE NOT IN THE "ELECTRIC EARDRUM"—
—WE'RE IN THE STREET.—AND WHAT MAKES YOU THINK THE "ELECTRIC EARDRUM" IS AN "OLD-FASHIONED SPOT"?
OH, BA-BY ... IT IS. THE "ELECTRIC EARDRUM" HAS BEEN "OUT" SINCE LAST WEDNESDAY. HOWEVER ... THE EVENING HAS JUST BEGUN. WAIT TILL YOU SEE THE "ELECTRIC EYEBALL."
THE "ELECTRIC EYEBALL" IS A DIFFERENT KIND OF ASSAULT ON THE SENSES. IT AFFECTS YOUR EYES AS WELL AS YOUR EARS.
FOR THE LAST HALF HOUR I'M TRYING TO MAKE IT WITH THIS CHICK AND YOU TELL ME SHE'S A PROJECTION?
IS THERE AN OPTOMETRIST IN THE HOUSE?
GO, BA-BY!
I'M N-NOT DANCING! I'VE GOT A SH-SHORT CIRCUIT IN MY ELECTRIC D-DRESS!
I'M GOING BACK TO OUR ELECTRIC TABLE AND ORDER AN ELECTRIC GIN FIZZ.
BUT DON'T SIT DOWN IN THE ELECTRIC CHAIR!
GOLLY! THE "ELECTRIC EYEBALL" IS ABSOLUTELY OUT OF SIGHT!
JUST AN APPETIZER, SWEETIE. THERE ARE SENSES AS YET UNTOUCHED. ARE YOU READY FOR THE EXPERIENCE OF YOUR LIFE? WE'RE GOING TO THE "ELECTRIC EYE, EAR, NOSE AND THROAT"!
(SNIFF) SOLLY! HOW GROOVY! —NOT ONLY SIGHT AND SOUND BUT SMELL!
DIG THOSE BOFFO NOSTALGIC AROMAS (SNIFF)! OOH! I JUST GOT A WHIFF OF DAMP CORDUROY KNICKERS ... RAINY DAYS IN SECOND GRADE!
(SNIFF) APPLE ON A STICK ... (SNIFF) ... OH MY GOD, AIRPLANE GLUE!
ELECTRIC EYE EAR NOSE & THROAT

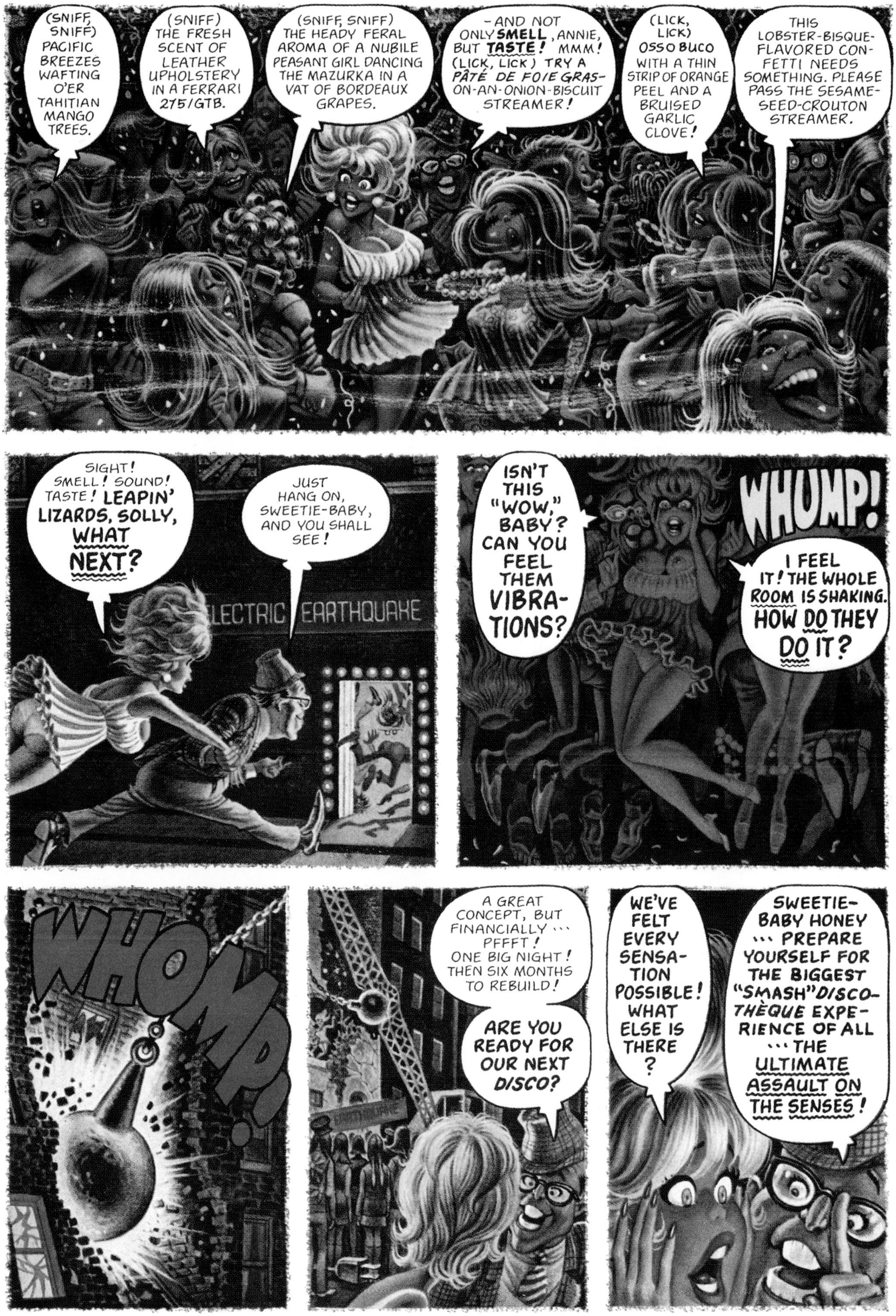
(SNIFF, SNIFF) PACIFIC BREEZES WAFTING O'ER TAHITIAN MANGO TREES.
(SNIFF) THE FRESH SCENT OF LEATHER UPHOLSTERY IN A FERRARI 275/GTB.
(SNIFF, SNIFF) THE HEADY FERAL AROMA OF A NUBILE PEASANT GIRL DANCING THE MAZURKA IN A VAT OF BORDEAUX GRAPES.
-AND NOT ONLY SMELL, ANNIE, BUT TASTE! MMM! (LICK, LICK) TRY A PÂTÉ DE FOIE GRAS-ON-AN-ONION-BISCUIT STREAMER!
(LICK, LICK) OSSO BUCO WITH A THIN STRIP OF ORANGE PEEL AND A BRUISED GARLIC CLOVE!
THIS LOBSTER-BISQUE-FLAVORED CONFETTI NEEDS SOMETHING. PLEASE PASS THE SESAME-SEED-CROUTON STREAMER.
SIGHT! SMELL! SOUND! TASTE! LEAPIN' LIZARDS, SOLLY, WHAT NEXT?
JUST HANG ON, SWEETIE-BABY, AND YOU SHALL SEE!
ELECTRIC EARTHQUAKE
ISN'T THIS "WOW," BABY? CAN YOU FEEL THEM VIBRATIONS?
WHUMP!
I FEEL IT! THE WHOLE ROOM IS SHAKING. HOW DO THEY DO IT?
WHOMP!
A GREAT CONCEPT, BUT FINANCIALLY ··· PFFFT! ONE BIG NIGHT! THEN SIX MONTHS TO REBUILD!
ARE YOU READY FOR OUR NEXT DISCO?
WE'VE FELT EVERY SENSATION POSSIBLE! WHAT ELSE IS THERE?
SWEETIE-BABY HONEY ··· PREPARE YOURSELF FOR THE BIGGEST "SMASH" DISCOTHÈQUE EXPERIENCE OF ALL ··· THE ULTIMATE ASSAULT ON THE SENSES!

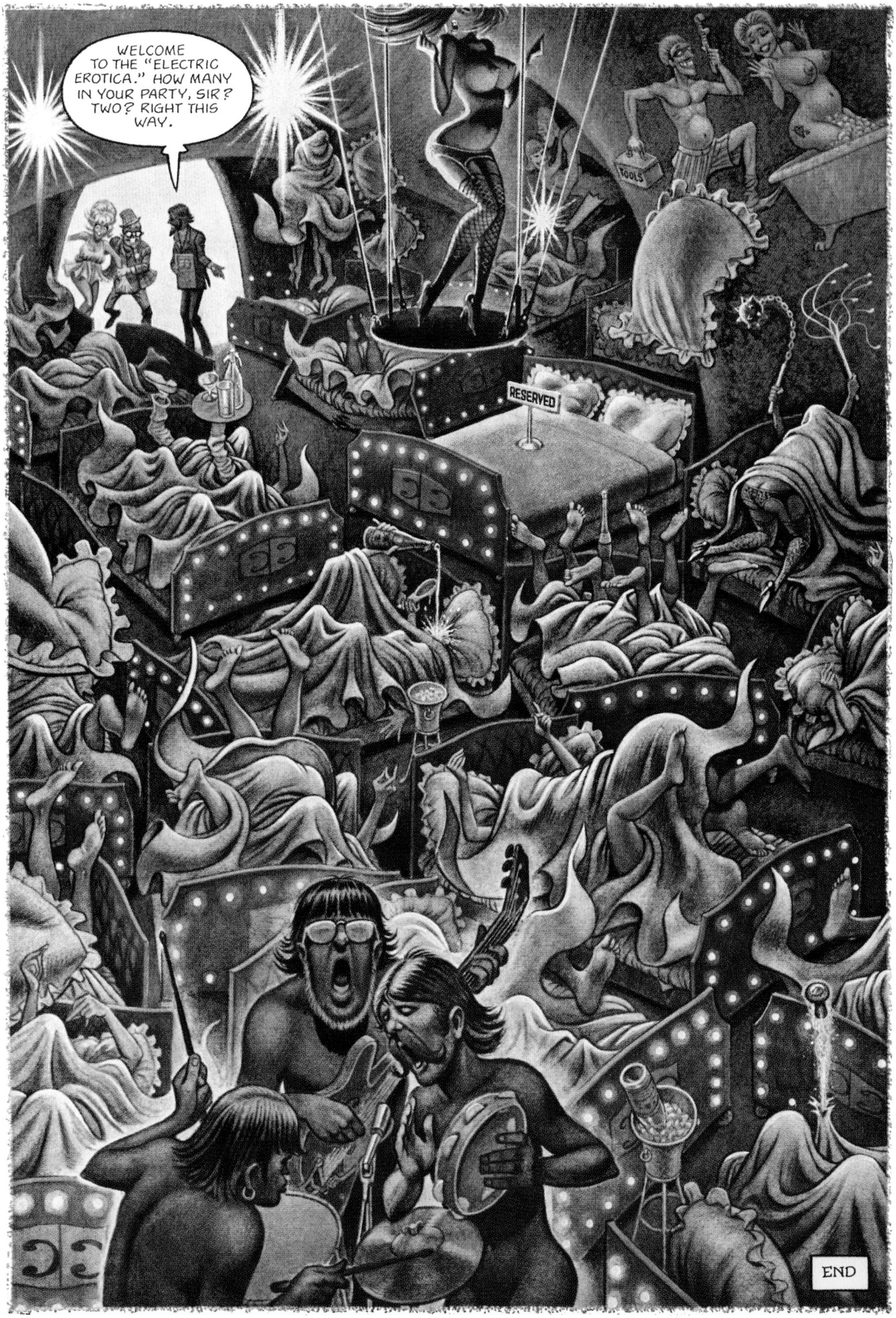
WELCOME TO THE "ELECTRIC EROTICA." HOW MANY IN YOUR PARTY, SIR? TWO? RIGHT THIS WAY.
RESERVED
TOOLS
END

Little Annie Fanny

BY HARVEY KURTZMAN AND WILL ELDER
WITH LARRY SIEGEL

REMEMBER THE OLD HOLLYWOOD FILMS WHERE THE GIRL WAS A VIRGIN UNTIL SHE GOT MARRIED (EXCEPT DORIS DAY, WHO WAS A VIRGIN **AFTER** SHE GOT MARRIED)? REMEMBER HOW, WHEN THE CLIMAX OF THE LOVE SCENE WOULD APPROACH, THE CAMERA WOULD PAN TO THE SKY?-- FADE OUT! CUT TO BREAKFAST! -- WELL, IN TODAY'S FILMS, NOBODY'S A VIRGIN, THE CAMERA NEVER PANS TO THE SKY AND NO ONE HAS **TIME** FOR BREAKFAST, AS FOR EXAMPLE: OUR HEROINE ACTING IN A NEW MOD FLICK UNDER THE DIRECTION OF THE GROOVY RICHARD LUSTER —

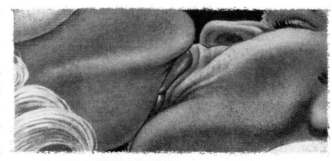

CUT!

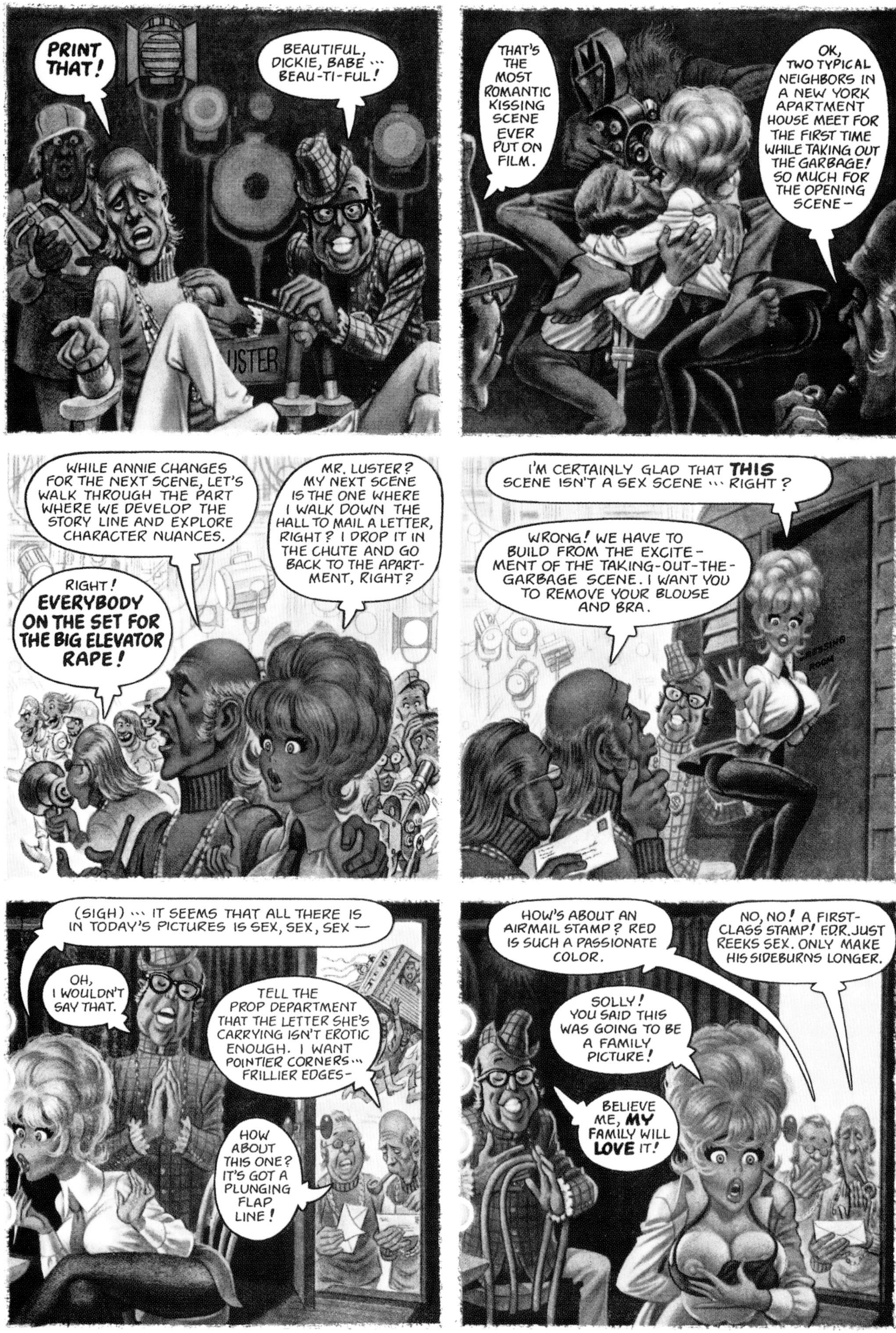
PRINT THAT!
BEAUTIFUL, DICKIE, BABE ··· BEAU-TI-FUL!
USTER
THAT'S THE MOST ROMANTIC KISSING SCENE EVER PUT ON FILM.
OK, TWO TYPICAL NEIGHBORS IN A NEW YORK APARTMENT HOUSE MEET FOR THE FIRST TIME WHILE TAKING OUT THE GARBAGE! SO MUCH FOR THE OPENING SCENE—
WHILE ANNIE CHANGES FOR THE NEXT SCENE, LET'S WALK THROUGH THE PART WHERE WE DEVELOP THE STORY LINE AND EXPLORE CHARACTER NUANCES.
MR. LUSTER? MY NEXT SCENE IS THE ONE WHERE I WALK DOWN THE HALL TO MAIL A LETTER, RIGHT? I DROP IT IN THE CHUTE AND GO BACK TO THE APARTMENT, RIGHT?
RIGHT! EVERYBODY ON THE SET FOR THE BIG ELEVATOR RAPE!
I'M CERTAINLY GLAD THAT THIS SCENE ISN'T A SEX SCENE ··· RIGHT?
WRONG! WE HAVE TO BUILD FROM THE EXCITEMENT OF THE TAKING-OUT-THE-GARBAGE SCENE. I WANT YOU TO REMOVE YOUR BLOUSE AND BRA.
(SIGH) ··· IT SEEMS THAT ALL THERE IS IN TODAY'S PICTURES IS SEX, SEX, SEX —
OH, I WOULDN'T SAY THAT.
TELL THE PROP DEPARTMENT THAT THE LETTER SHE'S CARRYING ISN'T EROTIC ENOUGH. I WANT POINTIER CORNERS··· FRILLIER EDGES-
HOW ABOUT THIS ONE? IT'S GOT A PLUNGING FLAP LINE!
HOW'S ABOUT AN AIRMAIL STAMP? RED IS SUCH A PASSIONATE COLOR.
NO, NO! A FIRST-CLASS STAMP! F.D.R. JUST REEKS SEX. ONLY MAKE HIS SIDEBURNS LONGER.
SOLLY! YOU SAID THIS WAS GOING TO BE A FAMILY PICTURE!
BELIEVE ME, MY FAMILY WILL LOVE IT!

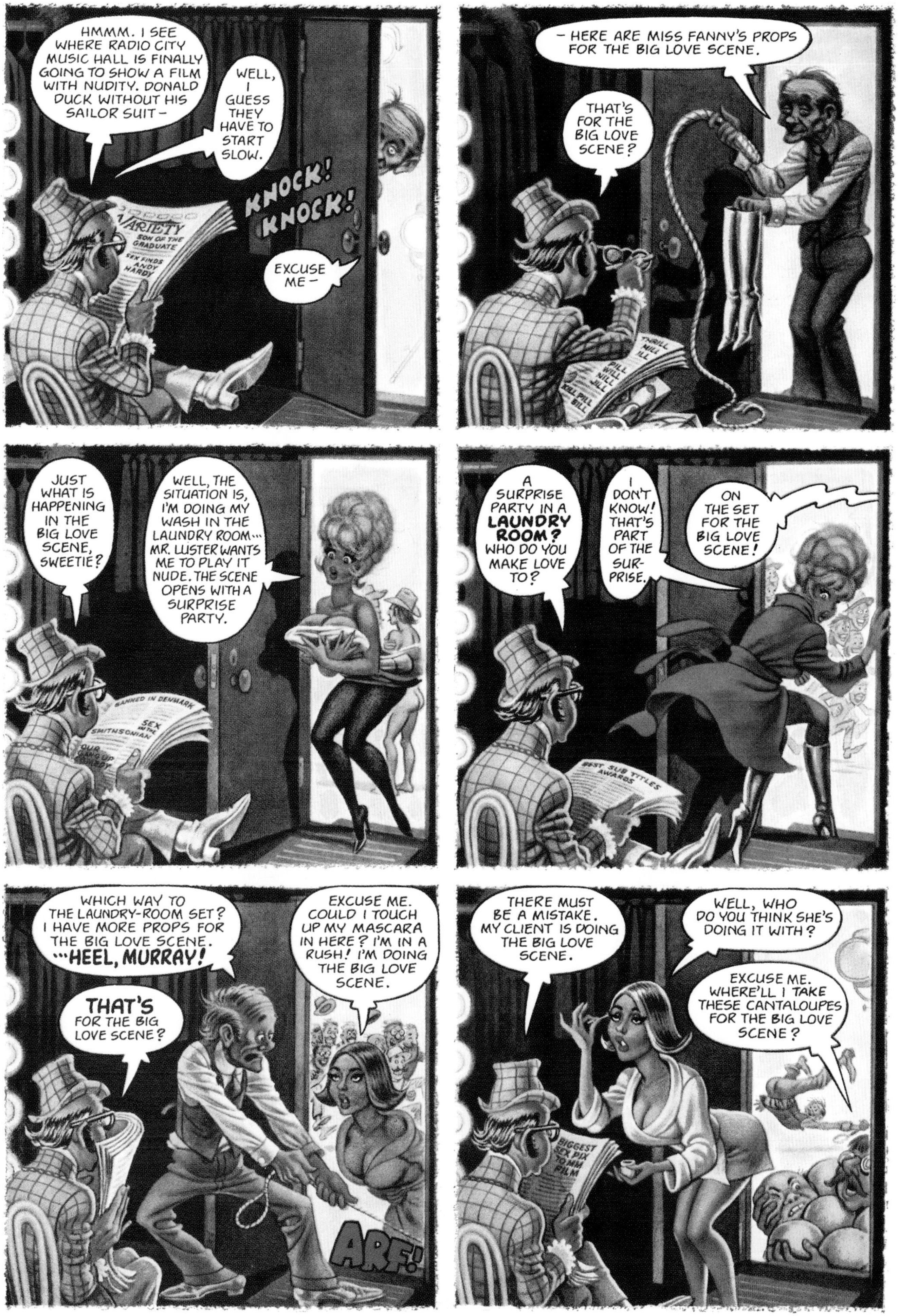
HMMM. I SEE WHERE RADIO CITY MUSIC HALL IS FINALLY GOING TO SHOW A FILM WITH NUDITY. DONALD DUCK WITHOUT HIS SAILOR SUIT –
WELL, I GUESS THEY HAVE TO START SLOW.
KNOCK! KNOCK!
VARIETY
SON OF THE GRADUATE
SEX FINDS ANDY HARDY
EXCUSE ME –
– HERE ARE MISS FANNY'S PROPS FOR THE BIG LOVE SCENE.
THAT'S FOR THE BIG LOVE SCENE?
JUST WHAT IS HAPPENING IN THE BIG LOVE SCENE, SWEETIE?
WELL, THE SITUATION IS, I'M DOING MY WASH IN THE LAUNDRY ROOM… MR. LUSTER WANTS ME TO PLAY IT NUDE. THE SCENE OPENS WITH A SURPRISE PARTY.
BANNED IN DENMARK
A SURPRISE PARTY IN A LAUNDRY ROOM? WHO DO YOU MAKE LOVE TO?
I DON'T KNOW! THAT'S PART OF THE SUR-PRISE.
ON THE SET FOR THE BIG LOVE SCENE!
BEST SUB TITLES AWARDS
WHICH WAY TO THE LAUNDRY-ROOM SET? I HAVE MORE PROPS FOR THE BIG LOVE SCENE. …HEEL, MURRAY!
THAT'S FOR THE BIG LOVE SCENE?
EXCUSE ME. COULD I TOUCH UP MY MASCARA IN HERE? I'M IN A RUSH! I'M DOING THE BIG LOVE SCENE.
ARF!
THERE MUST BE A MISTAKE. MY CLIENT IS DOING THE BIG LOVE SCENE.
WELL, WHO DO YOU THINK SHE'S DOING IT WITH?
EXCUSE ME. WHERE'LL I TAKE THESE CANTALOUPES FOR THE BIG LOVE SCENE?
BIGGEST SEX PIX

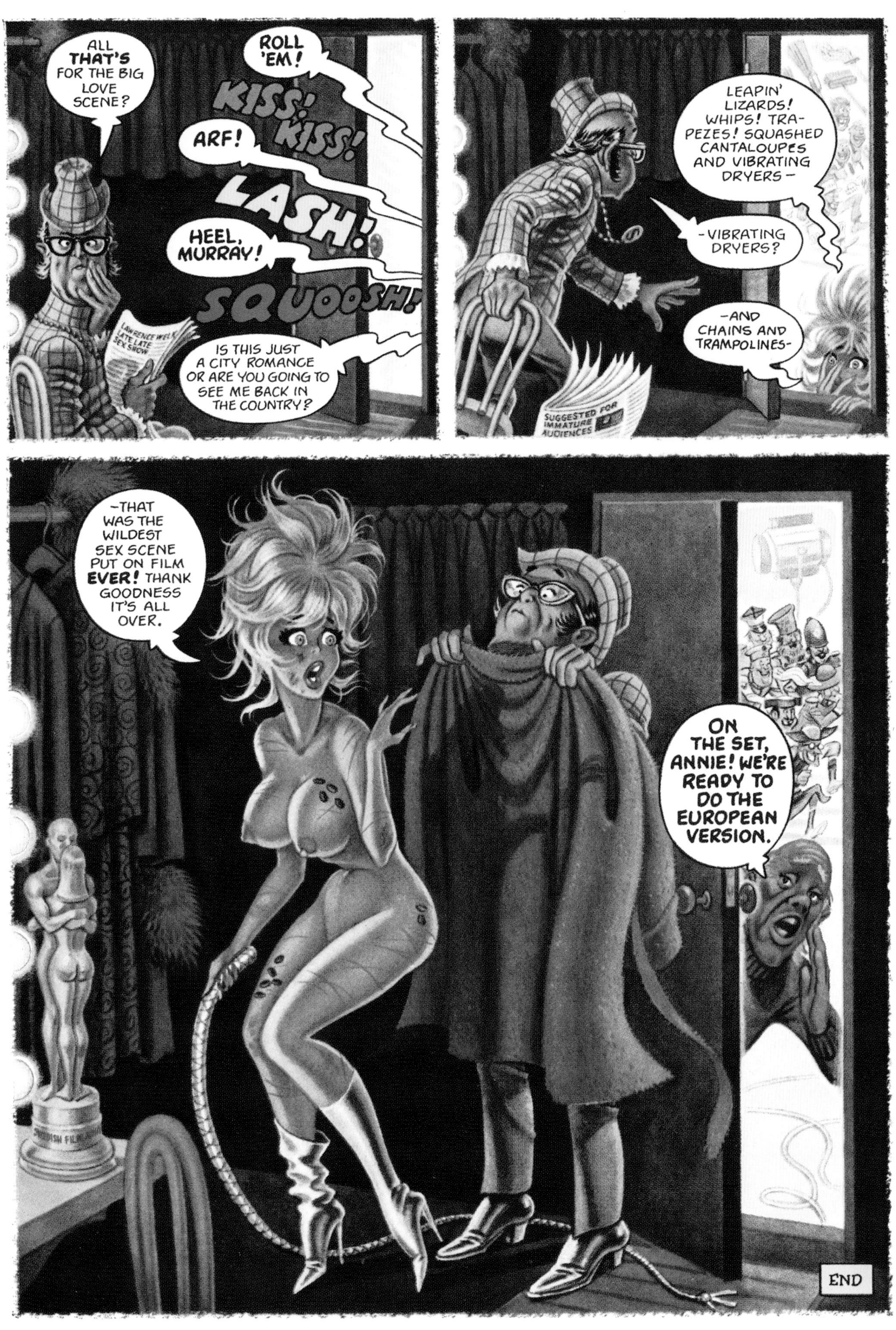
ALL **THAT'S** FOR THE BIG LOVE SCENE?
ROLL 'EM!
KISS! KISS!
ARF!
LASH!
HEEL, MURRAY!
SQUOOSH!
LAWRENCE WELK LATE LATE SEX SHOW
IS THIS JUST A CITY ROMANCE OR ARE YOU GOING TO SEE ME BACK IN THE COUNTRY?
LEAPIN' LIZARDS! WHIPS! TRA-PEZES! SQUASHED CANTALOUPES AND VIBRATING DRYERS—
—VIBRATING DRYERS?
—AND CHAINS AND TRAMPOLINES—
SUGGESTED FOR IMMATURE AUDIENCES
—THAT WAS THE WILDEST SEX SCENE PUT ON FILM **EVER!** THANK GOODNESS IT'S ALL OVER.
ON THE SET, ANNIE! WE'RE READY TO DO THE EUROPEAN VERSION.
END

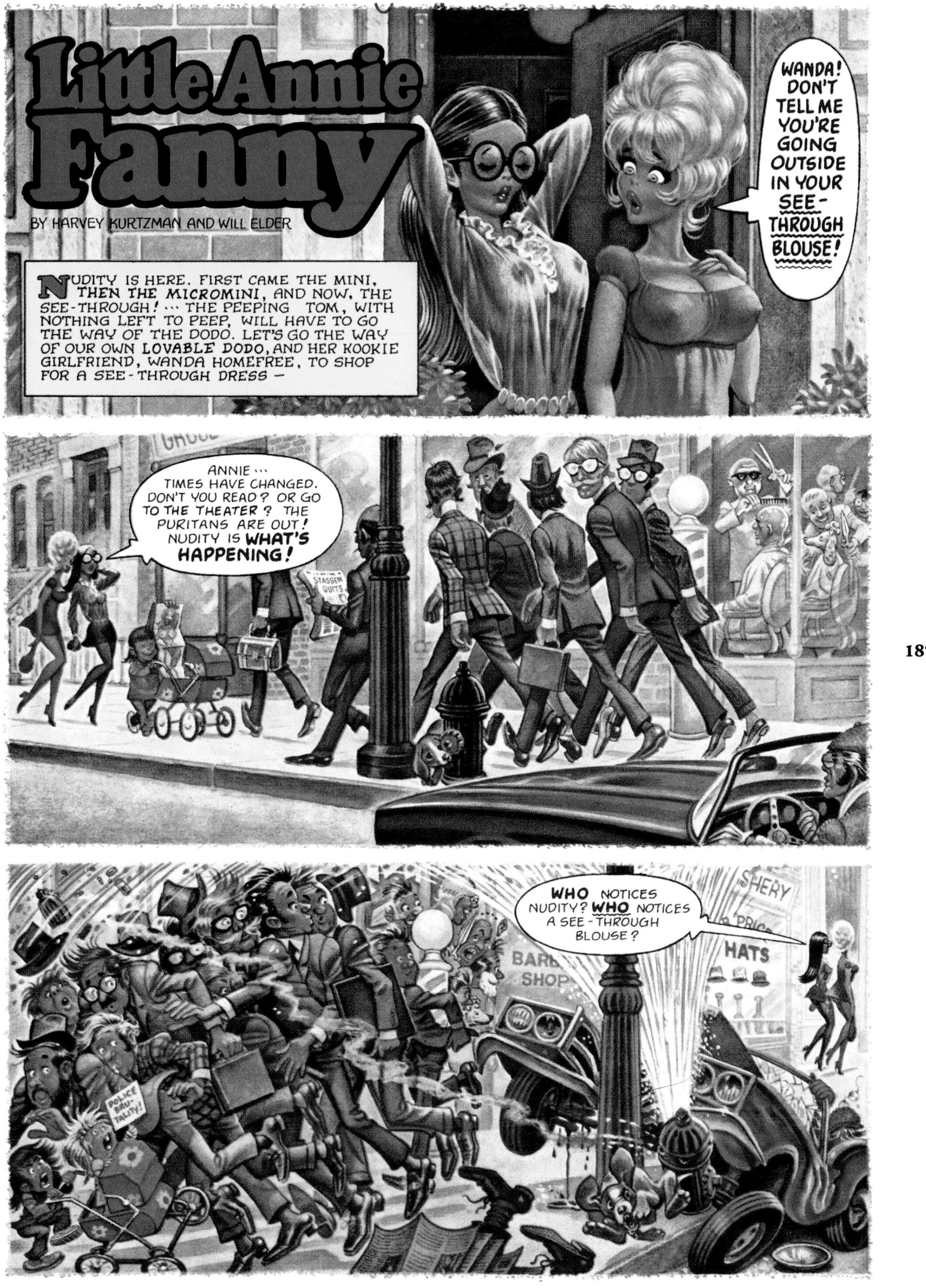
Little Annie Fanny
BY HARVEY KURTZMAN AND WILL ELDER
NUDITY IS HERE. FIRST CAME THE MINI, THEN THE MICROMINI, AND NOW, THE SEE-THROUGH! ··· THE PEEPING TOM, WITH NOTHING LEFT TO PEEP, WILL HAVE TO GO THE WAY OF THE DODO. LET'S GO THE WAY OF OUR OWN LOVABLE DODO, AND HER KOOKIE GIRLFRIEND, WANDA HOMEFREE, TO SHOP FOR A SEE-THROUGH DRESS —
WANDA! DON'T TELL ME YOU'RE GOING OUTSIDE IN YOUR SEE-THROUGH BLOUSE!
ANNIE ··· TIMES HAVE CHANGED. DON'T YOU READ? OR GO TO THE THEATER? THE PURITANS ARE OUT! NUDITY IS WHAT'S HAPPENING!
WHO NOTICES NUDITY? WHO NOTICES A SEE-THROUGH BLOUSE?

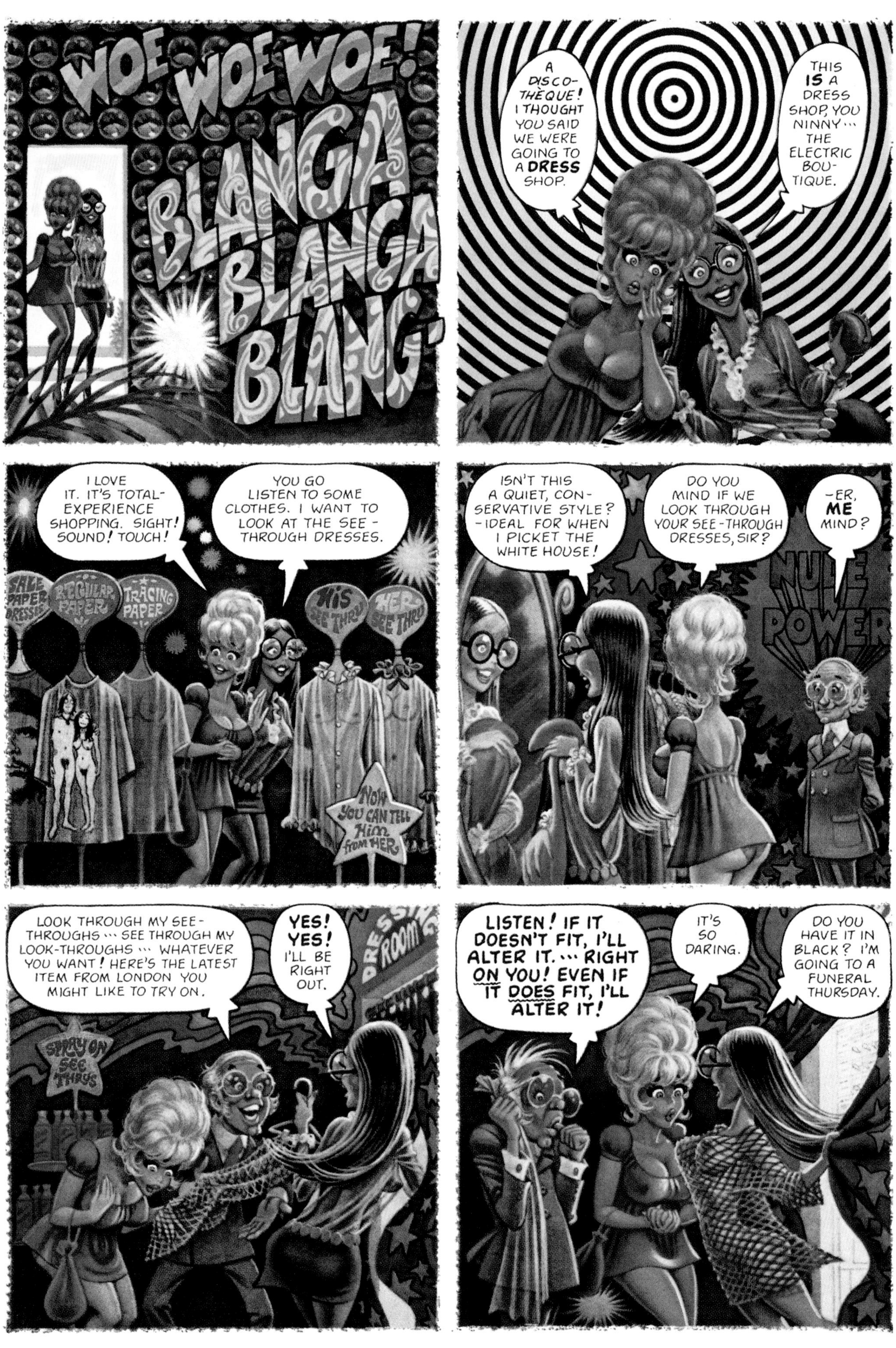
WOE WOE WOE WOE!
BLANGA BLANGA BLANGA BLANG-
A DISCO-THÈQUE! I THOUGHT YOU SAID WE WERE GOING TO A DRESS SHOP.
THIS IS A DRESS SHOP, YOU NINNY··· THE ELECTRIC BOU-TIQUE.
I LOVE IT. IT'S TOTAL-EXPERIENCE SHOPPING. SIGHT! SOUND! TOUCH!
YOU GO LISTEN TO SOME CLOTHES. I WANT TO LOOK AT THE SEE-THROUGH DRESSES.
SALE PAPER DRESSES
REGULAR PAPER
TRACING PAPER
HIS SEE THRU
HER SEE THRU
NOW YOU CAN TELL HIM FROM HER
ISN'T THIS A QUIET, CON-SERVATIVE STYLE? -IDEAL FOR WHEN I PICKET THE WHITE HOUSE!
DO YOU MIND IF WE LOOK THROUGH YOUR SEE-THROUGH DRESSES, SIR?
-ER, ME MIND?
NUDE POWER
LOOK THROUGH MY SEE-THROUGHS ··· SEE THROUGH MY LOOK-THROUGHS ··· WHATEVER YOU WANT! HERE'S THE LATEST ITEM FROM LONDON YOU MIGHT LIKE TO TRY ON.
YES! YES! I'LL BE RIGHT OUT.
DRESSING ROOM
SPRAY ON SEE THRUS
LISTEN! IF IT DOESN'T FIT, I'LL ALTER IT.··· RIGHT ON YOU! EVEN IF IT DOES FIT, I'LL ALTER IT!
IT'S SO DARING.
DO YOU HAVE IT IN BLACK? I'M GOING TO A FUNERAL THURSDAY.

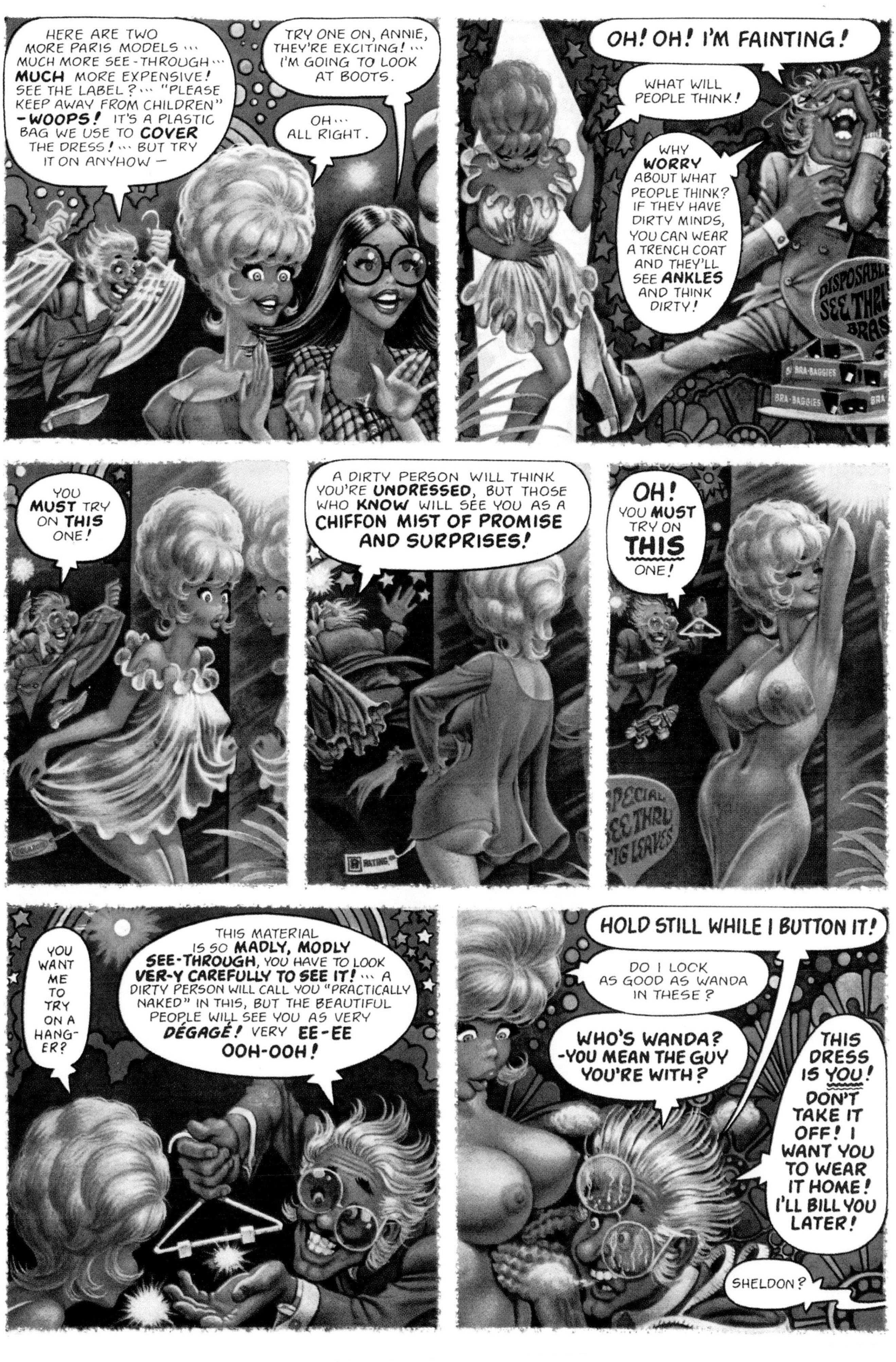

HERE ARE TWO MORE PARIS MODELS ... MUCH MORE SEE-THROUGH ... MUCH MORE EXPENSIVE! SEE THE LABEL? ... "PLEASE KEEP AWAY FROM CHILDREN" -WOOPS! IT'S A PLASTIC BAG WE USE TO COVER THE DRESS! ... BUT TRY IT ON ANYHOW —
TRY ONE ON, ANNIE, THEY'RE EXCITING! I'M GOING TO LOOK AT BOOTS.
OH ... ALL RIGHT.
OH! OH! I'M FAINTING!
WHAT WILL PEOPLE THINK!
WHY WORRY ABOUT WHAT PEOPLE THINK? IF THEY HAVE DIRTY MINDS, YOU CAN WEAR A TRENCH COAT AND THEY'LL SEE ANKLES AND THINK DIRTY!
DISPOSABLE SEE THRU BRAS
BRA-BAGGIES
YOU MUST TRY ON THIS ONE!
A DIRTY PERSON WILL THINK YOU'RE UNDRESSED, BUT THOSE WHO KNOW WILL SEE YOU AS A CHIFFON MIST OF PROMISE AND SURPRISES!
OH! YOU MUST TRY ON THIS ONE!
SPECIAL SEE THRU FIG LEAVES
YOU WANT ME TO TRY ON A HANGER?
THIS MATERIAL IS SO MADLY, MODLY SEE-THROUGH, YOU HAVE TO LOOK VER-Y CAREFULLY TO SEE IT! ... A DIRTY PERSON WILL CALL YOU "PRACTICALLY NAKED" IN THIS, BUT THE BEAUTIFUL PEOPLE WILL SEE YOU AS VERY DÉGAGÉ! VERY EE-EE OOH-OOH!
HOLD STILL WHILE I BUTTON IT!
DO I LOCK AS GOOD AS WANDA IN THESE?
WHO'S WANDA? -YOU MEAN THE GUY YOU'RE WITH?
THIS DRESS IS YOU! DON'T TAKE IT OFF! I WANT YOU TO WEAR IT HOME! I'LL BILL YOU LATER!
SHELDON?

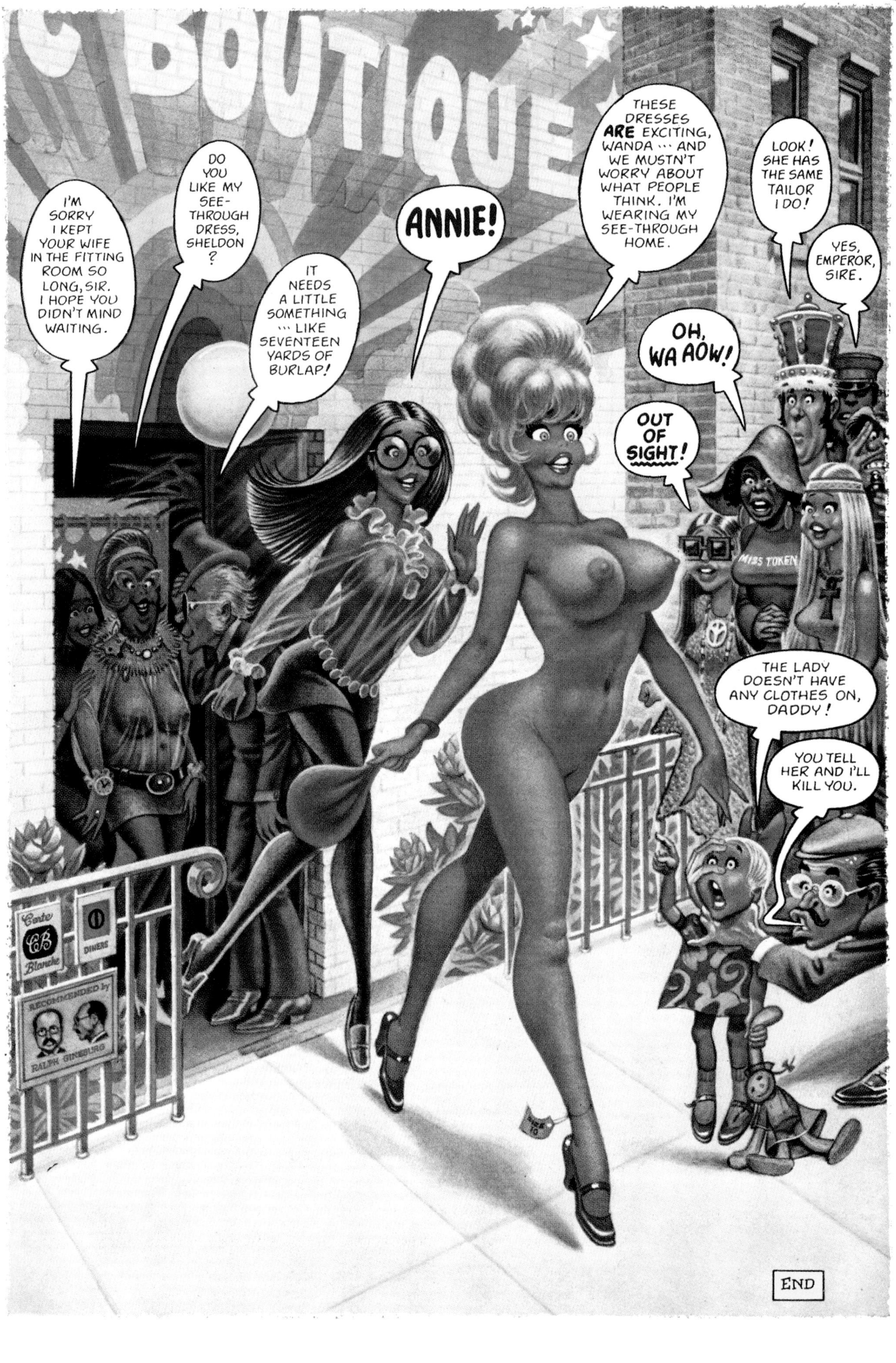
BOUTIQUE
I'M SORRY I KEPT YOUR WIFE IN THE FITTING ROOM SO LONG, SIR. I HOPE YOU DIDN'T MIND WAITING.
DO YOU LIKE MY SEE-THROUGH DRESS, SHELDON ?
IT NEEDS A LITTLE SOMETHING ··· LIKE SEVENTEEN YARDS OF BURLAP!
ANNIE!
THESE DRESSES **ARE** EXCITING, WANDA ··· AND WE MUSTN'T WORRY ABOUT WHAT PEOPLE THINK. I'M WEARING MY SEE-THROUGH HOME.
OH, WA AOW!
OUT OF SIGHT!
LOOK! SHE HAS THE SAME TAILOR I DO!
YES, EMPEROR, SIRE.
MISS TOKEN
THE LADY DOESN'T HAVE ANY CLOTHES ON, DADDY!
YOU TELL HER AND I'LL KILL YOU.
Carte Blanche
DINERS
RECOMMENDED by
END

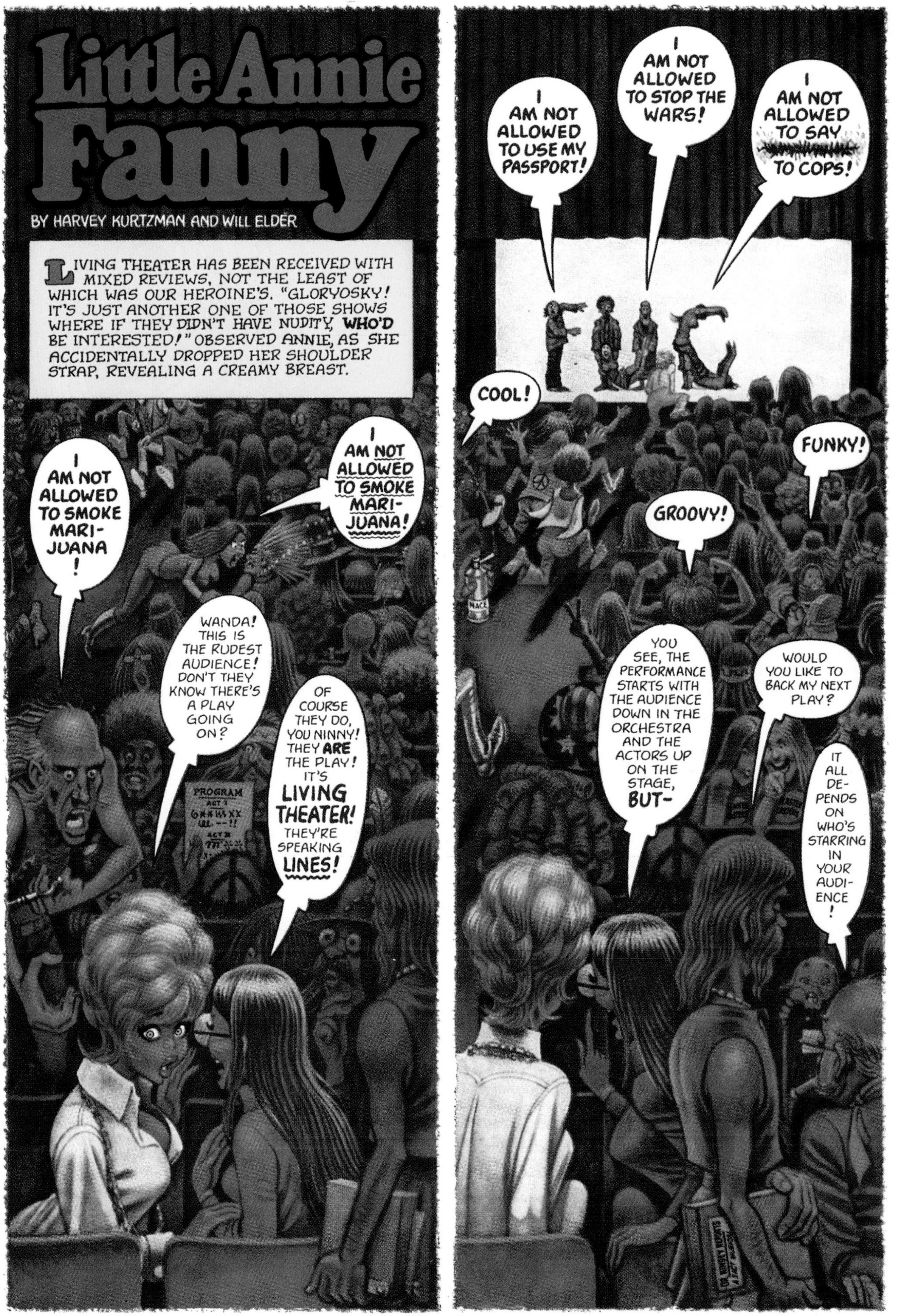
Little Annie Fanny
BY HARVEY KURTZMAN AND WILL ELDER
LIVING THEATER HAS BEEN RECEIVED WITH MIXED REVIEWS, NOT THE LEAST OF WHICH WAS OUR HEROINE'S. "GLORYOSKY! IT'S JUST ANOTHER ONE OF THOSE SHOWS WHERE IF THEY DIDN'T HAVE NUDITY, WHO'D BE INTERESTED!" OBSERVED ANNIE, AS SHE ACCIDENTALLY DROPPED HER SHOULDER STRAP, REVEALING A CREAMY BREAST.
I AM NOT ALLOWED TO SMOKE MARIJUANA!
I AM NOT ALLOWED TO SMOKE MARIJUANA!
WANDA! THIS IS THE RUDEST AUDIENCE! DON'T THEY KNOW THERE'S A PLAY GOING ON?
OF COURSE THEY DO, YOU NINNY! THEY ARE THE PLAY! IT'S LIVING THEATER! THEY'RE SPEAKING LINES!
PROGRAM
I AM NOT ALLOWED TO USE MY PASSPORT!
I AM NOT ALLOWED TO STOP THE WARS!
I AM NOT ALLOWED TO SAY [redacted] TO COPS!
COOL!
FUNKY!
GROOVY!
MACE
YOU SEE, THE PERFORMANCE STARTS WITH THE AUDIENCE DOWN IN THE ORCHESTRA AND THE ACTORS UP ON THE STAGE, BUT-
WOULD YOU LIKE TO BACK MY NEXT PLAY?
IT ALL DEPENDS ON WHO'S STARRING IN YOUR AUDIENCE!

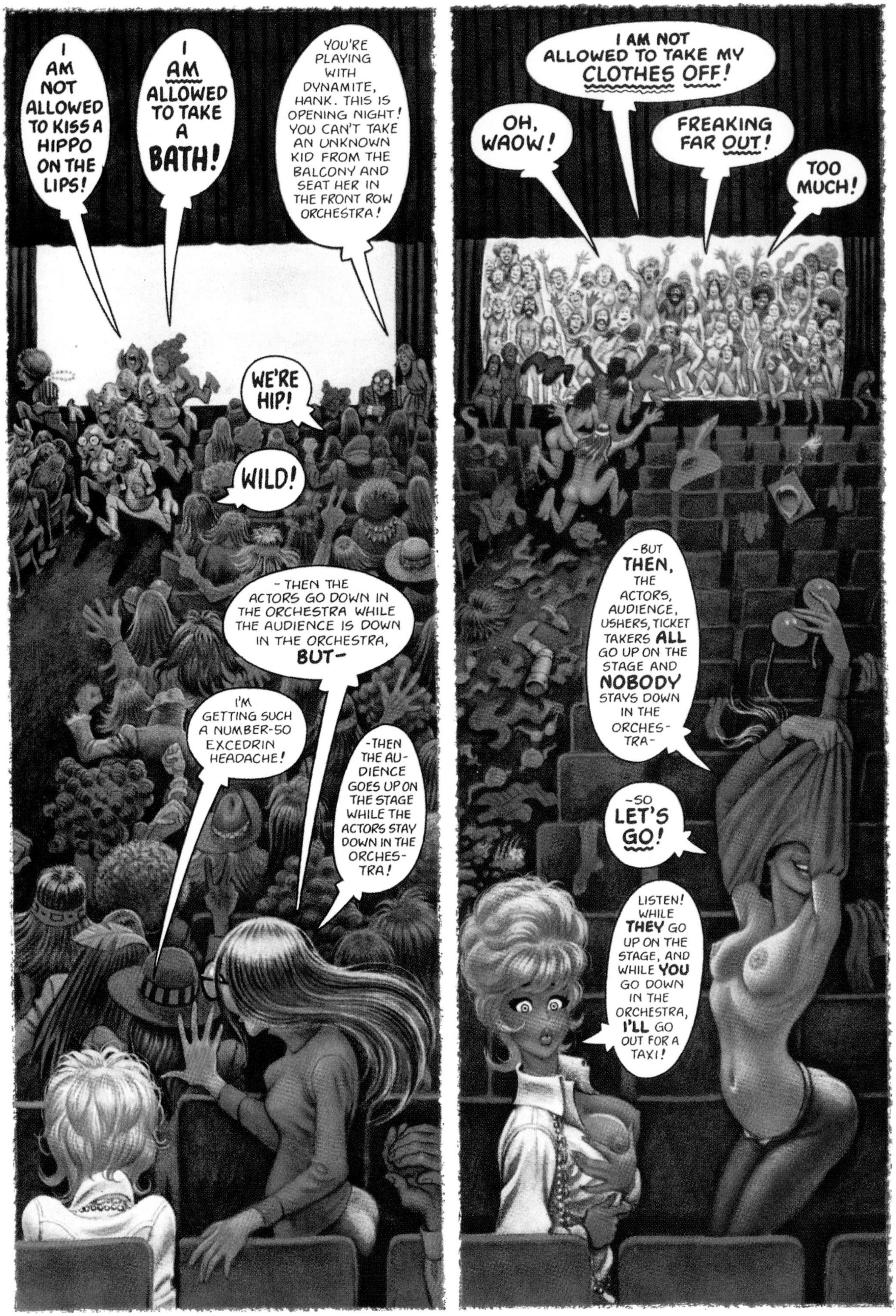
I AM NOT ALLOWED TO KISS A HIPPO ON THE LIPS!
I AM ALLOWED TO TAKE A BATH!
YOU'RE PLAYING WITH DYNAMITE, HANK. THIS IS OPENING NIGHT! YOU CAN'T TAKE AN UNKNOWN KID FROM THE BALCONY AND SEAT HER IN THE FRONT ROW ORCHESTRA!
WE'RE HIP!
WILD!
-THEN THE ACTORS GO DOWN IN THE ORCHESTRA WHILE THE AUDIENCE IS DOWN IN THE ORCHESTRA, BUT-
I'M GETTING SUCH A NUMBER-50 EXCEDRIN HEADACHE!
-THEN THE AUDIENCE GOES UP ON THE STAGE WHILE THE ACTORS STAY DOWN IN THE ORCHESTRA!
I AM NOT ALLOWED TO TAKE MY CLOTHES OFF!
OH, WAOW!
FREAKING FAR OUT!
TOO MUCH!
-BUT THEN, THE ACTORS, AUDIENCE, USHERS, TICKET TAKERS ALL GO UP ON THE STAGE AND NOBODY STAYS DOWN IN THE ORCHESTRA-
-SO LET'S GO!
LISTEN! WHILE THEY GO UP ON THE STAGE, AND WHILE YOU GO DOWN IN THE ORCHESTRA, I'LL GO OUT FOR A TAXI!

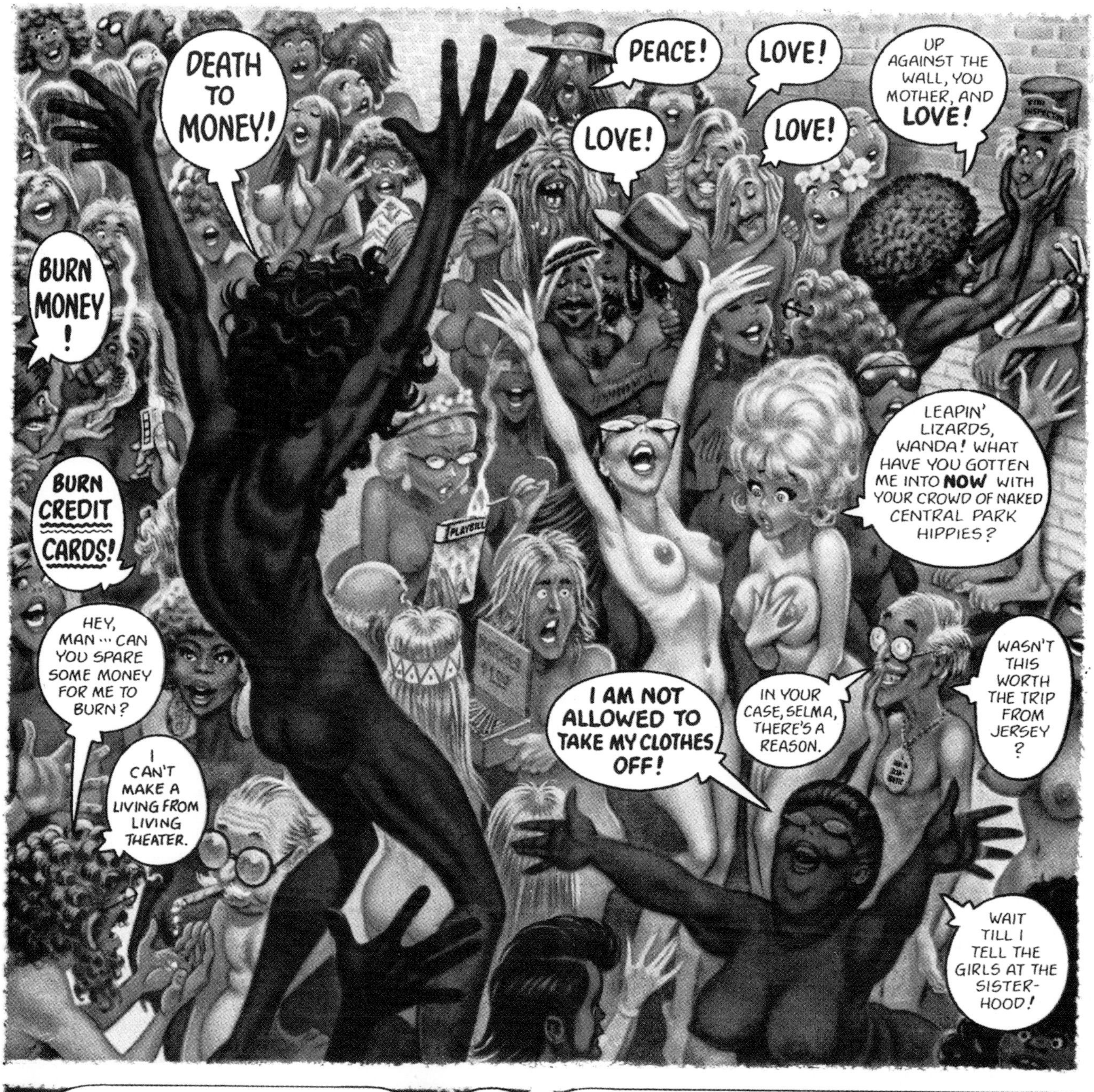
DEATH TO MONEY!
PEACE!
LOVE!
LOVE!
LOVE!
UP AGAINST THE WALL, YOU MOTHER, AND LOVE!
BURN MONEY !
LEAPIN' LIZARDS, WANDA! WHAT HAVE YOU GOTTEN ME INTO NOW WITH YOUR CROWD OF NAKED CENTRAL PARK HIPPIES?
BURN CREDIT CARDS!
HEY, MAN ... CAN YOU SPARE SOME MONEY FOR ME TO BURN?
I CAN'T MAKE A LIVING FROM LIVING THEATER.
I AM NOT ALLOWED TO TAKE MY CLOTHES OFF!
IN YOUR CASE, SELMA, THERE'S A REASON.
WASN'T THIS WORTH THE TRIP FROM JERSEY ?
WAIT TILL I TELL THE GIRLS AT THE SISTER-HOOD!
PLAYBILL

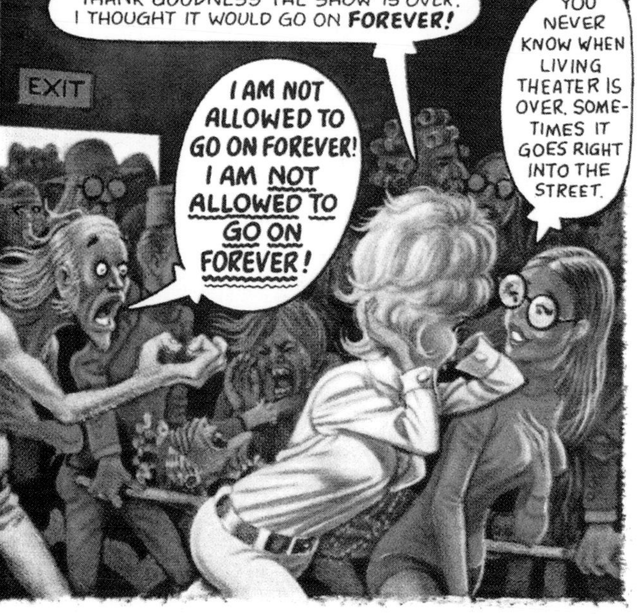
THANK GOODNESS THE SHOW IS OVER. I THOUGHT IT WOULD GO ON FOREVER!
YOU NEVER KNOW WHEN LIVING THEATER IS OVER. SOME-TIMES IT GOES RIGHT INTO THE STREET.
EXIT
I AM NOT ALLOWED TO GO ON FOREVER! I AM NOT ALLOWED TO GO ON FOREVER!

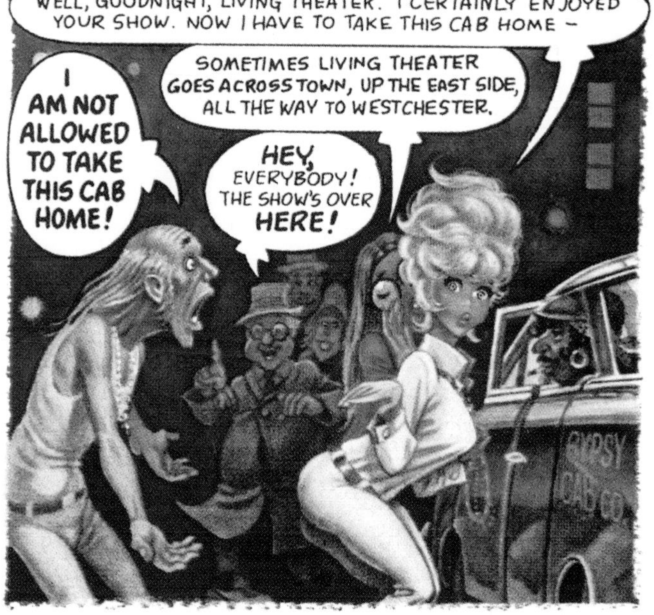
WELL, GOODNIGHT, LIVING THEATER. I CERTAINLY ENJOYED YOUR SHOW. NOW I HAVE TO TAKE THIS CAB HOME –
SOMETIMES LIVING THEATER GOES ACROSS TOWN, UP THE EAST SIDE, ALL THE WAY TO WESTCHESTER.
I AM NOT ALLOWED TO TAKE THIS CAB HOME!
HEY, EVERYBODY! THE SHOW'S OVER HERE!

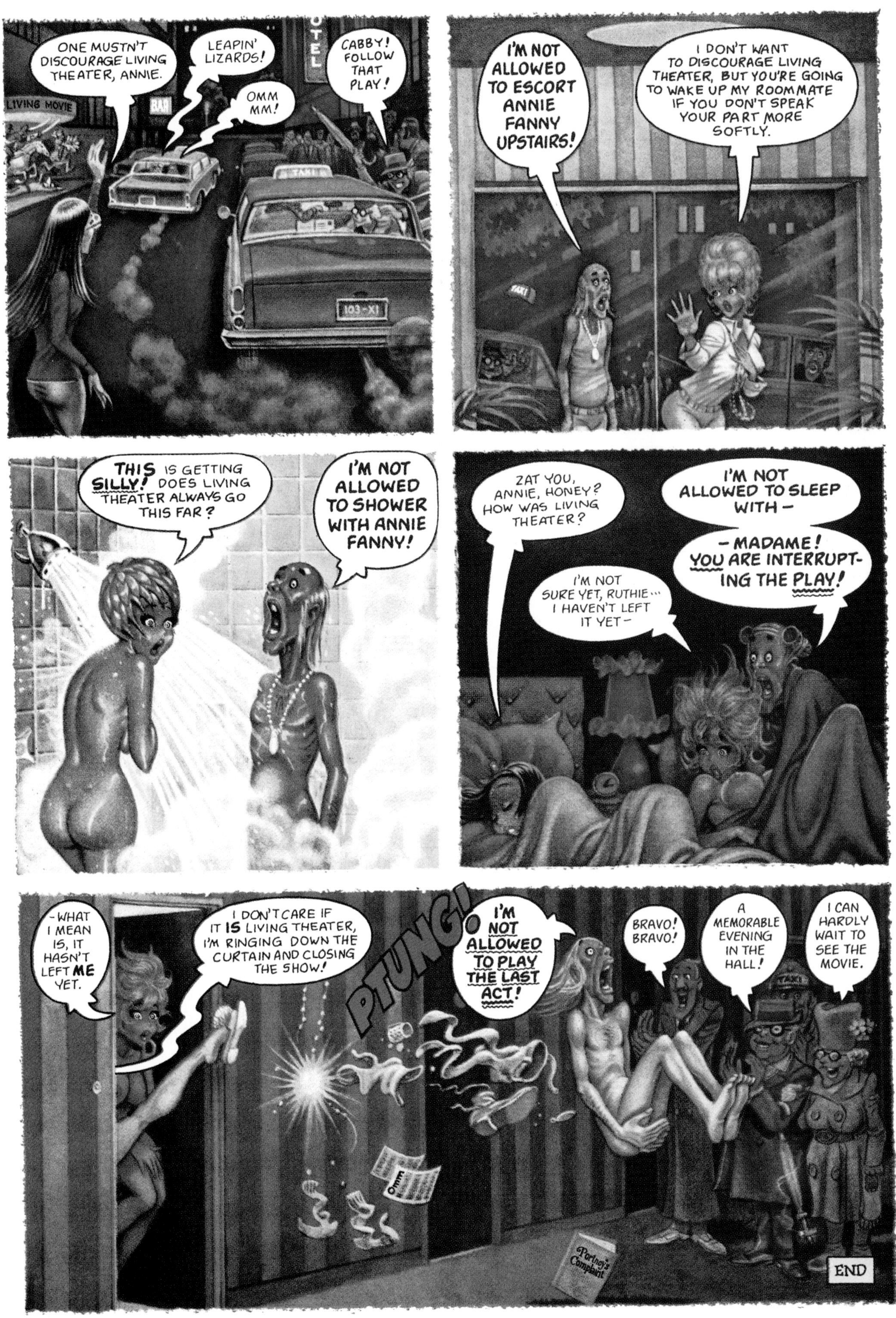
ONE MUSTN'T DISCOURAGE LIVING THEATER, ANNIE.
LEAPIN' LIZARDS!
OMM MM!
CABBY! FOLLOW THAT PLAY!
OTEL
LIVING MOVIE
BAR
TAXI
103-X1
I'M NOT ALLOWED TO ESCORT ANNIE FANNY UPSTAIRS!
I DON'T WANT TO DISCOURAGE LIVING THEATER, BUT YOU'RE GOING TO WAKE UP MY ROOMMATE IF YOU DON'T SPEAK YOUR PART MORE SOFTLY.
THIS IS GETTING SILLY! DOES LIVING THEATER ALWAYS GO THIS FAR?
I'M NOT ALLOWED TO SHOWER WITH ANNIE FANNY!
ZAT YOU, ANNIE, HONEY? HOW WAS LIVING THEATER?
I'M NOT SURE YET, RUTHIE... I HAVEN'T LEFT IT YET-
I'M NOT ALLOWED TO SLEEP WITH-
-MADAME! YOU ARE INTERRUPTING THE PLAY!
-WHAT I MEAN IS, IT HASN'T LEFT ME YET.
I DON'T CARE IF IT IS LIVING THEATER, I'M RINGING DOWN THE CURTAIN AND CLOSING THE SHOW!
PTUNG!
I'M NOT ALLOWED TO PLAY THE LAST ACT!
BRAVO! BRAVO!
A MEMORABLE EVENING IN THE HALL!
I CAN HARDLY WAIT TO SEE THE MOVIE.
Portnoy's Complaint
END

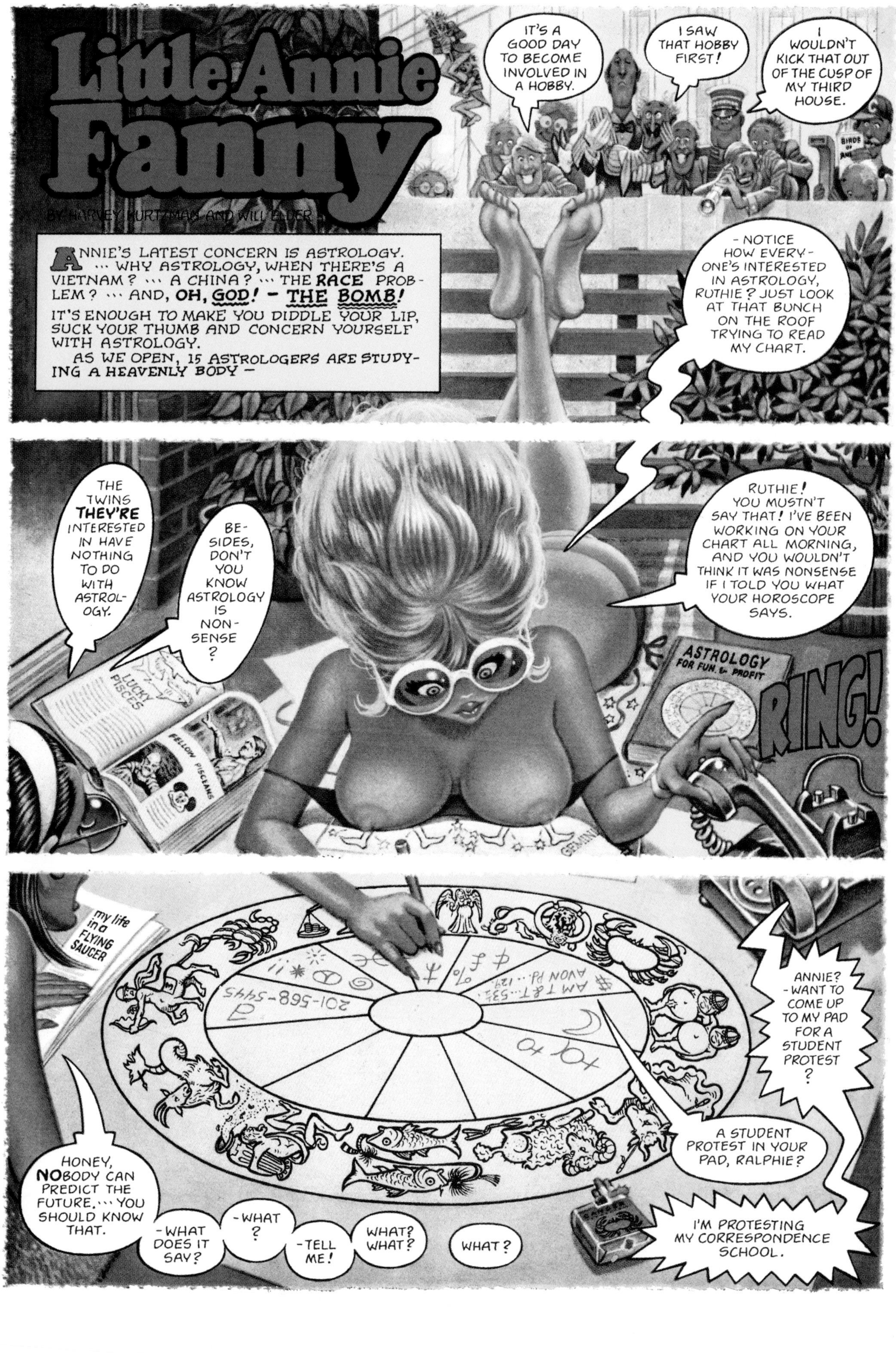

Little Annie Fanny
BY HARVEY KURTZMAN AND WILL ELDER
IT'S A GOOD DAY TO BECOME INVOLVED IN A HOBBY.
I SAW THAT HOBBY FIRST!
I WOULDN'T KICK THAT OUT OF THE CUSP OF MY THIRD HOUSE.
ANNIE'S LATEST CONCERN IS ASTROLOGY. ... WHY ASTROLOGY, WHEN THERE'S A VIETNAM? ... A CHINA? ... THE **RACE** PROBLEM? ... AND, **OH, GOD! – THE BOMB!**
IT'S ENOUGH TO MAKE YOU DIDDLE YOUR LIP, SUCK YOUR THUMB AND CONCERN YOURSELF WITH ASTROLOGY.
AS WE OPEN, 15 ASTROLOGERS ARE STUDYING A HEAVENLY BODY –
– NOTICE HOW EVERYONE'S INTERESTED IN ASTROLOGY, RUTHIE? JUST LOOK AT THAT BUNCH ON THE ROOF TRYING TO READ MY CHART.
THE TWINS **THEY'RE** INTERESTED IN HAVE NOTHING TO DO WITH ASTROLOGY.
BESIDES, DON'T YOU KNOW ASTROLOGY IS NONSENSE?
RUTHIE! YOU MUSTN'T SAY THAT! I'VE BEEN WORKING ON YOUR CHART ALL MORNING, AND YOU WOULDN'T THINK IT WAS NONSENSE IF I TOLD YOU WHAT YOUR HOROSCOPE SAYS.
LUCKY PISCES
FELLOW PISCEANS
ASTROLOGY FOR FUN & PROFIT
RING!
my life in a FLYING SAUCER
ANNIE? – WANT TO COME UP TO MY PAD FOR A STUDENT PROTEST?
A STUDENT PROTEST IN YOUR PAD, RALPHIE?
HONEY, **NO**BODY CAN PREDICT THE FUTURE. ... YOU SHOULD KNOW THAT.
– WHAT DOES IT SAY?
– WHAT?
– TELL ME!
WHAT? WHAT?
WHAT?
I'M PROTESTING MY CORRESPONDENCE SCHOOL.

196

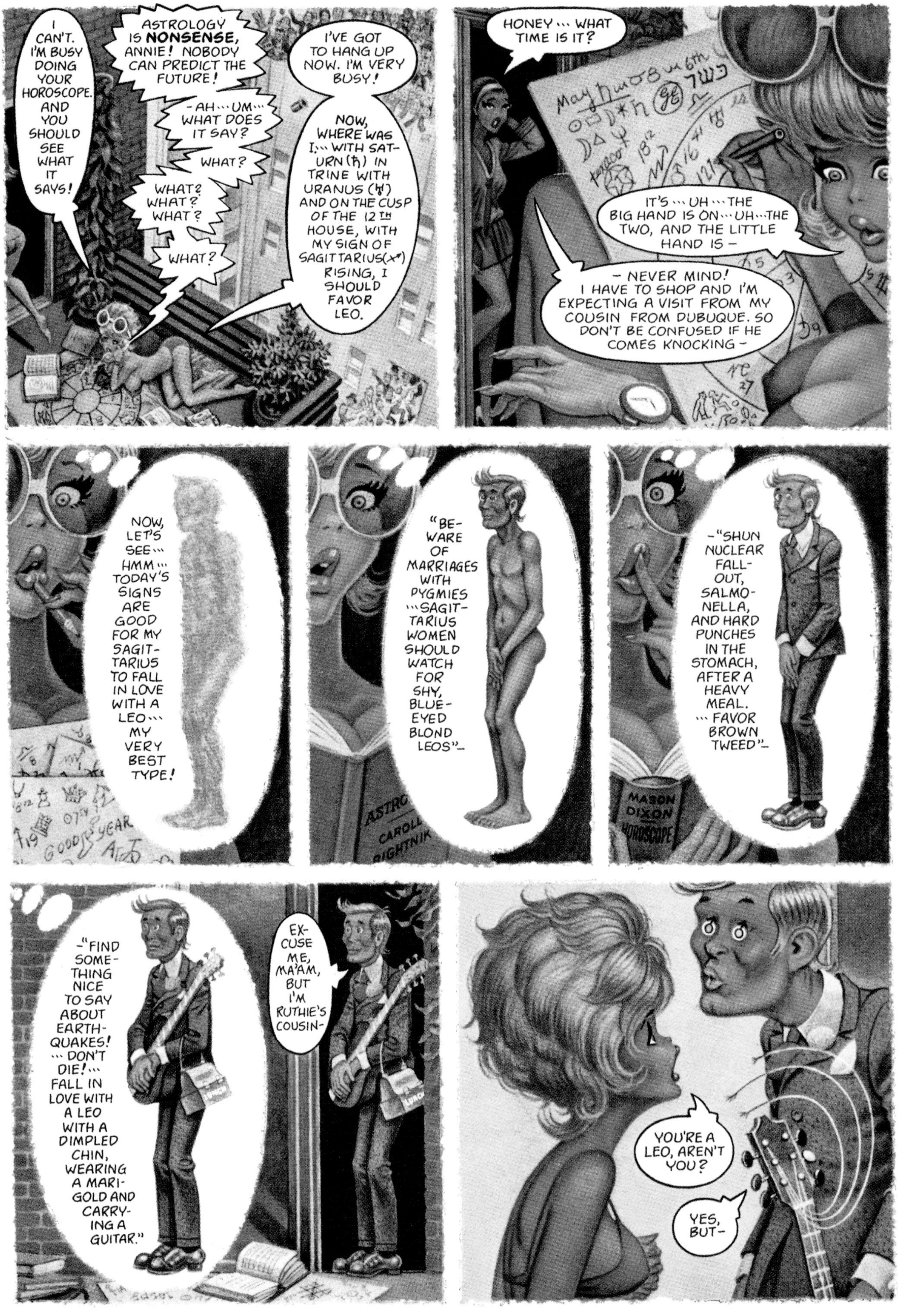
I CAN'T. I'M BUSY DOING YOUR HOROSCOPE. AND YOU SHOULD SEE WHAT IT SAYS!
ASTROLOGY IS **NONSENSE,** ANNIE! NOBODY CAN PREDICT THE FUTURE!
-AH··· UM··· WHAT DOES IT SAY?
WHAT?
WHAT? WHAT? WHAT?
WHAT?
I'VE GOT TO HANG UP NOW. I'M VERY BUSY!
NOW, WHERE WAS I··· WITH SATURN (♄) IN TRINE WITH URANUS (♅) AND ON THE CUSP OF THE 12TH HOUSE, WITH MY SIGN OF SAGITTARIUS (♐) RISING, I SHOULD FAVOR LEO.
HONEY··· WHAT TIME IS IT?
IT'S··· UH··· THE BIG HAND IS ON··· UH··· THE TWO, AND THE LITTLE HAND IS –
– NEVER MIND! I HAVE TO SHOP AND I'M EXPECTING A VISIT FROM MY COUSIN FROM DUBUQUE. SO DON'T BE CONFUSED IF HE COMES KNOCKING –
NOW, LET'S SEE··· HMM··· TODAY'S SIGNS ARE GOOD FOR MY SAGITTARIUS TO FALL IN LOVE WITH A LEO··· MY VERY BEST TYPE!
"BEWARE OF MARRIAGES WITH PYGMIES ···SAGITTARIUS WOMEN SHOULD WATCH FOR SHY, BLUE-EYED BLOND LEOS"–
–"SHUN NUCLEAR FALL-OUT, SALMONELLA, AND HARD PUNCHES IN THE STOMACH, AFTER A HEAVY MEAL. ··· FAVOR BROWN TWEED"–
MASON DIXON HOROSCOPE
–"FIND SOMETHING NICE TO SAY ABOUT EARTHQUAKES! ··· DON'T DIE! ··· FALL IN LOVE WITH A LEO WITH A DIMPLED CHIN, WEARING A MARIGOLD AND CARRYING A GUITAR."
EXCUSE ME, MA'AM, BUT I'M RUTHIE'S COUSIN-
YOU'RE A LEO, AREN'T YOU?
YES, BUT-

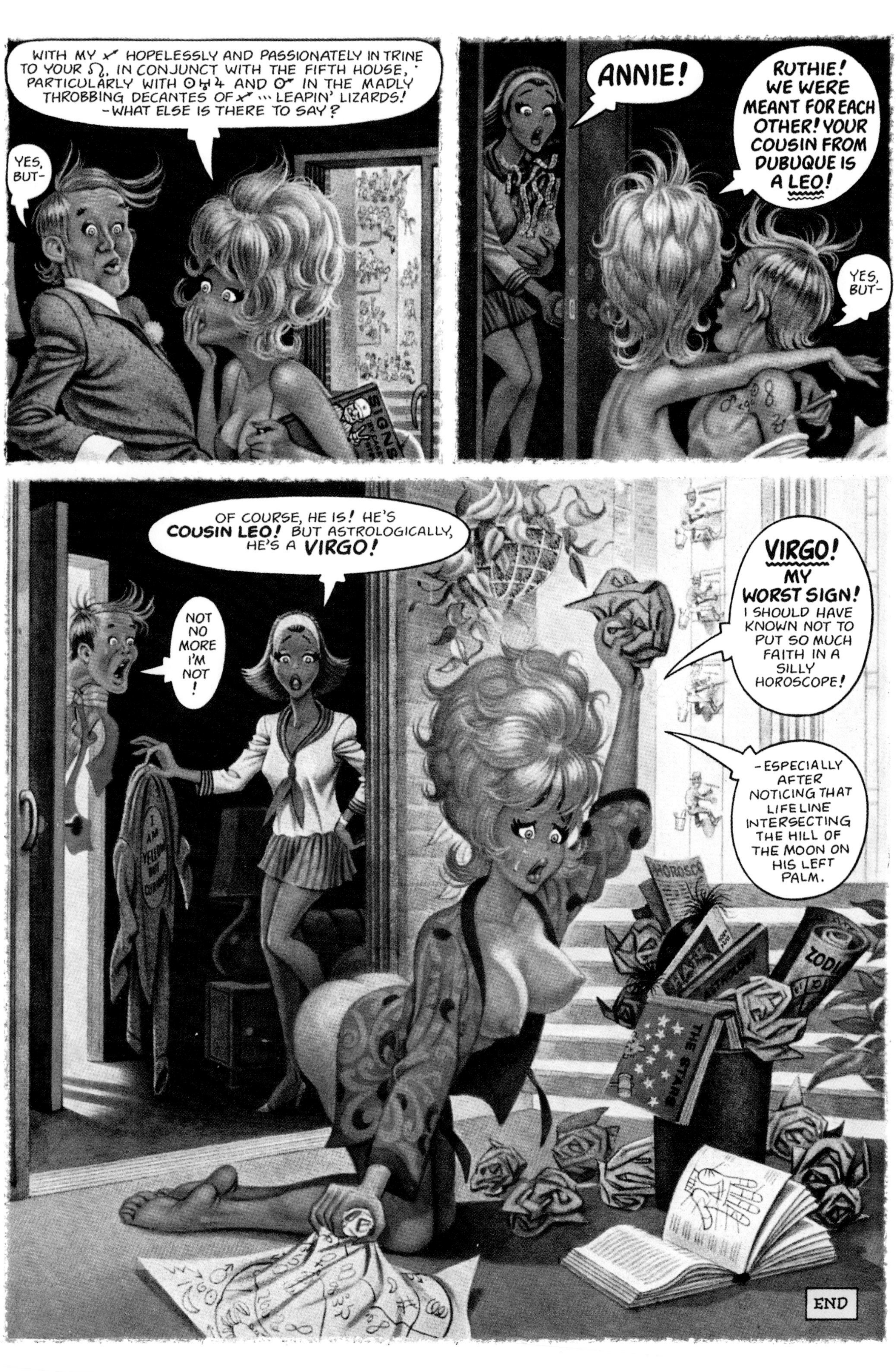

WITH MY ♐ HOPELESSLY AND PASSIONATELY IN TRINE TO YOUR ♌, IN CONJUNCT WITH THE FIFTH HOUSE, PARTICULARLY WITH ☉♅♃ AND ♂ IN THE MADLY THROBBING DECANTES OF ♐ ... LEAPIN' LIZARDS! -WHAT ELSE IS THERE TO SAY?
YES, BUT-
ANNIE!
RUTHIE! WE WERE MEANT FOR EACH OTHER! YOUR COUSIN FROM DUBUQUE IS A LEO!
YES, BUT-
OF COURSE, HE IS! HE'S COUSIN LEO! BUT ASTROLOGICALLY, HE'S A VIRGO!
NOT NO MORE I'M NOT!
VIRGO! MY WORST SIGN! I SHOULD HAVE KNOWN NOT TO PUT SO MUCH FAITH IN A SILLY HOROSCOPE!
-ESPECIALLY AFTER NOTICING THAT LIFELINE INTERSECTING THE HILL OF THE MOON ON HIS LEFT PALM.
END

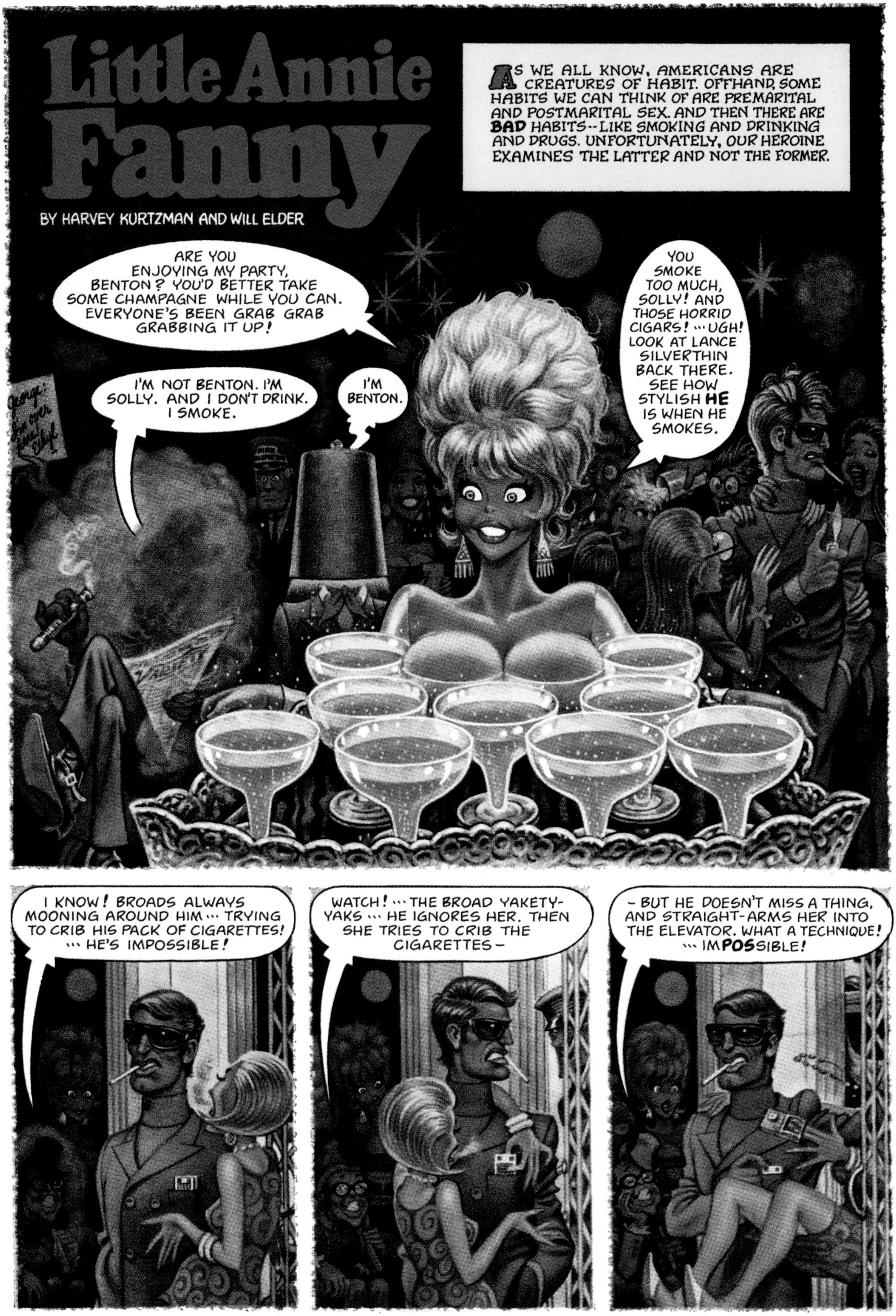
Little Annie Fanny
AS WE ALL KNOW, AMERICANS ARE CREATURES OF HABIT. OFFHAND, SOME HABITS WE CAN THINK OF ARE PREMARITAL AND POSTMARITAL SEX. AND THEN THERE ARE BAD HABITS--LIKE SMOKING AND DRINKING AND DRUGS. UNFORTUNATELY, OUR HEROINE EXAMINES THE LATTER AND NOT THE FORMER.
BY HARVEY KURTZMAN AND WILL ELDER
ARE YOU ENJOYING MY PARTY, BENTON? YOU'D BETTER TAKE SOME CHAMPAGNE WHILE YOU CAN. EVERYONE'S BEEN GRAB GRAB GRABBING IT UP!
I'M NOT BENTON. I'M SOLLY. AND I DON'T DRINK. I SMOKE.
I'M BENTON.
YOU SMOKE TOO MUCH, SOLLY! AND THOSE HORRID CIGARS! ... UGH! LOOK AT LANCE SILVERTHIN BACK THERE. SEE HOW STYLISH HE IS WHEN HE SMOKES.
I KNOW! BROADS ALWAYS MOONING AROUND HIM ... TRYING TO CRIB HIS PACK OF CIGARETTES! ... HE'S IMPOSSIBLE!
WATCH! ... THE BROAD YAKETY-YAKS ... HE IGNORES HER. THEN SHE TRIES TO CRIB THE CIGARETTES –
– BUT HE DOESN'T MISS A THING, AND STRAIGHT-ARMS HER INTO THE ELEVATOR. WHAT A TECHNIQUE! ... IMPOSSIBLE!

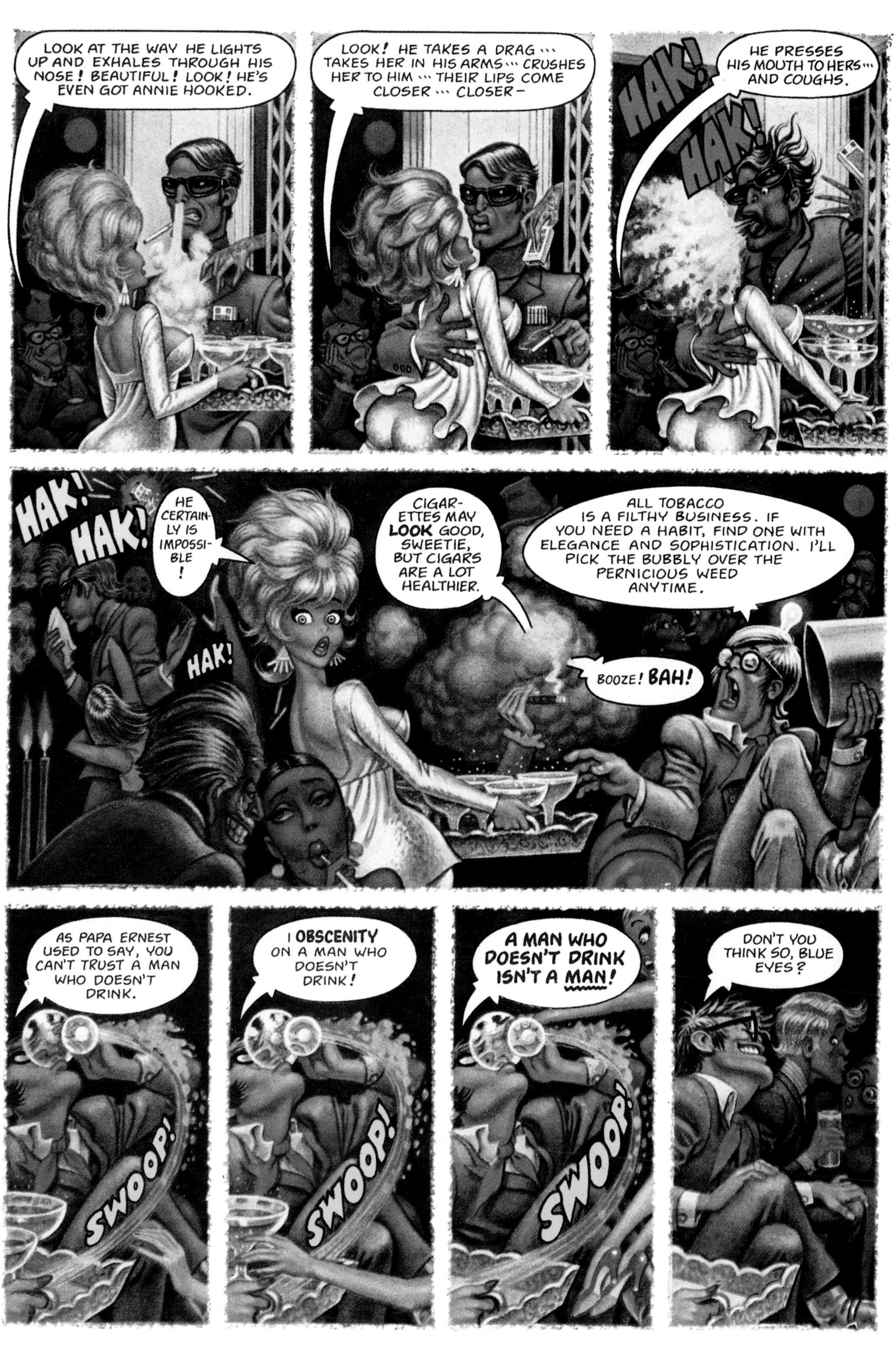
LOOK AT THE WAY HE LIGHTS UP AND EXHALES THROUGH HIS NOSE! BEAUTIFUL! LOOK! HE'S EVEN GOT ANNIE HOOKED.
LOOK! HE TAKES A DRAG ... TAKES HER IN HIS ARMS ... CRUSHES HER TO HIM ... THEIR LIPS COME CLOSER ... CLOSER –
HAK!
HAK!
HE PRESSES HIS MOUTH TO HERS ... AND COUGHS.
HAK!
HAK!
HE CERTAINLY IS IMPOSSIBLE!
HAK!
CIGARETTES MAY LOOK GOOD, SWEETIE, BUT CIGARS ARE A LOT HEALTHIER.
ALL TOBACCO IS A FILTHY BUSINESS. IF YOU NEED A HABIT, FIND ONE WITH ELEGANCE AND SOPHISTICATION. I'LL PICK THE BUBBLY OVER THE PERNICIOUS WEED ANYTIME.
BOOZE! BAH!
AS PAPA ERNEST USED TO SAY, YOU CAN'T TRUST A MAN WHO DOESN'T DRINK.
SWOOP!
I OBSCENITY ON A MAN WHO DOESN'T DRINK!
SWOOP!
A MAN WHO DOESN'T DRINK ISN'T A MAN!
SWOOP!
DON'T YOU THINK SO, BLUE EYES?

199

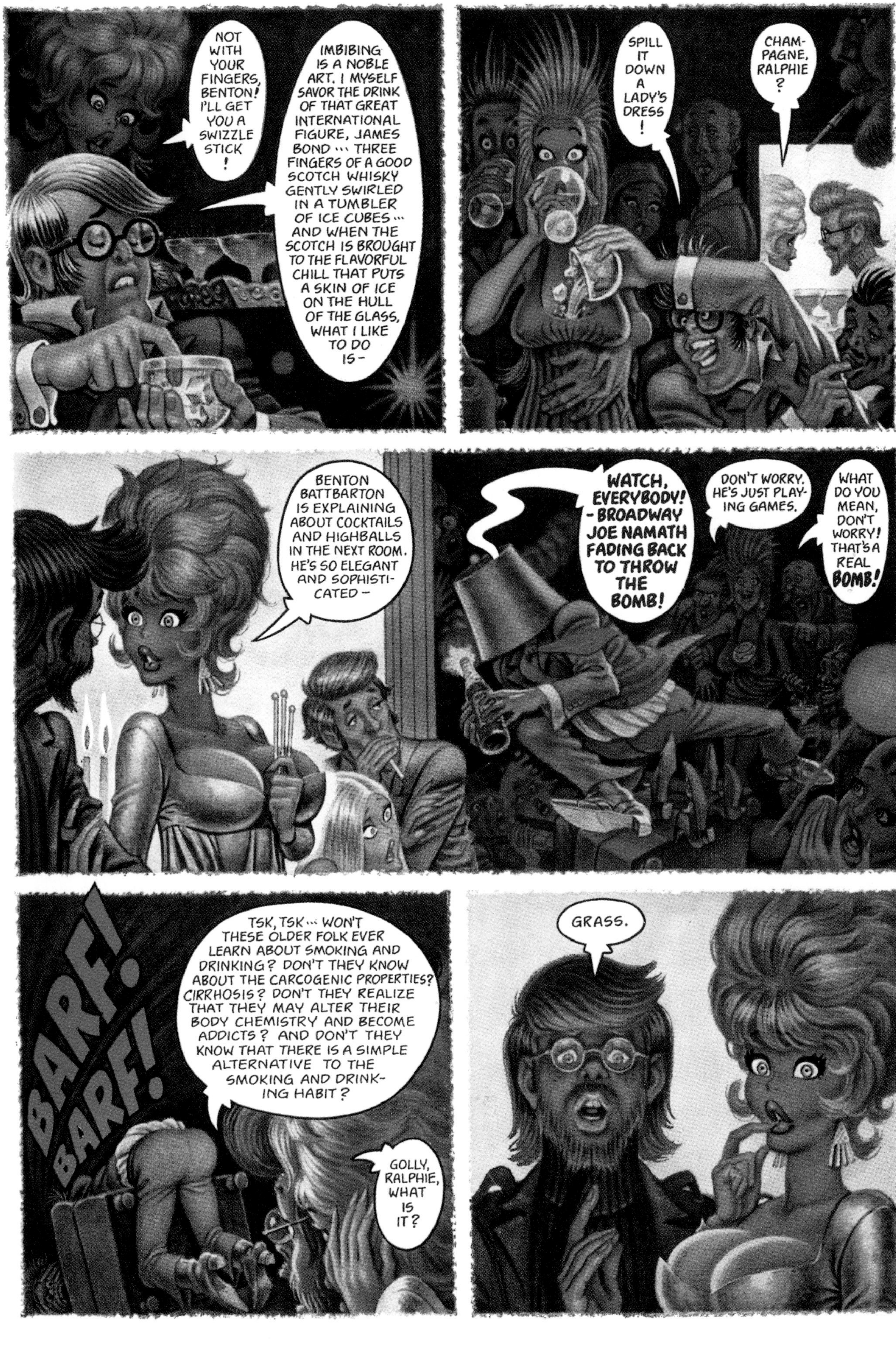

NOT WITH YOUR FINGERS, BENTON! I'LL GET YOU A SWIZZLE STICK!
IMBIBING IS A NOBLE ART. I MYSELF SAVOR THE DRINK OF THAT GREAT INTERNATIONAL FIGURE, JAMES BOND ... THREE FINGERS OF A GOOD SCOTCH WHISKY GENTLY SWIRLED IN A TUMBLER OF ICE CUBES ... AND WHEN THE SCOTCH IS BROUGHT TO THE FLAVORFUL CHILL THAT PUTS A SKIN OF ICE ON THE HULL OF THE GLASS, WHAT I LIKE TO DO IS–
SPILL IT DOWN A LADY'S DRESS!
CHAMPAGNE, RALPHIE?
BENTON BATTBARTON IS EXPLAINING ABOUT COCKTAILS AND HIGHBALLS IN THE NEXT ROOM. HE'S SO ELEGANT AND SOPHISTICATED–
WATCH, EVERYBODY! - BROADWAY JOE NAMATH FADING BACK TO THROW THE BOMB!
DON'T WORRY. HE'S JUST PLAYING GAMES.
WHAT DO YOU MEAN, DON'T WORRY! THAT'S A REAL BOMB!
BARF! BARF!
TSK, TSK ... WON'T THESE OLDER FOLK EVER LEARN ABOUT SMOKING AND DRINKING? DON'T THEY KNOW ABOUT THE CARCOGENIC PROPERTIES? CIRRHOSIS? DON'T THEY REALIZE THAT THEY MAY ALTER THEIR BODY CHEMISTRY AND BECOME ADDICTS? AND DON'T THEY KNOW THAT THERE IS A SIMPLE ALTERNATIVE TO THE SMOKING AND DRINKING HABIT?
GOLLY, RALPHIE, WHAT IS IT?
GRASS.

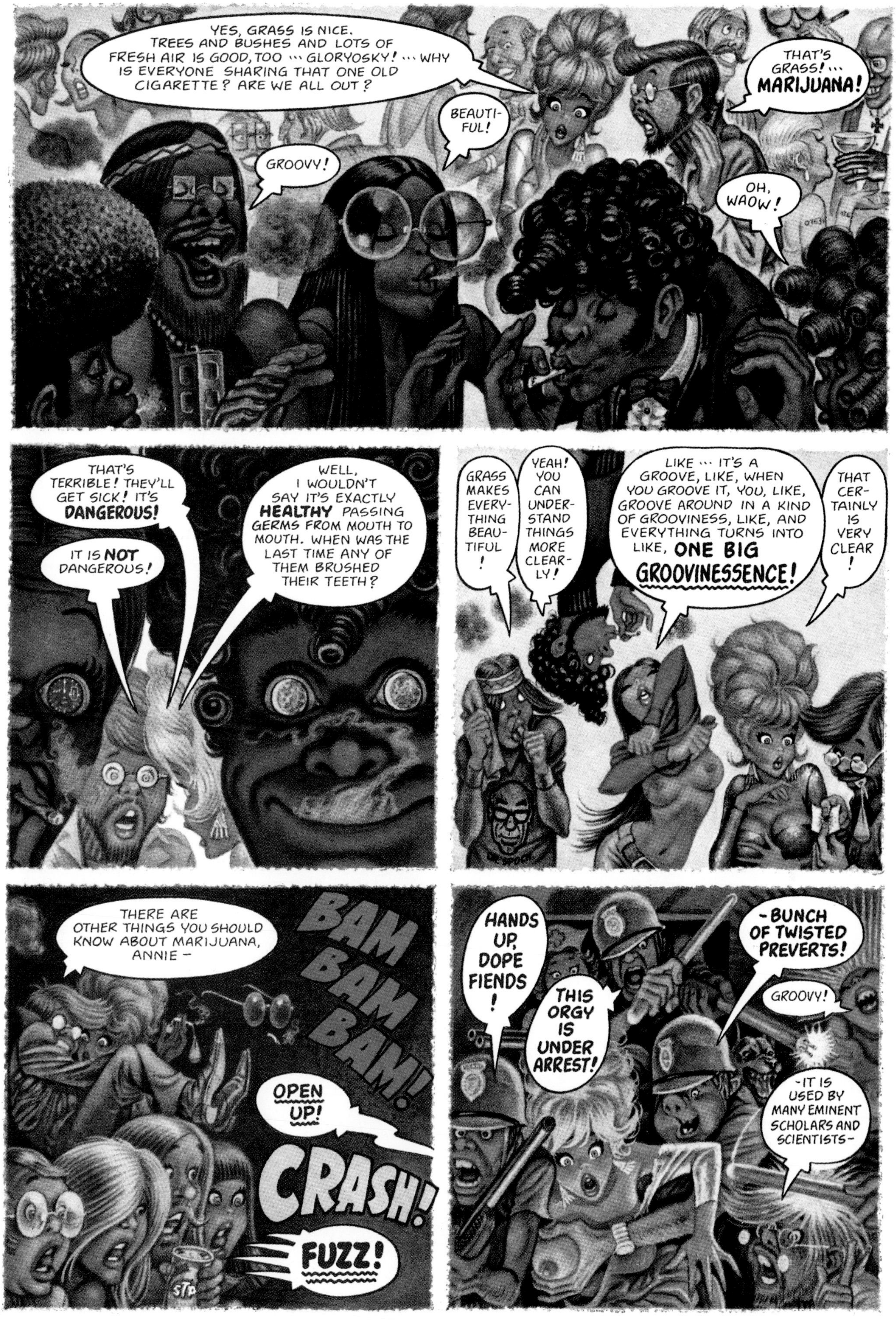
YES, GRASS IS NICE. TREES AND BUSHES AND LOTS OF FRESH AIR IS GOOD, TOO ··· GLORYOSKY! ··· WHY IS EVERYONE SHARING THAT ONE OLD CIGARETTE? ARE WE ALL OUT?
THAT'S GRASS! ··· MARIJUANA!
BEAUTI- FUL!
GROOVY!
OH, WAOW!
THAT'S TERRIBLE! THEY'LL GET SICK! IT'S DANGEROUS!
IT IS NOT DANGEROUS!
WELL, I WOULDN'T SAY IT'S EXACTLY HEALTHY PASSING GERMS FROM MOUTH TO MOUTH. WHEN WAS THE LAST TIME ANY OF THEM BRUSHED THEIR TEETH?
GRASS MAKES EVERY- THING BEAU- TIFUL!
YEAH! YOU CAN UNDER- STAND THINGS MORE CLEAR- LY!
LIKE ··· IT'S A GROOVE, LIKE, WHEN YOU GROOVE IT, YOU, LIKE, GROOVE AROUND IN A KIND OF GROOVINESS, LIKE, AND EVERYTHING TURNS INTO LIKE, ONE BIG GROOVINESSENCE!
THAT CER- TAINLY IS VERY CLEAR!
THERE ARE OTHER THINGS YOU SHOULD KNOW ABOUT MARIJUANA, ANNIE –
BAM BAM BAM!
OPEN UP!
CRASH!
FUZZ!
HANDS UP, DOPE FIENDS!
THIS ORGY IS UNDER ARREST!
-BUNCH OF TWISTED PREVERTS!
GROOVY!
-IT IS USED BY MANY EMINENT SCHOLARS AND SCIENTISTS-

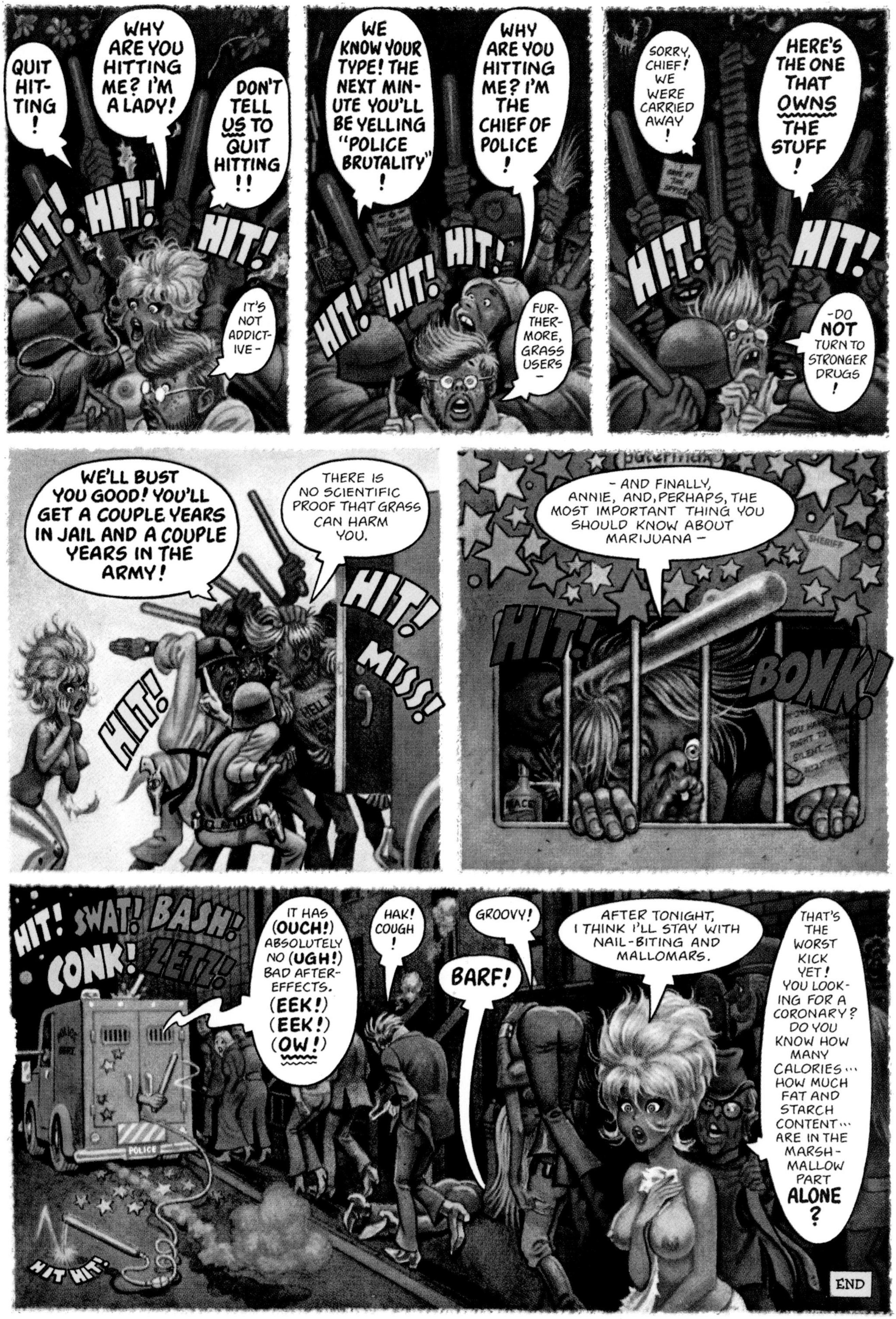
QUIT HIT-TING!
WHY ARE YOU HITTING ME? I'M A LADY!
DON'T TELL US TO QUIT HITTING!!
HIT! HIT! HIT!
IT'S NOT ADDICT-IVE –
WE KNOW YOUR TYPE! THE NEXT MIN-UTE YOU'LL BE YELLING "POLICE BRUTALITY"!
WHY ARE YOU HITTING ME? I'M THE CHIEF OF POLICE!
HIT! HIT! HIT!
FUR-THER-MORE, GRASS USERS –
SORRY, CHIEF! WE WERE CARRIED AWAY!
HERE'S THE ONE THAT OWNS THE STUFF!
HIT! HIT!
–DO NOT TURN TO STRONGER DRUGS!
WE'LL BUST YOU GOOD! YOU'LL GET A COUPLE YEARS IN JAIL AND A COUPLE YEARS IN THE ARMY!
THERE IS NO SCIENTIFIC PROOF THAT GRASS CAN HARM YOU.
HIT! MISS!! HIT!
– AND FINALLY, ANNIE, AND, PERHAPS, THE MOST IMPORTANT THING YOU SHOULD KNOW ABOUT MARIJUANA –
HIT! BONK!
HIT! SWAT! BASH! CONK! ZETZ!
IT HAS (OUCH!) ABSOLUTELY NO (UGH!) BAD AFTER-EFFECTS. (EEK!) (EEK!) (OW!)
HAK! COUGH!
GROOVY!
BARF!
AFTER TONIGHT, I THINK I'LL STAY WITH NAIL-BITING AND MALLOMARS.
THAT'S THE WORST KICK YET! YOU LOOK-ING FOR A CORONARY? DO YOU KNOW HOW MANY CALORIES... HOW MUCH FAT AND STARCH CONTENT... ARE IN THE MARSH-MALLOW PART ALONE?
HIT HIT!
POLICE
END

THE ORIGINS of LITTLE ANNIE FANNY

By Denis Kitchen

Little Annie Fanny would seem to be the *least* likely cartoon character to have begun as a male. But before we get to the delicate subject of two-dimensional sex changes, a little history is in order. In 1954 Harvey Kurtzman invented a revolutionary satire comic book-turned-magazine, *Mad*, which soon became a publishing sensation. He was the editor. He contributed art. He wrote scripts. He designed page layouts. And he gathered around him some of the finest cartoonists ever. But he didn't own the publication. *Mad* was owned by William Gaines, the publisher of E.C. Comics.

In 1954 another cartoonist invented a revolutionary magazine which became a publishing sensation. He too wrote, laid out pages, and gathered brilliant talent around him. Hugh Hefner, of course, also owned his magazine.

Hefner was sending a finished issue of *Playboy* to press when he discovered an early *Mad* on a Chicago newsstand. He contacted Kurtzman and the two quickly developed a mutual respect and friendship. In early 1956 Kurtzman, in part encouraged by Hefner, felt confident enough to demand a large equity stake in *Mad*. The astonished Gaines refused. Hefner, waiting in the wings, promptly hired Kurtzman along with Will Elder, Jack Davis, Al Jaffee, Arnold

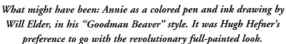

'LITTLE ANNIE FANNY'

What might have been: Annie as a colored pen and ink drawing by Will Elder, in his "Goodman Beaver" style. It was Hugh Hefner's preference to go with the revolutionary full-painted look.

Roth, Russ Heath (all names familiar to readers of "Little Annie Fanny"), and others to create a slick, full-color satire magazine that was eventually named *Trump*. Kurtzman and his staff made full use of *Playboy*'s resources to create the most lavish satire magazine America had ever seen.

The launch in early 1957 was not an immediate success. Start-up magazines typically need time to become profitable, but Hefner, at that early stage of what would become an empire, was not able to sustain the considerable losses, and the noble experiment failed after only two issues. The core of Kurtzman's hardy crew reformed. Using their own meager resources, they independently launched a low-rent satire comic-turned-magazine called *Humbug* in late 1957. Despite the partners' fierce determination, long hours, and fine work, *Humbug* suffered from bad production quality and even worse distribution. With resources exhausted, *Humbug* failed the following year. The band of zany cartoonists then went in different directions. Kurtzman throughout 1958 made a series of feature proposals to *Playboy*, all of which were rejected. By the end of December Kurtzman gave up on any further pitches. In a brief letter to Hefner he wrote:

> I got the "beat" article back, and for several reasons, I'm sorry it didn't work out. I'm sorry I've disappointed you again, and I'm sorry at what I sense to be the final flicker of our association, which has existed, like all associations, on the basis of some mutual activity. Trying to create for *Playboy*, I've a blind spot that I don't think I can ever overcome.

Hefner immediately sent Kurtzman a candid but reassuring reply:

> I don't believe the problem we've been faced with is really a blind spot where *Playboy* is concerned, Harv. You went through a pretty low period near the end with *Humbug* and after it died, and I think that very much influenced your sense of humor and your ability to be critical about it. The only real problem with the work you've submitted to us is that it hasn't been funny. It really hasn't. And in a more critical time, you would have recognized that yourself, I'm sure.
>
> I feel certain, too, that with things moving ahead now for you, the old sharpness will return. There is really no great gap in our senses of humor—I think I have proven that I dig your work by investing $100,000 in it [*Trump*] and by running a nine-page portfolio on it in *Playboy* [December 1957]. I bow to no one in my appreciation for H. Kurtzman.

Mad, and the others were extremely successful, undergoing numerous reprints. But William Gaines switched the paperback rights to Signet Books, leaving a large hole in Ballantine's humor line. Ballantine was prepared to do *Trump* paperbacks,

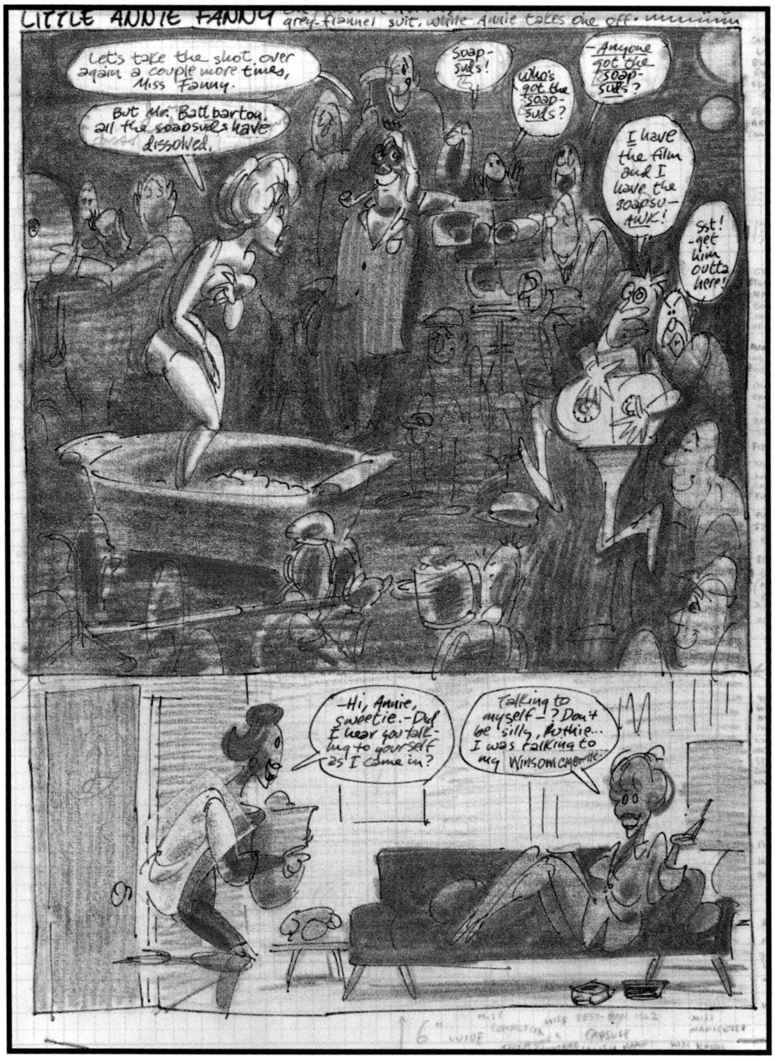
LITTLE ANNIE FANNY
grey-flannel suit, while Annie takes one off.
Let's take the shot over again a couple more times, Miss Fanny.
But Mr. Ballbarton, all the soapsuds have dissolved.
Soap-suds!
Who's got the soap-suds?
-Anyone got the soap-suds?
I have the film and I have the soapsu-AWK!
Sst! -get him outta here!
-Hi, Annie, sweetie.-Did I hear you talking to yourself as I come in?
Talking to myself-!? Don't be silly, Ruthie... I was talking to my

Kurtzman's original layout for the first episode of "Little Annie Fanny" was done on cardboard graph paper, with the six pages stapled together to form a little book, which Hefner would lay open and mark up. Once Hefner approved these, Kurtzman created significantly larger layouts, along with color guides for Elder. A full story metamorphosis can be seen in the second volume.

Encouraged, Kurtzman continued his communication with Hefner, but decided to seek more immediate and pragmatic outlets for his talent. Ian Ballantine was a pioneer and visionary in the growing paperback publishing field. Ballantine Books published the first four *Mad* paperback collections. *Mad Reader*, *Utterly* had that magazine succeeded, and he did publish *Humbug Digest*, which didn't do nearly as well as *Mad*. But he recognized Kurtzman's inherent genius and approached him in the spring of 1958. Ballantine wanted something original from the creator of *Mad* and was willing to give Kurtzman carte blanche. Kurtzman leaped at the opportunity. The result was *Harvey Kurtzman's Jungle Book*, published in 1959. It was the first paperback consisting entirely of original art. *Jungle Book* contained four distinct satires, all brilliant, in pen and wash. Kurtzman's experiences in publishing coalesced in "The Organization Man in the Grey Flannel Executive Suite," a jaundiced look at the magazine business. In this story he introduced a character named Goodman Beaver. Beaver's first name came from two sources. Kurtzman's hand-lettered introductory text—everything in *Jungle Book* is done by hand—describes Goodman as "fresh and eager ... full of intellect, ideals, and moral convictions, with a burning enthusiasm to create new things ... good things ... for his fellow man." Goodman is literally a good man. But the ultimate duality of the story required a darker inspiration and it came from Martin Goodman. This Goodman was a cynical schlock publisher whose holdings included the kind of men's magazines that *Playboy* ultimately drove under, crossword puzzle magazines, and Timely Comics, which evolved into Marvel. Kurtzman worked early in his career for Timely/Marvel (where Goodman's teenage nephew, Stan Lee, ran the shop). Kurtzman's continued fascination with *Playboy* can be seen in the "Organization Man" story. Goodman, a newly hired editor, meets a fellow editor, modeled after Hugh Hefner, who creates the ultimate centerfold: it unfolds to near billboard size. But Goodman Beaver in this debut story ultimately turns from "good man" to bad, and the character could have easily ended there. He did remain dormant for a while. *Jungle Book*, despite its legendary status among many today, was a commercial failure. Ballantine cancelled a planned follow-up paperback with Kurtzman. Kurtzman produced a steady variety of material for *Pageant*, *Madison Avenue*, *TV Guide*, and other publications, but continued to correspond with Hefner and *Playboy* executive editor Ray Russell. Kurtzman still wanted to produce features

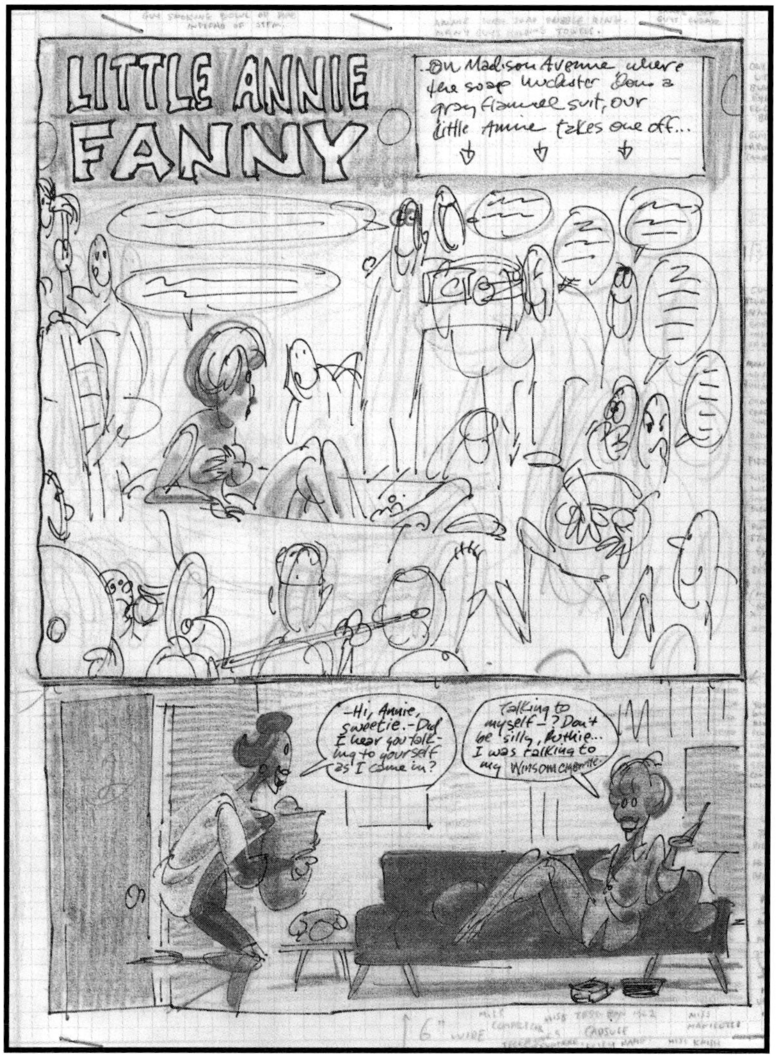
LITTLE ANNIE FANNY
On Madison Avenue where the soap huckster dons a gray flannel suit, our little Annie takes one off...
Hi, Annie, sweetie.—Did I hear you talking to yourself as I came in?
Talking to myself—? Don't be silly, Ruthie... I was talking to

Based on feedback from Hefner, Kurtzman drew a new, sketchier version of the first panel, attaching it over the first. Note the three staples across the top of the page. A heavy crease below the staples allows this leaf to fold up, so one can still view the original layout beneath.

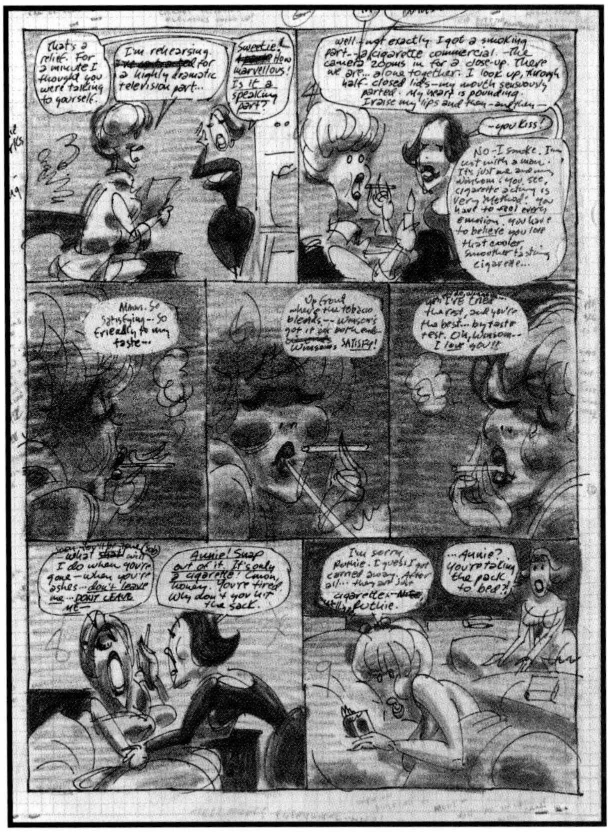
That's a relief. For a minute I thought you were talking to yourself.
I'm rehearsing for a highly dramatic television part..
Sweetie! How marvellous! Is it a speaking part?
Well.. not exactly. I got a smoking part--a cigarette commercial. -The camera zooms in for a close-up. There we are... alone together. I look up, through half-closed lids—my mouth sensuously parted. My heart is pounding. I raise my lips and then—and then—
—you kiss!
No-I smoke. I'm not with a man. It's just me and my Winsom! You see, cigarette acting is very Method! You have to feel every emotion. You have to believe you love that cooler, smoother tasting cigarette...
Mmm. So satisfying-- So friendly to my taste--
I've tried the rest, and you're the best... by taste test. Oh, Winsom-- I love you!!
I do when you're gone—when you're ashes... don't leave me... DON'T LEAVE ME—
Annie! Snap out of it. It's only a cigarette! C'mon, honey. You're tired. Why don't you hit the sack.
I'm sorry, Ruthie. I guess I got carried away. After all... they are just cigarettes—
...Annie? You're taking the pack to bed?!

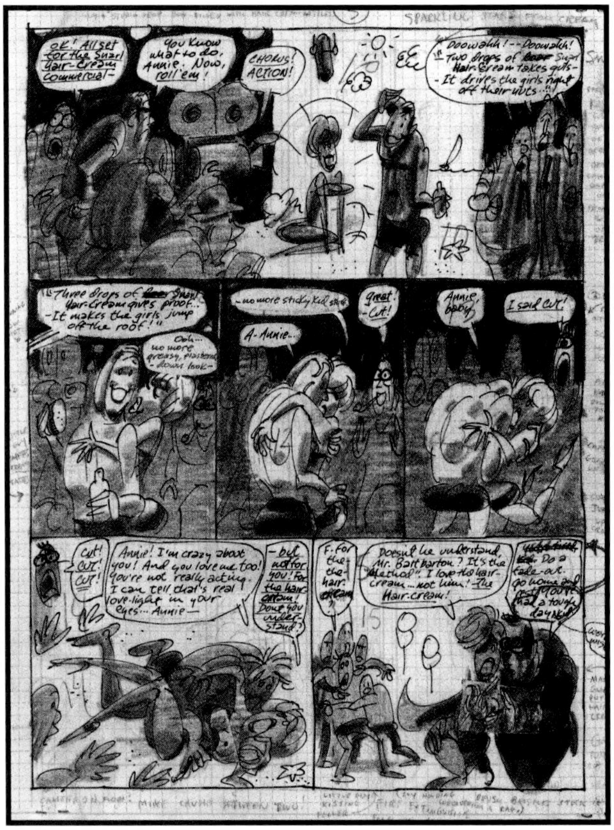
OK! All set for the Snarl Hair-Cream commercial—
You know what to do, Annie. Now, roll 'em!
CHORUS! ACTION!
Doowahh!--Doowahh! "Two drops of Snarl Hair-Cream takes guts- -It drives the girls right off their nuts..!!"
"Three drops of Snarl Hair-Cream gives proof... -It makes the girls jump off the roof!"
Ooh... no more greasy, plastered-down look-
A-Annie..
Great -Cut!
Annie, baby,
I said CUT!
Cut! CUT! CUT!
Annie! I'm crazy about you! And you love me too! You're not really acting. I can tell that's real love-light in your eyes... Annie—
—but not for you! For the hair cream! Don't you under-stand?
F-For the-the-hair-cream?
Doesn't he understand, Mr. Bartbarton? It's the "Method". I love the hair-cream... not him! -The Hair-cream!

Everything from lighting to balloon placement was dictated in these initial layouts, modified by the larger, subsequent layouts. Elder added background gags, worked out color schemes based on Kurtzman's guides, and slaved over the rendering, which grew more lavish as the strip matured.

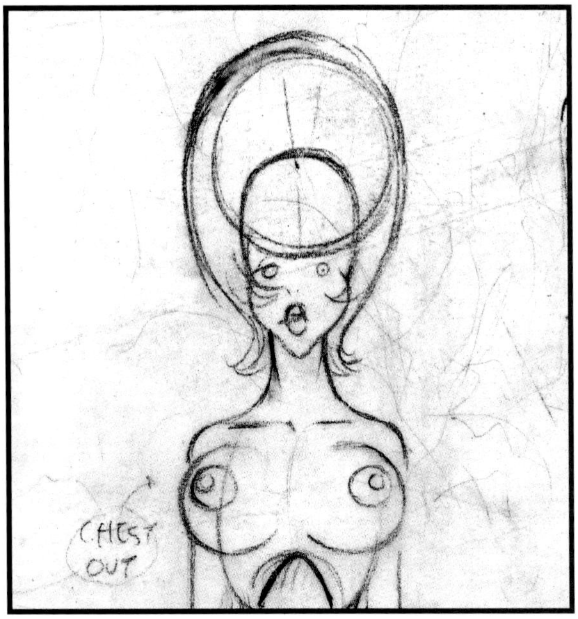
CHEST OUT

Kurtzman's informative perspective study comes from the back of a page from the unfinished Bleatles story (pages 217-220).

for the magazine and *Playboy* wanted more visual humor. Russell, in a February 1960 letter to Kurtzman, said,

> Hef and I both strongly feel there is great value in the comic strip form for us. Comic strips have a basic, immediate appeal to many levels of readership … They are bright, colorful, easily assimilated … dramatic and tell a continuous narrative. Big problem, of course, is to adapt this technique to something that would have meaning for *Playboy*, and be defensible and justified in our pages. We certainly don't want anything even remotely resembling what Bill Gaines was doing there for a while, that "pictofiction" crap … Satire seems to be the only solution. If *Mad* never existed, stuff like your old "Flesh Garden" and similar parodies would have been perfect for us … good

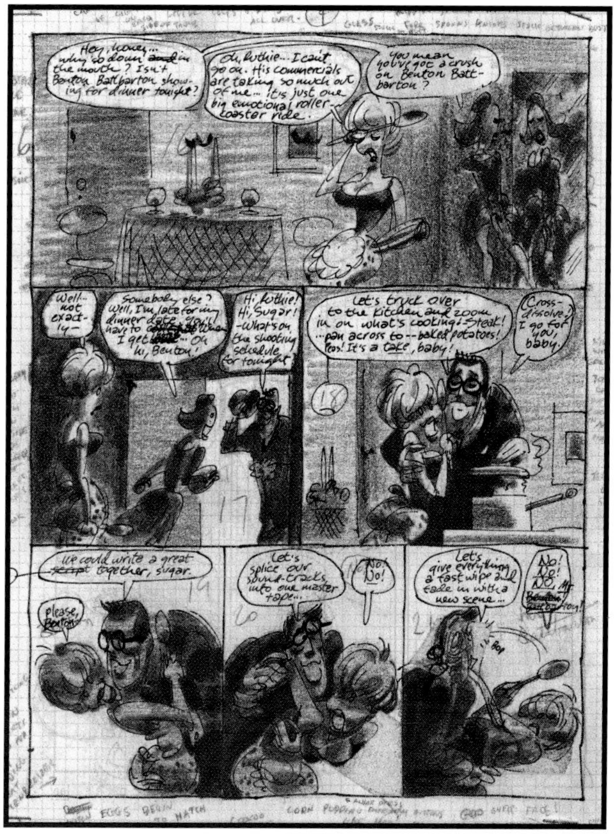
Hey, honey... why so down in the mouth? Isn't Benton Battbarton showing for dinner tonight?
Oh, Ruthie... I can't go on. His commercials are taking so much out of me... it's just one big emotional roller-coaster ride.
You mean you've got a crush on Benton Battbarton?
Well– not exactly–
Hi, Ruthie! Hi, Sugar! –What's on the shooting schedule for tonight
Let's truck over to the kitchen and zoom in on what's cooking!–Steak! ..pan across to– –baked potatoes! Peas! It's a take, baby!
(Cross-dissolve) I go for you, baby.
We could write a great together, sugar.
Please, Benton
Let's splice our sound-tracks into one master tape...
No! No!
Let's give everything a fast wipe and fade in with a new scene...

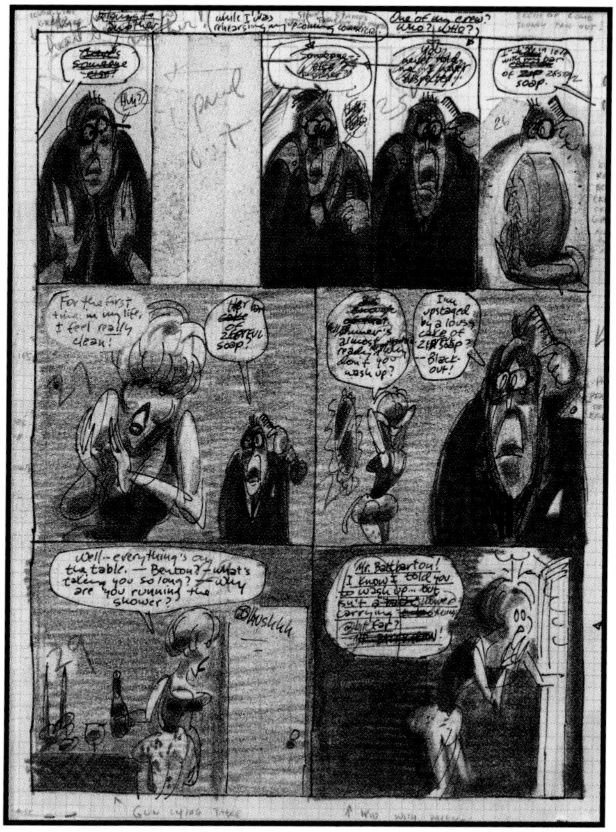
One of my crew? Who? Who?
Huh?
For the first time in my life, I feel really clean!
soap?
I'm upstaged by a lousy cake of soap? –Black-out!
Well– everything's on the table. –Benton? –What's taking you so long? –Why are you running the shower?
Mr. Battbarton!

Kurtzman's layouts maintained this level of detail throughout the feature's history. This sort of initial planning was a trademark of his from his early days at EC Comics on the war titles and the original Mad.

draftsmanship, action, sexy girls in brief costumes, and (last but not least) satire. The presence of satire has twofold importance: satire for its own sake, and (we are really getting to the point now) satire as an excuse or rationale for a slick magazine to be publishing a comic strip.

Russell went on to say, "In *Jungle Book*, you did a thing on the gray-flannel-suit-organization-man syndrome; that was going in the right direction for us. You did a thing on television private eyes; that too was very close to the bull's eye." But, as before, subsequent Kurtzman proposals failed to hit the mark, though the two sides were clearly attracted to each other. Kurtzman continued to freelance for others, including, with some guilt, *Playboy*'s rival *Esquire*.

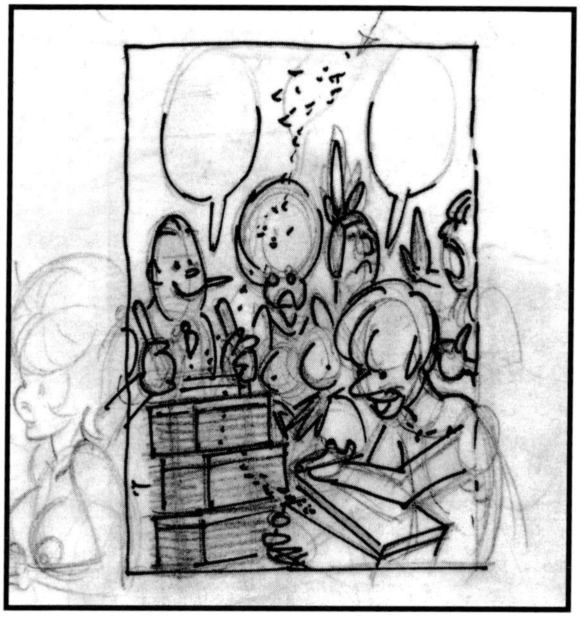

This drawing, also from the back of a Bleatles page, shows Kurtzman revising a panel composition. Both of these drawings can be seen, as realized by Elder, on the unfinished pages.

Kurtzman created a number of brilliant one-shots around this period, including "The Grasshopper and the Ant" for *Esquire*, but found the market narrowing for work he created himself. Kurtzman, discouraged, effectively abandoned his solo efforts. In 1960 he entered into a business partnership with publisher James Warren to create and edit yet another satire magazine, *Help*! The new magazine attracted Kurtzman's usual crew of zany cartoonists (and opened the door for a new generation of underground cartoonists including Robert Crumb and Gilbert Shelton). Its highlight was a series of five new Goodman Beaver adventures. This time Kurtzman wrote and laid out the stories, but the finishes, in masterful pen, were by Will Elder. In the new incarnation Goodman shed his dark side and became a modern Candide. *Help!* had a loyal but never large audience. It was not on financially solid ground. By September 1961 Kurtzman confessed to Hefner that he "might be looking for work soon." He asked if he could pick up on the thread left by Russell a year and a half earlier to create "a strip for *Playboy* à la old *Mad*." Kurtzman sent the earliest Goodman Beaver strips and offered *Playboy* the first opportunity to publish the Superman and Sea Hunt parodies. In November 1961 Hefner responded favorably to Goodman, but he also made it clear that the strip, as it existed, was not right for *Playboy*. Nonetheless he asked Kurtzman to explain his ideas behind Goodman Beaver and added, "Maybe there is a way of launching a similar series on a guy that can somehow be related to *Playboy*, and who has all manner of misadventures related to various subjects." Kurtzman sent the explanation:

> Goodman Beaver's reason for being is, I wanted a

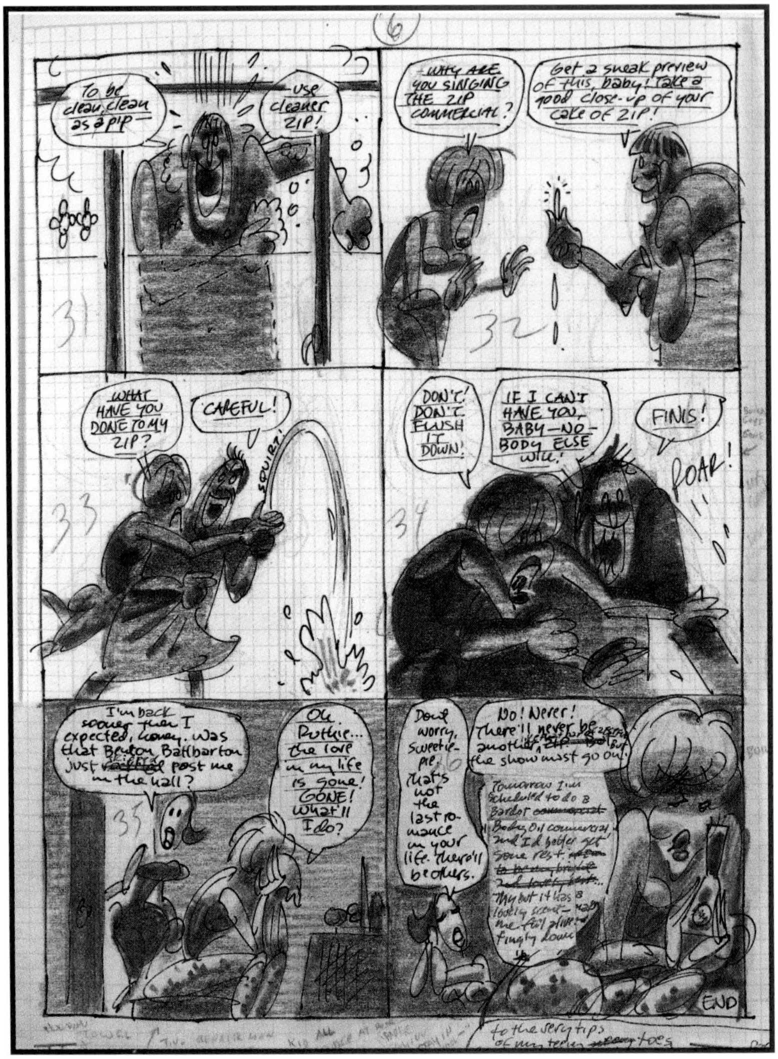
To be clean, clean as a pip
use cleaner ZIP!
WHY ARE YOU SINGING THE ZIP COMMERCIAL?
Get a sneak preview of this, baby! Take a good close-up of your cake of ZIP!
WHAT HAVE YOU DONE TO MY ZIP?
CAREFUL!
SQUIRT!
DON'T! DON'T FLUSH IT DOWN!
IF I CAN'T HAVE YOU, BABY—NOBODY ELSE WILL!
FINIS!
ROAR!
I'm back sooner than I expected, honey. Was that Benton Battbarton just post me in the hall?
Oh Ruthie... the love in my life is gone! GONE! What'll I do?
Don't worry, sweetie-pie. That's not the last romance in your life. There'll be others.
No! Never! There'll never be another. But the show must go on!
END

Kurtzman also changed this original layout for the final page. Note that the first four panels did not yellow with age the same as the bottom of the page. The toilet gag was left out at Hefner's request.

> character who could be foolish and at the same time wise ... naive, yet moral. He innocently partakes of the bad while espousing the good. That way, I can simultaneously treat with foibles and ideals. Goodman Beaver is a lovable, good-natured, philosophical idiot. He's restless. He wanders and can show up anywhere.

He's young and can get involved in sexy situations. (That last sentence was for you.)

A week after this explanation Kurtzman wrote Hefner again.

"ZEST-FUL is first in every pull- It cleans you; body, mind and soul."
"No need to clean between each meal- One cleaning gives that ZESTFUL feel!"
Why are you singing the ZESTFUL commercial?
—just borrowed your bar of ZESTFUL, honey, so's I could get some of it to rub off on me, appeal-wise. Now maybe we can do a close-up.
My bar of ZESTFUL. LOOK OUT!
MY ZEST-FUL!!
WOOPS! There it goes... quick zoom out the window!
Not even with a pinkie baby. I'm like in the ZESTFUL commercial- clean! clean! clean! Body, mind and soul. —Ooh I do believe I'll get home to bed before I catch a chill. Mum wouldn't like that.
I'm back sooner than I expected, honey. Was that Benton Battbarton just past me in the hall?
Oh Ruthie... the love in my life is gone! GONE! What'll I do?
Don't worry, sweetie-pie, that's not the last romance in your life. There'll be others.
No! Never! There'll never be another... But the show must go on.
END

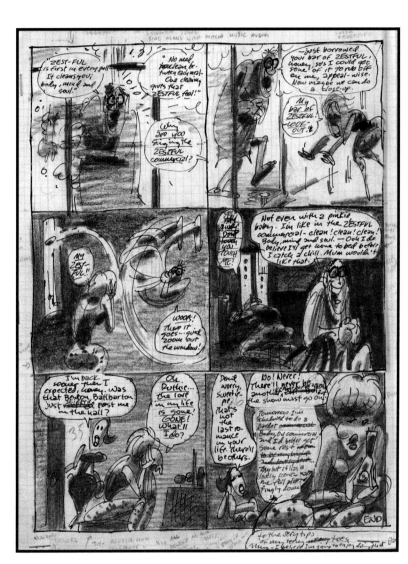

Once again staples attach a revised leaf, this time bound at the side of the page. Readers should compare these layouts to the final versions on pages five through ten of this volume.

You suggested in your Nov. 7, '61 letter that "Maybe there's a way of launching a similar series (to Goodman Beaver) ... that can somehow be related to Playboy ..." What would you think of a girl character, roughly modeled along the lines of Belle Poitrine-Lace, etc. ... very very roughly, whom I could apply to my kind of situations?

Six silent weeks went by while Kurtzman continued to toil on *Help!* and further adventures of Goodman, during which time yet another proposal of Kurtzman's was rejected by Hefner, whose correspondence backlog was often considerable. Then, the day after Christmas, Hefner replied to Kurtzman's suggestion. "I think your notion of doing a Goodman Beaver strip of two, three, or four pages, but using a sexy girl ... is a bull's eye. We can run it every issue." Months of correspondence, calls, and meetings at the Chicago mansion followed, to determine the feature's name, the art technique, the desired frequency, and the plot possibilities. But they had at last reached a basic meeting of the minds.

Help! No.13 (February 1962) contained "Goodman Goes Playboy," a tongue-in-cheek parody of Hugh Hefner's supposed Roman orgy lifestyle, written and drawn well before Hefner's "bull's eye" letter. Hefner, though he was literally depicted as the devil in this story, was quite amused. Not amused at all was Archie Comics, whose wholesome characters were depicted being seduced by the *Playboy* lifestyle. Archie sued *Help!* for copyright infringement.

Kurtzman's partner and financial backer in the magazine, James Warren, did not want to litigate with Archie. For a detailed history of the full travesty see the introduction to *Goodman Beaver* (Kitchen Sink

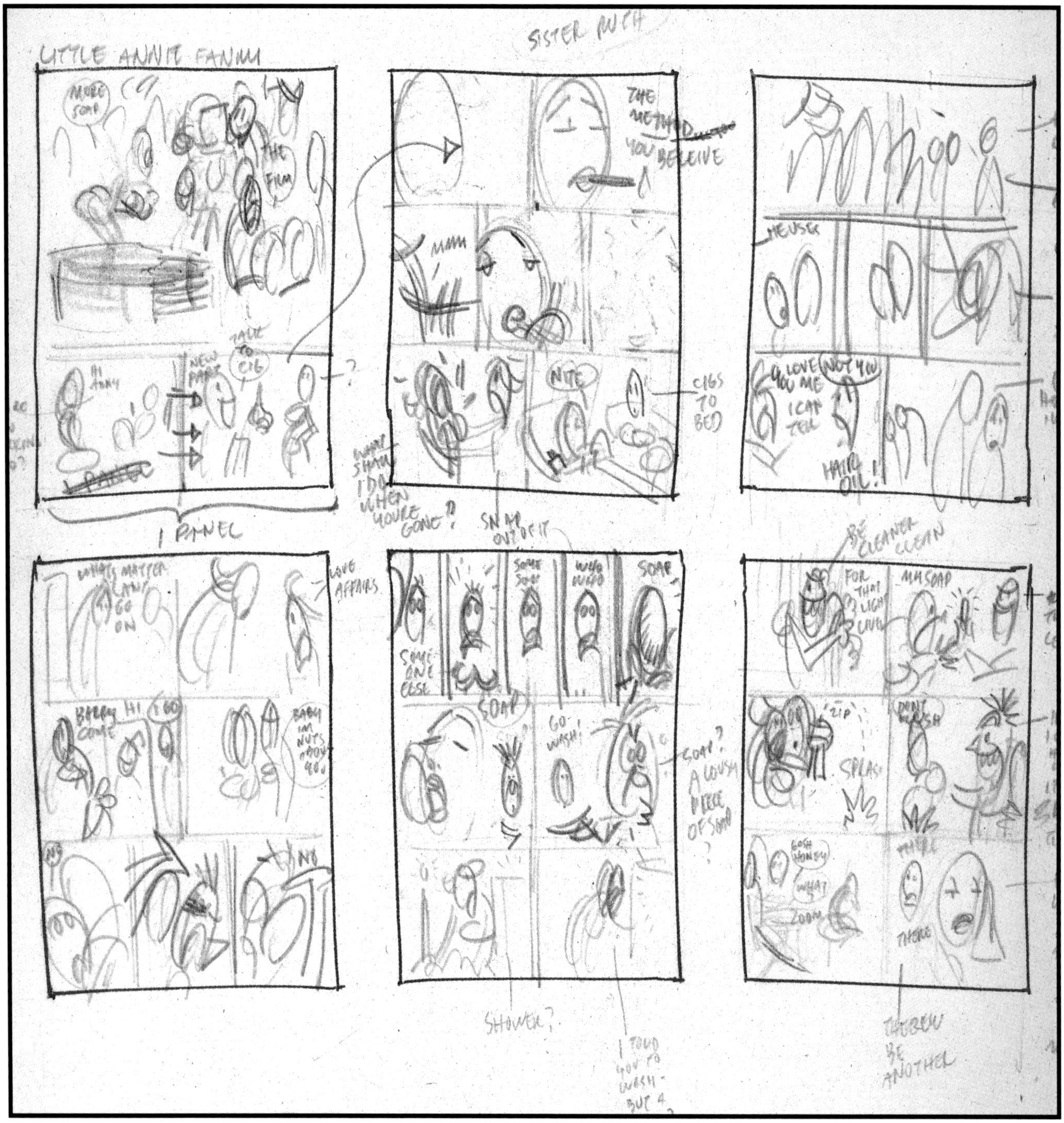
LITTLE ANNIE FANNY
MORE SOAP
THE FILM
HI FANNY
1 PANEL
CIGS TO BED
HAIR OIL!
SOAP
GO WASH!
SHOWER?
ZOOM
THERE

Kurtzman worked out the general pacing and action of the story in "thumbnail" drawings, representing his very first visual thoughts. The pencil roughs presented on pages 204 to 209 would follow this smaller, less detailed version. Kurtzman created thumbnails like the one above for every story he was involved with at E.C. Comics and **Mad**, *and for many of his "Little Annie Fanny" stories.*

Press, 1984). Warren's quick settlement and his reluctance to fight Archie's weak legal case on principle made Kurtzman all the more comfortable with his decision to join *Playboy*. He continued to simultaneously produce *Help!* (which lasted till 1965) while developing, with Will Elder, the new feature for *Playboy*. Kurtzman suggested the new strip could be painted in the "outlineless" style Elder used in a Sgt. Bilko Camel cigarette take off in *Trump*. But he expressed a preference for the feature to be drawn in

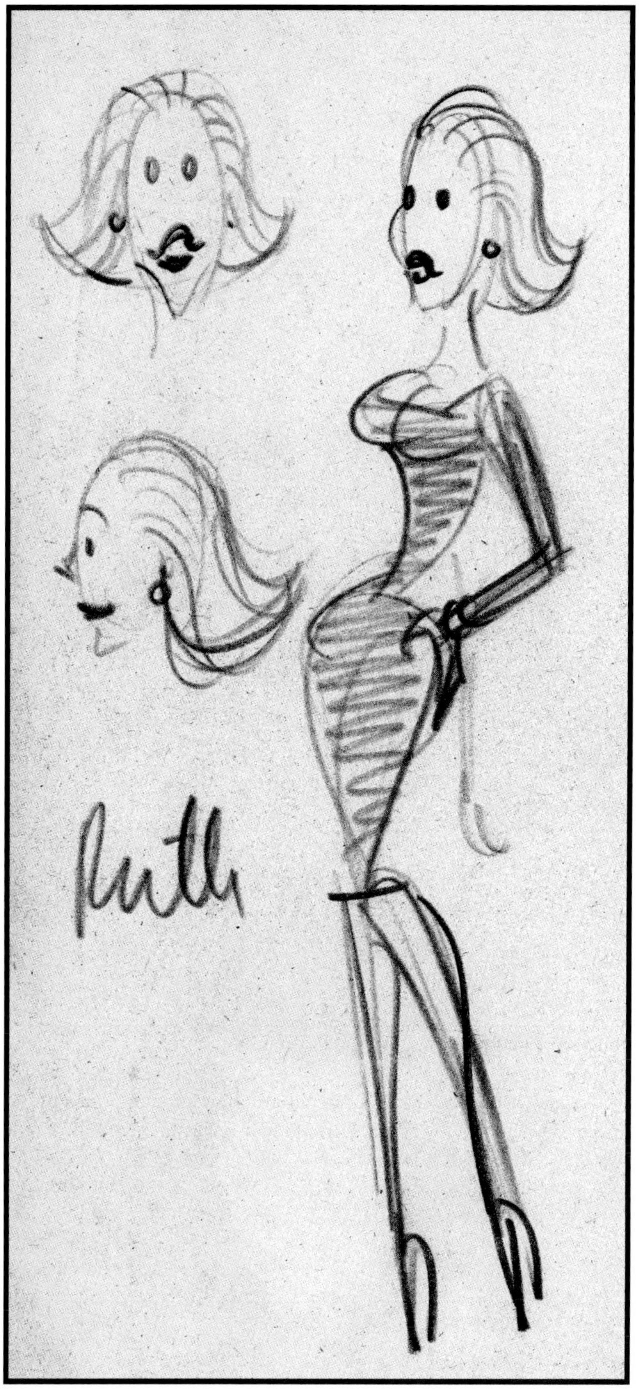
Ruth

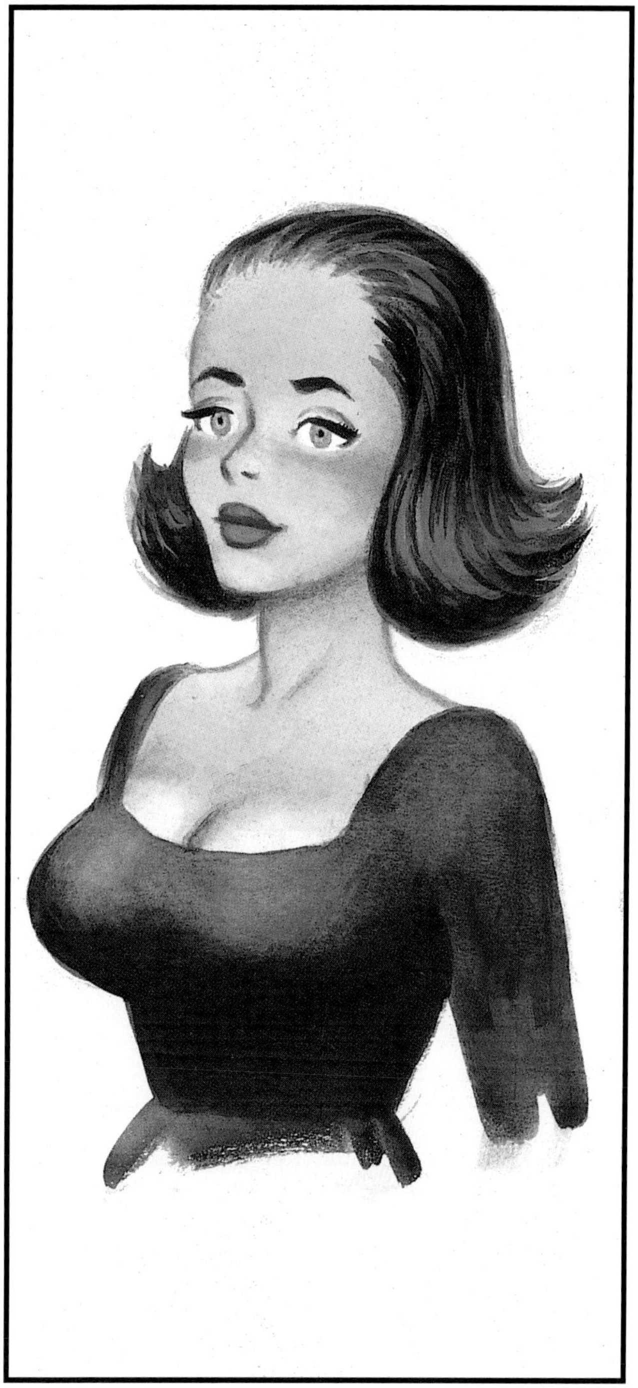

Kurtzman's first sketch of Ruthie, in the style that he drew his **Jungle Book** *in, gives a general sense of her character, which Elder refined significantly in his full-color design. Ruthie was a mainstay of the strip through its entire twenty-six year run.*

the same style as "Goodman Beaver … where he [Elder] India-inks the hell out of it," with flat comic-book color behind the solid black lines. Hefner's preference for Elder's fully painted Sgt. Bilko style in *Trump* prevailed. Kurtzman's initial name suggestions included "The Perils of Zelda," "The Perils of Irma," "The Perils of Shiela," and even "Little Mary Mixup" before he and Hefner settled on "Little Annie Fanny."

In the October 1962 *Playboy* "Little Annie Fanny" made her debut. Hardly anyone noticed the sex change. ♥

Story titles in most cases are from Harvey Kurtzman's notes.

1.) *Pages 5-10.* **"Madison Avenue"** (October 1962). The initial episode depicts Annie as a TV commercial model. We meet two characters who will become recurring cast members: **Annie's roommate Ruthie** (her sister in the original concept), and Annie's first boyfriend, advertising executive **Benton Battbarton**. His name is derived from two of the prominent advertising agencies of the time: Benton & Bowles, Inc. and Batten, Barton, Durstine & Osborne. As early as 1958, (post-*Trump* magazine) Kurtzman pitched the germ of the opening panel in this excerpt of a long letter to Hugh Hefner. "I know you don't watch too much TV, but right now there's a rash of bathtub commercials ... with a girl in the tub full of suds, and she's in love with a cake of soap. The only thing that occurs to me is a panel gag situation where they're trying to shoot a commercial and someone keeps letting the water out." Annie and Benton in this debut episode are so caught up in client products and advertising jargon that their relationship plays second fiddle. In Kurtzman's rough draft, the soap on the last page does not fly out a window but into the toilet. However, toilet humor of this kind did not have a place in *Playboy*. This first episode is also, thankfully, the last time we see Annie smoking cigarettes. Quitting in 1962 placed her well ahead of the curve for most Americans.

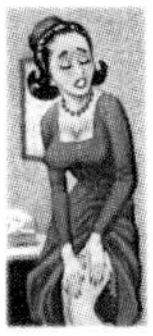

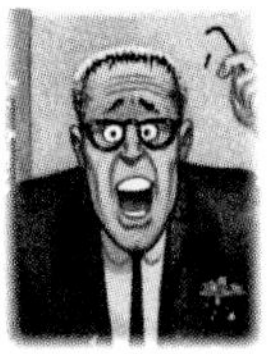

2.) *Pages 11-14.* **"Playing Doctor"** (November 1962). Long before *E.R.* and *Chicago Hope* two popular medical shows dominated TV: *Dr. Kildare*, starring Richard Chamberlain in the title role, with Raymond Massey as Dr. Gillespie; and *Ben Casey*, starring Vince Edwards, with Sam Jaffe as the wizened old Dr. Zorba. Pushing the wheelchair is actor Lew Ayres, who played the lead in the first several Hollywood versions of *Dr. Kildare*. In the wheelchair is actor **Lionel Barrymore**, who played a chair-bound Gillespie in the earlier film series. In several backgrounds we see actor Richard Boone, best known for his role in *Have Gun, Will Travel*, but who also starred in TV's *Medic*. Visual homage of this type was a regular undercurrent in "Little Annie Fanny." The character Avacado framing the story is based on pop-photographer Richard Avedon.

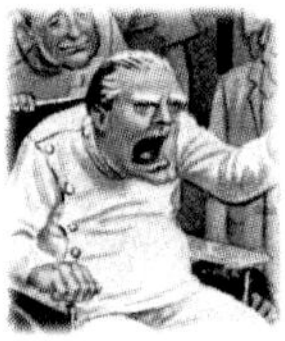

3.) *Pages 15-18.* **"Christmas Office Party"** (December 1962). **Ralphie Towzer** is introduced as Annie's newest boyfriend. Ralphie is the painted version of Kurtzman and Elder's earlier black-and-white character Goodman Beaver, the good-hearted, earnest, but naive character featured in several *Help!* magazine adventures (including, ironically, a satire on *Playboy*). To differentiate him slightly from Goodman and to emphasize that he is an intellectual, Ralphie is given playwright Arthur Miller's eyeglasses and pipe. Benton Battbarton, Richard Avacado, and smarmy actor Peter Lorre make cameo appearances at the office party thrown by the J. Walter Huckster Ad Agency (after J. Walter Thompson). The relative decadence of the party is made clear by Ralphie's reference to *La Dolce Vita*, the celebrated Federico Fellini film all the rage the previous year. It is underscored by the presence of Italian actor **Marcello Mastroianni**, astride a woman from a memorable scene near the end of that film, and actress Anita Ekberg (holding the cat). The woman standing on the desktop and the fur-draped woman on the floor are also straight out of the movie. A limp-wristed Liberace, not so subtly holding fruit, takes center stage in the large party panel.

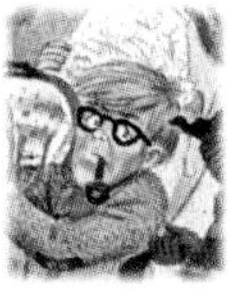

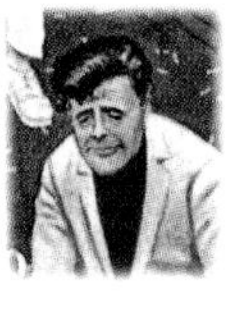

4.) *Pages 19-24.* **"Sugardaddy Bigbucks"** (January 1963). Since Annie's name and her frequent expression "Leapin' Lizards!" are derived from "Little Orphan Annie," it is no surprise that other elements of that classic Harold Gray newspaper strip became the subject of parody. Here Orphan Annie's protector, noble capitalist Daddy Warbucks, transforms into **Sugardaddy Bigbucks**, a more rapacious breed of businessman, who became a recurring character despite the seemingly fatal last panel. Warbucks' mysterious assistant The Asp becomes The Wasp. Punjab, Warbucks' giant right-hand man from India, becomes Shazam (a name taken from the comic book *Captain Marvel*), who quickly disposes of TV G-man **Robert Stack and his "Untouchables."** The brash "college kids" at the party are Robert and Edward Kennedy, then regarded as especially young political figures riding their older brother John's coattails. Bigbucks' "wall-building blocks" are helping to build the then-newly constructed Berlin Wall. "Billie" is convicted Texas businessman /swindler Billie Sol Estes whose connections to Vice President Johnson embarrassed the Kennedy administration. The gagged characters toward the end include French President Charles DeGaulle, Ralphie Towzer, Jiggs from the strip "Bringing Up Father," Anita Ekberg, Avacado, and the trademark character from Dutch Boy Paints (gagged with a paint brush).

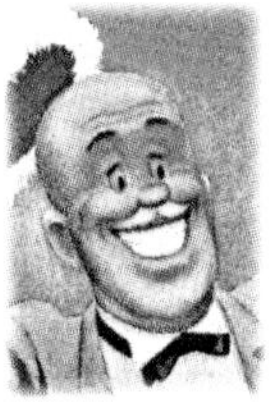

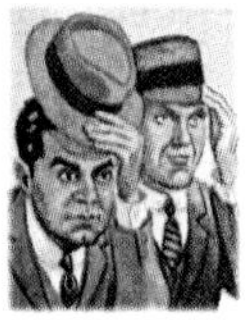

5.) *Pages 25-28.* **"Films, Italian Style"** (March 1963). We meet Annie's "nervy" agent **Solly Brass**, based on the actor Phil Silvers, indelibly typecast in his role as the fast-talking and ever-scamming lead on TV's *Sgt. Bilko*. The "ponytail" Annie is affixing in the opening panel comes from a package from Eddie Arcaro, famous horse jockey. Familiar faces abound. Marcello Macaroni (Mastroianni) repeats his horseback scene. Sugardaddy Bigbucks appears in the second panel wall photo with 1964 Republican presidential candidate Barry Goldwater. Associating Goldwater with the unscrupulous Bigbucks makes Kurtzman's political position clear. Meanwhile a man steals a bike (and later a moped) in a background homage to the groundbreaking Italian film *The Bicycle Thief*, and actor Robert Stack and his Mafia-busting agents from *The Untouchables* return to keep a wary eye on all the Italians present.

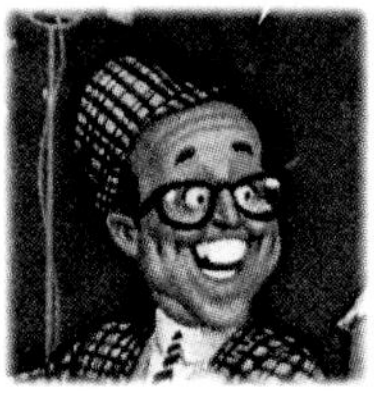

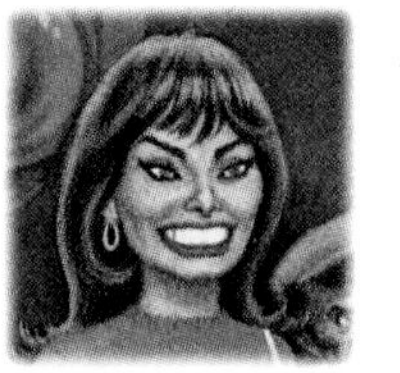

6.) *Pages 29-31.* **"The Unhappy Comic"** (April 1963). Solly books Annie as a "straight man" to **Freddy Flink**, a struggling comedian based on comic actor Fred Gwynne (*Car 54, Where Are You?*). The audience in the opening page is replete with actual stand-up comics. From the top: Shelley Berman utters his trademark line to a stewardess; Mort Sahl talks to Adlai Stevenson, failed presidential candidate cum ambassador; Jonathan Winters (sitting with his female alter ego Maude Frickert) is on the phone with Bob Newhart, whose early shtick was based on phone conversations; black comedian Dick Gregory drinks Jim Crow; Mike Nichols is with Elaine May; and Lenny Bruce hypnotizes a malt. Bruce reappears

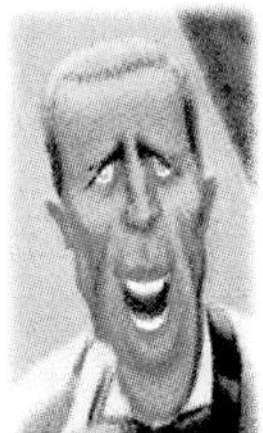

half-naked, handcuffed, and sitting with a *Henry Miller Dictionary*, referring to his profanity and arrests for obscene performances. Freddy's final punchline refers to the recent Cuban Missile Crisis. In a rare example of stealing his own jokes, Kurtzman recycled the identical gag on the front cover of his May 1963 *Help!* magazine.

7.) *Pages 32-33.* **"Kennedy Jokes"** (May 1963). Annie quickly rejoins comedian **Freddie Flink**. This time Kurtzman's satiric sights were on presidential impersonator Vaughn Meader and his debut album, *The First Family*. Cleverly poking fun at Kennedy, his heavy Boston accent, and contemporary politics, the album broke all-time sales records. Within six months Kennedy was assassinated and Meader was a quickly forgotten one-hit wonder. This still-sensitive Annie story was not included in the 1966 Playboy Press compilation. Note Richard Nixon, who was defeated by Kennedy in the 1960 presidential election, waiting tables in the second panel.

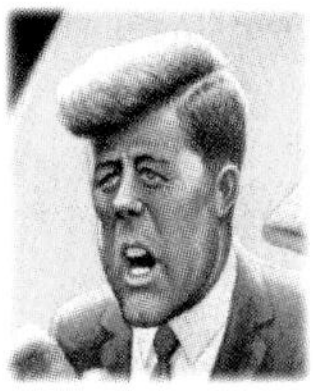

8.) *Pages 34-35.* **"Fifty Mile Hike"** (July 1963). This episode was prompted by President Kennedy's call for Americans to become more physically fit, as the artwork took on a lusher, more defined look.

9.) *Pages 36-39.* **"The Artist"** (September 1963). Annie models for **Duncan Fyfe Hepplewhite**, a starving painter (he eats rooftop pigeons) in the classic style, who's forced to become a counterfeiter to survive. On Hepplewhite's wall in the splash panel is a parody of Rembrandt's *The Anatomy of Dr. Tulp*. Instead of the master's Dutch surgeons we see Vince Edwards, Richard Chamberlain, Richard Boone, Raymond Massey, Sam Jaffee, Lew Ayres, and Lionel Barrymore, last seen in "Playing Doctor" (November 1962). Other fine-art parodies substitute Elizabeth Taylor, Richard Burton, Elvis, and TV cowboys for the original subjects. Making a third appearance is Robert Stack, who's quickly become the strip's all-purpose cop.

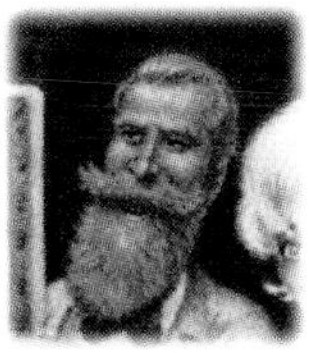

10.) *Pages 40-43.* **"The Talent Contest"** (November 1963). From Kurtzman's preliminary notes: "The whole gag is predicated on [a] girl who believes bedding is talent and is naive enough to believe she'll be tolerated." In the final version, **Wanda Homefree**, Miss Greenwich Village hardly comes off as naive. Mr. Backus, the nearly blind handyman, is based on the nearly blind animated cartoon character Mr. Magoo, whose voice was dubbed by actor Jim Backus (best known as Thurston Howell III on *Gilligan's Island*). Herb Sparks is Bert Parks, the longtime emcee of the Miss America contests. Casey Stengel, manager of the then-hapless New York Mets, makes a fitting scouting appearance as the worst talent is demonstrated.

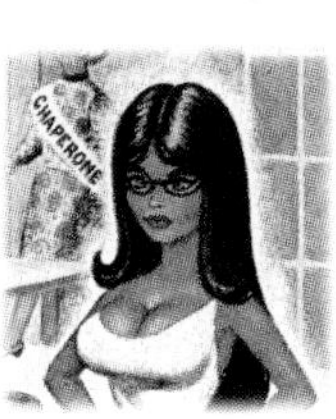
CHAPERONE

11.) *Pages 44-50.* **"Yuletide One-Upmanship"** (December 1963). Benton Battbarton is back with a Christmas office party to rival a Roman orgy. Marcello Mastroianni can be seen once more riding a woman à la *Dolce Vita*. A new recurring character is introduced: **Huck Buxton**, a rival within the advertising agency and a competitor for Annie's affections. Gap-toothed Buxton is modeled on the British comic actor Terry Thomas. At the bottom of the final panel are caricatures of Russ Heath, Elder, Kurtzman, and Hugh Hefner, along with characters from earlier episodes. This is the only time we see the creative team behind the curtains. At seven pages, this is the longest installment of "Little Annie Fanny."

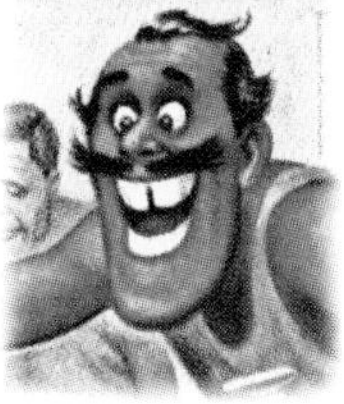

12.) *Pages 51-56.* **"The Set Jets to South America"** (January 1964). The smiling wall photos of **the Kennedys** on the opening page may strike some readers as being in questionable taste given the date of this story. But *Playboy*, like all newsstand magazines, is on sale at least a full month before the printed cover date. This issue was probably at press when Kennedy was killed on November 22, 1963. Bigbucks' South American staff includes German-accented brats **Hans and Fritz** from the classic newspaper strip "The Katzenjammer Kids," and German stereotype director/actor **Erich Von Stroheim** (with monocle). This strip has a distinct look because of illustrator Arnold Roth's considerable contribution.

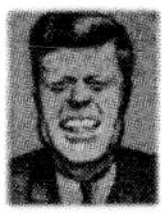

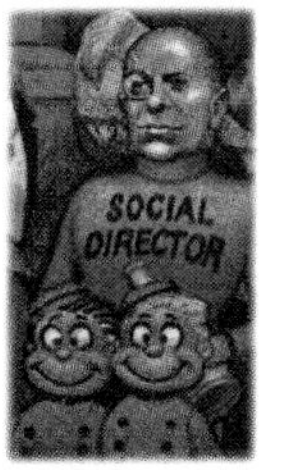
SOCIAL DIRECTOR

13.) *Pages 57-61.* **"Annie Joins the Peace Corps"** (April 1964). This story kicks off the only three-part Annie adventure, which was set in the South Pacific. The boys in the opening panel (and the girl in the second panel) are dead ringers for **Marlon Brando**. The actor starred in the 1962 remake of *Mutiny on the Bounty* as one of a handful of men stranded for years with native women in the South Pacific. After the filming of *Bounty*, Brando bought an island off Tahiti, and the paparazzi made much of his preference for the native women over Hollywood starlets. "Adam Clayton Powell Travel Agency" on the porter's T-shirt refers to the controversial Harlem congressman notorious for taking junkets (and perhaps other things). The two native women in the opening right background are from the Paul Gauguin painting, *Tahiti Women by the Mango Tree*. Chief Boola Goldluau is Arizona **Senator Barry Goldwater**, the leading contender for the Republican presidential nomination. The boy talking to the Brando kid in the first panel of the second page is modeled after Clark Gable, who played Brando's character in the 1935 version of *Bounty*. A detail from Gauguin's *Spirit of the Dead Watching* appears behind Ralphie in the third panel of the second page. The signed photos in the hut on the second page are Hollywood references. Jon Hall and Dorothy Lamour appeared throughout the thirties and forties in various South Seas adventure films. The figure on the prow of the canoe paddled by Goldluau on the last page is Captain Bligh (actor Charles Laughton) from the 1935 *Mutiny on the Bounty*.

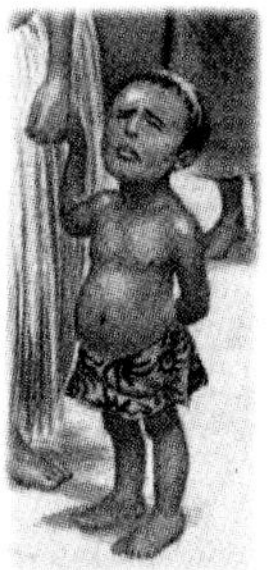

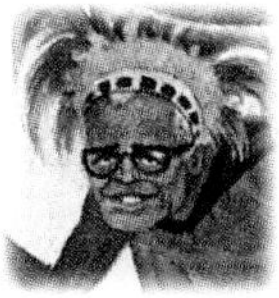

14.) *Pages 62-66.* **"Alone on a Desert Isle"** (July 1964). Part two finds Annie and Ralphie stranded. Ralphie is holding The *Rubaiyat of Omar Khayyam*, whose most famous lines explain the other props:

> Here with a Loaf of Bread beneath the Bough,
> A Flask of Wine, a Book of Verse—and Thou
> Beside me singing in the Wilderness—
> And Wilderness is Paradise enow.

They aren't alone for long. The first boat that lands contains Nelson Rockefeller, then Governor of New York, who'd campaigned for the 1964 Republican presidential nomination; a clearly subordinate and shifty-looking Richard Nixon prior to his political comeback; and Goldwater, still as tribal chief Goldluau. His remark, "I always believe in going back!" refers to Goldwater's ultra-conservative views (i.e., going back in time). Subsequent boats bring **Captain Hook** from Disney's *Peter Pan*, the Hunchback of Notre Dame, and communist leaders Vladimir Lenin and—dancing together—**Nikita Khrushchev and Fidel Castro**. The two kids with poles at the bottom of the second page are from *Lord of the Flies*. Standing to the right is Robinson Crusoe, with Friday underfoot. Many of the disreputable seafarers are drawn by Paul Coker Jr., in a style very distinct from Elder and Heath. The raft of survivors on the third page is based on Theodore Gericault's masterpiece, *The Raft of the Medusa*, one of Elder's favorite paintings, which he parodied again on the cover for *Snarf* No. 10 in 1987. Its timing and the fact that Kurtzman originally titled the story "Convention" underscore the strong political focus of this episode. The Republican National Convention convened in San Francisco in July 1964.

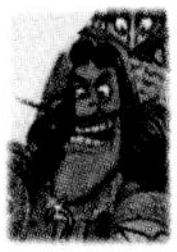

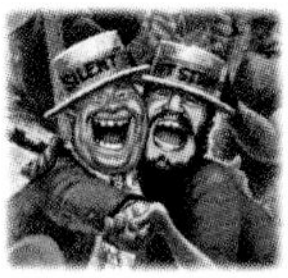

15.) *Pages 67-71.* **"Lost at Sea"** (September 1964). The final South Pacific installment manages to satirically navigate the sensitive waters of America's rising racial tensions. The black man begging to be rescued is, of course, Reverend **Martin Luther King, Jr**. The most prominent sailor denying King passage is Governor George Wallace, the staunch segregationist who personally blocked the University of Alabama entrance to enrolling black students. Black Muslim leader **Malcolm X** helms the large ship that rescues King. To the left is attorney Roy Cohn, whispering in the ear of his cohort, the late redbaiting Senator Joseph McCarthy (both in blackface). Kurtzman had previously parodied Cohn and McCarthy's joined-at-the-hip relationship through the House UnAmerican Activities hearings in issue 17 of Kurtzman's revolutionary *Mad* comic book. To the right, are recently converted Black Muslim boxer **Muhammad Ali**, wearing a crown, and blackfaced Chinese dictator Mao Tse-Tung. At the top of the fourth page Ali holds a telegram from Charles DeGaulle stating, "I recognize you." This is a reference to the French president's independent foreign policy, often in defiance of his American "ally." When the Black Muslims are revealed to be nothing more than Nazis in the final panel, the German "kids" Hans and Fritz (in blackface) make a return appearance. The uniform in the "farm tools" box bears Hitler's initials. Shuffling actor/racial stereotype Stepin Fetchit tries on Hermann Goering's oversize Luftwaffe uniform while Rev. King symbolically leaps overboard to take his chances with the sharks. This is the first episode in which *Mad* artist Al Jaffee lends a hand.

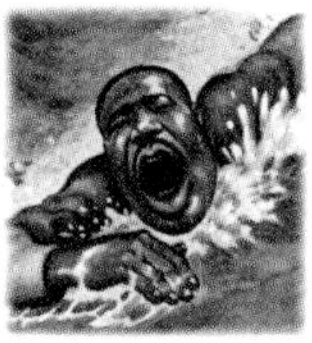

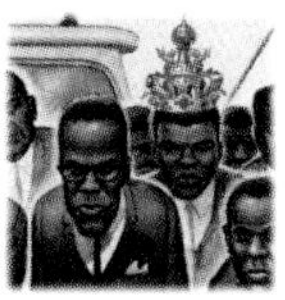

16.) *Pages 72-74.* **"Gun Fun"** (October 1964). Rival ad execs Huck Buxton and Benton Battbarton square off again, this time to see who has the best and biggest gun. The episode works both on the surface and as a Freudian metaphor, and the satire remains fresh and topical nearly four decades later. The hand of Jack Davis is clearly seen assisting Elder and Heath.

17.) *Pages 75-79.* **"Astronaut Annie"** (December 1964). This outer-space political spoof allows Kurtzman to indulge in one of his favorite targets: the comic strip ***Flash Gordon***. From November 1951 to April 1953 Kurtzman wrote and laid out the daily newspaper strip (pencilled by Frank Frazetta and inked by Dan Barry). In 1954 Kurtzman (with Wally Wood) created the brilliant parody "Flesh Garden" in *Mad* No. 11. Flash also served as a running sub-plot in Kurtzman and Elder's "Dragged Net!" in *Mad* No. 3. In 1958 he produced a Russian twist, "Flyashi Gordonovich," with Jack Davis, for his ill-fated *Humbug* magazine. When Kurtzman began speaking at colleges in the early '70s his talk was titled, "Why Flash Gordon Uses His Sword Instead of His Zap Gun." And in 1972 he drew a feminist parody of Flash Gordon for the cover of *Snarf* No. 5. In "Astronaut Annie," Flash himself is absent until the final two panels, where he is depicted as actor Buster Crabbe, who played Flash in the movie serial. However, Flash's nemesis Ming of Mongo (Ming the Merciless) leads a pack of Chinese commie hawk men straight out of an Alex Raymond strip. Astronaut O'Kaye's cap (inside his space-walk air bubble) is from the original outer-space strip, *Buck Rogers*. Back at the Pentagon Defense Secretary Robert McNamara orders the lights shut off while actor **George C. Scott** reprises his role as General "Buck" Turgidson from the just-released *Dr. Strangelove*. Actor Peter Sellers appears in the background in all three of his roles from the same film. Sterling Hayden, who played General Jack D. Ripper, is also visible. The Russian lettering on Bigbucks' banner translates to "Merry Christmas."

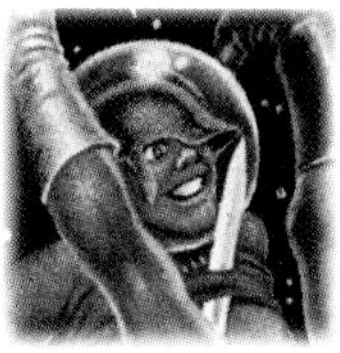

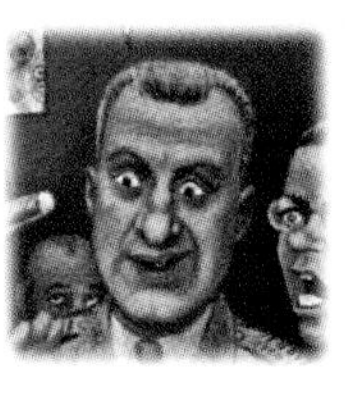

18.) *Pages 80-85.* **"From Annie with Love"** (January 1965). At this early stage of the seemingly never-ending James Bond adventure films, Sean Connery is 007 and the specific film parodied is *From Russia with Love*, with oblique references to *Dr. No* and *Goldfinger*. The fourth (oval) face on Annie's centerfold is body builder Charles Atlas. The lecturing Russian is Andrei Gromyko, then the USSR's foreign minister. The Smersh lantern slide is circa 1930. The bearded fellow ("Ptooie!") is the pre-revolution villain Rasputin. The short female comrade is Rosa Klebb (actress Lotte Lenya in the film). Smersh agent **Ivan Flamyink** (actor Robert Shaw in the film) takes his name from Ian Fleming, the creator of James Bond. Bond's contact, based on Q from the film series, is a caricature of John Foster Dulles, Secretary of State in the Eisenhower administration. The oversized club with the spike going through it is a cartoon convention most closely associated with cave-dwelling Hairless Joe from *Li'l Abner*. With the exception of the key characters' faces—and the full Annie—by Will Elder, virtually all of the characters and backgrounds are painted by Jack Davis, who was capable of working very quickly. Kurtzman was constantly looking for the right combination of talent to meet *Playboy*'s desire for greater frequency.

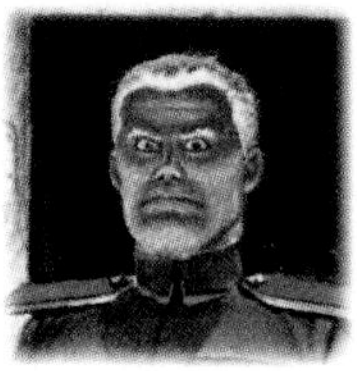

19.) *Pages 86-88.* **"Thunderballing"** (February 1965). The Bond spoof continues, as master of the feminine form Frank Frazetta joins Heath and Elder on the art finishes and the result is a particularly sensuous Annie. In the large battle panel a boat labeled *Tonkingulf* is exploding, sending Asians flying. This is a reference to the incident in Tonkin Gulf that officially ignited the Vietnam War. The "Hi-Octane" **tank with a tiger tail** extending out is based on Humble Oil/Esso (later Exxon) gasoline ads of the day whose tag line was "Put a tiger in *your* tank!" The final panel refers to the long-running White Rock mineral-water ads featuring a nymph overlooking a cliff.

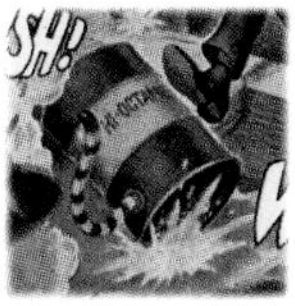

20.) *Pages 89-93.* **"The Topless Suit Case"** (May 1965). Designer Rudi Gernreich's headline-garnering invention of the topless bathing suit inspired this episode, which opens with an unmistakable Frazetta rendering of Annie's lower half. The vast majority of the artwork from the second page on is by Jack Davis. The half-buried campaign poster in the opening panel is the strip's last word on candidate Barry Goldwater, who was buried in a landslide in the November presidential election. Solly's remark about "Lena the Hyena" refers to the ugliest woman in the world, whose face was selected in a widely publicized art contest held in 1946 by cartoonist Al Capp in his *Li'l Abner* strip. (The hideous winning portrait of Lena, drawn by Basil Wolverton, was selected by judges Boris Karloff, Salvador Dali, Frank Sinatra, and Capp.) The second and third cops in the first court panel are, respectively, actors Fred Gwynne (last seen as comedian Freddie Flink in episode 6) and Joe E. Ross, a.k.a. officers Muldoon and Toody on *Car 54, Where Are You?* Dixon Mason is TV's famous defense attorney Perry Mason (actor **Raymond Burr**) who almost never lost a case. The show's trademark was the dramatic last-minute courtroom confession, often by an unlikely suspect, as parodied here. The figure saying "Take my case! Take my case!" in the fourth courtroom panel is Teamster Union President Jimmy Hoffa, a frequent target of federal prosecutors. The law firm of Defender and Defender is based on the popular TV show *The Defenders*, starring **E. G. Marshall** as attorney Lawrence Preston and Robert Reed (later famous as the father on *The Brady Bunch*) as his attorney son Kenneth. The plump atheist Mrs. Gridge is Madalyn Murray (later Madalyn Murray O'Hair) who successfully challenged the constitutionality of prayers in school. The "M Green Stamps" held by destitute Robert Reed are based on S&H Green Stamps given by certain retailers with purchases. Consumers could eventually redeem a full book of S&H stamps in 1965 for two dollars cash. The uniformed Nazi, Mr. Rockhead, is George Lincoln Rockwell, then head of the American Nazi Party, which frequently challenged community efforts to block its members from public demonstrations. Buying a hotdog amidst the lynch mob is Deputy Barney Fife (actor Don Knotts) from *The Andy Griffith Show*. The attorney hired by Sugardaddy Bigbucks to save Annie at the end is real-life hired gun Melvin Belli.

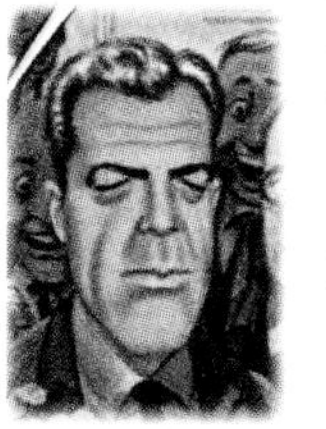

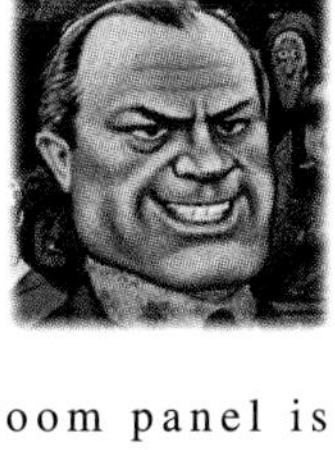

21.) *Page 94-98.* **"The Surfers"** (July 1965). The bathing beauties, including Annie, are again the unmistakable work of Frank Frazetta, while most of the rest of this story is clearly painted by Jack Davis. The Ford woody wagon in the third panel is driven by now-obscure cartoon character Harold Teen (who reappears in the crowd on the second page). The "Star of India" line in panel 4 refers to the celebrated robbery of the famous sapphire by "beach boys" in 1965. The antique calculating device held by Ralphie on the last page is a slide rule.

22.) *Pages 99-103.* **"Seven Days with Mae"** (October 1965). Nuclear threat "doomsday" movies were the subject of this episode, specifically the Hollywood productions *Seven Days in May*, *Dr. Strangelove*, and the made-for-TV *Fail-Safe*. Bursting through the door in the splash panel is actor **Kirk Douglas**—here wearing corporal's stripes—who played Colonel "Jiggs" Casey in *Seven Days in May*. Solly's comment about "19th Century-Fox Studio being torn down to make way for a supermarket" is true. That was the actual fate of the 20th Century-Fox lot. Behind Douglas in panel 2 are actual generals George Marshall, Dwight Eisenhower, and Douglas MacArthur. Producer Joe Laverne is fashioned after novelty songster ("Hello Mudduh, Hello Fadduh") Allan Sherman. **Peter Sellers** plays the President in his *Dr. Strangelove* personae Merkin Muffley (last seen in episode 17). On page three Annie encounters actor Burt Lancaster, who played General James M. Scott in *Seven Days in May*. G.H.Q. is "Pentagon talk" for general headquarters, and "comsymps" is shorthand for communist sympathizers. The *Fail-Safe* pilot Wayne Welch is actor **John Wayne**. Welch is a reference to Robert Welch, founder of the ultra right-wing John Birch Society. Though President Johnson was cut from the cast, his vice president, Hubert Humphrey, remains as a "stand-in" on the fourth page. Federico Moffundzallo (Fellini) returns as the director. Larry Siegel, for the first time, contributes a script, heavily edited by Kurtzman, and is credited. Once again the primary character faces (other than the President) and the full Annie are by Elder, and Jack Davis illustrates the rest.

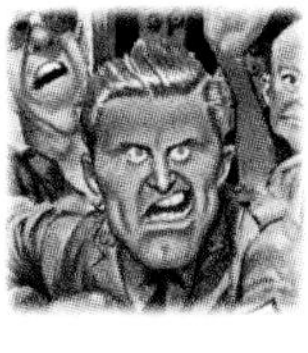

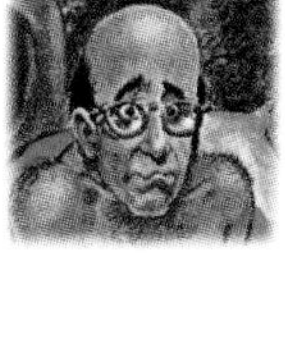

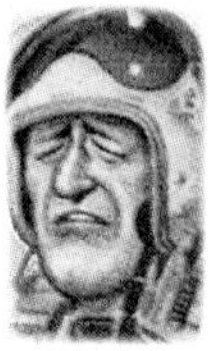

23.) *Pages 104-107.* **"Annie Meets The Bleatles"** (December 1965). Harvey Kurtzman called the group "The Bootles" in his first draft. The wavy pop art featured in the opening panel is a variation on similar canvases by Julian Stanczak, but credited in this story to familiar forger Duncan Hepplewhite. Producer Joe Levine from the previous Hollywood parody returns for an opening line cameo. Sugardaddy Bigbucks' complaint about the U.S. post office deliberately printing millions of misprinted stamps to dilute the value of an accidental imperfection that reached the market is what actually happened with the 1965 Dag Hammarskjold commemorative stamp. Though The Beatles were a huge international hit by 1965, the forty-one-year-old Kurtzman could not tell them apart. On the second page Paul is introduced as John, George is introduced as Paul, and John is introduced as George. Only the more unusual-looking Ringo is correctly identified. One might assume the error was a deliberate attempt at humor, especially since the Beatles' names do match the faces on the personalized boxer shorts seen on the third page. Not only would such humor appear pointless, but Annie's failure to acknowledge the wrong introductions is inconsistent with her fan role. Kurtzman's straightforward preliminary instructions to Elder include incorrect identifications and his tight pencil roughs repeat the same errors. In a November 30, 1965 letter to Kurtzman, several weeks after publication of "The Bleatles," Hefner noted, "By the way, Harv, one of our British bunnies currently in training here at the Chicago [Playboy] Club, informs me that, while she thoroughly enjoyed our Beatle satire in the December issue, when the four boys are introduced at the beginning of the adventure, the only one that we've got correctly named is Ringo. Sounds like your usually expert research fell through." How such flagrant errors got by Kurtzman and Hefner—both legendary perfectionists—and *Playboy's* proofreaders is nothing short of remarkable. One also wonders why the errors were not corrected in Playboy Press' large *Little Annie Fanny* book collection in 1966. In addition, the caricatures of the Beatles in this episode are not nearly as dead-on as we have come to expect from Elder, suggesting a lack of inspiration.

Interestingly, Kurtzman and Elder took another—and far better—satirical whack at the Beatles following the enormous success of *Sgt. Pepper's Lonely Hearts Club Band*, and the band members' dramatic hippie transformation. In August 1967 the Beatles met Maharishi Mahesh Yogi and came under his influence. By February 1968 all four Beatles (with their wives and girlfriends) traveled to India, joining devotee actress Mia Farrow, to study Transcendental Meditation with their charismatic guru (who took one-quarter of his disciples' earnings monthly). The rock icons' spiritual odyssey received worldwide publicity. During this period Kurtzman, Elder, and Davis were hard at work on a story wherein our buxom heroine meditates with "The Bleatles" and "life-long celibate" Maharishi Berayogi (a play on New York Yankee catcher Yogi Berra). Not surprisingly, the Bleatles in the plot lust for Annie, the guru breaks his vow of celibacy, and Robert Stack returns in an irresistible India pun on *The Untouchables*. In the unfinished four pages which survive, presented in this volume on pages 215 through 218, we see superb Elder caricatures of the Beatles, as well as Annie at her finest. Unfortunately, the story was aborted. By April 1968, following the guru's alleged attempted seduction of Mia Farrow, the last of the Beatles had deserted the Maharishi. The premise of the Annie story was dead. It dramatically demonstrates the danger inherent in wedding a labor-intensive art form to the demand for topical humor. Nonetheless, the frozen-in-time unfinished pages give us a unique opportunity to see how "Little Annie Fanny" pages are constructed. Working from Kurtzman's precise layouts, Jack Davis (in this instance) pencilled the full story. Elder, with Kurtzman's color guides, painted the complete Annie on every page, along with Bigbucks, Stack, about half of the Beatles' appearances, and the full backgrounds on seven panels. Davis, according to Kurtzman's notes, was to have illustrated most of the remaining space when the team suddenly abandoned the no longer topical adventure. The masking tape is intended to peel away to reveal white panel gutters which would be carefully retouched to create the distinctive fuzzy panel edges, with hand-lettering by Bob Price as the final step.

24.) *Pages 108-113.* **"Battbarton's Holiday Spirit"** (January 1966). Kurtzman originally wrote and laid out this story for the December 1964 issue but it was bumped to run the more topical two-part James Bond parody, with Annie's New Year's Eve resolution an integral part. Again Elder focuses on principal characters' faces and the full Annie while Davis does all the other characters and backgrounds.

25.) *Pages 114-116.* **"On the Brooklyn B.M.T."** (March 1966). This brief story, written in December 1964, was Kurtzman's reaction to the moral questions raised by the notorious murder of twenty-eight-year-old Kitty Genovese in Queens, NY. Numerous witnesses in the high-density neighborhood saw Ms. Genovese or heard her screams as she was repeatedly stabbed, but not one lifted a finger to intervene or to call the police. Kurtzman—like most New Yorkers and Americans—was appalled by the new urban attitude of not wanting to get involved. The "Beautify America" billboard refers to first lady **Ladybird Johnson**'s personal crusade to rid America of "ugly billboards." The irony here is that both Ladybird and husband Lyndon were regarded as, er, rather unattractive.

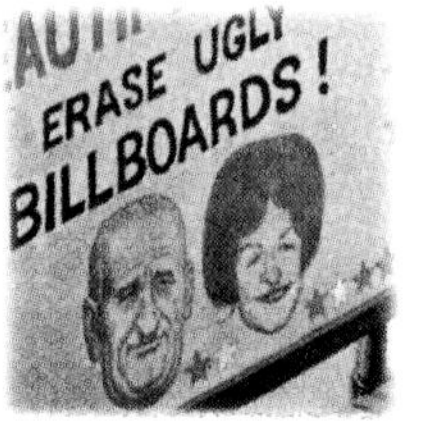
ERASE UGLY BILLBOARDS!

26.) *Pages 117-121.* **"Annie in TV Wasteland"** (May 1966). Writer Salinger Fiengold is, of course, patterned after reclusive author **J. D. Salinger** (*Catcher in the Rye*). Solly takes Fiengold to meet "Aubrey Aubrey, Programming President of ABS-TV," based on James Aubrey, programming chief of CBS-TV. Aubrey axed *Playhouse 90*, the Tiffany Network's most prestigious program, and instead stressed sitcoms, many of them mindless. Aubrey is drawn as the acerbic arch-conservative editor and columnist (and later host of TV's *Firing Line*) William F. Buckley. His "Abe Lunkhead" concept is a reference to the popular TV monster shows *The Addams Family* and *The Munsters*. "Abe's Gang" and the Civil War death-camp Andersonville are sarcastic references to the popular *Hogan's Heroes*, which concocted humor from a Nazi P.O.W. camp. "The Man from L.U.N.K.L.E" is a play on *The Man from U.N.C.L.E.*, a Bond-inspired spy drama. The villains marked "SNICC," surrounded by "SNIK" sound effects, refer to SNCC (commonly pronounced "SNIK"), which stood for the Student Non-Violent Coordinating Committee, a radical civil-rights and anti-war organization headed by firebrand Stokely Charmichael. "Lincolnbaloo" is based on the teen-oriented music show *Hullabaloo* and its rival *Shindig*.

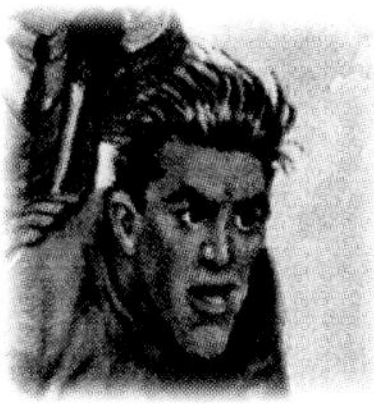

27.) *Pages 122-125.* **"Annie Under the Sheets"** (July 1966). Wanda Homefree, the talent contestant from episode 10, returns in her first co-starring role as she and Annie land in the middle of a Ku Klux Klan rally. The longhaired fellow holding the spiked club (see episode 18) is hillbilly Hairless Joe from *Li'l Abner*. The Exalted Newt who is exposed as an embezzler is **Robert Shelton**, then the Grand Imperial Wizard of the KKK. The image of the Imperial Lizard as a Jew in Nazi dress may now seem inexplicable, or in very poor taste, but it is a specific reference to the publicized exposure of Dan Burros, a self-loathing Jew and member of the inner circle of George Lincoln Rockwell's American Nazi Party. Burros killed himself the day after he was outed by the *New York Times* in 1964.

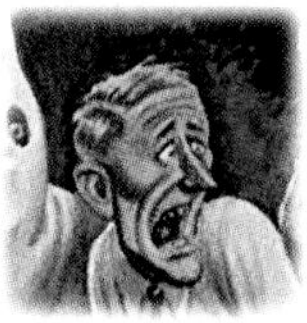

28.) *Pages 126-130.* **"Euphoria-in-the-Pines Resort"** (September 1966). The scene opens with one of only two double-page spreads of all the Annie stories. In this panoramic scene of sight gags we see a few familiar faces: Katzenjammer brats Hans and Fritz are back, putting lobsters, frogs, an octopus, and dry ice in the pool; Wanda Homefree tans her

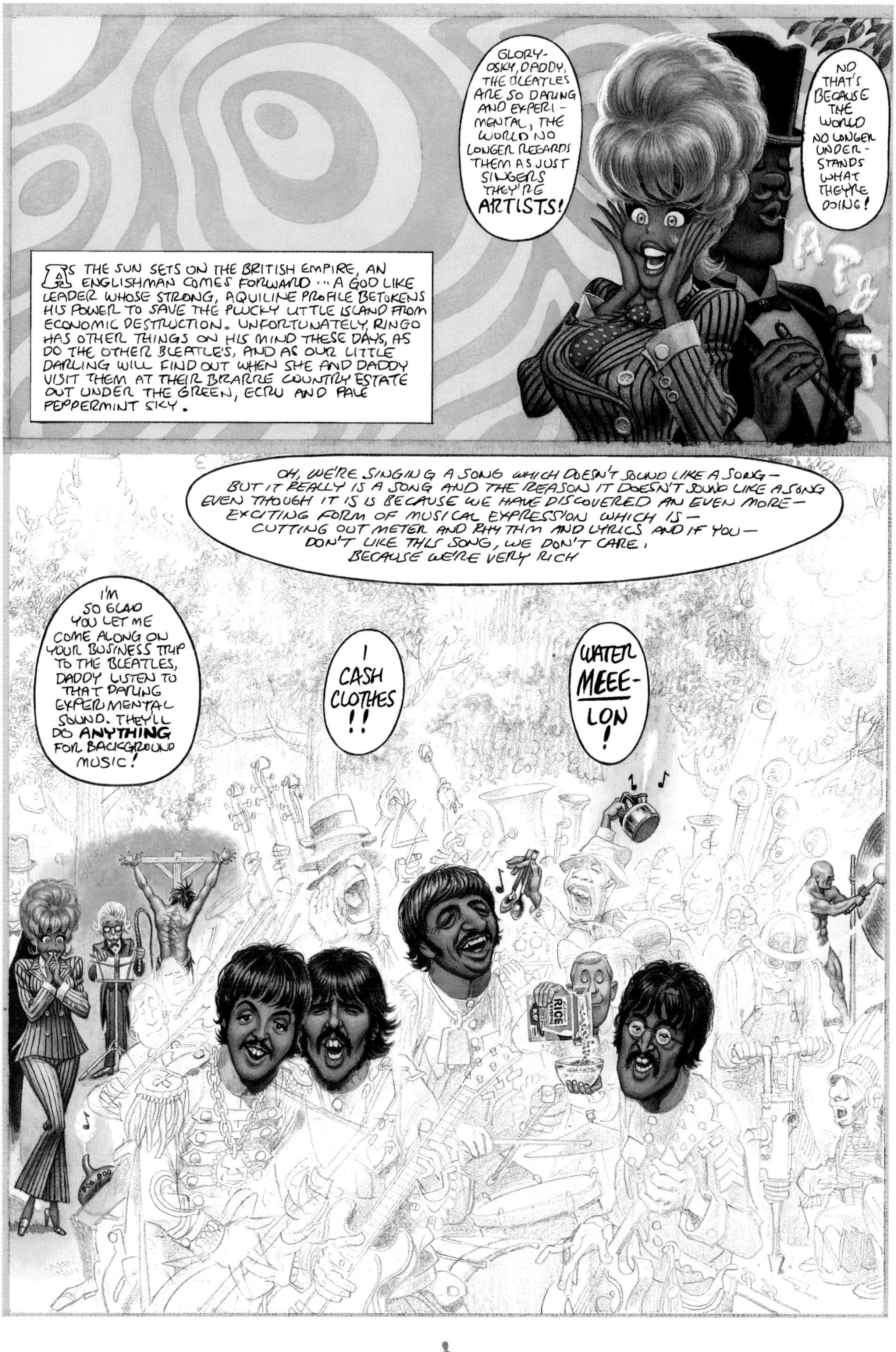

AS THE SUN SETS ON THE BRITISH EMPIRE, AN ENGLISHMAN COMES FORWARD ... A GOD LIKE LEADER WHOSE STRONG, AQUILINE PROFILE BETOKENS HIS POWER TO SAVE THE PLUCKY LITTLE ISLAND FROM ECONOMIC DESTRUCTION. UNFORTUNATELY, RINGO HAS OTHER THINGS ON HIS MIND THESE DAYS, AS DO THE OTHER BLEATLE'S, AND AS OUR LITTLE DARLING WILL FIND OUT WHEN SHE AND DADDY VISIT THEM AT THEIR BIZARRE COUNTRY ESTATE OUT UNDER THE GREEN, ECRU AND PALE PEPPERMINT SKY.
GLORY-OSKY, DADDY, THE BLEATLES ARE SO DARING AND EXPERI-MENTAL, THE WORLD NO LONGER REGARDS THEM AS JUST SINGERS THEY'RE ARTISTS!
NO THAT'S BECAUSE THE WORLD NO LONGER UNDER-STANDS WHAT THEY'RE DOING!
OH, WE'RE SINGING A SONG WHICH DOESN'T SOUND LIKE A SONG— BUT IT REALLY IS A SONG AND THE REASON IT DOESN'T SOUND LIKE A SONG EVEN THOUGH IT IS IS BECAUSE WE HAVE DISCOVERED AN EVEN MORE— EXCITING FORM OF MUSICAL EXPRESSION WHICH IS— CUTTING OUT METER AND RHYTHM AND LYRICS AND IF YOU— DON'T LIKE THIS SONG, WE DON'T CARE, BECAUSE WE'RE VERY RICH
I'M SO GLAD YOU LET ME COME ALONG ON YOUR BUSINESS TRIP TO THE BLEATLES, DADDY LISTEN TO THAT DARLING EXPERIMENTAL SOUND. THEY'LL DO ANYTHING FOR BACKGROUND MUSIC!
I CASH CLOTHES!!
WATER MEEE-LON!
RICE

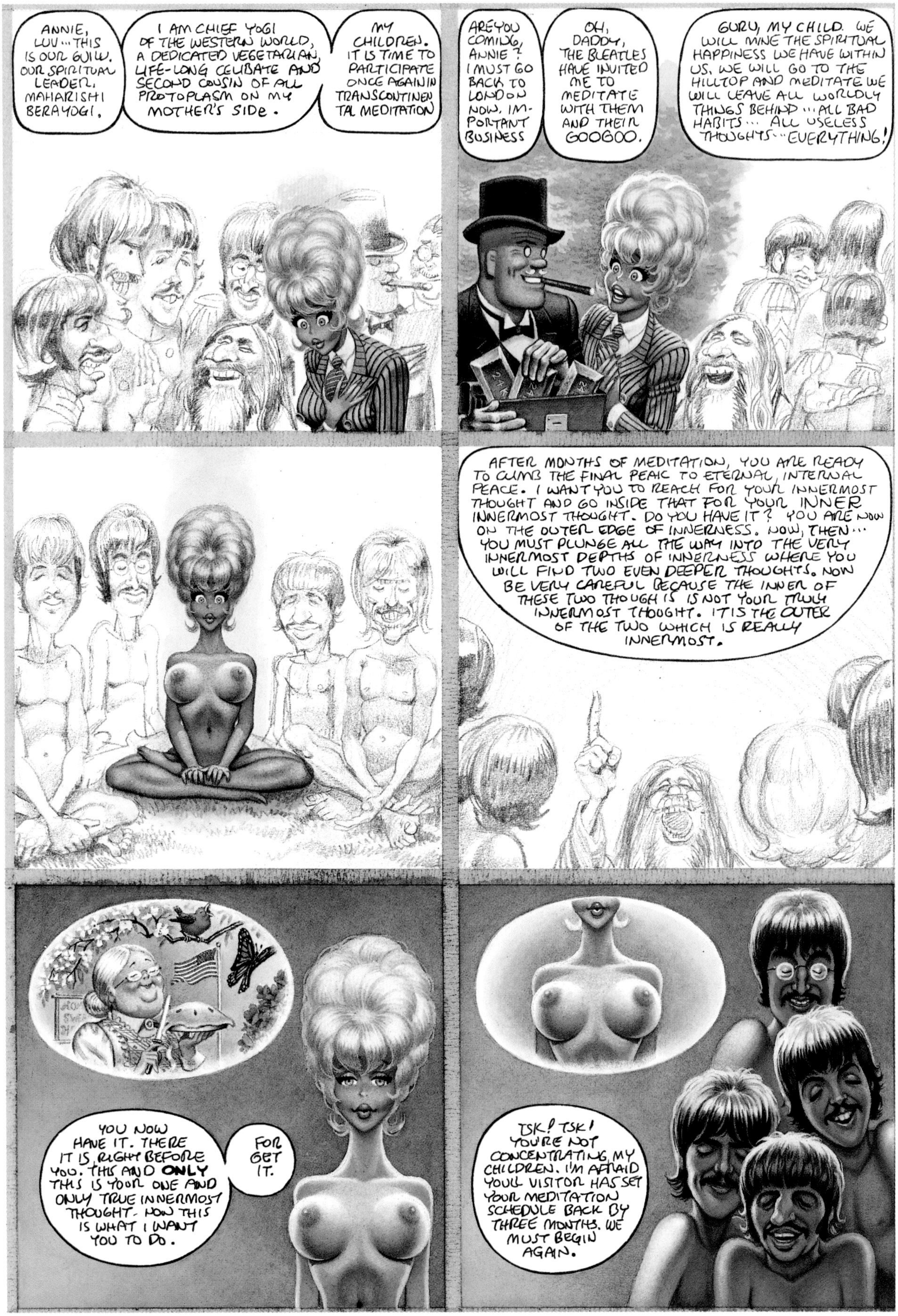

ANNIE, LUV... THIS IS OUR GUIW. OUR SPIRITUAL LEADER. MAHARISHI BERAYOGI.
I AM CHIEF YOGI OF THE WESTERN WORLD, A DEDICATED VEGETARIAN, LIFE-LONG CELIBATE AND SECOND COUSIN OF ALL PROTOPLASM ON MY MOTHER'S SIDE.
MY CHILDREN. IT IS TIME TO PARTICIPATE ONCE AGAIN IN TRANSCONTINENTAL MEDITATION
ARE YOU COMING, ANNIE? I MUST GO BACK TO LONDON NOW. IMPORTANT BUSINESS
OH, DADDY, THE BLEATLES HAVE INVITED ME TO MEDITATE WITH THEM AND THEIR GOOGOO.
GURU, MY CHILD. WE WILL MINE THE SPIRITUAL HAPPINESS WE HAVE WITHIN US. WE WILL GO TO THE HILLTOP AND MEDITATE WE WILL LEAVE ALL WORLDLY THINGS BEHIND... ALL BAD HABITS... ALL USELESS THOUGHTS... EVERYTHING!
AFTER MONTHS OF MEDITATION, YOU ARE READY TO CLIMB THE FINAL PEAK TO ETERNAL, INTERNAL PEACE. I WANT YOU TO REACH FOR YOUR INNERMOST THOUGHT AND GO INSIDE THAT FOR YOUR INNER INNERMOST THOUGHT. DO YOU HAVE IT? YOU ARE NOW ON THE OUTER EDGE OF INNERNESS. NOW, THEN... YOU MUST PLUNGE ALL THE WAY INTO THE VERY INNERMOST DEPTHS OF INNERNESS WHERE YOU WILL FIND TWO EVEN DEEPER THOUGHTS. NOW BE VERY CAREFUL BECAUSE THE INNER OF THESE TWO THOUGHTS IS NOT YOUR TRULY INNERMOST THOUGHT. IT IS THE OUTER OF THE TWO WHICH IS REALLY INNERMOST.
YOU NOW HAVE IT. THERE IT IS, RIGHT BEFORE YOU. THIS AND ONLY THIS IS YOUR ONE AND ONLY TRUE INNERMOST THOUGHT. NOW THIS IS WHAT I WANT YOU TO DO.
FOR GET IT.
TSK! TSK! YOU'RE NOT CONCENTRATING, MY CHILDREN. I'M AFRAID YOUR VISITOR HAS SET YOUR MEDITATION SCHEDULE BACK BY THREE MONTHS. WE MUST BEGIN AGAIN.

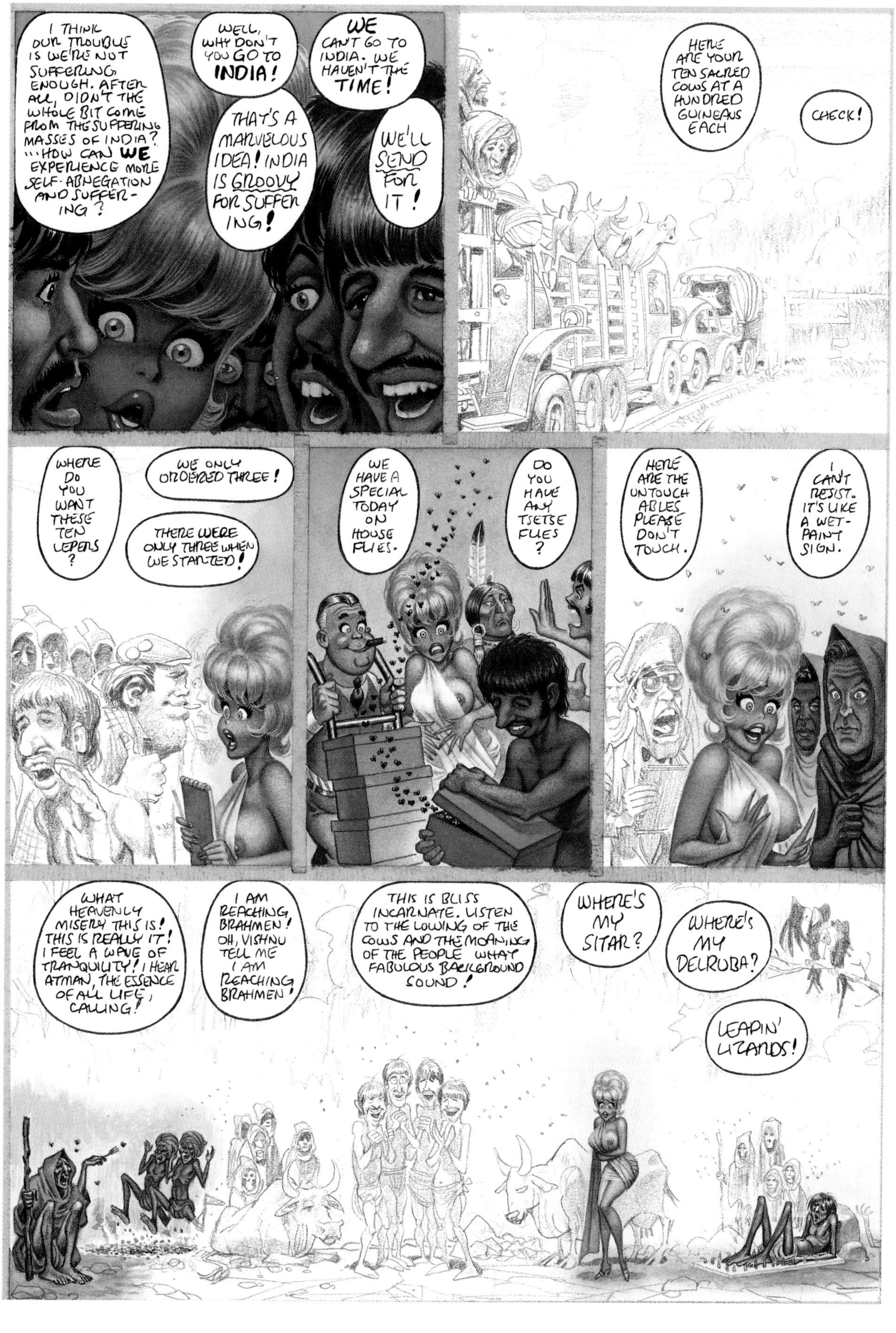
I THINK OUR TROUBLE IS WE'RE NOT SUFFERING ENOUGH. AFTER ALL, DIDN'T THE WHOLE BIT COME FROM THE SUFFERING MASSES OF INDIA? ...HOW CAN WE EXPERIENCE MORE SELF-ABNEGATION AND SUFFER-ING?
WELL, WHY DON'T YOU GO TO INDIA!
WE CAN'T GO TO INDIA. WE HAVEN'T THE TIME!
THAT'S A MARVELOUS IDEA! INDIA IS GROOVY FOR SUFFER ING!
WE'LL SEND FOR IT!
HERE ARE YOUR TEN SACRED COWS AT A HUNDRED GUINEAUS EACH
CHECK!
WHERE DO YOU WANT THESE TEN LEPERS?
WE ONLY ORDERED THREE!
THERE WERE ONLY THREE WHEN WE STARTED!
WE HAVE A SPECIAL TODAY ON HOUSE FLIES.
DO YOU HAVE ANY TSETSE FLIES?
HERE ARE THE UNTOUCH ABLES PLEASE DON'T TOUCH.
I CAN'T RESIST. IT'S LIKE A WET-PAINT SIGN.
WHAT HEAVENLY MISERY THIS IS! THIS IS REALLY IT! I FEEL A WAVE OF TRANQUILITY! I HEAR ATMAN, THE ESSENCE OF ALL LIFE, CALLING!
I AM REACHING BRAHMEN! OH, VISHNU TELL ME I AM REACHING BRAHMEN!
THIS IS BLISS INCARNATE. LISTEN TO THE LOWING OF THE COWS AND THE MOANING OF THE PEOPLE WHAT FABULOUS BACKGROUND SOUND!
WHERE'S MY SITAR?
WHERE'S MY DELRUBA?
LEAPIN' LIZARDS!

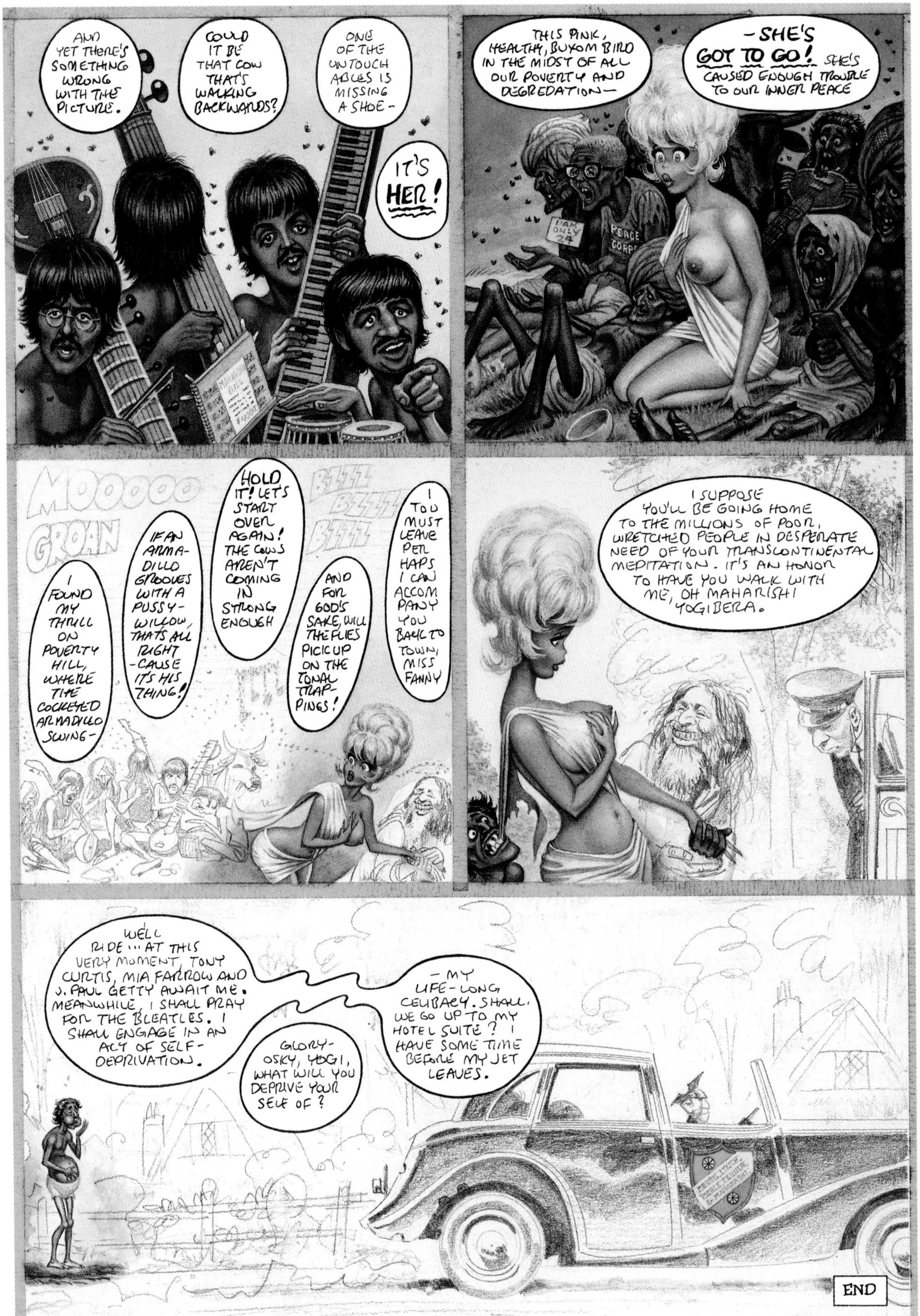
AND YET THERE'S SOMETHING WRONG WITH THE PICTURE.
COULD IT BE THAT COW THAT'S WALKING BACKWARDS?
ONE OF THE UNTOUCH ABLES IS MISSING A SHOE-
IT'S HER!
THIS PINK, HEALTHY, BUXOM BIRD IN THE MIDST OF ALL OUR POVERTY AND DEGREDATION—
-SHE'S GOT TO GO! SHE'S CAUSED ENOUGH TROUBLE TO OUR INNER PEACE
MOOOOO
GROAN
BZZZ
BZZZ
BZZZ
I FOUND MY THRILL ON POVERTY HILL, WHERE THE COCKEYED ARMADILLO SWING-
IF AN ARMA-DILLO GROOVES WITH A PUSSY-WILLOW, THAT'S ALL RIGHT -CAUSE IT'S HIS THING!
HOLD IT! LET'S START OVER AGAIN! THE COWS AREN'T COMING IN STRONG ENOUGH
AND FOR GOD'S SAKE, WILL THE FLIES PICK UP ON THE TONAL TRAP-PINGS!
I TOO MUST LEAVE PER HAPS I CAN ACCOM PANY YOU BACK TO TOWN, MISS FANNY
I SUPPOSE YOU'LL BE GOING HOME TO THE MILLIONS OF POOR, WRETCHED PEOPLE IN DESPERATE NEED OF YOUR TRANSCONTINENTAL MEDITATION. IT'S AN HONOR TO HAVE YOU WALK WITH ME, OH MAHARISHI YOGIBERA.
WELL RIDE... AT THIS VERY MOMENT, TONY CURTIS, MIA FARROW AND J. PAUL GETTY AWAIT ME. MEANWHILE, I SHALL PRAY FOR THE BLEATLES. I SHALL ENGAGE IN AN ACT OF SELF-DEPRIVATION.
GLORY-OSKY, YOGI, WHAT WILL YOU DEPRIVE YOUR SELF OF?
—MY LIFE-LONG CELIBACY. SHALL WE GO UP TO MY HOTEL SUITE? I HAVE SOME TIME BEFORE MY JET LEAVES.
END

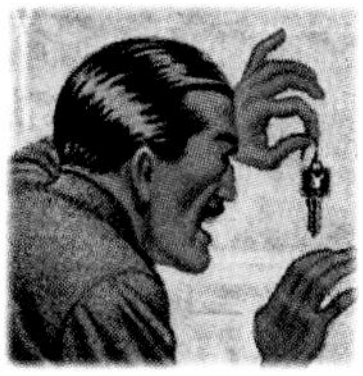

breasts; and Salinger Fiengold runs the theater group. Patients in the therapy group include Vincent Van Gogh (with bandage over ear), a vampiric Batman (accused in *Seduction of the Innocent* of pederasty), and Captain Kangaroo, also once accused. Dr. Manduck, who takes Annie onto a rowboat, is based on the cartoon character **Mandrake the Magician**. Watching from shore is outdoorsman Mark Trail, another daily comic-strip character. The key Manduck uses to hypnotize Annie is a Playboy Club key. The resort on the other side of the lake is populated by surgeons including Rex Morgan, M.D. and some we've seen before: Ben Casey, the two Dr. Gillespies, and Dr. Kildare.

29.) *Pages 131-134.* **"Hoopadedoo Show"** (October 1966). Annie is a dancer on the Hoopadedoo Show (*Hullabaloo*) which showcases contemporary musical talent. Elvis, **Dylan**, and Little Anthony are all parodied, and Sonny and Wanda,

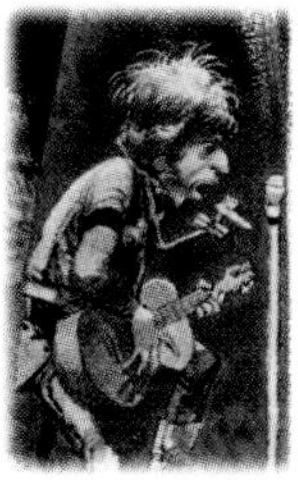

though not caricatures, are clearly inspired by Sonny and Cher. William F. Buckley returns as CBS head James Aubrey, who rejects Solly's self-immolating protest group. Self-immolation by Buddhist monks and nuns in Vietnam (as well as the occasional American) was the ultimate anti-war "protest" at this time. "The Cleans" poster depicts the bald Mr. Clean trademark in triplicate. The "Coming" poster to the right pictures Kickapoo Joy Juice bootleggers Hairless Joe and Lonesome Polecat from *Li'l Abner*.

30.) *Pages 135-138.* **"Greenback Busters"** (December 1966). The Greenback Busters are of course the reigning NFL champion Green Bay Packers. Annie's comment about "our star quarterback" is a pun on the Packers' actual quarterback Bart Starr. Paul Horny is halfback Paul Hornung, renowned for his after-hours adventures. "Johnny Uneeda of Baltimore" is Johnny Unitas, quarterback of the then Baltimore Colts. Bigbucks' plan to sell the Busters to "complete strangers" in Boise is mere plot device, but Wisconsin's other beloved franchise, the Milwaukee Braves, was moved in 1966 to Atlanta in an equally cynical bottom-line maneuver.

31.) *Pages 139-142.* **"High Camp"** (January 1967). Pop-culture references abound as Benton Battbarton shows Annie

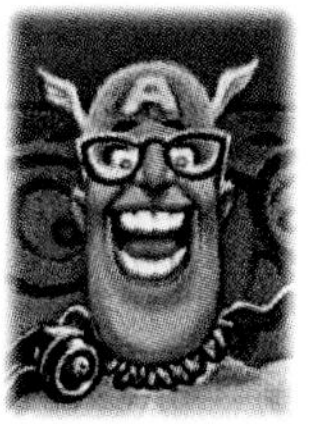

his collection of nostalgic "camp" items. A large Phantom pop-art poster by Ray Moore adorns Benton's wall along with the Roy Lichtenstein silk-screens *Pistol* and *Sweet Dreams, Baby!* An oversize Andy Warhol soup can is on the floor next to a Popeye *Thimble Theatre* throw rug. Beneath his '30s radio and aviator cap is a row of Big Little Books, including *Buck Rogers*, *Li'l Abner*, *Terry and the Pirates*, and *Alley Oop*. A blowup of Krazy Kat, Offisa Pup, and Ignatz hangs above the sofa. The ribbon-like objects on the left of this panel are once-popular hard candies glued to paper. RCA Victor's trademark dog listens for "his master's voice" next to a turntable while Battbarton reads a vintage *Human Torch* comic. In the next panel Benton inexplicably reads of Superman's girlfriend Lois Lane from a *Batman* comic. Annie's "*Marvel*-ous!" and Benton's "*Mar*-velous fantasy!" remarks refer to the popular Marvel Comics revival of the day. The pennants are from obsolete baseball teams: the Philadelphia Athletics became the Kansas City A's in 1955, then moved again to Oakland in 1967. The St. Louis Browns became the Baltimore Orioles in 1954. In the background of the same panel is the smiling face that graced the entrance to the Coney Island amusement park, and we see James Montgomery Flagg's World War I recruiting poster with

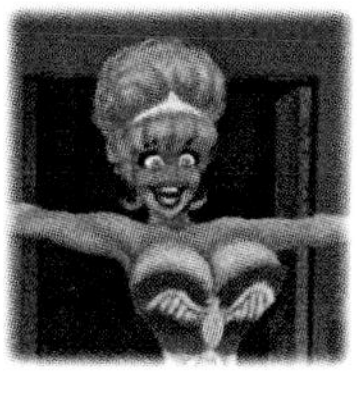

Uncle Sam. The Major America and Wondrous Woman costumes are of course based on **Captain America** and **Wonder Woman**. Battbarton changes in a phone booth à la Clark Kent.

32.) *Pages 143-147.* **"Las Vegas Kidnapping"** (May 1967). Kurtzman and Siegel's satiric arrow

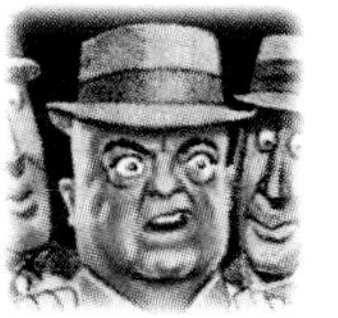

is aimed at the Federal Bureau of Investigation's emphasis on agents' appearance and moral fitness, as well as Nevada's then-unique climate of legalized gambling and prostitution. Addressing the straight-laced agents is long-standing FBI director **J. Edgar Hoover**, who prided himself and his agency on being paragons of virtue. Hoover's briefcase overflows with "Crimestoppers," a sidebar crime-solving feature of the *Dick Tracy* comic strip. Agent Squarechin is based on comedian Dick Van Dyke. Las Vegas mainstay **Frank Sinatra** performs, with pals Dean Martin and Sammy Davis Jr. watching. The threesome (with Peter Lawford and Joey Bishop) formed the core of the hipper-than-hip Rat Pack. Martin's notorious consumption of alcohol fuels his drinking-

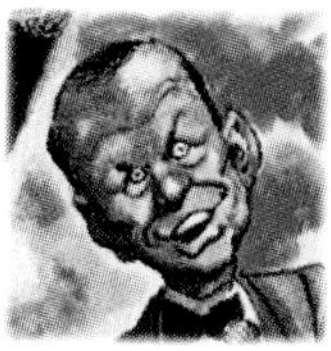

joke comment. Davis' Jewish joke comment stems from his conversion to Judaism. To the left is Sinatra's third wife, actress Mia Farrow. To the right is a poster for evangelist Billy Graham, an improbable visitor to immoral Las Vegas. The old timer at the bar who lost track of time was at the casino since the Chicago World's Fair in 1933, or possibly 1893. Kurtzman originally planned Dr. Neutrino to look like heavy-browed physicist Edward Teller, but Hefner thought it would be more amusing to make the doctor "a rather effeminate fellow... an apple-cheeked Truman Capote type." The kidnappers are Cuban. Though not caricatures, Raul is Fidel Castro's brother and Che is Che Guevara. Actor Efrem Zimbalist Jr. played Inspector Lew Erskine on TV's *The F.B.I.* Lamont Cranston was the alter ego of The Shadow. Hoover's lectures about moral cleanliness and the obscenity of a naked woman were humorous only for their seeming exaggeration in 1967. They since take on a new dimension with the revelation that Hoover, hypocritically, was a longtime closet queen, and his inseparable FBI lieutenant, Clyde Tolson, was his presumed lover.

33.) *Pages 148-150.* **"Americans in Paris"** (August 1967). Benton Battbarton is cast, uncharacteristically, as a prudish American tourist in Paris, a role that would seem tailor made for another of Annie's boyfriends, reserved intellectual Ralphie Towzer. In an otherwise lightweight plot, Larry Siegel's final "gag," involving an unprovoked attack on two women, presumably evoked giggles in the freewheeling late '60s, but appears offensive in today's more sensitive climate of gender relations. However, the pure aesthetics here reach new heights thanks to the unadulterated

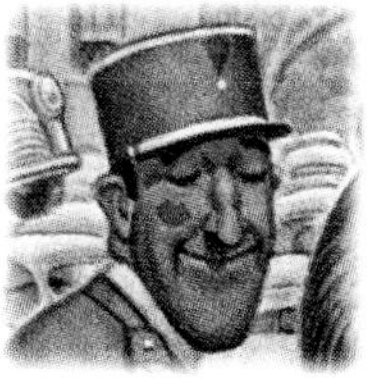

hand of Will Elder. Collaborating artists on "Little Annie Fanny" signed the final pages on episodes 8 through 16, though none received first panel credits—a sensitive issue—until episode 17. Payment records indicate that Russ Heath and Warren Sattler, though uncredited, assisted on episodes 2 through 7. Thus, though he has always been the principle artist, "Americans in Paris" is, remarkably, Will Elder's first solo effort since the debut. And, in the vernacular of this episode, it is a tour de force. Elder demonstrates his consummate skill, showing incredible growth as a color illustrator since the relatively primitive first "Annie" five years earlier. To take nothing whatever away from Heath and Jack Davis (geniuses in their own right), it's a joy to see Elder's primary characters blend seamlessly with his own backgrounds and secondary characters into one cohesive and delectable whole.

34.) Pages 151-154. **"The Ultimate Kick"** (September 1967). It was inevitable, on the heels of San Francisco's celebrated "Summer of Love" in 1967, that Kurtzman would tackle LSD, free love, and other hedonistic elements of the hippie phenomenon. This is the first of several episodes inspired by the '60s subculture. The University of Bookless, California is based on the University of California's Berkeley campus, an epicenter of radical student activity. Indian nuts (nutmeg) and morning glory seeds, cited by Ralphie, are natural hallucinogens sometimes used as alternative trips, or when pure LSD is not available or affordable (both, however, have unpleasant side effects). Professor Timothy Clearly is, of course, the onetime Harvard researcher **Timothy Leary**, the high priest of LSD, who popularized use of the controversial

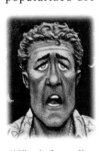

drug and encouraged adherents to "turn on, tune in, and drop out." "Chain-in" is an invented term in this strip, but campus protesters did often chain themselves together during sit-ins to make it more difficult for police to disperse them. It was also more newsworthy. The cartoon swearing symbols emanating from the window of a "curse-in" (another invented term) is a reference to the "free-speech movement" spearheaded by student Mario Savio on the Berkeley campus in 1964. In the window are actors Richard Burton and Elizabeth

Taylor, reflecting their recent expletive-filled roles in Who's Afraid of Virginia Woolf? The license plate on Ralphie's car, SNCC, stands for the Student Non-Violent Coordinating Committee.

35.) Pages 155-159. **"Booby Doll"** (December 1967). James Bomb returns as a showroom guard for the Dinkywinky Toy Co. (there was a Dinky Toy Co.). One of the Raggedy Ann and Andy dolls in the background is based on beat poet Allen Ginsberg. Also in that first panel, Bomb refers to the onrush of Bond clones,

including Napoleon Solo in The Man from U.N.C.L.E., Dean Martin's spoof character Matt Helm, James Coburn's films Our Man Flint and In Like Flint, and even comic-strip heroine Modesty Blaise. Toy tycoon J. P. Dinkywinky is modeled after veteran actor **Walter Pidgeon**. The toys in the background of the large splash are torn from headlines of the day: wiretapping was a controversial tool of the FBI; the "Li'l Communist Punching Bag" has the face of China head Mao Tse-tung; the counterfeiting kit labeled "War on Poverty" comes from one of President Lyndon Johnson's most celebrated social programs; and Zip Guns are primitive (but functional) handmade pistols associated with '50s juvenile delinquents. The small Annie look-alike "Booby Doll" is based on Mattel's franchise Barbie doll.

Barbie, for most of her prosperous career, has had a very ample bosom. Her traditional hourglass figure has more recently been altered to resemble

that of an actual female. This story wasn't Kurtzman's first satirical look at the shapely doll. In the May 1965 issue of Help! he ran "Christopher's Punctured Romance," a long fumetti ("photo funny") about a man (portrayed by pre-Monty Python John Cleese) obsessed with his daughter's Barbie. Other sight gags: When industrial spy **Israel Bomb** leaps out a window, the skyscraper being built in the background is constructed of then-popular Tinkertoys. The "Twiggy" doll is named for the exceptionally thin British actress. Lyndon Johnson's face appears in the crowd on the fourth page wearing a "Real Mask Toys" button. Dinkywinky's chief rival, Mendel, is modeled after actor Lee J. Cobb. Like episode 33, this story is rendered solely and exquisitely by Will Elder.

36.) Pages 160-163. **"The Master-Testers Institute"** (January 1968). Kurtzman and crew can't resist a few more pokes at the burgeoning hippie subculture. Annie finds her new roommate Wanda Homefree in bed with Neanderthal-like **Grok** (from Robert Heinlein's Strangers in a Strange Land) the Guru. Grok sucks on the hose of a hookah—pictured in panel 2—a water pipe used to smoke pot or hashish.

The spray can of Oxygen is an apparent reference to the perpetually smoke-filled room, while the Ken-L Ration (dog food) Burger on the wood-burning stove implies a poverty level. Wanda

and Annie's East Village pad is decorated with psychedelic posters, including beat poet Allen Ginsberg as Uncle Sam, and various references to "Be-Ins," the more pacifist hippie version of sit-ins. A poster of LSD guru Timothy Leary hangs above the bed on the second page. The rock group "The Fuggy Electric Mothers" is derived from three separate music groups of the day: The Fugs, The Electric Prunes, and Mothers of Invention. Military uniforms, displayed here in a shop window, were an ironic fashion statement in the anti-war environment. A closed barber shop refers to hippies' lengthy and sometimes unruly hair, and the "Crazy Button Shop" reflects the prevalence of "message" buttons (the bottom one unconvincingly states "Hugh Hefner is a Virgin"). Wanda's many sex partners leads us to the primary target of this satire: sex research. In the 1960s Dr. William H. Masters and Virginia E. Johnson were famous as the world's foremost sex researchers. The obfuscatory language attributed to "Master and Tester" in this story is not far from reality. Masters and Johnson's prose was technical, never titillating. When Annie and Wanda enter the "Master-Testers" Institute there is a book entitled Ethel Kennedy and the Pill. As a strict Roman Catholic, Ethel presumably never used the pill (she and husband Robert had eleven children). On Master's wall in the same panel is Flemish artist Jan van Eyck's Giovanni Arnolfini and His Bride. Aside from the fact that the bride is pregnant, this may be presumed to be a visual pun on "master" artist or masterpiece. "Kinsey," named by Annie's middle-aged putative co-star, is the 1940s sexologist Alfred Kinsey. Master's "Think Strasberg!" directive is a reference to famed acting coach Lee Strasberg. In the final scene a bemused Johnny Carson watches from the TV screen.

37.) *Pages 164-168.* **"Unionized Cruise Ship"** (March 1968). Ruthie (absent since a cameo in episode 16) is back as Annie's roommate—or cabin-mate—on a luxury cruise ship. Ruthie's opening comment refers to the Katherine Ann Porter book and 1965 film *Ship of Fools*, in which a cruise ship became a microcosm representing the post-War world—but the stress here is on the word fools. The ex-roller derby star in the second panel is actor **Lee Marvin** (Tenny in *Ship of Fools*). Heavy-browed and bespectacled "Mr. Mike Powers Magoony" is AFL-CIO union head George Meany. Part of his fictionalized name is derived from the nearsighted cartoon character Mr. Magoo, and "Powers" implies Meany's significant influence at a time when unions wielded considerably more power than today. Kurtzman's original pencil layout called for this character to be Teamster President Jimmy Hoffa, which would have been more in character with the premise. All hurricanes in 1968 were named after women, and the names suggested here—Arthur, Bruce, and Clifford—were not considered manly men's names. In other words, this is a gay joke. When Annie goes on deck, sunning to the left is embattled Congressman Adam Clayton Powell, smiling as he reads a subpoena. Nonchalantly walking the deck is cartoon sailor Popeye (last spotted in the rowboat with George Wallace in episode 15). Also returning, for "Gala Night," is toothsome **Bert Parks** as emcee Herb Sparks, last seen in "The Talent Contest." Cruise entertainers tend to be unknown or over-the-hill, and this ship obviously features the latter: a sign behind Annie's head says, "Tonite, Kay Kyser and his Band starring Ish Kabbibble." The butler serving No Doz to bored cruisers is typecast British actor Arthur Treacher (later known as sidekick to TV talk-show host Merv Griffin). Getting bonked by a paper-mâché ball at the bottom of the third page is author (and eventual hurricane) Truman Capote. Dousing a dowager with a seltzer bottle (and wearing a "Make War Not Love" button) is returning film director and über-German Erich Von Stroheim. In the third panel of the fourth page the disheveled older couple are better known, when sober, as the straight-laced models for Grant Wood's *American Gothic*, who previously appeared in "Sugardaddy Bigbucks" (January 1963). The ship's captain is Charles Laughton (Captain Bligh in the 1935 version of *Mutiny on the Bounty*). The giant wave thrashing the cruise ship on the left side is from the 1831 Japanese print *The Hollow of the Deep Sea Wave of Kanagawa* by Hokusaï. The New York Newspaper Typographers Union may strike contemporary readers as particularly obscure, especially since typographers are long extinct. But in the '60s this aggressive union instigated several lengthy newspaper strikes, which probably created a special annoyance for New Yorkers Kurtzman and Elder. That Kurtzman skewered unions at all would have shocked his parents, regular readers of *The Daily Worker*.

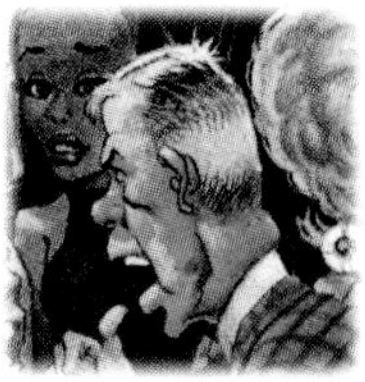

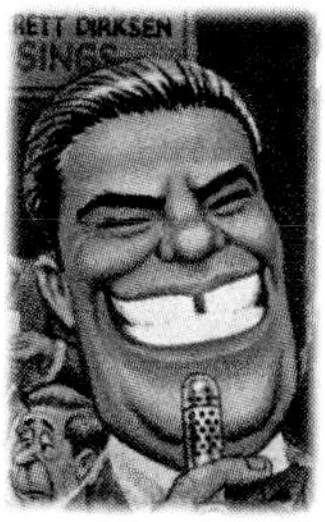

38.) *Pages 169-173.* **"Annie at the Olympics"** (June 1968). The "Viva Tijuana Brass" button Annie's agent Solly Brass shows the Mexican policeman refers to the popular American band headed by Herb Alpert. At the racetrack, Charles DeGaulle is leaping the hurdles, prompting a sideline commentator to say, "Won't he ever learn to delegate authority?" This reflects the American perception that the French president was an imperious leader. The Chinese runner going the opposite direction of other hurdlers is an apparent reference to Communist China's backward status. Jokes about Russia and Israel refer in part to the Russian military equipment abandoned in droves by their retreating Arab allies during the 1967 desert war with the Israelis. The lead runner with an eye patch is based on Moishe Dayan, Israel's celebrated one-eyed general. The Swedish pole vaulter landing on women's chests instead of sawdust reflects the prevalent view that Sweden was the world's most sexually liberated country. The Bulgarian shot putter is heaving his own ball and chain, symbolic of Bulgaria's status as a Soviet satellite. Bigbucks' suggestion that **Russia's runner** might actually be a man is based on the belief that Eastern Block competitors sometimes passed male athletes off as females to gain an advantage. In 1966 Polish sprinter Eva Klobukowska was prevented from further Olympic competition and forced to return her medals when she failed a chromosome gender test, even though she passed a gynecological test. This subject was a running joke at the 1968 Olympics, particularly with regard to any large, unattractive, or highly muscled Soviet bloc female athlete. Wilma Malibu's first name comes from America's top female runner, Wilma Rudolph. The announcement about the United Arab Republic (a short-lived political union of Syria and Egypt) and Georgie Jessel is a commentary on the Jewish entertainer's reputation as a major fundraiser for Israel bonds. The Divorce O-Mat machine refers to Mexico's reputation for quick, cheap divorces. Svetlana Stalin, daughter of the late USSR dictator, had recently defected to America and written a successful book about her life, which explains her brother's presence here. U Thant, cheering on each team, was the Secretary General of the United Nations, hence neutral. The crowd around U Thant includes a ring-necked Ubangi tribeswoman (these, presumably, are Olympic rings), Ethiopian emperor Haile Selassie sitting next to a lion (part of his lengthy official title was Lion of Judah), and five Fidel Castro look-a-likes—decoys to spare the Cuban leader from reputed CIA assassination attempts.

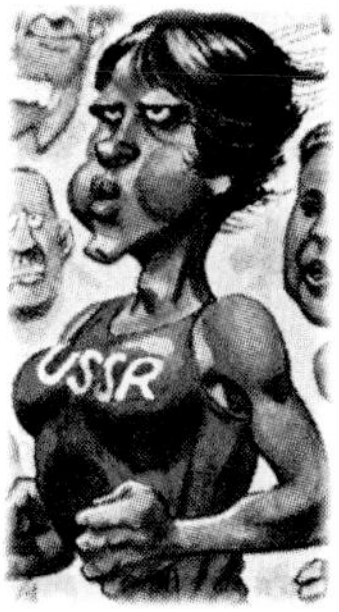
USSR

39.) *Pages 174-178.* **"The Real Howard Hews"** (December 1968). By 1968 fastidiously reclusive billionaire Howard Hughes was the source of intense media curiosity. In 1966 he had moved to the Desert Inn in Las Vegas (where there were no state taxes) and set up elaborate security measures to protect his privacy. Even his closest business executives were unable to see him in person. His great wealth and hermit mystique set up this Annie Fanny adventure. After CBS Newscaster Walter Cronkite, columnist Drew Pearson feels the blackjack blows of The Wasp and Shazam. The examining nurse's remark, "Mr. Hews is deathly afraid of contamination," is true. Hughes required a spotless environment and touched everything with a Kleenex tissue. His lieutenants playing with a giant Monopoly game attest to his extensive real estate holdings. The hangar panel represents his long association with the aircraft industry, as a daring aviator, an airplane designer, and as the owner of Trans-World Airlines. The huge airplane in the hangar is his pet World War II project: the all-wood Hercules, nicknamed the "Spruce Goose." It quickly proved obsolete and only made one brief flight, piloted by Hughes. The topless swinging stewardess he is credited here with designing is a reminder of Hughes' pre-recluse days as a notorious womanizer. The Hollywood set for "Son of the Outlaw" refers to Hughes'

days as a moviemaker (he owned RKO Studios). Hughes' most famous film, *The Outlaw*, is best remembered for actress Jane Russell's bountiful cleavage. The impeccable stand-in that Annie meets is based on actor **Gregory Peck**. The "Dickie Nixon Make-Up Kit" on the desk is an old joke recalling Richard Nixon's lack of make-up during the first televised presidential debate in 1960. Other stand-ins for Hews include loquacious toastmaster George Jessel, U Thant, and playboy actor **Warren Beatty**. And, of course, the final gag is that clever capitalist Bigbucks is the ultimate stand-in; he is the "real" Howard Hews.

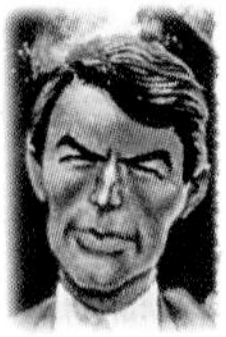

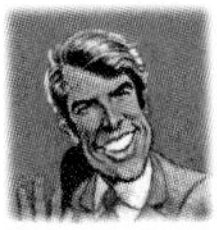

40.) *Pages 179-182.* **"Discothèques"** (February 1969). The original concept featured Benton Battbarton as Annie's guide and date, but Hugh Hefner suggested Solly Brass as a more logical purveyor of the Discothèque scene. The oval photos inscribed "love" on Annie's wall in the opening panel show that she is an equal-opportunity girlfriend: the men pictured are General William Westmoreland and Ho Chi Minh, opposite combatants in Vietnam.

41.) *Pages 183-186.* **"Annie the Actress"** (April 1969). Agent Solly Brass, wearing a briefly popular Nehru jacket and a dollar-sign medallion, lands Annie a major role in a "mod flick" directed by Richard Luster, based on Richard Lester (*A Hard Day's Night, Help!*). The *Variety* headlines Solly is perusing range from the real—"Pill Will Nill Jill" is a spoof on the famous *Variety* headline "Hix Nix Stix Pix"—to the wildly improbable "Lawrence Welk Late Late Sex Show." The actress touching up her mascara provides the first hint of lesbian activity in "Little Annie Fanny" (of course it's *just* a movie). The statue of **Oscar** embracing an equally nude female figurine is labeled "Swedish Film Award" as another wink at Sweden's pre-eminent position in the erotic film world at the time. In the late '60s Hollywood often added sexier scenes for the much more permissive European film market, which explains Luster's final call for the "European version."

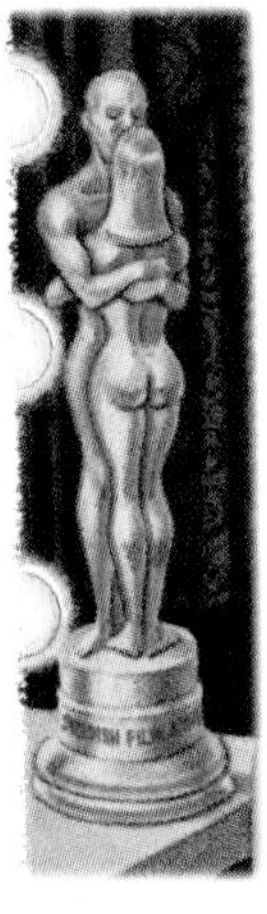

42.) *Pages 187-190.* **"See-Through Dress"** (July 1969). Like the earlier topless swimming suit, see-through dresses were a brief (ever so brief) fashion statement in the late '60s, as were disposable paper dresses, also pictured. The left dress displays the familiar face of Cuban revolutionary Che Guevara, while the middle paper dress shows the naked **John Lennon and Yoko Ono** from their recently released *Two Virgins* album cover. See-through His & Her outfits in the same panel are a bemused reference to the late '60s "unisex" look, in which fashion-conscious men and women dressed in look-alike jackets, vests, and accessories (and which inspired an episode in our second volume). Ralph Ginsberg was a controversial publisher jailed for publishing the "obscene" *Eros* magazine, hence the mug shots on the final page. Since the punchline is a transparent retelling of "The Emperor Has No Clothes," it is nice to see the original emperor on the scene, as well as a clever variation on the innocent child who spills the beans.

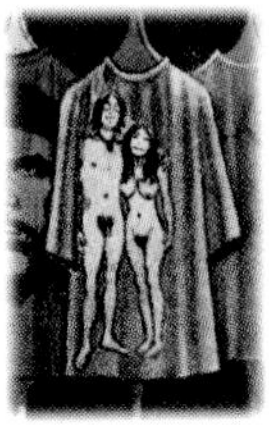

43.) *Pages 191-194.* **"Living Theater"** (October 1969). The improvisational Living Theater troupe, founded in the early '60s by directors Julian Beck and his wife Judith Malina, served as cultural shock troops in the mid and late '60s. Avante-garde actors mixed with the audience, took off their clothes, shouted obscenities, and involved the audience in anti-war and anti-materialism chants. The anarchistic performances would frequently end in a cacophonous din. The balding, longhaired man in the opening panel is Beck. Actors spelling "FUC" on stage is the closest the strip comes to using that four-letter word. The infamous Plaster Caster sisters are depicted in the same panel, no doubt scouting for candidate penises. The actor on page three who says he can't make a living from Living Theater is telling the truth. On a lengthy European tour (with no advance bookings) the actors learned to live on four dollars per day. Annie, fleeing the theater, gets into a "Gypsy Cab," a term used for unlicensed taxis, but in this case the driver is actually a gypsy. When Ruthie finally kicks Beck out of their apartment, a copy of **Philip Roth's *Portnoy's Complaint*** is among the exiting debris. Roth, obsessed with all things sexual, is the subject of a future Annie adventure.

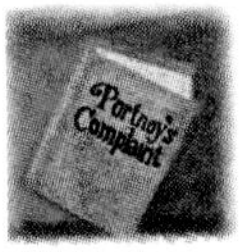
Portnoy's Complaint

44.) *Pages 195-197.* **"Astrology"** (December 1969). As Sagittarius Annie takes an interest in astrology, her friends scoff, but are intensely interested in their own signs' futures. The opening chapter on "Lucky Pisces" pictures Adolf Hitler (actual), the Creature from the Black Lagoon (water sign), and Mickey Mouse. The nearby article on flying saucers confirms Kurtzman's own level of belief. The sign symbols on the circular **Zodiac chart** are superficially accurate but twisted. Annie carries a book called *Signs*, but the author is baseball manager Casey Stengel, shown flashing a peace sign (or is that a sign to steal second?). The message on the jacket Ruthie hands to her cousin Leo, the newly deflowered Virgo, refers to the 1967 Swedish film *I Am Curious, Yellow*, which was prosecuted for obscenity in at least three states.

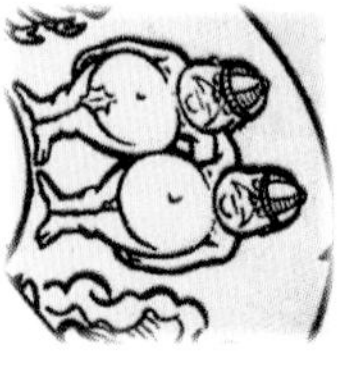

45.) *Page 198-202.* **"Marijuana"** (January 1970). Ralphie has dropped his Arthur Miller horn rims in favor of the wire-rimmed glasses worn by fashionable hippies, and he now sports long hair and a beard. As Ralphie tries to explain, logically, that smoking marijuana has no harmful side effects, he is beaten to a pulp by **overzealous cops**, the real target of the satire. The hope-less-looking fellow to the left of Benton's lampshade in the opening panel is the fire inspector. The thumb-sucking hippie clinging to a security blanket is wearing a Dr. Spock sweatshirt. Pediatrician Benjamin Spock was America's foremost advice giver when baby boomers were being raised. Many blamed his "overly permissive" philosophy for the whole hippie phenomenon. The partially obscured slogan on Ralphie's shirt as he is being shoved into the paddy wagon is "Hell No, We Won't Go," a mantra of draft-dodging anti-Vietnam War activists. In the next to last panel, as puffy-lipped Ralphie is being battered by a police baton, floating above his head are stars, the traditional cartoon convention denoting pain. But in a final hippie indignity these stars are in the style and coloration of pop artist Peter Max, whose trademark signature and © symbol can just be made out above Ralphie's voice balloon. ♥

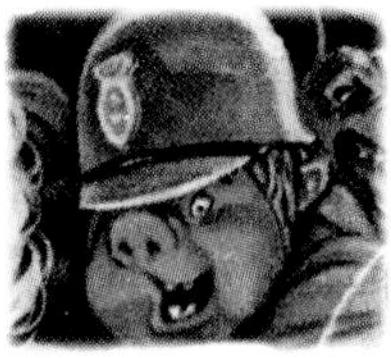